KU-002-720

THE MAKING OF
THE HABSBURG MONARCHY
1550–1700

---◆---

An Interpretation

R. J. W. Evans

CLARENDON PRESS · OXFORD

This book has been printed digitally and produced in a standard specification
in order to ensure its continuing availability

OXFORD
UNIVERSITY PRESS

Great Clarendon Street, Oxford OX2 6DP

Oxford University Press is a department of the University of Oxford.
It furthers the University's objective of excellence in research, scholarship,
and education by publishing worldwide in

Oxford New York

Auckland Bangkok Buenos Aires Cape Town Chennai
Dar es Salaam Delhi Hong Kong Istanbul Karachi Kolkata
Kuala Lumpur Madrid Melbourne Mexico City Mumbai Nairobi
São Paulo Shanghai Singapore Taipei Tokyo Toronto

with an associated company in Berlin

Oxford is a registered trade mark of Oxford University Press
in the UK and in certain other countries

Published in the United States
by Oxford University Press Inc., New York

© R. J. W. Evans 1979

The moral rights of the author have been asserted
Database right Oxford University Press (maker)

Reprinted 2002

All rights reserved. No part of this publication may be reproduced,
stored in a retrieval system, or transmitted, in any form or by any means,
without the prior permission in writing of Oxford University Press,
or as expressly permitted by law, or under terms agreed with the appropriate
reprographics rights organization. Enquiries concerning reproduction
outside the scope of the above should be sent to the Rights Department,
Oxford University Press, at the address above

You must not circulate this book in any other binding or cover
and you must impose this same condition on any acquirer

ISBN 0-19-873085-3

Cover illustration: the Loretto church and monastery in Prague:
begun 1626, carillon 1694, facade by the Dientzenhofer family) c. 1720.

CROYDON COLLEGE
LIBRARY

COPY 06 118 7616

CLASS 943·603 EVA

3 8017 00118 7616

DAW
3/06
£24.99

THE MAKING OF
THE HABSBURG MONARCHY

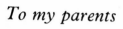

To my parents

Preface

Many historians, in a dozen languages, have sought to explain why the Habsburg Monarchy declined and fell; none has ever seriously investigated the causes of its rise. Hence this book. Hence also the limitations of this book, since the first word on a subject cannot evidently also be the last.

Of course, some intelligent summary accounts exist for the period I have chosen, along with a number of impressive older studies concentrated upon foreign policy. There are lively specialist traditions in ecclesiastical, constitutional, legal, and cultural history, and there is good recent work on economic developments. Local history possesses a voluminous literature, much of it associated with the dozens of excellent scholarly journals which have long flourished throughout the area. But three crucial elements have, I think, been lacking in previous approaches. The first is a consistent account of the Central European Counter-Reformation and its concomitant socio-economic changes, which provided the framework for a new structure of power and a new set of attitudes. The second is a balanced view of the Monarchy as a whole, especially of the interaction between regions and central government, since the consolidation of the Habsburg state rested essentially on a series of bilateral agreements between the rulers and their mightier subjects. The third is an understanding of intellectual evolution from the Renaissance to the Baroque, for the enhanced authority of the dynasty depended at least as much upon mentalities as upon institutions.

There are thus (if a crude geometrical metaphor be excused) three dimensions to this study, corresponding to the three equal parts of the text: a lengthwise section through the material; a transverse section; and a sounding in depth. Yet the subject does not permit of any watertight compartments, and the political, social, and cultural threads which wove a casual juxtaposition of territories into a powerful and reasonably stable commonwealth cannot readily be disentangled. Nor can chronological limits represent more than approximate guide-lines: hence the terminal dates which eschew any precise identification with reigns or regimes. The book is—as its sub-title indicates—merely one way of looking at an immensely rich and complex tapestry. Many of its conclusions must be regarded as highly tentative. It attempts to provide a tolerably comprehensive introduction, but not, needless to say, a complete picture. The reader may be surprised at the prominence accorded to certain issues: magic, for instance, which I define in a very broad sense. But he will assuredly be no less conscious of how much I have left out.

For some topics—popular culture is a good example—my neglect may be excused by the fact that no adequate body of secondary work yet exists. Elsewhere the omissions are more deliberate. I have written little about wars and armies, diplomacy and foreign relations, partly because information can already be found in other places, partly because the less familiar social and intellectual fields appear to offer a larger and more coherent set of explanations. It is manifestly important that at a crucial moment in 1620 Spain sent support for Emperor Ferdinand II while France did nothing to help the Bohemian rebels; that the Turks and Louis XIV both miscalculated during the 1680s; that Prince Eugene saw eye-to-eye with the duke of Marlborough. Yet there are also good reasons within the Central European evolution why those episodes should have yielded such weighty consequences—and the more contingent the event, the less can or should the historian build upon it. When the distinguished Austrian student of the period, Oswald Redlich, wrote a two-volume narrative of Habsburg politics from the Peace of Westphalia to the death of Charles VI, he called the first book *Die Weltmacht des Barock 1648–1700*, and the second *Das Werden einer Grossmacht 1700–40*. The titles, perfectly apposite, nevertheless contain an irony which was no doubt unconscious. How the 'world-power of Baroque' could precede the 'great power' of the Austrian army is one underlying theme of the present investigation.

*

I have profited from the kindness of many people while preparing this book. They range geographically from the staff of the Bodleian Library in Oxford, so unfailingly helpful and considerate, to the priest at Gheorgheni (Gyergyószentmiklós of old) who gave me a rare volume on the history of his community, the Armenian Catholics of Transylvania. Many colleagues, in England and abroad, have been generous with advice and encouragement: it would be invidious to name some of them and not others. To my family, in a hundred different ways, I owe the greatest debt of all.

Brasenose College, Oxford   R.J.W.E.
May 1978

Contents

Note on terms and names

1. No proper nomenclature exists for the political entity whose consolidation is the subject of this book. Observers, then and later, commonly described it as 'Austria', but the usage, at least when extended beyond the diplomatic and military relations between the dynasty and the rest of Europe, is incorrect and mischievous. I have preferred the terms 'Habsburg lands' and 'Habsburg Monarchy'; if it be objected that either phrase could conceivably, until 1700, be applied to the territories of the Spanish crown as well, the reply must be that they were not (and are not) in fact normally so employed. 'Habsburg Monarchy' is indeed, *par excellence*, a nineteenth-century expression, but not so exclusively as to sound anachronistic here. So is 'Habsburg Empire', which I have not used, in order to avoid any confusion with the German, or Holy Roman, Empire, *das Heilige Römische Reich deutscher Nation*, which the Habsburgs also ruled for the whole period under consideration, and to which large parts of their own patrimony owed ultimate allegiance. Some of the complexities issuing from this dual sovereignty are touched upon below in chapters five and eight. At the same time it should be borne in mind that 'Bohemia' and 'Hungary' were by no means simple notions either to contemporaries; a few of their underlying intricacies are indicated in chapters six and seven. The reader may detect one piece of geographical licence: since the expression 'Central Europe' does not, in English, denote a precise area, I have made a virtue out of necessity by defining it, politically, as co-extensive with the Habsburg Monarchy, and culturally as co-extensive with the seventeenth-century world of imperial Counter-Reformation which embraced much of southern Germany too.

2. Many locations in Central Europe, from the largest city to the smallest village, carry two or more names in different local languages, and it is often difficult for the historian to choose between them. I have tried to use those which are either most familiar to a Western readership or most authentic for the circumstances of the

time, but the result cannot claim to be altogether consistent. The Austrian lands present few problems: except in the south, the German word was appropriate then as now (though it is worth observing that neighbouring peoples might employ a radically different vocabulary—thus the Upper Austrian Schlägl is Drkolná in Czech; the Carinthian Klagenfurt is Celovec in Slovene; even Vienna itself is known to Hungarians as Bécs). In Bohemia and Moravia the first language of state, at least at the beginning of the period, was Czech, but some places, especially those in an area of German settlement, wear their German names more naturally. Silesia, with its predominantly Germanic character, is a special case; there the contemporary Czech equivalents (like Vratislav for Breslau) would represent an absurd mystification, the present-day Polish equivalents (including Wrocław for Breslau) an equally absurd anachronism. Historic Hungary, divided today between six different countries, is naturally more complicated. During the sixteenth and seventeenth centuries the Habsburg kingdom used Latin and Hungarian (Magyar) for official purposes, with German as the normal written tongue in many towns; Croatia used Latin and Croat; Transylvania used Hungarian and Latin, with German as the official language of its Saxon citizens. Other vernaculars (Romanian, Ruthene, Serbian, Slovak) possessed no formal legal status. I have tried to steer a common-sense course through this jungle: thus Hungarian Pozsony seems the only appropriate name for the then capital of the kingdom rather than the German Pressburg or the modern Slovak coinage, Bratislava, but I have spared the reader the Magyar mouthful of Nagyszombat for its university centre, in favour of the German form, Tyrnau. There is a glossary of more important variants at the end of the book; lesser ones have been registered only in the Index. A further appendix contains brief hints about the pronunciation of Czech and Hungarian words.

3. Personal names in Central Europe raise similar problems; here again the selection of one form rather than another may convey— however unintentionally—a political or cultural judgment. After considerable reflection I decided to use native, and not Anglicized, Christian names on almost all occasions, even where these might appear strange (Jiří and István, for example), but the choice

between rival variants (German or Czech, Magyar or Croat, and so on) must remain tentative. Thus in Bohemia surnames are divided very roughly according to nationality, but I have allowed German Christian names to predominate from about 1650; in Hungary most families have been spelled after the Magyar fashion. It should be remembered that many sixteenth-century Humanists and seventeenth-century priests answered more readily to Latinized surnames than to any vernacular equivalent. A final word is required about styles of nobility. German usage, with the particle 'von', needs no introduction, and I have retained it here (omitting 'von' where the noble in question also held an aristocratic title). In Czech 'von' was rendered by the preposition 'z', governing a genitive case, with consequent inflection of the following predicate. Such forms I have Anglicized as painlessly as possible: thus 'z Vrtby' as Vrtba, but 'z Lobkovic' as Lobkovic instead of the original 'Lobkovice'. Both German and Czech nobles (more especially the latter) can on occasion confuse the historian by a separation of family name from title: the clan of Bořita z Martinic, for instance, gradually became known as 'Martinic'; but such difficulties, less formidable than in England or France, are best left for the genealogist to unravel. Hungarian practice was different, quite apart from the habitual inversion of all Magyar names which English historians have traditionally observed in the single case of Bethlen Gábor. Hungarians indicated nobility by means of one or more adjectival 'forenames' deriving from the original grant of territory and employed only on formal occasions. Thus the rebel leader, Count Ferenc (Francis) Rákóczi, who took his predicate from a small village in the north-east called Felsővadász, appears in Hungarian parlance as felsővadászi gróf Rákóczi Ferenc. Such forenames have little scholarly use except for distinguishing separate branches of certain families, and I have included them only in the Index.

Abbreviations

Archives, libraries, periodicals, and some works of reference

Acta SS.	see Bibliography: *Acta Sanctorum*
ADB	*Allgemeine Deutsche Biographie*
Anal. Praem.	*Analecta Praemonstratensia*
AÖG	*Archiv für Österreichische Geschichte* (originally: *Archiv für Kunde Österreichischer Geschichtsquellen*)
AUC, Phil. et Hist.	*Acta Universitatis Carolinae, Philologica et Historica*
AUC, HUCP	*Acta Universitatis Carolinae, Historia Universitatis Carolinae Pragensis*
Aug.	*Augustiniana*
BČH	see Zíbrt in Bibliography
BÉ	*A Bécsi Magyar Történeti Intézet Évkönyve* (*Jahrbuch des Wiener Ungarischen Historischen Instituts*)
BL	British Library, British Museum, London
Bod.	Bodleian Library, Oxford
Bp.	Budapest (as place of publication)
ČČH	*Český Časopis Historický*, 1895–1948; cf. *ČsČH*
ČČM	*Časopis Českého Muzea* (originally *Časopis Muzea Království Českého*)
ČL	*Český Lid*
ČMM	*Časopis Matice Moravské* (vols. lxxviii–lxxxvi entitled *Sborník Matice Moravské*)
Coll. Franc.	*Collectanea Franciscana*
ČsČH	*Československý Časopis Historický* (since 1953)
DNB	*Dictionary of National Biography*
Egy. Kt.	Egyetemi Könyvtár (University Library), Budapest
HHStA	Haus-, Hof- und Staatsarchiv, Vienna
HJ	*Historisches Jahrbuch*
HZ	*Historische Zeitschrift*
ItK	*Irodalomtörténeti Közlemények*
Jbb. f. Natö. u. Stat.	*Jahrbücher für Nationalökonomie und Statistik*
Jb. d. St. Klnb.	*Jahrbuch des Stiftes Klosterneuburg* (new series since 1961)
Jb. f. Lk. v. NÖ	*Jahrbuch für Landeskunde von Niederösterreich* (originally *Blätter des Vereines f. Lk. v. NÖ*)
JGGPÖ	*Jahrbuch der Gesellschaft für Geschichte des Protestantismus in Österreich*
LK	*Levéltári Közlemények*
MHVSt	*Mitteilungen des Historischen Vereins für Steiermark* (cf. *ZHVSt*)

MIÖG	Mitteilungen des Instituts für Österreichische Geschichtsforschung (between 1923 and 1942: Mitteilungen des Österreichischen Instituts für Geschichtsforschung)
MIT	A Magyar Irodalom Története, ed. I. Sőtér, i–vi (Bp. 1964–6)
MKSz	Magyar Könyvszemle (new series since 1892)
MOöLA	Mitteilungen des Oberösterreichischen Landesarchivs
MÖStA	Mitteilungen des Österreichischen Staatsarchivs
MVGDB	Mitteilungen des Vereins für Geschichte der Deutschen in Böhmen
MVGStW	Mitteilungen des Vereins für Geschichte der Stadt Wien
NDB	Neue Deutsche Biographie
OL	Országos Levéltár (National Archives), Budapest
ÖNB	Österreichische Nationalbibliothek, Vienna
OSN	Ottův Slovník Naučný, i–xxviii (Pr. 1888–1909)
OSzK	Országos Széchenyi Könyvtár (National Széchenyi Library), Budapest
ÖVjschr. f. Kath. Theol.	Österreichische Vierteljahresschrift für Katholische Theologie
Pr.	Prague (as place of publication)
RMK	Régi Magyar Könyvtár, ed. Károly Szabó, i–iii (Bp. 1879–98)
SbAPr	Sborník Archivních Prací
Sb.d. bayr. Akad. d. Wiss., ph.-ph.-h. Kl.	Sitzungsberichte der bayrischen Akademie der Wissenschaften, philosophisch-philologisch-historische Klasse
Sb. d.k. Akad. d. Wiss., ph-h. Kl.	Sitzungsberichte der kaiserlichen (later: österreichischen) Akademie der Wissenschaften, philosophisch-historische Klasse
SbH	Sborník Historický
SbH (Rezek)	Sborník Historický (ed. A. Rezek), 1883–5
SbHKr	Sborník Historického Kroužku
SbMM	see ČMM
Str.	Strahov Library, Prague
Str. Kn.	Strahovská Knihovna
Stud. u. Mitt.	Studien (originally: Wissenschaftliche Studien) und Mitteilungen aus dem Benediktiner- und Cisterzienserorden
Sz	Századok
TSz	Történelmi Szemle
TT	Történelmi Tár (originally Magyar Történelmi Tár)
UK	Universitní Knihovna (University Library, now part of the State Library), Prague
V.	Vienna (as place of publication)
VČAVSlU	Věstník České Akademie pro Vědy, Slovesnost a Umění
Vjschr. f.S.u. WGesch.	Vierteljahrsschrift für Sozial- und Wirtschaftsgeschichte
VKČSN	Věstník Královské České Společnosti Nauk (třída filosoficko-historicko-filologická)

Zbl. f. Biblw.	*Zentralblatt für Bibliothekswesen*
ZHVSt	*Zeitschrift des Historischen Vereins für Steiermark* (since 1906; earlier *MHVSt*)
Zschr. f. Kath. Theol.	*Zeitschrift für Katholische Theologie*
ZVGAS	*Zeitschrift des Vereins für Geschichte und Altertum Schlesiens* (later *Zeitschrift für Geschichte und Altertum Schlesiens*)

Religious orders

Can. Reg. = Canonici Regulares	Canons Regular (Augustinian Canons)
O. Barn. = Ordo Barnabitarum	Barnabites
O. Carm. (Disc.) = Ordo [Fratrum] Carmelitarum (Discalceatorum)	(Discalced) Carmelites
O. Cart. = Ordo Cart(h)usiensis	Carthusians
O.Cist. = [Sacer] Ordo Cisterciensis	Cistercians
O. Crucig. = Ordo Crucigerorum (cum Rubea Stella)	Crusaders (with a Red Star)
O.E.S.A. (Disc.) = Ordo [Fratrum] Eremitarum Sancti Augustini (Discalceatorum)	(Discalced) Augustinian hermits (i.e. friars)
O.F.M. (Conv.) = Ordo Fratrum Minorum (Conventualium)	(Conventual) Franciscans (Minorites)
O.F.M. Cap. = Ordo Fratrum Minorum Capuccinorum	Capuchins
O.F.M. Obs. = Ordo Fratrum Minorum Observantiae	Observant Franciscans
O. Minim. = Ordo Minimorum	Minims
O.P. = Ordo Praedicatorum	Dominicans
O.Praem. = Ordo Praemonstratensis	Premonstratensians
O.S.B. = Ordo Sancti Benedicti	Benedictines
O.S.M. = Ordo Servorum Mariae	Servites
O.S.P. = Ordo Scholarum Piarum	Piarists
O.S.P.P.E. = Ordo [Fratrum] Sancti Pauli Primi Eremitae	Paulines (*Pálosok*)
O. Teut. = Ordo Teutonicus	Teutonic Knights
S.J. = Societas Jesu	Jesuits

Bibliographical Preface to Third Impression

This book first appeared in 1979, and research for it was largely completed by 1976. Much good work on the issues which it addresses has been published in the intervening years. It would be good to take proper account of that work here, as of the criticisms and suggestions made by reviewers. But thorough rewriting is not possible, so I must restrict myself—besides correcting some smaller errors—to an indication of the most significant contributions which have come to my attention, adhering roughly to the ordering of subject-matter within my text.

The international position of the Habsburg Monarchy in the early modern period (**Prologue**) attracted attention during the 1980s especially through the tricentennial commemoration of its decisive victories over the Turks at Vienna (1683) and Budapest (1686). Among the substantial body of literature thus generated may be noted: *Der Sieg bei Wien*, ed. P. Broucek (V.-Warsaw 1983); *Les Relations franco-autrichiennes sous Louis XIV. Siège de Vienne*, ed. J. Bérenger (St Cyr-Coetquidan 1983); *Studia Austro-Polonica*, iii (Cracow 1983); *Acta Historica Academiae Scientiarum Hungaricae*, xxxiii (1987); *Österreich und die Osmanen*, ed. E. Zöllner and K. Gutkas (V. 1988). Many writers on this subject make more play than I do with the significance of the Turks for Austrian state-building, whether as aggressors to be resisted or even as a model to be imitated (cf. K. Vocelka in *Südostforschungen*, xxxvi [1977], 13–34). Despite the obvious impact of the Ottoman Empire as an external agent, I am more struck by the fact that major Habsburg initiatives of an absolutist kind—the institutional reforms of Ferdinand I, the *Verneuerte Landesordnung* in Bohemia, the naked attack on Hungarian liberties in the 1670s—coincided with periods of reduced Turkish pressure. But the subject certainly needs amplification (cf. now H. Rabe in *Zeitschrift für Historische Forschung*, xvii [1990], 373–5). The collected essays of H. Sturmberger, *Land ob der Enns und Österreich* (Linz 1979), provide a general survey of international political developments over the period. Sturmberger is especially perceptive on the role of the estates, about which useful contributions are now gathered together in *Crown, Church and Estates. Central European Politics in the Sixteenth and Seventeenth Centuries*, ed. R. J. W. Evans and T. V. Thomas (London 1991). For the reign of Ferdinand I (**Chapter 1**) see now P. S. Fichtner, *Ferdinand I of Austria. The Politics of Dynasticism in the Age of the Reformation* (New York 1982). For Maximilian II: F. Edelmayer, *Maximilian II, Philipp II und Reichsitalien* (Stuttgart 1988); Edelmayer is also editing part of Maximilian's correspondence. Cf., on Lazarus Schwendi, R. Schnur in *Zeitschrift für Historische Forschung*, xiv (1987), 27–46. The spread of the Reformation in the *Erblande* is addressed in two helpful works by G. Reingrabner, *Adel und Reformation* (V. 1976), and *Protestanten in Österreich* (V. 1981). For Protestant education in Austria see also G. Heiss and A. Kohler in *Wiener Beiträge zur Geschichte der Neuzeit*, v (1978), 13–123. On the spread of Calvinism, especially in Hungary, I have assembled some information and literature in *International Calvinism, 1536–1715*, ed. M. Prestwich (Oxford 1985), 167–96. On sectarians in East-Central Europe see two valuable collections of conference papers: *Antitrinitarianism in the Second Half of the 16th Century*, ed. R. Dán and A. Pirnát (Bp.-Leiden 1982); and *Socinianism and its Role in the Culture of the 16th–18th Centuries*, ed. L. Szczucki *et al.* (Warsaw 1983).

Some new bibliography on the culture of late humanism and Mannerism, and on the reign of Rudolf II as a whole, is indicated in the second edition of my *Rudolf II and his World* (Oxford 1984), vi–xi. To this should now be added: *Prag um 1600. Kunst und Kultur am Hofe Rudolfs II* (Freren 1988); a further volume, *Prag um 1600. Beiträge zur Kunst und Kultur am Hofe Rudolfs II* (also Freren 1988); and T. Da. C. Kaufmann, *The School of Prague. Painting at the Court of Rudolf II* (Chicago 1988). Also useful are some of the chapters in *Renaissance Humanism: Foundations, Forms and Legacy*, ed. A. Rabil (3 vols. Philadelphia 1988), and *Studien zum Humanismus in den böhmischen Ländern*, ed. H.-B. Harder and S. Wollman (Cologne 1988). J. Pánek, *Výprava české šlechty do Itálie v letech 1551–2* (Pr. 1987), establishes an important linkage between travel and cultural receptivity. For Hungary see especially *Szenci Molnár Albert és a magyar későreneszánsz*, ed. S. Csanda and B.

Keserű (Szeged 1978), and M. D. Birnbaum, *Humanists in a Shattered World. Croatian and Hungarian Latinity in the 16th Century* (Columbus, Ohio 1986).

Aspects of the early Counter-Reformation (**Chapter 2**) are addressed in *Crown, Church and Estates* (above). See also J. Rainer's work on Khlesl in *Römische Historische Mitteilungen*, v (1961–2), 35–163, and in *Römische Quartalschrift für christliche Altertumskunde und Kirchengeschichte*, lix (1964), 14–35; the documentation on Hungarian Jesuits in *Monumenta antiquae Hungariae*. Vol III: *1587–92*, ed. L. Lukács (Rome 1981; cf. below, p. 49 n. 19), and *J. Argenti iratai, 1603–1623*, ed. E. Veress (Szeged 1983); and, on the first generation of Tridentine priests in Bohemia, J. Jarošová, 'Knihy svěcenců obnoveného pražského arcibiskupství', *Sborník Národního Muzea v Praze*, ser. C, xv (Pr. 1970, *recte* 1975).

The changing political situation in Bohemia is illuminated in several important contributions by J. Pánek: a splendid new edition of Václav Březan, *Životy posledních Rožmberků* (2 vols. Pr. 1985), with an associated major new joint biography, *Poslední Rožmberkové, velmoži české renesance* (Pr. 1989); *Stavovská opozice a její zápas s Habsburky, 1547–1577* (Pr. 1982); and arts. available in German in *Historica* (Pr.), xxv (1985), 73–120, and *MIÖG* xcvii (1989), 53–82. The Czech originals of these arts., along with other relevant contributions, are in the journal *Folia Historica Bohemica*. J. Janáček, *Rudolf II. a jeho doba* (Pr. 1987), is an extended and attractive political biography, strongest on the Bohemian side. The distinctiveness of events in the sister-province of Moravia is underlined by J. Válka, *Přehled dějin Moravy*. Vol. II: *Stavovská Morava, 1440–1620* (Pr. 1987). For the crisis in Hugnary after the turn of the century see A. Molnár, *Fürst Stefan Bocskay als Staatsmann und Persönlichkeit* (Munich 1983), who publishes some of Bocskai's correspondence. K. Benda, in *European Studies Review*, vii (1978), 281–304, gives a helpful summary of the disordered situation there.

Several significant essays in *Crown, Church and Estates* (above) consider the issues raised by the confederations and the revolt of 1618. See also the new edition, by J. Janáček, of Pavel Skála ze Zhoře, *Historie česká. Od defenestrace k Bílé hoře* (Pr. 1984); an important collection of Moravian documents, ed. L. Urbánková, *Povstání na Moravě v roce 1619* (Pr. 1979), complementing those ed. by her father, F. Hrubý (below, p. 71 n. 72); and arts. by

J. P. Kučera and J. Jurok in *Studia Comeniana et Historica*, xxviii (1984), 5–74. On Habsburg policies in the 1620s there is nothing new in J. Franzl, *Ferdinand II* (Graz 1978); but R. Bireley, *Religion and Politics in the Age of the Counterreformation: Emperor Ferdinand II, William Lamormaini SJ, and the Formation of Imperial Policy* (Chapel Hill, NC 1981) is a major reconsideration; cf. *Acta S.C. de Propaganda Fide Germaniam spectantia, 1622–1649*, ed H. Tüchle (Paderborn 1962), and J. Hanzal on Bohemia in *Muzejní a Vlastivědná Práce*, xii (1974), 22–34. The latest re-examination of the wider context of the Thirty Years War is *Krieg und Politik, 1618–48. Europäische Probleme und Perspektiven*, ed. K. Repgen (Munich 1988).

Social changes in the period of upheaval after 1600 (**Chapter 3**) have been studied for Austria by K. MacHardy and others in *Wiener Beiträge zur Geschichte der Neuzeit*, viii (1981), 48–157. The development of landed property in Bohemia in the decades before 1618 has attracted more good arts. in *Folia Historica Bohemica* and a monograph by V. Ledvinka, *Úvěr a zadlužení feudálního velkostatku v předbělohorských Čechách* (Pr. 1985). Cf., for the post-1620 situation, P. Čornej and O. Felcman in *ČsČH* xxviii (1980), 559–87. Good new material on social differentiation and religious allegiance among the Hungarian nobility appears in a dissertation by P. Schimert, whose publication is awaited. On peasant revolts see *Aus der Geschichte der ostmitteleuropäischen Bauernbewegungen im 16.–17. Jahrhundert*, ed. G. Heckenast (Bp. 1977); and on peasant society, H. Rebel, *Peasant Classes. The Bureaucratization of Property and Family Relations under Early Habsburg Absolutism* (Princeton 1983), a somewhat opaque work. V. Zimányi, *Economy and Society in Sixteenth and Seventeenth Century Hungary, 1526–1650* (Bp. 1987)provides an accessible survey; for Austria see E. Bruckmüller, *Sozialgeschichte Österreichs* (V. 1985). The history of the University of Prague in these years has been covered in a series of arts. in the journal *AUC HUCP*; while reviving intellectual life in Hungary is illuminated in a handsome book by B. Holl, *Ferencffy Lőrinc* (Bp. 1980). See also below, on Pázmány.

Religious consolidation under Leopold I (**Chapter 4**) is further documented with statistical material from Bohemia by E. Čáňová, in her edition of *Nejstarší zpovědní seznamy, 1570–1666* (Pr. 1973), and in *SbAPr* xxix (1979), 20–55; and with visitation reports of

Hungarian archbishops by E. Bouydosh, in *Slovak Studies* (Cleveland-Rome), v (1965), 7–98. I had missed an earlier source collection for Croatia: *Vrela i prinosi. Fontes et studia historiae Societatis Jesu in finibus Croatiae*, ed. M. Vanino, i–xii (Zagreb 1932–41). For an interesting case-study see C. A. M. Mooney, *The Servite Germanic Observance, 1611–1668* (Rome 1976), and L. M. Foster, *Theology and Theologians in the Servite Germanic Observance, 1636–1783* (Rome 1978). For popular education in Hungary see I. Mészáros, *Népoktatásunk 1553–1777 között* (Bp. 1972). The important imperial confidant, Hippolito da Pergine, has at last found an interpreter, A. Coreth, in *MÖStA* xxxi (1978), 73–97; while the study by R. Gherardi, *Potere e costituzione a Vienna fra Sei e Settecento* (Bologna 1980), is revealing both about the absolutist plans of some of Leopold's advisers, and (though only implicitly) about their total impracticability. J. A. Mears's reflections on Habsburg military reform in *Central European History*, xxi (1988), 122–41, are useful, but inconclusive.

Aspects of the notion of Austria (**Chapter 5**), in the wider and narrower senses, are explored in *Österreich: von der Staatsidee zum Nationalbewußtsein*, ed. G. Wagner (V. 1982). Cf. the last work by Friedrich Heer, *Der Kampf um die österreichische Identität* (V. 1981); and the interesting analysis of provincial separatisms at the very beginning of our period by G. R. Burkert, *Landesfürst und Stände. Karl V., Ferdinand I. und die österreichischen Erbländer im Ringen um Gesamtstaat und Landesinteressen* (Graz 1987). Sturmberger (above) is helpful on the status and development of Upper Austria. For Styria see K. von Moltke, *Siegmund von Dietrichstein. Die Anfänge ständischer Institutionen und das Eindringen des Protestantismus in der Steiermark* (Göttingen 1970), and W. Schulze, *Landesdefension und Staatsbildung. Studien zum Kriegswesen des innerösterreichischen Territorialstaates* (V.-Cologne 1973). Other provinces have been less well served, but there is an important study of religious change in Salzburg: F. Ortner, *Reformation, katholische Reformation, und Gegenreformation im Erzstift Salzburg* (Salzburg 1981). K. Müller, 'Habsburgischer Adel um 1700: die Familie Lamberg', *MÖStA* xxxii (1979), 78–108, is a useful example of the investigation of lineage.

The latest compendium on the history of Bohemia after the White Mountain (**Chapter 6**), *Přehled dějin Československa*. Vol. I, part 2:

1526–1848, ed. J. Purš and M. Kropilák (Pr. 1982), brings little that is new, while its bibliography confirms the paucity of recent work. But there are significant contributions by P. Čornej, in *AUC, Phil. et Hist.* (1976), i. 165–94, on the structure of land-holding, and by M. Volf, in *SbAPr* xxvii (1977), 3–49, on the domestic policies of Liechtenstein. For the rise of that family as a whole see *Liechtenstein. Fürstliches Haus und staatliche Ordnung*, ed. V. Press and D. Willoweit (Vaduz-Munich 1987). T. M. Barker, *Army, Aristocracy, Monarchy. Essays on War, Society and Government in Austria, 1618–1780* (New York 1982), provides fresh material about Bohemian military families, especially Piccolomini and Lobkovic; on the latter, P. de Gmeline, *Histoire des princes de Lobkowitz* (Nancy 1977), is amateur but informative. See also J. Macek on Kaspar Kaplíř in *MÖStA* xxxvii (1984), 73–119; and F. Hrubý, *Lev Vilém z Kounic, barokní kavalír* (Brno 1987). J. Veselý, in *SbAPr* xxix (1979), 56–110, clarifies the relationship between Bohemia and the Reich.

Work on the Church and on Baroque culture in Bohemia long had to be sustained by scholars operating, or at least publishing, in exile: see M. Součková, *Baroque in Bohemia* (Ann Arbor, Mich. 1980), a kind of literary odyssey; and cf. Kalista below. But all that has now begun to change. For indications of the new agenda see J. Kučera and J. Rak, *Bohuslav Balbín a jeho místo v české kultuře* (Pr. 1983); R. Zuber, *Osudy moravské církve v 18. století.* Vol. I: *1695–1777* (Pr. 1988); and *Studie Muzea Kroměřížska* (1989), with new contributions on the Piarists. Cf. W. Eberhard in *Römische Quartalschrift für christliche Altertumskunde und Kirchengeschichte*, lxxxiv (1989), 235–57. J. Válka, *Česká společnost v 15.–18. století.* Vol. II: *Bělohorská doba* (Pr. 1983), is a significant survey of society and culture; while for some very broad reflections on the position of Bohemia in the Habsburg Monarchy in the early modern age, see my chapter in *Conquest and Coalescence: The Shaping of the State in Early Modern Europe*, ed. M. Greengrass (London 1991), 134–54.

Volume V of the new massive general history of Hungary (**Chapter 7**), *Magyarország története, 1526–1686*, ed. Zs. P. Pach and A. R. Várkonyi, i–ii (Bp. 1985), now covers its period in nearly 2,000 pages, including 128 of close-printed bibliography. With its successor, *Magyarország története, 1686–1790*, ed. Gy. Ember and G. Heckenast, i–ii (Bp. 1989), it represents an indispensable handbook. Research has continued to concentrate productively on the decades of international and civil war from the 1660s. A. R. Várkonyi, *A rejtőzködő Murányi Vénus* (Bp. 1987), is a fascinating and ingenious reappraisal of the antecendents to the Wesselényi conspiracy. For the conspiracy itself and the constitutional struggle which followed it, see L. Benczédi, *Rendiség, abszolutizmus és centralizáció a 17. század végi Magyarországon, 1664–1685* (Bp. 1980), and *A Thököly-felkelés és kora*, ed. Benczédi (Bp. 1983); cf. also F. Theuer, *Tragödie der Magnaten* (V.-Cologne 1979), and the property inventories in *Monumenta historica familiarum Zrinski et Frankopan*, i, ed. R. Modrić (Zagreb 1974). Wider issues are addressed by B. Köpeczi in *Staatsräson und christliche Solidarität. Die ungarischen Aufstände und Europa in der zweiten Hälfte des 17. Jahrhunderts* (V.-Cologne 1983); while Várkonyi's collected essays, *Magyarország keresztútjain* (Bp. 1978), throw light on economic and ideological aspects of the years of turmoil. Of many publications to commemorate the tricentary of the birth of Ferenc II Rákóczi, the last and most important was *Rákóczi-tanulmányok*, ed. B. Köpeczi *et al.* (Bp. 1980). The contributors to *From Hunyadi to Rákóczi. War and Society in Late Medieval and Early Modern Hungary*, ed. J. M. Bak and B. K. Király (New York 1982) pursue mainly military themes (cf. vols. cited above on the 1680s).

The Church has come off less well, but I. Bitskey's *Humanista erudíció és barokk világkép: Pázmány Péter prédikációi* (Bp. 1979), and his short biography, *Pázmány Péter* (Bp. 1986), announce a welcome revival of interest in the Hungarian Richelieu, on whom the dissertation by Schimert (above) is now awaited. See also the last work of the late Librarian of Pannonhalma, J. L. Csóka, *Geschichte des benediktinischen Mönchtums in Ungarn* (St Ottilien 1980); T. Vanyó in *Soproni Szemle* (1979), 20–38, 113–30, 211–27, with good information from ecclesiastical records; and L. Lukács, *A független magyar jezsuita rendtartomány kérdése és az osztrák abszolutizmus, 1649–1773* (Szeged 1989). For Transylvania the major work of synthesis, *Erdély története*. Vol. I: *A kezdetektől 1606-ig*, ed. L. Makkai and A. Mócsi. Vol. II: *1606-tól 1830-ig*, ed. Makkai and Z. Szász (Bp. 1986), is now available in abridged German trans. as *Kurze Geschichte Siebenbürgens*, ed. B. Köpeczi *et al.* (Bp. 1990); while the late Zs. Trócsányi's *Erdély központi kormányzata, 1540–1690* (Bp. 1980), an important piece of administrative history, sheds light on the nature of absolutism in the principality.

The role of the Habsburgs as emperors in Germany (**Chapter 8**) is treated, directly or indirectly, in numerous studies by V. Press. Among them are his contributions to five collections which are all of general relevance to this topic: an issue of *Journal of Modern History*, lviii (1986); *Klientelsysteme im Europa der frühen Neuzeit*, ed. A. Mączak (Munich 1988); *Vorderösterreich in der frühen Neuzeit*, ed. H. Maier and Press (Sigmaringen 1989); *Stände und Gesellschaft im Alten Reich*, ed. G. Schmidt (Stuttgard 1989); and *Crown, Church and Estates* (above). One aspect of imperial influence is discussed by U. Eisenhardt, *Die kaiserlichen privilegia de non appellando* (Cologne 1980); and Habsburg connections with individual states emerge, *inter alia*, from G. Schnath, *Geschichte Hannovers . . . 1674–1714*, i–iii (Hildesheim-Leipzig 1938–78), F. Jürgensmeier, *Johann Philipp von Schönborn und die Römische Kurie* (Mainz 1977), and G. Christ, *Studien zur Reichskirche der Frühneuzeit* (Stuttgart 1989).

For cultural linkages see R. J. W. Evans in *Central European History*, xviii (1985), 14–30, and the reflections on the 'Baroque' age of the German universities by N. Hammerstein in *Studia Leibnitiana*, xiii (1981), 242–66. K. Jaitner, in *Wolfenbütteler Beiträge*, vii (1988), 273–404, places the special case of Pfalz-Sulzbach in a broad intellectual context. *Handbuch der historischen Stätten Schlesiens*, ed. H. Weczerka (Stuttgart 1977), provides a very useful guide to the politics and culture of Silesia. In Germany the Habsburgs reaped far more positive benefit from the Ottoman threat than in Austria, especially during the early part of our period: see the outstanding study by W. Schulze, *Reich und Türkengefahr im späten 16. Jahrhundert* (Munich 1978). Later developments in this sphere, touched on in numerous '1683–1983' contributions, have not, so far as I am aware, been comprehensively investigated.

The world of Baroque learning in the Danubian lands (**Chapters 9–10**) is now attracting somewhat more attention. Most important are several studies by S. Sousedík: *Valerianus Magni. Versuch einer Erneuerung der christlichen Philosophie im 17. Jahrhundert* (St Augustin 1982); on Arriaga in *Studia Comeniana et Historica*, xxvi (1983), 20–61 (also in Spanish in *Ibero-Americana Pragensia*, xv |1981|, 103–46); on Marci in *Studia Comeniana et Historica*, xxxiii (1987), 58–86; and, on Bohemian Scotists, *Jan Duns Scotus . . . a* *jeho čeští žáci* (Pr. 1989). For Magni see also the reflections of C. Vasoli in *Italia, Venezia e Polonia*, ed. V. Branca and S. Graciotti (Florence 1980), 79–112, and the massive bibliography by J. Cygan (Rome 1989), who also prints the fullest MS life. On Caramuel see D. Pastini, *Juan Caramuel: probabilismo ed enciclopedia* (Florence 1975); on Schyrl see A. Thewes, *Oculus Enoch* . . . (Oldenburg 1983). Kepler, of course, continues to fascinate historians of science; cf. the recent work of J. Field, as in *Archive for History of Exact Sciences*, xxxi (1984), 189–272, on his astrology, G. König, 'Peter Lambeck, Bibliothekar Kaiser Leopolds I.', *MIÖG* lxxxvii (1979), 121–66, is a limited treatment; whereas P. Preiss, *Boje s dvouhlavou saní. František Antonín Špork a barokní kultura v Čechách* (Pr. 1981), respresents a major critical reassessment of this significant and controversial figure.

The subject of Baroque popular culture (**Chapter 11**) is in the process of being rediscovered by new research. Witch-trials are particularly prominent. The pioneering investigations for Hungary by the late F. Schram (cf. below, p. 399 n. 44) were completed with his *Magyarországi boszorkányperek, 1529–1768*, vol. iii (Bp. 1982), which brings additional trial proceedings and a conspectus of the whole phenomenon. That is now supplemented by lively chapters in G. Klaniczay. *The Uses of Supernatural Power. The Transformations of Popular Religion in Medieval and Early Modern Europe* (Cambridge 1990). For Austria see the important essays in *Hexen und Zauberer. Die große Verfolgung: ein europäisches Phänomen in der Steiermark*, ed. H. Valentinitsch (Graz-V. 1987), and H. Dienst, *Hexen und Zauberei in den österreichischen Ländern* (V. 1987). For Bohemia see B. Šindelář, *Hon na čarodějnice* (Pr. 1986). Cf. also the major treatment of Bavaria: W. Behringer, *Hexenverfolgung in Bayern* (Munich 1987). An important source for this and other aspects of popular heterodoxy in the Bohemian lands is the continuing edition of *smolné knihy* (cf. below, p. 403 n. 52): see especially *Krevní kniha městečka Bojkovic*, ed. A. Verbík (Uherské Hradiště 1971); *Černá kniha města Velké Bíteše*, ed. Verbík *et al.* (Brno 1979); *Smolná kniha městečka Divišova z let 1617–1751*, ed. J. Pánek (Pr. 1977); and id. in *Středočeský Sborník Historický*, xii (1977), 129–81, xiii (1978), 87–195, xiv (1979), 71–109. On poverty, sickness, etc., literature has started to burgeon: e.g. the vol. on 'Alltag im 16. Jahrhundert', ed. A. Kohler and H. Lutz, *Wiener Beiträge zur Geschichte der*

Neuzeit, xiv (1987). Cf. the earlier, very detailed study by E. Nowotny, *Geschichte des Wiener Hofspitals* (V. 1978). For a challenging new interpretation of Jewish–Gentile relations see J. I. Israel, *European Jewry in the Age of Mercantilism*, *1550–1750* (Oxford 1985).

The broader horizons of the Baroque's 'world mission' in Central Europe (**Chapter 12**) encompassed a man whose career, only touched on here, continues to attract attention: Križanić. See *Život i djelo Jurja Križanića*, ed. R. Pavić (Zagreb 1974); *Juraj Križanić, Russophile and Ecumenic Visionary*, ed. T. Eekman and A. Kadić (The Hague 1976), with materials on his relation to Kircher, Caramuel, etc.; and *Juraj Križanić: sabrana građa*, ed. I. Golub (Zagreb 1983). Fresh documentation of Serbian relations with Rome has been begun by M. Jacov (ed.), *Spisi Kongregacije za propaganda viere u Rimu o srbima*, *1622–44*, vol. i (Belgrade 1986). For Bohemian missionaries see R. Grulich, *Der Beitrag der böhmischen Länder zur Weltmission des 17. und 18. Jahrhunderts* (Königstein im Taunus 1981), and some chapters in *Česká touha cestovatelská: cestopisy, deníky a listy ze 17. století*, ed. S. Binková and J. Polišenský (Pr. 1989). On the Vasa episode in Breslau: G. Ćwięczek, 'Królewicz Karol Ferdynand Waza jako biskup wrocławski', in *Studia z historii kościoła w Polsce*, ii (Warsaw 1973), 7–269. The intellectual world of Baroque art and literature, especially in Bohemia, formed a lifelong preoccupation of the distinguished Czech historian, Zdeněk Kalista (1900–82): his last work, *Tvář baroka* (Munich 1982), affords a retrospect as well as many new suggestions.

Some early eighteenth-century ramifications of the themes treated here (**Epilogue**) may now be approached through a political biography by C. W. Ingrao, *In Quest and Crisis: Emperor Joseph I and the Habsburg Monarchy* (West Lafayette 1979). Charles VI remains neglected, but cf. the massive and controversial analysis of his artistic patronage by F. Matsche, *Die Kunst im Dienst der Staatsidee Kaiser Karls VI.*, i–ii (Berlin-New York 1981). For detailed bibliography of the age of Maria Theresa and Joseph II see *Österreich im Europa der Aufklärung. Kontinuität und Zäsur in Europa zur Zeit Maria Theresias und Josephs II*, i–ii (V. 1985). I have sketched some aspects of the cultural evolution in *Das achtzehnte Jahrhundert und Österreich*, ii (1985), 9–31. Finally, there are two works which, though their concern is basically the society of Maria Theresa's time and its material circumstances, reveal much of relevance for an earlier period: E. Hassenpflug-Elzholz, *Böhmen und die böhmischen Stände in der Zeit des beginnenden Zentralismus. Eine Strukturanalyse der böhmischen Adelsnation um die Mitte des 18. Jahrhunderts* (Munich 1982), and especially P. G. M. Dickson, *Finance and Government under Maria Theresia, 1740–1780*, i–ii (Oxford 1987).

Brasenose College, Oxford   R.J.W.E.
January 1991

Prologue

Three great changes remoulded Central Europe in the early part of the sixteenth century: one gradual; one sudden; the third a sudden stroke with gradually unfolding implications. First came the impact of the Renaissance, which had reached the cultivated entourage of King Matthias Corvinus in Hungary well before 1500. Soon the restored values of classical civilization took deeper root: men like Conrad Celtes animated university circles from Freiburg to Cracow with the new standards; prosperous burghers encouraged trade in books and works of art; rulers and their mightier subjects sustained the manner—if not always the exuberance—of the Corvine court. Native talents began to emerge: Janus Pannonius and then Bohuslav of Lobkovic, two of the great neo-Latin poets; Cuspinian, Gelenius, and other scholars; the architect Benedikt Rejt and the painters of the Danube school; the artists who clustered around Emperor Maximilian I. The style and character of the Renaissance, however, were international; a Catholic Humanism which, while urging reform in some directions, operated within the existing framework of belief.

Around 1520 a second international movement launched a much more violent assault on traditional attitudes: the Reformation. Lutheranism proved immediately effective, and though it drew on a variety of local fears and discontents—the turmoil of Turkish advance, the legacy of Hussite ideas, urban critique of the German church, the ingrained dissent of Alpine valleys, the chiliastic expectations of some popular preachers—nevertheless it followed a remarkably similar course throughout the region. Within a decade Protestant teachings could be heard everywhere, from guarded *sola fides* by the castle precinct in Buda or Prague to Anabaptist rantings in Tyrolese wayside pulpits. Initially the message seemed hostile to all secular culture, the fervour and fundamental stance condemning new learning no less than monkish scholasticism. But very quickly Humanists and Reformers found common ground in a range of

activities from Biblical exegesis to popular education, and their
meeting was to be far more than a merely temporal coincidence.

Meanwhile the same unsettled years witnessed a political turning-
point: the coming of age of the Habsburg dynasty. Having by 1519
secured themselves, in the person of Charles V, as rulers over
Germany and Spain, the Habsburgs were well placed to exploit the
extraordinary windfall of the battle of Mohács in 1526. For the ill
wind which blew the childless Louis II of Bohemia and Hungary to
destruction at the hands of Suleiman the Magnificent among the
swamps of the middle Danube allowed the Habsburgs, in the person
of Charles's younger brother Ferdinand, to add that dual sovereignty
to their inherited lands (*Erblande*) of Austria. And Ferdinand, one
of the family's shrewdest, most resilient characters, willingly took
up the task of bringing order to his patrimony. As yet a 'Monarchy'
in the heart of Europe existed only *in posse*: where imperial
government (to which Ferdinand at length likewise succeeded)
meant conflict with the separatist desires of German princes and
close liaison with Spanish interests, Austrian rule demanded minute
attention to immediate provincial grievance; where Bohemian
kingship brought the problems of a country long cast into resentful
isolation from its neighbours, the Hungarian crown embroiled its
wearer in crippling campaigns against the Ottomans and in the
strange ways of Magyar nationhood. The extent of Habsburg
success in harnessing such disparate elements would depend in
good measure on the policies they adopted towards Renaissance and
Reformation.

By 1550, with its new intellectual, religious, and political points
of departure given, Central Europe embarked on a protracted and
highly complex period of transition, a 150-year era which was
simultaneously 'early modern' (as historians west of Vienna would
say) and also 'late feudal' (as their colleagues further east now
insist). Nowhere else did modern and feudal not only overlap, but
actually coalesce. Two different kinds of evolution were competing
to modify local horizons and time-honoured particularism: one
tended to integrate Central Europe ever more into broad continental
developments; the other tended to create a distinct Central
European entity, independent without and interdependent within.
At first, roughly during the sixteenth century, Renaissance and
Protestantism dominated, thoroughly international movements in

a comparatively open society; Habsburg power, with its implication of distinctive sovereignty for the area, appeared largely formal, an accident of place and genealogy. In the end, however, Habsburg authority, and with it a comparatively closed society, became firmly established, triumphing over the vestiges of Renaissance and the ruins of Protestantism. Nevertheless the dynasty only triumphed thanks to a universal (imperial) ideology and a revived cosmopolitan (Catholic) Church, while the currents of thought and faith which it vanquished would later return—ironically enough—in the guise of nationalist (i.e. localist) oppositions.

Such, in confusing brevity, are the main lines of the historical process which this book will seek to describe and analyse. Ultimately the Monarchy was made by Baroque and Counter-Reformation; the decisive years for its formation lay in the seventeenth century. For nearly a hundred years after 1526 the self-sufficiency of the different regions remained very great: diets, administrative bodies, social fabric, traditional loyalties, old ways of thinking. Neither Ferdinand nor his immediate successors seriously threatened it. By the same token those dynamic elements which hinted at the birth of a new commonwealth were less tangible: the beginnings of cultural symbiosis, the myriad subtle attractions of the Habsburg court. Yet as the genesis of Baroque must be sought in Renaissance, of Counter-Reformation in the movement instigated by Luther; so our investigation must start before 1600: with a brief Golden Age, peaceful, prosperous, and expansive on the whole, when the Danube lands—with the blessing of their rulers Maximilian II and Rudolf II—belonged perhaps more nearly to Western Europe than at any other time before or since.

Part One

THE GENERAL EVOLUTION

CHAPTER I

The false dawn, 1550–1600:
Renaissance and Reformation

By the middle of the sixteenth century the ethos of the Austrian Habsburg lands was Protestant. That cannot be a precise statement; rather it indicates what religion was *not*. Catholic observance ebbed away: vestments were stored up or sold, relics and hallowed observances decried, sacraments no longer revered. Reformation embraced both town and country: while burghers willingly adapted to the freer climate, landowners strengthened their influence over the rural Church, acquiring some of its lands in fief or by outright purchase, and peasants showed no conspicuous devotion to the old priesthood. Where the distinction between town and country was blurred innovations made an especially dramatic advance: in mining settlements, among the mobile population of artisans and traders. The authority of Catholic precept decayed fast; in everything from choice of Christian names to wording of epitaphs the new fashion dominated. Visitations of the archdiocese of Salzburg reveal lamentable conditions. A provincial synod held in 1549, though it assembled what remained of lustre in the hierarchy of the old Church and enacted stringent decrees on discipline, dogma, and general order, met with resistance from all sides, or else was ignored altogether. Scripture everywhere came to be preached in a popular idiom and vernacular Bibles passed from hand to hand; everywhere, that is, except for those large areas which had no spiritual ministration of any kind.[1]

Clearest sign of all: the monasteries, repositories of Catholic tradition and privilege, atrophied. Not merely in Hungary, where the Turkish wars destroyed many and gave rapacious nobles a free hand to disturb the rest; not merely in Bohemia, where the coenobites had barely survived the Hussite troubles and their

---

[1] T. Wiedemann, *Geschichte der Reformation und Gegenreformation im Lande unter der Enns*, i–v (Pr.–Leipzig 1879–86), i, 132–94 and *passim*; K. Eder, *Glaubensspaltung und Landstände in Österreich ob der Enns, 1525–1602* (Linz 1936), 80 ff. J. Loserth, 'Die salzburger Provinzialsynode von 1549', *AÖG* lxxxv (1898), 131–356.

situation was still perilous; but also in Austria, with its many and prosperous religious houses. In 1563 Lower Austria had 122 monasteries—with 463 monks, 160 nuns, 199 concubines, 55 wives, and 443 children.[2] Twenty years after the first Salzburg synod a second was prepared by the Italian Dominican Ninguarda, but the hopelessness of its task emerges from the friar's own observations on the abysmal conditions among regular clergy. Most houses were now largely denuded of inmates, or sustained a residual colony of Italians. When Ninguarda's colleague, Cardinal Commendone, visited the great monastery of St. Florian in 1569 he found no one who could even converse in Latin; the same happened at Wilten, near Innsbruck, in 1578. Vorau had sixteen canons in 1528, only one by 1545; Lambach sank from nine monks to one between 1534 and 1554; the Premonstratensian foundation of Schlägl was likewise reduced by 1566 to one inhabitant, its married Lutheran prior; in that year the new administrator to Göttweig found no monks there at all.[3]

Not only did a climate of laxness prevail, quite alien to the ideals of chastity and asceticism, but many clergy positively espoused Protestant tenets. Klosterneuburg, with all its incorporated parishes, was clearly Protestant under the Humanist provost Hübner and his successor Hintermayr; so was Wilhering in Upper Austria. At Admont, remote among the Styrian Alps, the rector of the monastery school taught the Lutheran catechism with full approval

[2] E. Tomek, *Kirchengeschichte Österreichs*, ii (1439–1648) (Innsbruck 1949), 221 ff. On Hungary in general: D. Fuxhoffer, *Monasteriologia Regni Hungariae*, ed. M. Czinár, i–ii (3rd edn. V.–Esztergom 1869). On Bohemia in general: A. Frind, *Die Kirchengeschichte Böhmens*, iv (Pr. 1878), 202–371. For particular views: S. E. Kapihorský, *Hystorya Klásstera Sedleckého* (Pr. 1630), 85 ff.; A. Zerlik, 'Das Stift Tepl in der Zeit der Glaubensspaltung', *Anal. Praem.* xxxvii (1961), 262–81; xxxviii (1962), 93–110; xxxix (1963), 70–131, 257–66, at 263 ff., 93 ff.

[3] K. Schellhass, *Der Dominikaner Felician Ninguarda und die Gegenreformation in Süddeutschland und Österreich*, i (Rome 1930), 46 ff. and *passim*; id., 'Felician Ninguarda's Visitationstätigkeit in den österreichischen Kronlanden von Ende 1572 bis März 1576', *Stud. u. Mitt.* xxiii (1902), 126–54; M. Mayr, 'Cardinal Commendones Kloster- und Kirchen-Visitation von 1569 in den Diöcesen Passau und Salzburg', ibid. xiv (1893), 385–98, 567–89. H. S. Szántó, 'Reformversuche im Stifte Wilten nach dem Konzil von Trient', *Anal. Praem.* xxxv (1959), 56–78, 227–64; *Ein Chorherrenbuch*, ed. S. Brunner (Würzburg–V. 1883), 658 f.; *Ein Benediktinerbuch*, ed. S. Brunner (Würzburg, n.d.), 187, 137 f.; N. Backmund, *Monasticon Praemonstratense*, i–iii (Straubing 1949–59), i, 308–10. For the decay of one of Austria's most celebrated medieval houses: I. Keiblinger, *Geschichte des Stiftes Melk* (V. 1851), 739 ff.

of his abbot, who was forced to resign in 1568 for patronizing profane learning. At Garsten two more Benedictine abbots were deposed, one of them leaving only a pair of colleagues behind and ending his life as an innkeeper. Few monasteries could boast their own, freely elected head: even Rein, oldest of the Cistercian houses, called in a secular administrator. Those chosen were often spendthift, like Steingaden of Zwettl, or Jakob von Sternowitz who frittered away what remained of Strahov's estates around Prague. Some properties were alienated within the Church—Ossegg and Žd'ár to the local bishop; others outside it, as Schlierbach to the Jörger family. Almost all the hundreds of houses in Hungary were deserted and secularized, not just under Ottoman pressure; its most historic community, the Benedictines at Pannonhalma, dispersed long before the Turks occupied their hilltop site in the 1590s.[4]

The principal political beneficiaries of Protestant advance were the estates: nobles and cities in the various territories. Freeing them from the rivalry of prelates, the new religion gave them an access of strength and confidence in their dealings with the still Catholic prince. It has often been asserted that they deliberately provoked the secularizing movement to this end, and equally often counter-asserted that the estates merely provided a vehicle for authentic popular disillusion. Neither proposition is adequate to the complexity of the process. In reality confusion was rampant, and much novelty grew out of sheer misunderstanding, as usage varied from parish to parish. Ministers and their flocks halted at different points on the road from an old to a new observance, guided by a blend of conviction and convenience. No central control could pull the ravelled threads together, since the dynasty—anyway weakened by this unprecedented disenchantment with sanctified authority—did not agree with the high clergy over the proper means of stemming

[4] F. Röhrig, 'Protestantismus und Gegenreformation im Stift Klosterneuburg und seinen Pfarren', *Jb. d. St. Klnb.* N.F. i (1961), 105–70, at 116–35; J. Stülz, *Geschichte des Cistercienser-Klosters Wilhering* (Linz 1840), 87 ff. E. Böhl, *Beiträge zur Geschichte der Reformation in Österreich* (Jena 1902), 260–3; *Benediktinerbuch*, 56 f. G. E. Friess, 'Geschichte des Benediktiner-Stiftes Garsten in Oberösterreich', *Stud. und Mitt.* ii (1881), 4, 251–66, at 253–8. *Ein Cisterzienserbuch*, ed. S. Brunner (Würzburg 1881), 381–3 (Rein), 580 f. (Zwettl), 303 ff. (Osek and Žd'ár), 414 ff. (Schlierbach). *Chorherrenbuch*, 565 f. (Strahov). L. Erdélyi and P. Sörös (eds.), *A pannonhalmi Szent Benedek-Rend története*, i–xii (Bp. 1902–12), iv, with much detail; summarized in *Benediktinerbuch*, 218 ff. Cf. R. Békefi, *Zirc ... története*, i–v (Pécs-Bp. 1891–1902), and *Cisterzienserbuch*, 522 ff.

the tide, while the forces of opposition were ill-defined, hesitantly led, and balanced one against another in their essentially provincial standpoints. As time passed, doctrinal unity among the Protestants proved ever more of a mirage, though—as we shall see—a uniform Renaissance culture profited rather than suffered from its absence.

★

Lutheranism had its easiest path to German-speakers, and preachers from Saxony soon began persuading their southern neighbours to follow the orthodoxy of Wittenberg. Lower Austria, especially its chief town of Vienna, was early convinced, but not until the 1560s did Protestant spokesmen feel a need to press for formal recognition of the new religion. At the diet of 1568 they elicited from Maximilian II a grant of free exercise of the Lutheran faith for nobles and their subjects. Church leaders, under David Chytraeus, now drew up an *Agenda*, or form of worship, which the emperor sanctioned four years later. In fact the movement had not made much official progress, since Maximilian regarded legal permission as an act of grace and refused to extend it to the towns. Moreover, disputes in the Lutheran camp cramped its style and no full organization was created.[5]

Meanwhile, across the river Enns, the Upper Austrians pursued a similar course, without being willing to join Vienna on a common platform. Indeed the estates at Linz fought a fight on three fronts: against the neighbouring bishop of Passau, against the Habsburg ruler, and against their overbearing compatriots in Lower Austria. They too gained verbal but not constitutional guarantees from Maximilian and squandered much energy on disputes over ubiquitism and original sin.[6] Further south, the provinces of Inner Austria: Styria, Carinthia, Carniola, were by the death of Emperor Ferdinand almost wholly Protestant in sentiment. Under the rule of Maximilian's younger brother Karl they demanded full legal

---

[5] The classic work on the Austrian Protestants is Bernhard Raupach, *Evangelisches Oesterreich*, i–iii (Hamburg 1741–4). Modern accounts are G. Loesche, *Geschichte des Protestantismus im vormaligen und im neuen Österreich* (3rd edn. V.–Leipzig 1930), 79 ff; and—briefer but fairer—G. Mecenseffy, *Geschichte des Protestantismus in Österreich* (Graz 1956), 50–61. Cf. V. Bibl, 'Die Organisation des evangelischen Kirchenwesens im Erzherzogtum Österreich unter der Enns 1568–76', *AÖG* lxxxvii (1899), 113–228; and below, pp. 53 f.

[6] Eder, *Glaubensspaltung*, esp. 113–21.

reception of the Augsburg Confession. A protracted and acrimonious debate ensued; it led to a pacification in 1572, then to a bitter diet at Bruck an der Mur six years later when the estates threatened to withdraw from all co-operation with the dynasty. Eventually they also achieved the required safeguards, which were extended to cover Lutheran observance in the towns as well as on the land, though again the assurance was only verbal and allowed of conflicting interpretations.[7]

Germans in Bohemia readily accepted Luther's teachings, and some of the Reformer's chief lieutenants worked among them, notably Johann Mathesius, the imaginative apostle of the miners in the Erzgebirge. But of course the whole of Bohemia was classic Evangelical terrain, and the movement soon showed that it could harness the latent energies of the Hussite legacy. Even in Austria Lutheranism attracted not only Germans but a substantial Slovene population in Carniola and along the valley of the Drava. Many Czechs took up Lutheran positions, though they tended still to seek the protection of their time-honoured 'Utraquist' label. At the stormy diet of 1575 Maximilian, faced with a temporary coalition of Protestant forces, promised not to disturb their worship. His stance was not constitutionally binding and the situation remained confused, orthodox Lutherans of both language groups being flanked by more traditional Hussites and the sterner doctrine of the Bohemian Brethren.[8] In Hungary too the doctrines of Wittenberg appealed first to Germans. The close-knit community of Saxons in Transylvania embraced them, not without wobbling for decades on major theological points; so did most of the German settlers in Upper Hungary. At the same time many Slovaks toed the

---

[7] J. Loserth (ed.), *Acten und Correspondenzen zur Geschichte der Gegenreformation in Innerösterreich unter Karl II und Ferdinand II*, i–ii in 3 vols. (V. 1898–1907), i; id., *Die Reformation und Gegenreformation in den innerösterreichischen Ländern im XVI Jahrhundert* (Stuttgart 1898), 141–204, 247–84; Loesche, *Protestantismus*, 234 ff.; Mecenseffy, op. cit. 61–5.

[8] F. Hrejsa, *Česká Konfesse, její vznik, podstata a dějiny* (Pr. 1912); Loesche, *Protestantismus*, 234 ff. In general: F. Hrejsa, *Dějiny křest'anství v Československu*, v–vi (1526–76) (Pr. 1948–50), a chronicle of ecclesiastical history with much useful detail; R. J. W. Evans, *Rudolf II and his World* (Oxford 1973), hereafter *Rudolf II*), 29 ff. (and 246 on Mathesius); and the most recent sketch: K. Richter in *Handbuch der Geschichte der böhmischen Länder*, ed. K. Bosl, i–iv (Stuttgart 1966–74), ii, 111–28, 167–76.

Evangelical line and Magyars scrutinized it carefully before passing, in general, to more radical solutions.[9] Lutheranism thus made a deep impression on Central Europe, but it never secured full dogmatic harmony in any one territory, let alone the kind of overall *rapport* between territories which would have assured it of political dominance. Many of its principal theorists, like Chytraeus of Rostock whom we have already encountered, were foreign preachers, and their efforts to press a clerical orthodoxy on the lay supporters of the faith—noble protectors, town councils, guilds—generated an added tension. Moreover, from the 1550s Lutherans felt the competition of Swiss models, as what began with individual questions to Bullinger, Bucer, or Beza on doubtful issues turned gradually towards a more thorough profession of Calvinism.

Calvinism made its greatest gains in Hungary. By 1570 it had largely won the debate among the Magyar population, especially on the great plainlands where shifting and imprecise borders marked the limits of Habsburg, Turkish, and Transylvanian authority. Its propagators organized a succession of synods in such centres as Debrecen, and its leaders: Kálmáncsehi, Méliusz, Huszár, above all Szegedi Kis, were men of real intellectual substance.[10] Some have seen the Hungarians' shift from the Confession of Augsburg to that of Geneva as an overt reaction against the Germanic associations of Lutheranism, even against a German language which few of them commanded readily; but the truth is more complicated. In fact large numbers of Magyars continued to attend Wittenberg University until their orthodoxy became suspect to the Saxon government, while their later loyalties were directed just as

---

[9] On the Saxons, most recently, E. Roth, *Die Reformation in Siebenbürgen*, i–ii (Cologne–Graz 1962–4); cf. F. Teutsch, *Geschichte der evangelischen Kirche in Siebenbürgen*, i–ii (Hermannstadt 1921–2), i. G. Bruckner, *A reformáció és ellenreformáció története a Szepességben*, i (Bp. 1922). In general: P. Bod, *Historia Hungarorum Ecclesiastica*, ed. L. W. E. Rauwenhoff *et al.*, i–iii (Leiden 1888–90), i, bk. 2, and M. Bucsay, *Geschichte des Protestantismus in Ungarn* (Stuttgart 1959), 33 ff.

[10] Bucsay, op. cit. 42 ff. is very brief. Best is I. Révész, *Magyar református egyháztörténet*, i (Debrecen 1938), esp. 97 ff. (on the theoretical debates). Much documentation in F. A. Lampe [really Pál Ember of Debrecen], *Historia Ecclesiae Reformatae in Hungaria et Transilvania* (Utrecht 1728), pt. 2, 101 ff., including synodal debates. L. Földvári, *Szegedi Kiss István élete és a Tisza-Duna mellékének reformációja* (Bp. 1894).

much towards Heidelberg and Basle as towards the Huguenot patriarchs of international Calvinism. Hungarian adherence to the new faith was anyway not clear-cut. In the west of the country discussion of the Eucharist and predestination long proceeded in a low key; even the more militant east went its own way, with home-grown politicians and a homespun theology only slowly penetrated by the precision of Genevan precept.[11]

In Bohemia too a substantial minority progressively adopted a Calvinism which came to maturity at the end of the century with the career of Amandus Polanus, a native of Troppau in Silesia, who succeeded his father-in-law Grynaeus as the leading theologian of Basle. Swiss influences were felt especially strongly among the congregations of Bohemian (or Czech) Brethren which alone preserved the authentic flavour of radical Hussitism. The Brethren had a sturdy and self-contained organization, well-established lay participation, a distaste for frills and ceremonies, along with narrowly-defined rules of personal conduct. At the same time they were not sympathetic to minute doctrinal argument or clear political commitment, and so they never accepted all the implications of West-European Calvinism, still less submerged their own identity in any common Protestant cause.[12] In Austria, though the number of Calvinists was smaller, they carried considerable public weight, since the most resourceful of the nobility seized on a faith which gave greater leverage to their programme of estates' domination. Georg Erasmus Tschernembl, who would lead this party after 1600,

---

[11] M. Asztalos, 'A wittenbergi egyetem és a magyarországi kálvinizmus', *BÉ*, ii (1932), 81–94, and id., 'A wittenbergi egyetem magyar hallgatóinak nyelvismerete a XVI században', *Egyetemes Philológiai Közlöny*, 1934, 1–11; criticized by Révész, loc. cit. and 'Szempontok a magyar "kálvinizmus" eredetének vizsgálatához', *Sz* lxviii (1934), 257–75; cf. id., *Méliusz és Kálvin* (Cluj 1936). G. Szabó, *Geschichte des ungarischen Coetus an der Universität Wittenberg, 1555–1613* (Halle 1941); and cf. below, pp. 26–31. B. Nagy in T. Bartha (ed.), *A Heidelbergi Káté jelentkezése, története és kiadásai Magyarországon a XVI és XVII században* (Bp. 1965), 19–91; and see below, pp. 54 f.

[12] On Calvinism in general: Hrejsa, *Dějiny*. E. Staehelin, *Amandus Polanus von Polansdorf* (Basle 1955). On the Brethren there is the contemporary view of Joachim Camerarius, *Historica Narratio de fratrum orthodoxorum Ecclesiis* (Heidelberg [1605]), esp. 145 ff., 263 ff.; the thorough narrative in A. Gindely, *Geschichte der Böhmischen Brüder*, i–ii (Pr. 1868); and the modern summary ed. R. Říčan, *Jednota Bratrská 1457–1957* (Pr. 1956), esp. 13–104 and 111–45. Various works by O. Odložilík are important, the last being *Jednota Bratrská a reformovaní francouzského jazyka* (Philadelphia 1964).

showed open enthusiasm for his French and Dutch co-religionists.[13]

Alongside the major confessions there flourished a multitude of sects. The Reformation's wilder offshoots took two directions in Central Europe. Popular Anabaptism, very widespread during the troubled 1520s, retreated afterwards into defensive communities of zealots who lived a simple peasant life of self-help and discipline. The Anabaptists enjoyed open toleration in Moravia and may have survived in considerable numbers elsewhere—though the evidence is very patchy—from the well-documented followers of Jakob Hutter to obscure radical groups hidden even from contemporary gaze. But observers were well aware of the variety of their teachings. One malicious commentator describes twenty-five different persuasions in Moravia alone, with such choice names as Adamites, Stablarians, Clancularians, Manifestarians, Demoniacs, Concubites, and Grubenhamerites.[14]

The second kind of sectarianism was led by intellectual extremists, especially those who rejected the doctrine of the Trinity. It developed more slowly, under the impact of exiles from Italy, striking local roots above all in eastern Hungary, where the remarkable Ferenc Dávid, having passed from Catholicism through Lutheranism to Calvinism, now produced a stirring rationale for complete denial of traditional beliefs. In Transylvania the Unitarians achieved influence and even respectability, though coherence was always at a premium. By the 1580s they had split into an exclusive, dogmatic sect which, inspired by Dávid, embraced a sort of Judaic Christianity, and a broader movement of reasoned scepticism.[15] The latter maintained links with like-minded groups in neighbouring Poland, as well as secretive feelers towards non-conformists in the Habsburg lands. The advanced freethinkers among Central European Arians: Dávid, Palaeologus, Francken, Dudith, fiercely controversial in their time, rescued from obscurity in our own,

[13] H. Sturmberger, *Georg Erasmus Tschernembl* (Linz 1953), early chs.

[14] A. Meshovius, *Historiae Anabaptisticae Libri 7* (Cologne 1617), 113–16. In general: G. H. Williams, *The Radical Reformation* (London 1962), esp. 165–76, 204–33, 410–14, 417–34, 670–84, 617–21; cf. the very different approach of C. P. Clasen, *Anabaptism, a social history* (Ithaca, N.Y. 1972).

[15] Révész, *Egyháztörténet*, 87 ff., 152 ff.; A. Pirnát, *Die Ideologie der Siebenbürger Antitrinitarier in den 1570er Jahren* (Bp. 1961), 161–87; J. Zoványi, *A magyarországi protestantizmus 1565-től 1600-ig*, op. posth. (Bp. 1977), 11–57, 101–37. On the extremists: S. Kohn, *Die Sabbatarier in Siebenbürgen* (Bp. 1894).

boldly adapted Protestantism to the philosophical ideals of the Renaissance and thereby extended the whole base of theological debate.[16]

*

The Austrian Habsburg territories thus supported a great range of religious opinion in the sixteenth century, from the Swabian *Vorlande* and the Tyrol, where Catholicism—after serious upsets— survived more or less intact,[17] to Transylvania, where the extremities of the Unitarians showed how far rethinking could proceed within the space of two generations. This diversity flowed in part, of course, from the different circumstances and attitudes of different confessional groups. Every Protestant Church laid due stress on schooling, to spread its own message as far as possible by means of instruction in the vernacular language. During its years of real confidence, after the middle of the century, the Reformation promoted discussion of all manner of new issues connected, however loosely, with the interpretation of Scripture.

Some of the educational fabric remained Catholic: Vienna University was not formally emancipated, Prague only partially so. Parish and monastic schools survived in places, reaching a *modus vivendi* with the prevailing climate.[18] But they were now supplanted by a network of far livelier institutions. Lutheran Austria drew on immigrants from the German academies to set up a system which, though uneven, seemed full of promise. The estates' schools at Linz

[16] D. Caccamo, *Eretici italiani in Moravia, Polonia, Transilvania (1558–1611)* (Florence–Chicago 1970) is most recent on their international links. For the Polish situation and the figure of Dudith see ibid., ch. 4, and Williams, op. cit. 639–69, 685–707, 733–63. On Palaeologus: *Rudolf II*, 108 f.; L. Szczucki, 'Jakub z Chios-Palaeolog', *Odrodzenie i Reformacja w Polsce*, xi (1966), 63–91; xiii (1968), 5–50; and I. Ch. Palaeologus, *Catechesis Christiana Dierum Duodecim*, ed. R. Dostálová (Warsaw 1971). On Francken: *Rudolf II*, 105; and L. Szczucki, 'Chrystian Francken', *Odrodzenie i Reformacja w Polsce*, viii (1963), 39–75. Cf. G. F. Lessing, 'Von Adam Neusern, einige authentische Nachrichten', in *Sämmtliche Schriften*, ed. K. Lachmann and W. von Maltzahn, ix (Leipzig 1855), 352–404.

[17] The position in the Vorlande (cf. below, p. 160) is too complicated and tangential to be surveyed here. The Tyrol had much Anabaptism and unrest in the 1520s, and some longer-lived Protestantism among the miners of the Inn valley; see the summary in Loesche, *Protestantismus*, 329–75. Its monasteries remained weak throughout the century, even Stams and Neustift, whose abbot gave refuge to Charles V in 1552 (*Cisterzienserbuch*, 433 ff; *Chorherrenbuch*, 429–31).

[18] e.g. the Rožmberk school at Český Krumlov: see J. Hejnic, *Českokrumlovská latinská škola v době rožmberské* (Pr. 1972).

and Vienna and the *Stiftsschule* at Graz pursued decent pedagogical goals with considerable efficiency, while the abler clergy stimulated interest at a local level, as a visitation of 1580 reveals.[19] In Bohemia Protestants of various hues vied with each other to advance the burgher schools which became so positive a feature of urban society there; while the Brethren tended to concentrate attention on smaller centres already dominated by their congregations. Fulnek, Velké Meziříčí, Ivančice, such places earned a reputation beyond the confines of the country for enlightened teaching combined with high standards of godliness.[20] In Hungary Calvinists led the field, establishing their own worthy seminaries at Debrecen and Sáros-patak, Pápa and Nagyvárad, and fighting off the challenge of the Unitarians within Transylvania.[21]

This thirst for education had its limits—the universities scarcely profited—and was certainly not free of prejudice. After all, it grew out of a belligerent, often selfish campaign against the old Church and was designed to sustain divergent justifications of the new ones. But the broadened theological spectrum brought, of necessity, a basic widening of horizons. By the end of the sixteenth century Protestant Central Europe had come to participate in all the main intellectual issues of the day. We can observe the process with

---

[19] There is much local historical material on schools, but little synthesis. See Loesche, *Protestantismus*, 90–4, 162–5, 227–30; Loserth, *Reformation und Gegenreformation*, 204–30, and id., *Die protestantischen Schulen der Steiermark im 16. Jahrhundert* (Berlin 1916); A. Dimitz, *Geschichte Krains*, i–ii (Laibach 1874–6), pt. 3, 155–83; K. Gutkas, *Geschichte des Landes Niederösterreich* (4th edn. St. Pölten 1973), 184 f., 211 f. Tomek, *Kirchengeschichte*, 348–90, *passim*, gives visitation evidence, based on Raupach.

[20] Z. Winter, *Život a učeni na partikulárních školách v Čechách v 15. a 16. stoletich* (Pr. 1901), a mass of undigested information; J. Holinková, *Městská škola na Moravě v předbělohorském období* (Pr. 1967); F. Palacký, 'Obyvatelstvo českých měst a školní vzdělání v 16. a na začátku 17. století', *ČsČH* xviii (1970), 345–68. There is much on individual schoolmasters in J. Hejnic and J. Martinek (eds.), *Rukověť' humanistického básnictvi v Čechách a na Moravě*, i—(Pr. 1966—). On the Brethren: J. Müller, *Die deutschen Katechismen der Böhmischen Brüder* (Berlin 1887), esp. pt. 4. They attracted foreign pupils, like the Austrian, Enenkel: A. Coreth, 'Job Hartmann von Enenkel', *MIÖG* lv (1944), 247–302, at 258 f. Cf. below, n. 22.

[21] V. Frankl, *A hazai és külföldi iskolázás a XVI században* (Bp. 1873), 3–192. Further bibliography in D. Kosáry, *Bevezetés a magyar történelem forrásaiba és irodalmába*, i–iii (Bp. 1951), i, 265–7. For a contemporary impression see S. Bagyary, *A magyar művelődés a XVI–XVII században Szamosközy I. történeti maradványai alapján* (Esztergom 1907), 121 ff. On Sárospatak: I. Mészáros in *Comenius and Hungary*, ed. E. Földes and I. Mészáros (Bp. 1973), 111–32.

Reformers like Johann Honter among the Transylvanian Saxons or Valentin Trotzendorf in Silesia—indeed Silesian schools laid the foundation for that province's remarkable Humanistic achievements. Most strikingly of all, we can follow the Bohemian Brethren in their progress from obscurantist sectarians to impassioned educators, the preceptors of Comenius, through the work of Jan Blahoslav, Esrom Rüdiger, and others.[22]

The further practical consequence of such variegated patterns of faith was a widespread *de facto* toleration: not a merit of the Reformation, but the very atmosphere in which it operated, tantamount to its lack of any clear focus. 'In affairs of religion everyone does as he pleases, and thus something like peace obtains between the parties,' observes one censorious Catholic, and the thought is seconded by a Lutheran: 'In Austria there is almost too much liberty in religion, since all those who have been banished from the rest of Germany for whatever reason flood to it with impunity.' 'At Prague, that populous and dirty place,' noted the Huguenot Prince de Rohan in 1600, 'there is no German sect of which one cannot find some trace.'[23] After the 1520s little religious violence broke out and serious persecution was very rare throughout the century, Ferdinand's attack on the Bohemian Brethren for a few years from 1547 being the clearest case. The traditional Catholic edifice still stood, partly because it enjoyed the protection of the dynasty, more importantly because no single Protestant group had the strength or organization to replace it.

The amorphous politico-religious situation meant that little effective censorship could be practised. Civil and ecclesiastical

---

[22] O. Wittstock, *Johannes Honterus, der Siebenbürger Humanist und Reformator* (Göttingen 1970). G. Bauch, *Valentin Trotzendorf und die Goldberger Schule* (Berlin 1921), and id., *Geschichte des Breslauer Schulwesens in der Zeit der Reformation* (Breslau 1911), both very detailed; cf. E. Michael, 'Die schlesische Dorfschule im 16. Jahrhundert', *ZVGAS* lxiii (1929), 227–61. On the broadening horizons of the Brethren there is much information in *Sborník Blahoslavův*, ed. V. Novotný and R. Urbánek (Přerov 1923); *Jan Blahoslav, předchůdce J. A. Komenského*, ed. S. Bimka and P. Floss (?Uherský Brod ?1973); A. Molnár, *Českobratrská výchova před Komenským* (Pr. 1956).

[23] V. Bibl, 'Die Berichte des Reichshofrates Dr. Georg Eder an die Herzoge Albrecht und Wilhelm von Bayern über die Religionskrise in Niederösterreich (1579–87)', *Jb. f. Lk. v. NÖ* N.F. viii (1909), 67–154, at 136; id., 'Organisation , 135 (quoting David Chytraeus in 1574); *Voyage de Duc de Rohan faict en l'an 1600...* (Amsterdam 1646).

authorities tried to control printing, but their successes before the end of the century were few.[24] Book production developed apace: not in the occasional great enterprise but, with its very dispersed resources, in a plethora of small concerns. Hungary had migrant printers alongside the sturdy burgher undertakings of Lutheran Bartfeld or Calvinist Debrecen. Bohemia had long-standing and sophisticated publishing at Prague beside little provincial operators. The presence of the dynasty at Vienna gave the Catholic side a disproportionate influence there, but false imprints and pseudonyms could easily be employed, and officials connived at booksellers filling their shops with imported literature. The Transylvanian Arians purveyed their wildly heterodox views through presses both domestic and foreign.[25]

Some remarkable vernacular religious publications saw the light of day against this background. The Bohemian Brethren issued a handsome and authoritative Czech version of Scripture from the tiny Moravian town of Kralice (first in six volumes, then collected together in a single volume). Gáspár Károlyi worked almost unaided against great odds to produce the earliest complete Magyar Bible in a small village church on the edge of the dusty Hungarian plain. A classic series of Slovene religious translations accompanied the

---

[24] T. Wiedemann, 'Die kirchliche Büchercensur in der Erzdiöcese Wien', *AÖG* l (1873), 215–520, at 215 ff. on the activities of the bishop of Vienna; R. Peinlich, 'Zur Geschichte des Buchdruckes, der Büchercensur und des Buchhandels zu Graz im 16. Jahrhundert', *MHVSt.* xxvii (1879), 136–73; F. Menčik, 'Censura v Čechách a na Moravě', *VKČSN*, 1888, 85–136, at 85 ff. The documents in F. Tischer, 'Příspěvek k dějinám censury za arcibiskupa Antonína Brusa', *Listy Filologické* xxxii (1905), 258–71, 376–9, also suggest a general lack of achievement. Cf. most recently G. Klingenstein, *Staatsverwaltung und kirchliche Autorität im 18. Jahrhundert* (V. 1970), 22 ff. *passim*.

[25] For Hungary, P. Gulyás, *A könyvnyomtatás Magyarországon a XV és XVI században* (Bp. 1931), is thorough; J. Fitz, *A magyarországi nyomdászat, könyvkiadás és könyvkereskedelem története*, ii (Bp. 1967), adds little. Cf. the interesting statistical information in G. Borsa, 'A XVI századi magyarországi könyvnyomtatás részmérlege', *Reneszánsz-Füzetek*, xxii (1973), 249–69, based on Borsa *et al.*, *Régi magyarországi nyomtatványok*, i (Bp. 1971). For Bohemia, J. Volf, *Geschichte des Buchdrucks in Böhmen und Mähren bis 1848* (Weimar 1928), gives a general picture; the details of Czech-language publications are in Z. Tobolka and F. Horák (eds.), *Knihopis českých a slovenských tisků*, ii—(Pr. 1939—, hereafter *Knihopis*). For Vienna: A. Mayer, *Wiens Buchdruckergeschichte*, i–ii (V. 1883), i (1482–1682), esp. the observations at 164–8; cf. the evidence in Wiedemann, 'Büchercensur', and R. J. W. Evans, *The Wechel Presses* (Oxford 1975), 31–7. The Arian texts are listed in *Régi magyarországi nyomtatványok*; cf. C. Sandius, *Biblioteca Antitrinitariorum* (1684, reprinted Warsaw 1967).

Reformation in Carniola. Everywhere the printed word was enlisted as an ally: significantly the Inner Austrian estates enshrined their concessions of 1578 in a flysheet, the so-called *Brucker Libell*, while those of Lower Austria flouted the law and created a press on which to issue the Lutheran *Agenda*.[26]

So far we have seen how coexistence followed from an uneasy balance of competing forces. Seen in this light, toleration was basically something external: it bespoke a dominance of secular forces and a want—for all the strident importunings from rival clergymen—of deep and divisive piety or commitment. All the same, coexistence and toleration possessed positive local sources of strength too. Multi-racial societies in Central Europe were perhaps less vulnerable to sudden disruptive passions in that age; a profound contrast to their nineteenth-century experience. Post-Hussite Bohemia had learned its own kinds of compromise, while Breslau, the capital of Silesia, housed a reasonably harmonious mixture of Catholic bishop, Lutheran burgherdom, and crypto-Calvinist, if not thoroughly unorthodox intelligentsia.[27] Many noble households in Hungary maintained both a priest and a preacher as late as the 1580s; Silesian pastors not only shared churches with the local Catholics, but continued to elevate the Host and wear the Eucharistic vestments. Some Transylvanian extremists took up a theoretical defence of toleration—that by Palaeologus is the best elaborated—which reflects their personal behaviour: the incorrigibly indecisive Francken was formally converted to Rome on four separate occasions. Even Turkish-occupied areas on the plain had a lively Protestant intellectual life.[28]

---

[26] *Bibli Česká*, i–vi (Kralice 1579–93); cf. M. Daňková, *Bratrské tisky ivančické a kralické* (Pr. 1951). G. Károlyi, *Szent Biblia* (Vizsoly 1590). There is a large specialized literature on the Slovene texts, e.g. T. Elze, *Die slowenischen protestantischen Druckschriften des 16. Jahrhunderts* (Venice 1896), and G. Stökl, *Die deutsch-slawische Südostgrenze des Reiches im 16. Jahrhundert* (Breslau 1940). G. A. Crüwell, 'Die niederösterreichische Reformations-Druckerei', *Zbl. f. Biblw.* xx (1903), 309–20; cf. Bibl, 'Organisation', 152 ff.

[27] Though this tolerance can be exaggerated, as recently by W. Eberhard in F. Seibt (ed.), *Bohemia Sacra* (Düsseldorf 1974), 222–35, and J. K. Zeman, 'The rise of religious liberty in the Czech Reformation', *Central European History*, vi (1973) 128–47.

[28] Révész, *Egyháztörténet*, 64 n.; H. Ziegler, *Die Gegenreformation in Scnlesien* (Halle 1888), 1–22, esp. 13 f. Palaeologus, op. cit., *passim*; cf. Pirnát, op. cit. 66 ff. On
(continued).

Spared full involvement in the bitter feuds which rent the west of the continent, the Habsburg lands tended to extract those aspects of the confessional debate consonant with the Humanistic principles imbibed by all its parties as their educational standards rose. Much common ground existed in a wide receptivity to classical learning, to a world of scholarly inquiry whose internal disagreements were not basically doctrinal ones. Major libraries were assembled which did justice to the gamut of late-Renaissance curiosity: Job Hartmann von Enenkel, for instance, bought 8,000 books, while theology formed only a small part of collections like those of the Hungarians Johannes Sambucus and Boldizsár Batthyány, of the emigrant Italian historian Giovanni Brutus and the powerful imperial minister Wolf Rumpf.[29] Erasmus was increasingly valued on all sides: he had anyway forged many links with Central Europe and spent most of his last years in the Habsburgs' university city of Freiburg. The place of Philip Melanchthon became even more central, the esteem of influential native Protestants far outweighing attacks on his moderate stance by preachers of the rival Flaccian inclination. His writings held sway most of all in Breslau and the other towns of Silesia which contributed so much to German culture during the sixteenth century.[30] In Hungary the prevailing Calvinism was kept from being doctrinaire by a strong lay element which built both on Philippist ideas from the Empire and on the Italian Humanism of Padua. This latter current proved especially

---

Transylvanian toleration, most recently: L.. Binder, *Grundlagen und Formen der Toleranz in Siebenbürgen bis zur Mitte des 17. Jahrhunderts* (Cologne–V. 1976), narrower than the title suggests. G. Kathona, *Fejezetek a török hódoltsági reformáció történetéből* (Bp. 1974) studies the Great Plain.

[29] Coreth, art. cit., for Enenkel; *Rudolf II*, 123–8 (Sambucus); Evans, *Wechel Presses*, 35 f. (Batthyány); B. Iványi, *Könyvek, könyvtárak, könyvnyomdák Magyarországon 1331–1600* (Bp. 1937), no. 207 (Brutus), and cf. ÖNB, MS. 5580, fols. 46–7. Rumpf's catalogue is ÖNB, MS. 15286, dated 1583 but including some later volumes, 1019 in all. Cf. R. Stumpfl, 'Bibliotheken der Reformationszeit in Oberösterreich', *Zbl. f. Biblw.* xlvii (1930), 317–23.

[30] I. T. Waldapfel, *Humanizmus és nemzeti irodalom* (Bp. 1966), 50–132, on Erasmus and Hungary. For Melanchthon: G. Loesche, *Luther, Calvin, Melanchthon in Österreich-Ungarn* (Tübingen 1909); I. Borzsák, 'A magyarországi Melanchthonrecepció kérdéséhez', *ItK* lxix (1965), 433–46; *Rudolf II*, 98 f. On Silesia: C. Grünhagen, 'Schlesien unter Rudolf II und der Majestätsbrief', *ZVGAS* xx (1886), 54–96, at 54 ff.; S. Tync, 'Z życia patrycjatu wrocławskiego w dobie Renesansu', *Sobótka*, viii (1953), 69–123; and the case study by A. W. J. Wachler, *Thomas Rehdiger und seine Büchersammlung in Breslau* (Breslau 1828).

powerful in Transylvania—the Chancellor Farkas Kovacsóczy is a good case in point—where it underlay also the secularizing thrust of the Unitarians.[31]

★

Still more striking are attitudes on the Catholic side. The Catholic Church was now a head without a body, but its upper echelons contained men whose range of interests paralleled those of their Protestant contemporaries. Amid the grim realities of embattled Hungary the hierarchy displayed a thoroughly Renaissance sophistication. Nicholas Oláh, primate of the country between 1553 and 1568, corresponded with Erasmus and compiled works on classical monuments and topography. His successor, Cardinal Antal Verantius, an outstanding diplomat, was likewise a prolific author with a historical bent; so were his protégés Ferenc Forgách and Miklós Istvánffy, whose chronicles form vital and balanced sources for the period.[32] Istvánffy (1538–1605), poet and Latinist, scholar and collector, illustrates many of the dominant traits of later Humanism; during the 1570s and 1580s he belonged to a regular circle of Catholic *literati* around Bishops Liszti and Radéczi. 'Liszti', wrote one acquaintance, 'is a Nicodemite: he thinks one way about religion, and speaks another.' Their episcopal colleague Zacharias Mossóczy, first codifier of Hungarian statute law, assembled a typical polyglot library of the day.[33]

---

[31] L. Szádeczky, *Kovacsóczy Farkas* (Bp. 1891), esp. 82 ff.; cf. Kovacsóczy's Lutheran colleagues Berzeviczy (E. Veress, *Berzeviczy Márton* (Bp. 1911)) and Szamosközy (Bagyary, op. cit., *passim*). V. Frankl, 'Melanchton és magyarországi barátai', *Sz* viii (1874), 149–84; D. Kerecsényi, *Humanizmus és Reformáció között* (Bp. n.d.); L. Makkai, *Histoire de Transylvanie* (Paris 1946), 172–4, 182 f.; A. Pirnát, 'Aristoteliánusok és antitrinitáriusok', *Helikon*, xvii (1971), 363–92.

[32] J. Csontosi, 'Adalék Oláh Miklós könyvtárához', *MKSz* viii (1883), 61–6; C. Albu and M. Capoianu (eds.), *Nicolae Olahus, corespondenţă cu umaniştii batavi şi flamanzi* (Bucharest 1974). A. Fortis, *Viaggio in Dalmazia*, i (Venice 1774), 137–44, and M. G. Kovachich, *Scriptores Rerum Hungaricorum Minores*, i–ii (Buda 1798), *passim*, on Verantius, whose *Opera Omnia* were edited by L. Szalay and G. Wenzel, i–xii (Bp 1857–75); cf. OSzk, MS. 2380 fol. lat. 1–3. Cf. *A magyar irodalom története*, ed. I. Sőtér, i–vi (Bp. 1964–6, hereafter *MIT*), i, 281–4. For the maverick Bishop Forgách: P. Sörös, 'Forgách Ferenc élete', *Sz* xxx (1896), 519–41, 634–48.

[33] K. Bóta, *Istvánffy Miklós* (Bp. 1938); J. Holub, *Istvánffy Miklós Históriája hadtörténelmi szempontból* (Szekszárd 1909) is wider than the title suggests. Cf. OSzK, MS. 3606 fol. lat. 1–3, described by J. Berlász in *OSzK Évkönyve*, 1959, 202–40. On Liszti, etc.: L. Brummel, *Twee ballingen 's lands tijdens onze opstand tegen Spanje* (The
(continued).

This kind of lukewarm Catholicism was by now quite out of step with Rome. No Hungarian prelate visited the Pope between 1553 and 1600, while those who travelled in the latter year, András Monoszlói and Faustus Verantius, both stood for moderation. Faustus, Antal's nephew, an intellectual of rare and curious gifts, accepted a bishopric with little enthusiasm, and his mistrust of orthodox Counter-Reformation thinking was still by no means unique in the episcopate: Demetrius Náprági affords a further belated example.[34] Elsewhere in Central Europe leading Catholics showed the same spirit of accommodation. Many gathered at the court of Stephen Báthory, initially in Transylvania and then at Cracow after Báthory acquired the Polish crown : from Brutus with his international contacts to more local luminaries like the physician-poet Ferenc Hunyadi.[35] At Prague Archbishop Antonín Brus, though he chaired the censorship committee at the Council of Trent, refused to attempt any severe prohibitions, and his own library betrays a man of much latitude. The see of Breslau had several incumbents of similar temper. In Austria we find bishops of Vienna from Faber to Neubeck restrained perhaps only by a lack of means from unfolding the Renaissance pomp exhibited by their metropolitans of Salzburg.[36] How many later monastic historians

Hague 1972), 33; L. Kubinyi, *Ioanni Listhio . . . Epitaphia* (Pr. 1577); G. Entz, *A magyar műgyűjtés történetének vázlata 1850–ig* (Bp. 1937), 12, 18 f. B. Iványi, *Mossóczy Zakariás és a magyar Corpus Juris keletkezése* (Bp. 1926), esp. 103-35; id., *Könyvek,* nos. 149, 198, 214, 216, 218.

   [34] K. Juhász, *A csanádi püspökség története, 1552–1608* (Makó 1935), 135–52, esp. 143 f.; cf. *Rudolf II,* 187, on Verantius. Monoszlói's will is in Egy. Kt., Coll. Hevenesiana, tom. xviii, fols. 388–413. F. Jenei, 'Az utolsó magyar humanista főpap: Náprági Demeter', *ItK* lxix (1965), 137–50.

   [35] In general : T. Csorba, *A humanista Báthory István* (Bp. [1944]); L. Biró in *Etienne Batory, roi de Pologne, prince de Transylvanie* (Cracow 1935), 47–70. J. M. Brutus, *Selectarum Epistolarum libri V* (Cracow 1583); cf. M. Papp, *Brutus J. M. és Báthory István magyar humanisták* (Bp. 1940). Hunyadi wrote poems in Hungarian and Latin : I. Weszprémi, *Succincta Medicorum Hungariae et Transylvaniae biographia,* i–iii (Leipzig–V. 1774–87), ii, 1, 86–92; G. Magyary-Kossa, *Magyar orvosi emlékek,* i–iv (Bp. 1929–40), iii, 1012.

   [36] On Brus; A. Skýbová, 'Knihovna arcibiskupa Antonína Brusa', *Knihtisk a kniha od husitství do Bílé Hory,* ed. F. Šmahel (Pr. 1971), 241–56; Menčík, 'Censura', 98 f.; F. H. Reusch, *Der Index der verbotenen Bücher,* i–ii (Bonn 1883–5), i, 314–21. Cf. K. Borový, *Antonín Brus z Mohelnice* (Pr. 1873), and S. Steinherz (ed.), *Briefe des Prager Erzbischofs Anton Brus* (Pr. 1907). J. Jungnitz, *Martin von Gerstmann, Bischof von Breslau* (Breslau 1898). On Austria : A. Lhotsky, 'Die Bibliothek des Bischofs

lament with incredulity (where they do not pass over in silence) a series of sixteenth-century abbots infected with Humanist passivity! How many princes of the Church prove by Tridentine standards remarkably receptive to heretical values!

The most prominent Catholic party of all was evidently the dynasty itself. Did not the whole spread of divergent confessions result from Habsburg debility? Certainly the ruling family possessed as yet few weapons with which to combat heterodoxy, but we must judge its position in the context of the climate of moderation I have already outlined. Although Ferdinand I's commitment to Rome did not waver, he had, like his brother Charles, no patience with overweening Papal claims. The mildly increased power which he wielded in his dominions—especially after the check to German Protestants and their Bohemian sympathizers in 1546–7—was intended to consolidate the position of a dynasty (or at least his own branch of it) above factions and countries. Moreover Ferdinand had some ear for the harmonies of Humanism: several of his advisers openly displayed Erasmian sympathies and approved of colloquy. Hence a logical culmination of his policy was the effort at the Council of Trent to authorize clerical marriage and the use of the chalice among the laity: those two grand symbols, one moral, the other doctrinal, of popular resistance to the old Church were not simply a gesture from weakness, but a real movement towards conciliation within the area of *adiaphora* (in the Philippist sense). On his death in 1564 Ferdinand even won the praise of the radical Anglican Edmund Grindal.[37]

This approach was continued by Ferdinand's eldest son. The Emperor Maximilian II is remembered as a tolerant ruler who early in life so favoured the Lutherans as to be suspected of apostasy, later in life maintained a frigid reserve towards both the Pope and his

---

von Wien Dr. Johann Fabri', *Festschrift für K. Eder* (Innsbruck 1959), 71–81; M. Mairold, 'Die Bibliothek Bischof Urban Sagstetters', *Carinthia I*, clxi (1971), 277–92. On Salzburg: H. Widmann, *Geschichte Salzburgs*, i–iii (Gotha 1907–14), iii, 1–271, *passim*; E. Tomek, op. cit. 428 ff.

[37] For such advisers as Witzel, Cassander, and Urban of Gurk see F. W. Kantzenbach, *Das Ringen um die Einheit der Kirche im Jahrhundert der Reformation* (Stuttgart 1957), 176–229; Böhl, op. cit. 109–36. On the chalice: G. Constant, *Concession à l'Allemagne de la communion sous les deux espèces*, i–ii (Paris 1923), i, chs. 2–6, a remarkable but little-known work. E. Grindal, *Concio funebris in obitum … Ferdinandi Caesaris* (London 1564), translated into Latin by John Foxe.

brother-in-law Philip II, and at the very end of life may still have
refused the Catholic sacraments. He disliked Spanish policy in the
Netherlands, the massacre of St. Bartholomew's Day, the excom-
munication of Queen Elizabeth.[38] What has been forgotten is the
corollary to that behaviour: Maximilian's patronage of a court
which, in its composition and mentality, represented the very image
of educated moderation. He had many gifts, among them a capacity
to inspire loyalty, a shrewd judgment in personal matters, and a
powerful grasp of intellectual issues. Maximilian's reign therefore
witnessed the climax of orthodox Humanism in Austria, with at its
apex his own entourage, a fraternity aptly described by one critic as
Hofchristen: 'aulic Christians'.[39] Certainly these men, from their
different backgrounds, were united in an unwillingness to press
confessional niceties. Even the emperor's military commander,
Lazarus von Schwendi, preached sweet reasonableness, as did his
principal advisers, Seld and Zasius.[40] Some, of course, were
moderates from conviction; others from lack of conviction. Perhaps
the distinction is not so important (like those which from
convenience we have etched into the very fluid religious map of
Central Europe). Rather they shared a vague desire to unravel the
deeper connection between classical and Christian learning, much
as Maximilian himself entertained a serious interest in ecclesiastical
historiography.[41]

★

Viennese Humanism in the 1560s and 1570s rested on conventional
principles: the primacy of Latin as a vehicle for elegant expression
and for recreating the virtues of classical civilization. Many of its
prime exponents held posts at the university, which as an institution

[38] H. Hopfen, *Kaiser Maximilian II und der Kompromisskatholizismus* (Munich
1895); W. Maurenbrecher, 'Kaiser Maximilian II und die deutsche Reformation',
HZ vii (1862), 351–81; V. Bibl, 'Zur Frage der religiösen Haltung Kaiser
Maximilians II', *AÖG* cvi/2 (1918), 298–426; M. Koch, *Quellen zur Geschichte des
Kaisers Maximilian II*, i–ii (Leipzig 1857–61), ii, 92–108; V. Bibl (ed.), *Die
Korrespondenz Maximilians II*, i–ii (V. 1916–21), *passim*, on relations with Philip II;
W. E. Schwarz, *Briefe und Akten zur Geschichte Maximilians II*, i (Paderborn 1889),
esp. no. cxxiii, on relations with the Papacy, Cf. *Rudolf II*, 84–6.

[39] Bibl, 'Eder', 97 ff., 125 ff., 143.

[40] W. Janko, *Lazarus Freiherr von Schwendi* (V. 1871); cf. J. Glücklich in *ČČH*
xviii (1912), 481–5. For Seld and Zasius see *ADB*, s.vv.

[41] V. Bibl, 'Nidbruck und Tanner, ein Beitrag zur Entstehungsgeschichte der
Magdeburger Centurien', *AÖG* lxxxv (1898), 379–430.

now stood directly under the court and partook of its catholic standpoint. Poetry was promoted with regular *eisteddfodau* presided over by the mathematician Paul Fabritius, the lawyer Peter de Rotis, the writer Elias Corvinus, and others; success could bring imperial favour and a title of *poeta laureatus*.[42] Discussion centred on questions of literature and inscriptions, morals and pedagogy, set in a firmly Aristotelian base. Andreas Camutius, author of highly formalistic works on intellect, love, and nobility, relates how Maximilian would enter into these debates. The textbooks of Nicholas Biesius have similar praise of his royal protector. More striking testimony comes from Stephen Pighius, who spent three years in Vienna as tutor to the young duke of Cleves, a nephew of the emperor, and whose own books display the same mixture of classical inspiration and Renaissance manners which he experienced at the Habsburg court.[43]

Some of this activity had lasting merits. Pighius and the Austrian Lazius produced important work on Roman history; Sambucus and the apostate bishop Andreas Dudith enjoyed European celebrity as Greek scholars; so did Nicasius Ellebodius, one of the Humanists at the nearby Hungarian capital of Pozsony (Pressburg), who continued to hold a prebend in the Catholic Church.[44] Efforts were made to secure the rising Justus Lipsius for Vienna and he went there on an extended visit; foremost among the local worthies noted in his carefully contrived autobiography is the imperial diplomat

---

[42] On the university in general: R. Kink, *Geschichte der kaiserlichen Universität zu Wien*, i–ii (V. 1854), i, pt. 1, 308 ff.; J. Aschbach, *Geschichte der Wiener Universität*, i–iii (V. 1865–88), ii–iii. G. Eder, *Catalogus Rectorum et illustrium Virorum Archigymnasii Viennensis* (V. 1559) documents the decline and the beginnings of revival. On the poets see also J. A. Bradish, 'Dichterkrönungen im Wien des Humanismus', *Journal of English and Germanic Philology*, xxxvi (1937), 367–83; and HHStA, RHR, Privilegia varii generis latinae expeditionis, fasc. 4.

[43] A. Camutius, *De Amore atque Felicitate* (V. 1574), ded.; id., *De Nobilitate* (Milan 1641), 233–5; cf. *Dictionnaire historique et biographique de la Suisse*, s.v. N. Biesius, *De Arte Dicendi* and *De Natura* (both Antwerp 1573), deds. S. Pighius, *Hercules Prodicius* (Antwerp 1587), 157–210; cf. *Biographisch Woordenboek der Nederlanden*, xv (1872), 313–15, and *ADB*, s.v. (inaccurate).

[44] Above, n. 29 (Sambucus). P. Costil, *André Dudith, humaniste hongrois* (Paris 1935), 223–339. T. Klaniczay, 'Nicausius Ellebodius és Poètikája', *ItK* lxxv (1971), 24–34; id., 'Contributi alle relazioni padovane degli umanisti d'Ungheria: Nicasio Ellebodio e la sua attività filologica', *Venezia e Ungheria nel Rinascimento*, ed. V. Branca (Florence 1973), 317–33. The group included Dr. Georg Purkircher, on whom see M. Kneifel, *Purkircher György* (Bp. 1942).

Busbecq, whose famous account of the Ottoman lands includes many antiquarian and linguistic digressions.[45] Indeed, philological interest shaded into a much more general curiosity. Many of Maximilian's protégés occupied the position of *Leibarzt*—physician-in-ordinary: Camutius and Biesius among those already mentioned. Some, like Guarinoni and Alexandrinus, made outstanding professional reputations, while Dr. Crato, most cultured and accommodating of Silesian Lutherans, became Maximilian's unshakeable confidant. Another *Leibarzt*, Rembert Dodoens, wrote pioneering books on the animal and vegetable kingdoms, as did the keeper of the royal gardens, Charles de l'Escluse or Clusius. Dr. Reisacher busied himself with astronomy, like Dodoens and Fabritius, who was a key figure in Viennese intellectual life. Such learned investigations married with the collecting passion shared by Maximilian and other sixteenth-century Habsburgs and with the involved Mannerist style of his artists; one of the great Renaissance antiquaries, Jacopo Strada, acted as imperial aesthetic counsellor.[46]

Maximilian's circle was fully cosmopolitan, attracting above all Italians and Netherlanders in search of recognition and untroubled working conditions; its contacts were correspondingly extensive. Best evidence of this appears if we dwell a little on the court librarian, Hugo Blotius. Blotius, a Dutchman, studied and taught at Louvain, Paris, Orleans, Basle, Strasbourg, and Padua before settling in Vienna from 1575. There despite some personal frictions—for he was a self-willed man—Blotius found the atmosphere congenial enough; in religious matters he could keep a low profile, probably adhering throughout his life to a mild Calvinism, and the Hofbibliothek, recently fortified with valuable Greek manuscripts from Busbecq and others, represented a major repository for scholars.[47]

---

[45] J. Lipsius, *Opera Omnia*, ii (Antwerp 1637), 159–62; Lipsius's special pleading—stressing his pious career and withdrawn, scholarly life—is discussed by G. Oestreich, *Geist und Gestalt des frühmodernen Staates* (Berlin 1969), 80–100. Cf. also Lipsius's letter to Maximilian, printed in his edition of Tacitus (Antwerp 1574), 3–8.

[46] Some of these men, especially Crato, Clusius, and Strada, are discussed in *Rudolf II*, chs. 3–4. On Dodoens, a major intellectual figure, there is no adequate biographical information.

[47] Best on Blotius's life is now L. Brummel, op. cit. 1–80. For the court library: J.

Blotius was evidently a respected member of the Humanist community. As such he shared its characteristic epistolary passion and kept careful lists of the addresses and titles of his friends. During the 1570s and 1580s especially correspondents wrote to him from all over Europe.[48] Some were old student acquaintances, like the lawyer Hubert Giffen, whose hundred extant letters document a busy career ending in Prague. Others were Austrian literary men: Sambucus, Busbecq, and Crato, who helped him to favour at court; the poets Calaminus and Porschius, Frenzelius and Arconatus; noble supporters too, among them Schwendi, whose son he tutored for a time.[49] Such posts as private preceptor were attractive to the academic, and Blotius also taught Bishop Liszti's rough-cast nephew. The pupil brought little joy, but the job forged links with Istvánffy, Ellebodius, and their friends at Pozsony, as well as with more isolated Hungarian scholars and noblemen in the country-side.[50] Among Bohemians he knew the wordy Silesian Monau, Codicillus and Kocín at Prague, and a number of provincial Humanists. German friends included Camerarius at Nuremberg, Hans Herwart at Augsburg, Crusius at Tübingen, Chytraeus and Caselius at Rostock, Reineck and Horstius at Helmstedt, Gruter at Heidelberg; together with Zwinger and several more scholars from Basle. Further afield Blotius kept in touch with his native land and with colleagues in France and England.[51]

Stummvoll (ed.), *Geschichte der österreichischen Nationalbibliothek*, i (V. 1968), 81–127. One example of a new collection of MSS. appears from ÖNB, MS. 9737[z15], fol. 202.

[48] Blotius's correspondence is in ÖNB, MSS. 9737[z14–18]; there is a hand-list of writers, and I shall not give full references in what follows. Cf. ibid. MSS. 9690, 9708, for lists of Blotius's friends.

[49] Little of this correspondence has been printed or even consulted. See G. Knod, 'Hugo Blotius in seinen Beziehungen zu Strassburg', *Zbl. f. Biblw.* xii (1895), 266–75; and cf. *Rudolf II*, ch. 4, *passim*. On Giffen, below pp. 58, 106.

[50] These connections are studied, and some letters printed, by F. Mencsik, 'A Páduában tanuló Blotz Hugó levelezése erdélyi és magyarországi barátaival', *Erdélyi Muzeum*, xxvii (1910), i; id. in *TT*, 1907; and J. Ernuszt, *Die ungarischen Beziehungen des Hugo Blotius* (Bp. 1943, separatum from *BÉ* x). Blotius knew the Transylvanians Berzeviczy, Kovacsóczy, and Gyulai in the 1570s. Interesting among his later contacts are the aristocrat, Imre Forgách, and the minister at Késmárk, Sebastian Ambrosius.

[51] This is only a small selection. The most important Frenchman was Duplessis-Mornay; Englishmen included Henry and Thomas Savile, Robert Sidney, and Henry Wotton.

Such names—and many more could be added—provide merely
the bare bones for an argument. They illustrate the scope of one
surviving correspondence based on Vienna; only some mention of
its contents can bring it back to life. Not that the contents were
often dramatic: the demands of elegant Latinity severely circumscribed their emotional range. Yet they convey much personal
information and, not infrequently, comments on political conditions
and current affairs, especially fears about any aggravation of
confessional strife. Platonic protestations of friendship and introductions for travellers give the authentic flavour of a sort of educated
freemasonry stretching from London to the Ottoman frontier. A
stream of visitors was entertained over the years at Blotius's lodgings
within the imperial Hofburg.[52]

The general progress of European scholarship bulks largest in
these letters, and though Blotius was himself no great innovator
there is good evidence of contemporary debates in classical studies,
history, and some branches of natural philosophy. At the same time
current publications on all kinds of subject receive much attention.
In 1576 and 1577, for example, the Czech legist Kocín seeks works
by Bodin, including the *Republic,* and some Italian edition of
Machiavelli, that great hammer of the Papacy. Authors dispatch
their own volumes to Blotius; printers engage the librarian's help
with their submissions for an imperial privilege. Meanwhile a
variety of professional services have to be rendered, from the
genealogical material requested by aristocrats to a transfer of books
for the banished Johannes Kepler, *en route* from Styria to Prague.[53]

*

The letters sent to Blotius illuminate an approved and sophisticated
Humanism which fitted the élite milieu of court and academy.
They belong with other contemporary correspondence: that of

---

[52] Current affairs are well represented in many letters from Crato and Monau, and
from Chytraeus in north Germany. *Amicitia* is proclaimed, for example, in ÖNB,
MS. 9737[214], fols. 170, 242, 321 f.; ibid.[215], fols. 74, 284; ibid.[216], fols. 56, 334;
ibid.[218], fol. 80. Beside Jan Kocín's letter of 11 June 1575 Blotius has noted:
'Doctissima et philosophica Epistola de suscipiendis oneribus et suscipiendo Vitae
genere' (ibid.[215], fols. 82 f.). Henry Wotton, one of the Camerariuses, and others
stayed with Blotius for months on end.

[53] Kocin: ÖNB, MS. 9737[215], fols. 173, 176, 192, 270. Privileges: ibid.[216], fols. 36,
110 f., 231; ibid.[218], fol. 121; etc. Aristocrats: ibid.[218], fols. 73, 158 f., 171, 176, 178,
184, 187; etc. Kepler: ibid.[218], fol. 144 (Prague, 5 Feb. 1601).

Languet, of the Camerarius family at Nuremberg, or—most lustrous of all—of Justus Lipsius, whose troubled religious stance so typifies the movement.[54] During the 1580s and 1590s Lipsius became the dominant figure in a network of contacts which embraced Central Europe from their base in the Low Countries. His letters, many published, even deliberately written with a view to publication, were the holy writ of the late Renaissance.[55] But these documents form only the peaks in a broad landscape: the wider horizons of European culture within which the Habsburg lands were gradually integrated. Stimulated by a sense of Protestant solidarity, the process developed apace under Maximilian, then continued under Rudolf II, who inherited his father's court and heightened the degree of receptivity. Only slowly would features of decay in the Rudolfine age grow apparent.

The evolution was one of mutual acceptance, a discovery of common factors within the international Renaissance. It is graphically exemplified in Calepinus's dictionary. No self-respecting scholar of the sixteenth century could do without that reference work which, still bearing the name of its long-defunct progenitor, who had originally conceived it as a mere word-book of Latin usage, passed through scores of editions under successive generations of editors. No old library of today lacks testimony to its lasting popularity. Progressively Greek, Italian, Spanish, French, and Hebrew equivalents were added; in 1568 German; two years later, Dutch. In 1585 a further major step was taken with the inclusion of three more languages: English, Hungarian, and Polish, and the huge polyglot thus obtained casts its own sidelight on cultural, even

[54] *H. Langueti ... ad J. Camerarium Patrem et ... filium ... Epistolae* (Groningen 1646); *The Correspondence of Sir Philip Sidney and H. Languet*, ed. S. A. Pears (London 1845, original edn. 1633). *Ioachimi Camerarii Epistolae familiae* (Frankfurt 1583); *Ioachimi Camerarii Epistolarum libri V posteriores* (Frankfurt 1595); *I. Bongarsi Epistolae ad Joachimum Camerarium* (Leiden 1647). Lipsius's letters are collected in his *Opera Omnia*, and in P. Burmann, *Sylloges Epistolarum a variis illustribus scriptarum*, i–v (Leiden 1727), i–ii. Cf. the complete conspectus of published and unpublished letters in A. Gerlo and H. D. L. Vervliet, *Inventaire de la correspondance de Juste Lipse 1564–1606* (Antwerp 1968).

[55] His Central European correspondents included Acidalius, Barvitius, Blotius, Busbecq, Clusius, Crato, Dudith, Ellinger, Mihály Forgách, Frenzelius, Giffen, Jerinus, A. G. Popel Lobkovic, Francesco Magni, Monau, Péter Révay, Nikolaus and Thomas Rhediger, Rimay, Sambucus, Ludwig Schwartzmaier, Richard Starhemberg, Wacker, Karel Žerotin, and several more in Cracow.

political, history.[56] The Central European vernaculars—Polish
standing also for its near relation Czech—make their appearance,
and no later than English, in polite international society; at the
same time all the new languages are still only appendages to the
Latin of the body of the dictionary, not a dog-Latin in dog-eared
quarto, but a Humanist Latin, enshrined in massive folio editions,
refined by an ever greater precision of definition and extension of
vocabulary. Hence the vogue for that neo-Latin verse whose Central
European exponents were second to none: Bruschius from Eger,
Corvinus at Vienna, the Silesian Lange, Carolides at Prague,
Simonides in Poland, Frischlin, who was called to run the school of
the Carniolan estates.[57]

In this two-way process of recognition the Habsburg lands held
some advantages. The basic decency of their political life and the
cultural expansion under dynastic leadership could attract immigrants from tenser parts of the continent. But the balance of profit
lay in the other direction. The book trade, for example, opened up
all sorts of distant prospects. Aspiring authors from Bohemia or
Hungary turned to publishers in Germany, Switzerland, and the
Low Countries; readers were served by foreign booksellers who set
up emporia at Vienna or Prague and carried on their commerce
across the frontier.[58] Still more decisive was travel for study abroad,
by-passing the old universities at Vienna, Prague, and nearby
Cracow, which had seen better days, despite the relatively tolerant

---

[56] There were ten- and eleven-language editions of Calepinus at Lyons in 1585,
1586, 1588, 1598; at Geneva in 1594; at Basle in 1590, 1598, 1605, ?1609, ?1615,
1616, 1627. See now A. Labarre, *Bibliographie du Dictionarium d'Ambrogio Calepino*
(Baden-Baden 1975). Cf. the *Teutsche Sprach und Weissheit, Thesaurus Linguae et
Sapientiae Germanicae*, i (A-G only) (Augsburg 1616), by the Hungarian German
Georg Henisch, which contains, besides German and Latin, equivalents in nine
other languages, including Czech, Polish, and Hungarian; and J. Turóczi-Trostler,
Magyar irodalom, világirodalom, i–ii (Bp. 1961), i, 17–72, for the international
reception of Hungarian.

[57] G. Ellinger, *Geschichte der neulateinischen Literatur Deutschlands im 16. Jahrhundert*, i–iii (Berlin–Leipzig 1929–33), ii, 192–8, 261–8, and *passim*. E. Herrmann, 'Der
Humanist Kaspar Brusch und sein Hodoeporikon Pfreymbdense', *Bohemia-Jahrbuch*, vii (1966), 110–27; for Corvinus and Carolides see *Rukověť*, ed. Hejnic and
Martinek, s.vv.; and ÖNB, MS. 9878. On Simonides and other Poles: J. Irmscher
(ed.), *Renaissance und Humanismus in Mitteleuropa und Osteuropa*, i–ii (Berlin 1962),
ii, 107–20, 139–48. On Frischlin: D. F. Strauss, *Leben und Schriften des Dichters und
Philologen Nicodemus Frischlin* (Frankfurt 1856).

[58] Evans, *Wechel Presses*, 20–37.

atmosphere in their student bodies and the excellence of some professors.[59] The vogue for higher education took deep root by mid-century, not only among the nobility whose sons could afford it, but in many towns where public funds were made available for the purpose. Alternatively commoners could defray the cost by acting as private tutors, sometimes for long periods, like the Moravian Opsimathes who spent most of the years 1598–1618 in this way.[60] Thus we encounter the characteristic duo of preceptor and pupil trudging the roads to the West, seeking out especially those centres where they can find an echo of their own uncommitted circumstances.

The first and greatest goal was Wittenberg, and vast numbers attended Luther's university for at least a short time. But Wittenberg became clogged with its own orthodoxy and, after a last hectic interlude under the reforming Elector Christian I, disowned the mild spirit of Melanchthon. Many Germans were satisfied with adjacent universities in Saxony, Brandenburg, and the Baltic: Jena, Leipzig, Frankfurt an der Oder, Königsberg, Danzig.[61] The other Habsburg nationalities looked increasingly to the Palatine university of Heidelberg, with its team of excellent professors, and the younger academies at Marburg, Strasbourg, Altdorf, and Herborn. All these were still open, as the sixteenth century ended, to religious peacemaking and freedom of opinion; all developed close links with the Habsburg lands. In Strasbourg the eirenical Matthias Bernegger,

---

[59] Kink, loc. cit.; V. V. Tomek, *Geschichte der Prager Universität* (Pr. 1849), 173 ff. L. Santifaller (ed.), *Die Matrikel der Universität Wien*, I—(Graz–Cologne 1954—), iii–iv (1518–1658) reveals the declining numbers, confirmed for Hungarians by K. Schrauf, *A bécsi egyetem magyar nemzetének anyakönyve 1453-tól 1630-ig* (Bp. 1902). But Silesian attendance seems, if anything, to have risen, albeit mostly from the episcopal lands (U. Hielscher in *Zeitschrift für Ostforschung*, xi (1962), 648–73).

[60] For a typical case see A. Luschin-Ebengreuth, *Studien zur Geschichte des steirischen Adels im XVI Jahrhunderte* (Graz 1875), 13–30. Opsimathes's travel-album is in BL, Egerton MS. 1220; cf. Odložilik, *Reformovaní*, 59–62.

[61] The Bohemian literature is listed in *Rudolf II*, 132 f. nn. For Hungarians see J. Bartholomaides, *Memoria Ungarorum qui in ... Universitate Vitebergensi ... studia confirmarunt* (Pest 1817); Frankl, *Iskolázás*, 202–319; and the bibliography in J. Herepei, *Adattár XVII századi szellemi mozgalmaink történetéhez*, i–iii (Bp. 1965–71), iii, 441–51. One interesting case is very drily examined by G. Kliesch, *Der Einfluss der Universität Frankfurt (Oder) auf die schlesische Bildungsgeschichte* (Würzburg 1961). On the role of Wittenberg in the late sixteenth century, cf. the important study by T. Klein, *Der Kampf um die zweite Reformation in Kursachsen, 1586–91* (Cologne–Graz 1962).

a native of Upper Austria, encouraged pupils from his homeland; at Altdorf Rittershausen and Rem helped a long succession of Bohemian visitors; Herborn attracted many Silesians. Those who professed a more open Calvinism might attend the Swiss universities: numbers of Czechs accepted the hospitality of Polanus at Basle and several members of families like the Moravian Žerotíns are recorded at Geneva.[62] Yet Geneva, like Wittenberg, represented a dogma with which the majority did not wish to be identified. The same was true of most Catholic universities, though that rule allowed of significant exceptions. Padua, above all, protected by the urbane mentality of Venice, proved a haven throughout the period. It trained both lawyers and doctors in profusion, as well as offering the flavour of advanced academic debate, by no means rigidly confined to a practical Aristotelianism, as has sometimes been asserted. Many of the Blotius circle studied at Padua; so did such pronounced opposites as Jessenius and Lobkovic among Bohemians, Berzeviczy and Kakas among Hungarians.[63]

Prolonged residence at a cultural metropolis would leave its distinctive imprint, but this was unusual. Generally students passed through several academies and were not indelibly marked by any one, rather by the common features of their experience. A good example is Albert Szenci Molnár, the Hungarian lexicographer, translator, and poet, who from 1590 attended Wittenberg, Heidelberg, Strasbourg, Basle, and Geneva, then moved to Italy, back to Heidelberg, and finally to Herborn and Altdorf in search of work.[64] Some extended their tour to the Netherlands—though the great era

[62] Heidelberg: Herepei, op. cit. i, 103–66. Strasbourg: J. H. Boecler, *Memoriae Philosophorum*, ed. M. Henning (Frankfurt 1677), 486–515, and *ADB*, s.v. 'Bernegger'; S. Eckhardt, *Magyar szónokképzés a XVI századi Strasszburgban* (Bp. 1944). Altdorf: H. Kunstmann, *Die Nürnberger Universität Altdorf und Böhmen* (Cologne–Graz 1963). Herborn: *Die Matrikel der Hohen Schule ... zu Herborn*, ed. G. Zedler and H. Sommer (Wiesbaden 1908). Geneva: Odložilik, *Reformovaní*, 13 f. and *passim*. Cf. in general Evans, *Wechel Presses*, 46 f.

[63] E. Veress (ed.), *A paduai egyetem magyarországi tanulóinak anyakönyve és iratai* (Bp. 1915); id. (ed.), *Olasz egyetemeken járt magyarországi tanulók anyakönyve és iratai* (Bp. 1941); A. Luschin-Ebengreuth, 'Vorläufige Mitteilungen über die Geschichte deutscher Rechtshörer in Italien', *Sb. d. k. Akad. d. Wiss, ph.-h. Kl.* cxxvii (1892), Abh. 2.

[64] *Szenczi Molnár Albert naplója, levelezése és irományai*, ed. L. Dézsi (Bp. 1898), with his diary and correspondence; cf. L. Dézsi, *Szenczi Molnár Albert* (Bp. 1897). Turóczi-Trostler, op. cit. ii, 109–55, adds little, but there are some further details in Herepei, op. cit. i, 5–53.

of the Dutch universities falls later—France and England. If Oxford and Cambridge probably received only perfunctory and confused notice, that is hardly surprising, given the strain of any journey which tried to include them. The young Silesian preceptor Paul Hentzner visited them on a four-year adventure from Strasbourg, Basle, and Geneva, via southern France and Paris, to Frankfurt am Main, Padua, Rome, and Naples in the 1590s.[65]

Foreign universities thus offered vocational courses combined with less tangible benefits. Their faculty stamp of medicine or law became increasingly important for a future career—interestingly enough, all the extensive theological training produced few serious Central European theologians at this time—while the years spent abroad brought introductions to men of like mind, who might be fellow-citizens of the Habsburg dominions. Their dual role reflects the anatomy of contemporary travel as both a practical and a theoretical activity. Travel had an evident expedience in an increasingly mobile world, and a distinct literature grew up to advise wayfarers on the best means of arranging a journey. Topographical handbooks abounded: one solicitous Belgian providing the Emperor Rudolf with minutely prepared itineraries tested against Ortelius and other leading authorities.[66] Many journeys, however, were dictated by pure curiosity. The numerous band of adventurous spirits who went to Constantinople and the Holy Land combined piety with a free-ranging pursuit of the exotic. One Austrian nobleman, not satisfied with the sights of the Ottoman Empire, voyaged on to Babylon, Goa, and Ceylon before returning through Persia, the Balkans, and Poland.[67]

These Renaissance travellers are a self-conscious breed. Travel for them is also an art: the *ars peregrinandi*, like its passive

[65] P. Hentzner, *Itinerarium Germaniae, Galliae, Angliae, Italiae* (Nuremberg 1612).

[66] Baptista van der Muelen, 'Descriptio Quinque Profectionum . . .', ÖNB, MSS. 8932–7 (six almost identical MSS. based on his travels between 1565 and 1582). For the mood in general see E. Trunz, 'Der deutsche Späthumanismus um 1600 als Standeskultur', *Deutsche Barockforschung*, ed. R. Alewyn (Cologne–Berlin 1965), 147–81, and S. I. Kovács, 'Justus Lipsius és a magyar késö-reneszánsz utazási irodalom', *Helikon*, xvii (1971), 428–36.

[67] Georg Christoph Fernberger in ÖNB, MS. 15434; cf. ibid. MS. 8135, fols. 69–72. Another very provincial nobleman *en route* for Constantinople finds it necessary to begin by describing Vienna! (Wolf Andreas von Steinach, ibid. MS. s.n. 3385, fols. 5–49). Other examples in R. J. W. Evans, 'Bohemia, the Emperor and the Porte, 1550–1600', *Oxford Slavonic Papers*, N.S. iii (1970), 85–106.

equivalent, the *ars epistolaria*. They compile little verse or prose
hodoeporica of their journeys and delight to see them printed. They
dilate on the merits of their undertaking. 'Not only those men are
wise', muses one Hungarian preceptor before setting off for
Wittenberg and the Rhine, 'who are versed in *literae humaniores*,
but much more they who add a knowledge of things in the world
around them, the theatre of human life, and have observed the
diversity of regions, customs, ways of living, and all the other
manifold things which are open to travellers.'[68] Such reflections,
with their stress on experiencing the splendid variety of creation,
belonged to the conventional wisdom of international Humanism.

Habits of cultivated intercourse during the decades after 1550 are
strikingly illustrated by the cult of the *Stammbuch* or album. Albums
flourished peculiarly in the Germanic world and adjacent lands:
they were collections of entries, usually motto and dedication, from
those encountered by the possessor on his travels; a formalized
repository of contacts and friendships.[69] For all the formality of the
genre, the *Stammbücher* which survive can tell us much about
educated society in Central Europe: its movements and attach-
ments; its preferred theological and classical authors; its cosmopolitan background. Latin naturally predominates in the inscriptions, but the medley of languages suggests a polyglot Calepinus,
with Czech and Hungarian entries a regular occurrence. Locations
range from the intimate, harmonious atmosphere of civic Breslau

---

[68] Quotation from I. Miskolci Csulyak in OSzK, MS. 656 oct. lat., intro. Other
Hungarian examples are: F. Hunyadi, *Ephemeron seu Itinerarium Bathoreum* (Cracow
1586); M. Forgách, *Oratio de Peregrinatione et eius Laudibus* (Wittenberg 1587), esp.
sig. C1–2; J. Decsi Csimor, *Hodoeporicon Itineris Transylvanici* (Wittenberg 1587),
discussed by J. Tardy in *Filológiai Közlöny*, xi (1965), 359–71. Large collections of
such works began to appear, like that by the Silesian, Nikolaus Reusner (Basle 1580).
Cf. above n. 43 (Pighius).

[69] General literature on albums: R. and R. Keil, *Die deutschen Stammbücher des 16.
bis 19. Jahrhunderts* (Berlin 1893); M. Rosenheim, 'The Album Amicorum',
Archaeologia, lxii (1910), 251–308; M. A. E. Nickson, *Early Autograph Albums in the
British Museum* (London 1970); E. Zöllner, 'Das österreichische Stammbuch des
konfessionellen Zeitalters und seine Bedeutung als Geschichtsquelle', *MÖStA* xxv
(1972), 151–68. Recent descriptions of individual albums include Zöllner, 'Aus dem
Stammbuch des Frh. Otto Heinrich von Herberstein', *MIÖG* lxiii (1955), 358–74;
id., 'Austriaca in der Stammbuchsammlung des Britischen Museums', *Österreich
und die angelsächsische Welt*, ii (V.-Stuttgart 1968), 345 ff.; Zs. Jakó, 'Miskolci
Csulyak István peregrinációs albuma', *Irodalomtörténeti Dolgozatok*, lxxi (Szeged
1972), 59–71.

to the exhilarating society of Europeans at Constantinople; from one bourgeois Moravian's experiences in bourgeois Prague to another's in Jacobean London.[70] Some are mainly social documents, filled with the commonplaces and the coats-of-arms of the nobility; some mainly intellectual ones, with quotations in Latin or Greek from famous professors and other aspiring scholars.[71]

Two albums may be taken to illuminate more sharply the theme of tolerant Humanism in the Habsburg lands and its international connections. The thoughtful Magyar theologian Imre Újfalvi travelled extensively in Germany during the 1590s and made friends with many leaders of the eirenical movement, before moving to Holland and meeting their Dutch equivalents, the early Arminians. Újfalvi's contacts cast important shafts of light on the tenor of Hungarian intellectual Calvinism at the turn of the century.[72] In the same decade a young Moravian nobleman, Zdeněk Waldstein, was studying first in Silesia, then at Strasbourg, where his companions included a wide cross-section of fellow-countrymen. To complete his education he then travelled through the Netherlands, England, and France to Italy: while his fascinating album records the names of Lipsius, Scaliger, Grotius, Mornay, Pacius, and other giants, the Lutheran Waldstein also visited Rome and observed it without prejudice.[73]

★

This was, therefore, a cultural Renaissance, uniform in its essentials, but operating on several levels of complexity. It embraced both

[70] Breslau: BL, Add. MS 19477 (Daniel, son of Daniel Rindfleisch, a prominent local Humanist). Constantinople: ÖNB, MS. s.n. 2973, a fascinating album, showing how many Westerners reached Constantinople, where its owner, Salomon Schweigger, was Protestant chaplain to the Habsburg resident around 1580. Moravians: BL, Egerton MS. 1216 (primitive); above n. 60 (Opsimathes).

[71] Contrast BL, Egerton MS. 1205 (Christoph Grundner), which belonged to a servant of the Upper Austrian Starhembergs, and ibid. MS. 1245 (Tobias Taufrer of Laibach), with its learned Latin tags, absence of crests, and signatures of Besold and Bernegger, Maestlin and Sebisch.

[72] B. Keserű, 'Újfalvi Imre és a magyar későreneszánsz', *Irodalomtörténeti Dolgozatok*, xli (Szeged 1968); id., 'Újfalvi Imre és az európai "későhumanista ellenzék"', ibid. liv (Szeged 1969); his album is OSzK, MS. 150 oct. lat.

[73] ÖNB, MS. s.n. 2607 (Zdeněk Brtnický z Valdštejna), a complement to the diary already used by B. Dudik, *Iter Romanum*, i–ii (V. 1855), i, 232–44; O. Odložilik, 'Cesty z Čech a Moravy do Velké Britanie v letech 1563–1620', *ČMM* lix (1935), 241–320, at 280–8; id., *Reformovaní*, 51–8; and (for the description of Rome) J. A. F. Orbaan, *Rome onder Clemens VIII* (The Hague 1920), 126–45.

active and passive members of the *Respublica litteraria*: from the
pinnacle of recognized authors who might hope to correspond with
Lipsius down to the ranks of those who were just—though in a
double sense—fellow-travellers.

Central European Humanism flowered late, with little real
originality, but a powerful urge to harmonize what others had
already created elsewhere. It rested on classical foundations: texts
and their transmission; language and its philological refinements;
Greek medical and Roman legal sources; the raw materials of
Biblical study. The corpus of Greek, Roman, and Christian
authorities supported a world-view still essentially Aristotelian, but
where continued dissection and reinterpretation of the various parts
had left an exceedingly shaky edifice. Above all Italian Platonism
had staked its claim, and even Hungary produced, in Peter
Lascovius, its poor man's Pico della Mirandola.[74]

The rapid sixteenth-century advance in learning and debate
brought a wealth of new questions. The inherited picture was
expanded, confronted with the evidence of discoveries and natural
observations, subjected to growing criticism on its peripheries.
Meanwhile it faced a challenge from within, as consonance among
traditional authors became ever more difficult to establish. Therein
lay the crucial issue, for many more Humanists sought complemen-
tarity than sought contradiction; most would willingly have settled
for that *concordia Platonis cum Aristotele* which Johann Jessenius—
to quote a Bohemian instance—looked towards in his edition of
Savonarola's *Natural Philosophy*.[75]

Thus we are brought to the central concern of late-Renaissance
thinkers: reconciliation of opposites in a harmonious ordering of all
knowledge. To that end they espoused reforms in logic, from the
analytical approach of Ramus to the synthetic art of Lull; they
.argued about method and constructed systems, often a conscious
blend of existing elements, as in the cosmology of Tycho Brahe or
the medical philosophy of the Paracelsans. Such order in variety

---

[74] Petrus Mon.[edulatus] Lascovius, *De Homine Magno illo in rerum natura miraculo et partibus* (Wittenberg 1585).

[75] Gir. Savonarola, *Universae Philosophiae Epitome*, ed. J. Jessenius (Wittenberg 1596), esp. 763–9. Cf., for Jessenius's originality, I. Farneti, 'Una scoperta nel campo degli studi savonaroliani?', *Atti della Accademia delle Scienze di Ferrara*, xxviii (1950–1) and separatum.

might be revealed through collections, organized displays of miscellaneous objects; through libraries, increasingly rationalized and catalogued; or more actively by means of travel. All threw light on the *Theatrum vitae humanae*: the term stands, a programme for the age, as the title of its most famous universal handbook. Theodor Zwinger's *Theatrum* headed many similar projects, among them the plans of Blotius—never realized—for a biographical lexicon of eminent men.[76] It is no accident that eirenical theology should have attracted this kind of mind, especially in the form of a stoic revival which seemed a bridge between pagan and Christian morality. Religious moderation belonged to a wider view of the metaphysical middle way, a way which should be all-inclusive rather than compromising.[77]

Of course, no single intellect could grasp the whole order of creation; even contemporaries—barring a few fanatics—appreciated that. Unity, the basic presupposition, must be demonstrated: no knowledge, so men assumed, could discountenance it; yet they increasingly felt the proof to be somehow hidden. In defence of a rational view they called on the irrational. The result was a highly intricate mixture of reasoned curiosity and unreasoned credulity which produced a surge in many kinds of occult study. Renaissance occultism played a vital role in Neoplatonic speculation which had its Central European advocates from the days of Marsilio Ficino's association with Matthias Corvinus. Astral magic, conjuration, and mystique were an essential part of the Platonic cult, and the serious belief—however paradoxical to later commentators—in esoteric revelation brought widespread enthusiasm for other ancient mysteries: the Egyptian oracles of Hermes Trismegistus, Zoroaster, Orpheus, the Sibyls, even the Jewish arcana of Cabalism, whose dissemination followed the deepening involvement in Hebrew as a language of Protestant theologians. A young Hungarian Humanist for example, Pál Gyulai, wrote a philosophical dialogue in 1571 which he sent off for Blotius's comments; his list of sources begins with Orpheus, Hermes, Plato, Aristotle, Plotinus, Iamblichus, and

[76] Zwinger's compendium first appeared at Basle in 1571. There are mentions of Blotius's plans in his correspondence: ÖNB, MS. 9737[214], fols. 313 f.; ibid.[215], fols. 10, 57, 68 f., 86, etc.; ibid.[216], fols. 266 f.

[77] See below, pp. 113 f.; *Rudolf II*, ch. 3; and the article by Klaniczay cited in the next note.

Proclus, and proceeds to Ficino, Pico, Agrippa, Albertus Magnus, and G. B. Porta. Gyulai's compatriot Lascovius quotes regularly from Plato and the Neoplatonists, the Cabala, *Pymander* and *Asclepius*, Pythagoras and Zoroaster.[78]

Such cases are typical; equally typical was the pursuit of astrology, both learned and popular. Indeed, the idea of a sympathetic interplay between upper and nether worlds belonged among those propositions which few contemporaries could or would refute. Needless to say, many Humanists rejected horoscopes; but even practical astrology found wide acceptance among the educated, with Tycho, or with Copernicus's pupil Rheticus, who lived the latter part of his life at Cracow and died in Hungary. Celestial manipulations formed a part of much system-building, like the wild but influential notions of Giordano Bruno which aroused interest in central Europe.[79] Astrology shaded into alchemy, and alchemy likewise—for all the vituperation surrounding it—flourished in cultivated society no less than with the charlatan. It became a passion from Rudolfine Prague to the Transylvania of Zsigmond Báthory. The poet Corvinus engaged in a long correspondence about transmutation with his patron Batthyány; Hieronymus Megiser, teacher, historian, and pioneer linguist, published books on alchemy and the parts of memory, prophecy and automata.[80]

These are again examples at random, the merest sketch for a first orientation. I have already discussed magic elsewhere and more will be said about it in the course of this book; for the present it must

[78] Gyulai in OSzK, MS. 2380 fol. lat., 2, 29–67. On him see A. Gárdonyi, 'Abafáji Gyulai Pál', *Sz* xl (1906), 894–906, and Gy. Szabó, *Abafáji Gyulai Pál* (Bp. 1974), who however regards the dialogue as lost (14 f.). Lascovius, op. cit., *passim*. Cf. in general, most recently, *Rudolf II*, chs. 6–7, and the important study by T. Klaniczay, 'A reneszánsz válsága és a manierizmus', *ItK* lxxiv (1970), 419–50 (also in French translation in *Acta Litteraria Academiae Scientiarum Hungariae*, xiii (1971), 269–314). Cf. below, chs. 10 and 12.

[79] Tycho: *Rudolf II*, 279 f. Rheticus: K. H. Burmeister, *Georg Joachim Rheticus 1514–74*, i–iii (Wiesbaden 1967–8). Cf. below, pp. 394–9. On Brunonians: *Rudolf II*, 229–34; for Bruno's Hungarian admirer, Mihály Forgách, see also L. Bártfai Szabó, *A Hunt-Pázmán nemzetségbeli Forgách család története* (Esztergom 1910), 491–4, and—most recently—*Forgách Mihály és Justus Lipsius levélváltása*, ed. T. Klaniczay (Bp. 1970).

[80] *Rudolf II*, 199 ff.; for Transylvania cf. the letter from Kovacsóczy to Simon Forgách, 20 July 1591, in *TT*, 1893, 42 f. (but contrast Bagyary, op. cit. 118). Corvinus: OL, Batthyány család levéltára, misszilisek, nos. 8056–133; Megiser: M. Doblinger, 'Hieronymus Megiser, Leben und Werke', *MIÖG* xxvi (1905), 431–78.

suffice to stress that no sort of clear distinction existed between Humanist and occultist. The two persuasions were often combined, and not infrequently viewed as identical. In the Habsburg case posterity has tended to link magic exclusively with Rudolf II and his notorious associates; but Maximilian's ostensibly level-headed court betrays many signs of it. Maximilian too received the dedication of Hermetic works, published and unpublished; he too had an interest in Nostradamus and patronized a series of astrological practitioners, Fabritius and Reisacher among them; he too kept Paracelsan doctors in his entourage and supported travelling adepts like Thurneysser.[81] Even the correspondence of the strait-laced Blotius reveals such matters, since the library in his charge contained tantalizing manuscripts on conjuration (like the celebrated *Picatrix*, of which Jacopo Strada also boasted a copy), secret writing, alchemy, divination by dreams, and the rest. Rudolf's obsession evidently did not spring from nowhere: one of his earliest astrologers, Elias Preuss, was well known to Blotius, at least via their common friend Franciscus Hippolyti of Hildesheim, an occultizing mathematician who even sent the librarian some verses in honour of his marriage. Another purveyor of *carmina gratulatoria*, one Matthias Zuber, found impeccably erudite employment—as translator of Greek alchemical manuscripts into Latin.[82]

★

The interpenetration of humanism and magic in later sixteenth-century Europe is a remarkable phenomenon, since the two traditions appear so mutually alien. It was not, of course, complete: men like Blotius must have had many reservations about the mystificatory leanings of their masters and the crudeness of some of

---

[81] Franc. Flussas, *Mercurii Trismegisti Pimandras utraque lingua restitutus* (Bordeaux 1574); Paul Skalich of Lika, 'Quadraginta Novem Librorum de Rerum Causis', ÖNB, MS. 10438, later printed in *Miscellanea de Rerum Causis . . .* (Cologne 1570); cf. below, pp. 353–6. Nostradamus: ÖNB, MS. 10717, predictions for 1565 translated at Maximilian's request. Fabritius and Reisacher: Aschbach, op. cit. iii, 187–94, 256–8; Mayer, op. cit. i, 356, 376, 456, 537, 569, 575, 596, 614, 621, 626–7, 637, 639, 641, 676, 690–2, 694, 697, 702–3, 811.

[82] Picatrix: ÖNB, MS. 9737^{z17}, fol. 140; ibid. MS. 5580, fol. 49; ibid. MS. 10101, fol. 3^r. Steganography: ibid. MS. 9737, fol. 12; cf. below, pp. 351–3. Alchemy: e.g. ÖNB, MS. 5580, fols. 51–2. Dreams: ibid. MS. 9737^{z17}, fol. 96, etc. Preuss and Hippolyti: ibid.^{z16}, fols. 57, 161; ibid.^{z17}, fols. 24, 31 f., 96; ibid.^{z18}, fol. 311*; ibid. MS. 10553, MS. 11449, fols. 6–11. Zuberus: ibid. MS. 11427; cf. J. H. Zedler (ed.), *Grosses Vollständiges Universal Lexicon*, i–liv (Halle–Leipzig 1732–50, hereafter Zedler), sv.

the occult's expositors. Zuber, while poring over the wayward
Hellenisms of his alchemical texts, left us hilarious marginal jottings
to convey his opinion of their philological, if not their philosophical
worth.[83] Yet an equally remarkable development of the period
exhibits similar features: the Mannerist style. At the root of
Mannerism lay a contradiction: frequently confident, virtuoso,
brilliant, extrovert—the veritable culmination of Renaissance
vigour, it nevertheless also manifested quite another face, showing
itself troubled and withdrawn, self-conscious and uncertain, heavy
in symbolism. Not only the strange art of Mannerist painters
belongs here—consider the heroic, but contorted, allusive canvases
of the Rudolfine masters; the duality penetrated every aspect of
culture. Emblem-books, for instance, were a Humanist commonplace, often used as a basis for albums; but the emblem possessed
profounder implications, finding its resonance in the mystery-
haunted temper of the day. To savour the world of emblems we
have only to take up the popular collection published by Sambucus
and read its weird, erudite preface.[84]

Sambucus was an ornament of Maximilian's and Rudolf's court,
and the social background of Mannerism was essentially courtly.
Princes and nobility entered fully into its display, exploring all the
aristocratic possibilities of this hothouse middle-European Renaissance. Many a fine chateau with classical porticoes, arcaded courts,
and inventive interiors bears witness, even today, to their taste:
Prague's Belvedere and Vienna's Stallburg, Opočno and Bučovice,
Jindřichův Hradec and Český Krumlov, Schallaburg, Rosenburg,
and Spittal an der Drau, Sárvár and Sárospatak ... At the same
time, castle-owners achieved no monopoly, for urban communities
also had a stake. Throughout the region citizens perpetuated their
accumulated wealth in civic buildings—from the grandeur of the
Landhaus at Graz to the intimacy of town-halls at Leutschau or
Bartfeld—and those characteristically wide, comfortable squares
where sometimes, as at Telč in Moravia, time has stood still ever
since. The unfolding of Mannerist forms and Humanist attitudes
in the Habsburg territories coincided with an era of prosperity

[83] Ibid. fols. 164ʳ, 174ᵛ, 197ᵛ, 224ʳ, etc. The comments, to make their point more
trenchantly, are in German.
[84] J. Sambucus, *Emblemata* (Antwerp 1564); cf., most recently, H. Homann,
Studien zur Emblematik des 16. Jahrhunderts (Utrecht 1971), 43–78.

which, as in Germany,[85] reached its peak by about 1550 and seems to have sustained itself through the rest of the century.

Economic growth rested on an exploitation of resources; primarily metals: Styrian iron and Idrian mercury, Tyrolean and Bohemian silver, Hungarian copper and gold; but also such staples as Hungarian cattle and wine, Bohemian wheat and flax. Some commodities were worked up and traded locally. More commonly, and more significantly, they were financed by outsiders and marketed at the great emporia of Germany.[86] Thus while Austrians published their books at Frankfurt, Frankfurters expanded their commerce with Austria; while Czechs trooped to Altdorf University, Nurembergers strengthened economic contacts with Prague; while Silesians and Lusatians travelled through Bavaria and Swabia, the major South German merchant houses developed the textile industry of their homeland. The export of Bohemian beer and fish went with German editions of local works on brewing and pisciculture, the latter—appropriately enough—compiled by a Catholic bishop and dedicated to members of the family of Fugger and their Hungarian associates the Thurzós.[87]

Entrepreneurship, and a primitive capitalism based on the

---

[85] The German case is debated, but see—in general—F. Lütge, *Deutsche Sozial- und Wirtschaftsgeschichte* (3rd edn. Berlin 1966), 335 and *passim*; and id., 'Die wirtschaftliche Lage Deutschlands vor Ausbruch des dreissigjährigen Krieges', in *Studien zur Sozial- und Wirtschaftsgeschichte* (Stuttgart 1963), 336–95. Cf. H. Kellenbenz in H. Aubin and W. Zorn (eds.), *Handbuch der deutschen Wirtschafts- und Sozial-Geschichte*, i (Stuttgart 1971), 414–64.

[86] F. Tremel, *Der Frühkapitalismus in Innerösterreich* (Graz 1954); id., *Wirtschafts- und Sozialgeschichte Österreichs* (V. 1969), 148–91; Gutkas, *Niederösterreich*, 168 ff. L. Makkai and J. Vlachovič in I. Bog (ed.), *Der Aussenhandel Ostmitteleuropas 1450–1650* (Cologne-V. 1971), 483–506, 600–27; cf. Vlachovič, 'Slovak copper-boom in the 16th and early 17th century', *Studia Historica Slovaca*, i (1963), 63–95. H. Braumüller, *Geschichte Kärntens* (Klagenfurt 1949), 281 f., 288 ff.; F. Gestrin, 'Économie et société en Slovénie au XVIᵉ siècle', *Annales ESC*, xvii (1962), 663–90, esp. 670 ff.; Zs. P. Pach, 'The role of East-Central Europe in international trade, 16th and 17th centuries', *Études Historiques*, 1970, 217–64.

[87] F. Lerner and J. Janáček in Bog (ed.), op. cit. 147–84, 204–28; G. Aubin and A. Kunze, *Leinenerzeugung und Leinenabsatz im östlichen Mitteldeutschland zur Zeit der Zunftkäufe* (Stuttgart 1940), esp. 271–89. T. Hagecius (Hájek), *De Cervisia, ejusque conficiendi ratione, natura, viribus et facultatibus* (Frankfurt 1585); J. Dubravius, *De Piscinis et Piscium naturis libri V* ([Zurich?] 1559). Dubravius's dedicatees were Anton Fugger and Ferenc Thurzó, Bishop of Nyitra, later a Protestant. On the Fuggers in Hungary see G. Wenzel, *A Fuggerek jelentősége Magyarország történetében* (Bp. 1882).

putting-out system, meant large profits for Fuggers, Thurzós, and their kind; but it could also bring tangible benefits to many a middling landowner or solid burgher, even to the hard-working peasant. For all the rise of the Atlantic seaboard and its colonial empires, trading within Europe expanded throughout the sixteenth century, and the heart of the continent was drawn into a broader commercial orbit. Even in Hungary, despite the ravages of the Turks, fatstock from the grasslands of the *Alföld* continued to feed the patricians of Venice, while the delicate flavour of Tokaj *Ausbruch* was first realized at this time and the little wine-exporting centres of the Upper Tisza region flourished as never before.[88]

In its economic foundations then, as in its religion, this Renaissance society was comparatively open. Indeed, more flexible attitudes were perhaps encouraged by the very predominance of monetary over natural transactions. Civic values mingled with courtly élitism. The nobility, like the dynasty, justified itself as Humanist maecenas: Nádasdys and Batthyánys in Hungary, Rožmberks and Žerotíns in Bohemia, Herbersteins and Starhembergs in Austria patronized scholars and printers, kept educated clergymen, and cultivated polite correspondence.[89] Rising commoners, for their part, sought nobility of spirit, that prime Humanist substitute for nobility of birth. The legions of university-trained lawyers and doctors knew their station, but felt that they inhabited an expansive world, with real scope for advancement; a view nicely conveyed by the ordering of their *Stammbücher*, where aristocrats enjoy pride of place, but have to acknowledge the same conventions as anyone else.

[88] O. Pickl in Pickl (ed.), *Die wirtschaftlichen Auswirkungen der Türkenkriege* (Graz 1971), 71–129; L. Makkai, *A magyar Puritánusok harca a feudalizmus ellen* (Bp. 1952), 23 ff.; id., 'Die Hauptzüge der wirtschaftlich-sozialen Entwicklung Ungarns im 15.–17. Jahrhundert', *Studia Historica*, liii (1963), 27–46, at 36. The ambitious study by I. M. Wallerstein, *The modern world-system, Capitalist agriculture and the origins of the European world-economy in the 16th century* (New York 1974), is neither well-informed nor well-directed in its Central-European sections.

[89] The subject is too large to be introduced properly here. For Hungary see, in general, B. Radvánszky, *Magyar családélet és háztartás a XVI és XVII században*, i–iii (Bp. 1879–96), and G. Tolnai, *Régi magyar főurak* (Bp. 1939?); and, for the particular case of the Nádasdys, *Nádasdy Tamás nádor családi levelezése*, ed. A. Károlyi and J. Szalay (Bp. 1882), *passim*. On Rožmberks and Žerotíns see *Rudolf II*, *passim*; cf., for another interesting Czech case, A. V. Šembera, *Páni z Boskovic a potomní držitelé hradu boskovického na Moravě* (V. 1870), esp. 108 ff.

*

To sum up: Renaissance and Reformation combined in Central Europe to produce a reasonably tolerant and uniform cultural climate. They also brought the climax of a centuries-old process of integration, such that the Habsburg lands became a major carrier of European civilization in the Mannerist age. As for the dynasty, its Humanism outran its Catholicism, while the collective weakness of its political rivals was at once cause and effect of that fragmentation of the Protestant camp which we have observed.

And yet Mannerist civilization was finely, too finely balanced. While its confidence, its subtlety, its thirst for reality, seem the acme of Renaissance learning and virtuosity, it bore also seeds of decay: intellectually it yielded no successful synthesis, or defence of the old unity of Christendom; materially its social base was insecure. This fragility is especially marked in Central Europe, where the whole movement blossomed so late. Indeed, by the reign of Rudolf II it was already living on borrowed time, with its large complement of refugees from fanaticism elsewhere.[90] At court the errant personality of the emperor turned the scales, and in an atmosphere of festering doubt his entourage grew withdrawn, esoteric, self-indulgent. And Rudolf—one significant detail—never travelled anywhere for pleasure.

In the Monarchy at large the situation deteriorated during the last years of the sixteenth century. Protestantism was well established; but where could it lead? Its fissiparity had been made evident to all. The stalemate between dynasty and estates might easily degenerate into political breakdown, and signs of licence were not wanting. No lasting economic solidarity had been achieved. Sectional interests conflicted, the more so when rising prices and threatened markets brought a crisis to entrepreneurs and rentiers. Pressures mounted on the mass of the peasantry, who have been largely absent from this chapter as they were largely absent from the Renaissance landscape. War against the Turks, renewed in 1593, meant disillusion, insolvency, and disorder. Above all a Catholic revival, set in motion decades earlier, had triumphed in neighbouring North Italy and Bavaria, and observers of the Austrian situation saw their chance. 'Our greatest good fortune is that no religion

---

[90] Especially from the Low Countries: M. E. H. N. Mout, *Bohemen en de Nederlanden in de zestiende eeuw* (Leiden 1975).

remains in Austria . . . but every preacher does things in his own style. With time people will notice, and call for the old ways again.'[91] Protestantism would need to be well defined and well organized in order to survive, as its leaders elsewhere in Europe had already shown. Many now expected a trial of strength in the Habsburg lands, and with the new century it was joined.

[91] Bibl, 'Eder', 111, quotation from 1580.

CHAPTER 2

The crisis, 1600–50:
religious and political

The Counter-Reformation of the Habsburg lands was not in its
origins a native growth. As with Lutheranism, we can date its
introduction reasonably precisely; indeed, we can assign the initial
spur to a single individual. In the early 1550s Peter Canisius led a
select band of Jesuits into Austria. He founded a college at Vienna
to be both a spiritual base for the young order and a teaching
establishment in the Catholic cause. Then he moved to Bohemia
and carried on the same work at Prague. Canisius soon returned to
Germany, but he kept his Austrian and Bohemian flocks under
constant surveillance: by the time of his death in 1597 there were
Jesuit houses at Graz, Innsbruck, Olomouc, and elsewhere.[1]

These early Jesuits were mainly foreigners—the first Bohemian
batch of twelve contained only one Czech. Often they came from
Bavaria, whose dukes Albrecht and Wilhelm had constructed by the
1560s a very important model for Catholic reform with a well-
drilled university at Ingolstadt, an Index, and a firm rejection of all
Protestant values. Now the Papacy, emerging victorious from the
Council of Trent, hastened to broaden its central European base. It
set up a permanent nunciature at the imperial court, as well as
tending the collateral Habsburg lines in Styria and the Tyrol; it
sent roving emissaries, like the apostolic commissioner Ninguarda,
to safeguard Roman interests in the Empire at large; it founded a
Collegium Germanicum and then a Collegium Hungaricum in Italy
to nurture direct missionary links. Philip II of Spain too tried to use
his Austrian contacts to promote a new orthodoxy of faith. Canisius,
the Curia, and Madrid planned nothing less than total reconquest.[2]

[1] O. Braunsberger (ed.), *Beati Petri Canisii SJ Epistulae et Acta*, i–viii (Freiburg
1896–1923), is monumental and immaculate. Cf. id., *Peter Canisius, ein Lebensbild*
(Freiburg 1917); A. Socher, *Historia Provinciae Austriae Societatis Jesu*, i (V. 1740),
esp. 28 ff., 50–2, 57 ff.; B. Duhr, *Geschichte der Jesuiten in den Ländern deutscher
Zunge*, i–iii (Freiburg–Regensburg 1902–21), i, 45 ff., 163 ff., 188 ff.
[2] Schellhass, 'Ninguarda'; V. Fraknói, *Magyarország egyházi és politikai összeköt-*

(continued)

What were the prospects for such an outcome? Far from sweeping
a receptive society, like Luther's movement, the Catholic revival
provoked resentment on all sides, not least among the small minority
which still adhered to the old faith and had no wish to break off its
dialogue with the rest of the community. Counter-Reformers
needed to breathe life into the shell of an army top-heavy with
reluctant officers—politicking prelates, a few aristocratic clans, a
leaven of court intellectuals—and having only the tattered remnants
of a rank and file among uncomprehending peasants and in a
handful of towns. They tackled the task in bold fashion, adopting
extreme postures and eschewing any truce. But there was, of course,
much more to their approach than any mere calculation of tactics:
they embodied a fresh spiritual mood which relished the challenge.

The first generation of Counter-Reformation leaders in the
Austrian *Erblande* all rose from modest circumstances. The eldest,
Georg Eder (1523–86), was a Bavarian lawyer who became rector
of Vienna University and made a distinguished career in Habsburg
service, helped by undoubted talent and good connections in
Munich rather than by his cantankerous religiosity. A friend of
Canisius, who tried to secure him a bishopric, Eder devoted his
literary œuvre, correspondence, and professional persuasiveness to
disinterested advocacy of the Roman cause.[3] His clerical counterpart
was Georg Scherer, born in the Tyrol in 1539, one of the earliest
Austrian Jesuits, later court preacher to the archdukes in Vienna,
an ingenious and indefatigable controversialist. Scherer's numerous
polemics against Lutheran ministers and apostate Catholics expose
a good deal of woolly thinking, and his collected works appeared in
print by the end of the century. In the southern provinces the prime
movers were two secular priests, Georg Stobäus and Martin
Brenner, both—like Eder—born in Germany, and both preferred
during the mid-1580s to poor and decayed bishoprics: Stobäus to
Lavant in Carinthia, Brenner to Seckau in Styria, whence they

tetései a Római Szent-Székkel, iii (1526–1689) (Bp. 1903), bk. 2, *passim*;
A. Steinhuber, *Die Geschichte des Collegium Germanicum in Rom*, i–ii (Freiburg 1895),
i; J. Köhler, *Das Ringen um die tridentinische Erneuerung im Bistum Breslau* (Cologne–
V. 1973), 89–156; B. Chudoba, *Spain and the Empire, 1519–1643* (Chicago 1952),
150–2 and *passim*. Cf. *Rudolf II*, 21 f., 34, 85 f.
[3] Bibl, 'Eder'; K. Schrauf, *Der Reichshofrat Dr. Georg Eder. Eine Briefsammlung
...*, i (V. 1904); Wiedemann, *Reformation*, ii, 143–58; E. Tomek, op. cit. 397 ff.

began firm missionary and visitatorial activity.[4] The youngest and most famous in the group is Melchior Khlesl (1553–1631), son of a Viennese baker, who rapidly acquired a whole clutch of ecclesiastical appointments: vicar-general throughout Lower Austria for the diocese of Passau, canon of Breslau, provost of Vienna Cathedral (and therefore chancellor of the university), *Hofprediger*, bishop of Wiener Neustadt, then administrator and later bishop of Vienna. The posts did not necessarily bring even prestige (consecration to the wretched see of Vienna was delayed until 1614), let alone wealth; but Khlesl's great strength lay in a commanding personality and a genius for clear statements which, secure in their own rather specious consistency, could cut through the hesitation of others.[5]

None of these men was popular, but each had some political *points d'appui*: they enjoyed a measure of official support and could profit from Protestant excesses, even though the latter might derive from their own provocation. Their first chance came in Styria, where Archduke Karl, spurred by marriage with a Bavarian Wittelsbach, took the profession of Catholicism more seriously than the rest of his family, and where a tense situation was created by the heated diet of 1578. Prince and estates soon fell out over the issue (unclarified to this day) of whether the towns had been verbally accorded full liberty of confession and Karl seized the opportunity to secure his own position by exerting pressure on the burghers, especially in Graz: despite protests to the imperial *Reichstag* he expelled certain preachers, like the stormy immigrant Jeremias Homberger, manipulated the membership of councils, and tried to enforce Catholic oaths of loyalty. By the end of the 1580s, backed by Stobäus, Brenner, and a forthright Papal nuncio, he had laid the

[4] G. Scherer, *Alle Schrifften*, i–ii (Klosterbruck 1599–1600); I have used the reprint, *Opera oder alle Bücher*…, i–ii (Munich 1613–14). Cf. Socher, op. cit. 428–30 and *passim*. J. Stepischneg, 'Georg III Stobaeus von Palmburg, Fürstbischof von Lavant', *AÖG* xv (1856), 71–132; L. Schuster, *Fürstbischof Martin Brenner, ein Charakterbild aus der steirischen Reformations-Geschichte* (Graz–Leipzig 1898), a huge and uneven volume.

[5] J. von Hammer, *Khlesls, des Cardinals*…*Leben*, i–iv (V. 1847–51), vol. i for this period, is a rambling political study with much important documentation which has never been superseded. Cf. T. Wiedemann, 'Beiträge zur Geschichte des Bisthums Wiener Neustadt', *Ö. Vjschr. f. kath. Theol.*, vii (1868), 241–66; viii (1869), 67–118; ix (1870), 359–74, at 67 ff.; E. Tomek, op. cit. 483 ff.

foundation for further advance by establishing a Jesuit university.[6] Meanwhile parallel moves took place in Lower Austria, where Archduke Ernst hearkened to the promptings of Eder, Scherer, and Khlesl. Again a few inflammatory pastors were exiled, notably Josua Opitz (another foreigner) from Vienna; again a legalistic attack on town administrations was initiated and a wedge driven between burghers and nobles. The regime sought to stem the tide of mass Protestantism in the capital by prohibiting the weekly exodus to castle chapels outside the city precincts.[7]

We should not exaggerate the achievement of this first phase of the Counter-Reformation in Austria, though many historians have done so, even the most distinguished spokesman for the Protestant side, Johann Loserth. It was decisive only in the particular circumstances of the Tyrol under Archduke Ferdinand's experienced rule.[8] Elsewhere committed protagonists like Eder had to admit privately that real progress was very slow. In the 1590s Inner Austria passed through an interregnum after the death of Karl which wiped out most Catholic gains; Vienna and Lower Austria were handed on from Ernst to the vacillating Matthias. Behind the scenes Emperor Rudolf in Prague did next to nothing to help, and with the resumption of war on the Ottoman frontier it seemed that the estates, still overwhelmingly Protestant and holding the provincial purse-strings, could only extend their power. Some signs exist of a broader Counter-Reforming mood: a few monasteries, mostly near the Bavarian border, recovered discipline and spirit, even pioneering a little Catholic printing, and Jesuit missions showed moderate success; but the overall picture remained bleak. When at the very end of the century young Archduke Ferdinand

[6] F. Hurter, *Geschichte Kaiser Ferdinands II und seiner Eltern*, i–xi (Schaffhausen 1850–67), i–ii; Loserth, *Reformation*, bk. 2; id. (ed.), *Acten und Correspondenzen*, i; H. Pirchegger, *Geschichte der Steiermark*, ii (Graz 1931), 445 ff.; Mecenseffy, op. cit. 71 ff. On Homberger, active also in Hungary, see F. M. Mayer, 'Jeremias Homberger', *AÖG* lxxiv (1889), 205–59.

[7] V. Bibl, 'Klesls Briefe an Kaiser Rudolfs II Obersthofmeister Adam Freiherrn von Dietrichstein', *AÖG* lxxxviii (1900), 475–580; id., 'Klesls Briefe an Herzog Wilhelm V von Baiern', *MIÖG* xxi (1900), 640–73; id., 'Erzherzog Ernst und die Gegenreformation in Niederosterreich', *MIÖG*, Ergänzungsband vi (1901), 575–96; Gutkas, *Niederösterreich*, 189 ff. *passim*; Mecenseffy, op. cit. 82 ff.

[8] Loserth, *Acten und Correspondenzen*, iia, intro, esp. p. v, and iib, intro, esp. pp. v–vi, contradict i, intro.; Dimitz, op. cit., pt. 3, 323–30 and *passim*, is better balanced. E. Tomek, op. cit. 453–80, on the Tyrol.

renewed the struggle, Bishop Brenner feared revolt on a Netherlandish scale.[9]

Brenner was wrong: for now the tide began to turn. Inspired by his Bavarian mother Maria, a formidably energetic dowager, by his Ingolstadt education, and by his recent trip to Italy, where at Loreto he swore a notorious vow to eliminate heresy throughout his territories, Ferdinand instigated a much more ruthless campaign to banish Protestants from all the towns of Inner Austria, close their churches and schools, and purge them from the administration. With the help of roving commissions under Stobäus, Brenner, and their pugnacious episcopal colleague Chrön of Laibach, he scattered the uncoordinated resistance of the urban estate, forcing pliant Lutherans like Johannes Kepler to flee, using violence against the refractory, such as Paul Odontius (again, not a native) who left us a vivid record of his tribulations.[10] Simultaneously the same kind of assault was launched in Upper Austria; there a major peasant rising, subdued in 1597, gave the Catholic authorities under *Landeshauptmann* Löbl the chance to implement a Counter-Reformation in the boroughs against the muted opposition of the intimidated nobility. In Lower Austria Khlesl likewise precipitated a clash, though with less devastating results.[11]

[9] For the 1590s: Loserth, *Acten und Correspondenzen*, iia, nos. 1–222. On the monasteries: C. Stengel, *Monasteriologia . . . O.S.B.* (Augsburg 1619), esp. 10 f., 30 f.; *Benediktinerbuch*, 401 f.; Friess, 'Garsten', 258–66; Röhrig, art. cit. 146 ff. There was a press, for example, in the small Franciscan house at Wimpassing (*Régi magyarországi nyomtatványok*, nos. 735–7, 862). On Jesuits: Socher, op. cit., esp. 325 ff., 371–4; there is much information in the published annual news-letter, like the *Litterae Annuae S.J.* for 1600 (Antwerp 1618), 426–44. Brenner's letter in ÖNB, MS. 13746, fols. 1 f.

[10] Hurter, op. cit. iv; Loserth, *Acten und Correspondenzen*, ii, with very copious documentation. P. Dedic, *Der Protestantismus in Steiermark im Zeitalter der Reformation und Gegenreformation* (Leipzig 1930), is just a useful summary. More evidence in G. Stobäus, *Epistolae ad diversos* (Venice 1749), an important source; Stepischneg, art. cit.; ÖNB, MS. 13746, fols. 3–7, etc.; Schuster, op. cit. 428 ff. and *passim*; Dimitz, op. cit., pt. 3, 273–314. On Maria: Hurter, op. cit. iii, and HHStA, Hausarchiv, Fam. Korr. A, Karts. 42–8. On Odontius: R. Leidenfrost, 'Zur Geschichte der Gegenreformation in Steiermark', *JGGPÖ* vi (1885), 54–80; cf. Stobäus, *Epistolae*, 128–30.

[11] Upper Austria: Eder, *Glaubensspaltung*, 249 ff.; M. Ritter, 'Quellenbeiträge zu einer Geschichte Rudolfs II', *Sb.d. bayr. Akad. d. Wiss., ph.-ph.-h. Kl.*, 1872, 237–72; V. Bibl, 'Die Religionsreformation Kaiser Rudolfs II in Oberösterreich', *AÖG* cix (1921), 377–433; Mecenseffy, op. cit. 89–106. Lower Austria: Wiedemann, *Reformation*, i, 498 ff.

*

Caution is still called for. These measures during the years around 1600, the second stage of Austria's re-Catholicization, were by no means conclusive. Among rural communities Protestantism remained largely intact; though expelled from the municipalities with a fork, it could easily grow back. A long and hazardous road lay ahead to restore Catholic uniformity. Yet the ultimate significance of the Austrian evolution appears if we turn to the processes unfolding *pari passu* in the Bohemian and Hungarian lands.

Bohemia's paradigm started from an even lower point. Not only did the Jesuits have to be introduced, but the corner-stone of the domestic hierarchy, the see of Prague, needed to be revived. The first archbishop since Hussite times, Antonín Brus, proved efficient and tactful rather than zealous in the face of many obstacles to the exercise of his office; neither his successor Martin Medek nor the few loyal aristocrats evinced a militant disposition. The Jesuits were more resolute and a good deal showier; their Prague college, the 'Clementinum', offered sound education for Protestant sons and a sophisticated missionary appeal to their parents. Its early ornament was Edmund Campion, who taught and preached with considerable success during the 1570s, then left the vicarious benefits of his willing martyrdom at the hands of a bloodthirsty English government. Campion's *Decem Rationes* soon circulated in the Habsburg lands as an outstandingly well-argued summary of the case for Counter-Reformation.[12] Moravia—the homeland of both Brus and Medek—preserved Catholic traditions slightly better, especially around the cathedral city of Olomouc. Its mild confessional climate could help as well as hinder the old faith and the Jesuits found fertile soil there for a college (settled in 1566) which soon achieved

---

[12] K. Borový, *Brus*, and id., *Martin Medek, arcibiskup pražský* (Pr. 1877), has much on the problems they faced. For the Jesuits: J. Schmidl, *Historia S.J. Provinciae Bohemiae*, i–iv (Prague 1747–59), i–ii; A. Kroess, *Geschichte der böhmischen Provinz der Gesellschaft Jesu*, i–ii (V. 1910–38), i; *Litterae Annuae* (1600), 445–77. Cf. in general *Rudolf II*, 34 ff., and most recently, Z. Kalista, 'Die katholische Reform von Hilarius bis zum Weissen Berg', in Seibt (ed.), op. cit. 110–44. For Campion the standard life by R. Simpson, *Edmund Campion, a biography* (2nd edn. London 1896) rests for the Bohemian period on Schmidl and his predecessor, Balbín (*Miscellanea Historica Regni Bohemiae*, decas i, bks. 1–8, decas ii, bks. 1–2 (Prague 1679–88), i, bk. 4, pt. 1, 189–96). There were early German or Central European editions of the *Decem Rationes* at Trier 1581, Ingolstadt 1583, Graz 1588, Trier and Würzburg 1589, Pr. 1592, V. 1594. Cf. the account (a contemporary copy?) of his martyrdom in ÖNB, MS. 11851.

university status. Further north, in Silesia and Lusatia, things looked far less promising and one of the few remaining pillars of the Catholic establishment, the long-suffering Dean of Bautzen, Johann Leisentritt, boldly tackled the Lutherans on their own ground of hymn-writing, amid desperate appeals for at least moral support from his distant superiors.[13]

From the 1570s there are occasional signs that the Bohemian Counter-Reformation is gathering momentum. On the lands of the Church its values could be propagated with increasing freedom, and the bishops of Breslau joined their colleagues at Prague and Olomouc in carrying out visitations, founding seminaries, and planting regular clergy. Some monasteries displayed stirrings of life and by the end of the century the Premonstratensians had bred three men of real spiritual endeavour. Two of them, Sebastian Freitag, a Renaissance cavalier once tutor to Rudolf II, and Sebastian Fuchs his successor, concentrated on cultural mission: their abbey at Bruck in southern Moravia had a printing-press, a seminary, and lively musical activity.[14] The third was a political priest, Johann Lohelius, Bohemia's Khlesl. Born of poor parents at Eger in 1549, Lohelius entered the neighbouring monastery of Tepl—one of the earliest to reimpose any discipline—then moved to Prague, studied with Campion, and took over the great but very decayed house of Strahov. His remarkably swift reform of Strahov led him on, by dint of continual visiting, pressure on capitular elections, and so forth, to a wider influence throughout Bohemia.[15]

---

[13] ÖNB, MS. 13559, a history of the Olomouc college in the 16th century. Cf. the detailed, but uncompleted study by B. Navrátil, *Jesuité olomoučtí za protireformace*, i (Brno 1916); and J. Radimský, *Jesuité v Olomouci 1567–1773* (Brno 1952). J. Leisentritt, *Catholisch Gesangbuch voller Geistlicher Lieder und Psalmen* ... (2nd edn. Bautzen 1584), esp. the dedications to Maximilian II (in German, reproduced from the 1st edn.) and to the nuncio Bonomi (in Latin).

[14] Köhler, op. cit. 157–248, for Breslau. W. Schram, 'Der Abt von Kloster-Bruck Freitag von Cziepiroh', *Zeitschrift des Vereines für die Geschichte Mährens und Schlesiens*, iii (1899), 312–24; M. Grolig, *Die Klosterdruckerei im Prämonstratenserstift Bruck a.d. Thaya, 1595–1608* (V. 1908).

[15] G. J. Dlabacz, *Leben des frommen prager Erzbischofs Johann Lohelius* (Pr. 1794); K. Pichert in *Anal. Praem.* iii (1927), 125–40, 264–83, 404–22, adds some details. There is correspondence from Lohelius and other material in Str. MS. DH III 49 for the years 1595–1603. On Tepl: Zerlik, art. cit. (*Anal. Praem.* xxxix (1963)), 7c–131. On Strahov: Str. MS. DJ III 2, pp. 109 ff.; and D. K. Čermák, *Premonstráti v Čechách a na Moravě* (Pr. 1877), 59–66. Another monastery which recovered in these years

(continued)

Meanwhile some aristocrats rallied to the cause: at the end of the
1590s Counter-Reformation began on the lands of Jaroslav Martinic
and—especially important—a select band of highly-placed converts
was won which included Vilém Slavata and Karl Liechtenstein.
Martinic, Slavata, and Liechtenstein would all have key roles to
play in later events.

Again we must not anticipate those events. In 1600 Bohemia
remained overwhelmingly Protestant: only two towns held to
Rome; most monasteries were still firmly marooned on the rocks.
A few peasants constrained into superficial alteration of their
allegiance seemed to make no more difference than the calculations—
material or spiritual—of a few educated men; and what was gained
when one magnate crossed the floor could as quickly be lost by the
indiscretion of another, like the fervent Jiří Lobkovic who for his
political pretensions had to live out his days in a royal prison.[16] As
in Austria, however, the years around 1600 brought a sea-change
and the next two decades were to prove decisive. Now a regular
cleric and a pair of aristocrats—one bishop, one politician—injected
real vigour into the Catholic offensive. Lohelius, forever nagging
and scheming, inspired a series of Tridentine measures which
culminated in the important synod held at Prague in 1605; Franz
Dietrichstein, elected to the see of Olomouc in 1598 despite much
local opposition, promptly undertook a provocative assault on
heresy in Moravia; Zdeněk Vojtěch Lobkovic (who, like Dietrichstein, had family connections with Spain) ingratiated himself at
court and as Bohemian chancellor persuaded Rudolf to dismiss his
Protestant advisers and renew mandates against the Bohemian
Brethren in 1602.[17] Dozens of villages and small towns throughout
the kingdom felt an ill wind of confrontation; Braunau, for example,
nestling with its old and enfeebled monastery in a fold of the
Sudeten mountains, received during the same year 1602 the

---

was Vyšši Brod (D. Kaindl, *Geschichte des Zisterzienserstiftes Hohenfurt in Böhmen*
(Hohenfurt 1930), 50 ff.).

[16] Pilsen and Budweis (Budějovice) stayed Catholic. Zlatá Koruna was probably
typical of the monasteries (F. Tadra in *Stud. u. Mitt.* xi (1890), 35–47). On Lobkovic:
M. Dvořák, 'Proces Jiřiho z Lobkovic', *ČČH* ii (1896), 271–92.

[17] F. Vacek, 'Diecēsni synoda pražská z r. 1605', *SbHKr* v (1896), 25–45. On
Dietrichstein and Lobkovic see *Rudolf II*, 68 f., 112, 286–8; both merit, though
neither has yet found, a serious biographer.

fractious abbot Wolfgang Selender whom we shall meet again as a protagonist of 1618.[18]

Hungary's case is different in detail, but strikingly similar in outline. There the initial obstacles appeared insuperable: many historic dioceses overrun by the Turks—the primate himself had to retreat from Esztergom to the sleepy market town of Tyrnau; the rest dominated by Protestants and even, in Transylvania, alienated to a succession of native princes, one of whom (uniquely in the annals of European monarchy) was actually a Unitarian. In 1560 Archbishop Oláh introduced the Jesuits: twelve missionaries, only one a Hungarian, who vegetated for a few years before retreating. Replanted a decade later in Transylvania the Society made a somewhat better showing, sufficient at least to earn from the estates a decree of banishment.[19]

Things began to improve when the hierarchy lent more active support. Its first major Counter-Reformation figure (since Oláh's modest initiatives seemingly made little impact) was Cardinal Drašković, who having appealed for moderation at the last sessions of the Council of Trent later turned into a vigorous critic of Calvinist pretensions. Earthier than the well-born Drašković, Miklós Telegdi worked his way up from peasant birth to become administrator of the vacant primatial see and backed his own unsophisticated polemical sermons with the far-sighted purchase of a printing-press for confessional literature.[20] Both Drašković and

[18] P. Skála ze Zhoře, *Historie Česká, 1602–23*, ed. K. Tieftrunk, i–v (Pr. 1865–70), esp. i, 71 ff., the classic story of these years, beginning—significantly—in 1602. For Braunau: *Benediktinerbuch*, 89 ff.; R. Schramm (ed.), 'Regesten zur Geschichte der Benediktiner-Abtei Břevnov-Braunau in Böhmen', *Stud. u. Mitt.* iii (1882), 4, 312–22; iv (1883), 1, 30–41; V. V. Tomek, *Příběhy kláštera a města Police nad Medhují* (Pr. 1881), 97 ff. Selender, a German from Regensburg, was imposed by the crown. Cf. the start of Counter-Reformation in nearby Troppau: A. Gindely, 'Beiträge zur Geschichte der Zeit Rudolfs II', *Sb. d. k. Akad. d. Wiss., ph-h. Kl.* xviii (1855), 17–62; G. Loesche, *Zur Gegenreformation in Schlesien*, i–ii (Leipzig 1915–16), i (Troppau, Jägerndorf).

[19] Socher, op. cit. 88–91, 138–40, 218–35, 270–6, 287–95, 336–53, 379–410; A. Meszlényi, *A magyar jezsuiták a XVI században* (Bp. 1931); L. Velics, *Vázlatok a magyar jezsuiták múltjából*, i–iii (Bp. 1912–14), i, 50–83. Massive documentation is now available in L. Lukács (ed.), *Monumenta antiquae Hungariae*, i–ii (1550–86) (Monumenta Historica S.J., ci, cxii, Rome 1969–76).

[20] Oláh's synods are in C. Péterfy, *Sacra Concilia Ecclesiae Romano-Catholicae in Regno Hungariae celebrata*, i–ii (Pozsony 1741–2), ii, 39–190. On Drašković see

(continued)

Telegdi died in 1586, but their work ushered in more fruitful years for Hungary's Catholics. Jesuits, now displaying greater local colour, returned to the north-western fringe of the country; one of them, István Szántó, drafted a serious programme of reconquest and worked on a Magyar Bible to rival Károlyi's Calvinist translation, while others laid the foundations for new Catholic schooling, albeit they had to lean heavily on the University of Graz across the Austrian border. In Transylvania some Jesuits clung on, and Alfonso Carrillo acted as chief adviser to the pro-Habsburg Prince Zsigmond Báthory during the 1590s.[21] Members of the high nobility protected these priests and might themselves contribute to the cause: Bálint Balassi (better remembered as an outstanding lyric poet) translated Campion's *Decem Rationes* into Magyar; Miklós Pálffy earned fame as a storming commander in the resumed war of attrition against the Ottomans.[22]

Nevertheless the historian of the Hungarian Counter-Reformation must guard against hindsight. Its base as late as 1600 remained even more circumscribed than in the *Erblande* or Bohemia: a handful of aristocrats; a sprinkling of secular priests, some almost unlettered; hardly any regulars beside the Jesuits who still lived on sufferance; a few books, but Telegdi's press soon ran out of money and authors. In Transylvania, where most had been ventured, the Catholic position crumbled when Zsigmond Báthory, a pathologically unstable character, delivered the province into years of such

---

I. Révész, *Kálvin legelső magyar támadója Draskovics György és Confutatiója* (Debrecen 1933); there is nothing adequate. On Telegdi: A. Fényi, *Telegdi Miklós* (Bp. 1939); for his press: B. Iványi-A. Gárdonyi, *A kir. magyar Egyetemi Nyomda története, 1577–1927* (Bp. 1927), 15 ff.; Gulyás, op. cit. 181–94; for his library: G. Nagy in *MKSz* v (1880), 37–50.

[21] Velics, op. cit. i, 83 ff.; *Litterae Annuae* (1600), 485 ff. On Szántó: Egy. Kt. Coll. Hevenesiana, tom. ix, fols. 1–16, printed in *Annuae Litterae S.J. de rebus Transilvanicis*, ed. E. Veress (Bp. 1921), 199–202; V. Fraknói, 'Egy magyar jezsuita a XVI században', *Katolikus Szemle*, i (1887), 385–433. His Bible was completed by Káldi, cf. below, p. 254. On Transylvania: E. Veress, *Carrillo Alfonz . . . levelezése és iratai* (Bp. 1906); id., *A kolozsvári Báthory-Egyetem története lerombolásáig 1603–ig* (Kolozsvár 1906, separatum from *Erdélyi Muzeum*, 1906); L. Szilas, *Der Jesuit Alfonso Carrillo in Siebenbürgen* (Rome 1966).

[22] I. Gál, 'Balassi Bálint Campianus-a', *ItK* lxxiii (1969), 578–85; on Balassi cf. below, p. 111. P. Jedlicska, *Adatok Pálffy Miklós a győri hősnek életrajza és korához* (Eger 1897), a vast compendium; Wenzel, op. cit. 66–70. Cf. the list of loyal families in F. Kazy, *Historia Regni Hungariae*, i–iii (Tyrnau 1737–49), i, 132.

chaos that the gentle reader is best spared any account of them.[23] What exists in 1600 is a springboard, which can be used on the threshold of the new century by a rising generation of activists. As in Bohemia, three personalities will dominate Catholic destinies over the next crucial period: a regular cleric and a pair of aristocrats, one bishop, one politician. The priest is Péter Pázmány (1570–1637), born a Protestant, converted by Szántó, who having joined the Jesuits and studied at Vienna and Rome is about to begin his career as Central Europe's greatest controversialist. The bishop is Ferenc Forgách (1564–1615), likewise a convert, shortly to be archbishop of Esztergom and to garner a rich harvest of noble souls into the bosom of Mother Church. The politician bears a name with special resonance for future Hungarian history: Miklós Esterházy, as yet only a youth in impoverished circumstances, but a recruit in the very year 1600 to the faith whose star will soon ascend as fast as his own.[24]

*

More even than their counterparts elsewhere, Hungary's Counter-Reformers now ceased to distinguish between confidence and foolhardiness. They compensated for the extra fragility of their position with an extra flamboyance of behaviour and in 1603–4 they propelled King Rudolf into three startling *coups* against their opponents: the trial of a prominent Lutheran magnate, István Illésházy, for sedition; the insertion into statute law, *motu proprio*, of a clause specifically prohibiting all discussion of religious grievances at the diet; and the forcible sequestration of Protestant churches at Kassa and a string of smaller boroughs.[25] Launched with minimal popular support (not even all Catholics approved), in

---

[23] Náprági became the first resident bishop for many years in 1598, then had to flee almost immediately; cf. Jenei, art. cit., and OSzK, MSS. 1146 fol. lat., 1496 fol. lat. There is no satisfactory account of these Transylvanian events in any language; even B. Hóman–Gy. Szekfű, *Magyar történet*, i–v (Bp. 1935–6), iii (by Szekfű), 315–23, seems to lose heart.

[24] V. Frankl, *Pázmány Péter és kora*, i–iii (Bp. 1868–72), i; M. Őry, *Pázmány Péter tanulmányi évei* (Eisenstadt 1970). P. Sörös, 'Forgách Ferenc a bíboros', *Sz* xxxv (1901), 577–608, 690–729, 774–818; K. Ackermann, *Forgách Ferenc* (Bp. 1918). F. Toldy (ed.), *Galántai Gróf Esterházy Miklós munkái*, i–ii (Pest 1853), esp. i, intro; Cs. Csapodi, *Esterházi Miklós nádor* (Bp. ?1942), 17 ff.

[25] Hóman–Szekfű, op cit. iii, 357 ff.; cf. *Magyar országgyűlési emlékek*, ed. V. Fraknói and A. Károlyi, i–xii (Bp. 1874–1917), xi, *passim*; A. Károlyi, 'A huszonkettedik artikulus', *Néhány történeti tanulmány* (Bp. 1930), 154–226.

the government's weakest quarter, this direct attack on all the gentlemen's agreements of the previous century represented the boldest stroke yet in the whole Central European campaign, and also the last straw. The Protestants finally responded in kind, and their protest, merging with general resentment at the brutal and inconclusive Turkish war, was dramatic. István Bocskai, previously a loyal general, led a mass army from Transylvania which overran the country and forced the Habsburgs to capitulate; by the treaties of Zsitvatorok and Vienna (1606) they settled with the Porte, acknowledged Bocskai as Prince of Transylvania, and promised free exercise of the main non-Catholic confessions.[26]

Under the shock of its failure in Hungary, the regime collapsed altogether between the intransigent visionary Rudolf and his mediocre but ambitious brother Matthias. Matthias, seeking any ally against the emperor, had to turn to the strongest forces in the ring: the Protestant estates throughout the Monarchy. In Hungary the reinstated Illésházy and György Thurzó led the opposition at a diet of January 1608 which, in return for electing Matthias king, gained a constitutional statement of the right to universal Protestant worship and further sweeping concessions, among them the expulsion of the Jesuits and Illésházy's nomination as palatine, a viceregal office which Rudolf had tried to suppress. The estates of Moravia and the Austrian duchies likewise took Matthias's side in order to demand their own pound of flesh: an explicit return to the code of practice agreed with Maximilian II in the 1570s.[27] The Bohemians and Silesians, bought off by Rudolf with promises in 1608, held out for even more; the following year they compelled him to sign the famous Letter of Majesty which amounted to a complete redress of grievances with institutional guarantees that the ruler would observe his obligations. A further, separate agreement, the *porovnání*, regulated remaining areas of friction

---

[26] K. Benda, *Bocskai István* (Bp. 1942). Bocskai died on the morrow of his triumph, plunging Transylvania into renewed strife. The treaty of Vienna is printed and analysed in R. Gooss, *Österreichische Staatsverträge: Fürstentum Siebenbürgen, 1526–1690* (V. 1911), 278–367.

[27] Hammer, op. cit. ii; Hurter, op. cit. v–vi; P. von Chlumecky, *Karl von Zierotin und seine Zeit*, i–ii (Brünn 1862); A. Gindely, *Rudolf II und seine Zeit*, i–ii (Prague 1862–5), i; Wiedemann, *Reformation*, i, 525–47. The continuation of the *Magyar országgyűlési emlékek*, ed. Kálmán Benda, will transform our understanding of these events in Hungary.

between the parties. Still worse followed in 1610–11 when Rudolf connived at the abortive attempt by his young cousin Leopold (brother of Ferdinand and bishop of Passau) to stage a military *coup d'état* in Prague.[28]

Though Rudolf cared much more for his thaumaturgic sovereignty than for any revealed religion, it was the Catholic temple which shook from his Samson-like orgy of self-destruction. Though Matthias had Bishop Khlesl as his closest confidant, the opportunistic manœuvrings of the archduke ignored all protests from Rome. The small minority of Catholics seemed to have suffered a disastrous loss of face and influence. In fact their defeats between 1604 and 1611 proved, like their successes before 1600, more apparent than real. They continued to make the political running and—as we shall see—the open crisis of authority in the end actually buttressed their position. By the same token the Protestants, who seemed to have permanent recognition of their majority status, were not really triumphant. Their situation too is full of paradox: now for the first time possessed of their 'freedoms', they feel the first need to organize in defence of them. And although the Catholic camp could muster comparatively few troops, its forces, hardened by adversity, were unlikely to melt away. Thus the Protestants had to put their own mass militia into order, and the exercise revealed weakness as well as strength.

Austria had made some progress during the sixteenth century towards the self-sufficiency of its Lutheran Church. Chytraeus, Polycarp Leyser, and other noted theologians helped organize it. Yet no superintendent was appointed, no proper internal discipline created. Habsburg unhelpfulness had something to do with this, but the real reason lay in the split between zealous Flaccians and accommodating Philippists. Should Martin Luther have the last word, especially about man's total wretchedness before God? Moderation, and the decline of the Flaccians by 1590, also meant victory for lay patrons and *laissez-faire*.[29] Moreover, militant preachers tended to come from Germany, importing their own

---

[28] For 1609: Skála, op. cit. i, 119–257; Gindely, *Rudolf II*, i, ch. 7; Grünhagen, 'Schlesien unter Rudolf II'. For 1610–11: Skála, op. cit. i, 264–329; Gindely, *Rudolf II*, 164 ff.; J. B. Novák, *Rudolf II a jeho pád* (Pr. 1935).

[29] In general, Böhl, op. cit., especially for the Flaccians; Bibl, 'Organisation'; Wiedemann, *Reformation*, i, 351–92.

rivalries and moving rapidly from place to place; in Styria that was
one potent factor in atomizing Protestant resistance to the
archdukes. Lack of local continuity, exacerbated by irregular
ordinations, left no clear framework on which to build when the
great opportunity came in 1608: in Upper Austria the Lutheran
estates were led by the Calvinist Tschernembl; below the Enns
their spokesmen (*Verordnete*) could never be sure quite how far to
go.[30]

Everywhere doctrinal uncertainty hindered cohesion. Bohemia's
Protestants agreed to differ in 1575; although they called up elected
representatives to protect the bargain made with Maximilian, the
role of these *defensors* remained ill-defined.[31] The only consistory
was still in the hands of traditional Hussites (Utraquists); hence no
coercion could be applied to the Lutheran majority, while the
censorious Brethren continued to mistrust its standards of discipline.
When the events of 1609 delivered the consistory into Protestant
hands, it was too late to repair the damage. The Letter of Majesty,
a political victory, could not efface the deeply-etched lines of
cleavage; in its shadow such groups as German-speaking Lutherans
and immigrant Calvinists began to strengthen their separate
identities.[32] In eastern Hungary the Protestant Churches had as
solid an ecclesiastical organization as troubled circumstances
allowed: congregations grouped into seniorates, seniorates into
superintendencies, with elected officers; though their arrangements
were not beyond controversy, as the disputes over Imre Újfalvi and
later over Puritanism reveal. In the main Habsburg area the process
took longer: only after the Csepreg colloquium in 1591 did the
Calvinists and Lutherans of the western borderland go their separate
ways, and the sixteenth-century *modus vivendi* survived even later
in the towns of Upper Hungary. Last of all to regularize their affairs
were the Lutherans of the north-western counties who met at the

---

[30] V. Bibl, 'Die katholischen und protestantischen Stände Niederösterreichs im
XVII Jahrhundert', *Jb. f. Lk. v. NÖ* N.F. ii (1903), 165–323. Much information on
Styria in Loserth, *Acten und Correspondenzen*, i, and (with exaggerations) in
Schuster, op. cit. 197 ff.

[31] R. Stanka, *Die böhmischen Conföderationsakte von 1619* (Berlin 1932), ch. 3. As
Budovec put the matter in 1609, it was like being invited to a banquet and given
nothing to eat. Cf. in general Hrejsa, *Česká Konfesse*, passim.

[32] R. Schreiber (ed.), *Das Spenderbuch für den Bau der protestantischen Salvatorkirche
in Prag* (Freilassing 1956); Mout, op. cit., ch. 5.

synod of Zsolna in 1610 under the leadership of Thurzó and his chaplain Eliáš Láni.[33]

The styles of Thurzó and Láni complemented each other: the cultured Renaissance magnate—son of an apostate bishop—educationalist, liberal churchman, and accommodating politician, prodigal alike as letter-writer and connoisseur, co-operated happily with the tough minister who (as an exact contemporary of Pázmány) well understood the need for confessional polemic and a close definition of ecclesiastical interests.[34] But such harmony was rare; more typically the likes of Thurzó ruled the roost alone. The Protestant cause fell into the hands of powerful families, such as the Jörgers in Lower Austria and the Žerotíns in Moravia, who exerted their political weight in 1608, then dominated the transitory bloom of the next decade. As the lay element finally won out, the tendency to doctrinal vagueness and a docile, uninspiring clergy could not be arrested. Church organization became estates' organization; hardly even that, since the isolation of the towns, which the Counter-Reformation had already seized on before 1600, was confirmed and, with the partial exception of Hungary, their representatives played no serious part in affairs. Still less were the lower orders allowed to contribute, and their betters conveniently forgot that Bocskai's original revolt had succeeded only with the help of the freebooting hajducks. This was the day, not of *Stadtprediger* or *Volksprediger*, but of *Burgprediger*.[35]

The events of 1608–9 filled Protestantism's noble leaders with a mixture of euphoria and unease. Suddenly they could look beyond

---

[33] Révész, *Egyháztörténet, passim*; Zoványi, *Protestantizmus*, 138–272. On Újfalvi, who brought back a measure of reformism from his European travels (cf. above, p. 31): Lampe, op. cit., pt. 2, 337 ff.; on the Puritans see below, pp. 268, 270. On Csepreg: A. Fabó, *Beythe István életrajza* (Pest 1866), 24 ff.; and Zoványi, op. cit. 246–72. S. Imre, *Alvinczi Péter kassai magyar pap élete* (Hódmezővásárhely 1898), 19 ff., for Upper Hungary, and see next note.

[34] *Gróf Thurzó György levelei nejéhez* ..., ed. E. Zichy, i–ii (Bp. 1876); Radvánszky, op. cit. ii, 104–14, 143–7, 149–225; B. Ila, 'Az első magyar evangelikus főiskola tervei', *Károlyi Árpád emlékkönyve* (Bp. 1933), 274–86; L. Gogolák, *Beiträge zur Geschichte des slowakischen Volkes*, i (Munich 1963), 56–62. J. Mocko, *Eliáš Láni ... a jeho doba* (Lipt. Sv. Mikuláš 1902).

[35] i.e. of 'castle-preachers', rather than 'town preachers' or 'popular preachers': Mecenseffy, op. cit. 141–7; H. Wurm, *Die Jörger von Tollet* (Linz 1955); Chlumecky, op. cit., *passim*. On the towns see below, pp. 81–5, and the literature cited there; for the hajducks see below, pp. 97–100.

local frictions and hope to subsume them in a larger alliance, risky but tantalizing, even a grand Central European confederation. During the crisis an impressive chain of close contacts was built up: Tschernembl, the strongest personality of all, and the Starhemberg brothers in Austria; Budovec and Rožmberk in Bohemia; the Žerotíns in Moravia; Illésházy and Thurzó in Hungary. Some—Tschernembl among them—wished to accord a special place to the now fully independent and Calvinist Transylvania. All cultivated links with the West and became an integral part of the international association directed from Heidelberg by Christian of Anhalt which took formal diplomatic shape in the Union of German Protestant princes.[36] The nature of this association has often been misunderstood by historians: it was far more a final tribute to the underlying force of late-Renaissance culture than a solid political front. Some of its members rebelled from a serious sense of Calvinist purpose: we can find elements of a vindication against tyranny in the activities of Bocskai and the influential Hungarian preacher Péter Alvinczi, of Tschernembl and the Starhembergs, of pro-Genevan Bohemians and Moravians like Budovec, Ruppa, or Opsimathes, not to say the *émigré* Polanus.[37] Others resisted the crown in a much more limited, traditional way. Between the two positions disagreement was unavoidable. Styrian Lutherans, having taken the advice of Wittenberg, declined to join the insurgents in 1608 and many Austrians felt grave scruples; Rožmberk in Bohemia began to drag his feet; when Karl Žerotín in Moravia did the same he was outflanked by his cousin Ladislav Velen; the deaths of Illésházy and then Thurzó left the mantle to the latter's fierier son Imre. Bocskai himself made as many enemies as friends through the excesses of his troops.[38]

---

[36] In general: Gindely, *Rudolf II*, i–ii. Much of the correspondence of these men is still unpublished, but some was printed by Chlumecky, op. cit. ii, and Sturmberger, *Tschernembl*, covers the ground well. Cf. I. Lukinich on Tschernembl's view of Transylvania in *BÉ* i (1931), 133–60.

[37] K. Benda, 'A kálvini tanok hatása a magyar rendi ellenállás ideológiájára', *Helikon* xvii (1971), 322–9, and id., almost the same article, in *Études Européennes, mélanges offerts a V.-L. Tapié* (Paris 1973), 235–43; Imre, op. cit. 50 ff.; Sturmberger, *Tschernembl*, 90 ff.; Stanka, op. cit., ch. 2; Odložilik, *Reformovani*, 35–9, 59–62, 103 ff.; F. Hrubý, 'Kalvinský theolog a bouře opavská r. 1603', *ČČH* xxxvii (1931), 593–601 (Polanus). For Opsimathes see below, p. 103, n. 55.

[38] K. Benda, 'Absolutismus und ständischer Widerstand in Ungarn am Anfang

Thus the Protestant estates could never overcome separatism: Moravians still distrusted Bohemians, Upper Austrians held aloof from Lower Austrians, and so forth. Indeed, they may ultimately have encouraged it by their nascent nationalist tendencies and stress on vernacular culture. The incompleteness of their co-operation would at length be laid bare during the great rebellion of 1618–20, while the belligerence of their ideology suffered continually from a strain of fatalism and chiliasm to which I shall return. Nevertheless, for all its debilities, the Protestant confederation briefly formed a real supranational grouping, reaching its acme perhaps at the general diet of Linz in 1614.[39] Humanist contacts were now turned to the service of political ends and some intellectuals, radicalized by changing circumstances, entered on a vigorous literary offensive. Such campaigns as the pamphlet war against the Jesuits, launched in the *Reich*, quickly spread to the Habsburg lands.[40] The clash between Protestant energies, so long restrained, and the set positions of the Counter-Reformation threatened the whole inherited notion of sovereignty in Central Europe.

*

Under this pressure from two armed camps the fragile imperial court disintegrated. The ageing Rudolf could not stomach what he regarded as wild and unprecedented Protestant claims, but he had no desire to create an equally alien Catholic theocracy. In truth the Rudolfine age was overtaken by events and its intellectuals faced a

des 17. Jahrhunderts', *Südostforschungen*, xxxiii (1974), 85–124, at 121 f.; Pirchegger, op. cit. 492 ff.; Loserth, *Acten und Correspondenzen*, iib, nos. 1772 seqq. *passim*; H. Sturmberger, 'Jakob Andreae und Achaz von Hohenfeld', *Festschrift Karl Eder* (Innsbruck 1959), 381–94. For Rožmberk and Žerotin see *Rudolf II*, 140–5; cf. F. Hrubý, *Ladislav Velen z Žerotína* (Pr. 1930). F. Kameníček (ed.), *Prameny ke vpádům Bočkajovců na Moravu* (Pr. 1894).

[39] A. Gindely, *Geschichte des dreissigjährigen Krieges*, i–iv (Prague 1869–80), i, 76–124; B. Ila, 'Az 1614-i linzi egyetemes gyűlés', *BÉ* iv (1934), 231–53. On cultural issues, cf. below, pp. 109 ff.; and on chiliasm, below, pp. 394–9.

[40] R. Krebs, *Die politische Publizistik der Jesuiten und ihrer Gegner in den letzten Jahrzehnten vor Ausbruch des dreissigjährigen Krieges* (Halle 1890); cf. *Speculum sive Theoria doctrinae Jesuiticae* ... (n.p. 1608), with interesting bibliography; M. Bohatcová, *Irrgarten der Schicksale* (Pr. 1966), nos. 5–9; J. Hrubeš, *Politické a náboženské rozpory v Evropě v dobové publicistice 1590–1617* (Pr. 1974), sows only confusion. A fine example of the radicalized intellectual is Johann or Jan Jessenius, on whom see J. V. Polišenský, *Jan Jesenský-Jessenius* (Pr. 1965), 59–78; and *Rudolf II*, 136–8.

situation where Humanism itself—the public profession of neutrality—came to be accounted heterodox. Counter-Reformation profited more from its decay. In 1591 Justus Lipsius returned 'from uncertain faith to certain heresy', as an Anglican correspondent of Blotius's put it. The near-coincidence of his conversion with that of Henri IV gave educated contemporaries much food for thought: suddenly the chief Protestant scholar and the bravest Protestant prince were both lost. Letters to Blotius document this shift, as in the messages from his fellow-countryman Cornelius Werdenborch, who served Jiři Lobkovic and tutored the future Cardinal Dietrichstein, or the stages by which Giffen announced his moves towards the Roman Church and a senior legal appointment in Prague. Blotius's successor, Sebastian Tengnagel, is already a close associate of the Jesuits, using his scholarship in defence of Papal claims.[41] One of the leading figures at court, Johann Matthias Wacker, while remaining devoted to the niceties of Humanist investigation (his correspondence contains lengthy discussion of classical charioteering), followed his friend Lipsius and embraced a resolute Catholicism. His protégé Scioppio went further, passing from erudite youth to rabid Curial propagandist in a few years after 1598. The letters which Scioppio wrote to his former colleagues, carrying first news of the burning of Giordano Bruno, afford striking testimony to a change of mood from free speculation to orthodox constraint.[42] Again the date is 1599–1600, that turning-point when the emperor was prevailed upon to dismiss so many of

---

[41] Lipsius: ÖNB, MS. 9737[717], fol. 158, letter from Henry Wotton. Werdenborch: ibid. fols. 236, 327. Giffen: ibid.[718], fols. 43, 55, 62, 68, 93, 104, 120, 130, 186. S. Tengnagel (ed.), *Complura monumenta hactenus inedita*, in *Gemina adversus Melchiorem Guldinastum Calvinianum replicatorem...Defensio* (Ingolstadt 1612), with ded. to Khlesl. On Tengnagel see Stummvoll (ed.), op. cit. 129–45; and his correspondence in ÖNB, MSS. 9737[r 1].

[42] ÖNB, MS 9734* contains some of Wacker's correspondence; cf. on him *Rudolf II*, 154–7, and Str. MS. DH III 49, fols. 80, 89ᵛ–90ʳ (letters from Lohelius). Scioppio's letters to Wacker are in ÖNB, ibid. fols. 18, 20, the latter (Rome, 19 Feb. 1600) describing Bruno's death in gloating, malicious terms. The detail agrees with Scioppio's well-known letter to their common friend Rittershausen (17 Feb. 1600), first published in *Macchiavellizatio, qua Unitorum animos dissociare nitentibus respondetur* ('Saragossa' = ?Kassa 1621), 30 ff., and often reprinted, as by [I. Oppenheim], pseud. J. Frith, *Life of Giordano Bruno the Nolan* (London 1887), 389–95. On Scioppio cf. *J. Bongarsi et G. M. Lingelshemi Epistolae* (Strasbourg 1660), 46–57, and M. d'Addio, *Il pensiero politico di Gaspare Scioppio* (Milan 1962), *passim*.

his earlier, more liberal advisers like Rumpf and the learned Protestant secretary of state Myllner.[43]

On Rudolf's death in 1612 the remnants of this entourage were swept away. Protestants, unable to dominate his counsels, had already looked elsewhere; ambitious Catholics had committed themselves to Matthias. In fact the two brothers were not so different in their basic politico-religious stance: Matthias just lacked Rudolf's profundity, his taste, his sense of mystery and dignity—in short, the very qualities which made Rudolf a remarkable, but also a remarkably unsuccessful, ruler.[44] Under Matthias the dynastic ideology of the Habsburgs emerges quite distinctly, an aulic Catholicism revivified by the example of Counter-Reformation, especially after 1600, yet never identical with it. As any courtier knew, the struggle between emperor and Pope had a long and involved history behind it; Reformation and Counter-Reformation simply lent a new twist. Let us take a preliminary look at the main issues of jurisdiction and control.

Sixteenth-century Habsburgs reserved their right to prevent Papal interference, even in matters considered purely spiritual by Rome. Thus they gave little sanction to the Tridentine decrees—although Drašković and others wished to proclaim them—and none to Inquisition or Index, not least because the dynasty's thinking on the key question of the chalice was firmly set against the uncompromising spirit of Trent and its local agents who blandly ignored even the Pope's temporary and qualified concessions over communion in both kinds.[45] The emperors resisted the growing influence of nuncios, both as acute diplomats and as spokesmen for Papal pronouncements, including that annual omnium gatherum

---

[43] On Rumpf cf. above, p. 16, n. 29 (library), and the letters to Blotius in ÖNB, MS. 9737[216], fols. 43, 59, 147; ibid.[218], fol. 53. J. Müldner, *Jan Myllner z Milhauzu*, ii (Pr. 1934), prints some of Myllner's interesting correspondence; (vol. i of this work, the biography, seems never to have appeared).

[44] Matthias remains a shadowy figure in the historical literature. Cf. most recently, on his relation with Rudolf in the earlier years, H. Sturmberger, 'Die Anfänge des Bruderzwistes in Habsburg', *MOöLA* v (1957), 143–88.

[45] Péterfy, op. cit. ii, 150 ff.; A. F. Kollár, *Historia Diplomatica Iuris Patronatus apostolicorum Hungariae Regum* (V. 1762), 256–74; id., *De Originibus et Usu perpetuo potestatis Legislatoriae circa sacra Apostolicorum Regum Ungariae* (V. 1764), 129–31 (but cf. below, p. 273 and n. 88 on those two works). For this whole paragraph: Fraknói, *Szent-Szék*, loc. cit.; cf. Wiedemann, *Reformation*, i, 291–324.

of directives to the faithful, the bull *In Coena Domini.* Bishops too
created a variety of tensions. Although they badly needed an
effective episcopal cadre in the provinces (and we shall see how
important a role this played in the eventual re-establishment of
order throughout Central Europe), the Habsburgs set impossible
standards of pliancy. Clashes took place even in the Tyrol; all the
more so in the Austrian duchies which belonged mostly to the
German diocese of Passau. A running fight developed between
Khlesl, as Passau's vicar-general, and the government, until a truce
was hammered out in the 1590s.[46] The largest issue here involved
presentation to bishoprics, which I shall discuss later and which was
no idle matter, even in the fallow years of the sixteenth century,
being raised—for example—at the time of Ferenc Forgách's election
to the see of Veszprém in 1587. Senior ecclesiastical preferment had
peculiar constitutional implications in Hungary where the prelates
formed, literally enough, a bench of bishops: titular dignitaries
most of them, their dioceses wholly or partly lost to the infidel, they
sat on the royal council and took a vital part in dynastic
government.[47] Rudolf was so fearful of rivalry (and so needful of
revenue) that he refused to nominate an archbishop of Esztergom
for the first twenty years of his reign.

The regular clergy posed further problems. Neither Rudolf nor
Matthias had any great sympathy for the Society of Jesus; even at
Graz and Innsbruck its impact on the dynasty can be exaggerated.[48]
And any revival of the older orders immediately raised questions of
sovereignty. What monastic life survived during the sixteenth
century fell clearly within the Habsburg sphere of influence. The
regime could sway elections, even install its own manager or bailiff.
Maximilian II formalized this state of affairs for his Lower Austrian

---

[46] J. Hirn, 'Der Temporalienstreit des Erzherzogs Ferdinand von Tirol mit dem
Stifte Trient', *AÖG* lxiv (1882), 353–98; J. Bücking, *Frühabsolutismus und
Kirchenreform in Tirol, 1565–1665* (Mainz 1972); Wiedemann, *Reformation,* ii, 362
ff.

[47] F. Galla, 'A püspökjelöltek kánoni kivizsgálásának jegyzökönyvei a Vatikáni
Levéltárbán', *LK* xx–xxiii (1942–5), 141–86; Fraknói, *Szent-Szék,* bk. 2, 196 ff.; id.,
A magyar királyi kegyúri jog Szent Istvántól Mária Teréziáig, i–ii (Bp. 1895–9), i, 274
ff. For Forgách: M. Kárpáthy-Kravjánszky, *Forgách Ferenc történetéhez* (Bp. 1938–
9, separatum from *Regnum*); the Pope withheld confirmation largely on grounds of
age. Cf. below, pp. 134 f.

[48] B. Duhr, *Die Jesuiten an den deutschen Fürstenhöfen des 16. Jahrhunderts* (Freiburg
1901), is right for the wrong reasons.

dominions by creating in 1568 the *Klosterrat*, an institution whose workings are still obscure and whose importance has not been adequately recognized: it represents the first step towards an imperial ecclesiastical policy operated with secular sanctions.[49] Of course, like other imperial bodies, the *Klosterrat* acted tentatively, fitfully, and inefficiently. Moreover, it provoked reaction, whether from whole communities—like the protracted though unavailing resistance of Klosterneuburg under provost Andreas Weissenstein, or from strong ultramontane politicians. Khlesl waged a furious war on the *Klosterrat* and its director, Wolf Unverzagt, from which he emerged with a large measure of success, although his own decisions on monastic matters were just as arbitrary.[50]

Yet there are other signs too of a rising generation of 'aulic Christians', who indeed serve Catholicism, but serve their own masters better, and have scope under Rudolf II to serve themselves best of all. We find in the professional ranks of Habsburg government the beginnings of a court étatism which originated perhaps among the bourgeois advisers to Ferdinand I. In Austria Löbl, the tough-minded reformer of Upper Austria, represents this tendency, along with such lawyers as Andreas Erstenberger and Ruprecht Hegen-müller; in Bohemia Lobkovic, for all his genuine fervour, and especially his unscrupulous deputy, Jindřich of Písnice. In Hungary Tiburtius Himmelreich, son of a burgher, exercised an importance quite out of proportion to his office of secretary and had some share in the *démarche* of 1604, while Istvánffy and even Faustus Verantius, sensing the futility of Humanist speculation, adopted similar positions.[51] These men were not fulfilling consistent Habsburg

[49] Wiedemann, *Reformation*, i, 195 ff.; Stülz, op. cit. 114–20, 127–9; Röhrig, op. cit. 135 ff.

[50] W. Jöchlinger, 'Andreas Weissenstein, erwählter Propst von Klosterneuburg, und sein Kampf gegen das Staatskirchentum', *Jb. d. St. Klnb.*, N.F. vi (1966), 7–135; Hammer, op. cit. i, 33 ff., 82 ff., 135 ff., 183 f. Examples of Khlesl's dictation in *Cisterzienserbuch*, 90 f., 582–4; *Chorherrenbuch*, 107 f., 229–31; C. Rapf, 'Die Abtbischöfe des Wiener Schottenstiftes im 17. Jahrhundert', *Festschrift F. Loidl*, i–ii (V. 1970), i, 255–300, at 256 ff.; cf. Wiedemann, *Reformation*, ii, 236–9.

[51] H. Goetz, 'Die geheimen Ratgeber Ferdinands I', *Quellen und Forschungen aus italienischen Archiven*, xlii–xliii (1963), 453–94; Wiedemann, *Reformation*, i, 459 ff. (Erstenberger). On Löbl and Hegenmüller see above n. 11, esp. Ritter, art. cit. and Eder, *Glaubensspaltung*, 410–13. On Pisnice: K. Stloukal in *Sborník prací věnovaných J. B. Novákovi* (Pr. 1932), 363–80. ÖNB, MS. 8579 contains some decisions handled

(continued)

policies, least of all those of the tergiversating Rudolf; but in an inchoate way they interpreted them and planted the seeds of a future development. Ultimately they were rivals to a traditional Roman-Catholicism, and while seeming to be its allies they harnessed its energies for their own purposes.

Thus Papal and dynastic Catholicism, notionally distinct, wove intricate patterns in these years and much of their interaction remains veiled and confused. Unverzagt, Khlesl's foe and Rudolf's confidant, was nevertheless a friend of the archduchess Maria in Graz; Himmelreich's son György became administrator of the monastery of Pannonhalma and devoted himself to the Benedictine cause; Lobkovic and his wife Polyxena, while retaining imperial favour, worked closely with the nuncios and the Jesuits of the Clementinum. Above all Khlesl pursued a double career: the self-appointed restorer of discipline in the Austrian Church against all the odds, he also planned Matthias's policies, including the strategic retreat of 1606–9. The fierce chancellor of the university who conceived its take-over by the Jesuits, he also played the peacemaker *vis-à-vis* the increasingly minatory demeanour of German Catholics. Despite delivering a major sermon against communion in both kinds in 1590, he continued to administer it for a further decade.[52] But judgment on Khlesl, one of Central European history's most intriguing figures, must await a full scholarly investigation.

*

Altogether we should beware of attempting to draw clear distinctions on slender evidence where contemporaries' vision of events was scarcely less blurred than our own. Yet in the Counter-Reformation interplay of Church and state the year 1600 appears once again to separate two stages of evolution. Before 1600, as we have seen, Catholic revival made only piecemeal progress, mainly independent of the Habsburgs, but sheltering under an archducal aegis wherever

---

by the obscure Himmelreich; cf. his earlier (1575–7) letters to Blotius in ibid. MS. 9737[z15], fols. 18, 22, 25, 38, 292; Sörös, art. cit. (*Sz* 1901), 596 f.; Hóman–Szekfü, op. cit. iii, 369; L. Szilágyi in *Emlékkönyv Domanovszky Sándor* (Bp. 1937), 556–60. Istvánffy was involved in the indictment of Illésházy (Holub, op. cit. 34–9).

[52] Unverzagt's letters to Maria are in HHStA, Hausarchiv, Fam. Korr., loc. cit. Rumpf also corresponded with her: Hurter, op. cit. ii, 544–8, 567–71; iii, 489–93, 533, 545–9, 554–5, 563–5. On the younger Himmelreich see Fuxhoffer, op. cit. i, 117–21; Erdélyi–Sörös (eds.), op. cit. iv, 75–85. For Khlesl cf. n. 5 above. The sermon (Wiedemann, 'Wiener Neustadt', 81–3) was later printed.

possible. Rome's representatives did not press points of friction and displayed a studied public deference towards Maximilian, even towards Rudolf, which has often misled historians. What cause, but fits of madness, could make His Majesty so uncooperative? In fact our most candid witness for the 1580s, Georg Eder, already harboured no illusions about the emperor's wilful unreliability.[53] Meanwhile the dynasty, impelled by a mixture of sentiment and calculation, used the old Church's resources and never quite abolished the status of Catholicism as most favoured confession.

After 1600 the climate changed, and a Roman movement of real fervour and originality achieved decisive advances in open disregard of Habsburg weakness. Forced to retrench, to work as a distinct 'party', its backers evolved a political determination which complemented their doctrinal commitment. Throughout the Monarchy Catholic estates came into being, a dissident minority of nobles working together with the local prelates. In Hungary Forgách and Pázmány shrewdly aligned their forces behind the national opposition at the diet of 1609. By supporting Thurzó as compromise candidate for the dignity of palatine, they extracted in return sweeping concessions for their Church which had seemed so near extinction at the time of Bocskai: lands were returned, the legal rights of clerics guaranted, Jesuit activity was soon tacitly permitted again.[54] In 1616 the contentious Pázmány, duly dispensed from his regular vows, succeeded Forgách as archbishop; two years afterwards the latter's convert brother Zsigmond followed Thurzó as palatine. In Bohemia Catholic diehards steadfastly refused to acknowledge Protestant equality: Lobkovic, Martinic, and Slavata never recognized the Letter of Majesty or the *porovnání*. Nor did Lohelius, who in 1612 became Archbishop of Prague and gained the additional power to present to all benefices situated on crown lands, a right exercised with equal firmness in Moravia by Cardinal Dietrichstein.[55]

[53] Bibl, 'Eder', 129, 132. Other evidence in *Rudolf II, passim*.

[54] A. Károlyi, 'Az ellenreformáció kezdete és Thurzó György nádorrá választása', *Sz* liii–liv (1919–20), 1–33, 124–63, an important article; *Pázmány Péter összegyüjtött levelei*, ed. F. Hanuy, i–ii (Bp. 1910–11), i, nos. 12–14; Fraknói, *Szent-Szék*, bk. 3, 268 ff.; Sörös, art. cit. (*Sz* 1901), 713 ff., 774 ff.; Velics, op. cit. ii, 3 ff. Cf., on Austria, Wiedemann, *Reformation*, i, 518 ff., 545–7; Bibl, 'Stände', *passim*.

[55] J. Vávra, 'Katolíci a sněm český r. 1608 a 1609', *SbHKr* i (1893), 3–28; Skála, i, 346–8 on Lohelius; Fr. Kameníček, 'Protireformační snahy Matyášovy na Moravě (1608–18)', *SbH* (Rezek), i (1883), 140–59, on Dietrichstein.

The political leadership took confidence from the internal strength of the movement, a cohesion helped by synods at Prague and Tyrnau and by the organizational abilities of Khlesl in Austria. Conversion of important persons proceeded apace: in Hungary, for example, where Pázmány and his hot-headed colleague Balásfi thundered out against the sectaries, the clergy won over György Drugeth of Homonna, the country's toughest military commander, while the rising star of Esterházy showed how much neophyte zeal could accomplish.[56] Monastic life (less easily indicted as the pursuit of mere ambition or fashion) likewise continued to recover. Lohelius and his Premonstratensian successor Questenberg at Strahov raised their house to a new eminence, expanding its judicial and economic, as well as spiritual power. So did the uncompromising Benedictine Selender at Braunau and Cistercian abbots in Austria like Alexander a Lacu at Wilhering, Johann Seyfried at Zwettl, and Simon Rupert at Lilienfeld. After a century of neglect some rebuilding began, as on the rock of Göttweig and at Rein, a few miles behind Graz.[57] One single generation of novices who entered Heiligenkreuz at this time fresh from the Collegium Germanicum in Rome proceeded to resuscitate a string of Austrian monasteries; among them was the Rhinelander Anton Wolfrad who later followed Khlesl as bishop of Vienna. Jesuit colleges were founded at Laibach, Klagenfurt, and Leoben, at Gorizia and Trieste, at Linz, Passau, and Krems; and other new or revived orders appeared: Capuchins, Augustinians, Servites, Camillians, Brothers of Mercy.[58]

---

[56] Vacek, art. cit.; Péterfy, op. cit., esp. ii, 190–218. I. Szabó, *Balásfi Tamás élete és munkái* (Bp. 1897). On Homonnai Drugeth, whose brother had fought with Bocskai, see Károlyi, 'Ellenreformáció', 5 f. (where his conversion is dated in 1608, though the *Litterae Annuae S.J.* for 1606, 557 f., suggest 1605); D. Angyal in *Sz* lxiii-lxiv (1929–30), 353–7; *MIT* ii, 35; and cf. below, p. 421. For Esterházy: Csapodi, op. cit. 22 ff.

[57] On Strahov and Braunau see below, pp. 218–21. Stülz, op.cit. 136 ff. (Wilhering); *Cisterzienserbuch*, 584–6 (Zwettl), 171 f. (Lilienfeld); *Benediktinerbuch*, 137–40 (Göttweig). On Rein: *Cisterzienserbuch*, 383 ff.; and cf. Hurter, op. cit. ii, 69–82.

[58] B. Gsell, 'Beitrag zur Lebensgeschichte des Anton Wolfradt', *Stud. u. Mitt.* iii (1882), 4, 334–45; iv (1883), 1, 41–8; 2, 255–67; A. Hopf, *Anton Wolfradt, Fürstbischof von Wien . . .* , i–iii in 4 vols. (but only 217 pp. in total) (V. 1881–4). It is an interesting sign of Counter-Reformation flexibility that both Wolfrad and his predecessor, a Lacu, passed from the Cistercians to the Benedictines to head the important abbey of Kremsmünster; cf. G. Wacha, 'Die Korrespondenz des Kremsmünsterer Abtes Alexander a Lacu mit den bayrischen Herzogen', *MÖStA*

In such ways the Catholic camp continued to take the initiative, outsmarting Protestant conciliators like Thurzó and outflanking moderates on its own side like Bishop Náprági or Adam Sternberg, the Grand Burgrave of Prague. The Protestant estates responded from those more advanced constitutional positions which they had so recently occupied. Now Matthias, pressed by his militant heir presumptive, Ferdinand of Styria, had to choose between them, and he was forced into alliance with Rome on the latter's terms. Pope and emperor, temporarily united, each sought to overturn the arrangements reached in 1608–9: the Church, because its faith could never be constrained by documents signed under duress; the dynasty, because Protestant rights were at best contracts agreed for a limited period, at worst pure graces of the sovereign. In 1618 their joint campaign issued in open confrontation. Two incidents illustrate clearly the contradictory nature of the Catholic programme at this point: on the one hand the provocation at Braunau (Broumov) and Klostergrab (Hrob) which led directly to the outbreak of the Bohemian revolt; on the other hand the high-handed arrest of Khlesl by Archduke Ferdinand which rendered any peaceful resolution of that revolt impossible.

Khlesl's downfall, however dramatic in itself (imagine Richelieu kidnapped by Gaston d'Orléans!), was perfectly logical: the old cardinal, still servant to the aims of an earlier phase of Counter-Reformation, is swept aside by men with a new vision of Catholic politics.[59] The Bohemian dispute, equally logical, nevertheless requires some brief explanation. The destruction of Protestant churches at Braunau and Klostergrab has conventionally been seen as a mere pretext for the Defenestration of Prague. So, in a sense, it was. Yet the issue of the two churches was protracted and crucial, since both places belonged to bastions of the Counter-Reformation: Braunau to the local monastery under its intransigent abbot Selender and Klostergrab to Archbishop Lohelius.[60] Protestants

---

xxvi (1973), 168–211. On the Jesuits: Duhr, *Geschichte*, ii, 1, 323–52; Dimitz, op. cit., pt. 3, 363–81. On the orders in general, Skála, op. cit. ii, 5, a jaundiced view; and below, pp. 123–33.

[59] Hammer, op. cit. iv, 78 ff., and ibid. Urkunden, nos. 865 seqq.; Hurter, op. cit. vii, 303 ff.

[60] Strictly speaking Klostergrab (Czech: Hrob or Hroby) had belonged to the Cistercian abbey of Ossegg, dissolved in 1580 and granted—pending some possible future restoration—to help endow the archbishopric. Cf. *Cisterzienserbuch*, 303 ff.

argued—following an old constitutional opinion—that all Church
land belonged ultimately to the crown; those who dwelt on it
therefore—by the terms of the 1609 *porovnání*—enjoyed freedom of
religious association and public worship. Catholics and the dynasty
denied their claim, on the grounds that Church land was only
protected, not owned, by the crown. In other words, it was the
Protestant side which appealed to the sovereign rights of the
monarch (much as contemporary Calvinist writers like Melchior
Goldast defended imperial interpretations of German law), the
Habsburgs who conceded those same rights to the Church of
Rome.[61] The paradox would not have amused Ferdinand I or
Rudolf II; nor—as the fate of Khlesl suggested—could it be long
sustained. It lasted just long enough to destroy Protestantism as a
political force in Central Europe.

Here is no place to study the rebellion and war of 1618–20 (though
it certainly deserves a modern treatment).[62] As insurgents the
Protestants continued to exhibit the same awkward mixture of
resolve and hesitation as earlier, the same kind of novelty which
masquerades as historical usage. We see their uncertainty in the
Defenestration itself, that tragi-comic charade which hoped to
eliminate by medieval means the two chief representatives (Martinic
and Slavata) of a king (Ferdinand II) so recently elected with an
overwhelming majority. We see it in the half-forthright, half-
apologetic justifications of the insurrection. The radical implications

---

[61] Gindely, *Rudolf II*, i, 353–5; id., *Dreissigjähriger Krieg*, i, 61 ff.; cf. the discussion
in J. Gebauer, *Die Publicistik über den böhmischen Aufstand von 1618* (Halle 1892), 5–
7. For Catholic views see C. Carafa, *Commentaria de Germania Sacra Restaurata*
(Cologne 1639), 57 f.; J. Svoboda, 'Die Kirchenschliessung zu Klostergrab und
Braunau und die Anfänge des dreissigjährigen Krieges', *Zschr. f. Kath. Theol.* x
(1886), 385–417. For Protestant views see *Gründtlicher Beweisz das die zu den
Geistlichen Güttern und Clöstern gehörige* [sic] *Unterhanen* [sic] . . . *gutt recht haben* (Pr.
1618); Skála, op. cit. ii, 11 ff., 259 ff. M. Goldast, *Monarchia S. Romani Imperii*, i–ii
(Hanau 1611–14), a work argued against by—*inter alia*—Tengnagel (above n. 41).

[62] Contemporary narratives in Skála, op. cit. ii–iv, and J. J. Beckovský, *Poselkyně
starých příběhův českých*, ii, in 3 pts. ed. A. Rezek (Pr. 1879–80), pt. 2. Far the best and
liveliest account is still Gindely, *Dreissigjähriger Krieg*, i–iii (not to be confused with
his later sketch of the whole Thirty Years War which was translated into English, i–
ii (London 1885)). Those who reckon Gindely a dry positivist historian should
read—or reread—his splendid description of the Defenestration (i, 237–99). The
most important recent development is the publication of the *Documenta Bohemica,
Bellum Tricennale illustrantia*, ed. J. V. Polišenský *et al.*, i—(Pr. 1971—), i–ii, with a
detailed new analysis by Polišenský in vol. i. He makes many of the same points in
The Thirty Years War, tr. R. Evans (London 1971).

of much of its pamphlet literature were muffled by its leaders, who thus narrowed support for the movement at home without creating any real European enthusiasm for their cause. Having expropriated the Jesuits and other prominent Catholics they hastened to proclaim a programme of religious toleration. The revolt enjoyed some military fortune which culminated in a famous episode when the rebel generalissimo, Count Thurn, came within an ace of capturing Ferdinand at Vienna, and this fired larger expectations. Ferdinand was deposed and the Elector Palatine, Frederick V, accepted the Bohemian crown; the prince of Transylvania, Bethlen Gábor, occupied most of Hungary. But although something like a great Central European confederation at length emerged, almost its only collective act was to christen the new monarch's infant son, Rupert of the Rhine.[63] Then splits between Lutherans and Calvinists, nobles and towns, combined with a lack of effective foreign support to make lasting success increasingly unlikely. Meanwhile, with Matthias dead and Khlesl detained in a Tyrolean monastery, Ferdinand could call up his own backers: the Pope, Spain, above all Bavaria with its well-drilled regiments under Count Tilly.

*

The victory of an international Catholic army on the White Mountain in November 1620 introduced a third phase of the Counter-Reformation. Ferdinand II, ruler of Inner Austria since 1596, King of Bohemia since 1617 and of Hungary since 1618, Holy Roman Emperor since 1619, was suddenly master in his own house. Both emperor and Pope saw the battle as a providential deliverance, and much was made of the miraculous role of a certain Carmelite friar and other heavenly portents: latest in a string of divine interventions since the angels had first arrested Martinic and Slavata in their plunge to otherwise certain death beneath the Hradschin.[64]

---

[63] Skála, op. cit. iv, 16–52.

[64] On P. Dominicus OCarmDisc (1559–1630), who died in the Hofburg at Vienna, see J. Caramuel Lobkovic, *Dominicus: hoc est venerabilis p. Dominici … virtutes, labores, prodigia …* (V. 1655); S. Riezler, 'Der Karmeliter P. Dominikus a Jesu Maria und der Kriegsrat vor der Schlacht am Weissen Berge', *Sb. d. bayr. Akad. d. Wiss., ph.-ph.-h. Kl.* 1897, 423–44. Cf. Beckovský, op. cit., pt. 2, 280–3, 287, 292–4, 304. Vilém Slavata, *Paměti*, ed. J. Jireček (Pr. 1866), 82 f., attributes his survival to a kind of angelic parachute. Cf. J. von Riegger (ed.), *Archiv der Geschichte und Statistik*, ii (Dresden 1793), 498 ff., for Martinic's account; and also F. Macháček, 'Defenestrace pražská r. 1618', *ČČH* xiv (1908), 197–211, 297–311, 436–51, esp. at 442–6.

Indeed, like the Defenestration, the 'Battle of the White Mountain' has a delicious ring of absurdity about it: an hour-and-a-half's skirmishing between makeshift armies on a featureless plateau just west of Prague. I have already stressed the disorder of the Protestants before combat was ever joined, whereas—given any adequate leadership—they could have resisted long afterwards, even in Bohemia. Why then did the engagement prove a turning-point (and in that sense at least it deserves the traditional appellation 'Mountain')? The answer lies in the reaction to it of the new emperor.

Ferdinand's view of politics on the morrow of the White Mountain may be summed up in a simple equation: Protestantism equals disloyalty. This identification of heresy with political opposition was his own; though notoriously faithful to a few chosen advisers, the emperor always retained his power of decision. From before 1600 he had been developing a theory of confessional absolutism: the Catholic monarch, prostrate before God, must become all-powerful over his own subjects. The legalistic approach, already adopted in Styria, that Protestants had never acquired real public rights, was now underscored by a theocratic one, that Protestants could not belong within society at all. The creed, disarmingly straightforward, would guide Habsburg attitudes well into the eighteenth century; but its implementation was far from straightforward and sometimes yielded surprising consequences. Rather, a tone of government had been set, with religious unity as a more fundamental goal than political unity. Ferdinand II willed the ends; neither he nor his successors were altogether in a position to will the means.[65]

The new stance amounted to a volte-face with immediate implications: it dealt a death-blow to moderate Protestants throughout the Monarchy. And historians have not commonly appreciated how many there still were in 1620. In the Bohemian lands some commanding figures in public life, especially Karel Žerotin, led eleventh-hour attempts to heal the breach between

---

[65] Hurter, op. cit. xi, 574–674, on the character of Ferdinand II; cf. Gindely, *Dreissigjähriger Krieg*, ii, 1–25, and F. Stieve in *ADB*, s.v. There is a good description of his 'absolutism' by H. Sturmberger, *Kaiser Ferdinand II und das Problem des Absolutismus* (Munich 1957); G. Franz in *Archiv für Reformationsgeschichte* xlix (1958), 258–69, is not significant.

estates and crown, and they had Silesian counterparts like Johann Christoph of Brieg and Hans Ulrich Schaffgotsch. Austrian nobles split disastrously over the question of allegiance to Ferdinand and many of them—Enenkel, for example—refused to rebel. Styria's Lutheran estates made no move at all.[66] In Hungary the Thurzó tradition was sustained by another member of the clan, Szaniszló Thurzó, elected palatine in 1622, as well as by such prominent politicians as Péter Révay; while eirenist, submissive views had considerable currency among Protestant intellectuals. Even many of the leaders who supported Bethlen in 1620: Imre Thurzó, Gáspár Illésházy, Ferenc Batthyány and his spirited Czech wife (a Lutheran Lobkovic), would have responded to any genuine overture from Ferdinand.[67]

This fund of goodwill the Habsburgs now chose to liquidate. The purge began in Bohemia, as direct retribution: in June 1621 twenty-seven fomenters of the revolt were executed and the rest had all their property confiscated. The symbolic concession of the chalice for the laity was now promptly and definitively withdrawn and larger measures soon followed: we have evidence that plans were already afoot to present the whole Protestant community with the alternatives of conversion or exile.[68] The attack commenced with

<hr/>

[66] For Bohemia: Gindely, *Dreissigjähriger Krieg*, i, 442–86; ibid. i, 366–72, 395–402, 430–6; ii, 37–51, on Žerotin; Skála, op. cit. iii, 121 ff.; Polišenský, *Thirty Years War*, 86 f., 101 f. For Silesia: C. Grünhagen, *Geschichte Schlesiens*, i–ii (Gotha 1884–6), ii, 162–85. On the cultured Johann Christoph of Brieg (1591–1639) see Krebs in *ADB*, s.v. For Austria: Gindely, op. cit. iii, 185–230; Bibl, 'Stände', 296–309; Luschin, *Studien*, 49 f.; Gutkas, *Niederösterreich*, 223 ff.; Coreth, 'Enenkel', 276 ff.

[67] R. Hrabecius, *Oratio Funebris in solennibus exequiis . . . D. Petri de Rewa* (Kassa 1623); S. Szilágyi, *Révay Péter és a szent korona* (Bp. 1875). M. Kubinyi, *Bethlenfalvi Gróf Thurzó Imre* (Bp. 1888), thin and sentimental; cf. L. Závodszky, *Thurzó Imre Gróf wittenbergi rektorsága* (Bp. 1912). L. Szádeczky (ed.), *Bethlen Gábor levelei Illésházy Gáspárhoz, 1619–29* (Bp. 1915). S. Takáts, *Zrinyi Miklós nevelőanyja* (Bp. 1917), esp. 48 ff., 105 f., on the Batthyánys. A further aristocratic example would be the unscrupulous György Széchy (I. Acsády in *Sz* xix (1885), 21–47, 116–25, 212–22, 306–15, at 27 ff.). Many Hungarian intellectuals held to the moderate positions of Bernegger at Strasbourg and David Pareus in Heidelberg; cf. below, pp. 112–15.

[68] Skála, op. cit. v, 81–142, and Beckovský, op. cit., pt. 2, 323–52, have differing views about the punishment of the rebels. Cf. Gindely, *Dreissigjähriger Krieg*, iv, 36–105; id., *Geschichte der Gegenreformation in Böhmen* (Leipzig 1894), 18 ff.; T. V. Bílek, *Dějiny konfiskací v Čechách po r. 1618*, i–ii (Pr. 1882–3), i, pp. xxxiv–lix. On the chalice (already eliminated everywhere else): Constant, op. cit. 742–68; Gindely, *Gegenreformation*, 108–11; V. Líva, 'Jan Arnošt Platejs z Platenštejna', *ČMM* liv (1930), 15–78, 293–336, at 61 ff.; Köhler, op. cit. 157–63. On Catholic plans: Bílek,

(continued)

the real 'sectarians', the Calvinist preachers, who could all be branded as guilty of sedition, at least implicitly, and who were expelled from the end of 1621. The Lutheran ministers speedily shared their fate, despite some half-hearted Saxon intercession, and within three or four years open Protestant worship had effectively ceased. The next stage, reached in 1625–6, brought pressure on townsmen to yield by means of reforming commissions and sharper forms of *force majeure*. Finally, in 1627, Ferdinand decreed a new constitution which explicitly established the one-confession state, and a few months later the government gave Protestant nobles six months notice to accept it or quit. Their peasantry, of course, faced the same prospect, except that many had only Hobson's choice.[69]

This methodical campaign was not made possible by the White Mountain alone. It harmonized closely with the startling military victories of the Habsburgs in Germany during the 1620s. The earlier expulsions coincided with the occupation of the Palatinate and the battle of Stadtlohn, the later onslaught with Wallenstein's still headier advance to the shores of the Baltic. Even so, to intend was not necessarily to implement; the Counter-Reformation encountered reactions which varied from surly external conformity to embittered resistance. By the standards of the time it was thorough and certainly tough. An ill-managed, profiteering government under Karl Liechtenstein gave no quarter, while in conditions of effective martial law a vicious *soldatesca* battened down on the entire population; the decade is rife with stories of brutality.[70] The

Reformace katolická neboli obnovení náboženství katolického v království českém po bitvě bělohorské (Pr. 1892), 20 ff.; Gindely, *Gegenreformation*, 88 ff.; A. Kroess, 'Gutachten der Jesuiten am Beginne der katholischen Gegenreformation in Böhmen', *HJ* xxxiv (1913), 1–39, 257–94; H. Grisar, 'Vatikanische Berichte über die Protestantisierung und die katholische Restauration in Böhmen zur Zeit Ferdinands II', *Zschr. f. Kath. Theol.* x (1886), 722–37.

[69] In general: Carafa, *Commentaria*, 98 ff. *passim*, and appendix; id., 'Relatione dello stato dell'Imperio e della Germania', ed. J. G. Müller, *AÖG* xxiii (1860), 103–449, at 239–58; Skála, op. cit. v (to 1623); Gindely, *Gegenreformation* (to 1627); Bilek, *Reformace katolická*; E. Denis, *Čechy po Bílé Hoře*, tr. and expanded by J. Vančura, i–ii (3rd edn. Pr. ?1921), i, bk. 1. Cf. below, pp. 118 f.

[70] In general: Gindely, *Gegenreformation*, esp. 214–36 on Kuttenberg; A. Podlaha (ed.), *Dopisy reformační komisse v Čechách z let 1627–9* (Pr. 1908). J. A. Comenius *et al.*, *Historia persecutionum Ecclesiae Bohemicae* (n.p. 1648), has some historiographical interest; as has [C. A. Pescheck], *The Reformation and Anti-Reformation in Bohemia*, i–ii (London 1845), ii. Specific cases: *Paměti Jana Jiřího Haranta ... 1624–1648*, ed. F. Menčík (Pr. 1897); G. Gellner, *Životopis lékaře Borbonia a výklad jeho deníků* (Pr.

regime struck hardest at the well-to-do, many of whom had to sell their estates for a pittance and grovel before the authorities. The towns suffered as corporate bodies for the sins of individual burghers; they fell into hopeless debt as the remaining citizens bore war levies piled onto the financial penalties for their rebellion.[71]

In Moravia events took the same course, with Cardinal Dietrichstein directing both the political operations and the spiritual mission. The day of reckoning approached for the Protestants of the *Erblande* too. Upper Austria, which under Tschernembl had made common cause with Bohemia, ranked likewise as conquered territory and was treated accordingly. The new policy, aggravated by the excesses of the occupying Bavarian troops, roused the peasantry to a revolt in 1626 which only hastened the banishment of all Protestants.[72] The Inner Austrians had only parleyed desultorily in 1619–20, but the changed situation gave Ferdinand an excellent pretext to complete the work he had begun thirty years earlier: between 1628 and 1630 some 800 Styrian, Carinthian, and Carniolan nobles went into exile. In Lower Austria, where a majority of the estates had remained loyal, their religious concessions were not formally abrogated. But the government expelled the preachers, completed an official Counter-Reformation in the towns, and generally exerted strong pressure on Protestant nobles to swim with the stream.[73]

In Hungary things were different. Confessional pluralism rested on constitutional guarantees which could not be slashed in two—as the Letter of Majesty literally was—by an unsympathetic sovereign. More important, the Hungarian opposition was able, with Tran-

---

1938), 112 ff.; E. Schebek, 'Zur Geschichte der Gegenreformation in Böhmen', *MVGDB* xiii (1875), 10–27.

[71] Bilek, *Dějiny konfiskaci, passim*; Polišenský, *Thirty Years War*, 133 ff. *passim*. Cf. below, ch. 6, for the political changes.

[72] Moravia: F. Hrubý (ed.), *Moravské korespondence a akta z let 1620–36*, i–ii (Brno 1934–7), with fascinating documents from the Žerotín, Dietrichstein, and Lobkovic archives; B. Dudík, 'Bericht über die Diöcese Olmütz durch den Cardinal Franz von Dietrichstein im Jahre 1634', *AÖG* xlii (1870), 213–31; and many documents in C. d'Elvert, *Beiträge zur Geschichte der Rebellion, Reformation, des dreissigjährigen Krieges und der Neugestaltung Mährens im 17. Jahrhundert* (Brünn 1867). Upper Austria: Carafa, *Commentaria*, appendix, 149 ff. (decrees); Loesche, *Protestantismus*, 172 ff.; F. Stieve, *Der oberösterreichische Bauernaufstand des Jahres 1626*, i–ii (Munich 1891), i, 32 ff. For the events of 1626 see below, p. 98.

[73] Inner Austria: Loserth, *Acten und Correspondenzen*, iib; Pirchegger, op. cit. 503 ff. Lower Austria: Wiedemann, *Reformation*, i, 591–624; ii, 250 ff.

sylvanian support, to mount a successful military defence of its positions. In 1620–1 the country came near complete secession and Ferdinand only clung on by concluding a disadvantageous peace with the erratic Bethlen at Mikulov in Moravia. During the 1620s, however, the political situation was retrieved somewhat, thanks to able diplomacy from Esterházy, who became palatine in 1625, and wily prelates like Miklós Dallos, Bishop of Győr. Two further indecisive campaigns established a *modus vivendi* with Bethlen, then the latter's death in 1629 removed the crown's most dangerous adversary. Meanwhile, unofficial Counter-Reformation continued in the Habsburg-controlled areas. Pázmány leaned on the royal boroughs, especially the capital Pozsony and the mining communities of Upper Hungary, to elect Catholic councils, while he and the Jesuits persuaded more members of the high nobility to rejoin the old faith: György Zrinyi, Ádám Batthyány, Mihály Károlyi, Miklós Wesselényi, András Balassa, even the sons of Szaniszló Thurzó.[74]

This single-minded onslaught on the heretics carried an equally momentous corollary: that Catholicism means loyalty. There is no doubt about Ferdinand II's own devotion to his Church and its ordained representatives; he carried personal piety to great lengths, widely reported and substantiated. His routine on waking included meditations and two masses, as well as kissing the floor five times in memory of Christ's five wounds. He would follow processions for hours, carrying a taper and bareheaded, even in pouring rain. A few months before his death he still sought the permission of his confessor to omit an hour's prayer before dressing when he had to rise at four o'clock for a journey.[75] That confessor, Guillaume Lamormaini, was also one of the emperor's closest confidants: the

---

[74] Csapodi, op. cit. 46 ff., on Esterházy; V. Frankl and K. Ráth, *Dallos Miklós győri püspöknek politikai és diplomatiai iratai, 1618–26* (Esztergom 1867). The Mikulov (Nikolsburg) and later treaties are given in Gooss, op. cit. 504 ff. Pázmány, *Levelei*, nos. 326, 329 seqq. *passim*, 343, 360, 386–7, 531, 538–9, 659, 906, 1010 (Pozsony); 390, 573, 582, 680, 791, 840 (mining towns); 561, 568, 576, 585, 595, 597, 682, 842 (to Ádám Batthyány). Cf. Kazy, op. cit. i, 131 f.; Fraknói, *Pázmány*, ii; A. Ipolyi, *Bedegi Nyáry Krisztina, 1604–41* (Bp. 1887), for the activities of Mátyás Hajnal SJ.

[75] Hurter, op. cit. xi, 575 f.; B. Dudík (ed.), 'Correspondenz Kaisers Ferdinand II und seiner erlauchten Familie mit P. Martinus Becanus und P. Wilhelm Lamormaini kaiserlichen Beichtvätern', *AÖG* liv (1876), 221–350, no. xli (Straubing, 25 Jan. 1637); Carafa, 'Relatione', 258 ff.

perfect example of a forward, international Jesuit who had taught in all parts of the Monarchy and played a major role as Counter-Reformer. In return for Ferdinand's favour Lamormaini propagated the Catholic virtues of his master, publicizing all the stories about his hatred of Protestant sin and delight in conversion, his charity and respect for the priesthood, his love of the Virgin and Saints, of the Eucharist and the Trinity.[76] These *Virtutes Ferdinandi II* laid the foundation for a very important dynastic political myth: the *pietas Austriaca*, a confessional re-interpretation of traditional precepts of wise government in terms of seventeenth-century absolutism. The faith and Christian merits of the house of Austria since the days of Rudolf I were paraded both as visual and as literary *topoi*. In the process of destroying most of their immediate enemies, the Habsburgs had apparently recovered their soul; better still, they had gained an ideology.[77]

*

During the euphoric 1620s dynasty and Church seemed perfect helpmates: all opposition in Central Europe, with the single exception of the Transylvanian state, lay cowed and ineffectual; Catholic armies under Tilly and Wallenstein occupied those parts of Germany which were not ruled by complaisant allies. Churches were simultaneously dedicated to Our Lady of Victories in Rome and Prague (the latter a building recently commissioned by the Lutherans and now sequestered); the new *Congregatio de Propaganda Fide* busied itself with spreading the faith in the Habsburg lands; the Pope's legate Carafa directed Counter-Reformation

---

[76] R. Stiegele, 'Beiträge zu einer Biographie des Jesuiten Wilhelm Lamormaini', *HJ* xxviii (1907), 551–69, 849–70; A. Posch, 'Zur Tätigkeit und Beurteilung Lamormains', *MIÖG* lxiii (1955), 375–90, a slight article; Dudík, 'Correspondenz', 228 ff. Lamormaini was the Belgian nephew of one of Rudolf's cooks and had studied or taught as a Jesuit at Olomouc, Vienna, Pozsony, Zsolna, Prague, and Graz. See also the next note.

[77] G. Lamormaini, *Ferdinandi II Virtutes* (Antwerp 1638), and many further editions or adaptations (as, for example, in *The Particular State of the Government of the Emperour, Ferdinand the Second* (tr. from Latin, London 1637), ch. 3). Cf. Kazy, op. cit. i, 317–36; A. Coreth, *Pietas Austriaca* (V. 1959); Sturmberger, *Absolutismus*; id., 'Der habsburgische 'Princeps in Compendio' und sein Fürstenbild', *Historica: Studien ... F. Engel-Janosi dargeboten* (V. 1965), 91–116. For artistic representations: Gy. Rózsa, *Magyar történetábrázolás a 17. században* (Bp. 1973), 81–106; A. Wandruszka, 'Ein Freskenzyklus der "Pietas Austriaca" in Florenz', *MÖStA* xv (1962), 495–9; Chicago, Newberry Library, Wing MS, fZW 1.696 (a magnificent example).

operations in the field, albeit not quite as omnipotently as he claimed. Priests flooded into Austria and Bohemia, many belonging to new orders, endowed with imperial privileges and grants of land. The Jesuits had free rein to suborn existing Protestant education and expand their own institutions at will.[78] The clerical estate of Bohemia, abolished by the Hussite wars, was reinstated, even given pride of place again over the nobility. With the Edict of Restitution in 1629, which proclaimed integral recovery of all Church lands lost in the *Reich* since 1555, the bold strategy appeared triumphant.

Yet the harmony of interest was brittle. 'All Catholics are loyal': any emperor knew this proposition to be by no means self-evident. Some Catholics had taken up arms against the Habsburgs in Hungary since 1604; a few had even been involved in the Bohemian revolt.[79] Rather Catholics must be made loyal, orthodoxy must be rephrased as political reliability. A slow development is under way which will reverse the situation of the years before 1620: as a kind of native Habsburg absolutism spreads its wings, the Papacy will be placed in the position of uneasy client. Moreover the whole military advance in the Empire had exceeded the bounds of the dynasty's ability to sustain it. Bavaria began to pursue independent aims; Wallenstein, anyway no friend of Viennese policies and eaten up with his own ambition, was hated by the electors who forced his dismissal on Ferdinand in 1630. Wallenstein's mantle of dictatorial generalissimo was promptly assumed by Gustavus Adolphus of Sweden, whose armies swept back across the contested German territories.

These events too made an immediate impact on the home front. It had been hard enough to suppress discontent during the 1620s, with widespread peasant disturbances and more co-ordinated resistance in parts of north-east Bohemia, Moravia, and Silesia—not to speak of Hungary. Now Saxon troops flooded into Bohemia, accompanied by many *émigrés*. Though their occupation proved brief (and possibly counter-productive to the Protestant cause), the

---

[78] H. Kollmann (ed.), *Acta Sacrae Congregationis de Propaganda Fide res gestas Bohemicas illustrantia, 1622–4*, i–ii (Pr. 1923–55); Carafa, *Commentaria*, and 'Relatione', *passim*. Cf. below, pp. 123–33.

[79] For Hungary see below, pp. 260 ff.; even Miklós Esterházy opposed the Habsburgs at the outset (Csapodi, op. cit. 20–2). In Bohemia Diviš Černín, for example, was a prominent rebel.

relapse laid bare deep tensions within the governmental fold. Wallenstein, recalled to fend off the menace of the Swedes and their allies, quarrelled with the court and plotted with Bohemian malcontents; Pázmány and Esterházy fell out, albeit less openly, over policy *vis-à-vis* Transylvania; the Jesuits and the older orders bickered about ownership of property and disputed the fruits of imperial favour; the Pope was alienated by Ferdinand's Italian policy and his lieutenants argued about the best way to convert a recalcitrant subject population.[80] All in all the early 1630s brought a major and in some ways permanent setback to the emperor's hopes. Then in 1634–5 the pendulum swung again: at the battle of Nördlingen the heir to the throne and his Spanish cousin won a personal triumph and paved the way for the peace of Prague which—as its name suggests—still represented a Habsburg-dominated settlement for those many princes prepared to sign it. But the dynasty was now reduced to a holding operation in Germany, and while it continued to press unrealistic claims there the Counter-Reformation at home could not be completed.

In 1637 Ferdinand II died and left his son with a roughly balanced ledger. The debits which Ferdinand III inherited are easier to itemize. In the international arena he faced a deteriorating situation: the debilitated realm of his Spanish cousin could no longer hold down an ambitious France, while Swedish power posed a direct and immediate threat. Bavaria and the Catholic ecclesiastical electors were unreliable, the Lutherans mistrustful. The Habsburg armies exhibited flagging morale and poor leadership, which the command given to Ferdinand II's younger son, Bishop Leopold Wilhelm, did nothing to alleviate. The burden of taxes and recruitment in the new emperor's own territories meant a general disarray which was soon exacerbated by further invasions. From 1639 until the Peace of Westphalia, Bohemia and Moravia were never free of enemy forces and sometimes deluged by them; with fine irony the Swedes

---

[80] Beckovský, op. cit., pt. 3, 105–203, for the events of 1631–2. We may note too— *en passant*—the tribulations of Habsburg Swabia at this time (W. E. Heydendorff, 'Vorderösterreich im dreissigjährigen Kriege', *MÖStA* xii (1959), 74–142; xiii (1960), 107–94). On Wallenstein: J. Pekař, *Valdštejn 1630–4* (2nd edn. Pr. 1933); and, most recently and readably, G. Mann, *Wallenstein*, tr. Ch. Kessler (London 1976). On Pázmány versus Esterházy see below, p. 260. P. Laymann, *Justa Defensio Sanctissimi Romani Pontificis, Augustissimi Caesaris* . . . (Dillingen 1631) is a long Jesuit excursus about the property squabbles.

made their headquarters during the 1640s in Leopold Wilhelm's episcopal city of Olomouc. The local population remained restless, not only in Hungary, where renewed war with Transylvania between 1643 and 1645 helped kindle again earlier antagonisms, but also in neighbouring regions like eastern Moravia, whose Wallachian highlanders had never been effectively subdued.[81] Thus true Catholic reform lagged far behind the idealist programme of the 1620s and at times providence seemed to have deserted the Habsburgs entirely: just before the disastrous battle at Jankau in 1645 the local statue of St. Wenceslas was found shattered in the church. The mass of the peasantry always hovered on the brink of sedition and heresy; during the last months of the war, as Archbishop Harrach of Prague privately admitted to Rome, large crowds of them flocked to outdoor Lutheran services sponsored by the Swedes.[82]

The credits were less tangible, but equally real. Ferdinand II's remarkable single-minded rise from obscure archduke to crusading emperor had acquired a momentum which would allow his intelligent and more flexible heir to consolidate the achievement once peace was re-established.[83] However incomplete, the Counter-Reformation was well on its way to becoming a dominant persuasion: court and chancery, monasteries and universities purveyed it; administrative posts fell almost exclusively to Catholics, even in Lower Austria, Silesia, and Hungary. Above all Ferdinand III enjoyed one great underlying advantage: his government now represented the only possible embodiment of order in Central Europe and must appeal to all who sought peace and recovery. A new generation had grown up, cut off behind the frontiers of an embattled Monarchy. When the Swedish general Königsmarck

[81] J. Pekař, *Kniha o Kosti*, i–ii (2nd edn. Pr. ?1936, original edn. 1910–11), i, 1–108, paints a telling picture of northern Bohemia in these years. Cf. Polišenský, *Thirty Years War*, 224 ff.; and below, p. 99, on the Wallachians. Lower Austria hardly fared better during the 1640s, and it suffered widespread destruction of property (Gutkas, *Niederösterreich*, 233–48).

[82] A. Podlaha, *Posvátná mista království Českého*, i–vii (Pr. 1907–13), vi, 105 (Jankau); O. Flégl, 'Relace kardinála Harracha o stavu pražské arcidiecèse do Říma', *VČAVSIU* xxiii (1914), 185–97, 227–43, at 228.

[83] The shrewd government of Ferdinand III has yet to find its historian, like the personality of this most neglected of all Habsburg emperors. M. Koch, *Geschichte des deutschen Reiches unter der Regierung Ferdinands III*, i–ii (V. 1865–6), covers only imperial politics to 1648. Stieve in *ADB*, s.v., is equally German-political.

invested the Old Town of Prague in 1648, its defences were manned with grim determination by a motley collection of Jesuit professors, students, monks, and burghers organized into Marian sodalities and guilds of Corpus Christi.[84]

The settlement then finally being reached at Münster and Osnabrück in Westphalia confirmed the Habsburg profit-and-loss account. The dynasty lost its political pre-eminence in the Empire, as the perfect sphere of *Kaiser* and *Reich* split into its component parts. That had been implicit in the whole tenor of German diplomatic activity by the 1640s, in the very summoning of a full conference of separate states; all the persuasion of Ferdinand's plenipotentiary and friend, Maximilian von Trautmannsdorf, could not alter it.[85] But in return the Habsburgs gained untrammelled sovereign authority over the *Erblande* and Bohemia, and the base for a similar long-term claim over Hungary. The doctrine of *cuius regio, eius religio*, already the ulterior justification for Ferdinand II's actions after 1620, now received formal sanction: with limited exceptions in Lower Austria and larger exceptions in Silesia (as well as in Hungary, no party to the peace treaty), the emperor had a free hand to complete the suppression of Protestantism, while other German rulers honoured the confessional map as it existed at the laboriously negotiated base-date of 1624.

The year 1648 itself, rather than the earlier events enshrined in it, forms the milestone on the other front which we have been examining. While Vienna celebrated a peace so hardly won, the Pope—as is well known—called down anathemas on all those responsible. Why were his denunciations so venomous? It is hard now to appreciate the extent of his chagrin, but at root the issue lay not with the Protestants, but between Rome and the emperor, as leader of Germany's Catholics. Even the Edict of Restitution,

---

[84] Bibl, 'Stände', for the Lower Austrian case. On Silesia cf. below, pp. 299 ff. There were still Protestants in *local* government in parts of Silesia and Hungary, but not among the great officers of state. The paradigm of a militant Hungarian prelate from the generation after Pázmány is György Drašković at Györ: B. Szabady, 'Draskovics György györi püspök élete és kora', *A Soproni Gimnazium Értesitöje*, 1936, 14–115. On 1648 in Bohemia: Beckovský, pt. 3, 368 ff., *passim*; A. Rezek, *Děje Čech a Moravy za Ferdinanda III až do konce třicetileté války* (Pr. 1890), 494–5??; cf. the hagiographic J. Svoboda, *Katolická reformace a marianská Družina v království Českém*, i–ii (Brno 1888), ii, 144–70.

[85] Koch, *Ferdinand III*, ii; F. Dickmann, *Der Westfälische Frieden* (Münster 1959).

promulgated without much consultation, had aroused friction; now the Pope saw his secular influence draining away to the profit of an emperor who reciprocated Curial fulminations in kind.[86] With Spain, France, and England already lost to various kinds of national Church, Central Europe had represented Rome's last great chance of exercising political controls outside Italy. Now the vertiginous programme pursued there since the 1560s had failed in its larger purpose.

At least there were compensations for the Papacy in the progress of the faith. Bohemian and Austrian Protestants had no compensation at all. Westphalia was their final blow: thus far they had continued to pin their hopes on the Swedes and other combatants.[87] As the return of Protestants to their homeland slipped from view as a war-aim, so their expectations in exile grew ever wilder. Some turned to eirenism, others to millenarian prophecy, others to a kind of global mysticism. Such attitudes were not merely a reaction to the privations of war; they were also the working-out of an inner evolution, the last stage in the decay of the Central European Reformation. Jan Amos Comenius and his disarmed colleagues carried with them to their refuges in northern Germany or Holland, in Britain or Transylvania or Poland, some portion of the battered legacy of late Humanism, refracted through that peculiar 'Rosicrucian' atmosphere of mixed radicalism and passivity which had settled over Protestant Germany during the years before 1618.[88]

In chapter four I shall take the story beyond 1648; but this sketchy narrative of events from 1600 has already raised more questions than it has answered. The first generation of seventeenth-century Catholics, whether tough politicians or clerics (or both), achieved great things: whence came their confidence and initiative? So did the same generation of seventeenth-century Habsburgs:

---

[86] K. Repgen, *Die Römische Kurie und der Westfälische Friede*, i (1521–1644) in 2 pts. (Tübingen 1962–5), in fact takes developments only from 1629; S. Sousedík, 'Jan Caramuel, opat emauzský', *AUC, HUCP* ix, 2 (1968), 115–38.

[87] B. Šindelář, *Vestfálský mír a česká otázka* (Pr. 1968) is a major study.

[88] On this mood among the émigrés see B. Mendl, 'Fridrich Falcký a české naděje pobělohorské', *ČČH* xxiv (1918), 77–119. There is good evidence in Harant's *Paměti*, esp. 34 f., 41–4, and Gellner, op. cit. See below, pp. 394–9, and literature cited there. For radicalism and 'Hussitism' among the exiles cf. the approach of E. Winter, *Die tschechische und slowakische Emigration in Deutschland im 17. und 18. Jahrhundert* (Berlin 1955).

were their victories—despite the weakness shown in 1609 and 1619—just the product of *force majeure*? Why could Protestantism not unite the estates? And what became of the towns? Did the peasantry play any significant part in the outcome of the crisis? How far were acts of conversion to Rome, especially those before 1620, a matter of rote or compulsion? We must now give some consideration to the social and intellectual framework of Central Europe during these same years.

CHAPTER 3

The crisis, 1600–50:
social and intellectual

The decades after 1600 brought not merely a military-political clash in Central Europe; they witnessed a deeper crisis of material circumstances and mentality. Economic depression gave an early indication of the changing situation. Some of its manifestations are well known: the inflation of the later sixteenth century, aggravated by governmental spending; spectacular bankruptcies in southern Germany, with a consequent tightening of credit; disorders in the Netherlands and France, and the expectation of troubles in the *Reich*. All sapped confidence and produced collective commercial difficulties. The Habsburg lands found themselves particularly hard-hit: some short-term factors can be linked with the major Ottoman war between 1593 and 1606 which brought devastation to Hungary, high taxes, devaluation, and reduced harvests, but the larger issues were of longer standing and flowed precisely from the previous expansion of trade. Having become participants in an international economy where they did not occupy a strong competitive or geographical position, the Central European territories proved peculiarly vulnerable to its vicissitudes.[1]

When did the slump set in, and how seriously? That is a complex question: thanks mainly to Marxist historiography we now have far more printed evidence than formerly, but consensus seems as distant as ever. Much depends on the area chosen for study—as Bohemia tended to hold up better than Austria, and Austria than Hungary; much depends too on terminology and emphasis. Yet it is clear that, however far back the antecedents of recession may be pursued, however much certain sectors remained buoyant (as in

---

[1] A point well taken by Marxist historians: Makkai, 'Hauptzüge'; id., 'Az abszolutizmus társadalmi bázisának kialakulása az osztrák habsburgok országaiban', *TSz* iii (1960), 193–223, esp. 211; Pach, 'East-Central Europe', esp. 253 ff.; J. Petráň, 'Středoevropské zemědělstvi a obchod v 16. a na počátku 17. stoleti, *ČsČH* xix (1971), 355–77; V. Zimányi, *Magyarország az európai gazdaságban 1600–50* (Bp. 1976), esp. 54 ff.

Germany) till the very eve of war, entrepreneurs experienced a disastrous reversal of fortunes about 1600. Mining, the leading branch of industry, makes the point graphically. Whereas Bohemian and Tyrolean silver had already begun to suffer severe competition from the New World, it was now joined by the widely ramified iron industry of Styria. Output from the Erzberg, which belonged to the crown, fell away sharply and threatened the livelihood of the flourishing founders and casters downstream at Steyr. By the early seventeenth century the copper mines of Upper Hungary experienced similar difficulties; soon war and Swedish rivalry added to their ruin.[2] Moreover, there was never any doubt where the Counter-Reformation stood in this process. The Catholic Church persecuted heretic silver miners at Schwaz as it scattered salters from the Salzkammergut and the sturdy Lutheran ironworkers of the Alpine valleys. One example may suffice for many others: Hans Steinberger, a prominent adviser to the exchequer about mining operations throughout the Monarchy, was imprisoned and exiled by Archduke Ferdinand in 1599, his large library consigned to the flames.[3]

Counter-Reformation stands here rather as symptom than as cause. Steinberger and his like were originally called in to arrest an existing decay which affected above all the urban communities of Central Europe. Recession tipped the scales against the towns, which had grown during the sixteenth century but remained exposed, their economic position unconsolidated. Lacking their own reserves of expertise and credit they depended heavily on international trade and finance. Altogether the towns of the Habsburg lands never developed a legal or constitutional base to match their commercial advance from the later Middle Ages; when

[2] L. Bittner, 'Das Eisenwesen in Innerberg-Eisenerz bis zur Gründung der Innerberger Hauptgewerkschaft im Jahre 1625', *AÖG* lxxxix (1901), 451–646; Tremel, *Frühkapitalismus*, 148–55; id., *Wirtschafts-und Sozialgeschichte*, 148–79; A. Hoffmann, *Wirtschaftsgeschichte des Landes Oberösterreich*, i (Salzburg 1952), 117–28. F. Fischer in Bog (ed.), op. cit., 286–319, investigates one trade which continued to flourish. Vlachovič, ibid., 600–27, for Upper Hungary. Cf., for Bohemia, J. Janáček, 'České soukenictví v 16. století', *ČsČH* iv (1956), 553–90; and the *compte rendu* by A. Mika, 'Sociálně ekonomická struktura českých zemí před třicetiletou válkou', i, *SbH* xxi (1974), 41–72; xxiii (1976), 37–78.

[3] Eder, *Glaubensspaltung*, 394 ff.; J. Kallbrunner, 'Hans Steinberger, ein Beitrag zur Geschichte der Montanwirtschaft im Zeitalter Rudolfs II', *Vjschr.f.S. u WGesch.* xxvii (1934), 1–27.

trouble came they had no political cards to play. Bohemia and
Hungary boasted numerous incorporated royal boroughs, subject
only to the crown: we know them best under German names like
Kuttenberg and Neusohl, Pilsen and Kaschau; while Austria had
some long-established urban centres besides Vienna, whose special
position I shall consider at a later stage.[4] In each province they
formed a separate estate with representation at the diet. But they
made no further progress towards autonomy during the sixteenth
century; far from it, they were frustrated at every turn.

The Habsburgs regarded the towns as revenue creators, and
exploited them for tax purposes while showing no understanding of
their larger problems; their free status was taken to mean merely
dependence on the newly-established royal Chamber or *Kammer*
and its officials. From the beginning of its rule in Bohemia and
Hungary the dynasty strove to reduce municipal privileges there,
and Ferdinand I took a long stride in that direction after 1547, when
the Bohemian estates showed defiance of him (however hesitantly)
during the Schmalkaldic War.[5] The success of the government's
thrust against the towns—striking by comparison with so much
failure and indecisiveness on other fronts—owed most to its
opponent's weakness. The urban estate comprised a motley
collection of municipalities large and small, mostly small (even
Prague, the greatest of them, was divided into four distinct cities).
They displayed little harmony of purpose or flair for negotiating;
they were loath to vote the expenses of delegations to court or diet.
Worse still, they found themselves deserted by the nobility, who
recognized no solidarity among the secular estates and allowed
burghers little role in their corporate organization with its
commissions and functionaries. A common front is as absent here
as against the Counter-Reformation, and from an earlier stage.[6]

---

[4] Bohemia had some thirty royal towns, plus the so-called dowry towns (*věnná
města* or *Leibgedingstädte*: Koniggratz (Hradec Králové) and eight others) which
belonged to the queen. Hungary possessed about twenty, though in both countries
the total fluctuated. They are indicated in *Školní atlas československých dějin*,
ed.I. Beneš (2nd edn. Pr. 1964), 12–13, and *Történelmi atlasz*, ed. S. Radó et al. (7th
edn. Bp. 1965), 12–13. On Vienna see below, pp. 191–4.
[5] K. Tieftrunk, *Odpor stavův českých proti Ferdinandovi I l. 1547* (Pr. 1872); and,
most recently, K. J. Dillon, *King and estates in the Bohemian lands 1526–64* (Brussels
1976), 111–40.
[6] J. Čelakovský, 'Úřad podkomořský v Čechách', *ČČM* li (1877), 3–31, 239–71,

The lords accepted the thesis that free towns belonged to the *Kammer* because it suited economic priorities of their own: not only were they pleased to see the boroughs bear a disproportionate share of the tax burden; they could also benefit at municipal expense.

The most important enterprise of the nobles was brewing, and manorial ales, retailed through a network of tied houses in the villages, entered into fierce competition with urban brewers during the sixteenth century. In some areas they encouraged crafts: textiles, pottery, glassmaking, metalwork, even supervised mining operations on demesne lands, using the labour of their own peasants, attracting artisans from elsewhere, always tending to undercut the costs of urban production.[7] More generally the nobles contested the legally guaranteed trading monopolies of the boroughs (the *Bannmeile* and the rest). The towns resisted as best they could; but lacking effective recourse to either diet or monarch, they faced a losing battle, the more so since their rivals could reply in kind. Against a local free town the lord could set his 'subject' town, the marketing centre on his private estates, whose inhabitants might live as well as most burghers without possessing any but very rudimentary rights of association. Such extensive demesne settlements, taking a slightly different form from region to region, their population only superficially urbanized, became a major feature of the economic scene throughout Central Europe.[8]

437–58, 557–80; id., 'Postavení vyslaných královských měst na sněmich českých', *ČČM* xliii (1869), 115–57; K. Gutkas, 'Landesfürst, Landtag und Städte Niederösterreichs im 16. Jahrhundert', *Jb. f. Lk. v. NÖ* N. F. xxxvi (1964), 311–19; Gindely, *Dreissigjähriger Krieg*, ii, 179–82; J. Janáček, 'Královská města česká na zemském sněmu r. 1609–10', *SbH* iv (1956), 226–51; Bibl, 'Stände', esp. 182–6; H. Hassinger, 'Die Landstände der österreichischen Länder: Zusammensetzung, Organisation und Leistung im 16.–18. Jahrhundert', *Jb. f. Lk. v. NÖ* xxxvi (1964), 989–1035. In Hungary the lords pressed harder for the rights of Protestant burghers (Benda, 'Absolutismus', 111 f.; cf. Bibl, 'Stände', 212 f., 224 ff., 252 ff., 304 f.) but granted them little political weight.

[7] Fr. Hrubý, 'Z hospodářských převratů českých v století XV. a XVI. se zvláštním zřetelem k Moravě', *ČČH* xxx (1924), 205–36, 433–69; J. Petráň, 'Pohyb poddanského obyvatelstva a jeho osobní právní vztahy v Čechách v době předbělohorské', *ČsČH* v (1957), 26–58, 399–447; H. Feigl, *Die niederösterreichische Grundherrschaft vom ausgehenden Mittelalter bis zu den theresianisch-josephinischen Reformen* (V. 1964), 144–54. Cf. the literature below, n. 15.

[8] Roughly speaking, the Austrian *Marktflecken* suggests a *commercial* halfway-house between town and country, the Czech *poddanské město* a *legal* one, the Hungarian *mezőváros* a *social* one. There are good examples of 16th-and 17th-century *Marktordnungen* in the *Österreichische Weistümer* (below n. 23), *passim*.

There are thus—if we recall our earlier survey of sixteenth-century culture—two ways of looking at the towns undei Habsburg sovereignty in about 1600. One viewpoint suggests considerable prosperity and real vigour: Prague, Vienna, and Breslau, at least, were great cities by any European yardstick; a number of other places, especially in Bohemia, maintained extensive foreign links and continued to grow until the outbreak of war; even some demesne towns seemed set to break the shackles of subservience, as the royal boroughs had done in previous centuries.[9] The other viewpoint allows us to discern that instability which would progressively cripple all urban communities in the seventeenth century: from 1618 they endured persecution, devastation, and indebtedness, and fell into a chronic decline as their much reduced populations faced an ever-growing burden of impositions and official interference. Tightly-knit municipal administrations outdid each other in pettiness and abuse of the restricted self-government which they still possessed. External markets disappeared, purchasing power ebbed away, and the boroughs sank behind their picturesque mouldering walls into a slumber from which they would only—at best—be awakened by the proddings of some cameralist commission a century later.[10]

The real issue lay at a deeper level: the towns of Central Europe ceased to be *bourgeois*. They lost any claim to represent distinct civic

---

[9] Z. Winter, *Kulturní obraz českých měst*, i–ii (Pr. 1890), with much miscellaneous information; cf. id., 'Přepych uměleckého průmyslu v měšťanských domech XVI. věku', *ČČM* lxvii (1893), 46–104. On Prague in particular: J. Janáček, *Dějiny obchodu v předbělohorské Praze* (Pr. 1955); R. Klier, 'Die Wettengel von Neuenberg', *Bohemia-Jahrbuch* xiv (1973), 43–80, studies one conspicuous commercial family.

[10] J. Klepl, 'Královská města česká počátkem 18. století', *ČČH* xxxviii (1932), 260–84, 489–521; xxxix (1933), 57–71, is the most thorough account. Bílek, *Dějiny konfiskací*, esp. i, pp. xcix–cviii; and F. Macháček, 'K hospodářskému stavu českých měst venkovských po válce třicetileté', *Práce věnované ... V. Novotnému* (Pr. 1929), 271–85, both have details of indebtedness. Cf. Denis, op. cit., i, bk. 2, 93–107; Hrubý (ed.), *Moravské korespondence*, i, esp. nos. 91, 118–20, 135, 138–41, 143–7; A. Klíma, *Manufakturní období v Čechách* (Pr. 1955), 21–8. On Austria: A. Luschin von Ebengreuth, *Österreichische Reichsgeschichte* (Bamberg 1896), 448–51. O. Placht, *Lidnatost a společenská skladba českého státu v 16.–18. století* (Pr. 1957), 156–216, presents a rather more positive view for later 17th-century Bohemia. J. Szücs, 'Das Städtewesen in Ungarn im 15.–17. Jahrhundert', *Studia Historica* liii (1963), 97–164, sees the roots of decay in Hungarian towns as early as the 15th century, but cf. the evidence in J. Macůrek and M. Rejnuš, *České země a Slovensko ve století před Bílou Horou* (Pr. 1958), ch. 2.

values and appeared as foreign bodies in an organic rural-based society, an impression fostered best of all wherever townsmen had actually once immigrated from abroad and still spoke a different language from the surrounding countryside, as through much of northern Hungary and parts of Bohemia's Czech hinterland. By the seventeenth century the estate of towns was not sufficiently integrated to play a political role of its own on the national level, not independent enough to assert an autonomous status. Burghers clung to a foothold in the constitution only as corporations; their claims to possess land or vote at the diet were collectively assimilated to the rights of any individual noble.[11] And while the noble could settle in a town on privileged terms, live there in an untaxed *Freihaus*, and lord it over local society, the occasional successful burgher (an Eggenberg or Henckel) would quite forswear his origins and turn into a landed aristocrat—at least, he would do so during the sixteenth century before such mobility became almost entirely restricted to commoners from abroad. The Habsburg lands lacked even those fainéant escutcheoned patriciates and shades of earlier intellectual vitality characteristic of the almost equally decayed *Reichsstädte* in southern Germany.[12] In sum: the new order of the seventeenth century held little place for the towns or for serious use of urban resources. The average town-dweller became more or less a peasant, tending his smallholding as well as plying his trade, unable to raise credit, and dreading the descent of the next imperial garrison.

*

The second great social antagonism divided lord and peasant. On the land, as in the towns, conditions throughout most of the sixteenth century were still tolerably stable and a high demand for

---

[11] J. Čelakovský, 'Stav městský na sněmě českém od l. 1692–1723', *ČČM* xliii (1869), 243–77; O. Brunner, 'Bürgertum und Adel in Nieder-und Oberösterreich', *Neue Wege der Sozialgeschichte* (Göttingen 1956), 135–54; Hoffmann, op. cit. 155–75. At the same time some limited migration evidently continued after 1620, especially from German areas into the Bohemian towns.

[12] On the Eggenbergs, Henckels, Berchtolds, Stürgkhs, Widmanns, and their Bohemian and Hungarian equivalents, see below chs. 5–8, *passim*; on foreigners, esp. pp.293–8. Cf. Luschin, *Studien*, 3–12. Makkai, 'Abszolutizmus', the only serious Marxist approach to the problem of absolutism's social base in Central Europe, seems to me to fall into contradiction: for where are the urban privileges and bourgeois financiers of whom he speaks (199 and *passim*)?

agricultural products brought signs of some general well-being.
The Bohemian peasantry grew in numbers, paid modest dues to its
landlords and government, owned considerable possessions in
clothes and furnishings, held substantial common property in land,
even took regular hot baths.[13] After the disturbed years which
culminated with the 1520s, when German events had some
resonance, especially in the Tyrol, Central European unrest seemed
largely confined to areas of Hungary where the Turks threatened
and memory lingered on of Dózsa's huge revolt in 1514, so bloodily
quelled.[14]

Yet here still larger changes were under way and made themselves
felt decisively during the period between 1600 and 1650. Again they
grew out of commercial opportunities: the expansion of trade, most
notably with Germany, in agricultural commodities—wheat, wine,
fish, cattle, sheep. The important thing is not expansion as such,
which could mean rewards for the whole rural sector, but the
direction taken by entrepreneurship. Only after about 1570 did a
major clash of interests become manifest between lords and
traditional peasant cultivators, a clash aggravated by the diminished
return, owing to inflation, from monetary rents which represented
the main feudal due in most of the Monarchy. Nobles adopted
various courses to safeguard their position. In Bohemia, the most
advanced region, they particularly developed techniques of estate
management, raising the yield of demesnes, employing trained
bailiffs to run home farms and supervise the tenantry, building
enormous fishponds to breed the famous native carp. These
activities they buttressed by creating trade monopolies, working up
their own resources, especially in breweries and distilleries; and
their private townships might be directed as much against village as

---

[13] Fr. Hrubý, 'Hospodářské převraty', 448–54, and id., 'Selské a panské inventáře
v době předbělohorské', *ČČH* xxxiii (1927), 21–59, 263–306, at 23–59; Gindely,
Dreissigjähriger Krieg, i, 146–9; K. Krofta, *Přehled dějin selského stavu v Čechách a na
Moravě* (2nd edn. Pr. 1949), esp. 158 f.; Pekař, *Kost*, ii, 143 ff.; A Míka, *Poddaný lid
v Čechách v první polovině 16. století* (Pr. 1960); J. Hanzal, 'Vesnická obec a
samospráva v 16. a na počátku 17. století', *Právněhistorické Studie* x (1964), 135–47;
J. Petráň, *Poddaný lid v Čechách na prahu třicetileté války* (Pr. 1964), esp. 146 ff.

[14] J. Macek, *Der Tiroler Bauernkrieg und Michael Gaismair* (Berlin 1965). Most
recently P. Blickle, *Die Revolution von 1525* (Munich 1975), has stressed the
radicalism of the rebels in 1525 and certain permanent gains which they made. For
the events of 1514: G. Heckenast (ed.), *Aus der Geschichte der ostmitteleuropäischen
Bauernbewegungen im 16.–17. Jahrhundert* (Bp. 1977).

against municipal enterprise. Wherever possible they would buy out peasant holdings and confiscate commons and water-meadows. By 1618 families like the Smiřickýs, who gathered together a vast acreage in the valley of the Elbe, were models of progressive landowners.[15]

Similar methods of *Gutsherrschaft* were applied in Austria and Hungary too; but there they formed a smaller part of the total strategy. In the *Erblande* exploitation of the demesne usually reached only an intermediate stage (described as *Wirtschaftsherrschaft* by some), whereby the lords took advantage of peasant production and marketed it as their own; a larger grievance of their tenantry was the unilateral raising of taxes on the sale and inheritance of holdings and the more efficient collection of other impositions.[16] Throughout the Habsburg lands a further weapon in the landowner's hands was compulsory labour service, normally though not invariably unpaid, and passing under a variety of names until the Czech term *robot* gained general currency. While the *robot* grew sharply in Bohemia and Austria, it found its classic home in Hungary, where agrarian relations remained by and large rather more backward. For reasons still not at all clear Hungary's nobles met the threat from falling real rents after the 1560s by means of drastically increased *robot* demands, in the shape of both field labour and domestic employment. They were foremost too, though not alone, in raising the payments exacted in kind, especially the lay tithe (the 'ninth') of the grain harvest.[17]

[15] Hrubý, 'Hospodářské převraty'; W. Stark, *Ursprung und Aufstieg des landwirtschaftlichen Grossbetriebs in den böhmischen Ländern* (Pr. 1934); A. Mika, 'České rybníkářství a problém počátků původní akumulace v českých zemích', *ČsČH* ii (1954), 262–71; F. Matějek, *Feudální velkostatek a poddaný na Moravě* (Pr. 1959); J. Válka, *Hospodářská politika feudálního velkostatku na předbělohorské Moravě* (Pr. 1962); J. Petráň, *Zemědělská výroba v Čechách v druhé polovině 16. a počátkem 17. století* (Pr. 1963). On the Smiřickýs: V. Pešák, *Panství rodu Smiřických v letech 1609–18* (Pr. 1940).

[16] A. Mell, *Die Lage des steierischen Unterthanenstandes seit Beginn der neueren Zeit bis in die Mitte des 17. Jahrhunderts* (Weimar 1896); G. Grüll, *Bauer, Herr und Landesfürst* (Linz 1963), 11–18, 33–49; Feigl, *Grundherrschaft*, 51 ff.; id., *Der niederösterreichische Bauernaufstand 1596/7* (V. 1972). Cf. Hoffmann, op. cit., 88–93; Tremel, *Wirtschafts- und Sozialgeschichte*, 132–48. Examples of Hungarian demesne farming in F. Maksay (ed.), *Urbáriumok, XVI.–XVII. század* (Bp. 1959), and intro. 20–33.

[17] Zs. P. Pach, *Nyugat-európai és magyarországi agrárfejlődés a XV.–XVII.*

(continued)

In the seventeenth century these processes continued apace, while war and persecution, above all in Bohemia and parts of Austria, tended to blur the earlier regional variation as well as differentiation within the peasant body itself: the mass of the rural population settled into what historians today often call 'second serfdom' (as distinct from the 'first serfdom' of the earlier Middle Ages). The expression has excited much debate, perhaps more than it deserves. In any event, the condition of the peasantry, except in the purely Alpine provinces where tenants had firm constitutional safeguards, clearly deteriorated so far that connotations of enserfment are not misplaced. That is confirmed by a vital corollary of the manifold other pressures: the restriction of rural mobility. Landowners made concerted efforts before 1600 to bind the peasant to the soil, though it is difficult to know how much success they achieved. In Hungary legislation culminated at the diet of 1608, when migration was effectively rendered impossible for those already subject to a lord. Drastic population loss during the recent Turkish war gave a decisive spur to these enactments, and when their own labour force shrank after 1620 the nobles of Bohemia and Austria reacted in the same way, giving teeth to existing controls over the communal and private life of their subjects.[18]

'Subjection' is the crucial idea. We should do wrong to imagine 'second serfdom' as a purely economic datum, or even an economic-cum-legal one. Its essence lay in the imposed authority of the manor or *Herrschaft*, a notion both concrete and abstract, at once the traditional unit of rural organization and also a theory of mutuality.[19]

---

században (Bp. 1963); Maksay (ed.) op. cit., 33 ff. On Austria: A. Mell in *MHVSt* xl (1892), 135–225; G. Grüll, *Die Robot in Oberösterreich* (Linz 1952). On Bohemia: Krofta, op. cit., 123–31; Válka, op. cit., *passim*. Strictly speaking the Czech word is *robota* (cognate with the common-Slavonic term—but not the normal Czech term— for 'work'). The Hungarian *kilenced* or 'ninth' was the 'second tenth' of the whole harvest; when the lord had also appropriated the ecclesiastical tithe he thus gained one-fifth of the crop.

[18] J. Varga, *Jobbágyrendszer a magyarországi feudalizmus kései századaiban, 1556–1767* (Bp. 1969), chs. 1–5, a major work. For Bohemia: Krofta, op. cit., 196 ff.; and, on attempts before 1620, Petráň, *Poddaný lid*, 188 ff.

[19] *Herrschaft* is Czech *panství* or *vrchnost*, Hungarian *uradalom* or *uralom*, depending on whether the physical or abstract notion is stressed. The latter was often also rendered in German as *Obrigkeit.* S. Adler, *Zur Rechtsgeschichte des adeligen Grundbesitzes in Österreich* (Leipzig 1902), is a legal and technical study. On the

Whereas *Herrschaft* had grown up through the Middle Ages as an intricate nexus of rights and obligations between protector and protected, it now changed its function, gradually but radically, and was transformed into a set of hierarchically ordered relations between ruler and ruled in tightly bound and regulated local communities.

Some of these relations took a primarily economic form: the life of the *Herrschaft* became enshrined in registers and collections of written instructions known (in Hungary at least) as *Urbaria*— precious sources of domestic information for the historian, oppressive and mystifying documents to the illiterate peasant.[20] Others were legal: noble landlords, who alone could exercise full *Herrschaft*, consolidated their jurisdictional position *viv-à-vis* both tenantry and the outside world. They dominated the local courts held in villages or manor-houses and the old communal institutions declined, village mayors and magistrates acting more and more as cheap servants of the lord to maintain order and deference. Antique procedures might survive, but a noble ethos invaded them, and the worst sufferers—comparatively speaking—could be those who clung to privileges at the margin of manorial society: wine-growers, miners, rivermen, foresters, travelling folk of all kinds. Though yeomen still served on the verderers' court at Buchlov, in the romantic highlands of southern Moravia, the tribunal now dispensed normal seigneurial justice, and their only remaining birthright was freedom from the *robot* while it sat.[21] The diets

evolution of *Herrschaft* see Feigl, *Grundherrschaft*; O. Brunner, 'Das "Ganze Hans" und die alteuropäische "Ökonomik"', *Neue Wege . . . 33–61;* K. Grünberg, *Die Bauernbefreiung und die Auflösung des gutsherrlich-bäuerlichen Verhältnisses in Böhmen, Mähren und Schlesien*, i–ii (Leipzig 1893–4), i, 36 ff.

[20] *Urbaria* went under a variety of names in the rest of the Monarchy. Many examples in Maksay (ed.), op. cit.; R. Marsina and M. Kušik (eds.), *Urbáre feudálnych panstiev na Slovensku*, i–ii (Bratislava 1959); J. Kalousek (ed.), *Řády selské a instrukce hospodářské* (*Archiv Český*, nos. 23–4) (Pr. 1906–8).

[21] For Austria: A. Stölzel, *Die Entwicklung des gelehrten Richterthums in deutschen Territorien*, i–ii (Stuttgart 1872), i, 142–65, 343–8; Luschin, *Reichsgeschichte*, 453–6 and *passim*; H. Demelius, 'Über Dorfversammlung und Herrschaftsgericht im 17. Jahrhundert', *Jb. f. Lk.v. NÖ* xx (1926–7), 2, 38–68; G. Wesener, *Das innerösterreichische Landschrannenverfahren im 16. und 17. Jahrhundert* (Graz 1963). For Bohemia: Hanzal, 'Vesnická obec', on 16th- century conditions; Pekař, *Kost*, ii, 117 ff.; W. Stark, 'Die Abhängigkeitsverhältnisse der gutsherrlichen Bauern Böhmens im 17. und 18. Jahrhundert', *Jbb. f. Natö. u. Stat.* clxiv (1952), 270–92, 348–74, 440–53,

(continued)

passed much anti-peasant legislation, often without any calculation
of immediate economic advantage, while the Habsburgs wielded a
negligible influence and the theoretical right of appeal to them
evidently availed little by the seventeenth century. All this went
with sanctions neither economic nor legal, but social and moral:
new concepts of ownership and altered expectations on either side;
the absolute sway of the lord and his values (how convenient and
how suitable that his serfs may no longer bear arms without express
permission!); extension of the *robot* in a thousand and one ever
more inefficient and degrading ways.[22]

Of course the rural picture over the whole of Central Europe is
one of bewildering complexity about which we still know much too
little. We should not paint it too black. The historian of immobility
in Hungary has pointed to a surprisingly large number of peasants
there who were never bound to the soil. Josef Pekař's wonderful
evocation of life around the castle of Kost in the leafy glens of the
'Bohemian Paradise' shows how tenants maintained basic levels of
dignity and security of inheritance. The *Weistümer*, those remarkable records of Austrian customary law, continued to be proclaimed
and codified into the eighteenth century, and cases resting on them
to be heard before village juries. It has even been possible for a
Marxist to deny the existence of second serfdom altogether.[23]

---

at 348 ff. For Hungary: F. Eckhart, *A földesúri büntetőbiráskodás a XVI.–XVII.
században* (Bp. 1954), esp. 8 ff., 156 ff. Cf. below, nn. 61–2. On Buchlov: A. Verbík
(ed.), *Černé knihy práva loveckého na hradě Buchlově* (Brno 1976), 9–39; in Upper
Austria the free peasants were forced into *corvée* (J. Strnadt, 'Materialien zur
Geschichte der Entwicklung der Gerichtsverfassung und des Verfahrens... des
Landes ob der Enns', *AÖG* xcvii (1909), 161–520, at 167 ff.).

[22] On the small part played by the ruler: Krofta, op. cit., 257–64; Feigl,
Grundherrschaft, 45–50; E. Varga, (ed.), *Úriszék, XVI.–XVII. századi perszövegek*
(Bp. 1958), 9 ff. A. Luschin-Ebengreuth, *Geschichte des älteren Gerichtswesens in
Österreich ob und unter der Enns* (Weimar 1879), esp. 184–7, exaggerates it; so does
Grünberg, op. cit., i, 28–35. On the later 17th-century evolution: ibid. 41 and *passim*;
Feigl, op. cit. 41–5 and *passim*; Klima, op. cit. 28–44, 59 f.; J. Kočí, 'Robotní
povinnosti poddaných v českých zemích po třicetileté válce', *ČsČH* xi (1963), 331–
40; J. Kašpar, *Nevolnické povstání v Čechách r. 1680* (Pr. 1965), ch. 3.

[23] J. Varga, op. cit. chs. 6–9. Pekař, *Kost*, ii, *passim*; cf. Placht, op. cit. 119 ff.
Österreichische Weistümer, var. eds., i– (V. 1870–), 18 vols. so far, covering most
of the country; cf. Stölzel, op. cit. i, 364–85; Feigl, *Grundherrschaft*, 28 f.; Wesener,
op. cit., esp. 121–3; H. Baltl, 'Die ländliche Gerichtsverfassung der Steiermark
vorwiegend im Mittelalter', *AÖG* cxviii (1951), 5–264. A Špiesz questions the
Marxist view in *Historický Časopis*, xv (1967), 539–58, and in *Historické Štúdie*, xvii

None the less by 1700 we can speak of fairly systematic subjection and impoverishment. The majority of Hungary's serfs clearly did count as *adstricti glebae*; Kost seems to have fared better than most places; *Weistümer* could hardly interfere with a lord's interest, and the competence of the commune, even in the *Erblande,* covered only inessentials, while village records such as the Silesian *Schöppenbücher* display unmistakable patterns of direction from above.[24] Entrepreneurial farming, where it survived—as on some cattle ranchlands in Hungary or the great estates of Bohemia—was bad enough for the peasant; generalized economic depression, exacerbated by war and high levels of state taxation, was worse. Rural society levelled downwards: on Wallenstein's old patrimony of Friedland, for example, 50 per cent of the inhabitants were landless *zahradníci* by 1680.[25] It had, as we shall see, only two recourses: the positive one of revolt, or at least disobedience; and the alternative, when that proved hopeless, of slipping away to create an equal problem for authority in the shape of a shiftless army of vagabonds.

*

So far I have shown something of the confrontation between nobles and townsmen, nobles and peasantry. But the third and final social opposition was generated within the noble estate itself: between the magnates and the rest of the privileged order. The number of really wealthy and important families had of course always been limited; they carried great weight at various times during the Middle Ages,

(1972), 47–61, though he was promptly sat upon by most of his Slovak colleagues; doubts about 'serfdom' are, of course, commonplace among non-Marxist historians—Grünberg has been a particularly influential spokesman for the more moderate view.

[24] *Österreichische Weistümer*, e.g. for Tyrol (vols. ii–v, xvii). One good example, among hundreds, of the authoritarian trend is a proclamation by Archduke Leopold, Bishop of Passau, for his estate of Königstetten, 1615 (ibid. ix, 77–85). The 'Weistümer' of Vorarlberg (ibid. xviii), are all really of this kind. Cf., for Bohemia, W. Weizsäcker, 'Weistümer aus Böhmen und Mähren', *Zeitschrift für Agrargeschichte und Agrarsoziologie*, ix (1961), 49–55. W. Meyer, *Gemeinde, Erbherrschaft und Staat im Rechtsleben des schlesischen Dorfes vom 16. bis 19. Jahrhundert* (Würzburg 1967).

[25] I. N. Kiss in Bog (ed.), op. cit. 451–82. On taxation: Pekař, *Kost,* ii, chs. 8–9; id., *České katastry 1654–1789* (2nd edn. Pr. 1932); F. de Bojani, *Innocent XI, sa correspondance avec ses nonces,* i–iii (Rome—Roulers (Belgium) 1910–12), iii, 6 ff. J. Kočí, *Odboj nevolníků na Frýdlantsku, 1679–87* (Liberec 1965), chs. 1–2, for Friedland.

never more so than in the disturbed conditions of the later fifteenth century. Now a more consolidated advance took place, firmly rooted in economic realities and social pre-eminence, to yield a permanent caste of aristocrats holding almost all the political strings and doubly relevant to the present argument: for they usually work with the sovereign rather than against him; and they display common characteristics which belie the extremely different traditions and milieus out of which they grew.

Great nobles profited most from the developments of the sixteenth century. Large estates had a greater scope for trading than small ones; they could ride the uncertainties of the market where necessary, even attracting runaway peasants from less flexible neighbours. Aristocrats enjoyed political weight through their senior role in the expanding organization of the estates and sufficient coercive power (though we should not exaggerate this) to lay hands on some defenceless Church lands. They exercised legal control, since effective jurisdiction over all serious cases belonged to the *Landgerichte* which were attached only to larger manors.[26] By the same token the lesser nobility began to lose its position, and while a few prominent members rose out of the class—Trčkas and Smiřickýs, Thurzós and Illésházys and Esterházys—many more disappeared or fell into penury, especially in Bohemia where the process was swiftest. Things were least clear-cut in Hungary, whose gentry retained strong influence over the county administration, hence to some extent over the patrimonial court or *úriszék*; but there too the magnates asserted their status, being recognized as a distinct chamber at the diet by 1608 and building up a large clientèle of retainers and private soldiers.[27] Throughout Central Europe the ostentatious new castles with their delicate arcading, while they

---

[26] Luschin, *Reichsgeschichte*, 193 f., 459, and *Gerichtswesen*, 103 ff.; Strnadt, art. cit. In Austria only certain *Landgerichte* were privileged to deal with the gravest crimes; in Hungary that does not appear to have been the case.

[27] Bohemia: A. Mika, 'Majetkové rozvrstvení české šlechty v předbělohorském obdobi', *SbH* xv (1967), 45–73, esp. 50 f., 63 f.; F. Matějek, 'Bilá Hora a moravská feudální společnost', *ČsČH* xxii (1974), 81–103, at 83–5 and *passim.* Hungary: B. Schiller, *Az örökös förendiség eredete Magyarországon* (Bp. 1900); A. Timon, *Ungarische Verfassungs- und Rechtsgeschichte* (Berlin 1904), 552 ff.; F. Eckhart, op. cit. 26 ff.; E. Varga (ed.), op. cit. 19 ff. Cf. for Austria: Luschin, *Reichsgeschichte*, 493–7; Feigl, *Grundherrschaft*, 37 f., 58, 256 ff.; Hassinger, 'Landstände', 999 ff. The whole process, of course, was a very slow one.

bore witness to Renaissance values, confirmed also in cultural and intellectual terms a growing social gulf.[28]

Some kind of aristocratic élite therefore had much running for it by the end of the sixteenth century. Who would be its actual members? That left more scope for contingency. Not, by and large, the greatest medieval families: some died out, either at a stroke, like the withered flowers of Hungarian chivalry cut down on the field of Mohács, or ebbing away like the Austrian Schaunbergs and Bohemian Rožmberks; others failed to adapt, among them the mighty lords of Rožmitál and Pernstein, who collapsed under mountainous debt. Rather certain middling clans made good, settled provincial nobles with an eye to the main chance and considerable good fortune. An excellent example are the Batthyánys who, originating in Croatia, brought together a complex of domains on Hungary's Austrian border: Güssing in 1524, Rechnitz and Schlaining in the 1540s, Körmend in 1604, Bernstein in 1644.[29] Habsburg favour evidently added a further degree of contingency— the dynasty could offer a public role, financial assistance, prestige (as Ferdinand I did for his protégé Ferenc Batthyány); but its activity was limited to that of a midwife, reinforcing a trend by assuring the loyalty of preferred individuals. Thus it did little to instigate (though it might smile upon) the marriages which began to tie together a 'Habsburg' aristocracy across frontiers: Zrinyi with Rožmberk and Kolovrat; Lobkovic with Batthyány, Hoyos, Starhemberg, Salm; Stubenberg with Kinský, Smiřický, Erdődy; Pálffy with Fugger, Mansfeld, Puchheim...[30]

Once again the sixteenth century had set in motion a process which would reach its conclusion during the decades after 1600, as the tide of opportunity for the new aristocracy rose to a flood, above all in Bohemia and Moravia. There by 1650 the estate of lords numbered only eighty-five families and a full 62 per cent of the total peasantry belonged to them. In Hungary the Batthyánys were

---

[28] Cf. above, p. 36. On magnate luxury cf. Radvánszky, op. cit. *passim*; Hrubý, 'Inventáře', 263–306; id. (ed.), *Moravské korespondence*, i, nos. 76, 82, 99, 173.

[29] V. Zimányi, *Der Bauernstand der Herrschaft Güssing im 16. und 17. Jahrhundert* (Eisenstadt 1962); ead., *A rohonc-szalonaki uradalom és jobbágysága a XVI–XVII században* (Bp. 1968), esp. 14–26.

[30] In general: H. I. Bidermann, *Geschichte der österreichischen Gesammt-Staats-Idee, 1526–1804*, i–ii (Innsbruck 1867–89), i, 17–20. Cf. below, pp. 169 ff., 204 ff., 246, for later developments.

maintaining some 800 soldiers as garrison alone and Güssing castle consumed 200,000 loaves and more than 100,000 litres of wine *per annum*.[31] Unstable times permitted a few careerists to advance their families onto the very highest rung of the ladder: Karl Liechtenstein, Zdeněk Lobkovic and his son, Franz Dietrichstein, Martinic and Slavata; along with one or two thorough parvenus: Eggenberg, Esterházy, and—in his own unique volcanic way—Wallenstein, the arriviste scion of long-established Czech nobility. These are names rich in associations for any student of the eighteenth-century, even the nineteenth-century Monarchy, and we shall return to them more than once. Again Habsburg policies confirmed the evolution by extending an earlier practice of generosity: army commands and court office, confiscated estates, the titles bestowed with unprecedented largesse in the 1620s.

Confirmed it; they did not *create* it. The relationship is epitomized by one further element in the triumph of the magnates: the establishment of a system of entail which ensured the continuity of the great estate and its owners from generation to generation. While the Habsburgs, like the ruling princes of Germany, moved hesitantly towards strict primogeniture within their own house, their leading subjects in the Monarchy took up the parallel legal device of *Fideicommissum* or *Majorat*, which spread to Central Europe from the Mediterranean lands after 1600 and resolved the uncertainties of previous customary inheritance, especially among the Slavs.[32] Every *Fideicommissum* had to be approved by the monarch—thus far the dynasty could show favour to its court

---

[31] Pekař, *Katastry*, 33; Placht, op. cit. 216 ff, esp. 230; Matějek, 'Bílá Hora', 85 ff. The figure for Bohemian lords in 1740 was 64 per cent (of which 95 per cent were owned by princes and counts): E. Hassenpflug, 'Die böhmische Adelsnation als Repräsentation des Königreichs Böhmen (1627–1740)', *Bohemia-Jahrbuch*, xv (1974), 71–90. at 85 f. For the Batthyánys: Zimányi, *Rohonc-Szalonak*, 45 f., 111–14 and *passim*.

[32] Strictly *Majorat* was only one kind, though the commonest, of *Fideicommissum*, whereby the entail passed through eldest sons. The first isolated examples appear before 1620 (Dohna 1600, Khevenhüller-Frankenburg 1605, and—according to *Ottův slovník naučný*, i–xxviii (Pr. 1888–1909, hereafter 'OSN'), iv, 823 f.—Bubna in 1608). See L. Pfaff and F. Hoffmann, *Zur Geschichte der Fideicommisse* (V. 1884), 26–32; V. Urfus, 'Rodinný fideikomis v Čechách', *SbH* ix (1962), 193–236. Hungary had some *Fideicommissa* from the 17th century, but there the traditional system of *ősiség*, or *aviticitas*, derived from Magyar tribal law, had much the same effect of rendering noble land inalienable. Mika, 'Rozvrstvení', shows how often large Bohemian estates were broken up in the 16th century.

nobility—but it rested on the existing wealth and status of the supplicant. By the reign of Leopold I the entailed latifundium emphatically called the tune within the world of *Herrschaft*; it is a telling detail that the serf could now be required to perform *robot* on any manor of his lord, not simply the one where he resided.[33]

Thus the temporary balance between monarch and estates, which made possible the age of Humanism in the sixteenth century, was upset not so much by any centralist policies of the former as by changing relationships within the latter. The divergent interests of the magnates inclined them to seek new allies. On one hand they rejoined the Catholic Church, that latifundian establishment which offered a haven from the increasingly strident opposition of their fellow secular estates. The ranks of the Catholic nobility, almost all aristocrats, before 1600 a mere remnant, now swelled apace; by 1631 Pázmány could publish a little handbook containing 'certain reasons which have moved many leading men to enter the bosom of the Roman Church'.[34] (I shall turn to this theme shortly.) On the other hand both magnates and prelates looked to the dynasty, particularly during the first two desperate decades of the seventeenth century. Historians have been puzzled by the significance of those years of *Bruderzwist*; but surely they were the rescue of the Habsburgs? For the political crisis proved a catalyst of new attitudes which rendered them indispensable. The emperors were saved by their own weakness, a paradoxical assertion only if we view the Habsburgs as masters of Central Europe's fate, rather than as its chief pawns who never had more than a limited authority to impose solutions. Hence similar evolutions in the dynasty's several territories are proof, not of any uniform absolutism, but of uniform underlying features in different parts of the Monarchy. The irony is nicer still if we recall that Rudolf II, besides being the most ineffectual of Habsburg rulers, also had the least love for haughty aristocrats. Rudolf perhaps came nearest to taking up some other

---

[33] Grünberg, i, 28.

[34] The list of Catholic nobles in 1600 would include some Lobkovices, Dietrichsteins, Pálffys, Erdődys, Draškovićes, and a few more, plus one or two families (like Hoyos) not yet fully native. Cf. the proportions shown by Fr. Dvorský in *SbH* (Rezek), ii (1884), 280–8, for Bohemia. P. Pázmány, 'Bizonyos Okok, mellyek erejétűl viseltetvén sok fő ember . . . az Római Ecclesiának kebelébe szállott' in *Összes munkái, magyar sorozat*, i–vii (Bp. 1894–1905), v, 307–42. Cf. below, p. 112.

social option on behalf of his family: he cultivated members of the
petty nobility, resided continuously in the liveliest urban centre of
his realms, even allowed some serious negotiations with the
discontented peasantry during the 1590s.[35] But these were half-
hearted gestures: the Habsburgs created no alternative buttress to
their power, and after 1620, emerging from the cul-de-sac into
which Rudolf and Matthias had led them, they accepted the lasting
alliance proferred by the new aristocracy.

★

Meanwhile the rest of society retreated into a passive resentment
punctuated with active revolt, revolt which served to cement more
firmly that ruling alliance. Lesser nobles and towns (already so
estranged) had little chance of success, though urban violence
formed part of the crisis after 1600 and we have some grounds for
linking both elements with the Bohemian revolt in 1618 and parallel
movements elsewhere in the Monarchy. Unrest erupted in Prague
during the Passau invasion of 1611 and again after the Defenestration. We can only guess at the extent of ferment beneath the surface
of municipal life; even Vienna was not entirely subservient: the
imperial family aroused widespread discontent when it fled the city
in 1683.[36] The evidence for 1618 is equally difficult to evaluate: by
no means all the ringleaders of rebellion were impoverished knights
or disaffected merchants—think of the immensely wealthy Smiřický
or the lordly Schlick; and not many were thoroughgoing Calvinists.
None the less those groups played a significant part, especially as
the revolt grew more radical. They were the ones prepared to risk
the Palatine gamble, though in doing so they fatally weakened the
base of their operations. The twenty-seven traitors executed in 1621
on the Old Town Square of Prague included seventeen burghers,
seven knights, only three lords.[37] Only in Hungary could the gentry

<hr/>

[35] A. Czerny, *Der zweite Bauernaufstand in Oberösterreich, 1595–7* (Linz 1890), 162
ff., 280 ff.; Sturmberger, *Tschernembl*, 68–77; G. Grüll, *Der Bauer im Lande ob der
Enns am Ausgang des 16. Jahrhunderts* (Linz 1969).

[36] Skála, op. cit. i, 283, 317 f.; Gindely, *Dreissigjähriger Krieg*, i, 300 f., 312–15;
Novák, *Rudolf II*, 151 ff. W. Sturminger (ed.), *Die Türken vor Wien in
Augenzeugenberichten* (Düsseldorf 1968), 48 f. Cf. below, p. 140.

[37] Gindely, *Dreissigjähriger Krieg*, iv, 36–105; cf. Placht, op. cit. 73–5. A few of the
leaders were killed earlier, or fled—and it was easier for the highly-placed to get away
(viz. H. M. Thurn). On the other hand two of the three executed lords—Budovec
and Harant—were recent creations.

and urban strongholds of Calvinism like radical Nagyvárad maintain a programme of resistance through fitful alliance with the princes of Transylvania who provided solid authority and a good bargaining counter.[38]

The more dangerous alternative lay in peasant uprising. Ultimately rural rebellion proved no better able to break the grip of the new ruling class since—besides its own inherent lack of cohesion—it usually in the end rallied even discontented knights and townsmen to the defence of whatever property they still possessed. But it raised the spectre of total anarchy, and significantly enough it too reached epidemic proportions in the years around 1600 after a comparative calm through most of the sixteenth century. That is particularly striking in the *Erblande* where a mounting sense of grievance led first to isolated violence in Upper Austria and Carniola, then between 1594 and 1597 to a concerted rebellion of Upper and Lower Austrian peasants who enjoyed considerable sympathy from local towns. The panic-stricken landlords wrought severe retribution.[39]

The same happened in Hungary, where calm had anyway been only skin-deep. The sentiments of Dózsa's 'crusaders', the *kurucok*, lived on, nourished by indigence, rapine, and visionary Protestantism, issuing in a preliminary wave of tumult about 1570 from Croatia to the mysterious 'black man' of Debrecen.[40] In the 1590s renewed Ottoman war brought disaster: not just military demands and conscription (factors which contributed to the Austrian insurrection) but complete devastation in many areas. Thousands of displaced peasants and disenchanted soldiers roamed the countryside, forming bands of 'hajducks'—irregular mercenaries—and creating their own ideology of resistance. The end of the war only compounded calamity: in a bout of uncontrolled ferocity

---

[38] On Nagyvárad: Makkai, *Puritánusok*, 140 ff. Cf. the troubles at Kassa in 1604, or at Eperjes in 1687, or along the upper Tisza in 1631–2 (below, p. 98).

[39] Upper Austria: Czerny, *Bauernaufstand*; Grüll, *Robot*, 97 ff.; Stülz, op. cit. 388–432. Lower Austria: K. Haselbach, *Der niederösterreichische Bauernkrieg am Ende des 16. Jahrhunderts* (V. 1867); G. E. Friess, *Der Aufstand der Bauern in Niederösterreich am Schlusse des 16. Jahrhunderts* (V. 1897, separatum from *Jb. f. Lk. v. NÖ*); Feigl, *Bauernaufstand*.

[40] The fullest description of Croatian events in 1573 is by Yu. V. Bromlej, *Krest'yanskoe vosstanie 1573g. v Chorvatii* (Moscow 1959); cf. I. Karaman in Heckenast (ed.), *Bauernbewegungen*, 335–40. On Debrecen see I. Révész, 'Debrecen lelki válsága 1561–71', *Sz* lxx (1936), 38–75, 163–203; and G. Heckenast in *TSz* vi (1963), 19–21.

reminiscent of the Russian Time of Troubles (with which it exactly coincides) the hajducks first supported Bocskai's revolt, then rebelled again to secure personal freedom for themselves. Their violence perhaps did more than anything else to bring together the Habsburgs and the major Hungarian nobles.[41]

Bohemia was spared serious tribulation a little longer, though sporadic incidents took place on the great estates, like the conflict between a villager called Kubata and the Lords of Hradec which became a *cause célèbre* in the Czech folk memory. But Bohemia led the way in the crescendo of unrest after 1618. A 'lament of the labouring people' issued in the 'troubled year of 1620' already indicates the degree of resentment at ever-mounting exactions. During the next decade popular revolt brought lasting chaos to whole provinces, especially in the north-east.[42] In Upper Austria a veritable peasants' war broke out in 1626 with the support of some towns and even nobles; it was at length suppressed by peculiarly distasteful means, only to revive six years later when foreign enemies of the Habsburgs again seemed within striking distance. Northern Hungary experienced a conflagration in 1631–2 as the serfs and the inhabitants of little wine-growing demesne towns along the upper Tisza felt the full impact of the new economic, social, and religious regime.[43]

---

[41] 'Hajdúk' is strictly the plural of 'hajdú' (originally a drover), but I follow established English usage. On them see I. N. Kiss in Pickl (ed.), op. cit. 273–96; and on their political significance: T. Wittman, *Az osztrák Habsburg-hatalom válságos éveinek történetéhez* (Szeged 1959), a stimulating, though confusing essay; L. Makkai, 'A hajdúk "nemzeti" és "függetlenségi" ideológiája', *TSz* vi (1963), 22–9 (and the comments of L. Nagy, ibid. 68–74); K. Benda, 'Der Haiduckenaufstand in Ungarn ... 1607–8', *Nouvelles Études Historiques* (Bp 1965), 299–313.

[42] Krofta, op. cit. 161–6; Válka, op. cit. 136–96; and J. Jirásek, *Poddaní na panství olomouckého biskupství v druhé polovině 16. století* (Pr. 1957), 65–71, indicate some pre-1618 evidence. On the case of Kubata (supposedly a clash over water-meadows) see Č. Zíbrt in *ČL* xiv (1905), 31–7, and id., *Bibliografie české historie*, i–v (Pr. 1900–12, hereafter *BČH*, iii, nos. 9956–10040. *Knihopis* no. 13895: *Pláč Robotných lidí* ('Wydán Léta bouřliwého, 1620'); 'robotný' means liable to *corvée*. For 1618–30: J. Koči, *Boje venkovského lidu v období temna* (Pr. 1953), chs. 1–2; J. Petráň, 'Matouš Ulický a poddanské povstání na Kouřimsku a Čáslavsku r. 1627', *AUC* 1954, no. 7, 43–64.

[43] Upper Austria: A. Czerny, *Bilder aus der Zeit der Bauernunruhen in Oberösterreich* (Linz 1876); Stieve, *Bauernaufstand*, who makes (pp. 67 f.) less of burgher or noble sympathy than does Czerny (pp. 12 ff.). Cf. Carafa, *Commentaria*, 253–5, 259 f., 264–6, 270. There were further disturbances there in 1636 (below, p. 399, n. 42), and 1648 (Czerny, *Bilder*, 273–98). Hungary: L Makkai, *A felsőtiszavidéki parasztfelkelés, 1631–2* (Bp. 1954); and id., *Puritánusok*, 161 and *passim*.

From 1648, as we shall see, that new order began to show more stability. But its foundations were still insecure in the very countryside with which it had identified itself so decisively. Isolated explosions continued in Austria and western Hungary; further east, serf and hajduck grievances were nourished by political malcontents and merged with the next phase of the military struggle against the Habsburgs.[44] In Bohemia the year 1680 brought the largest disturbance yet: a campaign of petitions and mainly passive resistance led by a blacksmith from Friedland. Having spread to affect almost half the country in some degree, it was hastily put down with needless—but characteristic—savagery.[45] Peasant revolt thus counterpoints the emergent Counter-Reformation world of entrenched *Herrschaft* to which the new authorities enforced subordination. Two special cases are instructive: the Wallachians or Vlachs, semi-nomadic frontier settlers of mountainous eastern Moravia, were reduced by a series of bitter military offensives during the 1630s and 1640s to the status of the neighbouring serfs; and the Chods, an equivalent group in the extreme west of Bohemia who held extensive traditional privileges, were likewise dispossessed with a combination of chicanery and force of arms which provoked them into a final full-scale uprising in the 1690s.[46] Yet in demanding conformity the authorities also precipitated a new kind of conscious non-conformity: an uprooted and submerged rural population.

The hajducks afford the first main indication of this process: casualties of endless war and economic repression, they grew into a distinctive feature of the Hungarian social scene, numbering some 100,000 by the mid-seventeenth century. Some proved indispensable, fighting in the service of Habsburgs and aristocrats—at least until their pay ran out; some acquired the rank of minor nobles—at

---

[44] Grüll, *Bauer, Herr . . .*, for Upper Austria; Karaman in Heckenast (ed.), *Bauernbewegungen*, for Croatia. L. Benczédi, 'A "vitézlő rend" és ideológiája a Thököly-felkelésben', *TSz* vi (1963), 33–43; J. Varga, op. cit. 104 ff.; I. Rácz, *A hajdúk a XVII században* (Debrecen 1969), ch. 7.

[45] Koči, *Boje*, ch. 3; id., *Frýdlantsko*; J. V. Šimák, 'Příspěvek k selské bouři r. 1680 . . .', *VKČSN*, 1899, no. xiv; J. Kašpar, 'Dvě studie k dějinám nevolnického povstání r. 1680', *AUC Phil. et Hist.*, 1958, I, 55–81; id., *Nevolnické povstání*, with details of the movement's extent. Cf. J. J. von Weingarten, *Codex Ferdinandeo-Leopoldino-Josephino-Carolinus* (Pr. 1720), 448–51.

[46] J. Dostál, *Valašská povstání za třicetileté války, 1621–44* (Pr. 1956); F. Roubík, *Dějiny chodů u Domažlic* (Pr. 1931), 229 ff., a minutely detailed study.

least for a time; the majority drifted along as a shifting and improvident mass always liable to exchange day-labouring for vagrancy and sedition. The wars of the later seventeenth century, which again brought ruin to many peasant households throughout Hungary, only exacerbated the situation and inaugurated the classic age of the bandit, whether the *betyár* of the Transdanubian forests or the *zbojnik* of the Carpathians.[47] In Bohemia and Austria too the spread of beggary already exercised observers before 1600 and now took on a new dimension in an age of strife and dislocation. Veritable armies of dangerous vagabonds came together, like the gangs of men called *petrovští* repeatedly proscribed by the Bohemian government after 1648; in Silesia hangmen were sent out to catch them and the solider peasantry lived in terror of arson and assault.[48] The smallish monastery of Baumgartenberg in Upper Austria received more than three thousand beggars in 1696 and the little province contained eight times that many voluntary or involuntary social outcasts. Similar figures could be calculated for most other parts of the Monarchy, where local officials were forced into continual action against bands of thugs and reprobates.[49]

★

The Counter-Reformation state met disturbance from below with a ruthlessness bred of fear. It undertook an equal and parallel

---

[47] Rácz, op. cit., covers the hajducks' 17th-century evolution, mode of life, and pattern of settlement. Cf., for the Carpathians, W. Ochmanski, *Zbójnictwo góralskie, z dziejów walki klasowej na wsi góralskiej* (Warsaw 1950); and V. V. Brabovets'kii, *Selyans'kii ruch na Prikarpatti* (Kiev 1962), who discusses Galician revolts from 1648 to Oleksa Dovbuš.

[48] Bohemia: Petráň, 'Pohyb', 430–9; id., *Poddaný lid*, 177–80, 227–40; Klíma, op. cit. 44–55; Placht, op. cit. 60 ff., 141 ff. Austria: Mell, *Lage*, 56–9. On the *petrovští*: Weingarten, op. cit. 266–8, 343–6; L. Baur (ed.), 'Berichte des hessen-darmstädtischen Gesandten J. E. Passer ... über die Vorgänge ... in Wien von 1680 bis 1683', *AÖG* xxxvii (1867), 273–409, at 295; A. Rezek, *Dějiny Čech a Moravy nové doby*, i–ii (Pr. 1892–3), i, 114–18, ii, 118–20; Klíma, op. cit. 58–61. For Silesia: P. Frauenstädt, 'Bettel-und Vagabundenwesen in Schlesien vom 16. bis 18. Jahrhundert', *Preussische Jahrbücher* lxxxix (1897), 488–509. For the similar situation in southern Germany see T. Hampe, *Die fahrenden Leute in der deutschen Vergangenheit* (Leipzig 1902), esp. 93 ff., with material from Nuremberg.

[49] Grüll, *Bauer, Herr* ... 55–7; cf. F. Loidl, *Menschen im Barock* (V. 1938), 97–105. Bohemian evidence in J. E. Schlenz, *Geschichte des Bistums und der Diözese Leitmeritz*, i–ii (Warnsdorf 1912–14), ii, 526 f. (for the abbey of Ossegg); E. Kittel, 'Kulturhistorisches aus Eger', *MVGDB* xvii (1879), 17–29, 284–91. Cf. below, pp. 412 ff. and, on the European background, H. Kamen, *The Iron Century, social change in Europe 1550–1660* (London 1971), chs. 10–11.

campaign to curb a different kind of dissent: the mental props to resistance, bred of intellectual pluralism and Humanist questioning. Government, aristocracy, and Catholic Church launched irregular attacks on this front before 1620, which were co-ordinated and swiftly extended thereafter. They were directed above all against education and printing.

The two ancient universities of Prague and Vienna formed prime targets. Prague's Carolinum was swept into an aggressively Protestant stance from 1609 by the explicit desire of the estates, well aware of its potential importance to them, and it collapsed with corresponding completeness on the morrow of the White Mountain. Its Jesuit rivals promptly forced it into their embrace and effected a decisive break with its Hussite past which all subsequent squabbles among Catholics over control could not undo. In Vienna subversion began earlier, as Khlesl sought to introduce Jesuit teachers and proposed large administrative reforms. The turbulent priest's programme was carried through by his monarch-rival and after 1620 Ferdinand II fused university with Jesuit academy under the sway of the latter.[50]

Existing higher education in the Habsburg lands had to be not only tamed, but also expanded and substituted for the study abroad so common in the era of Humanism. Jesuit universities flourished at Graz and Olomouc by 1600; thereafter they were complemented by further foundations at Tyrnau (which took over Graz's role for the lands across the Leitha) and Innsbruck, quasi-universities at Linz and Kassa, and a network of colleges especially strong in Austria and Bohemia.[51] Only Hungarians retained, besides some freedom to travel, a modest alternative source of schooling in their increasingly straitened and defensive Calvinist academies and a few Lutheran *Gymnasia*. Elsewhere Protestant institutions yielded totally to the new system and educational standards for the population as a whole fell away: most of all in the towns, perhaps

---

[50] V. V. Tomek, *Geschichte*, 251 ff.; Kink, op. cit. i, pt. 1, 346 ff. See below, p. 221 and n. 60, on the squabbles.

[51] J. Andritsch, *Studenten und Lehrer aus Ungarn und Siebenbürgen an der Universität Graz* (Graz 1965), a valuable study; cf. below, pp. 124–6. Freiburg im Breisgau was a Habsburg university, but *sui generis* and not under consideration here; the Jesuits never took control of it.

rather less sharply at parish level, though we have next to no detailed research to fill out the picture.[52]

Still more instructive is the fate of printing. As we saw, the Habsburg lands participated fully both in the intellectual debates of the *Reich* and then in its confessional arguments—especially over the Jesuits—during the bitter years after 1600. A wave of books and pamphlets spread diverse points of view through Central Europe with a mounting pungency of expression. The principal focus of attention was Bohemia, where Rudolfine Prague had supported a sophisticated publishing industry in several languages. Some of its printers moved to open sympathy for the Protestant cause, notably Samuel Adam Veleslavín (son of the country's greatest Humanist publisher) and Daniel Karl von Karlsberg.[53] Moreover, lively presses appeared in the provinces: the enterprise of Heník Waldstein and his assistant Andreas Mizera at Dobrovice, for example, or that of Martin Kleinwechter who issued more than sixty works at Königgrätz between 1614 and 1620. Some of the fare now offered was distinctly bold and mordant: witness the *Lázeň španělská* of about 1600, a satire on the defeat of the Spanish armada. Western Hungary's wandering printers, like Johann Manlius and his successor Imre Farkas, showed something of the same spirit and produced a regular stream of controversial matter for their Protestant employers.[54]

This development reached its climax during the Bohemian revolt and the first campaign of Bethlen Gábor. The war spawned an important pamphlet-literature, from news-sheets and proclama-

[52] J. Hanzal, 'Nižší školy v Čechách v 17. a 18. století', *Muzejní a Vlastivědná Práce*, x (1972), 152–70; contrast the opinion of J. Prokeš in *Československá vlastivěda*, iv (Pr. 1932), 538, 541 f. Cf. the information in A. T. Vanyó, *A katholikus restauráció Nyugatmagyarországon* (Pécs 1928), 88–101; and J. Házi, *Die kanonische Visitation des Stefan Kazó ... in den Jahren 1697–8* (Eisenstadt 1958), 16–18, on Catholic schools in western Hungary.

[53] Above, pp. 20 ff., 56 f. No satisfactory history of Bohemian printing exists; cf. Volf, op. cit. 86–96, and the full list of Czech titles in *Knihopis*.

[54] K. Chyba, 'Dobrovická tiskárna', *Ročenka Universitní Knihovny v Praze*, 1958, 54–97; J. Johanides, 'První knihtiskárna v Hradci Králové', *Str. Kn.* iv (1969), 66–90. J. Kolár (ed.), *Zrcadlo rozděleného království* (Pr. 1963), 130–50, prints the *Lázeň španělská*; cf. ibid. 157–98. On Manlius: A. Sennovitz, *Manlius János* (Bp. 1902); and Gulyás, op. cit. 210–22. The Farkas editions, produced at Keresztúr and Csepreg from 1611 into the 1640s, are noted in K. Szabó, *Regi magyar könyvtár*, i–iii (Bp. 879–98, hereafter *RMK*), i (Hungarian-language), and ii.

tions to appeals in various emotional registers. Justifications of the estates and vilifications of the Catholics predominate, most concealing both author and place of publication or bearing such transparently false imprints as 'Zaragoza'. And Western Europe was scoured for intellectual support: the decade before 1620 saw Czech translations of John Jewel, William Perkins, Savonarola, De Dominis, Duplessis-Mornay, and Calvin's *Institutes*; as well as versions of the classics of old Bohemian liberty: the constitution of Charles IV, Dalimil's *Chronicle*, the history of the Hussites.[55]

Such literature represented an obvious threat to order and the government made increasing efforts to eliminate it. Confiscation and book-burning were a stock-in-trade of the Austrian Counter-Reformation from its earliest days; here Bishop Brenner amply deserved his name.[56] The first substantial Bohemian case took place in 1602, when a small-time author and printer called Sixt Palma Močidlanský was imprisoned and banished for libels against the Catholic Church and the dynasty. In 1615 Waldstein and Mizera suffered for issuing a defamatory political work. Then came the authorities' real opportunity after 1620, and the ideologists of Counter-Reformation: Carafa, Lamormaini, and the Jesuits, provincial commissioners, and the rest, seized their chance not only to ban the publicity of their rivals but to manufacture their own.[57] No doubt they genuinely desired to convince—they were even swift to turn satire to the Habsburg cause; but more effective weapons (as other contemporary ecclesiastical establishments like the Anglican discovered) were blunter. Revived Catholicism worked

---

[55] Gebauer, op. cit.; A. Markus, 'Stavovské apologie z roku 1618', *ČČH* xvii (1911), 58–74, 200–17, 304–15, 421–35; Stanka, op. cit., chs. 4–5. These pamphlets had a wide dispersion; cf. the collection in Bod. Diss. K 211–13; and below, p. 267 and n. 76. Jewel: *Knihopis*, no. 3558; Perkins: ibid. 6994–8; Savonarola: ibid. 15234; De Dominis: ibid. 2062; Mornay: ibid. 5948–9; Calvin: ibid. 1406, whose most enthusiastic propagator was Jan Opsimathes (see M. Bohatcová in *Gutenberg-Jahrbuch*, 1974, 163–5); Charles IV: *Knihopis*, no. 3778. On Dalimil, the Hussites, and others, cf. Evans, *Wechel Presses*, 49 f.

[56] ÖNB, MS. 13746, fols. 13 f.; Wiedemann, 'Büchercensur', esp. 285 ff.; Socher, op. cit. 75, 142; Hurter, op. cit. iv, 252; Bibl, 'Erzherzog Ernst', 581 f.; E. Tomek, op. cit. 409 f., 461 f., 475 f.

[57] A. Škarka, 'Ze zápasů nekatolického tisku s protireformací', *CCH* xlii (1936), 1–55, 286–322, 484–520. In the gruesome case of Waldstein and Mizera dog ate dog: Waldstein having his accomplice executed, and thus escaping with a fine (Chyba, art. cit.). Carafa, *Commentaria*, 176 f. and *passim*; Grisar, art. cit. 729; Podlaha (ed.), *Dopisy*, no. 223 (pp. 232–4).

through 'official' presses with near-monopoly status and suppressed
any free market in books. At Graz the Widmanstetter dynasty was
already installed by 1600. In Vienna Gregor Gelbhaar and Matthias
Formica were the only significant entrepreneurs, and their concerns
united in 1640 when Cosmerovius took over from Gelbhaar as
Hofbuchdrucker and married Formica's widow.[58] In Prague the
Veleslavín press, the main outlet for the Carolinum, was confiscated
and turned into a strictly regulated Jesuit undertaking. In Hungary
the new university of Tyrnau set up a publishing house with
equipment, some of which had come in a devious way from the
earliest abortive settlement of Viennese Jesuits, some, via a devout
and enterprising royal secretary, from one of the famous printers of
Rudolfine Prague. *Habent sua fata typi!*[59]

★

Thus a system of controls forced conformity from the intellectual,
as from the lower classes. It was helped by the internal discipline of
the Catholic Church, especially of its religious orders, the leading
sector in the Counter-Reformation, which imposed their own
censorship on errant members much more effectively than any civil
government could.[60] But just as social change and the breakdown
of the estates prepared the way for a compact between magnates and
dynasty, so developments which began during the sixteenth century
and accelerated thereafter inclined intellectuals too towards a
voluntary alliance. While the age of Humanism and Protestantism
saw a great rise in the number of university-educated commoners,
it was strong enough only to bring into being a new social stratum,
not to emancipate it fully. Again we see the narrow base of the

---

[58] Bohatcová, *Irrgarten*, esp. nos. 55 seqq.: Kolár (ed.), op. cit. 217–26 (satires). In
England no printers were permitted outside London, Oxford, and Cambridge
between 1586 and the later 17th century. On Widmanstetter: J. Benzing, *Die
Buchdrucker des 16. und 17. Jahrhunderts im deutschen Sprachgebiet* (Wiesbaden 1963),
154 f.; Andritsch, op. cit. 279–88. Mayer, op. cit. i, nos. 961–1094 (Gelbhaar), 1097–
1191 (Formica), 1266–1617 (Matthias Cosmerovius, a Pole by origin).

[59] K. Beránek, 'Z dějin akademické tiskárny v Praze', *AUC, HUCP* vi (1965), 2,
91–100; Menčik, 'Censura', 107 ff.; Volf, op. cit. 96 ff. Cf. id., 'Dějiny novinářství v
Čechách v l. 1657–1718', *ČČH* xxx (1924), 74–94, 237–48, for the *lack* of newspapers
in Bohemia. On Tyrnau: Iványi–Gárdonyi, op. cit. 15–45 (some of its equipment
once belonged to Telegdi: cf. above, pp. 49 f.); F. Jenei, 'Ferenczffy Lőrinc
nyomdájának történetéhez', *MKSz* lxxvii (1961), 297–308.

[60] Cf., in general, Duhr, *Geschichte*, ii, pt. 2, 362 ff.; iii, 531–4. For the important
case of Bohuslav Balbín see the documents in F. Menčik, 'Petr Lambeck a Balbínova
Epitome', *VKČSN*, 1889, 182–202, and below, pp. 230 f.

Habsburg Renaissance, highly dependent on an expansive dynasty and nobility and their patronage, the more so when the towns failed to provide lasting material support or civic values.

What avenues lay open to the ambitious intellectual in these circumstances? One possibility, of course, was a career in the Church, Catholic rather than Protestant. I shall come back to that complex issue. Clearer to follow are the ways in which the rising secular disciplines of law and medicine attached themselves to court and aristocracy. Throughout Europe, as is well known, Humanism encouraged a professional caste of jurists who rediscovered Roman procedures, introducing the written records and sophisticated arguments demanded by the more intricate litigation of the early modern period. In the Habsburg lands lawyers seemed politically progressive for a time: Protestants, deriving advanced ideas from their foreign travels, pleading the causes of estates and towns. Examples are the Viennese Schwarzentaler and De Rotis, or the Bohemian school from Všehrd to Kocín.[61] But by 1600 the climate began to change and different implications emerged. Learned legists reacted more and more against the illogical, incoherent common law and the traditional interplay of local interests which it mirrored. They turned—now usually as Catholic converts—to serve the individual magnate, with his endless suits, his *Landgericht*, his *Fideicommissum*; more especially they turned to serve the ruling house. Not only could they gain influence and preferment through Habsburg courts, particularly the Aulic Council, with its bench reserved for doctors, and the Bohemian appeal court at Prague, founded in 1548, which employed first four, then eight, and eventually ten doctors, and after 1628 demanded professional qualifications from all its noble members as well; a law degree might be very helpful in administrative bodies such as chanceries (which anyway exercised certain judicial functions).[62]

---

[61] Stölzel, op. cit., is an excellent overall view, though he concentrates on the situation in Hesse. Luschin, *Reichsgeschichte*, 364 ff.; E. Ott, *Beiträge zur Receptions-Geschichte des römisch-canonischen Processes in den böhmischen Ländern* (Leipzig 1879), chs. 8–9, 11; J. Klabouch, 'Die humanistische Jurisprudenz in den böhmischen Ländern', J. Irmscher (ed.), op. cit. ii, 279–303; Aschbach, op. cit. iii, 258–60 (De Rotis).

[62] Ott, op. cit., esp. ch. 10; J. Klabouch, *Osvícenské právní nauky v českých zemich* (Pr. 1958), 24–9, an important study. On the Prague appeal judges see also

(continued)

One of the earliest to make his peace with the Catholic establishment was Blotius's friend Giffen. Others followed during the crucial years between 1600 and 1630 or 1640. Let us take a random sample of three: Otto Melander (1571–1640), born in Hesse, educated at Wittenberg and a Latin poet of some merit, the *éminence grise* behind Bohemia's constitutional revolution after 1620; Matthias Prickelmayr (died in 1656), son of a peasant, Austrian chancellor throughout the reign of Ferdinand III; Isaac Volmar (1582–1662), of Swabian Protestant stock, sometime professor at Freiburg, who like Prickelmayr ended his life as a baron and represented Austria at the Peace of Westphalia.[63] As the seventeenth century progressed these successful jurist intellectuals tended, like Melander, to have been born across the frontier inside the German *Reich* (another point to which we shall return). Some found their *métier* in restoring university legal faculties at Vienna and Prague, and opening new ones at Olomouc and Tyrnau, which now—besides providing opinions in difficult cases—had the firm purpose of breeding future generations of attorneys loyal to Church and state. The Bavarian Christoph Kyblin (1617–78), for example, ennobled for his share in the defence of Prague against the Swedes, became the leading academic lawyer in Bohemia.[64]

Let us not mistake this situation: such men evidently enjoyed the protection of Habsburg government, which made their careers possible and paid them well, especially in the chanceries. But the process was a two-way one: lawyers, like aristocrats, turned to strong aulic authority as an ideal, and moulded it according to their

---

J. C. Auersperg, *Geschichte des königlichen böhmischen Appellationsgerichtes*, i–ii (Pr. 1805), esp. ii, with their careers; F. Rachfahl, *Die Organisation der Gesamtstaatsverwaltung Schlesiens vor dem dreissigjährigen Kriege* (Leipzig 1894), 220–58.

[63] On Giffen, above, pp. 23, 58. Melander: Ott, op. cit. 264–7; O. von Gschliesser, *Der Reichshofrat 1559–1806* (V. 1942), 206–8; *ADB*, s. v. (brief). There is nothing on Prickelmayr, but cf. Bidermann, op. cit. i, 103 f. Volmar: *ADB*, s. v. (lengthy); K. von Wurzbach, *Biographisches Lexikon des Kaiserthums Oesterreich*, i–lx (V. 1856–91, hereafter 'Wurzbach'), li, 269 f.

[64] Klabouch, *Právní nauky*, 29 ff.; *OSN*, s. v. 'Kyblin'; F. Eckhart, *A jog- és államtudományi kar története 1667–1935* (Bp. 1936). In Hungary common law retained greater influence both inside and outside the university (cf. below, p. 151) its most celebrated 17th-century commentator being János Kitonics, whose *Directio methodica processus judiciarii juris consuetudinarii inclyti Regni Hungariae* first appeared at Tyrnau in 1619. See also below, pp. 179 f. (Abele), 294 (Windhag, Hocher), 297 (Blume).

own lights. By joining the system they helped it to work. The stamp they set on forms of justice buttressed the claims of government in a variety of ways: appeals procedures, public prosecutors, efforts at codification.[65] No less significant, probably, for the overall stability of the Monarchy were the corresponding very slow changes in basic notions of legality.

A characteristic case is the elimination of feud as a legitimate means of redress, open—albeit not in the same degree—to high and low alike. Noble feud, that typical facet of fifteenth-century Central Europe, was gradually restrained: by the 1560s Emperor Maximilian II could brand the atavistic troublemaker Wilhelm von Grumbach a pure rebel and murderer; by the 1660s, thanks to new bonds of allegiance between the crown and its chief vassals, it had ceased to operate in the *Reich*, Austria, or Bohemia (except perhaps in transmuted form as the right to wartime plunder). Predictably it survived longest in Hungary, where those bonds of allegiance were so much weaker; there a prominent aristocrat, Imre Balassa, could defy Leopold I's government for months on the grounds of individual *jus resistendi*. Even after the 1680s the just feud lived on as a *de facto* collective privilege of the Hungarian nobility.[66] At a lower level the desperate weapon of peasant challenge (*Absage*) was still invoked sporadically into the seventeenth century, within the village community and even against the lords, but outlawed by the authorities it gradually came to appear a mere anti-social vendetta, though we may perhaps see traces of its spirit carried over to the rising folk hero of the avenging bandit.[67] A tell-tale pendant to the decline of feud is the attack on a more curious kind of customary

---

[65] On law codes: Luschin, *Reichsgeschichte*, 367 ff.; Strnadt, art. cit. 188 ff., 227 ff. But cf. below, p. 167, n. 21.

[66] O. Brunner, *Land und Herrschaft* (5th edn. V. 1965), 1–110. On Grumbach: Koch, *Quellen*, i, 8–85; a Moravian case in Dillon, op. cit. 63 f. On looting as legitimate deprivation: F. Redlich, *De Praeda Militari: looting and booty 1500–1815* (Wiesbaden 1956). On Balassa: V. Bogišić (ed.), *Acta coniurationem P. a Zrinio et F. de Frankopan nec non F. Nadasdy illustrantia* (Zagreb 1888), 55 ff.; T. A. Vanyó, *A bécsi nunciusok jelentései Magyarországról 1666–83* (Pannonhalma 1935), 27 ff. *passim*. The example of László Liszti (below, p. 382) is not very different; both eventually came to a bad end. The extraordinary story of a Hungarian robber-baron on a grand scale, eventually brought to justice in 1601, is told by A. Komáromy, 'Thelekessy Mihály (1576–1601)', *Sz* xxiv (1890), 468–84, 544–67, 617–43, 696–725, 775–804.

[67] Brunner, *Land und Herrschaft*, 66 ff.; Grüll, *Robot*, 67–73. One defence against witchcraft accusations seems to derive from the same source (cf. below, p. 412).

self-help: the *Schmähbrief* or open libel, employed to shame an offender, especially debtor, into an admission of guilt. Lawyers and emperors combined to condemn this traditional practice, which called into question both the proper channels of judicial recourse and the ruler's powers of censorship.[68]

The same evolution as among jurists seems to have taken place among qualified physicians. I shall dismiss them very summarily: the social history of Central European medicine is in its infancy. Medical doctors likewise tended to be progressive in the sixteenth century: many imbibed the radical Aristotelianism of Padua; one, Johann Jessenius, emerged as the foremost academic spokesman for the Bohemian revolt and had his tongue cut out and quartered in 1621. Thereafter the changed nature of patronage constrained them into a conservative role which anyway they seem increasingly to have welcomed. Successful physicians could rise to membership of two overlapping official bodies. They could serve at court, attending either directly on the imperial family (as a well-paid *Leibarzt*) or merely on the courtiers in general (as a less well-paid *Hofarzt*). Such *Leibärzte* and *Hofärzte* would normally belong to the university medical faculty, which included in addition a growing number of other teaching doctors—thirty-five at Vienna by the 1660s.[69]

Between them court and universities dominated the practice of medicine as thoroughly as did senior jurists that of advocacy, and a chain of command stretched down through provincial medical officers and army surgeons to the local apothecary or blood-letter.[70] Leading physicians might have either native or foreign origins. The

[68] J. S. Brunnquell (pres.), *De Pictura Famosa et de specie Iuris Germanici, pacto nimirum, quo maiores nostri, sub pictura famosa ... sese obligarunt* (Jena 1733), esp. 23–5, 34–60; I. L. Klüber, *De pictura contumeliosa commentatio* (Erlangen 1787). Kleist's *Michael Kohlhaas* is a marvellous literary depiction of anachronistic feud, including the elements of placards and magic.

[69] The imperial court lists (*Hofstaaten*) indicate these doctors: e.g. ÖNB, MS. 12388, fols. 20–2; ibid. MS. 14071, fols. 12–14. The terms *Leibmedicus* and *Hofmedicus* were also often used. J. Zwelfer, *Discursus Apologeticus* (V. 1668), sig. + + 2 r.

[70] *Acta Facultatis Medicae Universitatis Vindobonensis*, iv–v (1558–1676), ed. L. Senfelder (V. 1908–10); *Geschichte der Stadt Wien*, ed. H. Zimmermann *et al.*, i–vi (V. 1897–1918), vi, 206–90, esp. 216 ff.; K. Kučera and M. Truc (eds.), *Matricula Facultatis Medicae Universitatis Pragensis 1657–1783* (Pr. 1968), with lists of approved apothecaries, barber-surgeons, midwives, even Jewish doctors; J. Macek and V. Žáček, *Krajská správa v českých zemích a její archivní fondy* (Pr. 1958), 71.

most influential *Leibarzt* of the mid-seventeenth century for example, Johann Wilhelm Mannagetta (1588–1666), came from a family well established in Lower Austria and his descendants, raised to the rank of baron, turned to employment in the Habsburg administration; while Mannagetta's successor in public esteem, Paul Sorbait, doyen of the Vienna faculty, was the fifth son of a Belgian woodcutter. Indeed, foreigners probably found the privileges increasingly attractive: witness the influx of Irish doctors like Jacob Smith of Balroe, who studied at Prague without knowing either German or Czech, took a chair there, and gained the coveted post of *Leibarzt*. Whatever their background, members of the medical profession rallied to the imperial side, and we shall meet them again in later chapters among its intellectual propagators.[71]

*

So far we have observed two interlocking aspects of the new system which took root under the Austrian Habsburgs during the earlier seventeenth century: a set of long-term material interests and a set of controls. There remains one further aspect yet more difficult to analyse: the mental and spiritual factors which disposed men to serve the Counter-Reformation state. I reserve detailed examination of Catholicism's intellectual world to the third part of this book, but something must be said here about the deeper sources of Protestant breakdown. It was by no means just a story of repression and exile, and—what matters most in the present context—the revival of loyalty to the Roman Church hung closely together with a fear of anarchy and extremism.

Protestantism stood vulnerable on three counts in the years after 1600: it could appear divisive, unhistorical, and radical. As we saw in the first chapter, the simple fact that Central Europe had not one Reformation but several is of prime importance. Now it displayed its negative side, for when a nebulous but seamless Protestantism gave way to several sharp-edged and recriminatory Protestantisms the moderates who were still uncommitted found themselves in a

[71] Wurzbach, s. v. 'Mannagetta'; and works in Mayer, op. cit. 1. On Sorbait: *Biographisches Lexikon der hervorragenden Ärzte aller Zeiten und Völker*, ed. A. Hirsch *et al.* (repr. Munich–Berlin 1962), s. v., and Mayer, loc. cit. L. Schmid, *Irští lékaři v Čechách* (Pr. 1968), 11–15 (Smith) and *passim*. Cf. below, esp. ch. 10; and the great stores of information about Hungarian physicians in Weszprémi, op. cit., and Magyary-Kossa, op. cit.

false position. Separation into distinct ecclesiastical bodies was more or less finally sealed by 1617 (the centenary of the Wittenberg theses),[72] yet the many degrees of opinion within Lutheranism and Calvinism and the further shadings beyond them left Protestant forces very disparate, while the urban community, their most cohesive base, gradually ceased to be an asset as the vitality of the towns ebbed away. That leads to the second weakness, for there is a real sense in which the tide of history ran for Protestantism during the sixteenth century and against it thereafter. Protestants had explained one crisis, after 1500, as the death-throes of a corrupted Church; yet now another crisis, no less severe, was brewing without any full resolution of the first. If Ottoman advance had betokened divine wrath in the 1520s, why could progressive elimination of the old observances not assuage it? The balance of argument among contemporaries—so much more aware of historicity than earlier generations—shifted powerfully in Central Europe after about 1590, in the face of renewed Turkish peril and civil disorder. Many Protestants, especially Lutherans, took refuge in Biblical rather than practical solutions: in prophecy and mysticism, eirenism and the arcane revelations of the Rosicrucian movement.[73] They were qualified for, at best, only passive resistance to the attacks of the Counter-Reformers.

The alternative response was militancy, and here too the years around 1600 mark a new departure: the last stage of Humanist emancipation in the Habsburg lands; a generation influenced by genuinely radical ideas from the West, mediated through the lively university atomsphere at Heidelberg, Altdorf, Herborn, Basle, or Strasbourg. We have not merely the swashbuckling Calvinism of (say) Tschernembl, but the continuing propaganda of Arians in Transylvania and Poland. Did not such ideas invite total social disorder? It was easy to see heretical elements in popular unrest: the Austrian revolts of the 1590s and 1620s owed something of their strength to tough and cogent Lutheran gravamina, just as Bohemian

---

[72] Krebs, op. cit. 93 ff. Cf., for Hungary, Kazy, op. cit. i, 130 f.; Kubinyi, op. cit. 43 ff. – but there some aristocrats, like the Thurzós, took part in both Lutheran and Calvinist festivities.
[73] This deserves fuller discussion elsewhere; but cf. above, p. 78, and below, pp. 257, 394–9.

revolts drew on more or less vaguely apprehended Hussite traditions. And extremer sects, like the *Springer* of Carniola, the 'black man' movement on the Hungarian plain, or the *Mikulášenci* (to which Sixt Palma belonged) encouraged all manner of nonconformity.[74] In fact such things rarely played a central political role: peasants sacked monasteries largely because the monks exploited them in a material way; the pastor Matouš Ulický did not really lead the *sans-culottes* of Kouřim in 1627. What matters is the *legend* of religious-inspired insurrection, which frightened so many contemporaries into considering again the more comfortable verities of the Roman Church. Uncompromising Counter-Reformation purges of Ana-baptists, 'Rosicrucians', and their like won widespread Protestant approval.[75]

Most Central European conversions whose spiritual background we can weigh hinged on these three arguments: Protestantism is partial, innovatory, destructive. Of course, they are no more than great commonplaces of the Counter-Reformation, repeated me-chanically enough as *topoi* from one printed apologia to the next, sometimes dictated verbatim by major Jesuit controversialists like Scherer, Pázmány, or Jodocus Kedd. But if they had not been found plausible, the Catholic campaign would never have caught fire, and on occasion the underlying convictions of converts shine through as (to take two examples from about 1590) in the deep religiosity of Bálint Balassi's last poems and the self-assurance of the

---

[74] The thesis that Lutheran sentiments lay at the heart of peasant insurrection was argued most outspokenly by Stieve, *Bauernaufstand*, for the events of 1626; but his case manifestly involves special pleading: a Bavarian historian seeking to prove that imperial Counter-Reformation and not Bavarian occupation inflamed the situation. Cf. Czerny, *Bauernaufstand*, and *Bilder*; A. Gindely, 'Die Gegenreformation und der Aufstand in Oberösterreich im Jahre 1626', *Sb. d.k. Akad. d. Wiss.,ph.-h. Kl.* cxviii (1889), Abh. 6; Eder, *Glaubensspaltung*, 394 ff., on the rising in the Salzkammergut. For Bohemia: A. Rezek, *Dějiny prostonárodního hnutí náboženského v Čechách,* i (Pr. 1887), where again the point is exaggerated; and id., 'Dva příspěvky k dějinám selských bouří a selského poddanství v XVII. století', *VKČSN,* 1893, no. 2, 3–11. Révész, 'Debrecen', 180–203, on the 'black man (György Karácsony) and his revolt. On the *Springer*: below, p. 407.

[75] Petráň, 'Ulický'. Zacharias Theobald, the historian of Hussitism, showed a typical Lutheran reaction to Protestant extremists: *Wiedertäuferischer Geist, das ist … bericht, was jammer und elend die alten wiedertäufer gestiftet und angerichtet, daraus zu schliessen, was man von den neuen genannten Weigelianern, Rosenkreuzern und pansophisten zu gewarten hab, weiln sie … einerlei Lehr führen* (Nuremberg 1623).

highly cultivated Canon Weissenstein at Klosterneuburg.[76] That is clearest of all immediately after 1600 in Hungary, where Catholic prospects appeared extremely dim. Yet Pázmány, who as late as 1609 himself still despaired at the hopeless state of the Church, could attribute sentiments to his imagined aristocratic interlocutor two decades afterwards about the uncertainty, the novelty, and the divisiveness of Lutheranism and Calvinism which must have rung true in many an embattled castle and manor-house. Not only there: the Reformed minister Mihály Veresmarty left us a detailed record of the soul-searching which brought him, via a close study of Campion and Bellarmin, to the same conclusion.[77]

Hungary affords the best terrain to introduce one further—and tentative—reflection, for Hungary was the last region of the Monarchy to partake fully in the atmosphere of the late Renaissance. Perhaps, after all, the character of Humanism and Mannerism, in their specifically Central European conditions, had something to do with the eventual recovery of Catholicism there. Converts to Rome took a lonely, often a bold decision, yet in some ways they took the decision *not to change*, to hold to a world with which Protestantism now seemed incompatible. The essence of that world (I oversimplify drastically) consisted in order and unity. Order is ultimately a metaphysical notion: maybe the return of hierarchy and the revival of scholastic methods made some appeal to systematic Humanists much as the very study of Roman law—quite apart from the quality of some of its Catholic commentators—tended to create a mental as well as a material disposition in favour of imperial authority. Certainly, on a lower plane, the years of trouble soon seem to have persuaded legal and medical minds of the merits of order and stability. The point is well illustrated by a forgotten little work of one Andreas Dalner, 'in inferioris Austriae Regimine advocatus', who in 1599 condemned the diabolical evil of sedition and called for its condign punishment. He clearly views public and private

---

[76] There are many examples of motives for confession, some very stereotyped, in A. Räss, *Die Convertiten seit der Renaissance*, i–xiv (Freiburg 1866–80); cf. below, p. 190 and *passim*. Balassi: *MIT* i, 448–81; Weissenstein: Jöchlinger, art. cit., esp. 12–14.

[77] Pázmány, *Levelei*, no. 15 (23 Mar. 1609); cf. above, p. 95 and n. 34. M. Veresmarty, *Megtérése históriája*, ed. A. Ipolyi (Bp. 1878); cf. Ipolyi, *Veresmarty Mihály élete és munkái* (Bp. 1875).

insubordination as quite literally the work of Satan, and makes much of the recent *lèse-majesté* of peasant leaders.[78]

Order had its ethical side, and the search for moderation and balance is reflected in the later sixteenth-century cult of stoicism, the last great Renaissance compromise between Christian and pagan inspiration. The stoic morality of discipline and resignation gained adherents in a climate of political uncertainty; its message of individual submission to a strong but clement ruler could attract all those dismayed by the fractured public affairs of Central Europe. This neo-stoic movement hinged on Lipsius, unofficial president of the academy of letters, whose writings about constancy and statecraft went into dozens of editions. They exercised an especially marked influence in Hungary, where intellectuals cultivated the virtues of serenity and self-control amid strife. Some were Protestants, like Bocskai's adherents Illésházy and Rimay, or the court *literati* around Bethlen Gábor; the first editions of Lipsius in Hungarian were translated by Bethlen's protégé János Laskai.[79] Yet after Lipsius himself returned to the Roman fold in 1591 his new brand of Catholic devotion was widely propagated. Some of his followers took the same course, among then the learned aristocrat Mihály Forgách who—as Pázmány tells us in a proselytizing tract— knew the Scriptures, Calvin's *Institutes*, and Lipsius's *Politica* almost by heart. Even Jesuits espoused stoicism: witness J.-B. Schellenberg's volume entitled *Seneca Christianus* which was translated into Hungarian for another aristocrat-convert, Ádám Batthyány.[80] Other adherents withdrew into a perplexed and subdued neutrality, supporting the Habsburgs as long as possible: good examples are the poet Rimay and his magnate friend Révay.

---

[78] A. Dalnerus, *Tractatus de Seditione* (V. 1599). Cf. Klabouch, *Právní nauky*, 69 ff., on civil law and scholasticism. Cf. below, ch. 9, on notions of order.

[79] *Rudolf II*, 95 f. J. Rimay, *Államiratai és levelezése*, ed. A. Ipolyi (Bp. 1887); id., *Összes művei*, ed. S. Eckhardt (Bp. 1955). Illésházy: *MIT* ii, 35 f.; cf. OL, Batthyány család levéltára, P. 1341, lad. 1, fasc. 19, Rimay to Illésházy, 7 Sept. 1606 (a reference I owe to the kindness of Kálmán Benda). *Laskai János válogatott művei magyar Iustus Lipsius*, ed. M. Tarnóc (Bp. 1970).

[80] Oestreich, op. cit., 101–56, esp. 122 f., 130 f., 136–8. Pázmány, 'Keresztyéni Felelet a megdücsöült Szentek tiszteletirül', in *Összes munkái*, ii, 321–501, at 327–34. Turóczi-Trostler, op. cit., ii, 156–218, esp. 184–6; *RMK* i, 882. The *Seneca Christianus* first appeared at Augsburg in 1637. There were Latin editions in Hungary in 1660, 1696, and 1700; and Hungarian editions in 1654, 1740, 1768, and 1770. Dalnerus, op. cit. 68 ff., also draws on Lipsius.

In either case the outcome was a firm theoretical stance in favour of deference to the prince and against rebellion: James I's *Basilikon Doron* appeared in Hungarian as early as 1612, while Guevara's *Horologium Principum*, written for Charles V, was rendered into Magyar by both a Catholic aristocrat and a Calvinist pastor.[81]

The preservation of order merged insensibly in the minds of the educated with the preservation of unity. Many Humanists feared an erosion of their cosmopolitan and Latinate values, and by 1600 the Catholic Church could appear the best guarantor of them. J. M. Wacker penned a typical erudite justification of his conversion in terms of the hallowed unity of scholarship when writing to a Silesian friend.[82] One of the Jesuit order's prime attractions at this time to intelligent young men was undoubtedly its dazzlingly international membership. The opening of Graz University was celebrated with sermons in eighteen different languages, fourteen of them mother tongues; Prague's Clementinum educated almost as many foreigners as Czechs before 1618; and the college at far-off Kolozsvár contained eighteen nationalities in the 1580s. The Central European careers of individual Jesuits like Lamormaini and Hurtado Perez, Alfonso Carrillo and Martin Becanus, William Wright and Robert Turner amply confirm the point.[83] This migration of personnel (among 269 professors at Graz only about forty stayed to die there) emphasized an absence of cultural frontiers; it was sustained by allowing the vernaculars a real but always subordinate place in the overall intellectual edifice. And the flair of the Jesuits was not restricted to externals: some true Humanist devotion to the classics survived among them during the seventeenth century, perhaps better than among local Protestants, as in the work of Bohuslav Balbín (who is so misleadingly remembered merely as a Bohemian patriot) or the first critical edition of Cosmas and Damian, the

---

[81] Gy. Szepsi Korotz, *BAZILIKON DŌRON, Az Angliai . . . Kiralynac . . . Fia tanitasaert irtt Kiralyi Ajandeka* (Oppenheim 1612). Cf. *MIT* ii, 41 f.

[82] ÖNB, MS. 9734', fols. 32–7. On Wacker, cf. above, p. 58.

[83] Schuster, op. cit. 222; M. Truc, 'Národnostní charakter jesuitské akademie pražské', *AUC, Phil. et Hist.*, 1958, 2, 49–68; Öry, op. cit. 17–19 and *passim*. On Lamormaini: above, p. 73 n. 76; Hurtado Perez was the first rector of Olomouc. On Carrillo: above, p. 50; on Becanus, or van der Beeck: Dudik, 'Correspondenz'. For Wright and Turner see *DNB*, s. vv., and Turner's *Posthumae Orationes* (Cologne 1615).

patron saints of physicians, published at Vienna in 1660 under the sponsorship of J. W. Mannagetta.[84]

Unity too possessed a deeper metaphysical meaning, embedded in the Renaissance cosmological scheme with its assumptions of harmony and perfect correspondence, and its sense of a hidden real world given expression through allusion and imagery. Here we may have the closest link between the crisis of Humanism and the emergence of a new Catholic intellectual establishment, for some clear continuity exists, in visual and literary terms, from the Mannerism of the sixteenth century to the Baroque of the seventeenth century in the Habsburg lands. That is a subject difficult to examine, especially given the disturbed conditions of the period; and stylistic considerations: the study of emblems, forms of public display, and so forth, are not central to the present theme.[85] Suffice it here to note one or two transitional figures: Christoph Lackner, jurist and loyal mayor of Sopron, and János Rimay, respected but melancholic diplomat, both prolific Protestant writers in the intricate, learned canon of international Mannerism; and their contemporaries, Mátyás Nyéki Vörös and Bálint Lépés, both Catholic priests who exploited the emotionalism of the proto-Baroque. Such examples come most naturally from Hungary, where the literary problems of late Humanism are currently receiving much attention.[86]

At root unity, whether of the sixteenth-century or of the seventeenth-century world-view, was preserved only by resort to occultism, and occult interests—as we shall see later—form the key area where in Central Europe earlier preoccupations were adapted rather than discarded. Magic had indeed to be purged and

---

[84] F. Krones, *Geschichte der Karl Franzens-Universität in Graz* (Graz 1886), 373 and *passim*; cf. below, pp. 187–9, 229 f., 253–5. B. Balbin, *Verisimilia Humaniorum Disciplinarum, seu judicium privatum de omni litterarum artificio* (Pr. 1666). S. Wagnereck and R. Dehn (eds.), *Syntagmatis Historici ... de tribus Sanctorum Anargyrorum Cosmae et Damiani nomine paribus, partes duae* (V. 1660), esp. ded. and pref.

[85] I have touched on these large issues elsewhere: *Rudolf II*, chs. 5 and 7.

[86] On Lackner: S. Payr, *Emlékezés Dr. Lackner Kristófról* (Sopron 1932); and the new biography by József L. Kovács (Sopron 1972). On Rimay: above, n. 79, and *MIT* ii, 15–29. On Nyéki Vörös: below, p. 250. Cf. T. Kardos, 'Adatok a magyar irodalmi barokk keletkezéséhez', *Magyarságtudomány*, i (1942), 63–93; T. Klaniczay, *Reneszánsz és barokk* (Bp. 1961), 303–39; *MIT* ii, 10–50, 123–49 (and B. Keserű's comments in *Acta Historiae Litterarum Hungaricarum*, vi (1966), 3–21).

refurbished, just as the symbolism surrounding Renaissance Habsburgs had to reappear in the orthodox guise of a '*pietas Austriaca*'; a different synthesis of rational and irrational had to be born out of religious and political intolerance. But we shall still be able to recognize the old striving after completeness of understanding. The achievements of the Habsburg Counter-Reformation between 1600 and 1650 may not have been quite as miraculous as enthusiasts imagined—their social determinants and material backing are all too evident; yet they undoubtedly drew heavily on men's *belief* in the supernatural.

CHAPTER 4

The consolidation, 1650–1700:
Leopold I and his Monarchy

After 1648 Central Europe's Counter-Reformation could be resumed with greater intensity, on a firmer base, and it continued to enjoy the wholehearted support of the emperors. Ferdinand III was no friend of the grand gesture, but he made no secret of his commitment to the new Catholic ideals, especially the cult of the Virgin. As a thank-offering for deliverance from the Swedes he raised an imposing Marian statue upon the most princely of Vienna's squares (Am Hof); at the same time he enforced an oath to the Immaculate Conception on all graduands and teachers of the universities, as well as on all privy councillors. The oaths, and the whole process, were taken a stage further by his successor.[1]

Leopold I, Ferdinand's younger son, received the kind of education which should fit him to assume the mantle of his pluralist uncle Leopold Wilhelm; when unexpectedly thrust as a callow youth into the role of emperor he displayed a richness of piety which rivalled the reputation of his grandfather. He practised all the works of charity, especially in giving copiously to the poor; he visited the monasteries of his capital three or four times every week. He heard several masses on each festival and attended special litanies during the days before and after; he undertook regular, well-publicized pilgiimages to the shrine of the Virgin at Mariazell.[2]

---

[1] E. Tomek, op. cit. 546. The present Marian column replaced the original in 1667. A similar *Mariensäule* stood on the Old Town Square of Prague from 1650 until 1919. Kink, op. cit. i, pt. 1, 379–82; Kazy, op. cit. ii, 210; Th. Fellner and H. Kretschmayr, *Die österreichische Zentralverwaltung*, Abt. I: 1491–1749, i–ii (V. 1907), i, 65 and n. The councillors' oath under Ferdinand II ended: 'so wahr mir Gott helfe'; Ferdinand III added: 'und alle lieben heiligen'; Leopold substituted: 'die gebenedeite mutter gottes Maria und alle liebe heilige'.

[2] [G. E. Rinck], *Leopolds des Grossen … wunderwürdiges Leben und Thaten* (Leipzig 1709), 97 ff.; [C. Freschot], *Mémoires de la cour de Vienne* (Cologne 1705), 101 f., 134–8; J. Burbury, *A Relation of a Journey … from London to … Constantinople* (London 1671), 26–8. A. Nyáry, *A bécsi udvar a XVII. század végén* (Bp. 1912), 99–115, describes also, *passim*, the kind of education given by Leopold to his own
(continued)

Genuine humility shines through Leopold's manuscript book of
private prayers ('Domine Dominantium, qui me vilem et ingratum
prae tantâ hominum multitudine elegisti, et ovibus tuis dilectis
imperare et praeesse voluisti . . . '), while the simple, equally private
homilies of a certain Domenico Signorini testify in a crude yet
eloquent way to the devout, even uplifting atmosphere of the court
chapel. The emperor set real store by the words of his preachers,
whether the Father Boccabella early in the reign who consoled him
on the death of his infant firstborn son, or the thunderous Marco
d'Aviano later.[3]

Under the aegis of Ferdinand III and Leopold, Catholicism
developed a characteristic peacetime *modus operandi*, drawing on
experience already gained in Bohemia after the White Mountain.
'Reformation commissions', comprising priests and officials in
equal numbers, toured the provinces, flanked by a soldiery which
served more to threaten than to chastise, though it was undoubtedly
used on occasions, especially in Bohemia.[4] The commissioners
enjoined people to submit to the Church, and demanded evidence
of their submission through the notorious tickets which were issued
to those making the obligatory Easter confession: fascinating
sources for the historian, such *Beichtzettel* are evidently unreliable
as a full statement of religious allegiance and left plenty of scope for
fraud.[5] This was, we might say, rough-and-ready injustice. It

younger son. P. Lambeck, *Diarium Sacri Itineris Cellensis* (V. 1666), also reprinted in
his *Prodromus Historiae Literariae* (Leipzig – Frankfurt 1710), ostensibly describes
the visit of 1665, but really gives us a disquisition on the Marian cult.

[3] ÖNB, MS. 11767: 'Viridarium animae ex Variis Authoribus Collectum', 1674,
fols. 29, 55, and *passim*; finely written by one Stephanus Zaręba. Domenico
Signorini: ibid. MSS. 11536 and 11612, *c.* 1700, the latter with a fuller ded. to
Leopold; the author was a man—as he tells us—'senza lettere nè ruditioni' (*sic*).
Privatbriefe Kaiser Leopold I an den Grafen F. E. Pötting, ed. A. F. Pribram and
M. Landwehr von Pragenau, i–ii (V. 1903–4, hereafter *Privatbriefe*), nos. 176, 180.
ÖNB, MS. 11613, contains sketches for sermons by Boccabella. On Marco d'Aviano
see below, p. 146.

[4] Bílek, *Reformace katolická*, 229–96; Rezek, *Dějiny*, i, 139 ff. On the instructions
and activity of earlier commissions: Carafa, *Commentaria*, 283–7, 296 ff., and
appendix, 85 ff.; Beckovský, op. cit., pt. 3, 50 ff.; F. Krásl, *Arnošt hrabě Harrach,
kardinál . . . a kníže arcibiskup pražský* (Pr. 1886), 33 ff. *passim*; V. Oehm (ed.),
'Protokol reformační kommisse, konané r. 1628 . . . ', *VKČSN*, 1897, no. 28; Podlaha
(ed.), *Dopisy, passim*; Gindely, *Gegenreformation*, 203–10, 252–4; Líva, 'Platejs';
Hrubý (ed.), *Moravské korespondence*, ij, nos. 47 seqq. *passim*.

[5] J. V. Šimák (ed.), *Zpovědní seznamy arcidiecése pražské z r. 1671–1725*, i, ix–xiii

weighed hardest on the lower classes, made an uneven impact in the towns, and treated the nobility with more circumspection, since public Counter-Reformation anyway relied for its enforcement on the private activity of willing Catholic landlords.

Lower Austria still had a large number of heretics, especially because its nobles enjoyed personal liberty of confession: 235 members of the estates proclaimed themselves Protestant in 1652 when the government restricted their right to employ non-Catholic retainers. The work of recovery now proceeded actively and we have a fascinating source for the campaign in the north-west part of the province. There a commission under the abbot of Altenburg and Baron Windhag secured over 22,000 conversions during a two-year period (we even learn their names)—some parishes acquired more new Catholic believers than old.[6] Meanwhile the Bohemian authorities exerted all kinds of suasion to gain the population for Catholicism without irreparably damaging economic life and driving the peasantry into rebellion or flight. Two protagonists of Counter-Reformation during the 1650s were veterans of the wartime period: Ernst Harrach, Archbishop of Prague since 1623, an effective and resilient prelate, and his gifted Capuchin friend Valerian Magni, who pursued one of several parallel careers as an indefatigable missionary organizer; the third was their vicar-general, the half-Spanish, half-Czech monk Juan Caramuel Lobkovic, a man in whom fixity of purpose went with an austere disregard for the niceties of conduct.[7] Whereas a renewed flood of tactical plans and mandates bears witness to their energy, it bespeaks also the continuing need for direction, and Harrach's confidential report to Rome in 1657, like the records of his protégé, Maximilian von Schleinitz at Litoměřice, depicted a Church still neglected and

---

(Pr. 1918–38), no more published, covers mainly the areas just west and east of Prague. Cf. Wiedemann, *Reformation*, v, 65 ff. *passim*; E. Tomek, op. cit. 544. On a case of fraud: Podlaha (ed.), *Dopisy*, no. 133 (pp. 138–40); Líva, 'Platejs', 322–7.

[6] ÖNB, MS. 7757, is a presentation copy for the emperor of the report of this commission. It was printed in a summarized form in *Hippolytus: Archiv für Diöcesan-Chronik und -Geschichte des Bisthumssprengels St. Pölten*, ii (1859), 277–83, 313–18, 349–56. Cf., in general, Wiedemann, *Reformation*, v, 25 ff. On Windhag see below, p. 294.

[7] On Harrach: Krásl, op. cit., esp. 66 ff., with much detail. On Magni: P. G. Abgottspon, *P. Valerianus Magni, Kapuziner* (Olten 1939); and below, pp. 217, 324. On Caramuel: Rezek, *Dějiny*, i, 150 ff., 165–70; Bílek, *Reformace katolická*, 229 ff.; and below, pp. 324 f.

impoverished. Protestantism went underground, but it was not easily buried.[8]

In the 1660s and 1670s attention switched east and north: towards Moravia, where the bishop of Olomouc sent teams of priests to root out heresy on his estates;[9] and above all towards Silesia. Silesia represents a special case: its Counter-Reformation was likewise long contemplated by militants and attempted piecemeal during the first half of the century, by means of intermittent persecution on royal and episcopal lands and the preference shown to Catholic officials. While the movement did enough to generate a stream of Protestant gravamina it could only proceed with real success after 1650. Now, despite nominal guarantees to Silesian Lutherans in the Peace of Westphalia, 600 of their churches were closed in the Habsburg-controlled hereditary duchies (Glogau, Schweidnitz-Jauer, Oppeln-Ratibor). Fines, Catholic appointments, expulsion of preachers, dragonnades, prohibition of Protestant marriage and burial: all reaped a brutal harvest, especially in the proud little towns of Upper Silesia like Troppau, Jägerndorf, and Leobschütz.[10] In 1675 the last native Piast prince died and his fiefs (Liegnitz-Brieg-Wohlau) faced the onslaught: more than a hundred Lutheran churches were eliminated, along with Calvinist services at the chapels of the former ruling house. By 1700 Silesian Protestants held only some 220 places of worship compared with over 1500 a century before. They defended grimly in their urban stronghold of Breslau and other semi-protected areas; elsewhere they clung on more by spirit than

---

[8] ÖNB, MS. 13321, with mandates for the years 1650–1, esp. (fols. 62–74) a 'Guett bedunkhen dess Cardinalss von Harrach' on the necessary *modus agendi*. Flégl, art. cit. 227–43; Schlenz, *Leitmeritz*, ii, 34–63, 148–88.

[9] [B. Balbin], 'Relatio progressus in extirpanda haeresi 1661–78', ed. A. Rezek, *VKČSN*, 1892, 203–57, with a total of 29,588 conversions; J. Chodníček and M. Kovář, 'Z katolických missií na Moravě a ve Slezsku v době reformace katolické', *SbHKr* v (1896), 108–56; vi (1897), 19–62.

[10] On the Silesian Counter-Reformation to 1650: Grünhagen, *Geschichte*, ii, 123–6, 153–7, 193 ff. esp. 213–30; Ziegler, op. cit. 23 ff.; H. Jedin, 'Eine Denkschrift über die Gegenreformation in Schlesien aus dem Jahre 1625', *Kirche des Glaubens, Kirche der Geschichte*, i–ii (Freiburg 1966), i, 395–412. Protestant grievances are well represented in *Antwort der Schlesischen Fürsten unnd Stände ... auff der Röm. Keys. Maj. Commissarien ... Werbung* (n. p. 1618); and *Warhaffter Abdruck ... der Römis: Kayserl: ... Mayest: ... abgegangenen Schreibens ... Und [der] darauff erfolgten Beantwortung* (n. p. 1634). For developments after 1650: Grünhagen, op. cit. ii, 317–28; Ziegler, op. cit. 93 ff.; and the case-studies in Loesche, *Zur Gegenreformation*, i, and ii (Leobschütz). On the political geography of Silesia cf. below, p. 196 n. 4.

by outward observance: throughout the hereditary duchies they possessed only three churches—known (ironically) as *Friedens-kirchen*—and even those had to be constructed of wood.[11]

Hungary was Silesia writ large. György Rákóczi's war against the Habsburgs resulted, at the treaty of Linz (1645), in a full confirmation of existing Protestant rights; in the circumstances, Counter-Reformation had to move more indirectly, working through sympathetic landowners, putting pressure on town councils and guilds, dividing Lutherans from Calvinists and ministers from their flocks.[12] Success was easiest in the west of the country, where the dynasty and great aristocrats could exercise strongest sway. By the later seventeenth century most people in counties like Sopron (Ödenburg) and Vas (Eisenburg) had been reconverted, and reasonably sophisticated religious life could flourish around churches which appeared well cared-for and well stocked with liturgical objects. Across the north of Habsburg Hungary things moved more slowly: Archbishop Szelepcsényi presented a detailed report to Rome of 64,029 conversions achieved in the single lustrum 1671–5, but we may well doubt the authenticity of his statistics. And when the Counter-Reformation experimented with more headstrong methods, as during the treason trials of the 1670s against leading preachers, its pastoral dividends proved paltry.[13] All the churches sequestered in the last bitter decades of the century brought back only bricks and mortar to the Roman faith, not souls.

Hungary best illustrates the incompleteness of the Catholic achievement. Protestants were indeed under siege, their security was progressively whittled away; but they still held important ground, and the series of constitutional settlements which culmi-

[11] Soffner, 'Die Kirchen-Reductionen in den Fürstentümern Liegnitz-Brieg-Wohlau nach dem Tode des Herzogs Georg Wilhelm', *ZVGAS* xx (1886), 121–56; D. von Velsen, *Die Gegenreformation in den Fürstentümern Liegnitz-Brieg-Wohlau* (Leipzig 1931); Ziegler, op. cit. 125 ff. These *Friedenskirchen*, churches of peace, a miserable fruit of the Westphalian settlement, stood outside the walls of Glogau, Schweidnitz, and Jauer.

[12] Details of the treaty in Gooss, op. cit. 715–805; and of the subsequent diet of 1647 in [P. Okolicsányi], *Historia Diplomatica de Statu Religionis Evangelicae in Hungaria* (n. p. 1710), appendix, 3–86. Cf. M. Zsilinszky, *A linczi békekötés és az 1647-i vallásügyi törvénycikkek története* (Bp. 1890).

[13] Vanyó, *Katholikus restauráció*; Házi, op. cit.; A. Meszlényi, *Szelepcsényi prímás és Északmagyarország rekatolizálása, 1671–5* (Bp. 1935), separatum from *Theológia*, ii), 16–22 and *passim*. Cf. below, pp. 237 f, 249 f.

nated in the Peace of Szatmár (1711) at length recognized their ineᵣ.ᵤᵢᵤᵤoility. In 1700 outlying parts of the country had been scarcely touched by Counter-Reformation, while ostensibly loyal areas like the bishopric of Győr needed continuous clerical vigilance. Even the royal capital of Pozsony presented a lasting challenge to the ecclesiastical authorities within forty miles of Vienna, and German burghers at Sopron, scene of the crucial diet of 1681, maintained a defiant Lutheranism whose influence radiated across the nearby Austrian border.[14]

Elsewhere too state Catholicism still faced opposition at the turn of the century. Silesia's Protestants gained a respite by the peace of Altranstädt in 1707, when the Swedish king intervened to confirm imperial privileges conceded sixty years earlier: now they could build six more churches—though still only wooden ones—in the hereditary duchies.[15] The rest of the Bohemian lands had their refractory heretics, encouraged by the crepuscular *Buschprediger* who entered surreptitiously from Saxony to hold forth before clandestine congregations in forests and upland glens. Confession-registers reveal many backsliders among the 'metallifossores' of north-western Bohemia, and the territory around Königgrätz in the east remained fertile soil for dissenters, often of a radical sectarian kind; vineyards near Prague harboured others. Persecution of them, somewhat reduced in the latter part of Leopold's reign, was taken up again under Charles VI with all the old vigour.[16] Even in Austria a residue of reprobates survived, both among the lower classes—usually artisans of the Alpine valleys—and, more seriously, as individual noble free-thinkers. Although a convert, Count Sigismund Friedrich Sinzendorf still wished to be buried in

---

[14] A. Kelemen, *Keresztély Ágost herceg katolikus restaurációs tevékenysége a győri egyházmegyében* (Pannonhalma 1931), 19 ff. (Győr); Baur, 'Passer', 307, 310, 312 f., 344, 372 f.; Mecenseffy, op. cit. 161. Nevertheless these Lutherans were very ready to be loyal, given a chance; e.g.: J. C. Barth, *Buda Recepta* (Regensburg 1686), a panegyric on Habsburg policy by a pastor from Sopron.

[15] The six new 'grace-and-favour churches' (*Gnadenkirchen*) were at Freystadt, Hirschberg, Landeshut, Militsch, Sagan, and Teschen: Grünhagen, *Geschichte*, ii, 396–409.

[16] Šimák, *Seznamy, passim*, esp. ix–x, 100 ff.; Rezek, *Prostonárodní hnutí*, 37 ff.; A. Podlaha, 'Úřední jednání konsistoře pražské ve příčině jinověrců v Čechách v letech 1730–47', *SbHKr* vi (1897), 83–114; id., 'Z dějin zápasu katolického náboženství s jinověrstvím v Čechách v letech 1700–56', ibid. vii (1898), 25–62; Koči, *Frýdlantsko*, 68–72.

Lutheran ground in 1678; another convert, Baroness Teufel (no less!), forced her coachman to deliver manure instead of attending confession and brought her dogs to howl at the local priest during the Eucharist.[17]

★

One of the greatest obstacles to Counter-Reformation throughout the seventeenth century lay in a chronic shortage of secular priests. Every contemporary report on Catholic prospects in Bohemia and Hungary laments the lack of qualified and capable incumbents and the correspondingly weak organization of parishes, many of which had known no curate since before the Reformation and could provide no financial support for one. In the 1640s well over half Bohemia's livings were vacant; around Chrudim, for example, 165 churches had only twenty-one priests. The situation was much the same in Hungary, where the Papacy had continually to dispense from Tridentine requirements in its fight against insufficiency of personnel.[18] Repair of this derelict human ecclesiastical fabric could only be gradual, and its most important consequence was the leading role played by regular clergy in the programme of re-Catholicization. Of 257 resident ministers for 636 Moravian parishes in 1635, the majority belonged to religious orders, and the proportion does not seem to have changed markedly at the end of the century. Between 1694 and 1710 the archbishop of Prague ordained 999 regulars against 674 seculars, and many among the former took charge of congregations.[19] The old orders: Benedic-

---

[17] Wiedemann, *Reformation*, v, 106 f., 122 ff. *passim*. See in general, Loesche, *Geschichte des Protestantismus*, 125–7, 199 ff., 260 ff.; Mecenseffy, op. cit. 186–90, 198 ff.; and articles by P. Dedic, in *Carinthia I*, 1948–50, 1952, 1955, 1957, 1960, 1964. One interesting case is examined by A. Meir, 'Der Protestantismus in der Herrschaft Paternion vom 16. Jahrhundert bis zum Toleranzpatent', *Carinthia I*, clxii (1972), 311–43.

[18] Bohemia: Podlaha, *Posvátná místa*, for many parishes quite forlorn into the 18th century; Krásl, op. cit. 216–37; Rezek, *Děje*, 130 ff.; Bílek, *Reformace katolická*, 254 ff.; Fr. Dvorský in *SbH* (Rezek), i (1883), 274–80. Quite a few of the early secular priests in Bohemia were Poles; cf. below, pp. 425 f. Hungary: F. Galla, 'Magyar tárgyú pápai felhatalmazások, felmentések és kiváltságok a katolikus megújhodás korából', *LK* xxiv (1946), 71–169; Kelemen, op. cit. 33 ff.

[19] Rezek, *Děje*, 153 ff. A. Podlaha, *Dějiny arcidiecése pražské od konce století XVII do počátku století XIX*, i, pt. 1 (1694–1710) (Pr. 1917. n. m. p.), 221 ff., 425 ff., contains much miscellaneous information. Cf. the lists of incumbents in id., *Posvátná místa*, and Šimák, *Seznamy*.

tines, canons regular, Cistercians, Premonstratensians, took a significant share in this work; but their activity, with its strong and differentiated local roots, is best reserved for consideration in the regional context of part two below. The brunt of the Counter-Reformation was borne by newer, more organically international orders of mendicants and clerks; above all it was borne by the Society of Jesus, which reached during the latter half of the seventeenth century its fullest extent and the peak of its influence in Central Europe.

Jesuits operated widely as missionaries, both singly and in groups. Teams of them tackled the recalcitrant peasantry of northern Moravia or served on the lands of proselytizing magnates in Upper Hungary. Individuals like the ascetic holy man Albrecht Chanovský and the rugged extrovert Kašpar Dirig made a more personal impact.[20] A few became martyrs to the cause and were invested with the halo of sanctity by their pious colleagues. Others formed shock troops for the confrontation with Protestants during the 1670s in Hungary; the vehemence of reprisals against their houses after that episode tells its own story.[21] Yet the Jesuits' real base lay behind the front-line, in a dense network of colleges and residences which stretched right across Central Europe from Swabia to Zagreb and Szatmár. In the *Erblande* they were already well organized by 1650, with fourteen colleges in all the main towns.[22] In the Bohemian lands they opened many new foundations during the century, whose very considerable wealth can be roughly assessed from the findings of the dissolution commissions after 1773. As

[20] Above, n. 9; B. Dudík, *Bibliothek und Archiv im fürsterzbischöflichen Schlosse zu Kremsier* (V. 1870), 46 f.; A. Podlaha, 'Z dějin katolických missií v Čechách r. 1670–1700', *SbHKr* iv (1895), 104–31. F. Krones, 'Zur Geschichte des Jesuitenordens in Ungarn 1645–71', *AÖG* lxxix (1892), 280–354 *passim*. [J. Tanner], *Vir Apostolicus, sue vita et virtutes Rev. P. Alberti Chanowsky SJ* (n. p. ?1658); A. Podlaha, 'Missie P. Kašpara Diriga v horách Krkonošských vykonaná r. 1679–80', *VKČSN*, 1900, no. 18.

[21] Matthias Tanner, *Societas Jesu usque ad Sanguinis et Vitae profusionem Militans . . .* (Pr. 1675), esp. 26 f., 58–60, 88–90, 102 f., 112–14, 146–8. F. Krones, 'Zur Geschichte Ungarns (1671–83) mit besonderer Rücksicht auf die Thätigkeit und die Geschichte des Jesuitenordens', *AÖG* lxxx (1893), 353–455; and cf. below, p. 250.

[22] The 16th-century colleges at Vienna, Graz, Innsbruck, Hall im Tirol, and Laibach, plus Klagenfurt (1604), Linz (1608), Passau (1612, a quasi-Austrian foundation), Leoben (1613), Gorizia (1615), Krems (1616), Trieste (1619), Judenburg (1621), Steyr (1630). Wiener Neustadt was added in 1674.

Silesia was tamed, some of the order's subtlest thinkers (Théodore Moretus and Christoph Scheiner, for instance) were sent to its nine colleges at Breslau, Neisse, Glatz, Glogau, Liegnitz, Oppeln, Sagan, Schweidnitz, and Troppau.[23] In Hungary the Jesuits expanded rapidly from the 1630s, bidding for the ground held by heretics in more and more provincial towns and never disheartened by the initial difficulties put in their way: good examples of their tenacity are the academies which developed at Győr and Kassa.[24]

Indeed the Jesuits' characteristic ambience was urban—albeit wherever they settled they contributed to the decay of burgher self-sufficiency and established their own nexus of patronage. They dominated not by force of numbers: in 1651 the whole Austro-Hungarian province contained no more than 870 full members of the Society (those having sworn the fourth vow of obedience to the Pope); in 1700 the number was 1,300. Rather they manipulated a web of influence which was spun largely from two threads: the excellent teaching in their colleges, and sensitive attention to the emotional needs of their audience. Once in possession of a near-monopoly over higher schooling, the order discharged its obligations honestly enough according to its own lights. Everywhere it ran *Gymnasia*, in six (or eight) chief centres universities as well: all offered a sound and essentially practical education, well modulated to the needs of the individual pupil, provided that pupil knew his place.[25] Nobles gained devoted tutorial guidance which would culminate in pompous, stage-managed disputations where they could pass off some professor's deferential wisdom as their own. At the same time deserving paupers had care lavished upon them: a hundred or so were studying at Graz in the later seventeenth century, while a French clerical visitor to Vienna lamented the instruction given to so many low-born students. Discipline was

---

[23] List of Bohemian colleges in J. Svátek, 'Organizace řeholních institucí v českých zemích a péče o jejich archivy', *SbAPr* xx (1970), 503–624, at 565–72; cf. below, p. 138 and n. 56. Much information about them in T. V. Bílek, *Statky a jmění kolejí jesuitských, klášterů, kostelů, bratrstev a jiných ústavů v království Českém od císaře Josefa II zrušených* (Pr. 1893), 7–139; and Duhr, op. cit. ii, 1, 353 ff.; iii, 212 f. Cf., in general, Schmidl, op. cit. (only to 1653); Kroess, *Geschichte*, ii (only to 1657).

[24] Krones, 'Jesuitenorden 1645–71'; Velics, op. cit. ii; G. Fejér, *De ortu et progressu Academiae Regiae Jaurinensis* (Győr 1819); J. B. Akai, *Initia Cassoviensis S.J.* (Kassa 1743).

[25] Duhr, *Geschichte*, iii, 184, and ii–iii, *passim*. Cf. above, p. 101 and n. 51.

fierce, but purposive: whereas censors applied firm standards, and
the notable mathematician Guldin was not even allowed to carry a
watch, well-subsidized university presses provided scope for him
and many others to publish on a broad range of topics.[26]
Altogether the Jesuits employed (as I have already suggested) an
intricate mixture of restrictions and temptations. They harnessed
both the calculations and the enthusiasms of the populace, especially
by encouraging the formation of lay societies or congregations to
cultivate sacred literature, drama, and music. Most famous were
the Marian sodalities, founded separately within each stratum of
society, such that larger towns might contain ten or a dozen, serving
charitable and convivial purposes as well as the public veneration of
the Virgin, even on occasion raising military legions to defend the
faith.[27] Power certainly contributed to the confidence of the Jesuits,
to their sense of divine favour and stress on the distinct, elevated
identity of their order. Matthias Tanner's works, illustrated by the
best artists of the Bohemian Baroque, on the global *res gestae* of his
confrères, are monuments to that mood. Yet they never lost the
common touch. Generation after generation of cunning and
effective polemicists made a direct appeal from pulpit and printed
page. With time, attacks on Protestantism gave ground to more
traditional homiletic themes, but the best Jesuit controversialists
remained at heart Counter-Reformers, and the continued need for
this genre illustrates the ultimate incompleteness of their achievement: as late as the early eighteenth century Johann Kraus
published a long series of German-language fulminations against
Lutheranism on the still-exposed Bohemian front.[28]

[26] Krones, *Universität Graz*, 299–307. The French observer was Freschot, op. cit.
22–7, a Benedictine and a snob. Duhr, op. cit. ii, pt. 2, 433 (Guldin). Cf. below, ch.
9, *passim*.
[27] Duhr, op. cit. ii, 1, 321, 335 f.; 2, 81–122; iii, 190 f., 642 ff. Svoboda, *Katolická
reformace*; F. Weiser, *Die Marianischen Congregationen in Ungarn und die Rettung
Ungarns 1686–9* (Regensburg 1891); and A. Mohl, *A Mária-kongregácziók története
különös tekintettel hazánkra* (Györ 1898), throw more light on the late 19th-century
Marian movement than on the 17th-century one. Cf. Rezek, *Děje*, 193–5; E. Tomek,
op. cit. 639 ff. For more examples of local societies see Podlaha, *Posvátná místa*, iii,
41–55, 176 f.; iv, 76–9; Schlenz, *Leitmeritz*, ii, 475 ff.; *Geschichte der Stadt Wien*, v,
299–312; and cf. Loidl, *Menschen im Barock*, 122–32.
[28] M. Tanner, *Societas Jesu ... Militans*; and id., *Societas Jesu Apostolorum Imitatrix
sive Gesta praeclara et virtutes eorum qui ... per totum Orbem terrarum speciali zelo
desudárunt*, i (Pr. 1694); huge volumes illustrated by Karel Škréta and J. G. Heinsch.

*

Jesuits had, of course, no monopoly of preachers or apologists, still less of popular moralizers. As the orders of friars revived, so the heritage of spiritual crusade which they had embodied in the Middle Ages revived with them. Much of the new vigour of Central European mendicants after 1600 was associated with stricter rules, first developed in Counter-Reformation Italy, then spread, usually from bases in Vienna, Prague, or Innsbruck, to smaller settlements throughout the Habsburg lands. I have space here only for the most salient features of this evolution.[29]

The Dominicans advanced in a steady, unspectacular way without ever quite attaining again their prestige of pre-Reformation days. While in Austria and Bohemia they reoccupied most of the houses which had been more or less deserted during the sixteenth century, establishing themselves in nearly thirty Bohemian centres by 1700 with a headquarters at the massive convent of St. Giles in the heart of Prague's Old Town, the once-proud Hungarian province passed into complete eclipse despite all efforts of the influential Sigismund Ferrarius at Vienna to have it resettled. Dominicans kept a place in teaching, with schools of their own and a toe-hold at the universities. But most of their intellectual thunder, along with their powers of censorship, was stolen by the Jesuits, and the imperial concession which exempted members of the order from the oath to the Immaculate Conception proved a hollow victory, especially as the Habsburgs were not prepared to revive any of the traditional Inquisitorial duties of the Preachers.[30]

A more distinctive role belonged to the Franciscans in their three

For Kraus: A. and A. de Backer and C. Sommervogel, *Bibliothèque de la Compagnie de Jésus*, i–x (Brussels–Paris 1890–1909, repr. 1960, hereafter 'Sommervogel'), s. v.; *Knihopis*, nos. 3381–5.

[29] Precise information is not easy to bring together; there are divergences in the sources and confusing provincial boundaries (cf. below, pp. 181, 251). I shall omit Further Austria altogether, and also most nunneries (but cf. below n. 58). M. Heimbucher, *Die Orden und Kongregationen der katholischen Kirche*, i–ii (Paderborn 1933–4), is an invaluable general guide; and Svátek, art. cit., an admirably authoritative survey for the Bohemian lands.

[30] Lists for Bohemia in UK, MS. XI A 1/b, fols. 2–63 (written in 1720); and Svátek, art. cit. 540–4. For Austria: S. Brunner, *Der Predigerorden in Wien und Österreich* (V. 1867). Hungary: S. Ferrarius, *De Rebus Hungaricae Provinciae O. P.* (V. 1637), pt. 4, by a professor in Vienna; B. Iványi, 'Bilder aus der Vergangenheit der ungarischen Dominikanerprovinz', *Mélanges Mandonnet*, ii (Paris 1930), 437–78, esp. 474–8. Kink, op. cit. i, pt. 1, 383 (oath).

branches: Observants, Conventuals, and Capuchins, rivals since the end of the Middle Ages. Though division within the order led to unedifying disputes about property rights, some sense of common origins lived on, as in the sumptuous *Chronicle* by Bernhard Sannig, one of the most prominent friars in Bohemia. Observant Franciscans had thriven greatly in Central Europe during the age of St. John Capistrano, who so electrified the campaigns against the Ottomans which reached their climax in the defence of Belgrade where he met his death in 1456. The legacy of Capistrano's commanding presence and severe exhortations enabled them, though sadly languishing, to survive the disasters of the sixteenth century, even in Hungary.[31] From about 1590 recovery was swift: a new church in Vienna; confirmation of privileges by Rudolf II; the internal reform of Hungarian houses; and during the Passauers' invasion of 1611, fourteen martyrs at Our Lady of the Snows in Prague *pour encourager les autres*. By the end of the seventeenth century there were twenty-four friaries in Austria, thirty-four in the Bohemian lands; further east a chain of mission stations ran from Croatia to a solitary historic outpost at Csiksomlyó in the shadow of the Transylvanian Alps. At one extreme the Observants maintained teams of priests working reasonably unhindered in the primitive conditions of Turkish Hungary (and 600 more in Bosnia); at the other they boasted solid theologians of international repute, especially in Prague, where Sannig and Amandus Hermann compiled huge tomes of a moral and devotional character.[32]

In Central European parlance the Observants are 'Franciscans'

---

[31] B. Sannig, *Chronick der drey Orden*, i–iii (Pr. 1689–91). Capistrano was canonized in 1724; on him see J. Moorman, *A History of the Franciscan Order to 1517* (Oxford 1968), 446–53, 466–72.

[32] Lists and history in V. Greiderer, *Germania Franciscana*, i–ii (Innsbruck 1777–81), i, 25–260 (Croatia and Carniola), 261–548 (Austria), 549–803 (Bohemia), 804–78 (Silesia); ii, 1–251 (Tyrol), 485–578 (Trent). For Austria see also P. Herzog, 'Cosmographia Franciscano-Austriacae Provinciae Sancti Bernardini Senensis', *Analecta Franciscana*, i (Quaracchi 1885), 41–213 (originally published in 1740). For Bohemia see also Svátek, art. cit. 548–50; C. Minarik in *Archivum Franciscanum Historicum*, xlii (1949), 159–71 catalogues the martyrs. For Hungary: Gy. P. Szabó, *Ferencrendiek a magyar történelemben* (Bp. 1921), 70 ff. (also 91 ff. on Bosnia, 104 ff. on Transylvania, 133–67 on Turkish Hungary); cf. below, p. 271 (Csiksomlyó). A. Hermann, *Tractatus Theologici*, i–iv (Cologne 1690–4), etc. Sannig's largest work was the *Schola Philosophica Scotistarum*, i–iii (Pr. 1684–5); cf. below, p. 320; and a long series of articles on Sannig's career by K. Minařík in *Časopis Katolického Duchovenstva*, lxi (1920)–lxxi (1930).

pure and simple; but their less strict brethren, the Conventuals—always called 'Minorites' in the Habsburg area—while initially overshadowed, likewise became a familiar part of the Baroque scene. The Conventuals' revival in the *Erblande* dated from 1621, with the nomination of a German instead of an Italian as provincial, and the reconstitution of their important house on Vienna's Minoritenplatz. At much the same time life began returning to their Bohemian friaries: to the beautiful church of St. James in Prague, to Litoměřice and Königgrätz, Pardubice, Boleslav, and others, and first steps were taken from across the Polish border to resettle the defunct Hungarian province. Within fifty years well over fifty houses functioned, most of them on traditional Franciscan sites.[33]

Still more successful were the youngest members of the family of St. Francis, the Capuchins, founded in Italy at the beginning of the sixteenth century. In terms of the international Counter-Reformation the Capuchins rose almost as spectacularly as the Jesuits: whereas they only moved outside Italy in 1574, by 1618 they numbered over a thousand houses and nearly 15,000 men. Their Central European progress was equally dramatic: called to Innsbruck by Archduke Ferdinand of Tyrol in 1593, they soon settled at Prague and Vienna under the forceful leadership of St. Lawrence of Brindisi who—like Capistrano reborn—took the cross to the battlefields of the Turkish war in 1601.[34] By 1625 they already had eighteen houses in the Tyrol, twelve in Styria, fourteen elsewhere in Austria and Bohemia, and through the century they continued to expand, reaching Silesia in 1654 and Hungary twenty years later, when enough speakers of the local languages could at last be brought together. By the turn of the century Capuchins were established at well over one hundred different places in the Habsburg lands and had won especial renown for two things: their abnegation of self

---

[33] Lists and history in G. E. Friess, 'Geschichte der österreichischen Minoriten-provinz', *AÖG* lxiv (1882), 79–245; Svátek, art. cit. 544–8; M. Knaisz, *Chronologo-Provinciale ordinis F. F. Minorum S. F. Conv. Provinciae Hungariae* (Pozsony 1803); cf. Gy. P. Szabó, op. cit. 126–9, and 201 ff. *passim*.

[34] Melchior a Pobladura, *Historia Generalis O. F. M. Cap.*, i–iii (Rome 1947–51), i, 92–7; ii, pt. 1, 56 ff. *passim*; cf. the articles in *Lexicon Capuccinum* (Rome 1951), cols. 153–5, 233–6, 774–5, 1647–8, 1710–15, 1735–7, 1814–17. For Austria see also E. Kusin, 'Die Anfänge des Kapuzinerordens im Erzherzogtume Österreich unter und ob der Enns (1600–30)', *Coll. Franc.* xxxix (1969), 245–81. On Lawrence of Brindisi, canonized in 1881, cf. *Rudolf II*, 90 f.

and the fervour of their preaching. Though they gave some names
to learning (notably Magni and Schyrl) the gaunt, bearded friars
in their sandals and peaked cowl earned general respect rather as
fearless ministers of the Word. From Lawrence of Brindisi to
Procopius of Templin and Marco d'Aviano they mediated between
the rarefied atmosphere at court—where many had the right of
entrée despite Jesuit jealousies—and the real world of the urban
poor whence most of them had originally been drawn: no priests
did more to render the spiritual values of the Baroque accessible to
ordinary people.[35]

The other long-established mendicant orders, Carmelites and
Augustinians, likewise split into more and less ascetic branches
during the Counter-Reformation period. Neither Calced nor
Discalced Carmelites, who together possessed some dozen houses,
made more than a local impact, though the barefoot whitefriars on
Prague's Little Side guarded in their church of Mary of Victories
a celebrated votive statuette of the infant Jesus, brought from Spain
and elaborately garbed in the Iberian manner.[36] The Augustinians
operated on a broader front, though they took a long time to recover
from their almost total collapse during the sixteenth century (they
were, after all, Luther's own order). Attempts to reform the handful
of houses which survived and their mostly Italian inmates proceeded
slowly after 1600: beginning in Styria and at Baden bei Wien, the
revival spread to embrace nearly forty friaries through Austria and
Bohemia (the bulk of them originally medieval foundations) and to
gain a foothold in Hungary at Lockenhaus (Léka) and later at Buda
and Pécs.[37] Meanwhile the Discalced Augustinians, once summoned

---

[35] Lists in Heimbucher, op. cit. i, 731 f. (Austria and Hungary); Svátek, art. cit.
551–3 (Bohemia). On the initial difficulties in Hungary: H. Frey, *Die Beziehungen
der Kapuziner zu Ungarn bis zur Gründung des ersten Klosters* (Bp. 1949). Cf. below,
pp. 324, 330–2 (Magni and Schyrl).

[36] Lists in Heimbucher, op. cit. ii, 69, 75 f.; Svátek, art. cit. 556–8, Cf. Krásl, op.
cit. 277 f., 314–20; V. Němec, *The infant Jesus of Prague* (New York 1958); and
above, p. 73.

[37] Lists in B. A. L. van Luijk, *Le monde augustinien du XIIIᵉ au XIXᵉ siècle* (Assen
1972), 28–9, 51–5; Svátek, art. cit. 553–5. History in X. Schier, *De Monasteriis
provinciae Austriae et Hungariae O. E. S. A. Succincta Notitia* (V. 1776); id., *Memoria
Provinciae Hungariae Augustinianae antiquae*, ed. M. Rosnak (Graz 1778);
U. Anzinger, 'Das Kloster der Augustiner-Eremiter in Baden', *Aug.* xviii (1968),
262–332. Detailed studies of the earlier years by J. J. Gavigan, 'The Augustinian
province of Bohemia-Austria 1604–36', *Aug.* xxi (1971), 151–217; id., 'Geschichte

to the Monarchy in 1623, showed an energy which belied their smaller numbers. Though the vanguard which took over their first church, St. Wenceslas 'on Zderaz' in the New Town of Prague, consisted largely of foreigners, they soon managed to oust their conventual brethren from the order's prize piece of real estate, the Augustinerkloster beside the imperial Hofburg, and banish them to a dusty suburb outside the gates of Vienna. Indeed the barefoot Austin friars, like the Capuchins, enjoyed strong Habsburg favour, and they repaid the debt in the person of Abraham a Sancta Clara, the great court preacher of Leopoldine Austria, whose unparalleled fame in the area is confirmed by 394 editions of his numerous writings before the year 1800. Augustinians came to perform a variety of functions from education to missionary and parish work.[38]

Several other resuscitated mendicant orders populated the Habsburg lands during the Counter-Reformation era. Each contributed something to the varied activities of the Church. A few served specific devotional purposes; Servites, completely extinguished by the Reformation, came to the Tyrol in 1612 on the invitation of Archduke Ferdinand's widow, then introduced their extreme version of the Marian cult elsewhere in the Monarchy: to Prague and the Rossau on the outskirts of Vienna; to western Hungary and provincial Moravia.[39] The austere Minims (or Paulines) occupied

der Völkermarkter Augustiner-Eremiten von 1550 bis 1616', *Carinthia I* clxii (1972), 207–26; id., 'Felice Milensio, Mitbegründer des Müllner Klosters', *Sacerdos et Pastor semper ubique: Festschrift F. Loidl* (V. 1972), 235–82. A minute account of the later period by id., *The Austro-Hungarian province of the Augustinian friars, 1646–1820*, i–iii (Rome 1975–7). For Hungary see also F. Fallenbüchl, *Az Ágostonrendiek Magyarországon* (Bp. 1943), 60 ff.

[38] Lists in Luijk, loc. cit.; Svátek, art. cit. 555 f. For the Prague house: UK, MS. XIX G 14, compiled in the mid-18th century, with lists of friars. For the Viennese house: J. J. Gavigan, 'The discalced Augustinians in Vienna', *Aug.* xx (1970), 495–580; and cf. id., 'Epistulae inter Priores Generales O. S. A. atque Imperatores Austriacos annis 1635–71 missae', *Aug.* xviii (1968), 425–513. On Sancta Clara: K. Bertsche, *Die Werke Abrahams a Sancta Clara in ihren Frühdrucken* (2nd. edn. V. 1961); and cf. below, p. 188. For the role in higher education: J. J. Gavigan, 'De doctoribus theologiae O. S. A. in universitate vindobonensi', *Augustinianum*, v (1965), 271–364; F. L. Miksch, 'Der Augustiner-Orden und die Wiener Universität', *Aug.* xvii (1967), 37–83.

[39] List and history in A.-M. Romer, *Servitus Mariana auspiciis Austriacis in Germaniae, Hungariae et Boemiae regnis reparata* (V. 1667), a thorough contemporary survey; Svátek, art. cit. 560 f.

a central site in Prague from 1626 with a church confiscated from the Lutherans and colonized twenty further towns, though on the whole—like the purely contemplative monks (Carthusians, Camaldulensians)—they made only a modest, symbolic impression.[40] More colourful were some coenobites with a caritative role: Brothers of Mercy (*Barmherzige Brüder*), brought from Italy to the Liechtenstein estates in 1605, soon set up their hospitals in Vienna and Prague (where they acquired the meeting-house of the Bohemian Brethren in the Old Town) and beyond, helped by a curious privilege from Ferdinand II for the exclusive sale of ice in the summer months; Camillians tended war-wounded on the battlefields of Hungary; Trinitarians, founded to ransom Christian slaves from Ottoman captivity, reached Austria—belatedly enough—in 1688 and before long were begging for alms in a score of Central European towns.[41]

Finally we must spare a few words for the remaining groups of more worldly conventual clergy ('clerks regular' is the technical expression) which grew out of the sixteenth-century Italian Counter-Reformation. Little needs to be said about them, so thoroughly did the Jesuits outstrip the rest throughout the Habsburg lands. Though the Barnabites had houses from the 1620s and produced some public figures, while the Theatines later built themselves a fine church and monastery on the slopes below Prague castle, neither became properly naturalized.[42] Only the Piarists,

[40]. The Minims are *Paulaner* in German, *pavláni* in Czech. Lists in Heimbucher, op. cit. ii, 50 f.; Svátek, art. cit. 561 f. History in UK, MS. XII G 2 (records of the Prague house at St Salvator in the Old Town, 1626–72); Krásl, op. cit. 322–32; J. Kadlec in *Časopis Společnosti Přátel Starožitnosti*, lviii (1950), 40–52. *Geschichte der Stadt Wien*, v, 248 f. Several leading 18th-century Czech intellectuals were Minims, including Procházka.

[41] On the Brothers of Mercy, or Brothers Hospitallers: J. de Deo Sobel, *Geschichte und Festschrift der österreichisch-böhmischen Ordensprovinz der Barmherzigen Brüder* (V. 1892), with much detail; cf. Mout, op. cit. 126, for Prague. The only literature I have found on the Camillians is Heimbucher, op. cit., I, 114–19, esp. 117 f. On the Trinitarians (known in Austria as *Weissspanier*): M. Gmelin, 'Die Trinitarier . . . in Österreich und ihre Tätigkeit . . .', *ÖVjschr. f. Kath. Theol.* x (1871), 339–406; cf. Zibrt, *BČH*, v, no. 30657.

[42] For Barnabites (in German also *Pauliner*) and Theatines (known in Czech as *kajetáni*): Heimbucher, op. cit. ii, 107 f., 101; Svátek, art. cit. 564 f.; Krásl, op. cit. 322 f., 334–6; *Geschichte der Stadt Wien*, v, 247 f. (Barnabites). Pio Cassetta de Olibano, the Italian called to run the Barnabite house on the Prague Hradschin, wrote *Speculum Ecclesiasticum*, i–ii (Pr. 1648–57), a good statement of clerical duties as understood by the Counter-Reformation.

with their mission of flexible popular education, enjoyed real success: their first communities outside Italy were founded at Mikulov, Strážnice, Lipník, Litomyšl, and Moravský Krumlov in Moravia, whence they expanded to similar small towns in Austria and Hungary. By the end of the century they had been admitted to Vienna, despite the vociferous objection of vested Jesuit and mendicant interests. But the great days of the Central European Piarists and their superb church of Maria Treu—arguably the finest Baroque church in Vienna—still belonged to the future.[43]

*

These orders were the cutting-edge of the international Counter-Reformation. Together with the monks we shall encounter in the next chapters they recreated the Catholic Church of Central Europe in the image of a great cosmopolitan movement. Setting—for the most part—high standards of personal conduct, they carried a direct and popular message which knew no political or geographical frontiers. Many of the foremost preachers, ascetics, and scholars, especially in the earlier years, were foreigners like Marco d'Aviano, whose *hwyl* could convulse the Viennese masses though they understood not a word of his Italian, or the Irish Franciscans (Hibernians) after whom one of the main streets in Prague is named.[44] Yet the Church militant was also a Church of state. Historians have often observed that Leopold, by virtue of his training for the priesthood, was a very clerical emperor; they have overlooked the corollary, that he would have made a very imperious cleric. Strong dynastic influences pervaded the whole fabric of Catholicism.

Religious orders felt a hand both paternal and firm. In many cases the Habsburgs were their original sponsors and protectors, bringing them first, perhaps, to Innsbruck and Graz in the days of Archduke Ferdinand of Tyrol and his like-named nephew of Styria, then after

[43] Lists in Heimbucher, op. cit. ii, 124 f.; Svátek, art. cit. 572–8. History in T. Wiedemann, 'Einführung der Piaristen in die Erzdiözese Wien', *ÖVjschr.f. Kath. Theol.* x (1871), 607–14; A. Horányi, *Scriptores Piarum Scholarum liberaliumque artium magistri*, i–ii (Buda 1808–9); G. L. Moncallero, *La fondazione delle Scuole degli Scolopi nell' Europa centrale al tempo del Controriforma* (Alba 1972); G. Sántha (ed.), *Epistulae ad S.Iosephum Calasanctium ex Europa Centrali* (Rome 1969, rectè 1977?). The Piarists had the backing of Valerian Magni and his brother Francesco (J. Cygan in *Coll. Franc.* xxxviii (1968), 364–72). Cf. below, pp. 187, 254.

[44] Baur, 'Passer', 345–8. On the Hibernians see below, pp. 217, 326.

1620 to Vienna and Prague. The more conspicuous the favour—on their death members of the ruling family left their heart (quite literally) with the Augustinians and their body with the Capuchins—the greater the opportunity for interference, and we can find much evidence of the dynasty imposing its will, as for example by restricting the right to free visitation from abroad. Above all the Jesuits owed so much to imperial help that they could scarcely resist official pressures, especially since their position excited such envy among fellow ecclesiastics. Thus their control over the universities, defended against the claims of the archbishop of Prague, the Austrian Dominicans, the Benedictines, and others, in fact allowed scope for increasing government involvement: civilian superintendents were installed at both Vienna and Prague by the 1650s and Jesuit censors had to work in collusion with the secular administration. Even the academic powers of the Society were never complete: emperors retained the privilege of granting degrees *motu proprio* and periodically availed themselves of it.[45]

The diocesan Counter-Reformation too fell a long way short of theocracy. Central European bishops were a body by no means independent of the dynasty. The Habsburgs nominated directly to the small sees founded in the *Erblande* in the later Middle Ages: Vienna, Wiener Neustadt, Laibach; to Trieste and the venerable but obscure Pedena (Piben) in Istria; to the refounded archbishopric of Prague and the dioceses carved out of it after 1650: Litoměřice and Königgrätz. As successors to St. Stephen they claimed apostolic powers of presentation and jurisdiction over Hungary, with its string of weird and wonderful titular offices like the bishoprics of Bosnia, Syrmia, and Zengg which lay deep in Ottoman territory, its richer pickings nearer at hand, and its newly-established Uniate Churches.[46] Elsewhere the Habsburgs pulled all the strings they

---

[45] Duhr, op. cit. ii, pt. 1, 541–53, iii, 397 f.; Tomek, *Geschichte*, esp. 282; K. Beránek, 'Správa a kancelář pražské university v době pobělohorské', *SbAPr* xix (1969), 189–240; *Geschichte der Stadt Wien*, vi, 77–84. On censorship cf. also Menčik, 'Censura', 116 f.; Klingenstein, *Staatsverwaltung*, 49–54. On degrees: HHStA, RHR, Privilegia varii generis latinae expeditionis, fasc. 3 (unfoliated and not chronological); cf. the sketch by A. von Wretschko, *Die Verleihung gelehrter Grade durch den Kaiser seit Karl IV* (Weimar 1910).

[46] Luschin, *Reichsgeschichte*, 184 ff.; A. Frind, *Die Geschichte der Bischöfe und Erzbischöfe von Prag* (Pr. 1873), 178 ff.; Schlenz, *Leitmeritz*, i, 145 ff.; J. Solař,

could: they exercised strong sway over the little suffragans (*Eigenbistümer*) of Salzburg on Austrian territory—Gurk, Seckau, Lavant; and considerable influence in Salzburg itself, Brixen, Trent, and Constance. The three trickiest sees were Passau (to which belonged most of Upper and Lower Austria though the city lay across the German border), Olomouc, and Breslau. There the dynasty sent special commissioners to press supposedly self-governing chapters to elect its own archdukes in the earlier seventeenth century, and reliable members of the aristocracy later.[47]

The largest duty of bishops was to implement the Council of Trent. This they tackled through regular synods—especially in Hungary; through seminaries and visitations; in general through tighter episcopal organization. But most Tridentine decrees had no official backing in the laws of the Monarchy and the government tried to tame the more headstrong prelates.[48] It co-existed with a succession of Hungarian primates, with the gorgeous but vulnerable archbishops of Salzburg, with Harrach of Prague, with Franz Dietrichstein and Karl Liechtenstein-Castelcorno of Olomouc. Liechtenstein, who harboured particularly grandiose designs (building himself a magnificent palace at Kroměříž and keeping dozens of court musicians), proved perhaps the most pugnacious adversary; his dispute with the Jesuits over censorship brought decades of skirmishing which involved dynasty and Curia on opposite sides.[49] Indeed, all these domestic conflicts between the

---

Dějepis Hradce Králové nad Labem a biskupství hradeckého (Pr. 1870), 318 ff. For Hungary: Fraknói, *Kegyúri jog*, i, 233 ff. *passim*; Galla, 'Püspökjelöltek', 156–60; and cf. below, pp. 256, 273. On the Uniate Churches see below, pp. 421–4.

[47] On Salzburg: below, pp. 279 f. Passau: M. Hansiz, *Germania Sacra*, i–ii (Augsburg 1727–9), i, a huge chronicle, with much attention to elections. Olomouc: *Rudolf II*, 34 f., 112. Breslau: H. Jedin, 'Die Krone Böhmen und die Breslauer Bischofswahlen 1468–1732', *Kirche des Glaubens* ... i, 413–53; Köhler, op. cit. 249 ff. The Habsburg incumbents at Passau were Leopold (1595–1625), Leopold Wilhelm (1625–62), Karl Josef (1662–4); at Olomouc: Leopold Wilhelm (1637–63), Karl Josef (1663–4); at Breslau: Karl (1608–24), Leopold Wilhelm (1655–63), Karl Josef (1663–4).

[48] Péterfy, op. cit. ii; I. Batthyány, *Leges Ecclesiasticae Regni Hungariae*, i–iii (Alba Iulia – Kolozsvár 1785–1827), i, *passim*. Cf. T. I. Vanyó, *De exsecutione decretorum Concilii Tridentini in Hungaria 1600–1850* (Pannonhalma 1933); and above, p. 59 n. 45. On the Prague synod of 1605 see Vacek, art. cit.; its *acta* were republished in 1650, 1684, and 1767 (Zíbrt, *BČH*, ii, no. 1116).

[49] Duhr, op. cit. iii, 425–39. There appears to be no study of Liechtenstein; cf.

(continued)

civil and the ecclesiastical power were ultimately conflicts between Vienna and Rome. Chronic problems of patronage, authority, and clerical immunity could only be patched up by a series of expedients. The Pope tended *de facto* to approve imperial candidates for high Church office; emperors tended to allow the promulgation of Papal bulls. Claims to Church land were resolved by compromise and by a readiness of the Habsburgs to return some property—on their own terms—to deserving religious institutions, as the history of former Benedictine possessions in Hungary demonstrates.[50] The most important case of compromise was the so-called salt treaty in Bohemia, by which the Papacy—over the head of some local interests—wrote off most of the estates alienated since Hussite times in exchange for one quarter-gulden excise on every barrel of salt; though this *gabelle* proved far from sufficient to restore the pristine autonomy of the clergy.[51]

Friction grew worse during Leopold's reign. Clashes over the appointment of cardinals and the niceties of privilege and protocol pepper the diplomatic correspondence. And part of the trouble was precisely Habsburg religious zeal; the nuncios sometimes deplore Leopold's excessive piety and fatalism, while the dynasty continues to intervene in matters spiritual: ordering prayers, decreeing feast days, approving votive images, and so forth.[52] Ironically relations deteriorated further at the very time of the great political alliance of Pope and emperor against the Ottomans in the 1680s and 1690s. The imposition of taxes and restrictions on the clergy raised issues

Dudík, *Bibliothek*, 56. It is interesting that the only clash between Breslau and the Habsburgs in the later 17th century took place when the chapter there sought to elect Liechtenstein (Jedin, 'Bischofswahlen', in op. cit. i, 442 f.).

[50] Fuxhoffer, op. cit. i, 179–311; cf. below, pp. 251 f. Not many abbeys passed into aristocratic hands; nor were many permanently retained by the Habsburgs: this whole question of the fate of Church lands needs full study.

[51] On the *Salzvertrag* of 1630: Krásl, op. cit. 499–513; Gindely, *Gegenreformation*, 307–26; H. Kollmann, 'O vlivu Propagandy na vznik t. ř. pokladny solní', *ČČM* lxxii (1898), 139–57; Abgottspon, op. cit. 36–46. Cf. the clash over annates in Lower Austria at this time (E. Tomek, op. cit. 543 f.), and above, pp. 59 f., for earlier issues.

[52] *Nuntiaturberichte vom Kaiserhofe Leopolds I*, i (1657–69), ii (1670–9), ed. A. Levinson, *AÖG* ciii (1913), 549–830; cxvi (1918), 497–728 (hereafter *Nuntiaturberichte*), at i, nos. 516–40, *passim*; ii, nos. 38 seqq. *passim*, 73 and 100 (on piety), 102, 137–9, 141, 155, 208–39 *passim*, 254, 271. See also Wiedemann, *Reformation*, v, 1–16; Luschin, *Reichsgeschichte*, 418–25. Cf. Weingarten, *Codex*, 650 f.; Kollár, *De Originibus*, ch 13.

of principle—and when the government could agree with the nuncio, Buonvisi, local ecclesiastics dug in their heels. Then differences over war aims compounded disagreement, and Leopold made no secret in private of his irritation. Even church silver was requisitioned: well could the emperor afford the devout velleity expressed in his will that it be speedily handed back by his successor, a successor who would soon actually be waging war on the Holy See.[53]

★

Except during a few years immediately after 1700 these quarrels fell well short of complete rupture; yet they have real importance. They show that co-operation between the Habsburgs and the Church was not the fruit of some pre-established harmony, but a balance struck in practice between two uneasy allies, each manœuvring to assert itself as the dominant partner. The balance was secured by a third, overlapping party: the aristocrats, who besides their links with the crown also had close links with the Church. Most of the higher secular clergy in Central Europe were well-born, and wherever possible bishoprics became consolidated as the seventeenth century progressed—perhaps after a Habsburg interlude—in the hands of loyal families: Harrach, Kolovrat, Waldstein, Breuner at Prague; Thun, Pötting, Lamberg at Passau; Breuner, Trautson, Harrach in Vienna; and so on. We find the same paradigm at Constance, whose diocese embraced much of Habsburg Swabia: Cardinal Andreas, morganatic son of Archduke Ferdinand, was followed by a Fugger, then by a *kaisertreu* Count Waldburg. Salzburg and its associated Alpine bishoprics compromised their independence by electing a succession of Austrian, mainly Tyrolese aristocrats: Lodrons, Thuns, Kuenburgs, later a rash of Firmians and Spaurs. Outside Hungary it became almost unknown for commoners to rise into the episcopate or its attendant cathedral chapters. What a contrast with the Middle Ages, or even with the feeble sixteenth

[53] M. Héyret (ed.), *P. Marcus von Aviano, sein Briefwechsel* ... ii (with Leopold I, 1680–99) (Munich 1938), 9–23, 35 f., 114 f., 142 ff., 259 f., 335–7, and *passim*; and much in the correspondence of Leopold and Sinelli (below, n. 73). Freschot, op. cit. 226–30, 248–53; Fraknói, *Szent-Szék*, iii, 381–492; Nyáry, op. cit. 40 f.; Bojani, op. cit. ii, 152–76; Vanyó, *Nunciusok*, nos. 154–61; Placht, op. cit. 246 f.; O. Redlich, *Das Werden einer Grossmacht* (4th edn. V. 1962), 35 (will). Cf. below, pp. 260 f., 308 and n. 78 (Aretin, esp. 546 ff.).

century, which could show such lustrous commoner bishops as
Faber, Nausea, and Khlesl, Brus and Medek, Liszti and Telegdi,
and the foundling Urban of Gurk![54]

The incumbents of the main sees possessed latifundia worthy of
any magnate and managed on occasion, though by no means always,
with equal efficiency: Olomouc and Esztergom are good examples.
The same held true for the larger monasteries—even those of the
world-shy Carthusians—and some mendicant houses. The comfortable Moravian friary of Alt-Brünn with its extensive estates
succeeded in surviving Hussites, Protestants, repeated devastation
during the Thirty Years War, and the secularizations of Joseph II
to earn unexpected international fame more recently as the site for
Brother Gregor Mendel's experiments in heredity.[55] Such institutions clearly had an economic commitment to the aristocratic ideal,
and in other ways too the bond between regular clergy and magnate
class was an intimate one. Noblemen did just as much as the
Habsburgs to introduce and sustain monastic orders. The Franciscans owed their resuscitation primarily to private patrons; almost
all the Jesuit colleges in Bohemia were founded by powerful
families: Rožmberk (Krumlov), Lobkovic (Chomutov), Hradec
and Slavata (Jindřichův Hradec), Waldstein (Jičín), Vřesovec
(Kuttenberg), Oppersdorf (Königgrätz), Schlick (Eger), Huerta
(Klatovy), Jeníšek (Březnice).[56] Not infrequently young aristocrats
donned the religious habit: most probably joined the Jesuits, among

---

[54] Vienna still elected commoners until 1639, Lavant until 1640, Laibach until
1641, Wiener Neustadt until 1669, Brixen until 1685. Otherwise the only exceptions
seem to be Sebastian Rostock at Breslau (1664–71), Sinelli at Vienna (1680–5),
Becker at Königgrätz (1701–10), and probably some bishops of the insignificant
Trieste and Pedena. On Hungary see below, p. 248. On Urban of Gurk (also
administrator of Vienna from 1563 to 1568): Wiedemann, *Reformation*, ii, 99–103;
and, most recently, J. Obersteiner, *Die Bischöfe von Gurk* (Klagenfurt 1969), 310–31.

[55] J. Jirásek, 'Růst pozemkového vlastnictví olomouckého biskupství v letech
1555–1636', *SbMM* lxxxi (1962), 182–90; Marsina–Kušík (eds.), op. cit. i, 278–408
(Esztergom). E. Friess, 'Zur sozialen und wirtschaftlichen Lage der gutsherrlichen
Leute am Fuss des Ötschers nach dem Bauernsturme', *Jb. f. Lk. v. NÖ*, N. F. xxi
(1928), 2, 172–88, on the demesne lands of Gaming, the largest Carthusian
monastery on German soil. C. d'E. Janetschek, *Das Augustiner-Eremitenstift
S. Thomas in Brünn*, i (Brünn 1898, n. m. p.), with much economic material. Cf.
below, pp. 183 f.

[56] Many examples among the Franciscan houses in Greiderer, op. cit.; Herzog,
op. cit.; Friess, 'Minoritenprovinz'. The other Jesuit colleges in Bohemia proper
(three in Prague, and Litoměřice) were established by the Habsburgs.

them Chanovský, the scion of old Bohemian nobility, and Baron
László Sennyey, who became chancellor of Graz and Tyrnau
universities; but other communities attracted their share.[57] Daughters of gentle birth regularly entered nunneries, and elegant
Damenstifte adorned the Austrian Baroque scene, some occupying
historic sites like the Nonnberg perched high above Salzburg and
the basilica of St. George inside Prague's Hradschin.[58]

At parish level the relation between Catholic magnates and their
Church was just as close, but more tense. The great power of a local
landowner extended beyond the right of advowson to financial and
social sanctions against any priest who aroused displeasure. That
could be a major brake on Counter-Reformation activity, more
particularly in Bohemia where visitations, conversions, and ecclesiastical jurisdiction generally, were often impeded with the
connivance of agents of the crown, and curates treated little better
than peasants. Wallenstein's calculated condescension found its
imitators.[59] Magnate attitudes to religion shared the same political
base—*mutatis mutandis*—as those of the Habsburgs: Baroque
Catholicism was far more tied than its medieval predecessor to both
dynastic government and the entrenched system of self-sufficient
Herrschaften; indeed the Church might at times seem little more
than estate-owners at prayer.

Yet just as the Habsburgs had their genuine *pietas*, so Catholicism
answered a deep spiritual need in their mightiest subjects, and we
find among them examples of real Leopoldine fervour. Aristocrats

---

[57] On Chanovský, above, p. 124; B. Iványi, *Báró Sennyey László ... római utazásai*
(Bp. 1929). More examples below, pp. 180 f., 215 f., 247, 253.

[58] In other respects nuns seem to have been only marginal to Counter-Reformation
society, and their life may not have been genuinely conventual, hence my neglect of
them here; though the teaching order of Ursulines had houses at Prague, Vienna,
Klagenfurt, Gorizia, Pozsony, Graz, Breslau, Innsbruck, and Olomouc by 1700
(Heimbucher, op. cit. i, 634–7), and the *Englische Fräulein* (Institute of Mary) built
their impressive convent at St. Pölten for the same purpose soon after 1700. Cf.
below, pp. 180, 193, 219 n 54, 220, 301.

[59] Rezek, *Děje*, 141–5, and *Dějiny*, i, 229–33; Podlaha, *Dějiny*, 251 ff., 431 ff.;
Schlenz, *Leitmeritz*, ii, 64–94, and esp. id., *Das Kirchenpatronat in Böhmen* (Pr. 1928),
254 ff.; Flégl, art. cit. 192–7; Házi, op. cit. 36–8. On Wallenstein: B. Duhr,
'Wallenstein in seinem Verhältnis zu den Jesuiten', *HJ* xiii (1892), 80–99;
A. Ernstberger, 'Johannes Nysius, eine Gestalt aus Böhmens Gegenreformation',
Franken-Böhmen-Europa, gesammelte Aufsätze, i–ii (Kallmünz 1959), i, 392–416;
G. Mann, *Wallenstein*, tr. C. Kessler (London 1976), 93 f., 243–8; and cf. his
relations with Magni, beautifully captured, ibid. 382–400.

needed conspicuous devotion to legitimize their families, in death as in life, and the social order which they dominated, perhaps also to expiate their own unnatural greatness. I shall return to this point more than once, and cite here only one textbook case of the young noble Florián Jetřich Žd'árský: converted just before the Defenestration of Prague and married to the daughter of Jaroslav Martinic just before the White Mountain, created count a few years later, Žd'árský founded the first Loretto on Bohemian soil in 1623 and his son endowed a Franciscan friary in the same outlying spot.[60] His example soon inspired others, above all the Lobkovices, whose monumental Loretto monastery behind the Hradschin remains one of the pearls of Prague's townscape. Altogether, despite frictions, the privileged religion and the privileged caste were firmly bound in a marriage of both convenience and conviction. If further proof be required, we may discover it in the behaviour of those who rebelled against the new establishment: Bohemian insurgents in 1680, Hungarian *kurucok*, Austria's disenchanted peasants and critics of government policy in 1683—all fell upon secular and clerical property with equal relish.[61]

*

During the long reign of Leopold I the Counter-Reformation in Central Europe was thus, outwardly at least, brought to fruition. Ecclesiastical and civil authorities combined to forge a new kind of unity. Historians of religious sociology have recently demonstrated how other establishments in early modern Europe—Catholic and Protestant alike—sought to impose firm standards of Christian morality and observance; they faced similar problems, particularly *vis-à-vis* refractory and primitive rural populations.[62] The Habsburg

---

[60] On Žd'árský: Podlaha, *Posvátná místa*, vii, 230–54; and *OSN*, s. v. Further examples below, pp. 215 f., 247.

[61] Examples of attacks on the Church in V. Schulz (ed.), *Korrespondence jesuitů provincie české z let 1584–1770* (Pr. 1900), nos. 111–69; J. V. Šimák, 'Chotěšovské zprávy o selské bouři r. 1680', *VKČSN*, 1900, no. 10; Kašpar, 'Dvě studie', 71 ff.; Grüll, *Bauer, Herr . . .* , 81–205; O. Redlich, *Die Weltmacht des Barock* (4th edn. V. 1961), 255; Sturminger (ed.), op. cit. 40 f., 48 f., 85, 88–91.

[62] J. Delumeau, *Le Catholicisme entre Luther et Voltaire* (Paris 1971), esp. ch. 4; J. Bossy, 'The Counter-Reformation and the people of Catholic Europe', *Past and Present* xlvii (1970), 51–70; id., 'The social history of confession in the age of the Reformation', *Transactions of the Royal Historical Society* 5th ser. xxv (1975), 21–38; E. W. Zeeden, *Entstehung der Konfessionen* (Munich 1965), 95 ff.

case is extreme; for here the whole assault came belatedly, and the obstacles: geographical, linguistic, cultural, political, were peculiarly intractable. Hence the imposition of a Church for the entire community, against loose-limbed medieval arrangements and sixteenth-century Protestant localism, remained in practice peculiarly incomplete. Yet this base was sufficient to allow the emergence, under Leopold, of a major European power. What politicians and diplomats called for convenience 'Austria' now began to operate quite distinctly from the two realms which until then had buttressed Habsburg sovereignty. On one flank, Spain fell into irreversible decline and although Leopold, like his predecessors, took a Spanish wife, he increasingly assumed the role of a dominant and distant cousin in the family partnership. By the 1660s, for the first time, Austrians (like the Jesuit Father Neidhart) wielded influence in Spain, rather than Spaniards in Austria.[63] On the other flank, the states of Germany after the Westphalian settlement developed their separate armies, diplomacy, and resources. The Monarchy of the Austrian Habsburgs, however, flourished to such good effect on its own that before Leopold's death in 1705 it proved able to sustain successful European wars on three fronts at once.

The external policies actually pursued by Leopold's Austria are well enough known, more so probably than any other subject treated in this book; it is no part of my purpose to add to the standard narrative accounts.[64] The reign falls, conveniently, into

[63] There appears to be no overall survey of these relations. For the marriage: A. F. Pribram, *Die Heirat Kaiser Leopold I mit Margaretha Theresia von Spanien* (V. 1891, separatum from *AÖG*, lxxvii). On Neidhard: *Privatbriefe, passim*; Duhr, *Geschichte*, iii, 823–35. Of course, individual Spanish ambassadors, like Borgomanero, could still wield influence, and some Spanish careerists such as Rialp shone briefly under Charles VI.

[64] For the reign as a whole: Redlich, *Weltmacht*, and the beginning of *Werden einer Grossmacht*. O. Klopp, *Der Fall des Hauses Stuart . . . im Zusammenhange der europäischen Angelegenheiten von 1660–1714*, i–xiv (V. 1875–88), though absurdly prejudiced (and despite its title), rests on the Viennese archives. There is now a serviceable introduction by J. P. Spielman, *Leopold I of Austria* (London 1977). For the later campaigns: A. Arneth, *Prinz Eugen von Savoyen*, i–iii (V. 1858); M. Braubach, *Prinz Eugen von Savoyen*, i–v (Munich 1963–5); and another serviceable introduction, with some new material, by D. McKay, *Prince Eugene of Savoy* (London 1977). For the eastern front see also the attractive book by E. Eickhoff, *Venedig, Wien und die Osmanen; Umbruch in Südosteuropa* (Munich 1970). None of these works is satisfactory on Hungary (Redlich was the best-informed); but nor is the standard Magyar account: Hóman–Szekfü, op. cit. iv (by Szekfü), 145–314.

two equal halves, divided by the dramatic events of the early 1680s: years of hesitant defence, looking more towards the west, but distracted by threats from the east; followed by years of resolute aggression, looking more towards the east, but distracted by threats from the west. The first period saw an inconclusive war against the Turks, then struggles against Hungarian malcontents, and finally combined belligerence from the Ottomans and Thököly's *kuruc* army which led to the siege of Vienna in 1683; meanwhile Austria sought a tentative accommodation with Louis XIV, only to react against the inflated pretensions of the French monarch. The second period brought almost unbroken triumph on the Danubian front: the liberation of Hungary and the harrying of the Turks into the northern Balkans, though renewed *kuruc* revolt under Ferenc Rákóczi then complicated the picture; while rivalry with France led to a showdown on the Rhine and the north Italian plain. The outcome, sealed eventually at Rastatt (1714) and Passarowitz (1718) was an Austria with more extended possessions than any other European state, stretching from Antwerp to the Romanian Olt, from Sicily to the monotonous marches of Lower Silesia.

If the diplomacy and campaigns are familiar, and some of the commanders belong among the most glamorous figures of Central European history—Charles of Lorraine and the 'Türkenlouis' of Baden, Ernst Rüdiger Starhemberg and Prince Eugene of Savoy, the real instigators of policy, with the emperor at their centre, remain far more obscure. Yet there is a wealth of evidence from which to construct a picture of Leopold and his immediate political entourage. Shrewd observers recorded their impressions at court: nuncios, Venetian ambassadors, emissaries from Germany, French and English travellers.[65] Not every contemporary historian was a

---

[65] The nuncios' reports have been published for the years 1657–79 in *Nuntiaturberichte*; cf. the additional material in Bojani, op. cit., and Vanyó, *Nunciusok*. Venetian reports exist in print only for the years 1657–61: *Venetianische Depeschen vom Kaiserhofe*, Abt. 2, vol. i, ed. A. F. Pribram (V. 1901); but the ambassadors' final relations give some picture of the general evolution: *Relationen Venetianischer Botschaften über Deutschland und Österreich*, ed. J. Fiedler, ii (V. 1867). G. von Antal and J. C. H. de Pater, *Weensche Gezantschapsberichten van 1670 tot 1720*, i–ii (The Hague 1929–34), excerpt mainly the matter relating to Dutch interests. The best individual views are Esaias Pufendorf, *Bericht über Kaiser Leopold, seinen Hof und die österreichische Politik 1671–4*, ed. K. Helbig (Leipzig 1862); and Pufendorf's diary:

paid hack; indeed, the two best descriptions of Leopold's rule were composed by sympathetic Protestants.[66] Above all we have the private correspondence of the emperor: thousands of handwritten polyglot letters addressed to his closest confidants—emissaries and stadholders, priests and librarian. Only a small proportion of them have ever been published (the most-cited edition contains, curiously, those sent to Leopold's least distinguished friend); the rest glower at the reader through a well-nigh impenetrable graphological jungle, the Latin script marginally less illegible than the German and Italian. Besides the letters can be set some personal memorials, like the little diary of an imperial journey to meet the German electors at Augsburg in 1689, with its calculations of the number of masses heard and its details of seating-plans (though not menus) at dinner.[67] From all these sources the character of Leopold stands revealed: devoutness going with a disarming gaiety; friendliness and immediacy with conscientiousness and pride. Here is a man well-informed, intelligent, and curious, but no freethinker; honest and correct, but pusillanimous and irresolute; thoughtful, immensely hard-working—witness the letters to his secretary, Marx von Bergh—and heavily reliant on advice which he treats, however, with some independence of spirit and without sense of obligation.[68]

[66] O. Redlich, 'Das Tagebuch Esaias Pufendorfs (1671–4)', *MIÖG* xxxvii (1916), 541–97; J. E. Passer from Hesse-Darmstadt: Baur, 'Passer'; the Marquis de Sébeville: G. Guillot, 'Léopold I et sa cour (1681–4)', *Revue des Questions Historiques*, xli (1907), 401–46 (rather less reliable); and an anonymous French report, ed. A. F. Pribram in *MIÖG* xii (1891), 270–96. Travellers include Edward Browne, *An Account of Several Travels through a great part of Germany* (London 1677), 71–116; Charles Patin, *Travels through Germany, Bohemia . . . and other parts of Europe* (London 1696), 3–34, 270–82; Casimir Freschot, op. cit.; and lesser lights like John Burbury, op. cit. Cf., in general, J. Bérenger, *Finances et absolutisme autrichien dans la seconde moitié du XVIIᵉ siècle* (Paris 1975). The important diary of Ignatius Lovina for 1698, though published in Hungarian paraphrase by Nyáry, op. cit., in 1912, has never been used by subsequent scholars.

[66] *The Life of Leopold late Emperor of Germany* (London 1706); Rinck, op. cit. Cf. N. Eisenberg, 'Studien zur Historiographie über Kaiser Leopold I', *MIÖG* li (1937), 359–413.

[67] The well-known *Privatbriefe* are nevertheless very revealing of Leopold and important for his policies. Some other series are indicated in the next notes; for Leopold and his *Hofbibliothekar* Lambeck see below, pp. 314 f. and n. 9. ÖNB, MS. 8906: 'Diarium Itineris Augustani et Negotiorum ibi actorum' (German and *manu proprio*).

[68] The best pen-portrait is by K. Heigel, 'Neue Beiträge zur Charakteristik Kaiser

(continued)

As we should expect, the emperor's advisers were selected almost exclusively from the dynasty's two great partners: aristocracy and Church; the only significant exceptions being a few commoners from Germany. In the earlier part of the reign the high nobility threw up a trio of dominant politicians: Johann Ferdinand Portia was mentor to the young Leopold and then an unprepossessing major-domo and first minister until his death in 1665; Johann Weickard Auersperg, the most powerful personality of Ferdinand III's last years, guided the new emperor to a secret alliance with France, but fell through his rather unsubtle attempts at dictation which culminated in intrigues for a cardinal's hat; Václav Eusebius Lobkovic, a key figure in both military and civil administrations, succeeded Portia as major-domo and pursued the accord with Louis XIV until it collapsed, and he with it.[69] Lobkovic's disgrace in 1674 left the field clear for a group of less-exposed confidants. Besides the parvenu Hocher they included a winsome new major-domo, Lamberg; the long-time president of the Aulic Council, Schwarzenberg; the accomplished courtier-general Montecuccoli; and a string of Leopold's favourite Bohemians, consistently neglected in the historical literature: Chancellor Nostitz, Grand Burgrave Martinic, and the ambassador Humprecht Jan Černín, with whom the emperor corresponded extensively in Italian.[70] Here too a break

Leopolds I', *Sb. d. bayr. Akad. d. Wiss. ph.-ph.-h. Kl.*, 1890, 1, 109–47, based on the correspondence with Pötting. Ninety letters to Marx (or Marst) von Bergh, 1681–92 (but none for 1685 or 1689), are in HHStA, Hausarchiv, Fam. Korr. A Kart. 13. Bergh worked in the imperial chancery between 1666 and 1673 (L. Gross, *Die Geschichte der deutschen Reichshofkanzlei von 1559 bis 1806* (V. 1933), 452).

[69] More about those mentioned in this paragraph below, chs. 5–8, *passim*. Ninety letters from Leopold to Portia, mainly 1662 and n. d., German, m. p., in HHStA, loc. cit. On Auersperg: A. Wolf in *AÖG* xx (1859), 289–304, 331–40; and G. Mecenseffy, 'Im Dienste dreier Habsburger. Leben und Wirken des Fürsten J. W. Auersperg', *AÖG* cxiv (1938), 295–508; cf. the characteristic letter from him to Leopold in HHStA, ibid. Kart. 12, fols. 2–5. On Lobkovic: A. Wolf, *Fürst Wenzel Lobkowitz* (V. 1869); cf. Redlich, 'Pufendorf', 571–4; *Privatbriefe*, ii, *passim*. Ninety-one of Leopold's letters to him, 1657–74, mainly German, were printed by Max Dvořák (ed.), 'Briefe Kaiser Leopold I an Wenzel Euseb Herzog in Schlesien . . .' *AÖG* lxxx (1893), 463–508 (the first published work of the great art-historian).

[70] Leopold's early letters to Černín, while the latter was ambassador in Venice, 1660–3, Italian, were printed by Z. Kalista (ed.), *Korespondence císaře Leopolda I s Humprechtem Janem Černinem z Chudenic*, i (Pr. 1936). The rest remain unpublished in the archive at Jindřichův Hradec; cf. Pekař, *Kost*, i, 167–72; *Listy úcty a přátelství*, ed. J. Klik (Pr. 1941), 297.

occurred in the early 1680s, when all these men died and a new generation took their place: again one parvenu, Strattmann; a handful of Austrian magnates, like the major-domos Dietrichstein and Harrach, the late convert Windischgrätz, and the saviour of Vienna, Starhemberg; more Bohemians: Chancellor Kinský and Grand Burgrave Sternberg, Chamberlain Waldstein and the shrewd diplomat, Dominik Andreas Kaunitz; Esterházy representing the loyal Hungarian nobility. Finally, after 1700, a further batch of counsellors came to the fore who anticipate the reign of Joseph I: the self-made Seilern, the Rhinelander Salm, the Bohemian Vratislav, another generation of Starhembergs, and the prickly but indispensable Eugene.[71]

The clergy exercised a more subtle influence on high policy, neither so sinister as ill-willed contemporaries claimed, nor so secondary as some positivist scholars have imagined. Jesuits were notoriously encouraged in the Habsburg entourage—fifteen of them worked at court in 1698. Most had purely spiritual functions, though a few could certainly sway the emperor on occasion: his cultivated tutor, Philipp Müller; later Franz Menegatti and the persuasive Friedrich Wolff.[72] The real intimates were not Jesuits, but two Capuchins. Emmerich Sinelli, apparently the son of a butcher at Komárom in Hungary, pursued a vertiginous career which ended with five years as a somewhat unwilling and gout-racked bishop of Vienna. Between 1668 and Sinelli's death in 1685 Leopold wrote him 623 holograph letters which survive (many more must be lost); they show that Father Emmerich stood closer to the emperor during that time than anyone else: his advice is sought on matters of every kind, from trivial appointments to the deployment of armies.[73] Sinelli was succeeded in Leopold's

[71] Leopold's unpublished correspondence with Sternberg, in Prague's National Museum, may well be of particular interest; cf. Placht, op. cit. 245. Some of it was used by Rezek, *Dějiny*, ii, 4 ff.

[72] Nyáry, op. cit. 99; Duhr, *Geschichte*, iii, 789–813.

[73] HHStA, Hausarchiv, Fam. Korr. A 14 (plus one more written by a scribe); all are in Latin, except two in German. Cf. Sinelli's letters to Pál Esterházy in OL, Eszterházy család levéltára, P. 125, (cs. 658), nos. 2476–2508, for the years 1679–84. There is no literature on Sinelli except G. Guillot, 'Le père Emerick', *Études Franciscaines*, xvii (1907), 641–58 (slight). Cf. Redlich, 'Pufendorf', 583 f.; Guillot, 'Léopold I', 435 f.; Antal–Pater, op. cit. i, 24, 41, 67, 75, 99, etc., 374; Bojani, op. cit. i, 67; ii, 168–71; iii, 1, 6, 8, 10, 13, 18 l., 23–5, 28 f. etc.; Galla, 'Püspökjelöltek',

(continued)

affections by the fiery Marco d'Aviano, another latter-day Capistrano, scourge of Turks and backsliding Christians, whose critical
epistles evoked apologetic and submissive responses from the
emperor until the friar's death in 1699. There were others too,
especially the music-loving Franciscan Hippolito da Pergine, a
minor-key Marco d'Aviano, to whom Leopold sent more than 200
letters (handwritten and unpublished, like those to Sinelli)
intermittently during the 1680s and 1690s; and—in a very different
mould—the extravagant Cardinal Kollonich: priest, aristocrat, and
soldier wrapped into one.[74]

★

Evidently Habsburg foreign political involvements under Leopold
received the broad sanction of both civil and ecclesiastical hierarchies
in the Monarchy. The actual terms of those involvements do not
here directly concern us; nor do fluctuations between an 'eastern'
and a 'western' orientation, or between 'Austrian' and 'imperial'
strategies: ultimately they are only epiphenomena on the domestic
development. But how was this international status sustained by the
society—or collection of societies—whose Counter-Reformation
evolution I have outlined so far? That is a question we shall be
addressing throughout the rest of the present book. The answer to
it has major political and cultural dimensions, which correspond to
the roles played respectively by government and court.

Since the Middle Ages the Habsburgs had possessed shadowy
organs of central government guided by senior officers at court,
especially the major-domo (*Obersthofmeister*). They were reconstructed and diversified under Ferdinand I, who created formal
bodies with salaried staffs.[75] Highest among them stood the Privy

---

173 n.; *Geschichte der Stadt Wien*, v, 272 ff. Sinelli is sometimes described as the son
of an immigrant Italian engineer; yet if that were so, we might expect him and the
emperor to correspond in Italian, and the Christian name Emmerich (Imre) is very
Hungarian.

[74] Héyret (ed.), op. cit., excerpts the d'Aviano correspondence and related
materials in German; it does not entirely supersede O. Klopp (ed.), *Corrispondenza
epistolare tra Leopoldo I Imperatore ed il P. Marco d'Aviano* (Graz 1888). The
emperor's letters to Hippolito da Pergine are in ÖNB, MS. 14717, mainly 1682–7 and
1689–93, Italian and m. p.; cf. the letters from Empress Eleonora, ibid. MS. 14855.
On Hippolito cf. Héyret (ed.), op. cit. i, 319; ii, 10 f., 115, 192f, 290. On Kollonich:
below, pp. 251 f.; on clerical advice see also below, p. 441 n. 55.

[75] In general: Fellner–Kretschmayr, op. cit., i–ii (history and documents);

Council, whose select membership met frequently (sometimes daily) to advise the ruler on important matters of state and prepared written reports under the normal chairmanship of the *Obersthof-meister*—still the best paid of Habsburg servants. For all its imperial associations, the Council openly supported dynastic Austrian interests at the time of the Thirty Years War; and in the later seventeenth century, streamlined as a so-called Privy Conference by the autocratic Lobkovic, it helped Leopold to take most of his crucial decisions.[76] The Council was flanked by two executive chanceries: imperial and Austrian. The former, under a vice-chancellor, exercised supreme control over the administration of the *Reich* and employed a large secretariat; the latter, founded—symbolically enough—in 1620, concentrated on the Habsburgs' own lands. Austrian chancellors: Werdenberg, Prickelmayr, Hocher, Strattmann, Seilern, became the most determined protagonists of undivided Habsburg sovereignty.[77]

Yet these institutions were far from being effective instruments of centralization. Instead of strengthening over the years, the Privy Council tended to decay: it grew unwieldy, with too many fainéant or incompetent councillors. By contrast with its lusty Renaissance origins, it turned into the preserve of an inbred aristocratic clique, and the formation of the Conference proved only a temporary palliative.[78] Worse still, the two chanceries were not partners but rivals, squabbling over areas of competence and prestige at court. Their struggle was not resolved in the seventeenth century, and it would be anachronistic to view the 'Austrian' chancery as a native organ, tailored to rule the Monarchy: it had not originally been

Bidermann, op. cit. i, better in detail than in its argument. Since the 1890s a number of constitutional histories of 'Austria' have been published, but the genre is a somewhat unsubtle one; Luschin, *Reichsgeschichte*, is still by far the best for this period. Cf. F. Walter, *Österreichische Verfassungs- und Verwaltungsgeschichte von 1500–1955*, ed. A. Wandruszka (V.-Cologne–Graz 1972), intro. O. Hintze, 'Der österreichische und der preussische Beamtenstaat im 17. und 18. Jahrhundert', *HJ* N. F. 1(1901), 401–44, is a thoughtful essay based on Luschin.

[76] H. F. Schwarz, *The Imperial Privy Council in the 17th century* (Cambridge, Mass. 1943).

[77] Gross, op. cit., esp. 41–76, a very thorough study. There is no history of the Austrian chancery, but see Fellner–Kretschmayr, op. cit. i, 139–73; Bidermann, op. cit. i, 34–8, 42 f., and nn.

[78] Schwarz, op. cit., appendix (with J. I. Coddington). The clique, it should be stressed, included descendants of erstwhile bourgeois councillors.

designed for that purpose, and much of its personnel came from Germany. It merely worked a modicum more smoothly than its imperial counterpart, which still fell partly under the nominal jurisdiction of the archbishop of Mainz. Moreover, neither body exercised any real sway in Bohemia or Hungary, where domestic chancellors jealously guarded their rights.[79] The Privy Council moved closer to possessing supranational powers, since it always contained Bohemian members and sometimes Hungarian ones; but here again traditional royal councils refused to be dislodged.

There existed two stronger and more distinctive central institutions: *Hofkammer* and *Hofkriegsrat*. The *Hofkammer*, or Court Chamber, managed Habsburg finances, both regalia and indirect taxes, and comprised a board of some fifteen councillors, including always a number of able, ambitious commoners, at the top of a quite ramified bureaucracy. From its inception in the sixteenth century the *Hofkammer* consistently broadened the scope of its activities: it soon laid a firm hand on the economies of the free towns; after 1620 it supervised the collection of revenues from Bohemia, still (despite war) the richest part of the Monarchy, and extended its tentacles across the Hungarian border. When the Turks had been expelled, it took over large tracts of the Great Plain (the so-called *Neo-Acquistica*) and deflected the profits from their exploitation or sale into the coffers of the imperial treasury. By Leopold's reign the *Hofkammer* was producing 'budget' statements of at least a rough accuracy; in the 1680s particularly, guided by a parvenu president, Christoph Abele, and the schemes of three celebrated cameralist advisers: Becher, Hörnigk, and Schröder, it gained new rules of procedure and sought to tap the long-neglected industrial resources of the Monarchy.[80]

[79] Fellner–Kretschmayr and Gross, loc. cit.; cf. below, pp. 211 f., 237–40, 294 f. The archbishop of Mainz was by ancient prescription arch-chancellor of the *Reich*, and the head of the imperial chancery acted in theory as his deputy; the origins of the 'Austrian' chancery lay in an attempt by Ferdinand II to sidestep the authority of Mainz. From the 1690s there was even a fifth chancery (Transylvania; cf. below, p. 272).

[80] A. Wolf, 'Die Hofkammer unter Kaiser Leopold I', *Sb. d. k. Akad. d. Wiss. ph.-h.-Kl.* xi (1853), 440–84; Fellner–Kretschmayr, op. cit., esp. i, 81–93; ii, 596 ff.; Bidermann, op. cit. i, 28–31, 37 f., 42, 44 f., and nn. (esp. pp. 111–14, 124–7, 130 f.); Bérenger, op. cit., *passim*; and cf. below, pp. 163 f. on cameralism. Some *Hofstaaten* with financial information are printed in Wolf, loc. cit.; cf. ÖNB, MSS. 12388, 14071.

Whatever extra finances the treasury could raise were promptly swallowed up by the Austrian army, and that army represented a second institutional bond between the various Habsburg territories. Throughout the seventeenth century it grew in size, reaching a total of some sixty regiments, plus artillery, garrisons, and the rest, for the campaigns of Prince Eugene. After 1648 it took on the classic 'absolutist' guise of a peacetime standing force. It was controlled by a War Council (*Hofkriegsrat*), a co-ordinating body of generals and officials, which organized all its dispositions from the Rhine to the Sava and Tisza. The *Hofkriegsrat* also maintained, as its private empire, the whole area of the *Militärgrenze*, the martial *cordon sanitaire* which ran along the Ottoman frontier, initially only in Croatia, later through the Banat and Transylvania as well. There the writ of Vienna was law, and even village communities lived according to military discipline.[81]

Again, however, we should not jump to conclusions. Neither treasury officials nor army officers achieved any decisive measure of centralization. The *Hofkammer* remained inefficient, even by the standards of early modern Europe; it functioned as a weak collegiate system, faced with a chronic deficit and encumbered by all manner of vested interests. Its president for twenty-four years after 1656, Count Sinzendorf, was at length, after years of rumour, convicted of embezzling some two million florins of government money.[82] Even then no proper structural reform took place; Becher and his

[81] O. Regele, *Der österreichische Hofkriegsrat 1556–1848* (V. 1949), is only a sketch; cf. Fellner–Kretschmayr, op. cit. i, 234 ff. E. Heischmann, *Die Anfänge des stehenden Heeres in Österreich* (V. 1925), is actually a study of nascent tendencies towards a permanent standing force before 1620, though the title suggests more. The fullest description of the 17th-century Austrian army is in *Feldzüge des Prinzen Eugen von Savoyen*, series I, i (V. 1876), a work edited collectively from the *Kriegsarchiv* in Vienna. Cf. T. M. Barker, *Double Eagle and Crescent* (New York 1967), 164–78; id., 'Military entrepreneurship and absolutism: Habsburg models', *Journal of European Studies*, iv (1974), 19–42, makes some observations on the role of foreign-born professional commanders. For the military frontier: G. E. Rothenberg, *Die österreichische Militärgrenze in Kroatien 1522–1881* (V.–Munich 1970), is thin on the earlier period.

[82] Bérenger, op. cit. 352–403 and *passim*, amply demonstrates the absence of any fiscal absolutism. He interestingly suggests (pp. 365–73) that Sinzendorf was no more crooked than anyone else, and fell because he had reforming plans. That seems unlikely, given the nature of contemporary gossip (e.g. *Relationen Venetianischer Botschaften*, ed. Fiedler, 133, 152, 171 f.); but if true it only places the rest of the *Hofkammer*, his successor Abele included, in an even worse light.

colleagues were probably—as we shall see—valued more highly as alchemists than as economists. Local chambers survived into the eighteenth century with their competences largely unimpaired: at Graz and Innsbruck; in Bohemia too—albeit its *komorníci* theoretically took their orders from Vienna—especially in the semi-autonomous Silesian duchies; in Hungary, where the *kamara* at Pozsony steadfastly refused to acknowledge Vienna as a superior instance.[83]

Bureaucratic frictions were matched by those inside the military cadres. The *Hofkriegsrat*, when it was not actually embroiled in disputes with the *Hofkammer*, suffered from the same kind of fragmented authority, which the establishment of a *General-Kriegs-Commissariat-Amt* and other sesquipedalian logistic departments during the wars against Louis XIV only exacerbated. The martial affairs of Inner Austria, and often of the Croatian sector of the border too, were handled by a subsidiary council at Graz, founded in the sixteenth century and undisturbed until the time of Maria Theresa. Hungary's levies and notoriously unruly frontier fortresses (*végvárak*) remained a law unto themselves. The rest of the army, much smaller than its French rival, formed really a congeries of separate commands, many regiments manned and paid by outsiders. In the circumstances, the *Hofkriegsrat* made little effort to impose an 'Austrian' stamp on such a variegated assemblage, not least because its emperors cut a distinctly unmilitary figure and its own membership was so cosmopolitan. The list of its presidents under Leopold includes Annibale Gonzaga, Montecuccoli, the Margrave of Baden-Baden, and Prince Eugene.[84]

One further sphere offered itself for those seeking to buttress royal sovereignty: the law. In two convergent ways the judiciary could seem to be moving towards greater Habsburg control. On the one hand, as confessional and political bickering hopelessly crippled Germany's supreme court, the *Reichskammergericht*, the emperor's own Aulic Council (*Reichshofrat*) in Vienna assumed mounting

---

[83] Bidermann, op. cit. i, 46, 49, and nn. (pp. 134 ff.). The relation between the *Hofkammer* and the Hungarian Chamber is well delineated in Th. Mayer, 'Das Verhältnis der Hofkammer zur ungarischen Kammer bis zur Regierung Maria Theresias', *MIÖG*, Ergänzungsband ix (1913–15), 178–263. Cf. the literature below, pp. 164 f., 212 f., 239 f.

[84] *Feldzüge des Prinzen Eugen*, 194–204; Regele, op. cit., *passim*; Klopp, *Haus Stuart*, i, 89 f., 179; ii, 51 f., 320–2.

importance. Though all its members were nominated by the dynasty and few of them were Protestant, the *Reichshofrat* handed down justice for both corporate bodies and individuals throughout the Empire.[85] On the other hand, the Austrian and Bohemian chanceries acquired during the seventeenth century the right to judge certain appeals from lower tribunals, and legally-trained royal servants had added scope for their activities on a few special appellate courts, notably that at Prague. Swift and condign punishment could be meted out to traitors, as Hungarian rebels discovered in 1671.[86]

Yet the legal system was even less unitary than the organs of government. The Aulic Council achieved success because Germans could have reasonable trust in its impartiality, that is to say precisely because it was a genuinely imperial body, not simply the expression of Habsburg territorial sovereignty. Indeed, it lost all its powers over the *Erblande* by 1700. And there was little consistent purpose about the jurisdiction of the dynasty in domestic cases either, little attempt to simplify or standardize the irregular mass of local courts and procedures. As we have already seen, changes in the social framework and the mentality of lawyers may have contributed more to the decay of traditional jurisprudence than did the promptings of Vienna. Significantly we encounter the strongest awareness of constitutional issues where the monarch's claims to sovereignty were most contested, in Hungary. The Habsburgs never found a publicist able to confound the regularly reprinted *Corpus Juris Hungarici* and *Tripartitum* of Werbőczi.

*

In sum: Habsburg political authority continued to hover awkwardly between the imperial and the provincial, unable and unwilling to detach itself from a Germany which still seemed vital to its raison d'être, inchoate as yet in the territories of immediate sovereignty. While a few of the dynasty's servants might invoke some ideal of total monarchy, the bulk of them in practice ploughed

[85] Gschliesser, op. cit. Only a few large territorial princes, such as Saxony and the Palatinate, possessed the *privilegium de non appellando* which protected them from the judgments of the Aulic Council. On the imperial Chamber Court: R. Smend, *Das Reichskammergericht*, i (Weimar 1911).

[86] Fellner–Kretschmayr, op. cit. ii, 498–533; cf. above, pp. 105–7. I have not seen F. Tezner, *Die landesfürstliche Verwaltungsrechtspflege in Österreich vom Ausgang des 15. bis zum Anfang des 18. Jahrhunderts*, i–ii (V. 1897–1902). On Hungarian rebels: below, pp. 246, 261–3; proceedings against them were controversial but effective.

a much narrower furrow. For ultimately government from Vienna was impossible without the complaisance of local interests: superficially at sessions of the diets, more substantially through the mechanism of the estates and all manner of scarcely-institutionalized channels, high nobles and prelates could strike bargains with their ruler over administration, direct taxation, recruits for the army, the dispensing of justice, the higher arcana of policy. Had Habsburg supremacy in Central Europe rested on government alone, it would have been very weak indeed.

Instead, central government was subsumed in a larger entity: the central court. Political operations were bound up with cultural ones. The role of the expansive Baroque court as a vehicle for quasi-absolutist regimes in early modern Europe has long been underrated by historians.[87] Counter-Reforming, aristocratic Austria provides the clearest example of how a set of values conspicuously embraced by the aulic entourage of the sovereign could create a set of responses in society at large. As the imperial household grew in numbers—a hierarchy minutely regulated under traditional noble officers—its ruling functions were complemented by display and symbolism which inspired (as they also reflected) loyalty to the imperial idea. Court festivities, carefully and lavishly prepared, celebrated all major occasions, and the literature of Habsburg eulogy, mediocre but influential, unfolded from Berger (1612) to Glabotsnig (1699) via dynastic historiographers like Khevenhüller and Gualdo Priorato.[88]

And here members of the dynasty found their true métier. Artistic patronage, even participation, came naturally to them, as an essential facet of their sovereignty. Until the mid-seventeenth

---

[87] J. Kruedener, *Die Rolle des Hofes im Absolutismus* (Stuttgart 1973), makes interesting general points, though his book is very sketchy and neglects the differences between French and Austrian types of court, the latter being much more evidently noble-based. P. Anderson, *Lineages of the Absolutist State* (London 1974), 299–327 on Austria, offers a highly intelligent argument, perceiving the formative role of 'Catholic ideology' in a way which belies his avowed Marxism. Cf. Oestreich, 'Strukturprobleme des europäischen Absolutismus', in op. cit. 179–96; and above, p. 85, n. 12 (Makkai).

[88] Elias Berger, *Trinubium Europaeum, hoc est De Societate Imperii Christiani inter Germanos, Hungaros, et Bohemos* (Frankfurt 1612); Caspar Glabotsnig, *Phosphorus Austriacus sive compendiosa Historia de Augustissimae Domus Austriacae Origine* (V. 1699); cf. below, p. 157, n. 2. See, in general, A. Coreth, *Österreichische Geschichtschreibung in der Barockzeit, 1620–1740* (V. 1950).

century they cultivated above all the fine arts, in a tradition whose
main stream derived from Maximilian I through Maximilian II
and Rudolf, while a subsidiary current—apt to be forgotten beside
the more obvious devotional concerns—flourished at Graz under
Archdukes Karl and Ferdinand. Ferdinand II's younger son
Leopold Wilhelm inherited the passion and built up an extraordinary
picture gallery which passed in turn to his nephew, Emperor
Leopold.[89] Although Leopold did not neglect the visual arts, the
creativity of his court centred on two other fields. One was literature,
mostly Italianate, for the emperor, like his father, was a keen turner
of verses in his preferred language. The other and greater enterprise
was music, on which both Ferdinand III and Leopold, themselves
highly competent performers and composers, spent profligately.
Leopold's correspondence abounds in references to it, including
practical arrangements and more studious matters, such as how to
procure manuscripts by Palestrina. Again the personnel was mainly
Italian, although we find notable exceptions, like the native Johann
Heinrich Schmelzer and the German organists Froberger, Pachel-
bel, Kerll, and Georg Muffat.[90]

Words and music came together with the rest of the arts in two
great synthetic achievements, alike commissioned by court, mag-

---

[89] On Graz: J. Wastler, *Das Kunstleben am Hofe zu Graz unter den … Erzherzogen
Karl und Ferdinand* (Graz 1897). For Leopold Wilhelm see K. Garas in *Jahrbuch der
kunsthistorischen Sammlungen in Wien*, N. F. xxvii (1967), 39–80; xxviii (1968), 181–
278; he left his nephew the emperor 'alle meine gemähl, statuas undt heydnische
Pfennig alss dass vornehmste undt mir das liebste Stuckh von meiner Verlassenschaft'
(ÖNB, MS. 14834, fols. 31–7). A. Lhotsky, *Die Geschichte der Sammlungen*, i–ii
(V.1941–5), i, 361–82, is rather brief on Leopold's collection.

[90] ÖNB, MS. 10073: 'Iconophylacium sive Artis Apellae Thesaurarium', Latin
poems about Leopold's pictures by F. ab Imstenraedt, ?1667. On emperors as poets:
HHStA, Hausarchiv, Fam. Korr. A 11, letters of Ferdinand III (e.g. 15 Jan. 1628,
20 July 1630, 24 Aug. 1642); Kalista (ed.), *Korespondence, passim*; there are Italian
poems dedicated to Leopold in ÖNB, MSS. 9984–6, 9997, 10007–8, 10137, 10148,
10169, 10176, 10196, 10202, 10234, 10249, 10263, 10302. Cf. M. Landau, *Die
italienische Literatur am österreichischen Hofe* (V. 1879), 10 ff. On music: H. Knaus,
'Die Musiker im Archivbestand des kaiserlichen Obersthofmeisteramtes (1637–
1705)', *Sb. d. ö. Akad. d. Wiss., ph.-h. Kl.* ccliv (1967), Abh. 1; cclix (1968), Abh. 3;
cclxiv (1969), Abh. 1; *Musik in Geschichte und Gegenwart*, iv (1955), cols. 36–8; viii
(1960), cols. 649–52; Kalista (ed.), *Korespondence*, esp. nos. 3–5, 7, 11, 15, 17, 21, 24,
27–8, 31, 41, 43–4, 61–5; HHStA, Hausarchiv, Fam. Korr. A 10–11, *passim*, and A
12, fols. 18 f. (P. P. Domenici, Rome, 27 Sept. 1681, on 'Giovanni Pierluigi').
Observers constantly comment on Leopold's devotion to music. Cf. below, pp.
339 f., 446.

nates, and Church, alike immortally associated with the age of Baroque in the Habsburg lands: the dramatic extravagance of opera; and its physical counterpart, the monumental architecture of the years around 1700. Their realm of display and allusion cannot yet be entered here. It mirrored an underlying intellectual concern: the commitment of the dynasty, its entourage, and increasingly the country at large to a distinctively Counter-Reformation world-view, which will form the subject of the last part of this book. Before that we must survey a different set of problems arising from the story of Habsburg consolidation in Central Europe. If unity was not forged by any simple political or military predominance of the ruler, how were the interests of central authority and regions actually harmonized? How far did the several Habsburg territories voluntarily submerge their identity? How far did international Catholicism and Baroque culture accommodate themselves to local conditions? Four case-studies follow: the Austrian hereditary lands; Bohemia; Hungary; and finally the Empire, where Habsburg claims to hegemony, more subtly phrased than during the Thirty Years War, could still prove surprisingly effective.

Part Two

THE CENTRE AND THE REGIONS

CHAPTER 5

Austria: the Habsburg heartland

Austria is not an easy term for the historian to handle. My use of it here as a synonym for the *Erblande*, the non-Bohemian and non-Hungarian lands ruled by the Habsburgs in direct sovereignty, represents only a convention, albeit one fortified by the latter-day creation of an Austrian Republic covering substantially the same area.[1] In one sense Austria was the whole Monarchy: it regularly meant the Habsburg dynasty, including the Spanish branch, and— loosely—the possessions of this 'house of Austria', which could be taken to embrace territories in northern Italy and the southern Netherlands. Thus in the apologetic works of Nicholas Vernulaeus, historiographer to the courts of both Madrid and Vienna.[2] Thus too, of course, in the commonplace, unthinking usage of later generations of foreigners. At the other extreme it signified a single duchy, which lay along the Danube between the eastern outliers of the Alpine chain, the forests of south Bohemia, and the foothills of the Carpathians, and which for all practical purposes became split into two along the line of the river Enns by the end of the Middle Ages. This duchy had acquired a distinct identity during the eleventh and twelfth centuries under the powerful family of Babenberg, who gained a series of privileges for it: full legal sovereignty, hereditary succession, freedom from most imperial obligations, and various ceremonial rights.

After the Habsburgs took over Danubian 'Österreich' about 1282, they gradually extended the meaning and privileges of Austria to embrace the other provinces they were acquiring in Central Europe:

---

[1] *'Erblande'* too was a fluid notion. After 1627 it became an open question whether the 'inherited lands' should include Bohemia; if they did, then the word corresponded more to the later 19th-century sense of 'Austria' as opposed to Hungary within the Dual Monarchy.

[2] N. Vernulaeus, *Apologia pro Augustissima … Gente Austriaca* (Louvain 1635). This sort of Habsburg propaganda was particularly strong in the Spanish Low Countries. Glabotsnig's book (above, p. 152, n. 88) was also based on an earlier Louvain edition.

Styria, the Tyrol, and so forth. At the same time they began to grace
members of the ruling house with the famous title of 'archduke',
apparently to denote their collective ownership of several different
duchies (interestingly enough, the term 'archduchy' never assumed
the same significance[3]). The Habsburgs insisted on these claims
with growing determination after the Golden Bull of 1356; denied
the status of electors, they none the less became in fact the most
independent rulers in the *Reich*. And they found documents to
justify their actions: the so-called *Privilegium Maius*, which, though
not acknowledged by Charles IV in the 1350s, was subsequently
confirmed by an emperor from within the family, Frederick III.[4]
There is one serious theoretical catch about the *Privilegium Maius*:
it was forged. In practice that did not matter, since scarcely anyone
suspected its authenticity, and anyway the Habsburgs as emperors
after 1438 could always bring pressure to safeguard their own
princely rights *vis-à-vis* the *Reich*. Much more important was the
fact that archducal powers over the complex of the inherited lands
remained thoroughly unconsolidated well into the modern period.

Austria was a patchwork of disparate territories, brought together
in largely piecemeal fashion, and some of the obstacles to its unity
are apparent from any map of Alpine Europe. Mountains blocked
communication, not only between north and south, but between
east and west as well. Worse still, the compact mass of the
archbishopric of Salzburg could interpose an almost complete
political barrier between the Tyrol and the provinces along the
Danube. Let us survey it briefly, beginning in the east. Most
prosperous, and quite populous for its size, was Lower Austria,
administered from Vienna, though Vienna lay by no means centrally
within it, and divided into four traditional districts (*Viertel*): two
'quarters' north of the Danube, on either side of the Manhartsberg;
and two more to the south, separated by the forbidding wilderness
of the Vienna Woods. Above the Enns, Upper Austria developed its
separate character and institutions, with common law and estates

---

[3] The 'archduchy of Austria' should presumably have been the whole of the
Erblande, or even the whole Monarchy, but it seems—certainly after 1500—rarely to
have been used in that way. Zedler (xxv, cols. 774ff.) and others equate it simply with
Lower and Upper Austria. The title of 'archduke' appears to have been employed
first by the dukes of Carinthia.

[4] A. Lhotsky, *Privilegium Maius, die Geschichte einer Urkunde* (V. 1957).

based on Linz. But it was weaker, and its constitutional status was not entirely beyond dispute, the line of the Enns still representing only a rough convention. Upper Austria also fell into quarters, whose frontiers fluctuated somewhat: Mühlviertel and Machland towards Bohemia; Hausruck and Traunviertel covering the upland terrain traversed by the rivers Traun and Enns.[5]

The next group of lands is Styria, Carinthia, and Carniola: Inner Austria, as they were regularly designated by the later sixteenth century (though a confusing earlier nomenclature still reckoned them part of 'Lower Austria'). Styria, an extensive province acquired by the Habsburgs in 1282, was reasonably cohesive and centred on Graz. Like Lower Austria, it tended to dominate its neighbours, but Carinthia and Carniola, gained in 1335, remained for most purposes quite distinct territories, with capitals (at Klagenfurt and Laibach (Ljubljana)), strong local loyalties, separate laws, government, and customs. Again, administrative subdivisions existed: Carniola, for example, being divided into 'Upper', 'Lower', 'Middle', and 'Inner'.[6] In the south, oddments of land led down to the Adriatic: the county of Istria, around Pisino (Mitterburg), added in 1374, and not to be confused with the coastal margravate of Istria, which belonged to Venice; Trieste and Fiume, annexed in 1382 and 1466, but confirmed in their traditional autonomies; Gorizia (eastern Friuli), acquired between 1500 and 1518 on the death of its independent rulers and after war with Venice. To the west, the Tyrol formed from 1363 a more compact block of territory, with its capital at Innsbruck, the third main focus (after Vienna and Graz) for Austrian politics. But Tyrol was *sui generis* in two ways: it displayed extreme localism, even parochialism, with little contact between the north and the south of

---

[5] There are good historical surveys of the various provinces (*Länder*) in *Handbuch der historischen Stätten: Österreich*, ed. K. Lechner and F. Huter, i–ii (Stuttgart 1966–70). For Lower and Upper Austria: M. Vancsa, *Geschichte Nieder- und Oberösterreichs*, i–ii (Leipzig-V. 1905–27), reaching only to 1522; Gutkas, *Niederösterreich*. The Viertel ob and unter dem Manhartsberg gradually became known as Waldviertel and Weinviertel respectively.

[6] For Styria: Pirchegger, op. cit. For Carinthia: Braumüller, op. cit. and earlier J. W. von Valvasor, *Topographia Archiducatus Carinthiae* (Nuremberg 1688). For Carniola: Dimitz, op. cit., and earlier Valvasor, *Die Ehre des Hertzogthums Crain*, i–iv (Laibach 1689). It is curious that this most outstanding of all Austria's historical geographies should be devoted to one of her smallest provinces.

the province, and each valley commanding its own loyalties; but it was also in a way unusually international, controlling a vital route across the Alps, close to Italy and the rich south German cities.[7]

West again and north-west, we pass to Habsburg property in Europe's most variegated region, the Swabian corner of the Empire, an inextricable maze of sovereignties and territorial configurations. The dynasty had originated here, in the undulating lowlands of northern Switzerland. By the sixteenth century it was quite driven from the lands of the Swiss Confederation, but it gained a congeries of other possessions over the years, in the desultory attempt to revive a 'duchy of Swabia'. They came to be known as the *Vorlande*, or Further Austria (though there is no precision of usage, even among historians).[8] Tolerably clear units were formed at either edge: to the west, the Sundgau and rights of overlordship in Alsace (until 1648), with the Breisgau and the city of Freiburg on the other side of the Rhine; to the east, the valleys and forests of Vorarlberg, adjoining the Tyrol, controlled by the towns of Bregenz, Feldkirch, and Bludenz. Between them lay Swabian Austria, where only a detailed historical atlas can help: four 'forest towns' (Rheinfelden, Laufenburg, Säckingen, Waldshut) and some surrounding land; the city of Constance, taken over in 1548; pieces of the Black Forest, including Triberg; the counties of Hohenberg and Sigmaringen; the landgravate of Nellenburg (a jigsaw of enclaves and outliers); some half-dozen towns along the upper Danube, with the margravate of Burgau beyond them; finally, a bewildering mixture of seigneurial and property rights designated (untranslatably) as the *Landvogtei* of Upper and Lower Swabia.

---

[7] The Adriatic area later became the 19th-century Austrian province of *Küstenland*. For Friuli as a whole: P. Paschini, *Storia del Friuli*, i–ii (2nd edn. Udine 1953–4), ii. For the Tirol: J. Egger, *Geschichte Tirols von den ältesten Zeiten bis in die Neuzeit*, i–iii (Innsbruck 1872–80), ii.

[8] F. Metz (ed.), *Vorderösterreich, eine geschichtliche Landeskunde* (2nd edn. Freiburg 1967), 47–65 and *passim*, is very helpful, with chapters on individual territories. J. A. Vann, *The Swabian Kreis* (Brussels 1975), 135 ff. *passim*, gives some examples of the extraordinary intricacy of overlordship. 'Vorderösterreich' and 'Vorlande' seem to be interchangeable expressions; both are frequently confused with 'Vorarlberg' and 'Österreich-Schwaben' (which were merely parts of the whole, the former more clearly defined than the latter), and both could also include the Tyrol. Under the dispensation of Maximilian I whereby the Austrian duchies, Styria, Carinthia, and Carniola were lumped together as 'Lower Austria', the *Vorlande* with Tyrol were designated 'Upper Austria'.

This was fragmentation run riot, but the rest of Austria preserved recognizable traces of similar features. In general, frontiers still fluctuated and some acquisitions were very recent. The Tyrol only rounded off its borders in the early sixteenth century: Rattenberg, Kitzbühel, and Kufstein were won from Bavaria in 1504; the Pustertal and Lienz from Gorizia in 1500; the Ampezzo area from Venice in 1516. The frontier between Upper Austria and Bavaria was still disputed, Maximilian I gaining the Mondsee region in 1506 (thus Michael Pacher's famous altarpiece at St. Wolfgang began its life in a *Bavarian* pilgrimage church), while isolated pieces of Habsburg land lay beyond, like the fortress of Neuburg am Inn, to sustain designs on the 'Innviertel' (only annexed by Joseph II as late as 1779). Continued Bavarian interest in Upper Austria is evident from Duke Maximilian's occupation of it during the 1620s. The line of the Hungarian frontier likewise lacked clarity, especially after the wars between Frederick III and Matthias Corvinus, when part of the area of the modern Burgenland became pledged to Lower Austria for nearly 200 years.[9]

Moreover a large number of enclaves remained. A few were those of lords owing allegiance to the emperor alone (not to the Habsburgs *qua* territorial princes): Schaunberg (Upper Austria) until the 1550s; Hardegg (Lower Austria); the lands of the Hohenems in Vorarlberg, including Lustenau and Schellenberg-Vaduz from 1613. Seefeld in Lower Austria was an imperial fief in the gift of the Hohenzollern family until 1779.[10] But most were Church lands: for not only did Austria owe preponderant allegiance to foreign ecclesiastical overlords (Salzburg, Passau, Trent, Constance, Chur, the disputed Aquileia, even the Hungarian see of Győr in part of Lower Austria), the same foreign bishops held estates there in full sovereignty from the early Middle Ages. Salzburg owned Gröbming (Styria), Sachsenburg, Althofen, Hüttenberg, and Friesach (Carinthia); Freising owned Waidhofen an der Ybbs (Lower Austria),

[9] A. Ernst, 'Zur Frage der von Ungarn an Österreich verpfändeten Herrschaften', MÖoLA v (1957), 387–412.
[10] These enclaves are described in *Handbuch der historischen Stätten*, ad loc. Cf., for the Schaunberg case: J. Stülz, 'Zur Geschichte der Herren und Grafen von Schaunberg', *Denkschriften der kais. Akademie der Wissenschaften, ph.-h. Kl.* xii (1862); O. Hageneder, 'Die Graftschaft Schaunberg', *MÖoLA* v (1957), 189–264; P. Feldbauer, *Der Herrenstand in Oberösterreich* (Munich 1972) 123–8.

Gross-Enzersdorf near Vienna, Innichen (Tyrol), and the substantial enclave of Bischoflack (Carniola); Bamberg possessed Villach, Wolfsberg, and Griffen (Carinthia). Oddest of all, the prince-bishopric of Brixen, though itself entirely surrounded by Austrian territory, consisted of eight different pieces of land in the southern Tyrol, some up to fifty miles from the cathedral city, as well as another substantial lump of Carniola (Veldes). Two villages in the Vorarlberg belonged as exempt jurisdictions to abbeys in Germany and Switzerland.[11]

All this diversity can be underlined by reference to racial and linguistic variations. Even among the German majority, long-standing differences of custom and dialect existed between the *Alemannen* west of the Arlberg and the descendants of Bavarian tribes east of it. To this day there are as many types of farmstead in Austria as provinces, some radically divergent in materials and design. While Teutons could be found in some numbers throughout the area—places as far south as Fiume (St. Veit am Flaum) boasted their distinctive German name—other peoples had their age-old settlements. French was spoken in Alsace, Romansch in remote corners of Vorarlberg, Ladin in south Tyrolese valleys, Slovene by a minority of Styrians and Carinthians and an overwhelming majority of Carniolans, Italian all around the southern periphery, from Bozen to Fiume, except in Friuli, whose population retained an unclassifiable local patois. Ethnographers could point to still further racial elements, such as the primitive, Romance-speaking Vlach tribesmen of Istria.

★

Vienna can hardly have known much about the Istro-Vlachs. Its central organs fought an unequal battle to give some cohesion to the *Erblande*. We have already met those two bodies which possessed an at least embryonic Austrian character: the Austrian chancery and the Court Chamber. Whereas the *Kanzler* and his staff really did little more than lend a certain Austrian dimension to supreme

---

[11] Blumenegg belonged to Weingarten between 1614 and 1802; St. Gerold belonged to Weingarten between 1614 and 1648, then to Einsiedeln until 1802. By the mid-16th century ecclesiastical rulers shared sovereignty over all these lands with the Habsburgs. The thorniest episcopal issue, unresolved for a further two hundred years, concerned the rights of the Venetian patriarch of Aquileia over Austria's southern confines (Paschini, op. cit. ii, 373–5, 384–9, 405 ff., 423 ff.).

decision-making, and a certain Habsburg dimension to the activities of provincial administrators and judges, the Chamber evolved a more far-reaching set of policies applicable to the whole region.[12] It managed a number of important industries. Salt for the domestic market was won from Hall in the Tyrol, the Istrian coast, and above all the crown preserve of the Salzkammergut (in Upper Austria and adjacent parts of Styria), where paternalist stewards regulated the lives of a workforce still tainted with Lutheranism, and special brine conduits supplied the boiling-pans at Ischl from the sombre fastnesses of Hallstatt and Aussee. Styrian iron production was handled, under official supervision, by a new and complicated holding enterprise called the *Innerberger Hauptgewerkschaft*. The rich mercury deposits at Idria, in Carniola, were taken in hand and exported throughout Europe. Wool manufacture, concentrated on Linz, had something approaching monopoly status from the 1670s, and employed over 4,000 workers in the earlier eighteenth century. Some of the royal forests were carefully husbanded, especially the Vienna Woods during the 1680s and 1690s.[13]

Behind this management lay increasingly the notion of commercial principle, mercantilism in a homespun Austrian guise. Its most influential spokesman was Philipp Wilhelm von Hörnigk, whose book *Österreich über alles, wenn es nur will* offered an overt manifesto for the economic self-sufficiency of the *Erblande*. A more imaginative apostle was Johann Joachim Becher, who set up silk farms in the Lower Austrian countryside and even a general house of trades in

---

[12] General surveys in K. and M. Uhlirz, *Handbuch der Geschichte Österreichs und seiner Nachbarländer Böhmen und Ungarn*, i–iv (Graz 1927–44), i, 295 ff.; Tremel, *Wirtschafts- und Sozialgeschichte*, 230 ff.; Hoffmann, op. cit, 175–224; Gutkas, op. cit. 265 ff.; E. Zöllner, *Geschichte Österreichs* (2nd edn. V: 1962) 278 ff.

[13] C. Schraml, *Das oberösterreichische Salinenwesen vom Beginne des 16. bis zur Mitte des 18. Jahrhunderts* i–iii (V. 1932–6). A. von Pantz, *Die Innerberger Hauptgewerkschaft, 1625–1783* (Graz 1906); I have not seen the earlier study by one Franz von Ferro (*sic*); cf. Metz (ed.), op. cit. 139–94. H. von Srbik, *Der staatliche Exporthandel Österreichs von Leopold I bis Maria Theresia* (V.–Leipzig 1907), despite its title, covers only the mercury and Hungarian copper trades (but very thoroughly). On the Linz *Wollenzeugfabrik*: V. Hofmann, 'Beiträge zur neueren österreichischen Wirtschaftsgeschichte', *AÖG* cviii (1919–20), 345–776, at 356 ff; its employees were not, of course, factory workers in the modern sense. On the *Wienerwald*: A. Schachinger, 'Das kaiserliche Waldamt und die Herrschaft Purkersdorf im letzten Viertel des 17. Jahrhunderts', *Jb. f. Lk. v. NÖ* xxix (1944–8), 167–272, complete to the last log.

Vienna.[14] Becher's younger associate, Wilhelm von Schröder, gave theoretical and practical support to the same causes, while some enterprise could be attracted and capital raised by granting privileges to outsiders: immigrant artisans, a few Protestant merchants, and the occasional court Jew, notably Leopold I's principal factor and banker, Samuel Oppenheimer, and his successor, Samson Wertheimer.[15] Yet the overall government achievement must be accounted slight. Much trading remained in the grossly inefficient and grasping hands of concessionaries—this so-called *Appalt* system embraced items as varied as tobacco, scythes, oysters, and carnival masks. Even the *Innerberger Hauptgewerkschaft* was still a private company, while Idrian mercury fell by the end of the period into the clutches of Dutch middlemen. Becher's projects scarcely outlived him, and he can have done little to scare the sturdy beggars of the capital. The great age of cameralism came only later, reaching Austria from active bases in eighteenth-century Germany; and even then it did not prove the engine for any overnight economic unification of the *Erblande*.

There was thus no effective central imposition of an Austrian identity. In fact the dynasty did not take the most elementary steps towards it. Branches of the ruling house set up at Graz and Innsbruck were extinguished only by genealogical accident: Graz with Ferdinand II; Innsbruck, its autonomy prolonged under his younger brother, when the latter's sons died out in 1665 and no other males remained besides Emperor Leopold. The morganatic sons of Archduke Ferdinand and Philippine Welser received rich apanages: Andreas in the Church, Karl in Further Austria. Moreover, separate administrative machinery survived still later, with governments and privy councils in Graz and Innsbruck, the chambers for Inner Austria and the Tyrol, and the active, independent war council in Graz which maintained the south-western section of the military frontier.[16] In remote areas the writ

---

[14] H. Hassinger, *Johann Joachim Becher, ein Beitrag zur Geschichte des Merkantilismus* (V. 1951), 138 ff.; two further documents on sericulture in OSzK, MSS. 637 and 965 fol. germ. Cf. below, p. 297, on the careers of Hörnigk and Becher.

[15] M Grunwald, *Samuel Oppenheimer und sein Kreis* (V. 1913); S. Stern, *The Court Jew* (Philadelphia 1950), 17–31, 85–93.

[16] For Tyrol before 1618: J. Hirn, *Erzherzog Ferdinand II von Tirol*, i–ii (Innsbruck 1885–8), a detailed internal history (ibid. ii, 369–420, on Karl and Andreas); id., *Erzherzog Maximilian, der Deutschmeister*, i–ii (Innsbruck 1915–36). For the later

of regional capitals ran further, for most purposes, than that of Vienna: Graz sent instructions over the Karawanken into the barren Slovene karstlands; Innsbruck was responsible for the whole of the *Vorlande*. Only the Austrian duchies stood directly under imperial sway. We cannot even think of this as a 'trialist' arrangement; for officials served the Habsburgs day by day in a strictly local capacity which they were neither eager nor encouraged to exceed. Saving the occasional employment of a stadholder as immediate representative of the sovereign, each province, large or small, had its lord-lieutenant (*Landeshauptmann*; in Lower Austria: *Landmarschall*) appointed by the prince to transmit decrees, preside over courts, and maintain order with the help of a deputy (*Landesverweser*; in Lower Austria: *Landuntermarschall*), a number of counsellors (*Regierungsräte*), and the administrators of local regalia (*Vicedome*), who mainly managed crown estates, but also exercised protective rights over Church land, Jews, travellers, and others.[17]

Provincial governments formed bodies of authority which during the eighteenth century would come to be called *Gubernia* and be used under Maria Theresa and Joseph II to spread a reform programme through the Monarchy over the heads of sectional interests. Before 1740, however, their role was different. They *enshrined* sectional interests, in a constitutional arrangement which can be neither called 'absolutist' nor identified as merely one stage in the transition to more efficient *gubernial* control. Two traditional restraints on princely sovereignty help to account for the limited extent of Habsburg intervention in the Austrian regions. The first was the *Landrecht*, the 'law of the land', whose evolution through the later Middle Ages—as the work of Otto Brunner has so persuasively shown—served to distinguish each *Land*, or province,

---

17th century: Egger, op. cit. ii, 434 ff., *passim.* V. Thiel, 'Die innerösterreichische Zentralverwaltung 1564–1749', *AÖG* cv (1916), 1–209; cxi (1929–30), 497–644, is very thorough on the institutions at Graz, both before and after 1619. Until 1635 'Lower Austria' (in Maximilian I's sense) actually had a *separate* Chamber (O. Brunner, 'Das Archiv der niederösterreichischen Kammer und des Vizedoms in Österreich unter der Enns und seine Bedeutung für die Landesgeschichte', *Jb. f. Lk. v. NÖ* xxix (1944–8), 144–66).

[17] Luschin, *Reichsgeschichte*, 189–92, 436, etc.; Gutkas, op. cit. 179 f., 244, 263; Brunner, 'Archiv'. There appears to be no full study of this subject.

and demarcate it from its neighbours.[18] The *Landrecht*, being divinely appointed, was held binding on all, including the ruler, and reflected a complex hierarchy of powers and mutual obligations. And the second restraining influence belonged to the very guarantors of the *Landrecht*: the provincial estates, which have rarely been accorded the attention they deserve in the political history of seventeenth-century Central Europe.

The estates, though their composition differed somewhat from *Land* to *Land*, always included clergy, nobility, and towns. In the Tyrol, Vorarlberg, and parts of Further Austria, communities of peasants also elected representatives. In practice, since the prelates were largely assimilated, the towns largely ignored, and the peasants a marginal and incohesive force, it was nobles who dominated, either as a single, consolidated estate, or more often as separate estates of lords and knights. Throughout the period these *Landstände* remained a crucial focus of local identity; it is striking how the few territories, in Swabia, which had previously lacked them, now witnessed their belated emergence.[19] Provincial diets bargained with the crown by offer and counter-offer, alternately discussing the princely propositions and advancing their own grievances, haggling over taxes and approving recruits. Far from abolishing any of them, the dynasty actually seems to have encouraged their local patriotism, perhaps from a fear of any revival of the general *Landtage* which so suited Protestant activists during the sixteenth

---

[18] Brunner, *Land und Herrschaft*, with an appendix (pp. 441–63) specifically on the evolution of the Austrian *Länder*.

[19] For the earlier period: ibid. 394–440, and Luschin, *Reichsgeschichte*, 160–84. There is a good general survey in Hassinger, 'Landstände' (rather fuller than id., 'Ständische Vertretungen in den althabsburgischen Ländern und in Salzburg', *Ständische Vertretungen in Europa im 17. und 18. Jahrhundert* (Göttingen 1969), 247–285). A. F. Pribram, 'Die niederösterreichischen Stände und die Krone in der Zeit Kaiser Leopold I', *MIÖG* xiv (1893), 589–652, is the only study set squarely in the later 17th century. A. Jäger, *Geschichte der landständischen Verfassung Tirols*, i–ii (Innsbruck 1881–5), ii, 1–2, covers the medieval evolution of the Tyrolean estates; Egger, op. cit. ii, *passim*, has much on the proceedings of 16th- and 17th-century diets there; N. Grass, 'Aus der Geschichte der Landstände Tirols', *Album H. M. Cam* i–ii (Louvain—Paris 1961), ii, 299–324, summarizes the Tyrolean evidence. N. Sapper, *Die schwäbisch-österreichischen Landstände und Landtage im 16. Jahrhundert* (Stuttgart 1965). P. Blickle, *Landschaften im Alten Reich* (Munich 1973), on the question of peasant estates in Tyrol (pp. 54–9, 159–254), Vorarlberg (74 f., 255–315), Habsburg Swabia (96–108), and the rest of *Vorderösterreich* (128–39).

and early seventeenth centuries. After all, centralized government could easily generate centralized opposition.

Yet diets as such did not form the real locus of estates' strength after 1620. Their meetings became irregular and thinly attended, their debates mediocre and mechanical. Rather, noble interests were protected by permanent provincial institutions and personnel. For continuous management of their affairs the diets elected well-paid delegates (*Verordnete*), responsible to themselves, who collected taxes, met the needs of defence, raised military levies, and so on. Moreover, candidates for the post of *Landeshauptmann*, whose duties included acting as princely commissioner to the diet, were nominated by the estates and answerable to them as well as to the ruler; thus they possessed a dual function in which local loyalties had full play. And the apparatus of seventeenth-century provincial control—the *Landschaft*, as it was loosely called—went much further: all kinds of experts (especially jurists), servants and concessionaries, customs and excise officials, teachers and doctors, printers and architects, even painters and cooks, were overseen and paid by the estates.[20] As administration grew more complex and taxation more ingenious, their share of government actually increased. At the same time the *Landrecht* found its active defenders, both among trained nobles and among the semi-autonomous legal officers attached to the *Landschaft*.[21]

This *modus vivendi* between court and country was no longer, of course, the organic medieval balance. Sixteenth-century contests left their mark: now the heritage of shared power gave way to a

---

[20] Luschin, op. cit. 440 ff. (a section which surely belies his view of estates' decline expressed ibid., 403–18); Pribram, 'Stände', 598 ff.; Thiel, art, cit. esp. 531 ff.; Hassinger, 'Landstände', 1019 ff. F. Popelka in F. Tremel (ed.), *Die Landeshauptleute im Herzogtume Steiermark* (Graz 1962), 30–2, is quite wrong to call the *Landeshauptmann* a mere '*Beamter*': in the 17th century his Carinthian equivalent was paid 2,000 gulden annually by the estates, only 500 by the crown, and the estates actually exercised legal control over his capital, Klagenfurt (Braumüller, op. cit. 302 f., 242 ff.). On the defensive function: W. Schulze, *Landesdefension und Staatsbildung, Studien zum Kriegswesen des innerösterreichischen Territorialstaates, 1564–1619* (V.– Cologne–Graz 1973).

[21] F. Wisnicki, 'Die Geschichte der Abfassung des Tractatus de Juribus incorporabilibus', *Jb. f. Lk. v. NÖ* xx (1926–7), 69–91; Luschin, op. cit. 351–64; cf. Thiel, art. cit. 588–95, on the office of the Inner Austrian *Kammerprokurator*. Estates' lawyers were basically conservative in their mentality; they shared common ground—though they might be in dispute—with spokesmen for more fully-fledged Habsburg positions (cf. above, pp. 105–7).

more conscious political alliance. The unspoken assumption behind
the bargain was a firm maintenance of *Herrschaft*, that fundament
of the Central European power structure whose consolidation in
this period we have already observed. Although in Austria the
manorial system still allowed some peasant self-government and
self-respect, it meant a rock-like invulnerability to outside interference. Individual *Herrschaften* were the irreducible units of fragmentation, their boundaries the basic constitutents of regional geography. Between Feldsberg and Eisgrub, Liechtenstein lands
straddled the Lower Austrian–Moravian frontier, taking next to no
account of its existence. When Esterházys and Batthyánys acquired
estates in the border region south-east of Vienna, they *ipso facto*
took the area back under the sovereignty of the Hungarian crown.[22]

In such matters the Habsburgs readily acquiesced. Their own
latifundia were run with full respect for the *genius loci*, *Vicedome* and
bailiffs often being drawn from the local petty nobility, courts
judging by common law, including a welter of particular jurisdictions: special tribunals for mines and wines, forests and rivers,
soldiers and Jews.[23] More significantly, the dynasty encouraged
private latifundia through the continuing alienation of crown lands.
In Lower Austria the bulk of the *Kammergut* was sold off between
1575 and 1625, and most of the rest later passed to Prince Eugene.
In Upper Austria crown estates—apart from the Salzkammergut—
had effectively disappeared by 1650. The Hohenems in Vorarlberg
were one powerful family among many who profited by this policy,
or lack of policy. Thus fewer and fewer Austrian peasants were
direct subjects of their sovereign, and the tentative measures taken
to protect them counted for little compared with the favour shown
towards landlords' interests. Divergent evolutions in Habsburg and
Venetian Friuli after 1500 are particularly instructive: the one area
dominated by a clique of so-called *strumieri* nobles, the other
safeguarding the rights of townsmen and tenantry.[24]

---

[22] Forchtenstein and Kobersdorf passed to Hungary in 1626, Hornstein and
Eisenstadt in 1647: Gutkas, op. cit. 244; *Handbuch der historischen Stätten*, i, 706
[23] Luschin, op. cit. 457–60; Metz (ed.), op. cit. 401–66.
[24] Tremel, *Wirtschafts- und Sozialgeschichte*, 248 f. For Lower Austria (which still
had a large extent of crown land in the early 16th century (Gutkas, op. cit. 151)):
Brunner, 'Archiv', 153. For Upper Austria: Stieve, *Bauernaufstand*, i, 3, 16–18;
Hoffmann, op. cit. 86. On the peasants see E. Patzelt, 'Bauernschutz in Österreich
vor 1848', *MIÖG* lviii (1950), 637–55; and above, p. 90. Paschini, op. cit. ii, 379 ff.

★

It might appear odd that seventeenth-century Austria lacked both strong government and strong opposition. In fact neither was necessary, and the occasional conflicts between princely commissioners and refractory diets involved little more than shadow-boxing. Beneath the constitutional surface dynastic and noble interests were hammered together in a series of workmanlike compromises and sealed with the stamp of Counter-Reformation. In Austria, as in the rest of the Monarchy, the crucial link was a rising group, small and close-knit, of aristocratic families whose compact with the like-minded dynasty would remain stable so long as the ethos of Catholic Baroque prevailed. Most had been Protestant; often conversion assured not only their political fortune, but a claim on the possessions of less dexterous members of the same house. All founded their pre-eminence squarely on landed property, which allowed them to dominate provincial administration and justice. They enjoyed a near monopoly of posts as *Landeshauptmann*, as *Regierungsrat*, as *Landrat* advising on the management of regalia; they controlled the local *Landgericht*, with its capital powers (*Blutbann*), and supervised its sessions in their own castles by the seventeenth century.[25] The estates of the magnates extended within their native region and beyond it; they thus formed a prime factor in countervailing the extremely centrifugal tendencies of Habsburg Central Europe. Many aristocrats purchased lands in several provinces, including Bohemia and sometimes Hungary; or at least they gained the right of naturalization, called *Landstandschaft* in Austria, *inkolát* in Bohemia, *indigenatus* (or *honfiusitás*) in Hungary, necessary for office and influence there. Their arrangements would be confirmed with one or more *Fideicommissa*, usually for the eldest son, while other members of the clan could be provided for at court, in the Church, in the army or diplomatic service.

All this found favour with the emperors: indeed, it parallels the Habsburgs' view of their own patrimony, cementing together a familial inheritance and later explicitly entailing it by the device of Charles VI's Pragmatic Sanction. Sometimes the favour extended to large grants of money and land, but these were not decisive, any

---

[25] Cf. above, p. 92, n. 26. In 1801 (when precise figures are available) there were 216 *Landgerichte* in Lower Austria, 100 in Upper Austria, 136 in Styria, 63 in Carinthia, 74 in Carniola and Istria (Luschin, op. cit. 193 f.).

more than that most obvious evidence of grace, noble titles, created an aristocracy. Rather they crowned the success of a limited number of families, most of whom were long established in some part of Central Europe. And no real inflation of honours took place: while between 1620 and 1720 212 newcomers joined the ranks of the Lower Austrian *Herrenstand*,[26] the 103 from within the province were mainly established notables, while the 109 outsiders were often only formally naturalized. But what had earlier been a comparatively open society, with regular movement up and down the scale and genuine feudal obligations, now turned into a more and more exclusive caste, perpetuating a few dozen potent aristocratic names till the very end of the Monarchy.

There no more existed an 'Austrian' nobility than an 'Austrian' government. But the *Erblande* were a common denominator between the *Reich* and the rest of the Monarchy, and as such they occupy an important place in the development of this social élite. The grant of titles and predicates was a very complicated matter, with fine shades of meaning now difficult to grasp. Basically two kinds lay in the Habsburg gift: imperial; and domestic—Austrian, Bohemian, Hungarian. In fact the categories overlapped considerably, and even contemporaries might be uncertain where 'Austria' stopped and the others began. Traditional imperial nobility had been distinguished by the conferment of immediate status (*Reichsunmittelbarkeit*), which went with possession of a territory subject only to the emperor and a voice—however insignificant—in the imperial constitution. That criterion was no longer very strictly applied, and the more imperial titles became a mere courtesy, the more they were sought after by lesser ranks, though the ultimate cachet remained a full sovereign principality, margravate, county, or lordship situated within the *Reich*. High nobles in Austria were thus a hybrid group, undergoing an increasingly elaborate process of differentiation.[27]

[26] Gutkas, op. cit. 234. Such figures need careful interpretation; cf. the garbled information about some 200 'new' aristocrats in *Status Particularis Regiminis ... Ferdinandi II* (n. p. 1637), 203–13, often repeated by later writers. Cf. above, pp. 93 f.; below, pp. 200 ff., 240 ff.

[27] Older titles in the Holy Roman Empire were tied to territories and could not be multiplied. Thus there were only seven ancient dukedoms, such as Saxony, besides the separate case of the less prestigious Silesian duchies (Wallenstein's dukedom of Friedland and Eggenberg's of Krumlov, like the later (1780s) Lobkovic dukedom of

Let us examine some paradigms of worldly success in seventeenth-century Austria.[28] The pinnacle of achievement was princely status, and before 1600 no Habsburg subject belonged in this category (except in so far as individual members of ruling houses from the *Reich* occasionally served and settled in Austria). The first to be elevated was Karl Liechtenstein (1569–1627). The Liechtensteins were a prominent family established in several of the Austrian lands, and although Karl's branch was not particularly well endowed, his father had already begun to consolidate a group of properties along the Lower Austrian–Moravian border. Karl's spectacular preferment displays three conspicuous features: marriage to a rich neighbouring heiress, conversion to Catholicism, and assiduous, unscrupulous service of both Rudolf and Matthias (a real feat of squaring the circle, since he did not entirely alienate either), as well as of Ferdinand II later. By 1608 he was a prince, then by 1613 Duke of Troppau in Silesia; during the 1620s, as governor of Bohemia, he made large acquisitions, including another Silesian duchy (Jägerndorf). His son, Karl Eusebius (1611–84), and grandson, Johann Adam (1656–1712), were both *primus inter pares* among the Austrian aristocracy of their time. Meanwhile Karl's brothers and fellow-converts, Maximilian and Gundakar, followed him in gaining the highest rank and riches through a politic dedication to the dynasty. One thing further was required to complete the panoply: the early eighteenth-century purchase by the Liechtensteins of Vaduz and

Raudnitz, were *Bohemian* titles). No more margraves or landgraves or territorial palsgraves came into being (the courtly *comes palatinus* was a different, and lesser dignity). New creations were either as princes (*Fürsten*), counts (*Grafen*), or barons (*Freiherren*), with a subdivision among the princes according to whether other members of the family could call themselves prince (*Prinz*) or merely count. The new prince did not need to possess a principality; it sufficed to own (or acquire) a county, which the emperor could elevate, by a legal fiction, to quasi-princely status (as a *gefürstete Grafschaft*). By the later 17th century it became possible to be made imperial count without owning landed property outside Austria at all (the *Reichsgrafen* von Windischgrätz are an early example), and that continued in the 18th century (cf. H. Gollwitzer, *Die Standesherren* (Stuttgart 1957), 37–9).

[28] This information is not easy to bring together. The essential source are the sixty volumes of Wurzbach, one of the most remarkable compendia ever written by one man: extremely well-informed and packed with detail, but diffuse, sometimes inaccurate or misleading, very much fuller of genealogical material in later than earlier volumes. Zedler likewise contains a mass of miscellaneous information, some of it almost contemporary. They may be supplemented, for certain families, by *OSN* (cf. below, p. 201, n. 14).

Schellenberg, two remote and impoverished, but sovereign territories within the *Reich* which, having assumed the name of their
new possessors, would—uniquely—outlive even the Habsburg
Monarchy itself.[29]

Three, briefly four, families joined the Liechtensteins in the
1620s. The Lobkovices, Dukes of Sagan, princely counts of
Sternstein, were, and remained, predominantly Bohemian; I shall
discuss them—and the Waldstein case, so soon revoked—in the
next chapter. The Dietrichsteins formed another ramified clan
whose most notable branch, much advanced by Adam Dietrichstein
as major-domo to Maximilian II, owned lands adjacent to the
Liechtensteins' in southern Moravia, while other lines inhabited
Lower Austria, Carinthia, and Styria. Adam's son Franz was the
Cardinal Bishop of Olomouc we have already met. His princely title
passed to a nephew, Maximilian, major-domo to Ferdinand III
from 1650 to 1655, whose son, Ferdinand Joseph, performed the
same office for Leopold I between 1683 and 1698. Meanwhile the
Lower Austrian Dietrichsteins reached the same rank via Gundakar,
imperial master of the horse and high chamberlain in the same
period.[30] The Eggenbergs are a different story: burghers at
Radkersburg in Southern Styria in the fifteenth century, leading
citizens and financiers of Graz, but still bourgeois, in the sixteenth.
Their status rose through Rupprecht (1546–1611), who commanded
Habsburg armies in the Low Countries and Hungary, then more
precipitately through Ferdinand II's close confidant and first
minister, the convert Hans Ulrich, created prince in 1623 and Duke
of Krumlov in Bohemia five years later. His son, Johann Anton,
besides owning vast tracts in Bohemia, Styria, and Carniola, bought
from Ferdinand III the county of Gradisca in Friuli, thus gaining
the accolade of immediate imperial sovereignty. But the family
made little use of it: Johann Anton died young and his two sons
squabbled over their spoils. Between 1713 and 1717, by a Baroque
gesture of fate, three generations of the house died out and the
Eggenbergs were extinguished in the male line, leaving only Hans
Ulrich's superb palace outside Graz as their memorial.[31]

[29] J. Falke, *Geschichte des fürstlichen Hauses Liechtenstein*, ii (V. 1877), is thorough,
especially on Karl (pp. 127–242).
[30] Wurzbach is brief, Zedler rather confusing; best is *OSN*, s.v.
[31] W. E. Heydendorff, *Die Fürsten und Freiherren zu Eggenberg und ihre Vorfahren*

The rest of the seventeenth century brought four more princely elevations. The last of them, the Hungarian Esterházys (1687) will concern us later;[32] the other three: Auersperg (1653), Portia (1662), and Schwarzenberg (1670), illustrate some of the features we have already discerned. The Auersperg were venerable nobility of Carniola, important, but dispersed into several lines, advanced to a larger significance by Ferdinand III's and Leopold's formidable minister, Johann Weickard (1615–77), who became Duke of Münsterberg and Frankenstein in Silesia and princely count of the Empire as ruler of Thengen in Swabia. Though Johann Weickart eventually overreached himself and lost favour at court, the family sustained its initiative over the next generations. Not so the Friulian Portias, thrust into prominence through Leopold's boyhood favourite, Johann Ferdinand (1606–65), and sovereign counts of Tettensee (also in Swabia) from 1689. The Portias too had every opportunity to exert influence, but like the Eggenbergs they made no further attempt to advance beyond an inherited social prestige. They lived quietly on for centuries in the grand Renaissance *palazzo* at Spittal an der Drau (Carinthia), originally built for Ferdinand I's Spanish protégés, the Salamancas, and acquired by Johann Ferdinand; in all that time they added nothing to it but their coat-of-arms.[33]

The Schwarzenbergs represent a different case again. By origin a German family with possessions in Franconia, they gained Habsburg gratitude through Count Adolf (died 1600), like Rupprecht von Eggenberg a hero of the Ottoman wars, his son

(Graz 1965), a useful summary. H. Zwiedineck-Südenhorst, *Hans Ulrich Fürst von Eggenberg* (V. 1880), is a disappointing biography of an elusive figure; cf. id., 'Ruprecht von Eggenberg', *MHVSt* xxvi (1878), 79–163.

[32] There were in fact two more princely creations in this period which have some reference to Austria: Piccolomini (1650), and Montecuccoli (1689)—the only military examples, besides Wallenstein (who was anyway a prince before he commanded in battle). But they only belong here marginally: neither was a Habsburg subject by birth, and neither family subsequently played any public role in the Monarchy. Piccolominis lived in Bohemia until the 1770s; the Montecuccoli princedom was established only for Raimondo's son, and it died with him in 1700.

[33] Cf. above, p. 144 and n. 69. I have found scarcely anything at all on the Auerspergs (they came too early in the alphabet for the mature Wurzbach); out cf. *OSN*, s.v. G. Probszt-Ohstorff, *Die Porcia, Aufstieg und Wirken eines Fürstenhauses* (Klagenfurt 1971), an interesting study, does not alter the impression of the Portias' profound lack of sparkle.

Adam (1584–1641), the imperial-minded confidant of the electors of Brandenburg, and their distant relation Georg Ludwig (1586–1646), a soldier and diplomat. Georg Ludwig acquired rich lands in Styria by a most remarkable marriage: in 1617, at the age of thirty-one, he became the sixth and last husband of Anna Neumann, then eighty-two years old, the immensely wealthy daughter of a mill-owner and aristocratic widow, a sort of Central European Bess of Hardwick. On his death these estates passed to the single surviving member of the family, Adam's son Johann Adolf (1614–83), president of the Aulic Council, major-domo, and prince of the Empire; then to two more only sons, Ferdinand (1652–1703) and Adam Franz (1680–1732). During this time the acquisitions continued through purchase and inheritance: by his death Adam Franz was ruler of three separate imperial counties (in Franconia, Swabia, and Westphalia), Duke of Krumlov as successor to the Eggenbergs, and owner of further Bohemian latifundia at Třeboň and Hluboká, not to speak of the Inner Austrian lands. He even approached a little too close to his sovereign, for Charles VI mortally wounded him with an accidental shot while they were hunting near Prague. 'It was ever my duty', Schwarzenberg exclaimed before expiring, 'to give my life for my sovereign.'[34]

*

The Schwarzenbergs (for all Adam Franz's death-bed deference) had evidently developed into a full-scale dynasty, and on that level these key elements in the Habsburg system of government deserve our attention. Like the ruling house they became centred on Vienna, but not narrowly 'Austrian'; they were poised between old provincial and new cosmopolitan ties. Much the same is true of the nobility which stood immediately below the princes on the ladder of preferment. There were perhaps 200 or so families of counts in the *Erblande* by the end of the seventeenth century. Almost all of them maintained some contact with the court and the Habsburg dynasty; most were designated honorary chamberlains in the imperial entourage. But a far smaller number played any active role

[34] A. E. Berger, *Felix Fürst zu Schwarzenberg* (Leipzig 1853), 3–150 (p. 134 for the story of Adam Franz's death); K. Schwarzenberg, *Geschichte des reichsständischen Hauses Schwarzenberg*, i(Neustadt a. d. Aisch 1963), 116 ff., on Johann Adolf and his heirs; A. Wolf, *Geschichtliche Bilder aus Österreich*, i–ii (V. 1878–80), ii, 146–97, on Ferdinand.

in the common affairs of Austria, and these would regularly be rewarded, during the eighteenth or early nineteenth century, by further grants of princely status.[35]

From the southernmost province of Carniola came the Lambergs, an extraordinarily prolific clan which spread into almost all the other crownlands, producing an archbishop of Prague at the beginning of the century, the young Joseph I's inseparable companion at the end, and an important imperial major-domo in between. Carinthia housed the Hochosterwitz branch of the Khevenhüllers, determined Protestants in their time, but restored to favour with the convert Ehrenreich (died in 1675), and the Orsini-Rosenbergs, one of whom was president of the *Hofkammer* during the 1680s. Friuli spawned the *strumieri* families of Colloredo, spreading to Bohemia in this period, and Thurn-Valsassina, whose tentacles reached throughout Inner Austria too (their more famous cousins of Thurn und Taxis remained primarily Italian and German-based).[36] Styria was dominated by (besides Eggenberg, Schwarzenberg, and a secondary Dietrichstein line) Stubenbergs, Herbersteins, Sauraus, Trautmannsdorfs, and Windischgrätzes. All had produced leading Protestants at the Reformation; all shed some members during the banishments of the 1620s; all recovered and flourished after their return to Roman Catholicism. The Herbersteins gave five lord-lieutenants to the province between 1556 and 1679, and their various lines gradually settled throughout the Monarchy. The Trautmannsdorfs used the leverage of Ferdinand III's intimate friend Maximilian to establish themselves northward in Austria and Bohemia, and produced a notable clutch of officers for the Habsburg armies. The Windischgrätzes had likewise expanded into Lower Austria: the convert Gottlieb (1630–95),

---

[35] Since these later princely elevations—like the 17th-century countly ones—usually reflect confirmation, in return for an appropriate money payment, of positions already acquired, I have included their dates in the index. All such pre-1806 creations were nominally extended to the Holy Roman Empire. Lists of chamberlains may be found in the *Hofstaaten*: e.g. *Status Particularis*, ch. 8; ÖNB, MS. 12388, fols. 11–20.

[36] Besides Wurzbach (who brings some order even into the near-impenetrable complexities of the Lamberg *Stammtafel*), there is B. Czerwenka, *Die Khevenhüller, Geschichte des Geschlechts* (V. 1867); cf., on Ehrenreich Khevenhüller's son, Sigismund Friedrich: Wolf, *Geschichtliche Bilder*, ii, 198–243; and M. Breunlich-Pawlik in *MÖStA* xxvi (1973), 235–53.

son of an *émigré*, became imperial vice-chancellor, and his son was president of the Aulic Council.[37] In the Tyrol and *Vorlande*, local empire-building bulked particularly large. Powerful families like Brandis, Spaur, and Wolkenstein looked to the perquisites of the Innsbruck administration and the Alpine bishoprics; while in Vorarlberg two sovereign imperial clans, Hohenems and Montfort, preserved and even (for a while) increased the autonomy of their miscellaneous territories and fiefs.[38]

Above all the duchies below and above the Enns, whose nobilities already overlapped greatly, even in the sixteenth century, threw up the families which consolidated their hold on Austria during the Counter-Reformation era. One of them was the Starhemberg, with its strong line in military heroes, above all the celebrated Ernst Rüdiger who defended Vienna in 1683, and Prince Eugene's deputy, Count Guido. Another was the Frankenburg branch of the Khevenhüllers, influential at court especially through the annalist and diplomat, Franz Christoph (1588–1650), and his grandson, Field Marshal Ludwig Andreas (1683–1744).[39] Both Starhembergs and Khevenhüllers had their fair share of Protestant rebels; so did the Sinzendorfs, whose generation of converts included Johann Joachim (died in 1665), Austrian chancellor between 1656 and 1665, and the notorious *Hofkammer* embezzler, Georg Ludwig, and—not to be confused with them!—the Zinzendorfs, who actually became more famous in their Saxon exile, though they also had a thriving Roman Catholic branch. In the case of the Kuefsteins, the

---

[37] Only Stubenbergs (J. Loserth, *Geschichte des altsteirischen Herren- und Grafenhauses Stubenberg* (Graz–Leipzig 1911)) and—less satisfactorily—Herbersteins (J. A. Kumar, *Geschichte der Burg und Familie Herberstein*, i–iii (V. 1817)) have found their historian, though Wurzbach is strong on them all. Cf. Wolf, *Geschichtliche Bilder*, ii, 89–145 for a Trautmannsdorf soldier (Sigismund Joachim); the absence of any biography of Maximilian Trautmannsdorf remains a great lacuna in the literature on Austria and the Thirty Years War.

[38] L. Welti, *Graf Kaspar von Hohenems 1573–1640* (Innsbruck 1963), mainly a family and cultural study; B. Lifka, 'Knižní dědictví Hohenembsů z Kunwaldu', *Str. Kn.* iv (1969), 152–81, is a pendant to it. See in general *Handbuch der historischen Stätten*, ii, 393–577, *passim*.

[39] The Starhembergs have attracted several biographers: A. Thürheim, *Feldmarschall Ernst Rüdiger von Starhemberg* (V. 1882); A. Arneth, *Das Leben des Grafen Guido von Starhemberg* (V. 1853); B. Holl, *Hofkammerpräsident Gundaker T. Starhemberg und die österreichische Finanzpolitik der Barockzeit* (V. 1976). On the Khevenhüller-Frankenburgs: Czerwenka, op. cit.; and Wolf, *Geschichtliche Bilder*, i, 113–71.

same individual was both Lutheran and Catholic politician: Johann Ludwig (1587–1657) led the moderate opposition to Ferdinand II in Lower Austria, then converted after the White Mountain and served the emperor as *Landeshauptmann* of Upper Austria. His successors followed the familiar road to latifundium and *Fideicommissum* (at Greillenstein). Even the Jörgers, most militant members of the Lutheran estates, recovered their ground by mid-century, and the convert Johann Quintin, grandson of the insurgent generation, rose to be vice-president of the *Hofkammer* and stadholder in Lower Austria.[40] Genetical chance extinguished the Jörgers soon after 1700, as it did the Trautsons, originally Tyroleans, major holders of court office between Maximilian II and Charles VI, and the historic house of Puchheim, whose name—as it were a trade-mark of quality, though they had been heavily implicated in the revolt of 1620—was assumed by the purchaser of their lands, the German imperial vice-chancellor, Karl Friedrich von Schönborn. But most of these families built for a long-term ascendancy, in both Austria and the rest of the Monarchy. The Harrachs, who had long ago originated in Bohemia, spread back there in the decades when Ernst Adalbert (1598–1667) was archbishop of Prague. The Althans, especially Michael Adolf, a convert in 1636, followed the Liechtensteins into the borderlands of Moravia. Breuners and Wurmbrands maintained their historical links with Styria; Abensberg-Trauns bought an immediate county in Swabia as early as 1658.[41]

The magnates thus had one foot in the provinces, the other in court service. Sometimes that service proved highly remunerative. We have already seen some examples of fortunes furthered thereby, and shall meet others in Bohemia and Hungary: one or two outstanding individuals make it possible for their successors to participate (if they wish) at the highest levels of Habsburg government. They receive handsome favours, culminating in imperial immediate status, which suited both sides, for the

[40] For the Kuefsteins: K. Kuefstein, *Studien zur Familiengeschichte*, i–iii (V.–Leipzig 1908–15), ii–iii, ancestor-worship of the best kind; and, on Johann Ludwig: Wolf, *Geschichtliche Bilder*, i, 238–305; and Wiedemann, *Reformation*, i, 614–16. For the Jörgers: Wurm, op. cit. (198–205 on Johann Quintin).

[41] There is little about these families outside the pages of Wurzbach, but *OSN* has a good article on Harrach. The Puchheims (or Buchheims) must be sought in Zedler, s.v. 'Buchaim'.

Habsburgs gained—besides the fees for patents of higher nobility—
a loyal voice in the *Reich*, even if they had to alienate Austrian
territory to do so, as with Gradisca, or Thengen, or the
Dietrichsteins' sovereign enclave of Tarasp in the Engadine. A
further and curious case is that of the Counts Paar, organizers of the
Austrian postal system and holders of the resonant title of *Obrist-
Reichs-Hof- und General-Erblandpostmeister*.

Yet the basic unit was always the family, and the family did not
suffer even if an individual fell from grace: witness the Auerspergs
and Lobkovices in the 1670s, even the Waldsteins in Bohemia after
1634 and Nádasdys in Hungary after 1671.[42] The Thurns and
Schlicks, suitably Catholicized, rose as high as the Martinices and
Slavatas whom they had been largely instrumental in defenestrating.
The Sinzendorfs easily survived the discomfiture of their arch-
peculator, Georg Ludwig; indeed, his son served as court chancellor
under Joseph I and Charles VI. Of course, families could be large
or small, and accidents of heredity played their part, the Schwarzenberg, for example, prospering by extreme concentration (seven
successive only sons), the Lamberg or Herberstein by an amoeboid
process of subdivision. But overall it was the gradual accumulation
from generation to generation of landed wealth and social prestige
which permitted the high aristocrats their remarkable dominance.
They alone could afford diplomatic missions and jobs at an often
insolvent court. They had the means and the incentive to indulge
a taste for conspicuous religion. They possessed the resources for
palaces and gardens, for festivities and art, for the whole grand
adventure of the Austrian Baroque.

There remained another nobility, regional and less conspicuous,
consisting mostly of barons and mere knights of the shire. It was
firmly entrenched, representing a (usually unarticulated) local
patriotism and a traditional view of *Herrschaft*. Two men illustrate
it at its best: Wolf Helmhard von Hohberg (1612–88), author of the
Georgica curiosa oder adeliges Landleben, with its intimate picture of
the customary landowner and his concerns; and Johann Weickard
von Valvasor (1641–93), whose mammoth *Ehre des Hertzogthums*

---

[42] On whom see below, pp. 205 f., 242. Karl Marx was surely wrong to regard the
entailed estate as destructive of family solidarity (see S. Avineri, *The social and
political thought of Karl Marx* (Cambridge 1968), 27–9).

Crain is unsurpassed as a loving portrait of an Austrian countryside and its inhabitants.[43] This nobility was stronger in some areas, especially the *Vorlande*, than in others, but it generally appears subservient, disorganized, and decaying. The fate of Protestantism helped to break its back—even Hohberg ended his days as an exile in Regensburg—and its mobility tended to be downwards: an increasing gulf opened up between high and low, especially as the towns no longer generated much of a rising stratum to bridge it. Few parvenus penetrated the Austrian establishment after 1620 and most of them were foreigners. Some German officials, mainly lawyers by training, made good and married well; some noble families immigrated, normally via the imperial army. The latter, if they settled permanently at all, rarely played any public role: that is true of St. Julien and St. Hilier (whose troops saved Ferdinand II from capture by the Protestants in 1619), of Montecuccoli and Tilly, and we shall meet the phenomenon again, on a larger scale, in Bohemia. Even earlier arrivals, like the Spanish Hoyos and Salamanca-Ortenburg, the favourites of Ferdinand I, and some of the Friulians, like Collalto and Attems, stood aside from politics.[44]

So far as native commoners were concerned, the world of open opportunities closed about 1620 with a last generation of self-made men such as Johann Baptist Verda, Count of Werdenberg, secretary to Ferdinand II and the first Austrian court chancellor, or the Kisls, who transformed themselves from burghers of Laibach to Counts of Gottschee within thirty years. Thereafter the number who rose to full participation in public life could probably be counted on the fingers of one hand: one was Christoph Ignaz Abele (1628–85), a less than dynamic president of the *Hofkammer*; another was Johann Walderode (1593–1674), an influential chancery secretary. These were infinitesimal rifts in the hierarchy, as was the one noble rebel

---

[43] O. Brunner, *Adeliges Landleben und europäischer Geist* (Salzburg 1949), chs. 1 and 4, on Hohberg. For Valvasor: P. Radics, *Johann Weikhard Freiherr von Valvasor* (Laibach 1910); Dimitz, op. cit. pt. 4, 35 ff.; Coreth, *Geschichtschreibung*, 153–5; cf. above, n. 6.

[44] On Germans from the *Reich* see below pp. 292–5. On Montecuccoli, cf. above, n. 32; the nephew of Johann Tserclaes Tilly installed himself at 'Tillysburg', a castle near St. Florian in Upper Austria, but the family died out with his grandson in 1724. The Salamancas only survived until the 1630s, and their successors at Ortenburg in Carinthia, local merchants grown rich in Venice, proved equally inconspicuous (G. Probszt, *Hans Widmanns Erbe, ein Beitrag zur Familiengeschichte* (Klagenfurt 1961)).

of the period: Hans Erasmus, Count Tattenbach, who mounted a trivial and totally unsuccessful putsch in Styria to coincide with the Hungarian conspiracy of 1670.[45] Otherwise the essentially social bonds between regional and central authority in Austria were everywhere consolidated.

*

Consideration of Austria's nobility leads naturally to a discussion of the Austrian Church, which presents the same dominance and expansiveness of character. In their upper echelons the two bodies overlapped closely: prelates formed the primary estate at all the diets, working with nobles to distribute the tax burden as painlessly as possible, and nobles became the arch-Catholic social group. As we have seen, places existed for aristocratic scions in the episcopate, where the more prestigious sees were theirs without question, and religious communities welcomed them, while successful abbots might hope for a patent of nobility. Some nunneries were highly fashionable, like Goess, near Leoben, and Sonnenburg in the Pustertal, which served the needs of unmarriageable daughters of the Styrian and Tyrolean nobility respectively, or Hall, founded by an archduchess as a decorous institution for well-mannered spinsters.[46] Other religious foundations benefited profoundly from noble support, especially mendicants and Jesuits, and aristocrats often maintained parish priests out of their own pocket, as well as exercising the works of charity. Again this is *family* piety, a kind of spiritual *Fideicommissum*, with much commemoration of ancestors, even expiation of their misdeeds, as Joseph Jörger, whose father was a Protestant *émigré*, joined the Cistercians at Lilienfeld, or Anton

---

[45] On Abele: *ADB* and *NDB*, s.v.; Bérenger, *Finances*, 376–8. He was the son of a converted Catholic citizen of Steyr, and had a brother with some literary pretensions who served as a mining official there. On Walderode, son of a Netherlandish immigrant: Gross, op. cit. 420–4. On Tattenbach: F. Krones, 'Aktenmässige Beiträge zur Geschichte des Tattenbach'schen Prozesses', *MHVSt* xii (1863), 83–113; cf. below, p. 363.

[46] J. Wichner, 'Geschichte des Nonnenklosters Goess', *Stud. u. Mitt.* xiv (1893), 15–39, 181–200, 333–51, 510–30; *Stift Göss, Geschichte und Kunst* (Graz 1961). Others of these nominally Benedictine convents were at St. Georgen am Längsee (Carinthia), Säben (southern Tyrol, from 1685 and rather more austere), Fiume, and Salzburg (on the Nonnberg); M. T. von Bolschwing, 'Die benediktinischen Nonnenklöster in Österreich, in H. Tausch (ed.), *Benediktinisches Mönchtum in Österreich* (V. 1949), 264–94, deals mostly with the last. Hall im Tirol was an unenclosed *Damenstift*. Cf. above, p. 139, n. 58, and below, n. 77.

Tattenbach, son of the executed Hans Erasmus, spent his life with their brothers at Rein.[47]

But the body of the Church was not noble; indeed, it was basically peasant, and we must ask of it the same question which we have already asked of the upper classes: how far did Catholicism bring together the different *Erblande* and reinforce loyalty to Habsburg government there? How far did it genuinely enjoy popularity? The Church was not Austrian in its boundaries: diocesan and territorial frontiers rarely coincided, and other divisions bore little relation to them. Friars had their 'Tyrolean', 'Styrian', 'Austro-Bohemian', 'Austro-Hungarian', even 'Austro-Moravian' provinces. The Society of Jesus, after much learned debate, split into a wine-consuming Austrian province and a beer-consuming Bohemian one, on the apolitical grounds that its members should not mix their drinks.[48] And the activities of these orders were international, pan-Monarchical, with Austria again a kind of common denominator, tied to both German and Habsburg developments. More specific to the *Erblande* was the autochthonous role of the old monasteries, or *Stifte*.[49] We earlier saw some evidence of their sixteenth-century decay and early seventeenth-century recovery; now is the time to give a more composite picture of those powerful institutions whose influence has survived in some degree down to our own day.

The Benedictines had over twenty houses in the Austrian provinces (with two more in Salzburg), but their importance lay in individual size and wealth rather than weight of numbers. All were medieval foundations, most dating from the eleventh to the thirteenth centuries. In Lower Austria there were the so-called *Schottenstift*, originally a Celtic monastery, in Vienna; Altenburg, hidden in the forests of the Waldviertel; the twin fortresses of Melk and Göttweig, commanding at either end the narrow passage of the Danube known as the Wachau; Seitenstetten to the west; and a smaller community at Klein-Mariazell in the Vienna Woods. Upper Austria contained the celebrated abbey of Kremsmünster, established in the eighth century by the Bavarian Duke Tassilo, and an even older foundation at Mondsee; Lambach above the river Traun,

---

[47] Wurm, op. cit. 168–70; *Cisterzienserbuch*, 181, 372.

[48] Duhr, op. cit. ii, 1, 315–17.

[49] *Stift* (plural *Stifte* or sometimes *Stifter*), 'a foundation', is the normal Austrian and south German word for a monastery (elsewhere *Kloster*).

and the twin houses of Garsten and Gleink. Styria had the large
monasteries of Admont and St. Lambrecht; Carinthia the slightly
smaller settlements at St. Paul, Arnoldstein, and the picturesque
lakeside village of Ossiach. Tyrol had monasteries at Marienberg
and St. Georgenberg (rebuilt in the eighteenth century at nearby
Fiecht), while the most famous Benedictine communities in the
Vorlande were Mehrerau beside Lake Constance, and St. Blasien in
the Black Forest, which possessed imperial immediate status after
1613.[50]

From the twelfth century onwards the reforming zeal of the
Cistercians had made an equally extensive contribution to the
Austrian countryside, especially to the remoter and, as yet,
unproductive upland areas. Their first foundation—nowadays the
oldest of all surviving Cistercian monasteries—was at Rein in Styria.
Thence the order spread, with its characteristic lines of filiation, to
Heiligenkreuz, Zwettl, and Lilienfeld in Lower Austria; to
Baumgartenberg and Wilhering in Upper Austria; to Sittich in
Carniola; to Viktring in Carinthia. Later came the renowned house
at Stams in the Tyrol, and further colonization of the provinces
lying to the east: Landstrass (Carniola), Engelszell (Upper
Austria), Neuberg (Styria), Säusenstein (Lower Austria), and an
unusual town abbey (the *Neukloster*) founded in Wiener Neustadt
by Emperor Frederick III. After 1620 the former Cistercian
nunnery at Schlierbach (Upper Austria) was sequestered from its
Protestant owners and given to male members of the order.[51]

Most distinctive of all were the numerous monasteries in Austria

---

[50] Details of the *Stifte* which survived Joseph II's secularization are very much
easier to come by than those of dissolved monasteries, and most of the former have
monograph histories. Outstanding treatments of Benedictine houses are Keiblinger,
op. cit. on Melk, H. Burger on Altenburg (i–ii, 1862–9), and J. Wichner on Admont
(i–iv, 1874–80). Convenient summaries in *Benediktinerbuch*, 10 ff. (dissolved houses),
40–83 (Admont and Altenburg), 117–217 (St. Georgenberg, Göttweig, Kremsmünster, Lambach, St. Lambrecht, Marienberg), 261–87 (Melk), 301–30 (St.
Paul), 368–449 (*Schottenstift* and Seitenstetten); and Tausch (ed.), op. cit. 36–70,
98–116. There were Benedictines at Gloggnitz on the Semmering, which belonged
to a Bavarian mother-house at Formbach. From 1636 there were also Spanish
Benedictines (*Schwarzspanier*) in Vienna. I have not attempted here or in succeeding
paragraphs to survey the *Vorlande*, most of whose abbeys were not subject to
Habsburg territorial jurisdiction.
[51] *Cisterzienserbuch*, 15 ff. (dissolved houses), 52–113 (Heiligenkreuz), 138–205
(Lilienfeld), 220–79 (*Neukloster*), 354–402 (Rein), 414–52 (Schlierbach and Stams),
498–521 (Wilhering), 542–603 (Zwettl). Cf. A. Sartorius, *Cistercium Bis-Tertium seu*

belonging to the regular canons of the Augustinian rule. This somewhat looser association of coenobites seems to have proved particularly congenial in the eastern Alps. The oldest abbeys stood at St. Florian, near Linz in Upper Austria, and at St. Pölten in Lower Austria. Soon the order spread elsewhere in the duchies: to the great and wealthy house of Klosterneuburg on the Danube above Vienna; to Herzogenburg and St. Andrä on the Traisen; to Waldhausen near Grein, Dürnstein in the Wachau, and St. Dorothea in Vienna; with a further clutch of properties (Reichersberg, Ranshofen, Suben) just across the Bavarian border in the Innviertel. In Styria and Carinthia the Augustinian canons settled at Vorau, amid the rolling hills north-east of Graz, at Stainz, Rottenmann, and Pöllau (the last as late as 1505), and formed the episcopal chapters of Seckau, Gurk, and St. Andrä in the valley of Lavant. They had Tyrolean houses at Neustift (Novacella) near Brixen, Gries near Bozen, and Wälschmichel, all in the south of the province. The stricter Augustinian order of Premonstratensians also made some progress in Austria; but they were more a feature of Bohemian Catholicism, as we shall see. Indeed, their abbeys at Geras-Pernegg (Lower Austria) and Schlägl (Upper Austria) were actually settled from across the border and continued to belong to the Bohemian *circaria*, while those at Wilten, just south of Innsbruck, and Griffen, the Bamberg enclave in Carinthia, maintained strong links with Bavaria.[52]

All these monasteries, so prosperous during the Middle Ages—when Melk, St. Florian, Klosterneuburg, and others enjoyed a European reputation—flourished with renewed vigour in the seventeenth century, such that the desperate Reformation decades came to seem in retrospect no more than a subdued interlude. Their wealth rested on *Herrschaft*: careful management of estates and effective control over a subject peasantry, with, by the end of the period, fifty to one hundred monks in each case directing a much

Historia Elogialis ... (Pr. 1700), 1091–1111, for a contemporary list; and Stülz, op. cit., for a detailed, but rambling study of Wilhering.

[52] *Chorherrenbuch*, 23–50 (St. Florian), 51–68 (dissolved houses), 200–63 (Herzogenburg), 271–366 (Klosterneuburg), 412–47 (Neustift), 638–80 (Vorau); *Benediktinerbuch*, 152–7 (Gries). For the Premonstratensians (whose houses, strictly speaking, are not 'abbeys', but 'canonries'): *Chorherrenbuch*, 91–413 (Geras), 496–511 (Schlägl), 681–715 (Wilten); Backmund, op. cit. i, 40 f., 53–5, 289–91, 305–10; iii, 517 f., 522 f., 585 f., 589 f.; and cf. below, pp. 220 f.

larger number of lay brothers and other employees. Monastic property tended to be more scattered than the aristocratic latifundium, but it represented an enterprise on a similar scale, capable of embracing industrial activity: sawmills, mining, brewing, and so on. Between 1623 and 1637 abbots of Kremsmünster and Lilienfeld were called by Ferdinand II to head the imperial *Hofkammer*. The exceptionally well-documented economic history of the Cisterian house of Velehrad in Moravia could serve for any of its Austrian counterparts. As late as the 1880s, Admont still owned ten castles and a wide variety of industrial concerns.[53]

Like the magnates, the *Stifte* strained even these ample resources to their limit—and sometimes beyond—by an orgy of conspicuous expense on architecture, art, and furnishings.[54] We tend today to associate this Baroque splendour above all with the earlier eighteenth century: we think of the grandeur of Prandtauer's Melk and the serenity of St. Florian; the imperial wing at Klosterneuburg and the monumental stairway of Göttweig; the exquisite libraries of Altenburg and Admont; the fishponds and observatory at Kremsmünster; the breathtaking Rococo of the churches at Wilhering and Neustift, Dürnstein and Ossiach. But often it is only a façade added to solid structures inherited from the years before 1700, like the princely titles liberally dispensed later to families already dominant by that date. Much rebuilding was completed in the seventeenth century: witness the work at Kremsmünster and Lambach; Geras and Schlägl; Lilienfeld, Schlierbach, and Zwettl; St. Lambrecht and St. Paul; the churches of the *Schottenstift*, Seitenstetten, Vorau, Garsten, Wilten. In many cases the existing fabric was simply remodelled in the spirit of later Baroque, or reconstructed following devastation, as at Heiligenkreuz after the Turkish ravages in 1683. All over Austria today such features as the florid stucco-work of the Carlones and other great *Comaschi* families

[53] Gutkas, op. cit. 216 f., 234. Hopf, *Wolfradt*, i, 15–31; the other prelate was Ignaz Kraft of Lilienfeld, made a baron by Ferdinand (*Cisterzienserbuch*, 172–5). R. Hurt, *Dějiny cisterciáckého kláštera na Velehradě*, i–ii (Olomouc 1934–8), a remarkably thorough account; *Benediktinerbuch*, 68 f. (Admont). Cf. A. Mell, 'Das Stift Seckau und dessen wirtschaftliche Verhältnisse im 16. Jahrhundert', *Stud. u. Mitt.* xiv (1893), 82–92, 255–65, 367–76; B. Gsell, 'Das Stift Heiligenkreuz und seine Besitzungen im Jahre 1683', ibid. iv (1883), 2, 284–94; 3, 81–9; 4, 330–43.

[54] There are useful brief surveys in F. Röhrig, *Alte Stifte in Österreich*, i–ii (V.–Munich 1966). Cf. below, p. 445, n. 63.

attest to the formation of a 'national' monastic style well before the end of the century.

The parallel between religious and aristocratic houses can be pursued a stage further. Of course, their points of departure were radically different. The monasteries tapped a great reservoir of talent and vocation throughout Austrian society: many of the leading abbots of the period came from peasant or artisan stock, and the ideal of contemplation was a thoroughly genuine spiritual response to the circumstances of the age. Moreover, there existed plenty of scope for neighbourly friction where a local lord claimed rights over the monks or coveted their possessions, as with the disputes between Eggenbergs and Cistercians across the border in Bohemia.[55] Yet both monastery and family were communities of interest, sustained by a sense of continuity, a pride in the past—especially in medieval achievements and respect for founders or ancestors—and a collective confidence in the future. Both were privileged corporations, their goods guaranteed by the sovereign and practically free from taxation. Above all the *Stifte*, no less than the magnates, had a public role to play, at the local and at the more national level.

This last point is worth developing. For all that the abbeys afforded a certain *centrum securitatis* to their inmates, they were far from pure asceticism.[56] They had strong local roots, the individual monastery being a more or less autonomous body, its identity moulded by place and tradition. They gave expression to the morality and piety of the day, displaying something of the earthiness as well as the simple faith of the rural population. Their role was anchored in pastoral activity. The continuing shortage and low calibre of secular clergy forced monks to run incorporated parishes

[55] F. Tadra (ed.), 'Regesten zur Geschichte des Cisterzienserstiftes Goldenkron, 1560–1660', *Stud. u. Mitt.* xiii (1892), 13–23, 237–44, 368–78; Kaindl, op. cit. 78ff. Cf. the three-cornered struggle between Batthyánys, Heiligenkreuz Cistercians, and Pázmány over the monastery lands at Szentgotthárd: Pázmány, *Levelei*, nos. 57, 317–18, 337–8, 342, 349, 413, 444, 467, 471, 499, 503–5, 507, 544–5, 552.

[56] Only three Carthusian monasteries survived the Middle Ages in Austria: Mauerbach, Gaming, and Aggsbach, all in Lower Austria (Gaming was the largest: cf. Friess, 'Soziale und wirtschaftliche Lage'); and there were not many more in the rest of the Monarchy, all of which formed part of the Upper German province of the order. None achieved prominence in this period, though the Austrian charterhouses gained ostentatious new buildings and (from 1670) representation among the Lower Austrian estates.

themselves, a very characteristic feature, not only of Austria's regular canons, but of its Benedictines and Cistercians since the Counter-Reformation.[57] More generally, regulars exercised greater influence than seculars; though clashing at times with bishops, monasteries tended to profit from the weakness of episcopal authority, since no major cathedral actually stood on Austrian soil. In Lower Austria the clerical estate consisted exclusively of heads of old monasteries (the few bishops being reckoned as lords), and usually the abbots co-operated reasonably harmoniously. Thus the *Stifte* grew into their larger political role: the Benedictines of Lower and Upper Austria, for example, formed themselves into a single congregation.[58] And they struck up an advantageous relationship with the Habsburgs too: despite some interference in capitular elections, the main impression is one of mutual aid. The monasteries assumed part of the mantle of dynastic mission, symbolized in their newly-built *Kaisersäle*, imperial suites, among which perhaps the most remarkable and extravagant example was to be at St. Florian, complete down to the preposterous bed for Prince Eugene in pseudo-Turkish Rococo. This was still no explicitly 'Austrian' solution. A large number of seventeenth-century monks, including more than half the abbots, came from abroad, mostly from the favourite Habsburg catchment area of southern Germany, like the cheerful and worldly Reginbald Möhner, who has left us a spirited account of the Benedictine houses where he stayed during the Thirty Years War.[59] But by 1700 monasteries had begun, semi-consciously at least, to wear a more native complexion in keeping with their key place in Austrian Baroque society.

*

Other aspects of the Counter-Reformation besides a revitalization of the *Stifte* strengthened 'Austrian' loyalties during the seventeenth

---

[57] Tausch (ed.), op. cit. 126–41.

[58] Gutkas, op. cit. 154; Hassinger, 'Landstände', 996–9; A. Dungel, 'Die österreichische Benediktiner-Congregation', *Stud. u. Mitt.* iv (1863), 1, 49–64; 2, 306–24; 3, 108–15; 4, 300–9. Premonstratensians tended to look more towards Prague.

[59] A. Czerny (ed.), *Ein Tourist in Österreich während der Schwedenzeit* (Linz 1874), prints Möhner's diary; G. Winner, 'Die niederösterreichischen Prälaten zwischen Reformation und Josephinismus', *Jb. d. St. Klnb.*, N. F. iv (1964), 111–27, esp. 126, on foreign abbots. Cf. Hopf, *Wolfradt*, for one of the most notable of them, born into a simple family at Cologne.

century. One was education, where the main Jesuit teaching system, which has already been described, created an enclosed structure, based on a series of university centres: Vienna, Graz, Innsbruck, Linz; and only magnates or those already committed to a religious life could cross frontiers for purposes of study. It was supplemented and to some extent rivalled by the schools of other orders. The Benedictines especially had renowned schools attached to some of their monasteries (Seitenstetten, Admont, Kremsmünster, Melk, and the *Schottenstift*), and even a university of their own at Salzburg, which proved increasingly attractive to clerics and nobles who sought a freer syllabus and an alternative set of authorities. Dominican pedagogues tried to re-establish their position at a local level, while the Piarists, first settled in Austria at Horn, north-west of Vienna, by Count Ferdinand Sigmund Kurz in 1657, began to lay the foundations for an impressive expansion in Central Europe.[60]

Such education, for all its attempts to woo the unprivileged, for all the fine distinctions between one theological tradition and the next, remained heavily conservative, suspicious of all influences from Protestant lands, and overwhelmingly Latinate. Its scheme left little scope for a German culture at all, let alone one attuned to the rich cadences of Austrian German. That was cultivated mostly by Protestant exiles like Katharina von Greiffenberg. But not entirely, for the Catholic establishment did bring forth some distinguished literary figures who wrote in both Latin and German, notably the Jesuit Jakob Balde, from Ensisheim, and the Benedictine Simon Rettenbacher at Kremsmünster.[61] Moreover, the Church fostered vernacular culture in one vital way: through popular preaching, which harnessed the resources of everyday speech, developed local motifs, and reflected local concerns. Sometimes entertainment dominated the pulpit, good stories rather than

[60] See, beyond the accounts of individual monasteries, A. Decker, 'Die benediktinischen Schulen in Österreich', in Tausch (ed.), op. cit. 117–25 (mostly about Seitenstetten); cf. below, pp. 279 f. for Salzburg University. Once again I leave out of account the *Vorlande* and Freiburg, with its semi-Jesuit university. On the Piarists see above, p. 133 and n. 43. Their major *Gymnasium* at Horn is chronicled by F. Endl, 'Geschichte des Gymnasiums der Piaristen zu Horn, 1657–1872', *Beiträge zur österreichischen Erziehungs- und Schulgeschichte*, ii (1899).
[61] For these figures, and literature on them, see W. Kosch, *Deutsches Literatur-Lexikon* (Bern–Munich 1963), s. vv. Cf. Brunner, *Adeliges Landleben*, 174 ff., on Hohberg and his friends; and Loserth, *Stubenberg*, 250–6, on Hans Wilhelm von Stubenberg, another literary exile.

Biblical texts. But a more purposeful tradition was also at work, at least since Scherer's powerful sermons at the chapel royal during the 1580s and 1590s.[62]

The leading later seventeenth-century preacher was the famous Abraham a Sancta Clara (1644–1709), born Ulrich Megerle, an innkeeper's son from Swabia. Sancta Clara's vivid sympathy for peasants, for lay communities and brotherhoods, drew on real experience of ordinary people and the nuances of their language. His sharp attacks on contemporary vices were mounted within a recognizably Viennese frame of reference.[63] Less well remembered is Procopius of Templin (1607–90), who converted to Catholicism in Prague, joined the Capuchins at Vienna in 1627, and worked throughout Central Europe, especially in the Austrian provinces. He preached incessantly, publishing his direct, pungent sermons in huge collections; less socially critical than those of Sancta Clara, they gain in poetic and visionary impact, and evidently struck an equally popular chord. Similar German homilies, with their fair share of dialect and local colour, must have resounded before congregations throughout Austria, to judge by the surviving literature in monastic libraries.[64]

Both Sancta Clara and Procopius encouraged local religious customs and popular observances. Thus the *international* devotional movement was realized in *particular* cults. Everywhere pilgrimages

[62] Baur, 'Passer', 329, for a typically droll preacher. Good examples of Scherer's style are the *Hofkapelle* sermons of 1594 entitled *Ein bewerte Kunst und Wundsegen ... damit man im Krieg nicht unten lige ...* (Ingolstadt 1595), reprinted with similar works in *Opera oder alle Bücher*, ii.

[63] Sancta Clara was actually born on Bavarian soil (cf. below, p. 292). His collected works were edited in 19 vols. (Passau–Lindau 1835–47); for a good sample of his style and themes see *Grammatica Religiosa quae piè docet declinare a malo, et facere bonum ...* (Salzburg 1691). The best guide to him, beside the standard biography by T. G. von Karajan (V. 1867), is Loidl, *Menschen im Barock*; cf. K. Helleiner, 'Das Bild der Wirtschaft und Gesellschaft bei Abraham a Sancta Clara', *MIÖG* lx (1952), 251-64 (slight); R. A. Kann, *A Study in Austrian intellectual history* (London 1960), 50–115; and the literature in Kosch, op. cit. s.v. 'Abraham'.

[64] Procopius was also a German. He is terrifying on hell and the Day of Judgment: *iudiciale, Purgatoriale et Infernale, Das ist ... Discursen oder Predigen vom Jüngsten Tag und Gericht ...* (Munich 1666); but he can also be very sweet, fresh, and naive: *Adventuale ac Natale Iesu Christi ... Hertzens-Frewd und Seelen-Lust im harten Winter ...* (Munich 1666). He has attracted little literature: see the life by V. Gadient (Regensburg 1912); and A. H. Kober in *Die Kultur*, xiv (1913), Hefte 2–4, and *Euphorion*, xxi–xxii (1914–18), Heft 3. Further good examples of the genre in many monastery libraries; e.g. Heiligenkreuz, MSS. 421, 453-4.

were sponsored, often in association with monasteries, as St. Lambrecht managed the great votive church at Mariazell, and Seitenstetten that on the Sonntagberg, Lambach the extraordinary Trinitarian church built in the early years of the eighteenth century at Stadl-Paura, and Rein that at Strassengel. A vast number of shrines sprang up, from major edifices to wayside calvaries, most of them no older than the Counter-Reformation itself. The cult of the Virgin clearly predominated over all others (as it did for Procopius, and indeed for Ferdinand III and Leopold I) and Mary was celebrated as Austria's national patron at Maria-Taferl, Maria-Dreieichen, Maria-Rasing, and the rest.[65] Other cults were more distinctive: St. Joseph joined Mary in the national pantheon from 1675 and was invoked by Leopold before the birth of his eldest surviving son. St. Leopold, a twelfth-century Margrave of Babenberg, combined spiritual and political virtues: his *cultus*, originating at Klosterneuburg, which he founded, became identified by the later sixteenth century with a more generalized Austrian *Landespatriotismus* and was further developed under the Emperors Leopold and Charles VI.[66] St. Florian, the first Austrian martyr, would protect one's own house against fire, while burning down the neighbour's; St. Coloman, a medieval Irish pilgrim hanged as a vagrant near Vienna, buried at Melk, was revered for his intervention in everything from cattle-plague to marital troubles. Most curious of all, the totally spurious St. Domitian (!), patron of Carinthia, who helped men to avoid disease and to catch fish, had high masses sung in his memory at Vienna, though his *gesta* rested on a confused medieval fabrication.[67]

---

[65] G. Gugitz, *Österreichs Gnadenstätten in Kult und Brauch*, i–v (V. 1955–8), is a fascinating source (ii, 87 ff., 115 ff., 188 ff.; iv, 197 ff., for places mentioned in the text). Cf. Wiedemann, *Reformation*, v, 186 ff.; E. Tomek, op. cit. 645–7; Gutkas, op. cit. 253 f. A typical smaller shrine is described by A. Erdinger, 'Maria Rasing', *ÖVjschr. f. Kath. Theol.* ix (1870), 251–94. On Procopius: A. H. Kober, *Die Marienpredigten des Procopius von Templin* (Münster 1916); for Ferdinand and Leopold see above, p. 117. For major Austrian calvaries see M. Lehmann, 'Die Kalvarienberganlagen im Donauraum', *Festschrift F. Loidl*, i–ii (V. 1970), i, 113–59, esp. 141–7.

[66] On Joseph: Loidl, *Menschen im Barock*, 32–4; Coreth, *Pietas*, 74 f. On Leopold, sainted in 1485: G. Wacha, 'Reliquien und Reliquiare des hl. Leopold', *Jb. d. St. Klnb.*, N.F. iii (1963), 9–25; Wiedemann, *Reformation*, ii, 500–5; v, 264–8. Charles VI planned to turn Klosterneuburg into an Austrian Escorial, one of the most colossal uncompleted enterprises of the Baroque (cf. below, p. 446).

[67] Florian: *Acta Sanctorum*, ed. J. Bolland *et al.*, i– (Antwerp, etc. 1643–   ,

(continued)

The cult of native saints was part of a larger identification of Catholicism with Austria. Had not Protestantism, as clerics claimed from the days of Scherer and Brenner onwards, always been a foreign body there? Like so many specious arguments, this one contained its grain of truth: around 1600, for example, two-thirds of Styria's ministers were immigrants. Certainly, the Counter-Reformation made a conscious attempt to purge all traces of the heretical past, though such cathartic rituals as mass processions to Hernals (once the bastion of Vienna's Lutherans) seem to have operated more on the level of popular orgy.[68] The notion of 'Catholic Austria' was partly an aspect of dynastic propaganda, celebrating the Habsburgs' achievements for the faith and stimulated by events in the 1680s; partly, though more fragilely, it tried to present the *Erblande* as the true, unsullied heart of the Holy Roman Empire. To this end German converts were paraded who had freely chosen to settle in Austria, and the arch-polemicist, Jodocus Kedd, doctored their *curricula vitae* to suit his apologetic purposes.[69] More effective was argumentation along historical lines, and by the end of the seventeenth century dozens of ecclesiastical chroniclers throughout the region cultivated a kind of *Catholicitas perennis*. Such historiography, among whose greatest exponents were the brothers Bernhard and Hieronymus Pez at Melk and Marcus Hansiz, author of the *Germania Sacra*, yielded many valuable studies of Austria's medieval Church. The Emperor Leopold, who fully shared its outlook, commissioned copies of the correspondence of Rudolf I, the founder of Habsburg power, in a spirit of family *pietas*.[70] In the process, however, the real Counter-

---

hereafter *Acta SS* and cited by month (of the feast-day) and vol.), May, i, 461–7. Coloman; ibid. Oct., vi, 342–57; cf. H. Pez, *Acta S. Colomanni* (Krems 1913). On 'Domitian', whose cause was taken up by the Jesuits at Millstatt, see R. Eisler, 'Die Legende vom heiligen Karantanerherzog Domitianus', *MIÖG* xxviii (1907), 52–116, esp. 105 ff.

[68] Schuster, op. cit. 202 f. C. Musart, *Nova Viennensium peregrinatio ... ad S. Sepulchrum in Hernals* (V. 1642); but cf. Freschot, op. cit. 48–51, for a jaundiced view of the marches to Hernals, a former Jörger castle made over to the cathedral chapter after 1620.

[69] On Kedd, who died at Vienna in 1657: Duhr, op. cit. ii, 2, 79 f., 413 f.; iii, 550 f.; Sommervogel, iv, cols. 958–77; and many examples of his influence in Räss, op. cit. (cf. above p. 112, n. 76). See also below, ch. 8, *passim*.

[70] M. Kropff, *Bibliotheca Mellicensis* (V. 1747), 515 ff.; Coreth, *Geschichtschreibung*, esp. 91 ff. Hansiz's *Germania Sacra* did not advance beyond the two Austrian dioceses

Reformation development came to be turned on its head: Austria is depicted as the guardian of Catholic orthodoxy, whereas in fact it was Catholic orthodoxy which created Austria. And 'Austrianness', on that basis, necessarily remained a somewhat imponderable quality.[71] Ultimately the Church, like the nobles, while reinforcing dynastic loyalty and local conformity, created only social and cultural, not institutional bonds between the two.

★

One more possible binding force within the *Erblande* has still to be considered: Vienna. Yet Vienna was not properly equipped to be an Austrian, rather than a Habsburg capital: history had linked it almost exclusively with its own province of Lower Austria, while its site, though strategic, was awkward. Surrounded by forests to the west and swamps to the east, it possessed only limited importance within the high-medieval Empire, becoming a—very minute—bishopric as late as 1469. During the decades around 1500 it enjoyed an age of prosperity and Humanist self-confidence, but wars against Hungary and the Ottomans posed a continual threat, and then, in 1522, the Habsburgs finally extinguished its independence.[72]

Thereafter Vienna, its administration packed with creatures and agents of the dynasty, fell totally under the domination of the Habsburg court.[73] The evolution was gradual and fairly accidental. During the fifteenth and sixteenth centuries several other cities, notably Prague, rivalled Vienna as imperial residences. After 1612 it came into its own, though Matthias still liked Linz better and even Ferdinand II, who had cause to be grateful for the loyalty of Viennese burghers in 1619, was buried at Graz. Now, with a retinue so large and pompous as almost to preclude lengthy travels (Leopold

of Passau and Salzburg and a *prodromus* to the description of Regensburg; he also edited the important reissue of Franz Christoph Khevenhüller's monument to the deeds of Ferdinand II, the *Annales Ferdinandei*, i–xii in 7 vols. (Leipzig 1721–6). ÖNB, MSS. 9351, 9720 (Rudolf I); cf. above, pp. 72 f. and n. 77.

[71] The interesting essay by A. Tibal, *L'Autrichien, essais sur la formation d'une individualité nationale* (Paris 1936), ch. 2, makes rather too strong a case.

[72] The definitive history, from the origins to 1740, is *Geschichte der Stadt Wien*, i–iv in 8 huge volumes. Ibid. ii, 2, 577–91 on the revolt and suppression of 1522. Cf. Tibal, op. cit., ch. 1.

[73] For the administration: *Geschichte der Stadt Wien*, v, 100–59; there were twelve senators, twelve magistrates (*Stadtgerichtsbeisitzer*), and seventy-six members of the plenary or 'outer' council (*Äusserer Rat*). Its workings were dominated, not by the figurehead mayor, but by the princely *Stadtanwalt*.

undertook thirty-nine, mostly short progresses during his long reign), the Habsburgs lived a sedentary life, and after the Turks had been repelled in 1683 their city assumed all the trappings of a proud *kaiserliche Haupt- und Residenzstadt*. That meant a further loss of true urban character, as a conservative patrician oligarchy mediated orders from above, and the common citizenry groaned under the standing obligation to find quarter for an ever-growing army of imperial servants.[74]

Thus the dynasty ruled—but again largely through aristocracy and Church. The imperial Hofburg was not very spacious; quite neglected for nearly a century between the 1570s and 1660s, it remained modest even into the eighteenth century, before the building of the new library, chancery, and riding school.[75] The aristocrats had two sources of influence: the court, and the government of Lower Austria (situated, aptly enough, in the Herrengasse), and their great power in the city was strengthened by the purchase of tax-free property there. Some large-scale construction began before 1683, like the old Starhemberg *Palais* on the Minoritenplatz—though earlier even Hans Ulrich von Eggenberg had possessed no regular house. After the siege came a wave of fine mansions: Dietrichstein and Herberstein, Strattmann and Questenberg, Liechtenstein and Schwarzenberg, Esterházy and Harrach, Batthyány and Batthyány-Schönborn, and others, none more spectacular than Prince Eugene's in the Himmelpfortgasse, begun about 1690. Meanwhile the first summer palaces, aping imperial *Lustschlösser*, were built just outside the walls in newly-respectable suburbs: Liechtenstein and Schwarzenberg again, Trautson and Paar, Schönborn and Althan, then Prince Eugene's monumental Lower and Upper Belvedere, completed in 1722.[76] And ecclesiastical

---

[74] On court progresses: R. Miller, 'Die Hofreisen Kaiser Leopolds I', *MIÖG* lxxv (1967), 66–103; cf. R. Lorenz, 'Reisen des Kaisers Leopold I und des Kurfürsten Max Emanuel im Türkenjahr 1683', *MIÖG* lii (1938), 295–312, at 306–12. J. Kallbrunner. 'Das Wiener Hofquartierwesen und die Massnahmen gegen die Quartiersnot im 17. und 18. Jahrhundert', *MVGStW* v (1925), 24–36.

[75] Many travellers remark on the lack of pretension of the imperial palace: e.g. Freschot, op. cit. 5 f. (but contrast Browne, *Account*, 76); cf. *Geschichte der Stadt Wien*, iv, 386 f., 407–9; and earlier, *Particular State*, sig. C3'.

[76] *Geschichte der Stadt Wien*, iv, 375–410, *passim*, esp. 401 f. On Eggenberg: Heydendorff, op. cit. 150–2. Many of these palaces survive, some under different names (thus the Dietrichstein later became Lobkovic).

architecture dominated the townscape no less, with St. Stephen's and its episcopal palace (archiepiscopal by the 1730s) right in the centre of Vienna. The Jesuits had three houses, at the university, Am Hof, and in the Annagasse, with some 270 priests in the 1660s, while other orders were ubiquitous: Discalced Augustinians, Minorites, and Barnabites beside the Hofburg; Benedictines, canons regular, Dominicans, Franciscans, Capuchins, Teutonic and Maltese knights elsewhere in the old town; Brothers of Mercy and barefoot Carmelites in the Leopoldstadt and Piarists in the Josefstadt, Calced Augustinians on the Landstrasse and Trinitarians on the Alserstrasse, Servites in the Rossau, Minims in Wieden, and sandalled Carmelites 'in the limepit'. Add to these the convents, including three houses of unregulated canonesses, two of Franciscans, Carmelites, and Ursulines, and the property owned by *Stifte* like Heiligenkreuz, Klosterneuburg, and Göttweig, and clerical hegemony is evident. Its ultimate symbol was visible on top of the Kahlenberg: the monastery of Camaldulensians, least profitable of orders, established by imperial fiat in 1628.[77]

From the slopes of the Kahlenberg the Christian armies surged down to relieve Vienna in 1683: and it is interesting that the last tiny loophole in Catholicism's domestic defences was finally closed that same year, when Protestant services at embassies were declared out-of-bounds to Austrian subjects.[78] But if the capital's 100,000 people shared one religion they displayed little uniformity in other ways. Vienna's population included men from all over the *Reich*, Bohemia, and Hungary; *émigrés* from the Balkans and Eastern Europe; soldiers, priests, and artists from the whole Mediterranean area and Catholic Western Europe. The variegated, polyglot city certainly associated itself with the Habsburgs, and the Habsburgs returned the compliment, learning to speak the local dialect with

---

[77] See, in general, *Geschichte der Stadt Wien*, iv, 247–53, 264 f. (estimates of numbers ibid. 258 and 264 n.); and Czerny, *Tourist*, 123–8 (for 1650). My list is roughly complete for the year 1700 or thereabouts. On the extensive urban possessions of the wealthy *Stifte* see, most recently, F. Röhrig, 'Die Klosterneuburger Stiftshöfe in Wien', *Jb. d. St. Klnb.*, N. F. ix (1975), 21–65. The canonesses (at Himmelpforten, St. Laurenz, and St. Jakob auf der Hülben) were likewise wealthy and had a strongly aristocratic tinge.

[78] Loesche, *Protestantismus*, 123. Today's Kahlenberg was actually called 'Sauberg' in the 17th century, while the modern Leopoldsberg next to it, with its church dating from the 1670s, went by the name of 'Kahlenberg'.

notorious relish. Yet growth as a multinational capital turned
Vienna away from any purely Austrian circumstances; to the very
end of the Monarchy, even beyond (and this is a political fact of
first importance), it remained in some measure estranged from its
hinterland.[79]

Seventeenth-century Austria, we may conclude, was neither a
nation, nor a political entity, but a working balance between the
international and the sub-national, between the cosmopolitan and
the provincial. Its Counter-Reformation establishment, while still
welcoming immigrants to fill the gap created by the expulsion of
heretics, became increasingly immobile and intolerant. None the
less, the new system possessed real roots in society and culture at
home, and it was not threatened from abroad, despite the 100,000
or so Protestant exiles who adopted a range of oppositional poses
from the religious revivalists around Count Zinzendorf at Herrnhut
to the Prussian Field Marshal Derfflinger.[80] The edifice of social
control and spiritual absolutism erected in the hereditary lands
affords a yardstick against which we can measure the less complete
solutions achieved elsewhere in Central Europe.

[79] One of the best-known, though not the best, descriptions of the imperial city is
by Mary Wortley Montagu, *Letters*, ed. R. Brimley Johnson (London 1906), 64 ff.
The bizarrest is definitely that by the Turkish traveller and tall-story teller, Evliyâ
Çelebi: *Im Reiche des goldenen Apfels*, tr. and ed. R. Kreutel (Graz 1957).

[80] Nikolaus Ludwig Zinzendorf, chief founder of the Moravian Brethren, was a
third-generation *émigré* in Saxony; but his two nephews, Ludwig Friedrich (1721–
80), and Karl (1739–1813), the last of his family, both converted to Catholicism,
returned to Austria, and became leading reformist politicians. Derfflinger (1606–
1695), born in Upper Austria of peasant stock, was a key figure in the creation of the
Prussian army (see *ADB* and *NDB*, s.v.).

CHAPTER 6

Bohemia: limited acceptance

The lands of St. Wenceslas were a simpler, more concentrated entity than the *Erblande*. Bohemia proper had been a single geographical unit since the ninth century with Prague as its natural centre, and subdivision into districts (*kraje*)—fourteen of them in this period[1]—bespoke little more than administrative convenience. Moravia formed a self-contained historical margravate, looking to its chief towns of Olomouc (Olmütz) and Brno (Brünn), the clerical and secular poles of its public life. There, as in Bohemia, two nationalities lived in reasonably well-demarcated juxtaposition: the Czech majority over most of the countryside, the German minority in towns and frontier regions. Certain institutions and customary practices progressively helped to bind together Bohemia, Moravia, and the other constituent parts of the kingdom: Silesia and the two Lusatias, Upper and Lower.[2] Nevertheless the basic political and ethnographical picture does not lack complexity: in western Bohemia, the region around Eger was ecclesiastically part of the diocese of Regensburg and constitutionally peculiar; in eastern Moravia, the boundary with Hungary ran across wild and ill-defined tracts and the upland settlers remained strongly idiosyncratic in their dialects and traditions.[3] Diversity was all the more characteristic of Silesia, which comprised a patchwork of some sixteen duchies, some controlled by the king, others by native princes who owed him merely a distant feudal vassalage. By 1600

[1] Pavel Stránský, *Respublica Bojema* (Leiden 1643), ch. 2; Balbín, *Miscellanea Historica*, i, bk. 3, 1–62. The 17th-century *kraje*, mostly named after towns, were: Boleslav, Königgrätz, Chrudim, Čáslav, Kouřim, Bechyně, Prácheň, Žatec, Litoměřice, Slaný, Rakovník, Podbrdsko, Vltavsko, and Pilsen; Bílek, *Dějiny konfiskací*, uses a slightly different list.
[2] J. Kalousek, *České státní právo* (2nd edn. Pr. 1892), 100 ff., 275 ff.; Rachfahl. op. cit. 134 ff.; and see the literature on Prague's court of appeal, above, p. 105, n. 62.
[3] For Eger see below, p. 299. J. Macůrek, *České země a Slovensko, 1620–1750* (Brno 1969), esp. 21 ff. Vlachs (Wallachians, on whom cf. above, pp. 76, 99), Lachs, and Hanáks were felt to be distinct racial communities.

only two native dynasties survived: the Poděbrad dukes of Münsterberg, and the Piasts at Liegnitz, Brieg, and Wohlau; during the century both died out and their lands escheated to the crown. Even so, jurisdictions continued to be very jumbled and one territory, the county of Glatz, enjoyed some kind of separate status; a situation not simplified by the presence, beside a dominant German population, of many Poles (or quasi-Poles) and some Czechs.[4] In truth Silesia, while sharing the essence of the Bohemian evolution, stands also a little apart from it; it forms a bridge to the rest of the German Empire, and I shall say more about it in chapter eight. The Lusatian duchies, occupied by Saxony as the price of her Habsburg alliance in 1620 and formally ceded fifteen years later by the Peace of Prague, do not belong here at all.

The seventeenth-century history of Bohemia and Moravia has often been made to appear, like their essential geography, simple and concentrated. After 1620, we are told, they experienced a political and social revolution; at their expense Counter-Reformation gained a classic victory. A Habsburg absolutism was imposed, Germanic and Viennese, alien to the Czechs, sullenly borne by the mass of a people ruined and denatured for the sake of imperial ambitions. That is a familiar tale in almost every text-book;[5] but it is basically a nineteenth-century tale, contemporary events and attitudes heavily overlaid by the pathos of a later nationalism. From the days of C. A. Pescheck it has remained much better known, both at home and abroad, than the only serious rival interpretation, itself equally Czech-patriotic and nineteenth-century in spirit: the

---

[4] It is difficult to be precise about the number of duchies in Silesia, since some had coalesced, or at least were normally ruled together, while others might be hived off as apanages for a limited period or sank to the level of a large *Herrschaft*. The 17th-century list appears to be, in Lower Silesia: Breslau and Neisse, Schweidnitz and Jauer, Münsterberg and Öls, Glogau and Sagan, Liegnitz, Brieg, and Wohlau; in Upper Silesia: Oppeln and Ratibor, Troppau and Jägerndorf, Teschen. Cf. below, pp. 299 ff. Although the 'dukes of Münsterberg' lived on until 1647, they were by that time in fact only rulers of tiny Öls (having sold Münsterberg to pay their debts), a circumstance which confused even the peacemakers at Westphalia!

[5] This presentation—while going back in some measure to the Protestant *émigrés*—really originated with Pescheck, op. cit. It was continued by—among others—Bílek, *Reformacé katolická*, etc.; Denis–Vančura, op. cit.; Prokeš in *Československá vlastivěda*, iv (Pr. 1932), 491–571; R. J. Kerner, *Bohemia in the Eighteenth Century* (New York 1932), 13 ff.; and it has been transmitted, with some modifications, into Marxist historiography. The latest summary, fair-minded but brief, is Richter in *Handbuch*, ed. Bosl, ii, 281–379.

Catholic apologia for the *res gestae* of the Bohemian Counter-Reformation.[6] We must now examine, in the light of the larger Central European patterns already sketched, how far this very negative view of Bohemia's development can be sustained.

There is no doubt about imposition and upheaval in the 1620s. Transfer of property took place on a staggering scale, even by the standards of a modern land reform. Bílek's statistics show that slightly more than one-half of all estates changed hands, and an even higher proportion of large ones. This was not, except in the case of the ringleaders of rebellion, naked legal expropriation, but it amounted to something very similar: property would often be temporarily confiscated, then compulsorily alienated in a buyers' market, or else returned dilatorily, grudgingly, and only in part. Indeed, the assumption of guilt went very deep: minor offenders found their lands converted into crown fiefs; even those willing to convert and declared innocent by commissions of retribution had to make a pious contribution to the Jesuit university.[7] Claims and counter-claims were still being haggled over at the end of the century. Individuals and whole communities which had played no part at all in the revolt were ruined. Many examples might be cited of a direct perversion of justice—Saxony could not protect the aristocrat Otto Heinrich Wartenberg from total loss, though he had express guarantees dating from before the White Mountain. Vengeance was largely wrought by a clique around Liechtenstein, including Wallenstein, Michna, the Jew Bassevi, and the Calvinist financier de Witte, which added financial swindle to its rapaciousness. The operation was, at best, only semi-Bohemian, and those who profited were foreign mercenaries and courtiers, while the long list of emigrants included names resonant throughout the country's Middle Ages and Renaissance.[8]

---

[6] All the existing relevant Czech Catholic literature was listed by J. Tumpach and A. Podlaha, *Bibliografie české katolické literatury náboženské, 1828–1913*, i–v (Pr. 1912–1923), esp. 1210 ff. Between the Wars the school of Josef Pekař adopted a similar standpoint.

[7] Bílek, *Dějiny konfiskací*, i, pp. cxlviii–cl and *passim*. E. Schebek, 'Die ferdinandeische Fundation', *MVGDB* xviii (1880), 161–81.

[8] Gindely, *Gegenreformation*, esp. 44–50 (on Wartenberg), and 327–64 (on the financial consortium); Bílek, *Reformace katolická*, 169–228. But the members of the *commissio executionis* and *commissio confiscationis* (listed by Bílek, *Dějiny konfiskací*, i, pp. xxxiv, lxi) were very largely Bohemians.

The climax of this process was a 'renewed' constitution (*Obnovené
zřízení zemské*; *Verneuerte Landesordnung*) decreed in 1627, over the
heads of the estates and their once-powerful diet, the *sněm*, which
had not been summoned since the fateful battle. To help him
prepare it, Ferdinand II called on both Bohemian and non-
Bohemian counsellors, and the latter's role was especially important:
the eight-man committee of 1625 included the Austrian chancellor,
Werdenberg, the imperial vice-chancellor, Stralendorf, and the
high-flying intellectual convert, Otto Melander, as well as the
naturalized Liechenstein (a Moravian subject, of course) and Otto
von Nostitz from Lusatia. That committee's findings were revised
by a smaller, *ad hoc* body including the heir to the throne,
Eggenberg, and Harrach (father of Prague's archbishop). Subdued
sněmy ratified the document for Bohemia during the bleak autumn
of 1627, then extended it to Moravia the following year. In 1640
certain modifications were introduced, largely to incorporate legal
judgments of a Roman and imperial hue.[9]

The main provisions of the *Obnovené zřízení zemské* may be
summarized under eight heads, as follows.[10] Firstly, the principle
of elective monarchy was abolished; the Bohemian crown became
hereditary in the house of Habsburg, and the venerable—and
lucrative—office of burgrave of Karlstein (where the regalia were
kept) was suppressed. Secondly, the clergy, politically impotent
since the Hussite wars, recovered their position as the first estate of
the realm. Thirdly, Rudolf's Letter of Majesty was abrogated and
all non-Catholic religions, except the Jewish, were declared illegal.
Fourthly, the sovereign was to be author of all legislation, a
stipulation soon mitigated when the diets regained some powers of
initiative in 1640. Fifthly, state functionaries, whether central or
local, must henceforth swear an oath to the king alone, no longer to

---

[9] Gindely, *Gegenreformation*, 467 ff.; Kalousek, op. cit. 391–434. On Melander cf.
above, p. 106. The other members of the larger committee were Wallenstein and the
lawyers Hillebrand (an aulic councillor, like Melander) and Hassolt (a Bohemian
appeal judge); of the revision committee: Slavata, Werdenberg, and Nostitz. For
the 1640 *declaratoria* and *novelly* see Kalousek, op. cit. 459–61; Rezek, *Děje*, 45–55.

[10] The text (Czech and German) was published by H. Jireček (ed.), *Constitutiones
regni Bohemiae anno 1627 reformatae* (Pr.-V.-Leipzig 1888). Cf. Kalousek, op. cit.
434 ff.; Denis–Vančura, op. cit. i, 1, 124 ff. J. Čelakovský in *OSN* vi (1893) contrasts
the pre-1620 situation (pp. 487–519) with the post-1627 one (519–39). The Moravian
document was somewhat different and marginally less severe.

the 'commonwealth of Bohemia' (*obec království českého*) as well, and all, from grand burgrave of Prague and Moravian *hejtman* downwards, could be replaced after five years. Sixthly, existing powers of the crown to hear appeals from any law court were strengthened. As a consequence of this and the previous point the Bohemian chancery, now operating from Vienna, gained added authority, and a new supreme tribunal was set up for Moravia with both administrative and judicial functions.[11] Seventhly, the king, not the estates, would in future control the *inkolát* and grant patents of Bohemian nobility, thus bypassing the reiterated requirement for his servants to be natives of the realm. Finally, the German language was raised to equality with Czech for all state purposes; and in fact only a German version of the new constitution appeared in print (though that was probably an accident).[12]

Like other key constitutional statements in Habsburg history: the *Privilegium Maius*, the Pragmatic Sanction, the *Ausgleich*—the *Obnovené zřízení zemské* by no means disposed of all issues in clear-cut fashion. It was not explicit about how to resolve possible conflicts between imperial Roman law and Bohemian common law; it adopted contradictory positions on the status of further, unmentioned aspects of the constitution: promises to confirm them may be set against the sovereign claim to 'extend, alter, and amend'. Yet, for all its involved language and its superficial adherence to the format of earlier *Landesordnungen*, it is a very severe document. It appears to change the whole character of public affairs in Bohemia and Moravia (Silesia was unaffected). Not totally, for the monarch had already been chief legislator, senior executive—nominating officers from a list presented to him, fount of justice, dispenser of nobility; but radically, since the dual system, whereby crown and estates balanced each other and perforce worked in partnership, seems to be destroyed.

---

[11] Fellner–Kretschmayr, op. cit. ii, 440–54, 474–98, for the Bohemian chancery; on the Moravian tribunal see below, n. 39. The grand burgrave (*Oberstburggraf, nejvyšší purkrabí*) of Prague, despite his name, was a kind of royal vicegerent throughout Bohemia proper, and not to be confused with the *hejtman* of Prague castle, a military appointment usually held by a knight.

[12] On the *inkolát*: A. Gindely, 'Die Entwickelung des böhmischen Adels und der Inkolatsverhältnisse seit dem 16. Jahrhundert', *Abhandlungen der k. böhmischen Gesellschaft der Wissenschaften*, ser. vii, 1, ph.-h. Kl. 3 (Pr. 1886). On the language: id., *Gegenreformation*, 484–7; Zíbrt, *BČH* iv, nos. 10338–60.

On paper the new *Landesordnung* came near to expressing what later Habsburg lawyers would call the principle of forfeiture (*Verwirkung*): the rebel province has lost all its rights, and what remains to it, remains by royal favour alone. The distinguished Czech historian, Anton Gindely, writing in the 1890s, certainly thought so; for him the Habsburgs now possessed the power freely to alter Bohemian public law, to abrogate all privileges not specifically confirmed, to drive a coach and horses through the country's traditional political arrangements. Ironically, most of his patriotic contemporaries took a different view: committed to their nineteenth-century assertion of the continuity of the Bohemian constitution, they were forced to argue that in theory the *Obnovené zřízení zemské* actually confirmed all privileges not abrogated.[13] It was the subsequent *practice* of government which turned Bohemia (so they thought) into a mere dependency of Vienna. But that, as I shall hope to show, is to reverse the relation between the new forms and their implementation, to mistake coach for horses. The Bohemian state coach was now, indeed, heavily stacked with Habsburg luggage; but the ruling house provided no new equipage to draw it. In fact the decades of turmoil between 1620 and 1650 disguise an autonomous domestic development running beside, and interacting with, the military and political authority of the Habsburgs and the strategy of their Counter-Reformation. A further set of causative factors, beginning earlier and continuing later, validated and impressed their own seal on the whole evolution. Again, as with Austria, I shall consider in turn the role played by aristocracy and Catholic Church, and the relations of each to the dynasty.

★

The rise of magnates is especially clear within the Bohemian nobility. The land settlement after 1620 hastened the elimination of the knights, many of whom emigrated or fell into such penury that those who remained lacked any collective influence, and the collapse of the towns, especially the royal ones. Curiously, the last great

---

[13] Gindely, *Gegenreformation*, esp. 471–3. Gindely had a German father and a Czech mother; his position lies close to that adopted—for more partisan reasons—by many Bohemian German historians. For the opposite view see (e.g.) Kalousek, loc. cit.; V. V. Tomek, *Sněmy české dle obnoveného zřízení zemského Ferdinanda II* (Pr. 1868), 1–12 and *passim*; and—in modified form—Denis-Vančura, loc. cit.

expression of Bohemia's pre-1620 social mobility was the chance to leave the country, and some 150,000 people trod the path into exile. By mid-century a much more closed caste occupied the summit of the new hierarchy.[14]

The first and most notorious beneficiary of Habsburg victory was the international *soldatesca*, which the dynasty paid off in estates for want of cash. Charles Bucquoy de Longueval (died in 1621), from Artois, was given lands in the south sequestered from the Švamberks (successors to the Rožmberks) even before the White Mountain. Baltazar Marradas (died in 1638), a Spanish soldier of fortune, descended with his mercenaries like leeches on the area around Pilsen, and gained the valuable castle of Hluboká, as did his fellow-countryman, Guillermo Verdugo, that at Doupov. Worst scourge of all, Martin Huerta (as he called himself, though really an impoverished petty noble from the Southern Netherlands) amassed extensive Bohemian properties. There were others during the 1620s: Julius Heinrich of Saxe-Lauenburg, who bought Ostrov (Schlackenwerth), with its rich mines; and a further convert from a north-German ruling family, Bruno von Mansfeld, who acquired Dobříš, having proved himself as devoted a supporter of the Habsburgs as his distant, lifelong Catholic cousin Ernst was their enemy; even the Rhenish clan of Metternich, whose new estate at Königswart, near Eger, would achieve fame only two centuries later.[15] A few court *arrivistes* from abroad likewise staked their claim: among them Francesco de Magni, or Magnis, and the two Questenbergs, Hermann and Gerhard, who had influential brothers in the Counter-Reformation clergy.

Yet the greatest court *arriviste* was local: Pavel Michna (died in

[14] The basic sources for what follows are articles in *OSN* (many by A. Sedláček), s.v.; some entries in Wurzbach; and the genealogical summaries from a 19th-century perspective in R. J. Meraviglia-Crivelli, *Der böhmische Adel* (Nuremberg 1886) and H. von Kadich, *Der mährische Adel* (ibid. 1887). Bílek, *Dějiny konfiskací*, contains much information, and there is good evidence of the state of land-holding by the 1650s in *Berní rula*, ed. K. Doskočil et al., i–iii, x–xiii, xviii–xix, xxiii, xxvi–xxviii, xxxi–xxxiii (Pr. 1950–5, n.m.p.), esp. i, 69–126 (by G. Čechová). Zibrt, *BČH* i, nos. 6068–23194, provides a vast bibliographical apparatus for noble families and their leading members, but very few have found serious historians, and some—especially those long-extinct—slip through the net entirely.

[15] Königswart (Kynžvart) was only an outlying possession for the family, though one Philipp von Metternich (died in 1698), a direct ancestor of the chancellor, was burgrave of Eger in the mid-17th century.

1632), once a chancery secretary, then *éminence grise* behind the consortium which debauched the country's finances in 1623, who rose to be Count of Vacinov (Weizenhofen), wealthy landlord, and builder of a large palace on the Little Side of Prague. And the greatest freebooter came from the ranks of the native nobility: Albrecht von Waldstein, known to the world as Wallenstein. His dizzy ascent through the 1620s to become imperial generalissimo, Duke of Sagan in Silesia and of Mecklenburg in the *Reich*, was founded on immense acquisitions of land and resources in Bohemia: a conglomerate of estates named after the castle of Friedland, though actually centred on the little town of Jičín (Gitschin). Let us not forget that he could style himself Prince of Friedland by 1623, Duke of Friedland by 1625, before ever he wielded the general's baton. Carefully rounded-off, administered, and nurtured, the richest lands in the valley of the Elbe belonged by the early 1630s either to Wallenstein, or to his close confidants and fellow-countrymen, Adam Trčka and Vilém Kinský.[16] So things might have remained, had not the 'accident' of Wallenstein's overweening ambition and suspicion of the court entailed the disgrace and murder of all three in 1634.

Only then did a second wave of rootless *condottieri* gain rich Bohemian pickings. They were led by two Italians: Octavio Piccolomini (1599–1656), Wallenstein's military successor, who took over the Trčka lands around Náchod; and Matthias Gallas (1584–1647), Habsburg war-chief by the 1640s, who settled at Friedland and Reichenberg (Liberec). Johann Aldringen (1588–1634), from Lorraine, one of the more gifted imperial commanders, received Teplitz as the price of his loyalty. And so it went on down to the Celtic fringe of actual assassins: John Gordon, garrison commandant at Eger on that fatal February day, Walter Butler, Walter Leslie, Walter Devereux.[17] The end of the war saw some further grants and purchases: for General Werth and his deputy, Johann von Sporck; for the military architect Pieroni; for the Huguenot Louis de Souches, who gallantly defended Brno against his former paymasters, the Swedes, in 1645 and later converted. But

---

[16] Bílek, *Dějiny konfiskací*, ii, 732–832; A. Ernstberger, *Wallenstein als Volkswirt im Herzogtum Friedland* (Reichenberg 1929); Polišenský, *Thirty Years War*, 181 ff., 197–200; Mann, op. cit. esp. 160–6, 181–6, 222–40.

[17] Bílek, loc. cit.; Mann, op. cit. 834–52, 865–9.

in sum the legend of vast acquisitions by a corps of cosmopolitan officers outstrips the reality. Moreover, their enjoyment of Bohemian possessions was rarely long-lived: the Souches lasted until 1736, Gallas, Piccolomini, and Questenberg until the mid-eighteenth century, Mansfeld until 1780, Leslie until 1802, Bucquoy and Sporck until the end of the Monarchy. But those families were the exceptions, and even they wielded little political influence; members, indeed, of the new ruling group, most proved inactive ones.[18]

The second category of aristocrats in seventeenth-century Bohemia was made up of loyal Catholic families, mostly established nobility, transplanted there from other parts of the Monarchy. Some of these were essentially soldiers of fortune, conspicuous among them the Tyrolean Christoph Simon von Thun, whose descendants dug themselves in for centuries around Tetschen and Klösterle, and several Friulian families: Colloredo and Collalto; the brothers Camillo and Paolo Morzin, who gained large holdings from the 1630s onwards; Francesco Clary and his son Geronimo, heir by marriage to the Aldringen fortune. We can find more evidence of overlap with the *condottieri* already discussed: Leslie had already settled in Styria; Aldringen's brother was bishop of Seckau; even the Gallases—though often taken for Spaniards—were actually rural nobility from the Habsburg Trentino. Yet, while such Central European immigrants may originally have settled in Bohemia by virtue of their military credentials, many others had little or no connection with the army. Their arrival was not necessarily bound to the events immediately after 1620 at all.

We have already encountered Liechtensteins and Dietrichsteins as major proprietors in pre-war Moravia. Their position was confirmed as outright dominance of the margravate by mid-century, and the Liechtensteins especially, given nearly limitless opportunities during Karl's governorship, made large purchases in Bohemia—more than had been bargained for even by the dynasty, which initiated lengthy (albeit half-hearted) litigation against his

---

[18] Perhaps the only important exceptions are Johann Wenzel Gallas, diplomat and viceroy of Naples, who died in 1719 (see, most recently, E. Jarnut-Derbolav, *Die österreichische Gesandschaft in London, 1701–11* (Bonn 1972), 171–529), and two Mansfelds who occupied high court positions simultaneously in the early 18th century; and even these were not really *Bohemian* politicians.

son.[19] Similarly the Thurn-Valsassinas were a Bohemian family both before and after the white Mountain, though they had to ride the proscription of Heinrich Matthias's branch. Whereas one or two of Austria's rising magnate houses burst upon the Bohemian scene without any genteel preliminaries, notably the Eggenbergs at Krumlov and the Trautmannsdorfs at Litomyšl, others possessed longer links with the country: Harrachs and Althans gained the *inkolát* before 1600; the cosmopolitan Salms began amassing lands in Moravia from 1604, the Styrian Rottals from 1612. Hungarian aristocrats too moved into Moravia: Forgách, Erdődy, Apponyi, Dóczy, Pálffy, Illésházy, even the nephew of Cardinal Pázmány. The Barons Serényi, having established a foothold there in 1614, advanced so far as to provide the provincial *hejtman* between 1655 and 1664.[20]

These families proved much more lasting and consequential than the footloose soldiery. They form the bulk of the foreigners who owned some two-fifths of Bohemia's peasantry in 1650, and their residence was often permanent.[21] But they exercised little power in their adopted country, especially in Bohemia proper, and for that kind of influence we must look elsewhere. However ragged its colours, however decimated its ranks, the old nobility of Bohemia still provided political leadership in the state.

*

The Bohemian *šlechta*—to use the Czech word is not to deny a German element within it—underwent the transition to an élite of magnates in extreme degree.[22] Again the process was in good

---

[19] Karl Liechtenstein had 3,672 Moravian subject families in 1618 (already more than anyone else), his son Karl Eusebius 9,349 in the 1640s (and his two brothers 3,906 and 2,204); by the 1690s the family possessed more than 19,000 peasant families there, some 20 per cent of the total. The Dietrichsteins had 1,652 in 1618 (excluding the bishopric), 5,628 in the 1640s, and more than 6,000 in the 1690s (Matějek, 'Bílá Hora', 83–5, 92, 94). Gindely, *Gegenreformation*, 360 ff.

[20] Macůrek, *České země a Slovensko*, 40; Pázmány, *Levelei*, nos. 535, 609, 674, 895, 907, 916, 935, 944, 994, 1009, 1032, 1056. On the Serényis: Matějek, art. cit. 93 f., Polišenský, op. cit. 247 ff.

[21] Placht, op. cit. 222 ff.; *Berní rula*, i–ii, *passim*. It also seems to be the case, as Placht points out (ibid. 259 ff.), that immigrant lords tended to settle in *German* areas.

[22] For what follows see—besides *OSN*, Wurzbach, Zedler, and (marginally) Meraviglia-Crivelli, op. cit. and Kadich, op. cit.—F. Vlasák, *Der altböhmische Adel und seine Nachkommenschaft nach dem dreissigjährigen Kriege* (Pr. [1866]), who studies

measure an organic one, begun well before 1620: while certain powerful houses fell away through natural wastage (Hradec (Neuhaus) in 1604, Rožmberk in 1611, Smiřický in 1627, Pernstein in 1631, Wartenberg in 1632, Trčka in the Eger bloodbath of 1634), others entrenched themselves ever more firmly with the triple guarantee of latifundium, Catholic orthodoxy, and fairly unswerving dynastic loyalty. By the late seventeenth century the inner circle seems to have comprised a mere ten families, almost all of which had once been infected with Protestantism, if not involved in the rebellion itself.

Primi inter pares came to the Lobkovices, a numerous clan which rode the disgrace of Jiří in the 1590s and the Lutheranism of its Hassenstein branch to emerge with unrivalled lustre through the intransigent Bohemian chancellor, Zdeněk Vojtěch, and his son, Václav Eusebius. Zdeněk Vojtěch (1568–1628), married to the vivacious and domineering heiress of the Pernsteins, was created prince in 1624 for his incalculable services to Ferdinand II. Václav Eusebius (1609–77), president of the War Council and chief minister to Leopold I, acquired the immediate county of Sternstein in the Empire in 1641, became Duke of Sagan in Silesia five years later (shades of Wallenstein!), and established an entail for the vast estates around Raudnitz on the Elbe. Though his fall from power briefly seemed to threaten sequestration and disaster, his son—a mediocre personality—retained all the family influence and married into the ruling houses of Nassau, Baden, and Schwarzenberg.[23]

The Waldsteins survived still rougher upsets: not only the heady career of the generalissimo Albrecht, but the pugnacious Protestantism of several other members, like the printer Heník, who perished in exile. Yet four generations of seventeenth-century Waldsteins held the highest offices of state at Prague and Vienna.

the fate of the whole pre-1620 nobility and finds a surprising measure of survival; and R. Procházka, *Genealogisches Handbuch erloschener Herrenstandsfamilien* (Neustadt a.d. Aisch 1973), with purely genealogical information about extinct families. Neither Vlasák nor Procházka includes Moravia. There are extensive family trees in Balbín, *Miscellanea Historica*, ii (cf. below, p. 215).
[23] There is an extraordinary lack of serious literature on this most powerful of old-Czech families. See Vlasák, op. cit. 63–6; *OSN*, s.v., and Wurzbach, s.v. 'Lobkowitz' (thorough). For Jiří and Zdeněk Vojtěch cf. above, p. 48; for Václav Eusebius, above, p. 144, and the life by A. Wolf cited there, and Z. Kalista, *Čechové, kteří tvořili dějiny světa* (Pr. 1939), 179–89.

Heník's cousin Adam (died in 1638), one of the leading Catholic advocates of political moderation both before and after 1620, became grand burgrave of the kingdom when that post re-emerged on Liechtenstein's death in 1627. His son Maximilian (who grew up under the wing of Albrecht) was master of the horse and high chamberlain to Ferdinand III; three of Maximilian's sons served Leopold, the youngest, Karl Ferdinand (1634–1702), likewise as high chamberlain and as major-domo to the young Empress Eleonora. He and his own son Karl Ernst (yet another high chamberlain) were also prominent diplomats. Meanwhile the fourth son of Maximilian ruled the archdiocese of Prague between 1676 and 1694.[24]

Perhaps—after all—some significance lies in the fact that the Waldsteins, while retaining possession of Albrecht's magnificent palace on the Little Side (which people still often called the *Palais* Friedland), were rarely, after 1634, given high *Bohemian* posts, with all their opportunities for intrigue. The reverse was true of two ancient Czech families much more prominent in their own country than outside it, and now bound by the peculiar ties which unite fellow-defenestratees: Slavata and Martinic. The rebel action on 23 May 1618 has commonly been accounted a tactical mistake, a piece of misguided victimization; but perhaps it erred only in so far as Vilém Slavata and Jaroslav Martinic escaped with their lives, for they were indeed formidable men and rightly marked as the leaders of Catholic extremism. After 1620, invested with the halo of martyrdom divinely averted (and granted uncommonly long careers, perhaps through the same agency), they dominated Bohemian politics: Slavata as chancellor from 1628 to 1652, Martinic as grand burgrave from 1638 to 1649. Both placed the enhanced family possessions on a secure and ordered foundation: the Slavatas, who, as heirs to the lords of Hradec, were second in riches only to the Lobkovices, around Jindřichův Hradec in the south; the Martinices around Smečno and Slaný west of Prague. Whereas Slavata's sons died comparatively young, Bernard Ignác

[24] Vlasák, op. cit. 69 f., and comprehensive treatment in *OSN* s.v. 'Valdštejn', and Wurzbach, s.v. On Heník, cf. above, pp. 102 f.; on Adam: Gindely, *Dreissigjähriger Kreig*, i, 382–6, 460 ff. *passim*. On Karl Ferdinand: Kalista, *Čechové*, 167–76. On Archbishop Johann Friedrich: M. Kinter in *ÖVjschr. f. Kath. Theol.* viii (1869), 525–72; ix (1870), 7–44, uncritical.

Martinic—once ransomed with his aged father from Swedish custody in 1648—became the foremost domestic politician of the next generation, grand burgrave for a remarkable span of thirty-four years from 1651. At the end of the seventeenth century, Slavatas and Martinices held an unassailable position in Bohemian society, one confirmed by a special superior status at the diet. Only human mortality could intervene: ironically paired again, they proved the only two families in this group not to survive as powerful dynasties until the end of the Monarchy. The Martinices died out in 1789, their name and possessions (like those of Gallas) being inherited by the Upper Austrian Clams; the Slavatas expired as early as 1712, when not one of Vilém's four prominent grandsons could produce an heir. The most important Slavata estates passed to the related Czech magnate family of Černín.[25]

The Černíns offer a classic paradigm of Reformation and Counter-Reformation vicissitudes: of three early seventeenth-century brothers, the eldest became major-domo to King Frederick and perished on the scaffold; the youngest, Heřman, an ambitious Catholic courtier, rose to be chief judge, high steward of Bohemia, and imperial diplomat, amassing a large fortune in lands (albeit lands devastated by war). His estates passed to the grandson of the middle, unadventurous brother. This grandson, Humprecht Jan (1628–82) was one of Leopold I's closest friends, a *grand seigneur* who commissioned the most monumental of all Prague's Baroque palaces; his own heir served as grand burgrave between 1704 and 1710. Similar success attended the Kinskýs, who in this period abandoned the original, less mellifluous form of their name: Vchynský. Of four Kinský brothers in the generation of 1618–20, two acted as rebel leaders, while a third, Vilém, was slaughtered with Wallenstein. But the eldest, Václav—although the arch-intriguer among them all—survived the crisis; his son married a

---

[25] *OSN*, s.v.; Wurzbach, s.v. 'Clam-Martinitz'; and Procházka, op. cit. 183–6, 281–6, are the only real sources. On Vilém Slavata and Jaroslav Martinic see also above, pp. 48, 63, 66 f.; *Rudolf II*, 69 and n.; and the correspondence between them printed by F. Tischer in *SbH* (Rezek), i (1883), 305–22; ii (1884), 32–7, 92–8; iii (1885), 193–202, 253–92, 360–4. For their special rank at the *sněm* (immediately behind them came the Waldsteins and Trautmannsdorfs; the Lobkovices—being princes—were a different case) see Gindely, *Gegenreformation*, 476 f., 500–3. The ransom paid in 1648 for the two Martinices amounted to 60,000 gulden (Rezek, *Dějiny*, i, 34). On Bernard Ignác, see below, pp. 231 f.

Portia, and his grandson, Franz Ulrich (1634–99), became one of the most significant courtier-diplomats of the Leopoldine era. Thus by 1700 the Kinskýs too were confirmed as both mighty aristocrats and devoted Habsburg servants: between 1683 and 1745 no less than four of them held the office of Bohemian chancellor.[26]

Four more families complete this select list. The Sternbergs—more Czech than German, despite the name—had produced in Adam (died in 1623) the chief Catholic conciliator of the years before 1618. Though his policies were outrun by events, his successors adapted themselves to changed circumstances. His son was made chief judge; his grandsons were characteristic representatives of the magnate culture of the Bohemian Baroque: Wenzel Adalbert builder of two elegant Prague palaces, on the Little Side and at Troya; Ignaz Karl a bibliophile and traveller. Adam's great nephew, Adolf Wratislaw, was a confidant of Leopold I and grand burgrave between 1685 and 1703; another branch of the family intermarried closely with the Martinices.[27] Equally ramified were the Kolovrats: their Libsteinský line, with entailed estates centred on Reichenau in north-east Bohemia, conspicuous above all in the *Hofkammer* president and grand burgrave, Ulrich Franz (1609–50), and his nephews Franz Karl, long-serving *hejtman* of Moravia, Ferdinand Ludwig, grand prior of the Maltese order, and Johann Wilhelm, postulated archbishop of Prague (who died before his consecration); the collateral line of Krakovský unfolded more fully in the eighteenth century. The Schlicks, long the chief landowners in north-west Bohemia and exploiters of the famous mines of

[26] Vlasák, op. cit. 50–5. The colourful 17th-century Černins have attracted two outstanding Czech historians: Pekař, *Kost*, esp. i, 121–76; Z. Kalista, *Mládí Humprechta Jana Černína z Chudenic, zrození barokního kavalíra* (Pr. 1932); id. (ed.), *Korespondence Zuzany Černínové ... s jejím synem Humprechtem Janem Černínem* (Pr. 1941); cf. id., *Čechové*, 203–11; and above, p. 144, n. 70. Heřman's mission to the Porte in 1644 is described by F. Tischer, *Die zweite Gesandschaftsreise des Grafen Hermann Czernin nach Constantinopel* (Neuhaus 1879). The equally colourful 17th-century Kinskýs seem to have been passed by, except for Kalista, *Čechové*, 193–200, on Franz Ulrich.

[27] J. Tanner, *Geschichte derer Helden von Sternen oder des ... Geschlechts von Sternberg* (Pr. 1732), pt. 2, written in the 1670s, reaches only to 1576. See also Vlasák, op. cit. 67–9; *OSN* s.v. 'Šternberk'; and Wurzach, s.v. On Ignaz Karl: UK, MSS. XVII A 25, IV D 11, VIII G 18 (travels); below, p. 314 (library). On Adolf Wratislaw: above, p. 145, n. 71. For information about the lesser, Holice line (which produced two bishops): V. Schulz (ed.), *Korespondence hr. Václava Jiřího Holického ze Šternberka* (Pr. 1898).

Joachimsthal, confirmed their position after the White Mountain, despite the arch-treason of Joachim Andreas, through his distant cousin Heinrich (died in 1650), field-marshal and president of the War Council. Heinrich initiated the usual process of founding a *Fideicommissum*; his grandson was Bohemian chancellor. Finally come the Nostitzes, a family of Lusatian and Silesian extraction, which spread across the Bohemian border both before and after 1620. The convert Otto enjoyed much royal favour as vice-chancellor of the kingdom from 1622 until his death in 1639. His nephews Otto and Johann Hartwig consolidated the advantage, the latter as chancellor from 1652 to 1683, constructing in the process one of Prague's most beautiful palaces and acquiring the sovereign county of Rieneck in Franconia.[28]

In Moravia the caste of historic families grew even smaller. Beside the Liechtensteins and Dietrichsteins, who so vastly extended their land-holding from bases in the south as to own one-quarter of the margravate by 1700 and shared with the Habsburgs the perquisites of Olomouc, most spacious of all bishoprics inside the Monarchy,[29] only the Kounices showed a real advance. While Oldřich of Kounice, the lord of Austerlitz, had been a firm Protestant, his orphaned son Lev Vilém (1614–55), brother to two rebels but converted and guided by Cardinal Dietrichstein, restored the family fortunes. Lev Vilém's son was Dominik Andreas (1655–1705), diplomat and imperial vice-chancellor. The next generation produced a bishop and a Moravian *hejtman*, and acquired the immediate county of Rietberg in the Empire. Then followed the famous chancellor, known to us in the German spelling of his name: Prince Wenzel Anton Kaunitz.[30]

Alongside this inner élite in the lands of the Bohemian crown

---

[28] Vlasák, op. cit. 56–60, 66 f. There is little on the Kolovrats (Ger.: Kolowrat) or Schlicks (Cz.: Šlik) beyond *OSN* and Wurzbach, s.vv.; but the Nostitzes have also G. A. Nostitz, *Beiträge zur Geschichte der Nostitz*, i–ii (Leipzig 1874–6); and lengthy treatment in V. Boetticher, *Geschichte des oberlausitzischen Adels*, ii (Oberlössnitz bei Dresden 1913), s.v. Cf. also *Rudolf II*, 232–6; unfortunately the official and family documents in *The Nostitz Papers*, ed. E. J. Labarre (Hilversum 1956), are examined only for their watermarks, and the result is useless for historical purposes.

[29] Franz Dietrichstein was bishop from 1599 until 1636, then Habsburg archdukes between 1637 and 1644 (above, p. 135, n. 47), and Karl Liechtenstein-Castelcorno (a collateral line) from 1664 until 1695. Dietrichstein's vicar-general, Jan Platejs (cf. below, p. 217) was elected in 1636 over the head of Archduke Leopold Wilhelm, but he died before his consecration.

[30] Vlasák, op. cit. 61–3; Procházka, op. cit. 137–43 (the Kaunitzes died out in
(continued)

stood an outer circle of middling aristocrats, comprising hardly
more than a further fifteen or twenty families.[31] Some tended to
decline during the period, like Berka of Dubá, one of the most
powerful Moravian clans about 1600, and aggressively Catholic in
two of its branches, but extinguished by 1706; Talmberk and
Řičanský; Vřesovec, sustained a little by the plunder of Vilém,
master of the mint during the 1620s; even Vrtba, which still
provided a grand burgrave between 1712 and 1734. Others were
gradually rising: Vrbna (Johann Franz Vrbna was Bohemian
chancellor from 1700 to 1705); Vratislav of Mitrovice, one of whose
number, the highly accomplished 'Count Wratislaw' at the court of
St. James's, arranged the diplomatic contacts between Marlborough
and Prince Eugene; Lažanský and Hrzán, and—in a more modest
way—Podstatský or Sedlnický. A few made startling recoveries
from deep complicity in the events of 1618–20. The descendants of
two executed noble ringleaders were readmitted to the establishment
as counts (one of them headed the government of Vienna during
the 1683 siege; another put down the revolt of the peasantry three
years earlier with an equally iron hand).[32] The Calvinist Žerotíns,
greatest house in the whole of Moravia before the revolt, hung on
through a single, subdued, Catholic branch. One or two major
native families of Silesia, primarily Schaffgotsch and Oppersdorf,
played a sufficient role in the kingdom at large to merit inclusion
here and round off the picture.[33]

1913); F. Hrubý, 'Český poutník v Assisi r. 1636', *ČČH* xxxii (1926), 283–98 (on
Lev Vilém); G. Klingenstein, *Der Aufstieg des Hauses Kaunitz* (Göttingen 1975). On
the Kaunitz estates see also J. Válka, 'Sociální poměry na uherskobrodském panství
v 17. století', *ČMM* lxxi (1952), 217–47; on Rietberg: G. Benecke, *Society and politics
in Germany, 1500–1750* (London 1974), 133–6.

[31] A certain number of families ranked as counts for all or most of the period 1620–
1720 appear to have had little or no public role: examples are Gutenstein, Hoditz,
and Bubna.

[32] On Kaspar Kaplíř, hero of the siege but grandson of a traitor, see F. Mareš,
'Hrabě Kašpar Zdeněk Kaplíř', *ČČM* lvii (1883), 3–45, 219–54; F. Houdek,
'Obránce Vídně proti Turkům ... v lidovém podání', *ČL* xxii (1913), 209–20;
Kalista, *Čechové*, 155–64. Christoph Wilhelm Harant, the hammer of the peasants
(Koči, *Boje*, 85–8; id., *Frýdlantsko*, ch. 3; Kašpar, *Nevolnické povstání*, 77), was son
of an *émigré*, Jan Jiří (cf. above, p. 70, n. 70, and Menčik in *ČČM* lxi (1887), 488–95),
and great-nephew of the arch-rebel, Kryštof Harant (cf. *Rudolf II*, 191–2, 278),
whose book of travels he had reissued in German translation (Nuremberg 1678),
with a fulsome dedication to Leopold I.

[33] Johann Ernst Schaffgotsch became grand burgrave from 1734 to 1747. Cf.
below, pp. 300 f.

★

This closely intermarried upper *šlechta*, as our genealogical sketches have already indicated, formed the political nation of Bohemia after 1620, as it had done on a far broader base before.[34] Its status was confirmed by the grant of titles from the Habsburgs, though again (compare the Austrian case) they were the gloss on a profounder evolution. Indeed, Bohemian aristocrats wielded conspicuous power, power out of proportion to their small numbers, in the imperial counsels at Vienna. For all Leopold's playful view of his 'rebellious Czechs', he numbered several of them among his closest friends. 'Bohemian' policies, tending to stress the interests of the Habsburg Monarchy rather than those of the *Reich*, even to the extent of a *rapprochement* with France, emerged during Lobkovic's presidency of the Privy Conference and culminated in the 1690s with the careers of Franz Ulrich Kinský and Dominik Andreas Kaunitz. They were then continued, in modified form, by Johann Wenzel Vratislav.[35]

The old noble families did not, for the most part, approve of the *Obnovené zřízení zemské* (even Zdeněk Lobkovic lamented it);[36] but it could not work without them, and through them it was *de facto* amended. The Habsburgs compromised with an aristocracy which at court represented the country and in the country represented the court, exercising an almost complete monopoly over the senior dignities of state. Between the battle of the White Mountain and the reforms of Maria Theresa no outsider held either of the two key offices: those of grand burgrave in Prague, and of Bohemian chancellor, resident mainly at Vienna, where the grandiose new chancery built for him shortly after 1700 by Fischer von Erlach shows how thriving was the institution. Much the same is true of the other posts whose occupants jointly acted, in the near-permanent absence of the monarch, as a lieutenancy council under the headship of the grand burgrave: high steward, high marshal,

---

[34] The point is taken, in a general way, by Placht, op. cit. 262 ff., and by Hassenpflug, art. cit.

[35] Disparagement in (e.g.) Kalista (ed.), *Korespondence*, no. 16: '[Bohemians] ordinariamente ... sono haimbtükisch [i.e. sly, treacherous]'. For the influence: above, pp. 144 f.; Kalista, *Čechové*, 179–223, *passim;* Klingenstein, *Haus Kaunitz*, 49 ff. On Vratislav as diplomat: A. Arneth, 'Eigenhändige Correspondenz des Königs Karl III von Spanien ... mit ... Grafen Johann Wenzel Wratislaw', *AÖG* xvi (1856), 3–224; Jarnut–Derbolav, op. cit. 36–170.

[36] Gindely, *Gegenreformation*, 449 ff., 504 f.

high chamberlain, chief justices of the realm and the court, president of the court of appeal, president of the Bohemian Chamber, the chief organ of economic policy. The only exceptions were a few lower offices still reserved to the knights—such as chief clerk or chamberlain of the royal boroughs—though here also old-established families had a stranglehold. Against them, the rise of the occasional bureaucrat like Johann Losy von Losimthal, Ferdinand III's controller of excise, cut very little ice, while the principle of royal appointment, and regular re-appointment, of state servants lost its force.[37] The statistics of royal commissioners to Bohemian diets between 1627 and 1698 tell their own story: in years of the full *sněm* two lords and one knight attended; in years of more limited assembly (*sjezd*) the grand burgrave alone represented the crown. In all a Martinic was present on twenty occasions, a Kolovrat on nineteen, a Sternberg on seventeen, Černín and Slavata on ten, Lobkovic on eight, Vrtba on seven, Vrbna and Kinský on six, Berka on four, Waldstein and Lažanský on three, Talmberk, Vratislav and Schlick on two, Nostitz on one; whereas the grand total for individuals recently settled in Bohemia is eight.[38]

These officers, with their attendant secretariats, formed the Habsburg administration in the Bohemian lands. Only one hesitant attempt was made to remove any part of it from native influence, in the shape of the new Moravian royal tribunal, which after 1636 sat under a *hejtman* regularly chosen from among families comparatively

[37] F. Roubik, 'Mistodržitelství v Čechách v letech 1577-1749', *SbAPr* xvii (1967), 539-601, esp. 580-8, with lists of the holders of these eleven posts, and of the other three which carried the rank of stadholder: burgrave of the *kraj* of Koniggrätz (reserved to a knight or burgher), master of the horse (a sinecure), and grand prior of the knights of Malta (see below, p. 222). Stránský, op. cit., ch. 14, describes their traditional functions; cf. Auersperg, op. cit. i, 26-8, 70, 75 ff., on the personnel of the court of appeal. For Losy's activities: Rezek, *Dějiny*, i, 346-64; ii, 159 ff.; cf. Zibrt, *BČH* i, no. 14365.

[38] These statistics are derived from the printed title-pages of dietal resolutions (*artikulové sněmovní*), reproduced in *Knihopis*, nos. 392-478. I have listed only the families already mentioned; for the sake of completeness we should add the semi-Polish Counts Rozdražov (four times), and the Bohemian Barons Hieserle (three times) and Laminger von Albenreuth (twice). The new arrivals were Thun (four times), Mansfeld, Colloredo, Trautmannsdorf, and Pötting (once each). In one exceptional year (1677), the lords were represented by two 'foreigners': Johann Friedrich Trautmannsdorf (son of Maximilian) and Leopold's old friend, Franz Eusebius Pötting, formerly ambassador in Madrid. The knightly commissioners—it need hardly be said—were still more solidly old-Bohemian.

newly introduced to the province. But that soon fell into confusion and inefficiency—and the man who did most to make it work was the thoroughly patriotic Maximilian Kaunitz.[39] If the high *šlechta* so dominated the Habsburg side of the constitutional equation, it is hardly surprising that they controlled the estates. As in Austria, these not only survived, but even increased their executive functions: diets met at least annually (fifty-nine times between 1648 and 1698), and their elected committees took the main responsibility for public order and tax-collection. A vast 'doomsday' survey of the country, known as the *berní rula* (1653–5), was actually commissioned and executed by the estates in order to safeguard their position *vis-à-vis* the royal Chamber.[40]

Local autonomies certainly faded away in Bohemia, whose nineteenth-century historians so bemoaned the collapse of its regions by contrast with the sturdy county structure of Hungary. Again, however, the main beneficiary was not the crown, but the great latifundium, freed from the meddling of towns and petty nobility. District *hejtmanships* tended to go to a penumbra of families on the edge of the highest society: Petřvaldský or Přehořovský, Deym of Střítež or Hieserle of Chodaw.[41] Nor did the *šlechta* suffer

---

[39] On this tribunal see Chr.d'Elvert, *Zur österreichischen Verwaltungs-Geschichte mit besonderer Rücksicht auf die böhmischen Länder* (Brünn 1880), 198–232; id., *Zur österreichischen Finanz-Geschichte mit besonderer Rücksicht auf die böhmischen Länder* (Brünn 1881), 209–55c, *passim*; V. Vašků, *Studie o správních dějinách a písemnostech moravského královského tribunálu z let 1636–1749* (Brno 1969); cf. J. Radimský, *Tribunál, sbírka normálií z let 1628–1782* (Brno 1956), intro. On Kaunitz, cf. Klingenstein, *Haus Kaunitz*, 79 ff. After Franz Dietrichstein (1620–36) the *hejtmanship* fell to a Salm (1637–40), then to a triumvirate of Liechtenstein, Rottal, and Francesco Magni (1640–3), and to Liechtenstein and Rottal alone (1643–55), then to Gabriel Serényi (1655–64), and—after a brief Dietrichstein interlude (1664)—to Franz Karl Kolovrat-Libšteinský (1664–1700), who was succeeded by a Thurn–Valsassina and an Oppersdorf.

[40] On the diets: Tomek, *Sněmy české*, mostly financial affairs; Rezek, *Děje*, and *Dějiny*, i–ii, with thorough discussion of their sessions. *Berní rula*, i, 13–67, esp. 37 f.; Pekař, *Katastry*, 4–56. Even Denis–Vančura (i, 2, 56 ff. *passim*) have to admit that no real 'centralization' or 'absolutism' existed under Leopold I; cf. Kalousek, op. cit. 463 ff.; Grünberg, op. cit. i, 108 ff.

[41] Every *kraj* had two *hejtmany* (hejtmen?), one a lord, the other a knight, who were traditionally confirmed in office each spring. B. Rieger, *Zřízení krajské v Čechách*, i–ii (Pr. 1889–92), i; Macek–Žáček, op. cit.; Rezek, *Děje*, 457–6.. This development has often been misunderstood; E. C. Hellbling, *Österreichische Verfassungs- und Verwaltungsgeschichte* (V. 1956), 253, even speaks of the 17th-century *hejtman* as an '*intendant*'.

from any serious economic *dirigisme*. Crown estates, few enough at the beginning of the seventeenth century, continued to be alienated throughout the period, and those that remained were almost all mortgaged. They brought ludicrously little return to the Bohemian *komora*, less still—after its mismanagement and corruption—to the treasury in Vienna.[42] Early mercantilist entrepreneurship, where it began to develop before 1700, was almost exclusively the brainchild of large landowners and their protégé projectors.[43]

With aristocratic management went aristocratic culture, full of opulence and display, and distinctly native in hue. By the 1650s, certainly by the 1700s, this was no longer substantially a Czech culture. The Czech language fell into decline, though it proved the casualty of a cosmopolitan atmosphere, not of official policy. Ferdinand III spoke it; Leopold made jocular efforts with it and insisted on sitting through sermons preached in it.[44] Czech continued to have precedence over German for proclamations and published decrees of the *sněm*; knowledge of it was still demanded for membership of the court of appeal. In Moravia it died of inanition: by the 1720s the Czech clerk to the tribunal simply had nothing to do. The aristocrats gradually abandoned it in favour of Italian and French, as well as German.[45] But to contemporaries linguistic considerations were secondary, and they remained consciously Bohemian. Genealogical studies enjoyed great vogue as a way of revealing ancient Slav ancestry, preferably royal, and links

[42] E. Maur, *Český komorní velkostatek v 17. století* (Pr. 1976), is most detailed. See also Balbín, *Miscellanea Historica*, i, bk. 3, 64 f.; Tomek, *Sněmy české*, 61–4; Rezek, *Dějiny*, i, 431; Bérenger, *Finances*, 300 f. Cf., for Silesia, Grünhagen, *Geschichte*, ii, 361 f.; and Rachfahl, op. cit. 264–6. Crown lands seem not to have yielded much over 1 per cent of the net royal revenue from Bohemia.

[43] Klíma, op. cit. 137 ff., 216 ff.; cf. below, p. 233 and n. 90. A little later, in 1715, the most famous of such magnate enterprises was founded, the Waldstein textile mill at Oberleutensdorf (Horní Litvínov). Some of the high nobles were also major creditors of the monarchy, especially the Černíns (Pekař, *Katastry*, 97 f.).

[44] Beckovský, op. cit., pt. 3, 440 f.; J. Muk, *Po stopách národního vědomí české šlechty pobělohorské* (Pr. 1931), 84 f.; Kalista (ed.), *Korespondence*, nos. 47, etc.; Placht, op. cit. 245.

[45] Klabouch, op. cit. 34; Vašků, op. cit. 29; Podlaha, *Dějiny*, 185; Pekař, *Kost*, i, 140–2, 164 f.; Muk, op. cit., esp. 103 ff. William O'Kelly, *Philosophia Aulica, juxta veterum ac recentiorum philosophorum Placita* (Pr. 1701, cf. below, pp. 326 f.), sig.)()()()(1ᵛ–4ᵛ, prints an anti-Aristotelean satire in its original French, 'eo lubentius, quod tota fere Nobilitas, in cujus gratiam hoc opus edidi, Gallicae linguae peritiam habeat'.

with the lustre of the medieval kingdom: the Jesuit Tanner's history of the Sternbergs is one example. A more celebrated Jesuit, Bohuslav Balbín, who had close links with the old nobility, prepared the project of a complete genealogy and anatomy of the *šlechta*, a grandiose, albeit unfinished enterprise. Balbín was quite ready to assimilate newer families to the old pantheon, including the Harrachs, for instance (who could, in fact, muster some distant relations among the local knightage), and even compiling spurious Czech origins for his patron, Count Lamberg.[46]

One important aspect of this antiquarianism was the concept of an aristocratic lobby within the *Bohemia sancta*, the temple of Bohemian Catholic saintliness. Medieval magnates had long been associated with private religious foundations, and it suited both spiritual and familial piety to see a continuance of these into the Baroque age: thus the Černíns basked in their descent from the Blessed Hroznata, one of the founders of Bohemian monasticism. Balbín lists many cases of nobles who either rose high in the Church or displayed personal sanctity.[47] Some of his examples are modern, and the contemporary *šlechta* exhibited a distinct leaning towards the ecclesiastical vocation and support for new religious institutions: a number of Kolovrats joined the Jesuits; Zdislav Berka became a Benedictine abbot and Benno Martinic a touchy provost of Vyšehrad; the semi-Polish Count František Rozdražov was an important Capuchin devotional writer; Sternbergs and Černíns paid much money and respect to the clerical profession; the pious endowments of Ferdinand II's friend, Václav Bruntálský of Vrbna would require a gargantuan footnote to enumerate.[48]

---

[46] Above, n. 27 (Tanner). Balbín, *Miscellanea Historica*, ii, bks. 1–2; a further eight volumes were planned; cf. O. Květoňová–Klímová, 'Styky Bohuslava Balbína s českou šlechtou pobělohorskou', *ČČH* xxxii (1926), 497–541; Muk, op. cit. 114 ff. Balbín came from a gentry family himself. On the Hřebenáři z Horochu (counts by 1706): Vlasák, op. cit. 85 f., and *OSN*, s.v. B. Balbín, *Epitome historica rerum Bohemicarum quam...Boleslaviensem Historiam placuit appellare* (Pr. 1677), sig.(b) 2ʳ (Lamberg).

[47] Schlenz, *Kirchenpatronat*, pt. 1; and F. Seibt, 'Land und Herrschaft in Böhmen', *HZ* cc (1965), 284–315, for the Middle Ages. Balbín, *Miscellanea Historica*, i, bk. 4, pt. 1, 54–8 (on Hroznata), 75 f., 155 f.; pt. 2, 101–3, 113 f., 116 f., 127–30, 149–70; ii, bk. 1, 34–49. Cf. Albert Chanovský, *Vestigium Boemiae Piae...* (Pr. 1659), 119 ff.

[48] On Martinic: V. V. Zelený, 'Tomáš Pešina z Čechorodu', *ČČM* lviii (1894), 1–22, 250–69, 471–97; lix (1885), 90–108, 226–43; lx (1886), 102–21, 331–57, 554–82,

(continued)

Evidently such things belonged to the style and career-structure of the age, but in Bohemia they were more than that. We can correlate them directly with a high sense of penitence for spectacular and frequently ill-gotten success. Wallenstein planted several religious orders on his lands and summoned Carthusian monks to solace him at his sylvan retreat of Valdice (a gesture beautifully evoked in a *Novelle* by Jaroslav Durych); flying high as usual, he even planned a bishopric for his duchy of Friedland, which would have allowed him to indulge in set-piece squabbles with the priesthood. Vilém Slavata turned by the end of his life into a mystic and spiritualist; it is a poetic accident that his family died out sixty years later with a general of the Carmelite order, Karel Felix, an intimate of Emperor Leopold who lived in Rome. The mood was easily captured by the new aristocracy, as by Franz Anton von Sporck (1662–1738), son of Johann, one of the most extraordinary noblemen of his time and donor of a bizarre Baroque foundation on his estate at Kuks. The sons of Johann Sigismund von Thun, nephew of Christoph Simon, included two archbishops of Salzburg and a bishop of Passau, as well as a Capuchin and a knight of Malta.[49]

★

Thus we reach the second bastion of Bohemian society and the other focus for native sentiment: the Church. That statement may seem difficult to reconcile with what we already know of an imposed Counter-Reformation. But (as we saw in chapter two) the new spiritual current already possessed local roots before 1620; while after the White Mountain it revealed a diversity which proved the

---

at 226–8. On Rozdražov: *Knihopis*, nos. 15000–6, though most of his works were in Latin. Sternbergs: Schulz (ed.), *Korrespondence jesuitů*, nos. 43–7, 49–50, 52–3, 55, 59, 73, 75–6, 79; Černins: Pekař, *Kost*, i, 166, etc; V. Kotrba, *Česká barokní gotika* (Pr. 1976), 53 f. On Vrbna: F. C. Khevenhüller, *Conterfet Kupfferstich*, i–ii (Leipzig 1721–2), ii, s.v.

[49] Mann, op. cit. 243–8; Schlenz, *Leitmeritz*, i, 37–44. On Vilém Slavata: Balbin, *Miscellanea Historica*, i, bk. 4, pt. 2, 130–4; cf. Mayer, op. cit. i, nos. 1272, 1315. On Karel Felix Slavata cf. *Listy úcty a přátelství*, ed. J. Klik (Pr. 1941), noting fifty indecipherable German letters to him from the emperor. On Sporck: H. Benedikt, *Franz Anton Graf von Sporck* (V. 1923), and J. Hanzal in *SbH* xxv (1977), 45–83. Motives, of course, were very mixed: witness the last Baron Leskovec, who joined the Premonstratensians after six marriages had failed to present him with an heir (Procházka, op. cit. 163–5). And as in Austria the body of the Church was non-noble—to the extent of 82 per cent of its priests in 1741 (Hassenpflug, art. cit. 85).

source of strength as well as weakness: the many mansions inside Baroque Catholicism offered scope for a distinctive Bohemian profile. Dispute raged even over the nature of the Counter-Reformation. The hard line of Carafa in the 1620s and Caramuel in the 1650s, pressing more the externals of religion and leaning on such groups as the firmly orthodox Italian congregation in Prague, conflicted at times with the gentler approach of Harrach, Magni, and their missionaries, who attempted to speak softly to the masses of the Slavonic population where a shortage of priests was chronic.[50] The lines of opposition were not clear-cut: Caramuel prided himself on a partly Czech ancestry, while Magni—a Milanese by birth—could be thoroughly internationalist when he chose: at one point he tried to secure a Bohemian bishopric for an Italian who spoke neither Czech nor German! In Moravia, Dietrichstein tended to occupy a middle position, as did the important Czech prelate, Jan Arnošt Platejs.[51]

Both sides had to rely heavily on cosmopolitan orders, above all Jesuits, Observant Franciscans, and Capuchins. But there again they found no seamless web: friction developed between the rampant Jesuits and the newly-introduced Hibernians (who also managed to quarrel with the local Franciscans); between Jesuits and the Piarists, spreading on their Moravian base from the mid-century; between Jesuits and the older orders; above all between Jesuits and Valerian Magni. The gifted Capuchin's appeal to oecumenical longings; his unwillingness to insist on extreme Papal claims; his intellectual powers and wide influence: all this made for a dangerous rivalry and a bitter, protracted feud.[52] Then came clashes between regulars and seculars. Secular prelates were

---

[50] Cf. above, pp. 118–21, and A. Rezek (ed.), 'Tak-zvaná 'Idea gubernationis ecclesiasticae' z času Kardinála Harracha', *VKČSN*, 1893, no. 3. The Italian congregation (which also formed a Bohemian branch) has its own historian: P. Rigetti, *Historische Nachricht sowohl von der Errichtung der Wellischen Congregation ... als auch des dazu gehörigen Hospitals* (Pr. 1773).

[51] Schlenz, *Leitmeritz*, i, 31 (Magni). For Platejs: Liva, art. cit.; Beckovský, op. cit., pt. 3, 13–24.

[52] On the Hibernians: B. Millett, *The Irish Franciscans 1651–65* (Rome 1964), 134–66. V. Magni, *Apologia contra Imposturas Jesuitarum* (n.p. 1659), explains the substance of the quarrel. Cf. his persuasive missionary work: *Judicium de acatholicorum regula credendi* (?Pr. 1628?, I have used the edn. at Cologne 1631), translated into English as *A Censure about the Rule of Beleefe practised by the Protestants* (Douai 1634).

marginally stronger in Bohemia than in Austria—at least after the establishment of new bishoprics at Litoměřice (1655) and König-grätz (1664)—but they stayed on the defensive, while payments to parish priests were always variable and usually meagre. During his long episcopate (1623–67) Harrach continually strove to assert his position, a task rendered no easier by squabbles about Prague's notional primacy over Olomouc. And wider animosities between clergy and laity only grew in intensity as outside threats declined: by the 1690s even the pious Černins were in contention with the Jesuits, and wartime stringencies clouded the relation between ecclesiastical and royal authority.[53]

Such oppositions could, in practice, act as a safety-valve. Often they involved a play of personalities rather than crucial issues of principle. At all events, the largest dualism, the polarity between universal and local Church, helped to strengthen the whole edifice. As in Austria, the old landed monasteries, with their incorporated parishes, had a great part in reconciling national with international. The Benedictines reasserted themselves so effectively that one of their abbots, Sobek of Bílenberk, having proved a very forceful tax commissioner for the estates during the 1650s, was chosen archbishop of Prague in 1668. Their activity emanated from Braunau (that *casus belli* of 1618), and led to the resettlement and rebuilding of historic houses at Rajhrad, near Brno—saved by Dietrichstein—and at Břevnov, outside Prague. Within the capital monks had been brought back to Charles IV's foundation called Emmaus as early as 1592 by Rudolf II; but Ferdinand II, charac-teristically finding their behaviour too lax, displaced the existing Benedictines into the Old Town and introduced the severe Spanish rule of Montserrat (the second abbot of these *Schwarzspanier* was the chameleon-figure of Caramuel, himself a former Cistercian). Both abbeys formed priories in the surrounding countryside, at Svatý Jan and Bezděz respectively. The list of Bohemia's Benedictine monasteries is completed by Kladruby, near Pilsen, and the ancient community revived on hallowed ground beside the river Sázava.[54]

---

[53] At the diet the archbishop, bishops, provost and dean of St. Vitus, and provosts of Vyšehrad and Boleslav preceded the abbots. On priestly stipends and circumstan-ces: Krásl, op. cit. 455–83 and *passim*; Podlaha, *Dějiny*, 465 ff. Placht, op. cit. 254 (Černins), and cf. above, pp. 135–7, 139.

[54] *Benediktinerbuch*, 84–99 (Braunau and Břevnov), 100–16 (Emmaus), 350–67

The Cistercians likewise maintained nine houses in the Baroque
period (with more in Silesia), and their recovery too moved from
a few centres which had weathered the Hussite and Lutheran
storms: from Vyšší Brod (Hohenfurt) and Zlatá Koruna (Goldenkron) hard against the Austrian border, from Plass in the German-
speaking west, from Zbraslav (Königsaal) in the wooded defile
upriver from Prague. Order and local pride were sufficiently
reinstated at Sedlec by 1630 to yield a published Czech-language
history of the monastery's vicissitudes; later its filial at Skalice was
recolonized. Ossegg—whose lands provided the other *casus belli* of
1618—was returned to the Cistercians by Ferdinand II and
developed gradually through the century into a focus for the culture
of north-west Bohemia and the site of the country's first textile
manufactory. In Moravia Velehrad and Žd'ár moved towards their
most pompous age, with a conscious re-creation of the medieval
splendour of Czech monasticism.[55]

The regular Augustinians had canonries in the Bohemian lands,
more modest imitations of those in Austria, none of them destined
to avoid dissolution under Joseph II.[56] In Bohemia, on the other

(Rajhrad); Bílek, *Statky*, 174–9 (St. Nicholas in the Old Town), 180–7 (Kladruby);
Podlaha, *Posvátná místa*, i, 117–26 (Sázava); ii, 47–61 (Svatý Jan); v, 10–21
(Břevnov); L. Helmling, 'Die literarische und künstlerische Tätigkeit im kgl. Stifte
Emaus in Prag', *Stud. u. Mitt.* xxv (1904), 655–75; Svátek, art. cit. 529–34. B. Dudík,
Geschichte des Benediktiner-Stiftes Raygern, i–ii (V. 1849–68), ii, is a very detailed
house chronicle of Rajhrad. Cf. also above, p. 49 n. 18 (Braunau and its filial at
Police); below, pp. 225 f. (Svatý Jan, Sázava and Emmaus). There were also
Benedictine nuns in a prominent convent within the royal castle (Bílek, *Statky*, 166–
74; Svátek, art. cit. 591 f.). On Sobek, cf. *Berní rula*, i, 41, 46, 53 f.

[55] Sartorius, op. cit. 976–1068, with long sections on Sedlec, Plass, and Ossegg;
Cisterzienserbuch, 125–37 (Vyšší Brod), 280–353 (Ossegg); Bílek, *Statky*, 191–213
(Sedlec, Zlatá Koruna, Plass, Zbraslav), 308–21 (Žd'ár, Velehrad; both among the
richest monasteries dissolved in the 1780s); Podlaha, *Posvátná místa*, iii, 65–91
(Plass), 276–308 (Zbraslav); F. Machilek, 'Die Zisterzienser in Böhmen und
Mähren', *Archiv für Kirchengeschichte von Böhmen-Mähren-Schlesien*, iii (1973), 185–
220; J. G. Středovský, *Sacra Moraviae Historia sive Vita SS. Cyrilli et Methudii*
(Sulzbach 1710), 608–23 (Velehrad); Klima, op. cit. 214–16 (Ossegg). Detailed
works: Kapihorský, op. cit. (Sedlec); Kaindl, op. cit. (Vyšší Brod); Hurt, op. cit.
(Velehrad); M. Zemek and A. Bartušek, *Dějiny Žd'áru nad Sázavou*, i–iii (Havlíčkův
Brod–Brno 1956–74), ii.; cf. S. Bredl, 'Eine Jubiläumsfeier im ehemaligen
Cisterzienser-Stifte Saar', *Stud. u. Mitt.* xv (1894), 623–35.

[56] At Karlov (in the New Town of Prague); Třeboň (Wittingau) and Forbes
(Borovany) in southern Bohemia, both recovered from the Jesuits in 1631; Olomouc,
Moravský Šternberk, and Fulnek (all in Moravia). See Svátek, art. cit. 523–5; Bílek,
Statky, 146–50 (Karlov).

hand, the stricter rule of St. Augustine, that conceived at twelfth-
century Prémontré, gained a particular ascendancy. We have
already discerned the first stirrings of Catholic revival at Tepl, then
at Strahov under Lohelius. Lohelius's successor proved equally
tough and single-minded: Caspar von Questenberg (died in 1640),
whose brothers were rising in the court service of Ferdinand II,
gave this 'mountain of Sion' (as the abbey was properly called) a
new spiritual and political status to match its fairy-tale physical
dominance over the city of Prague. He augmented the number of
canons, hardened discipline, and pressed for the rights of his order
at national and international level, achieving most of what he
wanted, though not all (Questenberg led the protest against the salt
treaty of 1630).[57] From Tepl and Strahov the Premonstratensian
recovery spread: to Želiv, resettled after 1620, and Milevsko; to the
Moravian houses of Bruck (Louka), already active before the White
Mountain, and Nová Říše, Hradiště outside Olomouc and Zábrdovice outside Brno (both of which had to be rebuilt after the Swedish
assault in 1645); to the semi-aristocratic convents of Chotěšov and
Doksany; to Schlägl and Geras-Pernegg across the Austrian
frontier, which maintained parishes within Bohemia and whose
restorers, like Martin Greysing of Schlägl, studied there; to Silesia
and the *Reich*.[58]

Two things lent added impetus to this mission. One was the cult
of the founder of the whole Premonstratensian order, St. Norbert,
whose relics were translated from Magdeburg to Strahov in 1627
amid great celebrations. Henceforth Norbert was numbered among

[57] Čermák, op. cit. 1–128, esp. 67–77 (Strahov), 355–91 (Tepl); *Chorherrenbuch*,
548–637; cf. C. Straka, 'Nejstarší kniha výslechů na práve kláštera Strahovského na
Pohořelci', *ČL* xvii (1908), 65–7, 116–18, 165–8, 224–8. On Questenberg: id.,
Albrecht z Valdštejna a jeho doba (Pr. 1911), despite its title; Str. MS. DJ III 2,
pp. 422–41 and *passim*; cf. Gross, op. cit. 418–20, on his brother Hermann. For the
Salzvertrag see above p. 136.
[58] On all these houses: Čermák, op. cit.; Backmund, op. cit. i, 276–323; Svátek,
art. cit. 525–8. *Chorherrenbuch*, 386–411 (Nová Říše), 512–47 (Želiv); Bílek, *Statky*,
275–84 (Doksany and Chotěšov), 348–62 (Bruck, Hradiště, Zábrdovice), indicates
the great wealth of the Premonstratensian houses dissolved in the 1780s. Podlaha,
Posvátná místa, ii, 278–84 (Chotěšov); there and at Doksany non-noble nuns were
admitted from the 16th century (cf. Čermák, op. cit. 171–3, 432 f.). L. Schuster,
'Martin Greysing, der zweite Gründer Schlägls, 1626–65', *Anal. Praem.* xxxiii
(1957), 217–58. See also, in general, the provincial chapter records edited by J. B.
Valvekens in supplements to *Anal. Praem.* xxxvi–xlii (1960–6).

the holy patrons of Bohemia, his name invoked in pilgrimage and baptismal register; and the fame of his new shrine spread as far as France, whose queen sought some dust from his bones, but received a polite refusal.[59] The second was the establishment of a seminary at Prague in 1637. This seminary of St. Norbert had its function as a focus for scholarly activity within the order; but it gained a larger importance in the context of Archbishop Harrach's campaign against the Jesuit monopoly of Bohemian education. Harrach used Premonstratensian teachers, along with some Cistercians (who also had their own college) and the hard-talking Hibernian fathers, as rivals to the Jesuit establishment, and thereby broadened the base of Counter-Reformation learning in the country. Thus Scotists were studied as well as Thomists, sceptics—even Jansenists—as well as realists, and the Premonstratensians developed a lively Baroque culture with a detectable patriotic flavour. Its greatest representative, whom we shall meet again, was Hieronymus Hirnhaim, abbot of Strahov between 1670 and 1681.[60]

Premonstratensians could only display native features within an international matrix. One Augustinian order, however, was purely Bohemian: the Crusaders with a Red Star. In fact the evocatively-styled *Ordo militaris Crucigerorum cum rubea stella* had begun as an association of medieval hospitallers ancillary to the Prague Franciscans, but it is characteristic of the aristocratic tendencies of the age that seventeenth-century Crusaders elaborated a legend of their chivalric origins in the Holy Land and neglected the commitment to healing in favour of monastic repose and the cure of souls. Before the Hussite wars the order grew to be one of the most significant ecclesiastical institutions in Bohemia, and it survived Protestant

---

[59] Str. MS. DJ III 2, pp. 350–69; Carafa, *Commentaria*, 275–7, 291–3; *Acta SS.* June, i, 871 ff.; C. Straka in *Anal. Praem.* iii (1927), 333–46.

[60] Str. MS. DJ III 2, *passim*; ibid. MS. DJ III 3, pp. 74–9, 166–70; ibid. MS. DJ IV 1: 'Annales Seminarii S. Norberti, 1637–1736'; F. Tadra, 'Počátkové semináře arcibiskupského v Praze', *SbH* (Rezek), ii (1884), 193–201, 270–9, 339–48; Krásl, op. cit. 158–98, 287–302, *passim*; Rezek, *Děje*, 87–121, 300–8; A. Soldát, 'Z dějin arcibiskupského semináře v Praze', *SbHKr* v (1896), 61–97; Flégl, art. cit. 240–2; Millett, op. cit. 142–4, 151–3. S. Bredl, 'Das Collegium St. Bernardi in Prag', *Stud. u. Mitt.* xiii (1892), 499–505; xiv (1893), 53–60, 212–21; xv (1894), 90–4, 297–306, describes the Cistercian college. Harrach also tried, less successfully, to assert his powers as chancellor of the Clementinum (Tomek, *Geschichte, passim*; Krásl, op. cit. 364–412). Cf. V. Bitnar, *Postavy a problémy českého baroku literárního* (Pr. 1939), pt. 3; and below, pp. 328 f. on Hirnhaim.

pressures with much of its extensive property intact. It probably benefited from the fact that between 1561 and 1694 its grand-master was also always archbishop of Prague: the expense of supporting him being balanced by an access of lustre and influence. Certainly Crusaders were prominent in the Counter-Reformation period: they controlled some hundred parishes on a network of scattered estates, more humanely managed than most; they built a stylish (suitably cruciform) Baroque church and residence in the very centre of Prague; under the leadership of Jiří Pospíchal (1634–99) they generated considerable local patriotism.[61]

The Crusaders with a Red Star were not the only representatives of their kind. Besides smaller-scale autochthonous offshoots from the same tradition of the medieval hospice, like the so-called Cyriacs, or Crusaders with a Red Heart, whose house at the church of St. Cross in Prague was revived by Ferdinand II and likewise attracted a largely Czech membership,[62] the Maltese and Teutonic Knights established themselves firmly in Bohemia. Whereas the latter remained a foreign body—their Moravian latifundia gave rise to endless jurisdictional disputes—the Knights of Malta possessed a domestic dimension. Indeed, after the Reformation their whole Germanic province became concentrated on Prague, where the grand prior was senior regular prelate at the diet and a permanent stadholder of the kingdom. For generations Bohemian magnates occupied the position (four Vratislavs between 1626 and 1721) and their fine palace in its leafy square ranks among the most graceful on the Little Side.[63]

---

[61] V. Bělohlávek and J. Hradec, *Dějiny českých křižovníků s červenou hvězdou*, i–ii (Pr. 1930); W. Lorenz, *Die Kreuzherren mit dem roten Stern* (Königstein im Taunus 1964). ÖNB, MS. s.n. 3338, lists (in Latin and Czech) the lands belonging to the Crusaders' hospital in 1610. On Pospíchal: A. Rezek, 'Paměti generála řádu křižovnického Jiřího Pospíchala z let 1661–80', *Zprávy o zasedání Královské České Společnosti Nauk*, 1880, 139–60, with extracts from his diaries; J. Hanzal, 'Jiří Ignác Pospíchal a jeho doba', *ČsČH* xix (1971), 229–57, a sympathetic study.

[62] The history of the Crusaders with a Red Heart can be reconstructed from UK MSS. VII A 9–11: a general chronicle written in 1756; annals from 1628–1780; and list of members (the last dean of the Prague house was a *Bohemian* called Antony Hill). On their church see I. Kořán, 'Cyriacky klášter a chrám sv. Kříže Většího v baroku', *Umění* xvi (1968), 173–95. There were also Crusaders with a Red *Cross* on Zderaz in the New Town.

[63] R. Zuber, 'Der Streit um das Patronatsrecht zwischen dem Deutschen Orden und dem Olmützer Bistum im 17. und 18. Jahrhundert', *Acht Jahrhunderte Deutscher*

*

Orders, old and new, thus sustained much of the edifice of Counter-Reformation Catholicism in Bohemia. Many of its features obviously conform to the Austrian pattern: educational system, popular preachers, and the circulation of sermons and devotional tracts by contemporary foreign authors like Martin van Cochem, with translations into Czech.[64] Marian worship and respect for St. Joseph were widely cultivated and found expression in hundreds of local votive pictures and sanctuaries.[65] Most famous was the Madonna of Stará Boleslav (Altbunzlau), whose remarkable peripatetic career during the war (stolen by a Saxon officer and returned in 1637; twice sent to Vienna and back again in the 1640s) enhanced its fame and won it the high esteem of Leopold I.[66]

This kind of devotion seems to have reached its peak in the mid-eighteenth century—ironically at a time when the Habsburgs themselves began to discourage it.[67] It made slower progress in Bohemia, since there, far more than in the *Erblande*, the re-creation of Catholic piety depended on a conscious assertion of the continuity of faith: the two centuries from Hus to the White Mountain were henceforth deemed merely an aberration. The struggle to confirm that premise manifested itself in a variety of ways. It added frenzy and drama to the extirpation of Protestantism after 1620: churches were reconsecrated, even fumigated; pilgrimages were instigated to

Orden in Einzeldarstellungen, ed. K. Wieser (Bad Godesberg 1967), 441–54; K. Wieser, *Die Bedeutung des Zentralarchivs des Deutschen Ordens für die Geschichte Schlesiens und Mährens* (Würzburg 1967). A. Wienand (ed.), *Der Johanniter-Orden, der Malteser-Orden* (Cologne 1970), esp. 352–7, 412–41, 613.

[64] This literature in Czech is exhaustively catalogued in *Knihopis*. Cochem, the popular Capuchin, became a favourite in Bohemia by the 18th century; see, for example, his *Žiwot Pána Nasseho Gezisse Krysta*, tr. E. Nymburský (Pr. 1698, etc.). Ignatius Loyola's *Spiritual Exercises* appeared in Czech in 1692 (*Knihopis*, no. 3355).

[65] Marian examples in Podlaha, *Posvátná mista*, iii, 21–7, 295–9; vii, 29–32, and *passim*; Denis–Vančura, op. cit., i, 2, 35 f., 53 f., 169–71 (tinged with patriotism); *Knihopis*, nos. 943, 4308–9; P. Knauer, 'Die Entstehungszeit des Marienwallfahrtsortes Wartha in Schlesien', *ZVGAS* li (1917), 164–217; J. Herzogenberg in Seibt (ed.) op. cit. 465–74. V. Ryneš, '"Imagines Miraculosae" doby pobělohorské', *ČL* liv (1967), 182–93, uses interesting reports from parish priests; E. Wiegand, *Die böhmischen Gnadenbilder* (Göttingen 1936), is more technical. For Joseph: Beckovský, op. cit., pt. 3, 310; Rezek, *Dějiny*, i, 227 f.; *Knihopis*, nos. 1403, 9547.

[66] Beckovský, op. cit., pt. 3, 260–4, 267, 275 f., 281, 351, 402–4; Balbin, *Epitome*, bks. 6–7; Pekař, *Kost*, i, 1 f., 168; *Knihopis*, nos. 264–5; and cf. below, p. 408.

[67] *Knihopis*, nos. 5655–901, 7083–110, 7183 seqq., 7872 seqq., 9921 seqq. Cf. the list of books owned at Outěnice, near Prague, in 1758 (Podlaha, *Posvátná mista*, v, 88–91).

the wonder-working battlefield; Corpus Christi processions expunged the memory of Hus's name-day (so conveniently adjacent in the calendar). Ferdinand II was narrowly persuaded not to raze the rebel Carolinum to the ground and build a home there for the public executioner. Slavata organized a theatrical ceremony at which the burghers of Hradec abased themselves before the verities of the Church of Rome.[68] At the same time medieval ideals were reinstated, a process which culminated symbolically with the unique architectural style of Bohemian Baroque-Gothic: the work of Giovanni Santini-Aichel at Žd'ár, Sedlec, Želiv, and above all secretive Kladruby, with its rib-vaults and fantastic pinnacles.[69]

Best prospects for the 'continuity thesis' lay in the notion of a *Bohemia sancta*. Here naturalized St. Norbert showed the way after 1620—as St. Vitus, whose relics gave the initial impulse to the construction of Prague cathedral, had done long before. But plenty of local talent was available too. There can be no question about the genuine patriotic sentiments attached to the name of St. Wenceslas, first Christian king of Bohemia. Wenceslas had been continuously venerated since his death in the year 923; his chapel in St. Vitus was the greatest jewel of the medieval kingdom. Feast-days for him and his mother Ludmila formed an established observance in the archdiocese of Prague, and Edmund Campion preached on the theme in the 1570s. One interesting example of sixteenth-century reverence for Wenceslas provides visual evidence that the charities attributed to the 'good king' by the Victorian hymn-writer were already valued then, although the historical Václav was no more than a golden youth at the time of his murder. After the White Mountain the cult of Wenceslas and Ludmila grew apace, formulated anew by the priesthood, encouraged by aristocracy and crown (Leopold gave the name to his eldest, short-lived son).[70] Not

---

[68] Pescheck, op. cit. ii, 12 ff.; Liva, art. cit. 48 f., 52, 64–6; Beckovský, op. cit., pt. 2, 313 f; pt. 3, 7. Gindely, *Gegenreformation*, 181, 79–81 (Carolinum and Slavata).

[69] Imaginatively reinterpreted by Z. Kalista, *Česká barokní gotika a její žd'árské ohnisko* (Brno 1970), and thoroughly surveyed by Kotrba, op. cit., incorporating much earlier studies by Z. Wirth. Cf. A. Angyal, *Die slawische Barockwelt* (Leipzig 1961), 19 ff.

[70] *Calendarium et Index Festorum et Ieiuniorum secundum usum Metropolitanae Ecclesiae Pragensis* (Pr. 1578), *passim*; Turner, *Posthumae Orationes*, 259–74 (Campion). ÖNB, MS. s.n. 2633: 'Icones Historici, Vitam et Martyrium St. Venceslai... designantes', illustrated for Archduke Ferdinand of Tyrol by Matthias

surprisingly, royal blood added to their pious merits in the eyes of contemporaries. Did not the same Přemyslid line also produce the Blessed Agnes, patroness of the first Bohemian Franciscans and Crusaders, whose body was providentially rediscovered in the 1640s?[71]

The other old-Bohemian saints were also mainly aristocratic. They included Prince Vojtěch (known to Germans as Adalbert), second bishop of Prague, missionary, martyr in 997, founder of the abbey of Břevnov; together with his brother Gaudentius. Their near-contemporary Günther (Vintíř) was a diplomat turned hermit, who died in the odour of sanctity. During the Middle Ages veneration for him centred on his burial-place at Břevnov; in the seventeenth century it shifted to the spot traditionally identified as his cell in the remote Bohemian forest, and a new chapel was built there. Hroznata, the greatest early benefactor of the Premonstratensians, likewise came of exalted stock, as did Hedwig, chief patroness of Silesia, and Hyacinth and his brother Česlav, founders of the Dominicans there, whose cult flourished anew from about 1600 (Hyacinth was canonized in 1594).[72] Such cults did not, however, just pander to the élite; they embodied real popular devotion, building after 1620 on traditions never entirely broken. One of the earliest of all Bohemian saints, Ivan—said to have been

Hutski of Křivoklát, 'artis pictoriae Pragae professor', is based on originals in the Wenceslas chapel of St. Vitus. J. Solimani, *S. Wenceslaus* (Pr. 1626), a tragedy; *Knihopis*, nos. 67, 4186, 13891, 16062-4 (Wenceslas); 3651, 13894 (Ludmila); *Privatbriefe*, nos. 143, 166; Muk, op. cit. 130 f.; Kotrba, op. cit. 69; *Acta SS.* Sept., vii, 770–844 (Wenceslas); v, 339–63 (Ludmila). Cf. the literature in Tumpach-Podlaha, op. cit., nos. B 1311–85, 1049–55; and—on Bohemian saints in general—Chanovský, *Vestigium*, 37–69.

[71] Balbín, *Miscellanea Historica*, ii, bk. 1, 7 ff. (who turns even the legendary ploughman Přemysl into a noble!). Beckovský, op. cit., pt. 3, 313–17; cf. Hanzal, 'Pospíchal', 243; and Tumpach-Podlaha, op. cit., nos. B 78–115. But Rome was not prepared to confirm the genuineness of Agnes's relics.

[72] Vojtěch: Matthias Bolelucký, *Rosa Boëmica sive Vita Sancti Woytiechi agnomine Adalberti* (Pr. 1668); *Knihopis*, no. 2094; *Acta SS.* Apr., iii, 174-205; Tumpach-Podlaha, op. cit. nos. B 1419–78. Günther: Chanovský, op. cit. 91 ff.; B. Piter, *Thesaurus absconditus* [i.e.] *S. Guntherus ... Vita et Miraculis ... illustratus* (Brünn 1762); G. Lang, 'Gunther, der Eremit in Geschichte, Sage, und Kult', *Stud. u. Mitt.* lix (1941-2), 3–83, esp. 69 ff.; *Knihopis*, no. 1819; ÖNB, MS. s.n. 40. Hroznata: above, n. 47. Hedwig: *Acta SS.* Oct., viii, 198–270 (thorough). Hyacinth: A. Bzovius, *Propago D. Hyacinthi Thaumaturgi Poloni ...* (n.p. 1606); *Acta SS.* Aug., iii, 309–79 (likewise thorough). Česlav: Bzovius, *Tutelaris Silesiae, seu De vita ... B. Ceslai Odrovansii commentarius* (Cracow 1608).

the son of a Croatian duke, though his life is very obscure—set up as an anchorite in a rocky cleft beside the Berounka, west of Prague. His shrine was taken over by Benedictines and visited by many leading Counter-Reformation figures. In the climate of Baroque spirituality his example inspired imitation: Joseph II suppressed no less than seventy-three (one source suggests eighty-three) hermits following the rule of St. Ivan.[73]

Another grass-roots Slavonic saint was Prokop (died in 1053), founder of the monastery at Sázava. The rehabilitation of Prokop represents an early act of Catholic revival: his relics were transferred in 1588 to Prague castle, apparently at the instigation of Rudolf II's sister Elizabeth.[74] Moreover, reverence of Prokop involved some sympathy for the whole idea of a Slavonic (rather than a Latin) liturgy, which he, as abbot of Sázava, had sought to propagate, and thus for the legacy of those misty apostles of the ancient Czechs and Moravians, Saints Cyril and Methodius. Though the message of Cyril and Methodius might appear dangerously schismatic when viewed from Rome—they had been ninth-century envoys of Constantinople—it was not entirely beyond the pale, especially in an age confident enough to believe that Catholicism might regain the loyalty of the Eastern Churches. The prospects of a recovery based on the Emmaus monastery in the New Town of Prague, established by Charles IV in direct continuation of Prokop's ideals, were blighted when the Benedictines of Montserrat took over its buildings, a clear case of the national aspect of religion defeated by the international. But the Cyrillo-Methodian tradition was cultivated at the Cistercian house of Velehrad, which supposedly stood on the site of their original activities, and whose abbot was senior regular prelate in Moravia. It found enthusiastic, if rough-hewn support from such writers as K. B. Hirschmentzel and J. J. Středovský.[75]

---

[73] C. Hostlovský, 'Memoria Subrupensis', ed. D. Kozler and L. J. Wintera, *Stud. u. Mitt.* i (1880), 4, 110–42; xi (1890), 296–306, 448–63, 613–32; Z. Kalista, 'Bedřich Bridel', *Annali dell' Istituto Universitario Orientale*, sezione slava, xiv (1971), 13–46, at 28–30. Lists of hermitages in Frind, *Erzbischöfe*, appendix 5; Bílek, *Statky*, 415–418; Svátek, art. cit. 587 f. One typical example in Podlaha, *Posvátná místa*, ii, 17–19.

[74] *OSN*, s.v. 'Prokop'; Kalista, 'Bridel', 37 f.; *Acta SS.* July, ii, 136–48; Tumpach-Podlaha, op. cit., nos. B 1198–1231.

[75] Středovský, op. cit. (with marvellously inappropriate illustrations). On Emmaus: L. Helmling, *Kurzgefasste Geschichte ... des Klosters Emaus* (Pr. 1903);

Seventeenth-century Bohemia produced no saints of its own: the somewhat dubious dean of Holešov, Jan Sarkander, who died at the hands of the Moravian rebels in 1620, is an exception who proves the rule.[76] It did, however, transform in the most celebrated and controversial fashion the memory of an earlier martyr: Jan of Nepomuk. There is no space here for details about 'Jan Nepomucký' or the furious debate which has raged about him for over two centuries. Suffice it to say that the saint was a real person, a fourteenth-century churchman who became vicar-general to the archbishop of Prague and was murdered by the king, either as a too-faithful keeper of the queen's confession or, more probably, as a turbulent priest. In the seventeenth century Catholics advanced Nepomuk as an orthodox antipole to his heretical contemporary fellow-Jan, Jan of Husinec; his canonization process began in 1675 and ended successfully in 1729, amid scenes of great festivity.[77]

Was Nepomuk, as many have believed, the perfect symbol of an imposed Counter-Reformation: an artifical counterweight to Jan Hus, even literally a non-person, foisted on a reluctant population by foreign authorities? The obvious Baroque enthusiasm for the saint should make us suspicious of this argument. Certainly Nepomuk was a counterweight to Hus: the search for continuity created that emotional need (and Hus himself,, after all, had acquired the attributes of sainthood in the eyes of many Czechs); but his cult was a native product, resting on a veneration of the

W. Pfeifer, 'Das Prager Emaus–Kloster—Schicksal einer Idee', *Archiv für Kirchengeschichte von Böhmen–Mähren–Schlesien*, ii (1971), 9–35, esp. 28 ff. A recent collective work: [J. Petr and S. Šabouk] (eds.), *Z tradic slovanské kultury v Čechách, Sázava a Emauzy* ... (Pr. 1975), adds nothing new for this period. On Velehrad: Machilek, art. cit. 192; B. Zlámal, 'Cyrilometodějstvi K. B. Hirschmentzla', *Slezský Sborník* xlviii (= viii) (1950), 57–67; and above, n. 55. Cf. below, pp. 421–4, on the Uniate Churches.

[76] Balbin, *Miscellanea Historica*, i, bk. 4, pt. 1, 206–8; bibliography in Zíbrt, *BČH* iv, nos. 6024–71; and Tumpach–Podlaha, op. cit., nos. B 858–82. A controversial figure, Sarkander has not always been admired.

[77] The argument about Nepomuk extends even to his name (Jan of Pomuk seems to be the proper form) and to his historical existence, though much of the confusion was introduced by a 16th-century Catholic writer who actually invented two different 'Nepomuks'. The man sainted for his death in 1393 (*recte* 1383) as a martyr to the sacrament of confession is largely fictional. J. Pekař, 'Tři kapitoly z boje sv. Jana Nepomuckého', *Z duchovních dějin českých* (Pr. 1941), 141–77, is very balanced. See, most recently, J. V. Polc and V. Ryneš, *Sv. Jan Nepomucký*, i–ii (Rome 1972), and the literature in Tumpach–Podlaha, op. cit., nos. B 734–853.

martyr's true or supposed virtues which dated back to the fifteenth
and sixteenth centuries. The time taken before his final canonization
may point to the limited extent of that original *cultus*; but it also
shows Rome's hesitation about approving it. Hagiography by Balbín
and others came first, even the poignant statue on the Charles
bridge in Prague which marks the presumed site of Nepomuk's
drowning. It need not matter to us whether the tongue of the
faithful confessor was really found uncorrupted when his tomb was
opened in 1719, so long as we respect the sincerity of those who
believed so.[78]

★

The story of Nepomuk—the rewriting of a Gothic legend—affords
the most fascinating case of interaction between new forces and old
roots in Bohemia, between Counter-Reformation propaganda and
spontaneous credence. The same admixture appears in Baroque
historiography as a whole: honest and serious, thorough but quite
uncritical, relating miracles with the same gusto as military exploits
of the old aristocracy, perceiving no difference between contemporary and medieval values. Its greatest writer was Balbín (1621–
88), who has left us in his unfinished *Miscellanea Historica* a piece
of outstanding scholarship, according to the standards of the time,
and also a remarkable source for the mentality of the period.[79]
Lesser Jesuits, like the brothers Tanner and Fr. Kruger, cultivated
the same interests. So did Balbín's friends in other orders, like Alois
Hackenschmidt, a Premonstratensian at Tepl, the Crusader Jan Jiří
Beckovský, author of a picturesque chronicle of Bohemia, and
Beckovský's superior, Pospíchal, who kept valuable diaries. Among
the secular clergy the leading figure was the tenacious and shrewd

---

[78] Perhaps the first printed work devoted to Nepomuk was by Jiří Plachý in 1641
(*Knihopis*, no. 13900), but monuments existed earlier (cf. F. Moryson, *An Itinerary*
(London 1617), i, 16). Balbín, *Miscellanea Historica*, i, bk. 4, pt. 1, 94–113; cf.
Knihopis, nos. 945–7. Good points are made by Kalista, *Barokní gotika*, 85 ff.; and—
on the cult of Hus—by J. Macek, *Jean Hus et les traditions hussites* (Paris 1973),
328 ff.

[79] The ninth book of the first *decas* of the *Miscellanea* was later published separately
as *Bohemia Docta*, ed. R. Ungar, i–ii (Pr. 1776–80). There is an uncritical life by A.
Rejzek, *Bohuslav Balbín, jeho život a práce* (Pr. 1908). It is characteristic of Balbín's
sense of nearness to the medieval past that he thought an obscure moralizing work
by a 14th-century Bohemian Carthusian worth publishing as a tract for his own
times (W. G. Storey, *The De Quatuor Virtutibus Cardinalibus ... of Michael the
Carthusian of Prague* (Salzburg 1972), 11 and n.).

Tomáš Pešina (1629–80), who devoted himself to writing the history of his native Moravia and his adopted domicile, the cathedral chapter of St. Vitus in Prague. Rather less ambitious were such parish priests as Středovský, who rose to the dignity of count palatine; Matyáš Bolelucký, the biographer of St. Vojtěch; and Jan Florián Hammerschmid, rector of the Týn church in Prague.[80] In the work of all these clerical intellectuals, study of the past overlapped with topography and a breathless receptivity to the wonders of creation. As we shall see, their view of human history is inseparable from their view of natural history, and divine intervention links the two.

Not only were Bohemia's intellectuals mostly priests. They were also mostly Czechs, and the Czech language evidently contributed to their patriotism. They sought a continued place for it, even went so far as to approve Protestant public figures who had cultivated it.[81] In fact the Counter-Reformation Church exercised no discrimination against Czech: there were many translations of improving works, and literature in the vernacular ranged from hagiography to the intense devotional poetry of Bedřich Bridel and the so-called St. Wenceslas Bible.[82] Some Dominican churches were instructed always to preach in Czech, and others must keep Czech-speakers available; candidates for the Crusaders with a Red Star had to know both languages; Jesuits rejected the suggestion that they favoured German; Sobek of Bílenberk while archbishop wrote pungent letters in Czech. The Prague consistory would only authorize priests who understood the language of their parish and,

[80] Hackenschmid·: A. Patera (ed.), 'Dopisy B. A. Balbína k opatu teplskému ... a knězi téhož kláštera Aloisovi Hackenschmidtu z l. 1664–7', *VKČSN*, 1888, 143–226; Schulz (ed.), *Korrespondence jesuitů*, nos. 82–3. Beckovský: op. cit., and the life of him by Rezek, ibid. pt. 3, pp. vii–xxxii. Pospíchal: above, n. 61. Pešina: Zelený, art. cit. Středovský: op. cit., and *Knihopis*, nos. 15766–7. Bolelucký: above, n. 72. Hammerschmid's main work: *Prodromus gloriae Pragenae* (Pr. 1723), abounds in fond information about all the monuments, especially ecclesiastical, of the city; cf. his *Hystorye Klattowská* (Pr. 1699), with much on the Marian cult.

[81] e.g. Balbín, *Bohemia Docta*, i, bk. 2, 314–17, 351–3, 364–7, and *passim*; Středovský, op. cit. 6f. The remarks are very guarded, of course.

[82] Selections in Z. Kalista (ed.), *České baroko* (Pr. 1940). On Bridel see also Kalista, 'Bridel'; and A. Škarka, *Fridrich Bridel nový a neznámý* (Pr. 1968). The Catholic Czech Bible—urged much earlier by Dietrichstein (Dudik, *Bibliothek*, 18)—finally appeared between 1677 and 1715, thanks to endowments collected by one of its translators, the Jesuit writer Matěj Václav Šteyer (on whom see *Knihopis*, nos. 15935–51, and J. Vlček, *Dějiny české literatury*, i–ii (3rd edn. Pr. 1940), i, 740 ff.).

if anything, was hesitant to recognize the needs of towns (like Budweis) where German grew steadily more popular. Many clerics still used both tongues: what a cruel irony for the Hussite tradition that such men were now described as 'utraquists'![83]

But Czech was under pressure, and intellectuals rallied to its defence. Středovský condemned its detractors, as did Pešina, whose first book appeared in the vernacular and had little success. Hammerschmid rejected a demand from the cobblers to have a German sermon on their patronal festival. Grammarians, above all the advocate Václav Jan Rosa, stressed the 'majestas et venustas linguae nostrae' and refurbished commonplaces—true or spurious—about the merits of the Slavonic tongues: they had been praised by Alexander the Great, urged on the sons of the German electors by Charles IV, used as a *lingua franca* in Constantinople; they combined great flexibility of expression with great geographical extension.[84] Prague even showed interest in the language of the Wendish peasants in Lusatia, and a grammar of it was produced by a Jesuit there. Most famous is the polemical apologia of Balbín in favour of Czech, suppressed by his superiors, and only published at the beginning of the national revival a century later.[85]

Nevertheless we should beware about dragging this debate (as the nineteenth century was apt to do) right out of its context. The apologia, uncharacteristic of most of Balbín's *œuvre*, represents no kind of '*narodnik*' manifesto. It simply laments the decline of one aspect of Bohemia's richness, mainly through neglect, a sentiment echoed in practical terms by the considerable numbers of burghers

[83] UK, MS. XI A 1/b, fol. 94^r; Lorenz, op. cit. 80; Rejzek, op. cit. 429–36; Schulz (ed.), *Korrespondence Václava ... ze Šternberka*, nos. 89–160 (Sobek); Podlaha, *Dějiny*, 264–7, 292–5. Cf. Denis–Vančura, i, 2, 167; and A. Míka, 'K národnostním poměrům v Čechách po třicetileté válce', *ČsČH* xxiv (1976), 535–60, at 550 ff.

[84] Středovský, op. cit. 5 f.: 'Sermo patrius Moravus ... multùm ab aetate hac Patriae nostrae injuriosa supprimitur'; Zelený, art. cit. 257 ff., 101 ff.; *OSN*, s.v. 'Hammerschmid'. V. J. Rosa, *Čechořečnost, seu Grammatica linguae Bohemicae* (Pr. [1672]), preface. Earlier spokesmen for such views included Thomas Reschelius (*Dictionarium Latinobohemicum* (Olomouc 1560)); Matthias Benešovský, Utraquist 'abbot' of Emmaus (1582–9), whose *Grammatica Bohemica* (Pr. 1577, copy in Bod.), preface, stresses the usefulness to the Habsburgs of the Czech language; and Peter Loderecker, Benedictine abbot of the same monastery (deposed in 1611).

[85] [J. Ticino?], *Principia linguae Wendicae, quam aliqui Wandalicam vocant* (Pr. 1679). B. Balbín, *Dissertatio apologetica pro lingua slavonica, praecipue bohemica*, ed. F. M. Pelzl (Pr. 1775); cf. Vlček, op. cit. i, 720–7.

and lawyers who manifested an equal unwillingness to abandon Czech. Support for one language did not necessarily involve any direct clash with the other: no serious racial tension can be found between Czechs and Germans in Bohemia either before or after 1620—the people's distaste for their new landlords is quite a different matter; nor were patterns of settlement significantly changed, as scholars have now belatedly come to recognize.[86] Still less did the Baroque intellectual's essentially Latinate world (of which Balbín was a fully-fledged member) countenance any kind of nationalist *ressentiment*. Rather, this intellectual patriotism rested heavily on the idea of a *Bohemia docta* (to adopt the title of another of Balbín's posthumous works) and went with infectious enthusiasm for the merits of the native land. Balbín lovingly describes its whistling fish, its beautiful gems, even a certain *avis Bohemica*; he is almost as proud of the gardens of the immigrant Saxe-Lauenburgs as of the historic royal fortress of Karlstein.[87]

Learned Bohemia thus comprised a national culture, subtly accommodated through *šlechta* and Church to the requirements of Habsburg rule. Bernard Ignác Martinic embodied it exactly, and he is an excellent symbol of it, especially since Martinic, although perhaps the most powerful political figure in the country during the decades after the Peace of Westphalia, has been remembered only as an enemy of Balbín. That issue was ultimately trivial: Martinic, a touchy character, indeed resisted the publication of Balbín's *Epitome Historica*, probably because (a good Baroque reason) he detected in it a slight to his own family; but he backed several of Balbín's colleagues, like Tomáš Pešina. In fact Martinic was devoted to the Church— a major patron of Franciscans, Servites, Theatines, Piarists—and to its culture. Well-educated and quite erudite, he corresponded with Caramuel, with the imperial librarian Lambeck, with Jesuits such as Athanasius Kircher; a great respecter of books, he wrote a history of Ferdinand III's campaigns, even (apparently)

---

[86] For the towns: Placht, op. cit. 204–11; and the documents printed in Macůrek, *České země a Slovensko*. For lawyers: Klabouch, op. cit. 36 f., 45–7. On nationalities see the two sensible revision articles by A. Míka, 'Národnostní poměry v českých zemích před třicetiletou válkou', *ČsČH* xx (1972), 207–29, and 'K národnostním poměrům . . .'.

[87] Above, n. 79. Balbín, *Miscellanea Historica*, i, bks. 1 and 3, *passim*. On Balbín's Latin interests cf. above, pp. 114f.

a general history of his own time. Friend, adviser, and wholehearted
admirer of Leopold I, his base of operations and mental frame of
reference yet remained firmly Bohemian.[88]

Martinic and his kind stand for a dual political and cultural
loyalty: to the Habsburgs, whose apotheosis was regularly celebrated
in both the visual arts and literature, even in such things as
disputation-placards and legal textbooks;[89] and to native inspiration, which lent the Bohemian Baroque an increasing popular
content. We can discern the same duality in Prague, now half-way
between capital city and provincial town. The face of Prague was
ruled by the shadow of the Habsburgs in their sombre, monumental
castle with its lieutenancy administration, whither Ferdinand III
and Leopold paid only occasional visits. It was also ruled by the
reality of its magnates' grand palaces, which, dotted on the slopes
of their superb quarters above the left bank of the Vltava, scarcely
have a visual equal in Europe, and its pompous churches, where
hundreds of priests in every imaginable habit and several different
languages ministered to a population still hardly smaller than that
of Vienna.

★

This balance, achieved at Prague and in the countryside, between
an international movement and its local manifestations, assured
comparative stability to the Counter-Reformation society constructed in Bohemia by 1700. But it left weaknesses. The first follows
directly from the nature of the bargain struck with the dynasty.
Ruling groups in the kingdom had not really surrendered power
and would resent any serious interference, whereas the Habsburgs
were gradually being driven to assert their authority more
effectively. For all the foot-dragging of the estates, the Bohemian

---

[88] I have found no literature at all on Martinic, beyond casual mentions; cf. Zíbrt,
BČH i, no. 14732. On his touchiness: Schulz (ed.), *Korrespondence jesuitů*, nos. 63–
5. On his dispute with Balbín: Květoňová–Klimová, art. cit. 504–11; Vlček, op. cit.
i, 725 f. On his patronage: Frind, *Erzbischöfe*, 216, 218; Zelený, art. cit. 107, 577;
Podlaha, *Posvátná místa*, vii, 143 ff., 181 ff.; Květoňová–Klimová, loc. cit.; Kotrba,
op. cit. 58; B. de Monconys, *Journal des Voyages*, i–ii (Lyons 1665–6), ii, 250 ff. On
his learned interests: below, pp. 317 f. 325, 331, n. 49, pp. 336, 438. His work about
Ferdinand III is in UK, MS. XI D 13, fols. 1–30, a copy, ?1630s; cf. F. Mareš in
MIÖG vi (1885), 310 f. Placht, op. cit. 244, 251 f. (Martinic and Leopold).
[89] O. J. Blažíček (ed.), *Theses in Universitate Carolina Pragensi disputatae*, i– (Pr.
1967–   ), pt. 1, fols. 1, 3; pt. 4, fols. 1–2, 4; pt. 5, fol. 2, etc.; [J. J. Weingarten],
Speculum Civium (Pr. [1675]), 37 ff.

lands still paid over 50 per cent of the Monarchy's total tax contribution. At the beginning of the eighteenth century the treasury's appetite was even more voracious, while the first signs appeared of a crude mercantilist planning of the economy.[90] Moreover, neither Bohemia's ancient nobles nor its prelates were quite treated as the equal of their Austrian counterparts. It is a small, but telling commentary that only Lobkovices, Kinskýs, and Kaunitzes were ever admitted to princely rank, while after 1695 the sees of Prague and Olomouc were as often filled with foreign clerics as with domestic.[91] The disloyalty of some aristocrats during the early 1740s, when Bavarian troops occupied the country, is directly proportionate to Habsburg disregard for their privileged position—and Bohemian patriotism, when under attack, could prove surprisingly attractive to more recently-settled families.

The second weakness was a more obviously grave one: the pressure exerted from without upon a system which served such limited social and intellectual élites. The deprived orders in Bohemia could only respond, not initiate, and their discontent, very massively demonstrated in 1680, was perforce directed against the establishment as a whole. Maybe they protested most of all against their new foreign landlords (it is curious that the most eloquent defence of the servile oppressed was penned by a Belgian Jesuit against an upstart Belgian estate-owner), but the combined impositions of dynasty, nobility, and Church formed their ultimate target, together with the immobile, hierarchical system which accompanied them. And Bohemia's peasants received even less practical consideration from

---

[90] But Pekař's argument (cf. above, p. 91, n. 25), that state taxation represented a worse burden for the peasantry than landlords' exactions has generally been thought exaggerated. Elements of early Habsburg economic centralization in Bohemia are discussed by A. F. Pribram, *Das böhmische Commerzkollegium und seine Tätigkeit* (Pr. 1898), and Klima, op. cit. 116 ff., 186 ff.; though such 'governmental' schemes of course had influential local supporters too.

[91] I omit the 18th-century princely elevations for two Bohemian-based, but immigrant families: Clary-Aldringen and Colloredo-Mansfeld (as well as for Liechtensteins, Dietrichsteins, etc.). The 18th-century archbishops of Prague (careers in Frind, *Erzbischöfe*, 231 ff.) were a Breuner, Kuenburg, Daniel Josef Mayer (a brief bourgeois episode, 1732–3), a Vratislav nominated but never consecrated, Manderscheid, Příchovský (ancient, but impoverished Czech nobility), and Salm-Salm. The bishops of Olomouc were Karl of Lorraine, then a Schrattenbach and Liechtenstein, two obscurer figures (Troyer and Egkh-Hungersbach), followed by a Hamilton and Colloredo–Wallsee.

the ruler than did their Austrian equivalents.[92] Meanwhile the army of resentful *émigrés*, though hardly more numerous than the Austrian exiles, lurked much closer at hand—many lived immediately across the Saxon border—and were less quickly assimilated into their foreign surroundings.

Bohemia on the threshold of the eighteenth century had almost healed the scars of the 1620s. The new edifice betrayed only minor internal divisions, and it exerted a real, albeit somewhat inscrutable, authority. But it was a more fragile solution than the Austrian one and might succumb to long-term threats. The issue of a major reconstruction had been side-stepped—no progress had even been made towards the institutional unity of Bohemia, Moravia, and Silesia—and old antagonisms could gradually revive in these, the richest of Habsburg possessions. Two pieces of symbolic evidence may clinch the argument: the pilgrimage church of the Servites on the White Mountain, begun shortly after the battle in 1620, took a full hundred years to complete;[93] while the Baroque décor in the Franciscan church of Our Lady of the Snows, though impressive, never quite reached to the top of its towering Gothic vault.

---

[92] The Jesuit was Jacques des Hayes, the tyrannical noble Count Guillaume Lamboy: Rezek, 'Dva příspěvky', 15–28. Some (e.g. Grünberg, op. cit. i, 127 ff.) have viewed Leopold's *robot* patent issued in 1680 (and printed ibid. ii, 3–10) as a significant step towards reducing peasant burdens, but Marxist historians (e.g. Klima, op. cit. 66–71) are surely right to question this interpretation. Cf. above, p. 168.

[93] Beckovský, op. cit., pt. 3, 62 f.; Podlaha, *Posvátná místa*, v, 21–9.

CHAPTER 7

Hungary: limited rejection

Hungary was at once very simple and very complicated: a kingdom long established and distinctive, with well-defined historical frontiers (mainly mountains or rivers), but also widely divergent forms of settlement and culture; a notion to any contemporary and a separate entry in his reference books, but a blurred notion and usually a second-hand entry.[1] Provisionally after 1526, firmly after 1541, the country split into three parts: Habsburg territories in the west and north; Turkish vilayets in a great wedge through the centre; and to the east, Transylvania, earlier governed by a voivode, now a more-or-less independent principality. The arrangement was never an entirely settled one, as boundaries continued to fluctuate and some areas lived under dual sovereignty or no effective sovereignty at all. Nominally, perhaps, the dynasty could claim that it exercised a single kingship, held in trust for a happier future; it—or rather the indigenous nobility—enforced some rights over subjects under Turkish rule. But in practical terms the Habsburgs controlled, for most of our period, not more than 30 per cent of the total area; indeed a declining proportion, since Ottoman advance only reached its fullest extent in 1664 with the capture of Nagyvárad and Neuhäusel, while seven counties were ceded to Transylvania in the 1620s and again in the 1640s, on top of the substantial districts—known in quaint lawyers' Latin as the *Partium*—pledged to the principality since 1570.[2]

[1] Information would have been found (for example) in Martin Schödel, *Disquisitio historico-politica de Regno Hungariae* (Strasbourg 1629); *Respublica et status regni Hungariae* (Leiden 1634), a well-known but feeble compendium; P. Heylin, *Cosmographie*, i–iv (London 1652), ii, 182–90.

[2] The seven north-eastern counties (Abaúj, Zemplén, Borsod, Bereg, Szabolcs, Szatmár, Ugocsa) passed for life to Bethlen Gábor (1621–9), and to György I Rákóczi (1645–8). The term *Partium* derives from the title assumed by the Transylvanian prince in respect of them: Dominus *Partium* Regni Hungariae. Few Western historical atlases have enough accuracy or detail to cope with Hungary; cf. *Történelmi atlasz*, pp. 12 f., 16 f.

Moreover, what the Habsburgs actually managed was highly variegated. Even the comparatively fertile and prosperous Trans-danubia had a rich blend of nationalities (besides the many Germans, Sopron county numbered far more Croat parishes than Magyar) and a succession of terrains from the swampy flatnesses of the Kisalföld along the Danube to the friendly undulations of the Őrség on the border with Styria. South of it lay the ruins of old Croatia, the self-styled triune kingdom of Croatia, Dalmatia, and Slavonia: long amalgamated with the rest of Hungary; truncated, ravaged, and displaced by the Turks; it yet clung to shreds of autonomy around its capital of Zagreb.[3] North and east stretched the arc of Upper Hungary (the *Felvidék*), peopled by Magyars, Slovaks, and Ruthenes in the countryside, Germans, Magyars, and Slovaks in the towns, the many local identities being enhanced by mountain ranges and fast-flowing rivers. Everywhere the seven-teenth century confused the picture further, bringing population flux, social dislocation, and a coarseness born of insecurity. These regional variations were no less in Transylvania, with its mixture of Magyars, Szeklers, Saxons, and Romanians. Only the vilayets of Buda, Temesvár, Eger, and Kanizsa had, through the heavy arm of economic and cultural oppression, eliminated much local colour; but the full history of Ottoman Hungary has yet to be written, and it will prove a tale of light as well as shade.[4]

One circumstance appears to introduce some clarity and a peg on which to hang arguments: the caesura of 1683; the siege of Vienna, followed by the expulsion of the Porte and the incorporation of Transylvania. Yet even the events of the 1680s (as I shall try to show in this chapter) provided at most a catalyst. Habsburg Hungary before 1683 formed the springboard for a renewed greater Hungary after 1683; the evolution was continuous, and the presuppositions were the same as elsewhere in the Monarchy, though the hindrances to the model were more formidable. Thus Hungary never came

---

[3] Vanyó, *Katholikus restauráció*, 60–3; Házi, op. cit., *passim*. As a result of Turkish advance Croatia was moved bodily north towards the Drava; much of its reduced territory came to form the Habsburg military frontier (cf. above, p. 149).

[4] The classic works on this subject are now somewhat antiquated: F. Salamon, *Ungarn im Zeitalter der Türkenherrschaft* (Leipzig 1887); S. Takáts, *Rajzok a török világból*, i–iv (Bp. 1915–28). There is some good recent literature: e.g. Kathona, op. cit.; and the *Studia Turco-Hungarica*, ed. Gy. Káldy-Nagy (Bp. 1974–   ).

near to being a political absolutism, either before or after the 1680s, despite the dynasty's most thoroughgoing attempt to impose it. The Habsburgs were used to compromise in Hungary. With the Turks they pursued round after round of negotiations, one-sided affairs until the 1590s, and hazardous for Austrian emissaries. *Vis-à-vis* Transylvania they signed treaties in 1538 and 1570 as with a junior partner and came very close during the 1540s, through the clerical diplomat, 'Friar George' Martinuzzi, to confirming the rights of royal overlordship there. Having encountered stiffer opposition from Stephen Báthory they seemed to taste success again with his nephew Zsigmond, married to a Styrian archduchess and guided by a resourceful Jesuit. But Zsigmond's stormy, disordered behaviour and the ravages of both sides in the latest Turkish campaigns created growing resentment; by 1608 Bocskai's revolt had victoriously reasserted all the claims of Transylvanian independence and Hungarian separatism. After 1613 Bethlen Gábor elevated Transylvania into a real Protestant alternative for the whole of Hungary and fought a sequence of indecisive wars against the Habsburgs in the 1620s. György I Rákóczi was more stolid, but he saw a chance to exploit grievances in the 1640s, and a further evenly-matched campaign ended with the terms of the *modus vivendi* vindicated.

But *open* compromise, especially with built-in Protestant freedoms, was not to the Habsburg taste. Precisely because their political control was so tenuous, they yearned to place it on a reliable base. By the 1670s they found their opportunity: a collapse of Transylvania through the wild ambitions of György II Rákóczi; a weakening of the Turks; then evidence of treason among the Habsburgs' own subjects. The execution of magnates after the Wesselényi conspiracy began a decade of arbitrary rule paralleling the events of the 1620s in Bohemia (and it is no accident that Lobkovic and Martinic were involved).[5] Though less pretext existed, the execution of policy was in some ways more consistent: the constitution was suspended and power placed in the hands of a *Gubernium* of foreigners, headed by Johann Kaspar von Ampringen, Grand Master of the Teutonic order, and dominated by Chancellor

---

[5] Wolf, *Lobkowitz*; Dvořák (ed.), art. cit., nos. 58–62; Bogišić (ed.), op. cit. 171 ff., 192 ff., 209 f.; Gy. Pauler, *Wesselényi Ferenc nádor és társainak összeesküvése*, i–ii (Bp. 1876), ii, 360 f. and *passim*. For the actual conspiracy see below, pp. 261–3.

Hocher. Persecution of Protestants, with Calvinist ministers in the front line, reached its height when some forty were condemned to the galleys, thus creating a first real martyrology for Hungary's anti-Catholic opposition.[6] The fate of the galley-slaves aroused also an international outcry, but otherwise these events are less well remembered than their Bohemian equivalent. The reason is not far to seek, for they ended in failure; indeed, they were thoroughly counter-productive. They called forth a new Bocskai in Imre Thököly and fanned the furious discontent of the next decades. In 1681 Leopold I had to recall the diet and re-establish the office of palatine. Military success between 1683 and 1686 against Turks and Thökölyites encouraged further pressure (again a Bohemian, Kinský, was influential); it included the mayhem of a Hungarian Judge Jeffreys, General Caraffa—the very name a manifesto of foreign dictation! Yet the diet of 1687 registered only nominal advances: while the estates forswore their right of free election and their medieval grounds for resistance, subsequent developments soon showed how much that was worth. In the 1690s more guarded moves, directed by the largely non-Hungarian Kollonich circle, towards absolute rule over the whole crown of St. Stephen, with centralized administration and economic management, provoked even more violent unrest. In 1703 rebellion broke out over most of Hungary and Transylvania under Ferenc II Rákóczi (grandson of György II) and temporarily deposed the Habsburgs altogether. Eight years later the treaty at Szatmár, between two exhausted parties, returned the country to a state of suspended over-animation.[7]

Thus the Hungarian constitution survived, and with it a series of estates' organs. The bicameral diet (*országgyűlés*), usually well-attended, albeit irregularly summoned, could dispute royal propo-

---

[6] *Life of Leopold*, 74 ff.; Krones, 'Zur Geschichte Ungarns (1671–83)', 359 ff.; Hóman–Szekfű, op. cit. iv, 179 ff.; Gy. Ember, *Az újkori magyar közigazgatás története Mohácstól a török kiűzéséig* (Bp. 1946), 107–12. Literature on the galley-slaves below, n. 32.

[7] The earlier events are carefully described in *Life of Leopold*, esp. 127–71, 197 ff. For the diets of 1681 and 1687: J. Bérenger, *Les 'Gravamina', remontrances des diètes de Hongrie de 1655 à 1681* (Paris 1973), 269–317; Okolicsányi, op. cit., appendix, 153–250. On the Rákóczi revolt: below, pp. 264–6. Hungary's General Caraffa was of the same Italian family as Bohemia's Cardinal Carafa, though the names are conventionally spelt slightly differently.

sitions and present its own hoary gravamina.[8] The palatine, lieutenant for an absentee monarch and chosen by the diet from among four royal nominees, executed the programme hammered out between sovereign and estates with the help of a *Consilium Locumtenentiale*. His deputy, the chief justice (*judex curiae* or *országbíró*) presided over the king's court of appeal, often known as *Tabula Septemviralis*, while a further tribunal, the *Tabula Regia*, functioned under a dignitary oddly named the *personalis*. The counties, with their administrative offices of *comes* (*főispán*) and *vicecomes* (*alispán*), their bench of magistrates, and their largely elective local organization, held far more power than counterparts elsewhere in Central Europe, and each sent two deputies to the diet.[9]

Of course the Habsburgs had *points d'appui* in Hungary, a mixture of traditional aspects of royal authority with some offshoots of the imperial administration. The shadowy chancery, directed by a high cleric, operated from Vienna. A Chamber in Pozsony ran the Habsburg regalia, especially the important mines of the *Felvidék*, and could be influenced from outside, partly by pressure from the Viennese *Hofkammer*, partly through the creation of a rival cameral organization in the Zips (Szepes) for the eastern counties. Neusohl copper made some recovery under direct Habsburg management in the mid-seventeenth century, until its export trade was again blighted by war. War Councils in Vienna and Graz ultimately controlled army pay and appointments, including fortress commands and the captaincies-general of six military regions. But the practical efficacy, sometimes even the competence, of such organs

---

[8] Timon, op. cit. 604 ff.; Bérenger, '*Gravamina*', 49–97. The published proceedings of the diet, *Magyar országgyűlési emlékek* (*Monumenta Comitialia Regni Hungariae*), extend as yet only to 1604; but cf. above p. 52, n. 27. In important ways the *országgyűlés* differed from diets elsewhere in the Monarchy (and in Croatia and Transylvania): a bicameral assembly, it had official members, bishops, and magnates in the upper chamber; county and town delegates, chapter representatives, and the deputies for absent bishops and magnates, in the lower.

[9] On the palatine: V. Frankl, *A nádori és az országbírói hivatal eredete és hatáskörének kifejlődése* (Pest 1863), early history; Ember, op. cit. 91–106; L. Papp, 'Eszterházy Pál kancelláriája', *LK* xx–xxiii (1942–5), 310–44. There seems to be next to no literature on the judiciary in this period, but see—on appeals from the free towns— I. Szentpétery, 'A tárnoki itélőszék kialakulása', *Sz.* lxviii (1934), 510–90. The word *personalis* (Hungarian: *személynök*) was another lawyers' corruption, from '*personalis praesentiae regiae in judiciis locumtenens*'. On the counties: Ember, op. cit. 520–41.

is difficult to ascertain. For most purposes Hungary's rulers until the time of Maria Theresa had to work through indigenous institutions: even the deferential state council, *Consilium Hungaricum*, remained basically an estates' body.[10]

★

On the surface, therefore, we have an uneasy balance between conflicting political aims. Deeper down, the Habsburg régime in Hungary subsisted on elements of a hidden compromise: a community of interest, here too, between dynasty, aristocracy, and Catholic Church. The traditional bearer of the constitution had been the nobility as a whole—nobles alone counted in conventional parlance as the *natio Hungarica*—and the caste was quite large and fluid during the Middle Ages. A major feature of the sixteenth and early seventeenth centuries was the emergence of a new magnate élite, assisted by royal favours and titles and by the right to individual representation in the upper chamber of the diet. But the magnates' real strength lay rather in a dominant socio-economic position won especially in Transdanubia, northern Croatia, and parts of the *Felvidék*.[11] Their activities ensured that the crisis years after 1600 would be resolved neither as feudal anarchy (contrast events in nearby Poland) nor as absolutism. These families— perhaps thirty or forty in sum—came to control higher administration, both national and local; they were *comites* and judges, guardians of the holy crown and counsellors; their private *banderias* maintained the lines against the Ottomans. Whereas in 1600 no more than a handful were Catholic (and most had derived some benefit from appropriated Church lands), after 1650 only a handful remained Protestant.

The inner circle of aristocrats was even more tightly circumscribed. Its membership seems to reduce itself, without undue simplification, to ten families, some of which we have already met.[12]

---

[10] See again the admirable work by Ember, op. cit. 75–91, 113–379, including a first serious investigation of the Szepes *kamara*. Srbik, *Exporthandel, passim,* for the copper mines. Cf. above, p. 150 n. 83.

[11] By the mid-17th century, according to a recent calculation, 37 per cent of Hungarian villages were in the hands of thirteen families (Benda, 'Absolutismus', 109 n.). Cf. above, pp. 91–4.

[12] The main work of reference is I. Nagy, *Magyarország családai*, 13 vols. in 8 (Pest 1857–68), though it is uneven, with many small errors, and poorly annotated. *Révai Nagy Lexikona*, i–xx (Bp. 1911–27), has some useful material; and much

The Esterházys were a unique phenomenon, an almost entirely parvenu line which rose to become the greatest of Hungary's nobility. Of course, they had a certain ancestry, as obsequious chroniclers took pains to demonstrate: one, with a perhaps misdirected enthusiasm, took it back to Attila. But by the sixteenth century the Esterházys lived as impoverished petty gentry in the shadow of powerful kinsmen. Only the career of Miklós, in the last mobile generation before 1620, transformed them.[13] Miklós (1583–1645) made a fortune as palatine, acquiring vast possessions around Eisenstadt and the near-impregnable fortress of Forchtenstein, and confirming the position of his house with a remarkable set of marital dispositions. Miklós himself took as second wife Krisztina Nyáry, the widow of Imre Thurzó, then wedded the son of his first marriage to her daughter, and the granddaughter of that first marriage to his own son by Krisztina. The latter son, Pál (1635–1713) likewise proved a highly astute politician, unflinchingly loyal to the Habsburgs, but with no hint of servility; his advance culminated in appointment as palatine at the fierce diet of 1681, a post which he held until his death. In 1687 the precedence of the Esterházys was confirmed by the title of prince of the Empire; and the plentiful progeny of Pál as well as of other branches in the clan ensured their continuing expansion, while a clutch of *Fideicommissa* laid an unshakeable material base. Pál built himself the first of the Esterházy mansions, that broad-shouldered palace at Eisenstadt which later would be so familiar to Josef Haydn.[14]

miscellaneous information, even about men who were not primarily writers, can be found in J. Szinnyei, *Magyar írók élete és munkái*, i–xiv (Bp. 1891–1913). Wurzbach is an honourable exception to the normal Austrian ignorance of things Hungarian: he uses Nagy, as well as independent information. There exist archival guides (*Levéltári leltárak*) for most of these families, produced in limited editions by the OL, and containing reliable skeleton histories. For the *sui generis* clan of Rákóczi, see below pp. 264 f.

[13] On Miklós Esterházy: above, p. 51 n. 24. His own father had made some social progress, becoming *vicecomes* of Pozsony county and having some highly-placed friends.

[14] On the Esterházys in general (the name can also be spelt 'Eszterházy'): *Trophaeum...Domus Estorasianae* (V. 1700), with crude portraits, brief biographies, and documents (including, sig. Ee4–Mm2, the princely diploma, which covered only the senior branch of the family). J. Eszterházy, *Az Eszterházy-család és oldalágainak leírása*, i–ii (Bp. 1901), is a comprehensive description. On Pál: L. Merényi and Zs. Bubics, *Herczeg Eszterházy Pál nádor*, i–iii (Bp. 1895–6), disappointing. On his mother: Ipolyi, *Nyáry Krisztina*; cf., for her first husband, who died young in 1622: above, pp. 56, 69.

By 1700 the Esterházys—like Liechtensteins in Austria and Lobkovices in Bohemia—were *primi inter pares*. Their rivals as owners of great estates in Transdanubia were the Batthyánys, Pálffys, and Nádasdys. The Batthyánys produced a series of ambitious and influential figures from Ferenc, the supporter of Ferdinand I, to Ádám (1609–59), convert and first count. Ádám's eponymous grandson, chief justice and ban (i.e. vicegerent) of Croatia, married a wealthy daughter of the Austrian Chancellor Strattmann, one of the more conspicuous unions of lineage and intellect in Habsburg history: their elder son became palatine, the younger—tutor to Joseph II—prince of the Empire; a grandson was primate of Hungary.[15] Pálffys and Nádasdys exhibit some similarity of development: both achieved prominence in sixteenth-century Habsburg service—one family Catholic, the other Protestant—while Miklós Pálffy and Ferenc Nádasdy were outstanding military leaders of the years before 1600 (helping their own prosperity by marriages to a Fugger and a Báthory respectively). Their successors maintained the impetus: Pál Pálffy, palatine in 1648, founded the inevitable *Fideicommissum* for his lands along the Austrian border; Ferenc Nádasdy (1623–71), the chief justice, following an equally inevitable conversion and marriage to Miklós Esterházy's daughter, added much of the surrounding countryside to his huge domains. At this point a dramatic divergence: whereas the next generation of Pálffys held high Hungarian court office, Nádasdy suddenly paid for leadership of the 1660s' conspiracy with his head and with confiscation of his lands. Yet the treason was surprisingly quickly redeemed; while Nádasdys never again quite enjoyed the favour lavished on the ultra-loyal Pálffys (the brothers Miklós (1657–1732) and János Pálffy (1664–1751) both became palatine), they continued to occupy high dignities in Church and state.[16]

---

[15] Genealogy in OSzk, MS. 95 fol. lat. (by Martin Kovachich, 1802); and see above, p. 93 and n. 29. This Eleonora (Lori) Strattmann became the bosom companion of Prince Eugene in his last years; one of her sons married another Strattmann, her niece.

[16] A huge article on the Pálffys in Nagy, op. cit.; cf. the mass of undigested documents in P. Jedlicska, *Eredeti részletek a gróf Pálffy-család okmánytárához* (Bp. 1910); and above, p. 50 n. 22. Maksay (ed.), op. cit. 175–239 describes the estates of the military commander of Pozsony castle, a Pálffy sinecure. There appears to be no history of the Nádasdys, but see ibid, 83–130, 241–77, for some of their lands.

A striking, but very understandable feature of the Hungarian situation was the direct involvement of the entire aristocracy in vital military operations. It is evident with those families whose genealogies we have already examined; all their estates lay within range of Turkish sallies and almost every able-bodied male played some part in warding them off. Again the Esterházys stand a little apart: both Miklós and Pál were rather organizers and financiers than commanders; even so, four Esterházys fell in a single skirmish in 1652.[17] Beleagured Croatia still more resembled an armed camp. There the most famous house was Zrinyi, with its warrior heroes Miklós IV, the defender of Szigetvár in 1566, and his great-grandson, Miklós VII (1616–64), scourge of the Ottoman lines along the Drava, inspired adventurer, and finest flower of Hungary's embattled frontier culture, in whom the line reached its apogee. The younger Miklós died as he had lived, savaged by a wild boar while hunting; and the mantle passed to his brother, Péter. But the latter, unequal in substance though equal in spirit, involved himself with the Wesselényi plot against the Habsburgs, and the family was extinguished shortly after.[18]

The Zrinyis had at least toyed with Protestantism; the Erdődys and Draškovićes preserved an unswerving Croatian loyalty to the Roman Catholic Church which brought much benefit to both. The Erdődys—like the related Pálffys—owed their original emergence from obscurity to the patronage of a kinsman, the Renaissance cardinal, Tamás Bakócz, who granted them their extensive lands in western Hungary. Between 1547 and 1693 they produced four bans of Croatia and a long sequence of pious testators. Cardinal Juraj Drašković (1525–86) performed a similar service for his family; his

---

[17] Examples of Miklós's involvement with the business of war in the 1620s and 1630s in OL, Eszterházy család levéltára, P. 108, cs. 453–70. For Pál: Zs. Bubics, *Eszterházy Pál Mars Hungaricusa* (Bp. 1895), an abstract of his account of the war of 1663–4; and cf., on the later campaigns, OSzK, MSS. 463, 502, 505 fol. lat., correspondence with the emperor and *Hofkriegsrat*. The bishop of Pécs preached a sermon on the four victims of 1652, and it was published (V. 1653) at Ferenc Nádasdy's expense.

[18] Zrinyi equals Zrinski in Croat and 'Serini' in the contemporary foreign approximation to the name. From the vast literature on Miklós VII, especially on his writings, see most recently T. Klaniczay, *Zrinyi Miklós* (2nd edn. Bp. 1964). Péter's daughter Ilona appears below (pp. 264 f.); his son Boldizsár was closely watched by the government, detained at the fortress of Kufstein, and died—apparently insane—without issue in 1704.

nephew Ivan (died in 1613) became ban and patron of the early Jesuits in Zagreb; his great-nephews were a palatine and a leading Counter-Reformation bishop. The Erdődys made themselves equally at home in court service besides: for all but seven years between 1684 and 1748 three members of the clan acted as president of the Chamber in Pozsony.[19]

Habsburg Upper Hungary was marginally less feudal than Croatia; it had no precise equivalent to the large-scale commercial enterprises of the Zrinyis. But there too three families stand out in the seventeenth century (in addition to the Esterházys, who also owned large tracts of land on the left bank of the Danube). The power of the Illésházys dated mainly from the spectacular career of István (1541–1609) who, despite deep friction with the Habsburgs, ended his life as count, palatine, and one of the country's richest landowners. István flourished as a firm defender of the Protestant cause, though that did not prevent his marrying into the Pálffys and the Erdődys and protecting an apostate nephew called Miklós Esterházy. His heir, Gáspár (1593–1648) maintained the same religious allegiance in more difficult times–we have already glimpsed him as a lukewarm adherent of Bethlen Gábor in the 1620s, loath to countenance any final break with the Habsburgs. After Gáspár's death his sons, Gábor and György, converted and helped strengthen the influence of Vienna along the broad valley of the river Vág.[20] A similar paradigm could confidently have been predicted for the neighbouring Thurzós of Bethlenfalva, where again the first seventeenth-century generation of a great Lutheran family returned

[19] Nagy and Enciklopedija Jugoslavije, s.v., on the Erdődys, marginally the oldest magnate family in this group (Hóman–Szekfű, op. cit. iv, 422). Bakócz (1442–1521) was archbishop of Esztergom from 1497. For the Draškovićes: above, p. 49, on Archbishop Juraj; and p. 77 n. 84, on the later prelate. Ivan married the daughter of Istvánffy and was one of the Hungarian translators of Guevara (Graz 1610, cf. above, p. 114); his son the palatine had the same Catholic fervour (Kazy, op. cit. ii, 105). See also Hrvatska Enciklopedija, v (Zagreb 1945), 245–50; and 'Szerémi', 'A Draskovichok trakostyani levéltárából', TT 1893, 342–60, 441–58. The Draškovićes later moved to Croat, rather than Magyar patriotism, hence my use of the Croatian form of the name; that language was certainly often used by Juraj (e.g. A. Apponyi, Hungarica: Ungarn betreffende, im Ausland gedruckte Bücher, i–iv (Munich 1903–27), no. 860, appendix).

[20] See above, pp. 51 f., 69; A. Károlyi, Illésházy István hütlenségi pere (Bp. 1883); Csapodi, op. cit. 51, 63. Marsina-Kušik (eds), op. cit. ii, 153–231, 251–79; Kazy, op. cit. ii, 161; Krones, 'Jesuitenorden 1645–71', 311–14 and nn.

to the Catholic faith; but the Thurzós died out in the male line in 1636.

The other domineering magnates of the *Felvidék* were Forgáches and Csákys. The brothers Ferenc and Zsigmond Forgách, as archbishop and palatine, had done much to aid Habsburg recovery after the revolt of Bocskai. Zsigmond's son Ádám (1601–81), field marshal and chief justice, created count in 1640, upheld the public status of the family, such that it was only slightly shaken by the rebellious actions of one of his sons, Simon (1669–1730). Similarly the Csákys, having migrated from Transylvania to Hungary, were sustained by a number of leading politicians—notably the chief justices László (died in 1655) and István (died in 1699)—against the more devious behaviour of other scions.[21]

With the kind of limited exception we shall consider below, these ten aristocratic houses proved loyal throughout the seventeenth century to the reality—not always the theory—of the Habsburg régime in the lands of St. Stephen. Necessarily so, since it could not function for long without them. They were not only *comites* in the counties, but *comites* by hereditary right, and they kept a firm hand on local administration, even though its executants had nominally to be elected. During the whole period between the re-establishment of the palatinate following Bocskai's revolt and its suspension by Maria Theresa in 1765 the office passed outside their charmed circle but once, and then to Ferenc Wesselényi (died in 1667), Count of Murány, who was only marginally inferior in rank.[22] The Wesselényis belonged to a group of families which grasped the reins of state rather more seldom. Some of them were long-established magnates entering a decline: Drugeth of Homonna and Széchy both died out in 1684; the Croatian branch of the Frangepans, hot-blooded peers of the Zrinyis, perished on the scaffold in 1671; the last of the Czobors squandered what remained of their fortune in

<hr>

[21] Cf. above, pp. 51, 63. The Forgáches have one of the best of Hungarian noble histories: Bártfai Szabó, op. cit. F. Deák, *Egy magyar főúr a 17. században, gr. Csáky István* (Bp. 1883); cf., in general, *A kőrösszegi és adorjáni gr. Csáky-család története,* i–ii (Bp. 1919–21).

[22] The Illésházys were actually *főispánok* in two counties, Trencsén and Árva. For the effective powers of the office see (e.g.) Ferenc Nádasdy's instructions to the administration of Vas in the 1640s (I. Nagy in Sz. v (1871), 52 ff.). No palatine was appointed between 1667 and 1681 (when Nádasdy and Szelepcsényi acted as deputies), or from 1732 to 1741 (when Francis of Lorraine deputized).

the mid-eighteenth century; Balassas and Nyárys, Perényis and Révays settled into merely provincial dominance. The rest were a small constellation gradually rising in the political firmament: Kohári (a miniature version of the Esterházys, from the upstart *Felvidék* politician and general Péter (died in 1629) to the last princely heiress who married Ferdinand George of Saxe-Coburg in 1817), Andrássy, Apponyi, Barkóczi, Dessewffy, Károlyi, Keglevich, Széchenyi, Zichy.

With these names, plus a few Transylvanian aristocrats and two pure eighteenth-century parvenus (Festetics and Grassalkovich), we have a fairly complete register of the families which guided Hungary into the age of Maria Theresa and beyond. The native élite possessed an international dimension. Intermarriage with nobles from elsewhere in Central Europe, not infrequent even before 1600, was now extended, the Pálffys leading the way. Hungarians settled in Moravia and Lower Austria—Ferenc Nádasdy's move across the border proved unwise in the circumstances, since he could be judged at his trial by Austrian law.[23] *Per contra*, many distinguished foreigners gained the Hungarian *indigenatus*, and some bought estates after 1683: Kaunitzes, Schönborns, Trautsons on one hand; mercenary interlopers from Prince Eugene to General Harrucker, son of a baker in Linz, on the other. But very few outsiders actually resided for long in Hungary, still less played a public role there. *Indigenatus*-statistics can be misinterpreted and the advent of a 'new nobility' much exaggerated. The point already made in the case of Bohemia needs reiterating, with greater emphasis, for Hungary.[24]

[23] Above, p. 93. The sons and grandsons of Miklós Pálffy and Maria Fugger married Puchheim, Mansfeld, Khuen, Harrach, Mollart, and Liechtenstein wives, and they began to have court weddings in Vienna (*Privatbriefe*, i, no. 187; ii, no. 215 (p. 14)). The Pálffys also moved into Lower Austrian estates (*Handbuch der historischen Stätten*, i, 312, 350, 370, 404). On Moravian immigrants see above, p. 204; another example (but probably at a later date) would be the branch of the Transylvanian Kálnokys which produced an Austro-Hungarian foreign minister, Count Gustav (1832–98).

[24] Eugene scarcely ever visited his property at Ráckeve; the Kaunitzes sold up in 1730 (S. Drkal, 'Kounický velkostatek na Slovensku na počátku 18. věku', *ČMM* lxx (1951), 298–347); Trautsons died out in 1775, as did Harruckers (Haruckerns), in their second generation. Many similar cases could be cited. Among the few to stay were the Schönborns (see below, p. 293). Cf. Hóman-Szekfű, op. cit. iv, 421. One typical case of exaggeration is in B. K. Király, *Hungary in the late 18th century* (New York–London 1969), 25–9; another by I. Sinkovics in *Sz.* cv (1971), 411.

*

There can be no doubt about the Hungarian magnates' influence over their branch of the international Catholic Church, or about their devotion to it. Almost all were recent converts, with the characteristic fervour of those having a past to redeem, and the sincerity of their religious beliefs is not impugned by the fact that there were good material and social reasons why they held them. Nor is it necessary (given my earlier analysis) to underline the aristocrat's powers of patronage, or rehearse a list of monastic foundations and ecclesiastical careerists (usually, but not always, younger sons). Let us consider merely the high piety of three of the century's dominant political figures.

Miklós Esterházy, sponsor of the Jesuit church and the new university at Tyrnau, organized his own disputations in Eisenstadt and composed a long defence of the Catholic religion which reveals a thorough reading of the patristic and more recent apologetic literature. The recipient of his treatise, his son-in-law Ferenc Nádasdy, developed an equal commitment and strengthened it by a visit to Rome in 1665. He instituted a particularly tough Counter-Reformation on his lands, setting up a printing-press to publish devout writings, and settling Augustinians at Lockenhaus and Servites at Loretto.[25] The latter place passed after Nádasdy's death to his brother-in-law, Pál Esterházy, who occupied a uniquely central position in the ecclesiastical as in the secular life of late seventeenth-century Hungary. Continuously active at the local level (the family owned nearly half the advowsons in Sopron county alone) he took thousands of his subjects on a pilgrimage to Mariazell in 1692 and introduced such penitential orders as the Camaldulensian hermits onto his estates. The author and promoter of a battery of works to advertise the Marian cult, Esterházy's correspondence reveals close contacts with many prelates. Six of his children entered the Church (so, predictably, did two of Nádasdy's).[26]

[25] Toldy (ed.), op. cit., prints the treatise by Esterházy. For Nádasdy: OSzK, MS. 1 duod. hung.: 'Diarium Itineris Romam', published in *TT*, 1883, 348 ff.; A. Mohl, 'Adatok Nádasdy Ferencz országbíró életéhez', *Sz*. xxxiv (1900), 616–27; Krones, 'Jesuitenorden 1645–71', 297 n. 2, 299, 320. On his press: K. Semmelweis, *Der Buchdruck auf dem Gebiete des Burgenlandes bis zu Beginn des 19. Jahrhunderts* (Eisenstadt 1972), 73–7. On his Augustinians: Gavigan, *Austro-Hungarian province*, i, 98–103; ii, 39–41, 181–3. On his Servites: A. Mohl, *Der Gnadenort Loreto in Ungarn* (Eisenstadt 1894), 33 ff.

[26] Vanyó, *Katholikus restauráció*, 85 ff.; Kelemen, op. cit. 46–50; Mohl, *Loreto*,

(continued)

At the same time, the Church was no aristocratic corporation. It offered the only chance for a lofty career to those of middling, even of lowest birth: Emmerich Sinelli is a classic example. In Hungary the episcopate remained distinctly less exclusive than elsewhere in the Monarchy, partly because most sees were impoverished (until the 1680s well over half, including the archdiocese of Kalocsa, existed in title only). Even the seventeenth-century primates of Esztergom trailed little purple: the well-connected Forgách was succeeded by the petty-noble Pázmány, then by Imre Losy (1637–1642), an obscure convert, György Lippay (1642–66), who left his family much less modest than he found it, György Szelepcsényi (1666–85), another petty noble, and György Széchenyi (1685–1695), who turned his kinsmen from marginal gentry into prominent Transdanubian landowners.[27] Only after the transitional figure of Count Leopold Kollonich (1695–1707) and the blue-blooded outsider, Christian August of Sachsen-Zeitz (1707–25), do the prime ruling families take over: Esterházy, Csáky, Barkóczi, Batthyány. Otherwise nobility rubbed shoulders with some very unsung pedigrees.[28] Yet high political office might be at stake. Until 1706 the Hungarian chancellor was always a prelate; the *Consilium Hungaricum* was packed full of bishops, and of abbots taking their style from dimly-remembered houses long swept away by the Turks; clerics even codified Hungarian law, and all higher courts contained representatives of the cloth.[29] The archbishop of

---

66 ff. The Marian works are listed in Bubics, op. cit. Cf. A. Angyal, 'Fürst Paul Eszterházy', *Südostdeutsche Forschungen*, iv (1939), 339–70; and the odd items in OL, Eszterházy cs. lt., P. 125, cs. 705, nos. 11931, 11935–7, 11956 (student exercises), etc. *Trophaeum . . . Domus Estorasianae*, pt. 1, nos. 123–6, 131–2, for the children.

[27] In general, N. Schmitth, *Archi-Episcopi Strigonienses compendio dati* (2nd edn. Tyrnau 1758). Pázmány's father may have been an *alispán*, but the case is not very clear. Lippay's father rose, rather like Himmelreich's (above, pp. 61 f.), as a royal secretary (Nagy, op. cit. s.v.; Marsina–Kušik (eds.), op. cit. i, 523). On the Szechenyis: L. Bártfai Szabó, *A gr. Széchenyi-család története*, i–iii (Bp. 1911–26).

[28] Several prestigious sees became mainly aristocratic in the 18th century: Eger, Vác, Győr; Pécs was dominated by foreigners for the first half of the century. Cf. L. Károlyi, *Speculum Jaurinensis Ecclesiae* (Győr 1747); J. I. Desericius, *Historia Episcopatus . . . Vaciensis* (Pest 1763); N. Schmitth, *Episcopi Agrienses*, i–iii (Tyrnau 1768); A. Ganoczy, *Episcopi Varadienses*, i–ii (V. 1776); J. Róka, *Vitae Vesprimiensium Praesulum* (Pozsony 1779); I. Katona, *Historia Colocensis Ecclesiae*, i–ii (Kalocsa 1800).

[29] 'High chancellor' was a mere title, always assumed by the primate; the 'cancellarius ordinarius' was another bishop, usually on the make; sometimes a third bishop might be appointed as vice-chancellor; see Ember, op. cit. 77–9, 113 f., with

Esztergom enjoyed many privileges, including extensive rights of ennoblement and legal immunity, the first vote in the upper chamber of the diet, and the dignity of *comes* in two separate counties. This political base allowed the Church to launch a strong Counter-Reformation assault which culminated, like Habsburg absolutist pressure, in the 1670s. While Leopold I naturally sought to use the priesthood as a spiritual arm in his own campaign, there is plenty of evidence to show how many independent initiatives were taken by the Catholic estates: prelates and magnates. Lippay had been a hammer of the Protestant boroughs since the 1640s, and his successor Szelepcsényi, deputy-palatine between 1670 and 1681, soon acquired the same reputation; Esterházy, Nádasdy, Wesselényi, the Illésházys and Erdődys, were all notorious for ruthlessness in the countryside. Wherever possible, heretical towns were denied their right of ecclesiastical presentation and heretical citizens compelled to contribute to the maintenance of a priest.[30] In 1671, Bársony, Bishop of Nagyvárad, published a tract which advanced three legalistic arguments against continued toleration: Catholic rights—though guaranteed by treaty—are being infringed; the agreements of 1608 and 1647, since the clerical estate always resisted them, were never approved by the whole diet; Hungary's Lutherans and Calvinists have diverged from the Augsburg and Helvetic Confessions, and innovation is not allowed. Thus Bársony and his fellows proclaimed Protestantism unconstitutional (contrast the treason-thesis of the dynasty).[31] Persecution reached its climax with the trial of the galley-slaves, and that episode was widely and correctly blamed less on Vienna than on the native Catholic camp.

---

lists of these and other counsellors. On the law: above, p. 17; the *Corpus Iuris Hungarici* was later expanded by the Jesuit Szentiványi (Hóman–Szekfü, op. cit. iv, 351).

[30] J. Korneli, *Quinque Lustra Georgii Lippai de Zombor* (Tyrnau 1722); M. Zsilinszky, 'Lippay György és a tokaji tanácskozmány', *Sz.* xx (1886), 400–24; Redlich, 'Pufendorf', 586–93; B. Obál, *Die Religionspolitik in Ungarn nach dem Westfälischen Frieden während der Regierung Leopold I* (Halle 1910), rather wild; Vanyó, *Nunciusok*, nos. 97 seqq. *passim.* Cf. above, nn. 25–6, on Nádasdy and Esterházy. For the towns: Á. Timon, *A párbér Magyarországon* (Bp. 1885), esp. 97 ff.; id., *Das städtische Patronat in Ungarn* (Leipzig–Bp. 1889), *passim.*

[31] György Bársony, *Veritas toti mundo declarata* (Kassa 1671, and later edns. in 1672, 1676, 1681, 1706, 1720?, 1725). There were several refutations: e.g. Okolicsányi, op. cit., appendix, 146–52.

When fortunes changed briefly in 1681–3, the Protestants' first thought was revenge on the Jesuits and the bloodthirsty episcopate, while Habsburg victory over the rebels promptly revived oppression from that quarter. Late seventeenth-century and early eighteenth-century diets imposed increasing restrictions on the public worship of 'Acatholics'.[32]

Nevertheless the long offensive did find considerable response: the other side of the coin is a real devotional resurgence within Catholicism, penetrating outwards from courts like the Esterházys' to the people at large. A vogue grew up for works of simple piety, sanctifying the basic truths proclaimed by Rome, either in a pure form, as with reissues of Thomas à Kempis, or poetically elaborated. One good example is the private spirituality—revealed by his prayer-books—and the public literary activity of Mátyás Nyéki Vörös (1575–1654): many editions appeared of his *Istenes énekek* (which included the finely-wrought religious verses of Balassi) and *Tintinnabulum*, with its vivid evocation of the four last things.[33] The mood was helped by a series of notable converts, from Mihály Veresmarty soon after 1600 to Fóris Ferenc Otrokocsi (1648–1718), in whom this Counter-Reformation reaped one of its most extraordinary fruits: the former galley-slave transformed into a fervent Catholic propagandist.[34] Such cases continued to be surrounded by a cloud of controversy. Veresmarty's warnings and threats, reprinted in the 1640s, brought sharp Protestant rejoinders, as did the widely-publicized apostasy of Johann Kircher, who had migrated from Tübingen to Upper Hungary. But Kircher's blunt and pugnacious opponent, Zacharias Láni, had much of the wind

---

[32] *A short Memorial of the … Sufferings of the Ministers … in Hungary* (London 1676); *A brief Narrative of the State of the Protestants in Hungary* (London 1677); *Life of Leopold*, 74 f.; Okolicsányi, op. cit., sig. a2ᵛ–c1ʳ; Lampe, op. cit. 447–96; Bod, op. cit. ii, 52–127. Cf. Hóman–Szekfű, op. cit. iv, 186–91; and the latest treatment: P. F. Barton and L. Makkai (eds.), *Rebellion oder Religion?* (Bp. 1977). On the aftermath: Krones, 'Zur ungarischen Geschichte (1671–83)', 397–444, *passim*.

[33] One of the translators of Kempis was Pázmány (*Összes munkái*, i, 207–370, first edn. V. 1624). For Nyéki Vörös: *Régi magyar költők tára*, ii (Bp. 1962), 400 ff., with life and poems. His prayer-book is ÖNB, MS. s.n. 2602, a beautifully illustrated MS. with notes by the possessor. On Balassi cf. above, pp. 111 f.

[34] Above, p. 112, on Veresmarty. His contemporarily published writings are *RMK* i, 431, 437, 697, 706, 721. F. F. Otrokocsi, *Examen reformationis Lutheri et sociorum eius* (Tyrnau 1696); etc. There is a life of him by F. Fallenbüchl (Esztergom 1899). For converts see also Krones, 'Zur ungarischen Geschichte (1671–83)', 393 f.

taken out of his sails when his patrons, the Illésházys, changed sides, and by the end of the century the flame of Protestant disputation burned lower. The most furious assault on Otrokocsi was penned, not in Central Europe, but in Oxford.[35]

Effective promotion of the Catholic cause owed most to a broad tradition: polemical, apologetic, and edifying, which stemmed from Pázmány. Learned but also direct, he gave his Church a maximum attractiveness as well as a keen cutting edge. The international orders offered a great opportunity to eager young spirits from a beleaguered country: study at the Collegium Hungaricum in Rome, perhaps, or the Pázmáneum in Vienna. Clever youths in the next two generations took advantage, then lent their shoulders to the wheel, like the Jesuit, Martin Szentiványi, who became rector of Tyrnau University.[36] Thus Hungary maintained intimate ecclesiastical links with the rest of the Monarchy. Provinces of orders were often undivided and exchanges of personnel took place—witness the early missions of the Piarists; Benedictine, Cistercian, and Premonstratensian houses in Austria and Bohemia took over lands recovered from the 1680s.[37] The highly controversial Cardinal Kollonich illustrates the point well. His family, originally from Croatia, was by the seventeenth century mainly Austrian, with fairly superficial Hungarian associations, including the *indigenatus*; Kollonich himself, the son of a spectacular convert, was born at Komárom, like Sinelli. His clerical career, begun among the knights of Malta (he remained one all his life), embraced Wiener Neustadt as well as Nyitra, Győr, Kalocsa, and Esztergom. President of the Pozsony Chamber in the 1670s, then

---

[35] Papistak meltatlan Uldözese a'Vallasert (n.p. 1643, reprinted [Várad] 1657), 55 ff., lumps Veresmarty together with Cardinal Carafa. Z. Láni, *Strigil Aetiologiae Kircherianae* ([Trencsén 1641]), a point-by-point confutation; cf. *RMK* ii, 517; Räss, op. cit. v, 546–94. Benjamin Woodroffe, *Examinis et Examinantis Examen, sive, Reformationis ... Defensio adversus calumnias F. F. Otrokocsi* (Oxford 1700).

[36] Steinhuber, op. cit., on the Collegium Hungaricum, which was soon united with the Collegium Germanicum. On the Pázmáneum: V. Fraknói, *A bécsi Pázmány-intézet megalapítása* (Bp. 1923). J. Serfőző, *Szentiványi Márton munkássága a XVII század küzdelmeiben* (Bp. 1942); cf. below, pp. 322 f.

[37] On the provinces, cf. above, p. 181; on the Piarists: below, n. 45. *Benediktinerbuch*, 407 f.; *Cisterzienserbuch*, 100–2, 527 ff.; Fuxhoffer, op. cit. ii, 94–9, 123–8. The Cistercian monastery of Zirc was acquired by Lilienfeld as early as 1659, and later passed to Heinrichau (in Silesia); see also Békefi, op. cit. Premonstratensians: *Chorherrenbuch*, 15–22, 144–99; Fuxhoffer, op. cit. ii, 3–68, *passim*.

the most thoroughly absolutist planner of the 1690s, Kollonich
proved an indispensable, but very awkward asset. And he was
succeeded as primate by a still more foreign body in the national
Church, a Saxon prince fresh from diplomatic activity in the service
of Vienna.[38]

*

The international movement by itself could not have persuaded
Hungarians. As elsewhere, it entered into a complex relationship
with a parallel native movement. Religious orders reasserted their
autochthonous character, above all the Benedictines at the archab-
bey of Martinsberg or—in modern parlance—Pannonhalma, south
of Györ. As old as Hungarian Christianity, first to recover from the
disasters of Protestantism and temporary capture by the Turks in
the 1590s, Pannonhalma was resettled after 1638 under one Pálfy—
a Cistercian from Heiligenkreuz, but the only Hungarian available.
Despite many vicissitudes it expanded and revived filials at Tihany,
Bakonybél, and Dömölk in the early eighteenth century. Since
Pannonhalma has received more historical attention than any other
monastery in the former Habsburg Monarchy (and probably in
Europe) I need not dwell on its story.[39]

Hungary possessed one entirely indigenous order. The Paulines
(*Pálosok*), or more properly hermits of St. Paul of Thebes (though
like the Augustinians they were not really eremitic), had been
regularized as an institution in the thirteenth century and spread by
the end of the Middle Ages to number over one hundred houses
within the lands of St. Stephen, with more in Poland and even
Germany. Decimated by the events of the Reformation, they clung
to the vestiges of life and to much of their property, and after 1600

---

[38] J. Maurer, *Cardinal Leopold Graf Kollonitsch, Primas von Ungarn* (Innsbruck
1887), a detailed biography. Kollonich's father, a soldier, was supposedly brought
back to the Church of Rome after miraculously recovering from temporary blindness
in 1621 (ibid. 10–13). His family died out in 1751 with Johann Sigismund, cardinal
archbishop of Vienna, grandson of a cousin of Leopold. Kollonich was president of
the *Neo-Acquistica* commission from 1688 and administrator of the *Hofkammer*,
1692–4; cf. Hóman–Szekfű, op. cit. iv, 243–9. On Archbishop Christian August:
below, p. 283.

[39] Erdélyi–Sörös (eds.), op. cit., cover the history of Pannonhalma and its
dependent houses in twelve huge volumes. For those without Hungarian, there is a
brief summary of the work by A. Schermann in *Stud. u. Mitt.* xxxviii (1917), 157–73,
398–408; cf. Fuxhoffer, op. cit. i, 7–157. The earlier Magyar name for this, the only
abbatia nullius in Central Europe, was (Szent-) Mártonhegy.

they found new animation, backed by the spirit of Trent, a new constitution, and a sequence of Croat generals.[40] The restored Paulines became a strong force in the Counter-Reformation at local level: they were the coenobites most closely bound up with Hungarian traditions ('Friar George' Martinuzzi, for example, had been one) and most favoured by the nobility, both as suitable recipients of benefactions and, in some important cases, as the foundation for an ecclesiastical career. Their general alone, along with the abbot of Pannonhalma, represented the regular clergy at the diet. They began to recolonize the rest of Central Europe, being introduced to Bohemia by Pešina and to Moravia by the Liechtensteins.[41]

Still more important for the Catholic crusade were initiatives in education and publishing which conformed with local needs. The Jesuits took the first step from 1635 with their university at Tyrnau and its printing-press. A very modest enterprise in its early stages, the academy soon gained a reputation for cheap, efficient, and patriotic teaching, while the flow of texts which it issued swelled into a flood by the 1690s. This pedagogy was, of course, Latin-based and largely unoriginal,[42] but Jesuits were not behindhand in cultivating the vernacular, and here again Pázmány proved the great innovator. His *Kalauz* in particular is a *tour-de-force* of controlled invective, from the introductory admonition that the reader forsake frivolous novelties to the concluding satire—800 folio pages later—on the incompetent arguments of his Protestant

---

[40] E. Kisbán, *A magyar Pálosrend története*, i–ii (Bp. 1938–40), is a thorough general history (i, 203 ff. on the recovery). For the 17th century see also *Fragmen Panis Corvi Proto–Eremitici seu Reliquiae Annalium O.S.P.P.E.* (V. 1663), covering events to 1663; N. Benger, *Annalium O.S.P.P.E. volumen secundum* (Pozsony 1743), with events between 1663 and 1727; F. Galla, *Marnavics Tomkó János boszniai püspök magyar vonatkozásai* (Bp. 1940); id., *A Pálosrend reformálása a XVII században* (Bp. 1941, both separata from *Regnum*). These Paulines are not to be confused with the Paulines = Barnabites.

[41] On nobles and the order: *Fragmen Panis*, 345 ff.; Benger, op. cit. *passim*; Kisbán, op. cit. i, 216 f., 239 ff., 285–9; Galla, *Pálosrend*, 107 f. Archbishop Imre Esterházy of Esztergom (1725–45) was a Pauline; so was Archbishop Pál Széchenyi, mentioned below (p. 265). Bérenger, *Gravamina*, 50 f. Zelený, art. cit. 14, 558 ff. (Pešina); *Fragmen Panis*, 364 f. (Liechtensteins). The order also bought a house in Rome; and cf. below, p. 426.

[42] The 18th-century Tyrnau press was notable for some of the very *last* Latin editions of obsolete treatises. For its Latin printing in this period see *RMK* ii; for its workings: Iványi–Gárdonyi, op. cit. 51 ff.

contemporaries, heavily buttressed with quotations from their writings. The brilliant blending of learned polemic with linguistic resource (as, for example, in the sections which seek to refute Protestant reliance on the authority of Scripture) has few parallels anywhere in Europe. It is, indeed, Pázmány's peculiar mastery over the Magyar language as a vehicle for Catholic truth which secures him a place among the greatest personalities of the Counter-Reformation, and yet has denied him international recognition of that place. Even when a famous Wittenberg theologian denounced the *Kalauz* at formidable length in Latin, Pázmány's blistering response was still couched in the earthy speech of the Hungarian peasant, while its precision and richness are remarkable for a man so caught up in affairs of state.[43]

Later Jesuits could never match Pázmány, but several, István Tarnóczy and András Illyés among them, were prolific in delivering and publishing the kind of homily which reached the common man, as well as in translating, mostly from Latin and Italian. Meanwhile the Catholic Bible translation by György Káldi confronted Calvinists on their own ground.[44] Equally productive, especially in preaching and books for the largely unlettered, were the Franciscans, while by the end of the century Hungarian schooling began to benefit from the strong commitment of the Piarists. Although the first members of that order only settled in the 1660s, it soon became a prime force in education, with deep local roots, and remained so until the twentieth century.[45] This activity naturally concentrated on Magyar, the main language of the nobility, and German, the main

---

[43] P. Pázmány, *Isteni Igazságra vezérlő Kalauz* (Pozsony 1613), esp. pt. 2, bks. 6–7. Id., 'A'Setét Hajnal-Csillag után bujdosó Luteristák Vezetője', in *Összes munkái*, v, 477–819, confuting Frederick Balduinus of Wittenberg. In the same year (1627) Pázmány still found time to compose instructions to estate bailiffs in his own hand: *Levelei*, nos. 394–7.

[44] *RMK* i, for these works. A. Illyés, *Megrövidittetet* [*sic*] *Ige az–az: Predikatios könyv*, i–iii (Tyrnau–V. 1691–2), is a serviceable introduction to the genre. S. Révai, *Káldi György életrajza, Biblia-forditása és Oktató Intése* (Pécs 1900); this translation was apparently begun by Szántó (above, p. 50). It is easy to forget, in the Central European context, that vernacular Bibles were actually prohibited (without special permission) by the Index (Reusch, op. cit. i, 333–6).

[45] Franciscans: Gy. P. Szabó, op. cit. Piarists: Horányi, op. cit., esp. i, 805–8; ii, 72–5, 103–5, 347–50; Gy. Balanyi et el., *A magyar piarista rendtartomány története* (Bp. 1943). Their first Hungarian house was opened at Privigye (Slovak: Prievidza; Ger: Priwitz) in the *Felvidék*. Earlier (1642) they had been brought to Podolin, one of the towns in the Zips region which were mortgaged to Poland.

language of the towns. But it did not discriminate: there is evidence of literature in Slovak, beginning with a translation of hymns in 1655, and the South Slav languages, for which Carafa acquired 'Illiricae litterae' as early as 1622.[46] We know that the rules of the Observant Franciscans provided for alternative election of Magyars and Slovaks, and much of Tyrnau society was thoroughly diglot. Pázmány's *Rituale Strigoniense* of 1625 appeared in four languages: Latin, Hungarian, German, and Slovak; while visitation reports reveal the extent of polyglot coexistence in western Hungary.[47]

The creation of a distinctive atmosphere and loyalties for the Hungarian Church under the aegis of universal Catholicism was much forwarded by the cult of saints and intermediaries. As in Austria and Bohemia, Marian worship is the most prominent feature of Counter-Reformation devotions. Pilgrimage places sprang up around miracle-working shrines: at Máriavölgy, near Pozsony, run by the Paulines; at Máriapócs, whose famous votive painting was later transferred to St. Stephen's in Vienna; at Boldogasszony (Frauenkirchen), founded by Pál Esterházy, with its fine Baroque church.[48] But again we have a Virgin conceived in the national image, for her cult was directly associated with the country's role as a bulwark against the Turks. Mary was seen as a kind of untouchable goddess, a divine protector against the infidel. In the towns Marian societies multiplied, especially where they were organized by the Jesuits, and although their influence on the

---

[46] *RMK* ii, 830, 1343, 1409, 1696, 2010; Carafa, *Commentaria*, 124; Kazy, op. cit. i, 203 f. Literature in Croatian is registered by I. Kukuljević Sakcinski, *Bibliografia hrvatska: tiskane knjige* (Zagreb 1860). By 1700 even Ruthene types were in operation at Tyrnau (Iványi–Gárdonyi, op. cit. 49).

[47] Gy. P. Szabó, op. cit. 81; E. Angyal, 'Česko-mad'arské a slovensko-mad'arské styky v době baroka', *Dějiny a národy* (Pr. 1965), 55–70, at 58–61; B. Varsik, *Národnostný problém trnavskej univerzity* (Bratislava 1938), esp. 22 ff.; I. Käfer in *Filológiai Közlöny*, xi (1965), 380–7. Cf. Pázmány, *Levelei*, no. 711; there was a Slovak translation of the *Kalauz* (see I. Käfer in *Helikon*, v (1959), 178–80). Above, n. 3 (Vanyó and Házi).

[48] L. Németh, *A Regnum Marianum állameszme a magyar katolikus megújhodás korában* (Bp. 1941), 58 ff.; Hóman–Szekfű, op. cit. iv, 121–4; K. Garas, *Magyarországi festészet a XVII században* (Bp. 1953), 25 ff. On Máriavölgy: Kisbán, i, 188–92; Galla, *Pálosrend*, 105 f.; L. Pásztor, 'A máriavölgyi kegyhely a XVII–XVIII században', *Regnum*, v (1943), 563–600. On Máriapócs: L. Juhász, *Bécs magyar emlékei* (V. 1972), 44 f. For Esterházy see above, n. 26. Joseph was also revered (Illyés, op. cit. i, 1–30); and at a later stage calvaries came much into vogue (Lehmann, art. cit. 136–42, 148, 150–6, lists some 250 substantial examples).

course of military events during the 1680s may well have been less than hagiographers would wish, none the less they tended to promote charity and encourage feelings of Catholic solidarity.[49]

The idea of a *Regnum Marianum* went with renewed veneration for Hungary's early saintly kings, who had made their land a haven of Latin Christianity under constant siege from the Orthodox and the pagans. The crucial figure was St. Stephen, warrior for *patria* and Catholicism. The mantle of Stephen suited the Habsburgs well: insistence on his apostolic rights over the Hungarian Church, supposedly granted by Pope Silvester II in the year 1000, could have consequences startlingly unwelcome to prelates and aristocracy alike, but in the seventeenth century no one pushed the doctrine to its limits; in fact it was ultramontanes like the Jesuit Inchofer and Bársony who expounded it. The popular *cultus* of Stephen, propagated in countless sermons, books, altarpieces, wall-paintings, and statuary, was much more straightforward, and his son Imre, who died young, partook of it: a Hungarian Wenceslas, though no martyr (like Zrinyi, he was slain by a boar).[50] The crown of martyrdom was borne rather by Stephen's confidant and Imre's mentor, Bishop Gellért, who was bound to a handcart and dispatched into the Danube from a great height in 1046. Stephen's relative and successor, Ladislas or László, also earned reverence as the paragon of a saintly national ruler: his cult flourished at Nagyvárad and Győr, and his feast-day was celebrated from the 1620s at Vienna University with Baroque pageantry and a ceremonial oration.[51] The gallery of lesser Christian heroes stretched from the early missionary Adalbert (*alias* Vojtěch, and shared with Bohemia), via the admirable St. Elizabeth, a princess from the house of Árpád, and her niece, the Blessed Margaret, who took the vows of a nun on the Danubian island named after her, to the

---

[49] Németh, op. cit.; cf. above, p. 126 n. 27.

[50] On the apostolic kingship cf. above, p. 134, and below, p. 273 and n. 88. M. Inchofer, *Annales ecclesiastici Regni Hungariae*, i, pts. 1-4 (Pozsony 1795-7), first published at Rome in 1644; *RMK* i, 1110 (Bársony). Illyés, op. cit. ii, 416-38, 560-79; iii, 21-60; *Acta SS.* Sept., i, 456-575 (Stephen—whose Hungarian feast-day, however, is 20 Aug.); ibid. Nov., ii, 1, 477-91 (Imre).

[51] Gellért (Gerard): ibid. Sept., vi, 713-27. László: Illyés, op. cit. ii, 249-70; iii, 60-80; S. Barta, *Ungarn und die Wiener Universität des Jesuitenzeitalters* (Bp. 1937), separatum from *BÉ* vii), 20 ff.; *Acta SS.* June, v, 315-27.

valiant crusading friar, St. John Capistrano, and the Jesuits slaughtered at Kassa in 1619.[52]

What began as a stress on the continuity of Catholic virtue broadened into a whole interpretation of Hungarian history, incorporating notions of hierarchy, order, and discipline freely adapted from the neo-stoics. This was a facet of the embattled culture of the Counter-Reformation which once more owed most to Pázmány. His refutation of the preacher Magyari in 1603 is the starting-point: the devilish message of Lutheranism has dissolved centuries of accumulated grace and precipitated Turkish conquest.[53] Again and again he returns to the particular situation of the early seventeenth century and scores points off the less adaptable Calvinist view of providence. Renewed concern for the medieval heritage came, naturally enough, from the older orders, but also from the Jesuits. It is striking how often Marian shrines were claimed—however spuriously—to date from the Middle Ages and to have miraculously survived Protestant iconoclasm. Yet the same urge brought also a first serious interest in source materials and led to the eighteenth-century Jesuit school of Hevenesi, Péterfy, Kaprinai, and Pray. It overlaps with the celebration of profane history stimulated by such men as Ferenc Nádasdy and Pál Esterházy, whose courts provided a real focus for native culture.[54]

★

I have outlined the makings of a 'system', an alliance—part-conscious, part-implicit—between the dynasty and the holders of secular and ecclesiastical power in Hungary. We must now turn to

---

[52] These and others are recorded in the *Ungaricae Sanctitatis Indicia* (Tyrnau 1692), translated as *Régi Magyar Szentség* (ibid. 1695), a work apparently by Gábor Hevenesi; and in the *Acta Sanctorum Ungariae* (ibid. 1743), drawn from the Bollandists, with an appendix on some homelier unofficial saints. Cf. Illyés, op. cit. iii, 1–21 (Adalbert); ii, 599–620; iii, 80–99 (Elizabeth); *Acta SS.* Jan., ii, 897–909 (Margaret, sainted in 1943); Pázmány, *Levelei*, nos. 502, 601, 624, 629–30, 700–1, 709. On Capistrano: above, p. 128.

[53] P. Pázmány, 'Felelet az Magyari István sárvári praedicatornak ... irt könyvére', *Összes munkái*, i, 13–192. On neo-stoics cf. above, pp. 113 f.

[54] On the first major Hungarian Jesuit historian, Gábor Hevenesi (1656–1715), friend of Kollonich and rector of the Viennese college, who left a large collection of MSS., see B. Hóman, 'Kishevesi Hevenesi Gábor', *Történetírás és forráskritika* (Bp. 1938), 337–51. *Mausoleum ... Regni Apostolici ... regum ... Ungariae* (Nuremberg 1664), directed by Nádasdy; cf. Rózsa, op. cit. 13–80, 107–20, and below, n. 66. The *Trophaeum ... Domus Estorasianae* was closely supervised, and probably partly written, by Esterházy.

the limitations of this system. Substantial pressure-groups rejected it from the outset. Protestantism lived on, and not only in the special circumstances of Transylvania and the comparative isolation of the north-east. Lutherans huddled together in most of the free towns, while Calvinists throughout the country had their parishes, districts, seniors, and superintendents, registered with a mixture of love and bitterness by the chroniclers of their tribulations.[55] With Protestantism survived the influence of Hungary's numerous gentry on provincial life: a 'country party' pursuing its grudges with grim determination through county administration and dietal representatives. Moreover, no proper stability existed beneath the surface: the large body of petty nobles shaded into free peasants, especially hajducks, privileged or unprivileged, then into migrant populations, shifted by war and economic distress, and bandit groups on the margin. Organized peasant resistance in the 1690s and 1700s contributed powerfully to the disorder of those years.

This remained an essentially fragmented opposition. It possessed one major piece of common ground: resentment at Germans (*németek*), a nebulous term embracing mainly the Habsburg armies, and administrators from the rest of the Monarchy and the *Reich*. They overbore the nobles, dismissed the local soldiery (especially after the peace of Vasvár in 1664), screwed taxes from the peasants and laid waste their livelihood. The antagonism was much more an elemental xenophobia nourished by material and psychological insecurity than a friction between nationalities. It did not normally extend to indigenous Germans; indeed, the latter were ironically thrown into the rebel camp by Habsburg religious intolerance.[56]

All this represented a substantial irritant to the grander strategy of the dynasty, but not a serious threat. More significant for our purposes are grave discords *within* the system. Magnates had an equal dislike of 'Germans', although the objects of their enmity stood rather higher up the social scale: warlords, presumptuous court officials. There was one important difference between them

[55] Lampe, op. cit., pt. 3; Bod, op. cit. iii, *passim*.

[56] *Venetianische Depeschen, passim; Relationen Venetianischer Botschaften*, ed. Fiedler, esp. 13: 'E veramente trà la Natione Onghera, e l'Alemana passa un Antipathia cosi grande, che il solo timore de'Turchi fà tollerare al Regno il Giogo Thedesco.' Further evidence of this mood in Hóman–Szekfü, op. cit. iv, 148 ff.; Bèrenger, '*Gravamina*', 67 f. R. F. Kaindl, *Geschichte der Deutschen in den Karpathenländern*, ii (Gotha 1908), 60 ff., on domestic German attitudes.

and their Austrian or Bohemian counterparts: throughout the seventeenth century, and even beyond, no Hungarian felt entirely at home in Vienna's corridors of power. And the Habsburgs and their immediate servants returned the mistrust. Scarcely any Hungarian was offered a major central post in our period, and such titles as privy councillor usually brought little more than prestige. The strange dress and unpronounceable names of the native aristocrats set them apart, and even the most ambitious among them continued, despite the hothouse atmosphere at court, to cultivate their own garden. They communicated with each other exclusively in Magyar—most knew little more of the German language than did their peasantry—and retained a full sense of the national past and its obligations, that past which they so glamorized in their fanciful genealogies.[57]

Pál Esterházy came nearest to assimilation; but he stood firm, like his father, on the role of the estates, even through the fraught years of the 1690s.[58] Let us consider two less obvious examples: during the reign of Ferdinand III Ádám Batthyány was a chief protagonist in the defence and the Counter-Reformation of the modern Burgenland, no more than sixty miles from Vienna. He regularly corresponded with the central government, especially with the War Council, in German and Latin (though admitting he needed a secretary to manage even the latter). But Batthyány's diary reveals only infrequent visits to the capital—perhaps once a year—and, while there, he might be kept waiting for three weeks without an audience.[59] Ádám Forgách too was a good servant of the

[57] Leopold made some strongly antipathetic comments in private about Hungarians, and not just after 1670: e.g. the remarks about 'quelle bestie dell'Ungari' in Kalista (ed.), *Korespondence* nos. 35, 38, 41 (all 1662). But such things are, of course, easily said (he does add that they are 'bestie al modo d'asini'). Cf. Vanyó, *Nunciusok*, pp. 14 f., 17, 55. The point about language is an obvious one, yet it has often been misunderstood. Latin too, though used for many official purposes, was hardly a living tongue to most of the nobility. For one typical example of ignorance: B. Grünwald, *A régi Magyarország* (Bp. 1888), 93 f. See also J. Bérenger, 'Latin et langues vernaculaires dans la Hongrie du XVIIᵉ siècle', *Revue Historique*, ccxlii (1969), 5–28; and id., '*Gravamina*', 23–8. Hungarian magnate costume, with *dolmány* and *mente*, long resisted the encroachments of international *haute couture*, and would make an interesting social study.

[58] Hóman–Szekfű, op. cit. iv, 237–9; cf. Csapodi, op. cit. 67 ff.

[59] OL, Batthyány cs. lt., P. 1315, cs. 1–3 (the foliation is very *ad hoc*). See cs. 2 for the (incomplete) travel-diary, 1644–54; cs. 1, fol. 25, for the ignorance of Latin; cs. 1, fols. 255–61, for the snub in Vienna. On Batthyány's Counter-Reformation see

(continued)

Habsburgs, despite temporary disgrace in 1663 when he allowed the fortress of Neuhäusel to fall to the Turks. He profited materially from his loyalty, and he enjoyed the friendship of Leopold's major-domo, Lamberg, even of Ampringen. But Forgách was appalled—at least privately—by the ill-considered policies of the 1670s. Both he and Batthyány show considerable recrimination over Vienna's neglect and incompetence; both appear to strive for distinctly cordial relations with the Rákóczis of Transylvania. Neither can have been entirely critical of the overtures made by magnates to Venice during the 1650s and later to France.[60]

The clergy's loyalty came under similar strain: a direct line of dissent stretches right back to the time of Rudolf II's unconstitutional actions after 1600. Pázmány, always true to the Habsburg alliance, never feared to voice disagreement, as with the forward policy adopted by Esterházy and Ferdinand II against Transylvania. Lippay was no less independent, while even Szelepcsényi and Tamás Pálffy, deputy-palatine and chancellor during the 1670s, resisted the naked exercise of court absolutism, and Sinelli did what he could for the counsels of moderation. The German background of Kollonich was nowhere more fiercely belaboured than among his fellow bishops: the primate, Szelepcsényi, for example, detested him.[61] When necessary, prelates could fall back on the Pope. We

above, p. 72, n. 74, and OL., Batthyány cs. lt. misszilisek, nos. 36158–67, 54896–8, mostly published by B. Iványi in *Körmendi füzetek*, iii (1943).

[60] Forgách's papers are in OL, Forgách család levéltára, P. 287, ser. II, cs. 40 (foliated in reverse order of dates); and ibid. P. 1883. Tributes to his loyalty: ibid. (P. 287), fols. 491, 481, 271. Neuhäusel affair: ibid. fols. 392–21 and (P. 1883) 103 ff. Letters from Lamberg: ibid. (P. 287), fols. 259, 233, 220, 189, 177 f.; from Ampringen, fols. 242–35, 218–12. Rákóczi: ibid. fols. 438 f. (an interesting letter). Habsburg criticism: esp. ibid. (P. 1883), fols. 108 f., '155–8' (*recte* 255–8), memorandum to Sinelli; cf. Bod, op. cit. ii, 66. For Venetian activity in 1659: *Venetianische Depeschen*, esp. nos. 119–34, 142 seqq.; *Relationen Venetianischer Botschaften*, ed. Fiedler, esp. 107 ff.

[61] Benda, 'Absolutismus', 114 f.; Pázmány, *Levelei*, nos. 429, 631, 644, 656, 838, 846, 860–1, 898–900, 911, 918–20, 924, 1065; cf. Csapodi, op. cit. 72 ff. Zsilinszky, 'Lippay'; and cf. below n. 65. Pauler, op. cit. ii, 57–9, 156 ff., 228 ff., 248 f., on Szelepcsényi's views in the 1660s; Meszlényi, *Szelepcsényi*, 7 f.; *Life of Leopold*, 77 f., 90; cf. Krones, 'Zur Geschichte Ungarns (1671–83)', 359 f. OL., Eszterházy cs. lt., P. 125 (cs. 658), nos. 2490–2508 (late 1683 and 1684), with Sinelli's hopes for the restoration of the kingdom of Hungary 'splendori pristino'; cf. Antal-Pater (eds.), op. cit. i, 270 f. On Kollonich: OL. Eszterházy cs. lt. P. 125 (cs. 658), nos. 3934–80 (letters from Szelepcsényi; esp. no. 3936; ibid. nos. 3899–3923 (letters from Széchenyi), esp. nos. 3921–3; ibid. nos. 2827–64 (letters from Kollonich), esp. nos. 2828, 2831–2; Vanyó, *Nunciusok*, no. 89.

have seen some chronic bones of contention between Vienna and Rome; and it is not surprising that the Hungarian Church should have been the most Curially-inclined in the Monarchy, just as Bohemia—with figures like Harrach and Magni—was potentially the most anti-Curial area. The Papacy had its own diplomatic course to pursue in Hungary: it might approve the centralizing drive of the 1670s (even congratulate Ampringen on resuming the Teutonic order's traditional mission against pagans!), but by the end of the decade it espoused mediation, then reverted to a strong Counter-Reformation line for the diet of 1681. The following year Szelepcsényi issued a formal condemnation of the new Gallican articles, which added to the storm of controversy in France. Of course, his attack suited the Austrian call to defence against Louis XIV; but historians seem to have overlooked the fact that its ultramontanism was also pointedly equivocal *vis-à-vis* the Habsburgs themselves.[62]

*

Out of this dual opposition from aristocrats and prelates, overlapping but not identical, deeply-felt but hesitant, grew Hungary's revolts against Habsburg authority after 1664. In that year, despite a Christian victory at Szentgotthárd over the Turks, the peace of Vasvár confirmed the Porte in its possession of more extensive Danubian territories than ever before, among them the historic city of Nagyvárad, whose famous equestrian statue of St. László, a miracle of the medieval kingdom once coveted by Rudolf II, was unceremoniously sunk in the river Tisza.[63] Leaders of the nation, with rare unanimity, railed at Vienna for its shameful diplomacy and insouciance There followed, as an immediate consequence, the so-called Wesselényi conspiracy, a very bizarre episode and an odd misnomer, a kind of *Fronde nobiliaire* with large dashes of slapstick.[64]

---

[62] Above, pp. 59–62, 133–7. *Nuntiaturberichte*, ii, nos. 203, 232, 250; Bojani, op. cit. iii, 426–79; Vanyó, *Nunciusok*, nos. 117 seqq., esp. 118. Szelepcsényi's statement is printed in Péterfy, op. cit. ii, 438–41; its impact is discussed by B. Zolnai, *A Gallikanizmus magyarországi visszhangja* (Bp. 1935, separatum from *Minerva*, xiii (1934)). Galla, 'Felhatalmazások', has interesting evidence of Papal policy towards Hungary *in spiritualibus*.

[63] On the battle at Szentgotthárd (called Mogersdorf by Austrian historians): G. Wagner, *Das Türkenjahr 1664, eine europäische Bewährung* (Eisenstadt 1964). A. Kampis, *A history of art in Hungary* (Bp.–London 1966), 73 f.

[64] Basic documents in F. Rački (ed.), *Acta coniurationem bani Petri a Zrinio et comitis Fr. Frangepani illustrantia* (Zagreb 1873); and Bogišić (ed.), op. cit. The most

(continued)

It was launched by the Croatian ban, Miklós Zrinyi, his patience with the Habsburgs finally exhausted, and by Archbishop Lippay, publicly outspoken in his abuse of the emperor and maddened at the loss of his estates around Neuhäusel. But both these men soon died, as did Wesselényi, the palatine, whose role in the movement never became more than peripheral. The plot was then taken over by Péter Zrinyi, his brother-in-law Fran Frangepan, and the chief justice, Nádasdy, with Machiavellian encouragement from the French ambassador, Gremonville, and from Protestant lesser nobles whose spokesman was a lawyer, István Vitnyédy.[65] Beside the hot-blooded Vitnyédy there is no doubt that Ferenc Nádasdy master-minded the malcontents. Contemporaries agree in stressing both his ambition and his great talents: a cultured and lively intelligence, he edited several volumes on the rights of the estates, one of them at his own press, then turned to eloquent appeals for a cleansing of Hungary from foreign influence.[66] Not even Nádasdy could breathe life into the 'conspiracy', whose amateurish plotting became an open secret both at home and in Vienna. Eventually, having heard the details of it from almost all the ringleaders in their periodic moods of contrition, Leopold had them arrested by stages in 1670. Fears of a genuine Protestant insurrection and Turkish involvement persuaded him—against his natural inclination—to order the execution of Nádasdy, Zrinyi, and

thorough treatment is Pauler, op. cit. Cf. Kazy, op. cit. iii, 37 ff.; Redlich, *Weltmacht*, 196–214; and some additional material in J. Bérenger, 'Francia-magyar kapcsolatok a Wesselényi-összeesküvés idején', *TSz* x (1967), 275–91. E. Lilek, *Kritische Darstellung der ungarisch-kroatischen Verschwörung und Rebellion, 1663–71*, i–iv (Celje 1928–30), is a harmless curiosity, which casts more light on academic frictions in inter-war Jugoslavia; by contrast G. Wagner, 'Der Wiener Hof, Ludwig XIV und die Anfänge der Magnatenverschwörung, 1664–5', *MÖStA* xvi (1963), 87–150, is disfigured by scurrilous anti-Hungarian polemic.
[65] On Lippay's attitude, blended of material and intellectual outrage (for he was a cultured patriot; cf. below, pp. 317 f.): Bogišić (ed.), op. cit. 7, 17 ff., 55; Pauler, op. cit. i, 21–3 and 82 n. He also sought a cardinal's hat (*Nuntiaturberichte*, i, nos. 149, 155). For Vitnyédy see J. Hörk in *Sz*. xli (1907), 289–320, 400–14, 502–17.
[66] Péter Révay, *De Sacrae Coronae ... Ortu [et] ... Fortuna* (V. 1652); id., *De Monarchia et Sacra Corona Regni Hungariae* (Frankfurt 1659); both reissued by Nádasdy. H. Verdyssen (ed.), *Articuli Universorum Statuum et Ordinum Inclyti Regni Hungariae, 1606–59* (Pottendorf 1668). F. Nádasdy, *Oratio az ország négy rendjéhez*, ed. E. Veress (Bp. 1896, separatum from *TT*). Cf. J. Vértesy, 'Nádasdy Ferencz mint iró', *Sz*. xxxviii (1904), 47–57. Opinions of him in *Privatbriefe*, ii, no. 258 ('Gwiss ist es, dass er origo omnis mali'); Bogišić (ed.), op. cit. 80 ff.; Pauler, op. cit. i, 29 ff.

Frangepan, and to move against their allies, actual or potential, among the gentry and burghers.

The Wesselényi conspiracy may appear a wild exception to the general argument of this book. Here we find the paladins of a magnate-Catholic élite engaged in *lèse-majesté*—and there is little doubt about their *formal* guilt, which they themselves more or less admitted! Yet on investigation it proves to conform to type, at least given the extra fragility of relations between the dynasty and Hungary. The existence of a privileged caste both made the plotting possible and also ensured its failure. Pampered but not courted, that caste was able to nurse rebellion while possessing neither the heart for a serious breakaway nor any understanding of political realities. Precisely because of the covert bond of high Counter-Reformation culture, Nádasdy could expect clemency from Leopold (whom he had regularly and regally entertained at his castles); precisely for the want of any overt political bond between Vienna and Hungary it could not be granted: indeed, all manner of improbable rumours were circulated about the dissidents' plans (like poisoning the emperor or burning down the Hofburg) and readily believed in Austria and abroad. Thus the same evidence was bound to be interpreted in two different ways, and the death sentences proved just as surprising to the magnates as they were obvious to most of the rest of Europe.[67]

The events of 1670–1 were made the pretext for the absolutist experiment in the next decade—Leopold frankly admits as much in his private correspondence.[68] Hence they brought ever more tumultuous resistance, led now by the Lutheran Thököly, who

[67] On the rumours cf. below, p. 381; some probably originated with loose-talking plotters. Most foreign writers condemned the conspiracy: e.g. C. Freschot, *Ristretto dell'Historia d'Ungheria* (Naples 1687), 155–95; *Life of Leopold*, 69; Rinck, op. cit. 554 ff., esp. 582–7; and, of course, translators of the official report of the proceedings, whose English version is *The Hungarian Rebellion, or an Historical Relation of the late wicked Practises of the three Counts . . .* (London 1672). But—as Rózsa rightly observes (op. cit. 123–8)— there is evidence of a deliberate Habsburg propaganda campaign to justify the sentences, moved by considerable fears of a wave of sympathy. The court composer, Alessandro de Poglietti, even wrote a *Toccatina sopra la ribellione de Ungheria*. The propaganda (though not perhaps the Toccatina) had its effect, and the conspirators have been consigned to historical limbo, irredeemably 'Magyar' to Habsburg sympathizers, yet not 'nationalist' enough for patriotic Hungarian historians. Cf. their pathetic pleas in (e.g.) OL, Eszterházy cs. lt. P. 125 (cs. 658), no. 3266; ibid. Forgách cs. lt. P. 287, ser. II, cs. 41, fols. 28–30.

[68] *Privatbriefe*, ii, no. 249 (Heiligenkreuz, 22 May 1670).

mobilized his co-religionists in the *Felvidék*: the *kurucok* come of age. But Thököly too was a magnate; his great-grandfather, once a rough cattle-dealer, had made the family fortunes in that mobile half-century before 1600. And Catholics were part of his milieu: his uncle became a convert; his wife was Ilona Zrinyi, daughter of Péter. In 1682–3, when Thököly's troops flooded Habsburg Hungary, most of the Catholic nobility threw in their lot with them.[69] By the same token, any lasting success was impossible without those Catholic supporters, as was soon shown when they reverted to Habsburg allegiance for the contest against the discountenanced Turks.

Exactly the same phenomenon presents itself, on a larger scale, with the last and most grandiose of the revolts: the Rákóczi rebellion of 1703–11.[70] To understand how Ferenc II Rákóczi came to dominate the culminating act in the drama of early-modern Hungary, we must look briefly at one more genealogy. The Rákóczis—Ragoczy or Ragotzi, as foreigners corrupted the name— were an established family of Transylvania, rising (yet again) on the eve of 1600 to stand among the senior nobility of the principality. Zsigmond (1544–1608) was temporarily elected prince in his old age; his son, György I gained the same position in 1630 and held it till his death in 1648. Parallel with their political advance went economic consolidation. Zsigmond gained large estates along the Polish border; György I added further latifundia in Upper Hungary, as well as the perquisites of personal government in Transylvania; his son was married to the last of the Báthorys, Zsófia, hence inheritor of another huge fortune. Even though György II's foreign political designs brought Rákóczi rule over Transylvania to an abrupt end, the family remained—beside the Esterházys—the most exalted and wealthy in Hungary. From the forests of Makovica down to the swamps of Ecsed and beyond they

---

[69] D. Angyal, *Késmárki Thököly Imre*, i–ii (Bp. 1888–9). Thököly took over the leadership of opposition from another magnate, Pál Wesselényi, cousin once removed to the palatine (on whom see Gy. Décsényi in *Sz.* xix (1885), 520–32, 614–20). For the term *kuruc* (or *kurutz*) see above, p. 97. At the time 'Thököly' was often spelt 'Tekeli', *vel sim.*

[70] The enormous secondary literature does not belong here; cf. Kosáry, op. cit. i, 435–72. The standard life is S. Márki, *II Rákóczi Ferencz*, i–iii (Bp. 1907–10); cf. Redlich, *Werden einer Grossmacht*, 108–55. Recent work has concentrated on international aspects of the story, especially B. Köpeczi, *A Rákóczi szabadságharc és Franciaország* (Bp. 1966, French version 1971).

could travel a hundred miles or more without quitting their private patrimony.[71]

The Rákóczis occupied a kind of middle-ground between the principality and the kingdom: resident and esteemed in both, they constituted the natural focus for anti-Habsburg patriotism in each realm. The short-lived Ferenc I (1645–76) took up where his father, György II had left off, becoming involved in the treasonable manœuvrings of the 1660s and marrying Péter Zrinyi's daughter Ilona (as her first husband); their son, Ferenc II (1676–1735) enjoyed a right of apostolic succession to the leadership of the *kuruc* army. Nevertheless the Rákóczis were also evidently magnates. Catholicism had been in the family since the 1620s with György I's convert brother Pál, chief justice of the kingdom. Zsófia Báthory, scion of a fervently Romanist house, was *persona gratissima* among the Hungarian prelates and second to none as a Counter-Reformer after her husband's death, beginning with the conversion of her own son, whose release from prison (and from possible execution) she managed to secure by intervention at Vienna in 1670. Ferenc II, after the defeat of his stepfather Thököly, actually received his education at a Jesuit college in Bohemia and lived out his young manhood amid the high culture of Vienna's international Baroque.

Thus Rákóczi carries the same stamp of the intelligent renegade courtier as does Nádasdy. At first he conspired equally idly against Leopold; then, committed to an Austrian dungeon (the same as had harboured his grandfather, Zrinyi), he escaped to raise the standard of national revolt. And who were his lieutenants? Catholics, almost to a man: Miklós Bercsényi, a refined, rich, and high-living noble, previously Habsburg commander in Upper Hungary; Sándor Károlyi, a leading landowner from the east; Antal Esterházy, a nephew of Pál; Simon Forgách, the younger son of Ádám; István and Mihály Csáky, two of the twenty-five children of chief justice István. In fact, initial Catholic sympathy for the rebellion was quite widespread, even among Jesuits and the Benedictines of Pannonhalma. The archbishop of Kalocsa, Pál Széchenyi, tried to mediate in 1704; although unsuccessful, he could at least see both sides of the argument.[72]

---

[71] On these estates: L. Makkai, *I Rákóczi György birtokainak gazdasági iratai, 1631–48* (Bp. 1954); Marsina–Kušik (eds.), op. cit. ii, 58–124.
[72] Again I cannot list bibliography for the other leaders of the revolt; but cf. K.

(continued)

In the end most Catholics returned to the Habsburg fold, and peace was negotiated by two magnates: Károlyi and János Pálffy. Of course, the prime motor of the uprising had lain elsewhere, in popular discontent and Protestant hatred. The peasants first encouraged Rákóczi to take the field; the Calvinist gentry elected him prince of Transylvania and sought to crown him king. But they alone could not deliver any decisive blow against the dynasty. Indeed, their growing predominance among the insurgents persuaded many members of the upper class and the Catholic intelligentsia to exchange, as in the 1620s and the 1680s, a half-hearted opposition for renewed lukewarm conformity. Rákóczi went into exile, wrapped himself up in a heavily French-inspired Jansenism quite remote from Hungarian traditions, and sought solace first at a Camaldulensian monastery in Paris. The declining years of melancholy reflection beside the Bosphorus are immortalized in the imaginative letters of his noble Catholic companion, Kelemen Mikes.[73]

*

That brings us to a consideration of Transylvania, Mikes's homeland and Rákóczi's strongest base. It must be short: the principality was an integral part of the Monarchy only from the 1690s; but it can be instructive, for it throws into relief the weaknesses and strengths of the entire Habsburg order in Hungary.[74] Transylvania stood in a curious position: almost completely autonomous (and more threatened from Istanbul than from Vienna during most of the period) it was yet bound by numerous ties to the crown of St. Stephen. No clear frontier existed, and much of eastern Hungary came under dual influence, especially on the estates of the Rákóczis—who held court mainly at Sárospatak—and in local towns

---

Thaly, *A székesi gr. Bercsényi-család, 1460–1835*, i–iii (Bp. 1885–92), ii–iii; and much documentation of the Károlyi family in *A nagykárolyi gr. Károlyi-család oklevéltára*, i–v (Bp. 1882–97), esp. v. On the religious issue: A Meszlényi, *II Rákóczi Ferenc felkelésének valláspolitikája és a jezsuiták* (Bp. n. d., separatum from *Regnum*); Erdélyi-Sörös (eds.), op. cit. iv, 123 ff; v, 57–60; cf., for a Protestant view, Bod, op. cit. ii, 322–40. For Széchenyi see Gy. Lánczy in *Sz*. xvi (1882), 273–99.

[73] Gy. Szekfű, *A száműzött Rákóczi* (Bp. 1913), is a shrewd, irreverent view. K. Mikes, *Összes művei*, ed. L. Hopp, i (Bp. 1966), a critical edition of the 'letters' from Turkey. The Rákóczis died out in exile with Ferenc II's two sons.

[74] There are very few general accounts, especially on the non-political side. J. Benkő, *Transilvania*, i–ii (V. 1778), is a very useful compendium; Makkai, *Transylvanie*, is the best narrative.

such as Debrecen, almost cut off from the rest of the country. Movement took place to-and-fro; some of the great families migrated or, like Csáky and Wesselényi, preserved two branches. Regular Magyar correspondence across the border shows common interests, while close contacts were maintained too among German communities: the leading Saxon politician of the early eighteenth century, Sachs von Harteneck, was the son of a burgher from the *Felvidék*. Transylvania had a county structure which, archaic and intricate, was arranged on the same principles as in Hungary; until 1659 the principality still sent observers to the royal diet.[75]

Thus Transylvania naturally represented, for those dissatisfied with life under the Habsburgs, the conscience of Hungary as a whole: the legacy of John Hunyadi and his son, Matthias Corvinus, who originated there; a truly native, elective régime. The tradition of resistance to Habsburg claims, periodically spilling over into belligerence, was advertised from Bocskai onwards as a struggle for political and religious liberties, the central strand in *kuruc* ideology. Major formulations are the apology for Bocskai, issued in 1605, and Alvinczi's *Querela Hungariae* of 1619. We should not (*pace* many Hungarian historians) take all the slogans too seriously, but they clearly offered an alternative set of values. They meant the survival, not only of Protestantism, but of confessional pluralism. Calvinism was the dominant faith, its sense of mission becoming a key factor in policy; but Lutherans survived as a minority group, now practically identical with the Saxon community, along with some Unitarians, even Sabbatarians, a sprinkling of Roman-Catholics, and a considerable population of Orthodox Romanians.[76] Links with Protestant Europe, snapped everywhere else by war and official pressure, were sustained in Transylvania. Indeed, the international role of Bethlen and the Rákóczis helped to bring her nearer to her foreign allies and sympathizers and to channel strong Dutch and English influences. They went with the continuance of

[75] On Sachs von Harteneck see the summary in F. Teutsch, *Die Siebenbürger Sachsen in Vergangenheit und Gegenwart* (Sibiu 1924), 126–30. For the constitutional position: Timon, *Verfassungsgeschichte*, 725 ff.; Bérenger, 'Gravamina', 48.

[76] The vindication of Bocskai appeared in English: *A Declaration of the Lordes and States of the Realme of Hungary* (London 1605, tr. from the French). The *Querela Hungariae* was printed in Hungarian, Latin, and German. The positive nature of toleration in Transylvania has been enthusiastically argued by some, e.g. by D. Angyal in *Sz.* lxiii–lxiv (1929–30), 591–600; cf. above, p. 15 and n. 28.

an urban culture: not at all a metropolitan ethos, but the life of the little boroughs of Transylvania and the humble *mezővárosok* of the Great Plain. Here Reformation pedagogy retained its hold, creating a stratum of Western-orientated lay intellectuals, taught by such exiles as Alsted and Comenius. Here, more even than in most of Germany, let alone the Habsburg lands, radical ideas could still flourish: most notably a Puritan critique of the established ecclesiastical and social order, but also certain aspects of Cartesian thinking, and the new theories of Bacon, Grotius, and Coccejus.[77]

Yet in many ways Transylvania ran a similar course to the rest of the Monarchy. In one key respect it outstripped the Habsburgs on their own ground: by the mid-seventeenth century it approached much closer to political absolutism. The development is a remarkable one, given the electiveness of the ruler and the religious compromises already entered into. It was helped by the *de facto* authority of the prince, who held most of the military, financial, and juridical strings of power; he and his court at Gyulafehérvár (Alba Iulia) could define their own sphere of influence and draw on the same sort of submissive neo-stoic literature which rallied to the Habsburgs. An estates' organization existed, based on the three 'nations' of Magyars, Szeklers, and Saxons, and the diet met very regularly; but (in the absence of any long tradition of precedent and authority) it depended heavily on the prince who summoned it. The very uncertainty of the situation, both at home and abroad, tended to predispose electoral assemblies in favour of a strong ruler.[78] This process advanced quickly from 1613, after Transylvania had passed through its own 'time of troubles', and Bethlen Gábor, by no means the semi-savage of traditional Western historiography, balanced his

[77] I intend to write more fully elsewhere about Transylvanian culture in the 17th century and its Western European connections. See most recently, on contacts, L. Demény and P. Cernovodeanu, *Relaţiile politice ale Angliei cu Moldova, Ţara Românească şi Transilvania în secolele XVI–XVIII* (Bucharest 1974). For the Puritans: J. Zoványi, *Puritánus mozgalmak a magyar református egyházban* (Bp. 1911), theological; Makkai, *Puritánusok*, social and economic.

[78] V. Biró, *Az erdélyi fejedelmi hatalom fejlődése* (Kolozsvár 1917), a perceptive essay. On the administration: Ember, op. cit. 380–516; cf. Benkő, op. cit. ii, 1–77. For the neo-stoics, cf. above, pp. 113 f. On the diet: Zs. Trócsányi, *Az erdélyi fejedelemség korának országgyűlései* (Bp. 1976). Transylvania is one of few parts of Europe with full published records of its 17th–century dietal proceedings: *Erdélyi országgyűlési emlékek* (*Monumenta Comitialia Regni Transylvaniae*), ed. S. Szilágyi, i–xxi (Bp. 1876–98).

natural deviousness with shrewd, tough, and quite enlightened policies , which included a kind of paternal mercantilism. Then the dynastic Rákóczis built upon his government and upon their own unrivalled private resources.[79]

The outcome could not, of course, be total absolutism. Sovereignty was shared with a high nobility which likewise won out from the 1600s onwards: a little later than further west, and less completely, but following the same trend, and helped by the hitching to Transylvania of the rich latifundia of the *Partium*. Many ennoblements took place during the wars, but the value of petty nobility declined steadily: one good example is the differentiation among the Szeklers, previously the most egalitarian society in Central Europe, and the enhanced prominence of such clans as Mikes, Kálnoky, Lázár, Mikó, and Apor.[80] When the Turks crushed Transylvanian independence in the years 1658 to 1662 and installed the fainéant Mihály I Apafi as prince, they left an oligarchy of established Magyar and Szekler families, more or less ancient in their provenance. Besides the ones just mentioned, these included Bethlen (the Keresd line, rather than the Iktár branch which produced Bethlen Gábor) and Bánffy of Losoncz; Kemény and Rhédey; Kornis and Gyulaffy; Telekis from the *Partium*, the nearest to arrivistes; and Hallers, unique examples of a transition from patricians of Nuremberg, through Saxon entrepreneurs, to landed aristocrats.[81] Chaos in the 1680s and 1690s, even more than

[79] Gy. Szekfű, *Bethlen Gábor* (Bp. 1929), esp. 152 ff.; Makkai, *Transylvanie*, 221 ff. E. Makkai, *Bethlen Gábor országalkotó politikája* (Bp. 1929), does not do justice to its title. For the Rákóczis as sovereigns: S. Szilágyi, *A Rákócziak kora Erdélyben* (Pest 1868).

[80] The Szeklers were originally a tribe used as frontiersmen by the early Hungarian state. By the 17th century they were largely assimilated to the Magyars, especially in language, but still preserved relics of their original military order and political privileges. It is not easy to find information on their social evolution. I have used, besides Nagy, op. cit., J. Benkő, *Imago inclytae ... Nationis Siculicae* (Nagyszeben–Kolozsvár 1791); L. Szádeczky Kardoss, *A székely nemzet története és alkotmánya* (Bp. 1927), esp. 107 ff., 214–59; and, most recent, S. Benkő, L. Demény, and K. Vekov (eds.), *Răscoala secuilor din 1595–6: antecedente, desfăşurare şi urmări* (Bucharest 1978), esp. 266–316.

[81] Much useful biographical information about ruling families is gathered together in the lists of *comites* of Transylvanian counties by M. Lázár in *Sz.* xxi (1887), 400–26, 518–28, 610–25, 700–15; xxii (1888), 33–41, 242–51, 334–48, 426–34, 505–22, 622–37, 730–9, 911–31; xxiii (1889), 30–41, 131–47, 229–37. See also Nagy, op. cit. The fascinating story of the Hallers of Hallerkő, *alias* Hallerstein, emerges from the article ibid., s.v.; cf. A. Kubinyi, 'Die Nürnberger Haller in Ofen', *Mitteilungen des*

(continued)

in the 1590s and 1600s, grew out of personality clashes within a very limited élite which would dominate the life of the principality, and sometimes of Hungary as a whole, for centuries to come.

The prince and the magnates sought greater social control, and in Transylvania too the key to this lay in the ecclesiastical situation. The seventeenth-century religious picture was no longer really liberal: Calvinism had become a state Church, its court preachers little better than house chaplains; Lutheranism was acceptable, but isolated and stagnant; the Unitarians were firmly restrained and their college at Kolozsvár showed few signs of animation. Once the spirit of Humanist accommodation faded away, only the letter of the constitution remained, and that proscribed all innovation. Not only Sabbatarians were persecuted, but heterodox Calvinists as well. Thus Puritanism suffered decisive rejection: Transylvania's authorities proved as antipathetic towards it during the 1650s as were the Habsburgs *vis-à-vis* their own radicals earlier. Having lost most of the battle over organization, it survived only in the interstices of a hidebound establishment, running into the sand of sterile theological disputes.[82] Mainstream Calvinism, with its episcopal structure, bore the stamp of deference, hierarchy, and conservatism.

Of particular concern in the present context is the state of Catholicism, which existed on sufferance throughout the golden age of Transylvanian independence. The Catholic community fell into a parlous decline by the early seventeenth century: in 1607 it numbered no more than forty priests (excluding Jesuits), most of them married, and saw no prospect of an appointment to the vacant see of Gyulafehérvár, where the episcopal palace had been occupied by the princely household. In this strange acephalous condition (somewhat akin to the state of Catholicism in the United Provinces), the Church could display no proper vitality. But it showed itself curiously tenacious, and even won a sort of official approval—evidently having less to fear than the Protestants from the

---

Vereins für Geschichte der Stadt Nürnberg, 1963–4, 80–128. Practically every one of the families mentioned was raised by the Habsburgs to the rank of count (not known earlier in Transylvania) between 1685 (Teleki) and 1714. Cf., on the oligarchy, Trócsányi, op. cit. 42 f. and *passim*.

[82] For the persecution of Sabbatarians: Kohn, op. cit. 295 ff. On the fate of Puritanism: Zoványi, *Puritánus mozgalmak*, 355 ff. This said, it should be added that some elements of Puritan morality remained influential, and that scarcely any of its advocates suffered extreme penalties for his opinions.

constitutional clause forbidding innovation. Bethlen Gábor permitted some Jesuit missionaries and schools, and maintained good relations with individual Catholics, while his nomination of an administrator (*vicarius*) on his own terms—forestalling any Habsburg candidate—may not have been entirely unacceptable to Rome. The Rákóczis extended the self-government of the 'Status Catholicus' in Transylvania and employed a few of its members in high positions.[83] After 1660 the Church broadened its spiritual base, aided especially by the Franciscans of Csik with their printing-press in the Szekler heartland, and a Catholic political group began to form around certain aristocrats (some of them converts): István Apor and Mihály Mikes, the Hallers and Kornises. Behind its recovery lay the larger cultural impact of the Habsburg world: neo-scholasticism and Jesuit education, Baroque learning and sentiment, which I shall touch on again in a later chapter.[84]

Thus by the 1680s the Transylvanian élite which was the inheritor of *kuruc* political traditions had grown increasingly ambivalent about them, and sought rather to safeguard its position in a country so near the edge of European civilization, but so proud of belonging within it. As will be remembered, no complete break with the rest of Hungary had ever occurred (for a few improbable years Zsigmond Báthory was actually brother-in-law to the future Emperor Ferdinand II); and so the Habsburg embrace could be attractive enough, given the right terms. The stages of accommodation are symbolized by two generations of the Teleki family: Mihály (1634–90), Apafi's chief minister, who, having campaigned for a French orientation, made a *volte-face* in the mid-1680s; and his son Mihály, who in 1689 translated an impeccably loyalist work

[83] V. Biró, *Bethlen Gábor és az erdélyi katholicizmus* (Cluj 1929); Kazy, op. cit. i, 104 f., 211 f., 265, 269–72, 299 f.; ii, 29–36; Révai, op. cit. 19, on Bethlen's subsidy for Káldi's Bible-translation; Szekfű, *Bethlen Gábor*, 192–5; F. Galla, 'A csiksomlyói ferencrendi kolostor viszontagságai Bethlen Gábor idején', *BÉ* iv (1934), 283–302; cf. *Nuntiaturberichte*, i, no. 91. Bethlen's widow, Katharina of Brandenburg, became a convert for a time; cf. below, p. 284. It may be recalled (p. 51 n. 23) that Transylvania had a resident Catholic bishop very briefly in the late 1590s.

[84] *RMK* i, 1188, 1253, 1273, 1328–9; cf. *MIT* ii, 319, on Kájoni. The best work on the Catholic revival, though a disorganized one, is V. Biró, *Apor István és kora* (Cluj 1935), on the powerful Transylvanian treasurer of the 1690s. Mihály Mikes (died in 1721), nephew of a Catholic chancellor of the principality under György II Rákóczi, was a supporter of the Rákóczi rebellion. Cf. below, ch. 9, esp. pp. 325–7, for the cultural background.

by an Austrian canon regular for the younger Prince Apafi.[85] The
flood of titles now issued by the Habsburgs for the Telekis and their
compeers were a mere appendage to the power of the aristocrats,
rather as, decades before, the ruling Rákóczis had been accorded
the style of princes of the Holy Roman Empire. And Catholics now
began to make the political pace in Transylvania, outrunning
Vienna's generous concessions to them in a way which fifty years
earlier, in the heyday of the Calvinist principality, would have
appeared wildly unlikely.

★

Let us, finally, take our stance in the years around 1700 and try
to draw conclusions. The Habsburgs have found just enough
support to seize the whole historic territory of the crown of St.
Stephen, as the Turks are rolled back to Belgrade, while the body
and spirit of Transylvanian separatism (young Prince Mihály II
Apafi and his chancellor, Miklós Bethlen) are held under close
surveillance in Vienna. But they have not found strength enough to
impose any kind of centralization in Hungary—not even the semi-
native variant proposed by that stormy petrel, Kollonich—while
Leopold's Diploma of 1690 for Transylvania retains, alongside the
native governor, a separate chancellor and treasurer for the
principality and too large a toleration to please local Catholics. The
peace of Szatmár will confirm the bargain, laying a foundation for
the country's more orderly eighteenth-century evolution. On the
one hand, the aristocracy is groomed for its magnificent gesture of
loyalty in 1741, and the Protestants are confined within narrow and
humiliating limits. On the other hand, a series of awkward
compromises are reached in the political and economic sphere: diet,
chancery, *Consilium Locumtenentiale*, courts and counties all continue with minimal modification, newly-recovered lands gradually
fall under domestic management, and a cryptic document known
as the Pragmatic Sanction comes to regulate relations between ruler
and ruled in a way calculated to generate far more heat than light.[86]

---

[85] The elder Teleki had earlier been responsible for the elimination of a strong
pro-Habsburg magnate group around Dénes Bánffy and Pál Béldi. Mihály Teleki,
Fejedelmi Lelek avvagy A'Jo Fejedelemnek Szükseges Ajandeki ... (Kolozsvár 1689),
from a Latin work by Adam Johann Weber of Neustift. This younger Teleki adhered
to the Rákóczi revolt, but his own son became a Catholic convert, further evidence
of the intricate loyalties at this time in Hungary.

[86] The modifications in Hungary's political institutions during the earlier 18th

Thus the arrangements I have examined in this chapter were considerably more fragile than those elsewhere in the Monarchy. Hungary after 1700 entered a period of full-scale Catholic Baroque florescence: the same religious and social intolerance, the same intellectual and educational preoccupations, the same buildings and paintings, as in the rest of Central Europe, all just a little belated. It is a meaning detail of delayed response that Stobäus's letter of 1598 to Archduke Ferdinand about how to destroy Protestantism in Styria was distributed at Tyrnau in 1714 for the instruction of new Hungarian doctors of divinity.[87] Yet the Habsburgs had little control over the movement, and it was threatened in two different ways. The continuing disruptive stance of Calvinist gentry and intellectuals would eventually lead to the liberal programmes of the Reform era and a fringe of more radical critics of the establishment. Much sooner than that, deep rifts were already appearing *within* the establishment. When Maria Theresa's librarian, Adam Franz Kollár—himself a native of Trencsén—wrote two learned Latin treatises in the 1760s to re-examine the nature of the crown's apostolic rights over the Hungarian Church, he flung the diet into a turmoil and barely escaped with an abject recantation.[88] There was, needless to say, some *arrière-pensée* about Kollár's, and the

century are conveniently summarized in H. Marczali, *Hungary in the Eighteenth Century* (Cambridge 1910), 329 ff. The Pragmatic Sanction was not, of course, merely (or even primarily) designed to resolve the constitutional problems of Habsburg Hungary, though that came to be its most important function—hence the absence of any properly objective treatment of it. Cf., in general, G. Turba, *Die Grundlagen der Pragmatischen Sanktion, i: Ungarn* (V. 1911).

[87] G. Stobaeus de Palmaburgo, *Historica Religionis Reformatio pennâ theologicâ*, ed. L. Tapolcsani (Tyrnau 1714), prints for the first time the guidance to Ferdinand (pp. 1–14), and the report of 1604 on the progress of Counter–Reformation (25–80). There are good summaries of high-Baroque culture in Hungary in Hóman–Szekfü, op. cit. iv, 366–416, and S. Domanovszky (ed), *Magyar művelődéstörténet*, i–v (Bp. n.d.), iv, 421–52 and *passim*.

[88] Kollár, *Historia Diplomatica*, and *De Originibus . . .* His defence of Habsburg powers of presentation, taxation, and so forth, *in foro ecclesiastico* is largely derived in a scholarly way, though undoubtedly fuelled by resentment at clerical and noble privilege. On the circumstances surrounding the Kollár-affair (not adequately recognized by historians) see F. Krones, *Ungarn unter Maria Theresia und Joseph II* (Graz 1871), pt. 1. The latest discussion of his ideas is a learned and curious article by D. Dümmerth in *Filológiai Közlöny*, xii (1966), 391–413. Other enlightened figures, like Bishop Batthyány of Transylvania (Batthyány, op. cit. i, 137 ff., 363 ff.), took Kollár's view of the authenticity of Silvester's donation to King Stephen, but eschewed his polemical tone.

empress's, investigation of sovereign claims; but the case serves to show how insecure was the foundation on which even existing co-operation between the Habsburgs and their Hungarian subjects rested. And when that base was called in question, the co-operation could only become progressively more difficult to sustain.

CHAPTER 8

The German Empire:
limited hegemony

Throughout the sixteenth and early seventeenth centuries the Habsburgs were continually occupied, often preoccupied, with German questions: the manifold problems of the *Reich* which spread away beyond the familiar confines of Austria and Bohemia as far as the Meuse, the North Sea, and the Baltic. Then 1648 brought a famous watershed, the failure of a direct military–political campaign to assert imperial authority. The princes of Germany now buttressed their liberties further at the diet of 1653–4, which settled the new constitutional mechanisms of a divided Empire, and during the protracted and unedifying dealings which preceded the election of Leopold in 1657.[1] Meanwhile the dynasty found compensation at home—underpinning the separate Austrian development allowed for by the *Privilegium Maius*; turning Bohemia's effective immunity from the *Reich* (and thus from the religious guarantees of Westphalia) against the very 'patriots' who had always appealed to it in the past; looking to a genuinely Danubian and Balkan foreign policy.

These points have often been made, and they were an essential precondition for any free-standing Habsburg commonwealth in Central Europe. Yet it is equally obvious that the Habsburgs still sought a German role. Integral Hungary was recovered largely by the accident of Ottoman miscalculation and decline. We have seen how little institutional evolution accompanied the changing position of the house of Austria. The dynasty itself was, in some irreducible sense, Germanic, and apt to become more so rather than less with the passage of time. Until the mid-nineteenth century it preserved

[1] J. S. Pütter, *An historical Development of the present Political Constitution of the Germanic Empire*, tr. J. Dornford, i–iii (London 1790), ii, 56–271. On the election, precipitated by the sudden death of Leopold's elder brother Ferdinand, who had already been confirmed as king of the Romans, i.e. heir apparent: A. F. Pribram, 'Zur Wahl Leopold I, 1654–8', *AÖG* lxxiii (1888), 81–222.

substantial rights of diplomatic interference across the frontier, if not of real hegemony.

The political power of the emperor in the Empire after the Westphalian settlement was by no means negligible. Some contemporary critics, like Chemnitz and Pufendorf, waxed polemical precisely because they still feared the long arm of Vienna and sought to restore the pristine harmony (as they imagined it) of the *Reich*.[2] Only later, under the impetus of nineteenth-century Prussian historiography, did such views degenerate into a serious misconstruction of the character of the old Empire and an underestimate of its institutional effectiveness. As we saw, the *Reichshofkanzlei* and the *Reichshofrat* were organs neither defunct, nor merely ancillary to a native Austrian or Bohemian administration. The chancery had fine new premises erected in the early eighteenth century at the centre of the Hofburg; their expansive façade, begun by one master of the Viennese Baroque, Hildebrandt, was completed by the other, Fischer von Erlach. The Aulic Council pronounced on some major constitutional disputes between states and within states.[3] The imperial diet might be stranded in permanent session at the free city of Regensburg; but at least it was stranded on the road to Vienna, and its endless negotiations, however wasteful of manpower, produced a certain body of legislation binding on all parties. It acted in economic matters, especially guild and coinage regulations and the major series of anti-French tariff measures inspired by J. J. Becher. It took military decisions about the raising of money and troops for imperial campaigns.[4]

Most significant were initiatives at a regional level. In some parts of the Empire the circles (*Kreise*) created by Maximilian I had very

[2] [Bohuslaw Philipp von Chemnitz], pseud. Hippolithus à Lapide, *Dissertatio de Ratione Status in Imperio Nostro Romano-Germanico* ('Freistadii' 1647); [Samuel Pufendorf], pseud. Severinus de Monzambano, *De statu Imperii Germanici* ('Geneva' 1667).

[3] Above, pp. 147 f., 150 f.; Gross, op. cit., and Gschliesser, op. cit., are both very thorough surveys. F. L. Carsten, *Princes and Parliaments in Germany* (Oxford 1959), esp. 111 f., 141 f., 144 f., 147 f., 295–7, 311–13, 331–4, 439–40, for important judgments of the Aulic Council.

[4] On economic policy: I. Bog, *Der Reichsmerkantilismus* (Stuttgart 1959); F. Lütge, *Reich und Wirtschaft* (Dortmund 1961); G. Benecke, 'The Westphalian circle, the county of Lippe, and imperial currency control', in J. A. Vann and S. W. Rowan (eds.), *The Old Reich* (Brussels 1974), 131–47. On military policy: Bérenger, *Finances*, 411–19; and see below, n. 70.

considerable vitality, and with the gradual proliferation of administrative tasks during the seventeenth century they (like estates'
organs within the Monarchy) actually extended their executive
functions. Princes, prelates, and cities in Swabia, Franconia, and
the Rhineland areas met regularly at *Kreistage* to vote taxes, settle
questions of recruitment and cantoning of armies, decide local legal
issues, arrange a common policy on public order and communications, even health and welfare. Not that the circles were creatures
of Habsburg authority, but imperial commissioners entered their
deliberations and ancient loyalties to the *Kaiser* gained nourishment
in the bosom of Germany's lesser rulers from fear of the ambitions
of the few large territorial states.[5]

There is a growing literature which can be consulted on the
federal structure of the *Reich* during the early modern period.[6] I
shall concentrate in what follows rather on the deeper resonance in
Germany of the Habsburg system and its values. For the role of
Vienna after 1648 needs to be elucidated, not purely in terms of
overt Habsburg motivation, but by attending to a background of
attitudes, the larger dynamics of a situation which could operate
more indirectly in Austria's favour. These complex sympathies had
deeper roots in some parts of the Empire than in others, as the years
after 1600 hastened an ideological division of Germany which the
years before 1600 had begun. Yet the outcome was not exactly what
might have been expected. At either end of the country we find
rising states with independent policies on a European scale. In the
north, Brandenburg built up a noteworthy military machine and—
equally important—showed a growing receptivity to Western ideas,
especially via the flexible world of the Dutch universities. In the
south, Bavaria, capitalizing on the *élan* of her Counter-Reformation
and emerging much strengthened from the Thirty Years War,

---

[5] Vann, *Swabian Kreis*, esp. chs. 1 and 6; Benecke, *Society and politics, passim*; R.
Wines, 'The imperial circles, princely diplomacy and imperial reform 1681–1714',
Journal of Modern History, xxxix (1967), 1–29.

[6] In addition to the works already cited, there is in English a major study of
constitutional issues by H. Gross, *Empire and Sovereignty, a history of the public law
literature in the Holy Roman Empire, 1599–1804* (Chicago 1973); and a remarkable
analysis of urban life in the provinces by M. Walker, *German Home Towns* (Ithaca
1971). Some recent German writing is discussed in Benecke, op. cit., ch. 3. Cf., for
an 18th-century view: T. C. W. Blanning, *Reform and Revolution in Mainz, 1740–
1803* (Cambridge 1974), esp. 1–38.

started to look more in the direction of Paris than of Vienna.[7] Despite various anti-French accommodations with the Hohenzollerns, despite continuing marriage alliances with the fellow-Catholic Wittelsbachs, both Brandenburg and Bavaria were ultimately rivals to the Habsburgs. But between Berlin and Munich stretched the broad band of middle Germany, from Swabia across Franconia and the central uplands to Thuringia and Saxony, an unconsolidated landscape with many small territories and thriving circle organizations. In these regions both ruler and subject tended to look to Vienna for support or advancement, and they frequently shared much the same kind of *Weltanschauung* as the Habsburg lands.

*

Directest channels of communication led from the imperial court to the ecclesiastical lands, that extensive and unique feature of the old *Reich*: some twenty-four well-endowed bishoprics and a similar number of immediate abbeys.[8] Bavaria had a foot firmly in this camp, since younger sons of the house of Wittelsbach ruled Cologne continuously for two centuries after 1583, as well as other north German sees. And periodic friction with ambitious and insubordinate clerics, evident during the war, became most pronounced when Mainz, under the remarkable clan Schönborn, tried to assert its dignity as arch-chancellor of Germany. Johann Philipp von Schönborn (elector from 1647 to 1673) and his active minister, Johann Christian von Boineburg, had an important share in forming the *Rheinbund* of 1658 whose stance was clearly anti-Austrian.[9] But the imperial office kept its sacral trappings; and anyway—as the Schönborns privately realized well enough—even Mainz's powers

---

[7] I cannot begin to assemble here the enormous literature on Brandenburg; but the point about openness and tolerance is often missed (cf. below, p. 307). For Bavaria: S. Riezler, *Geschichte Baierns*, i–viii (Gotha 1878–1914), vii–viii.

[8] The bishoprics, excluding those sees controlled by Austria, Salzburg, France, Switzerland, or the Protestant powers, were: Mainz, Cologne, Trier, Salzburg itself, Bamberg, Würzburg, Liège, Münster, Osnabrück, Paderborn, Hildesheim, Worms, Speyer, Basle, Constance, Chur, Eichstätt, Augsburg, Regensburg, Passau, Freising, Brixen, Trent, and Strasbourg until the 1680s. Among the most powerful of the abbeys were Kempten, Fulda, Ellwangen, and Corvey.

[9] G. Mentz, *Johann Philipp von Schönborn*, i–ii (Jena 1896–9); A. L. Veit, *Kirchliche Reformbestrebungen im ehemaligen Erzstift Mainz unter Erzbischof Johann Philipp von Schönborn* (Freiburg 1910). Cf. L. Gross, op. cit. *passim*, esp. 49 f., 59–61, on Vienna's refusal to appoint either Boineburg or (later) his son as imperial vice-chancellor.

were only reflections, hierarchically derived from those of Vienna, so that the *modus vivendi* could never be entirely abandoned. The Habsburgs, provided they did not strive after total hegemony, had plenty of scope for influence.

By the later seventeenth century the emperor (not the Pope) was directly involved in all elections to vacant Catholic bishoprics. Following a practice evolved with sees in the Habsburg lands, particularly Breslau and Olomouc, his commissioner became an indispensable legal and ceremonial figure, exercising no veto, but usually able to place the necessary weight behind an approved candidate. Ecclesiastical lords did not have to bend the knee in any very overt fashion. At Constance, for example, a concordat signed in 1629 guaranteed episcopal jurisdiction against everyday civil interference.[10] Yet there were mediate ways of bringing pressure to bear: the existence of ecclesiastical enclaves and diocesan rights in the *Erblande*—however much it compromised the domestic sovereignty of the dynasty—gave leverage for the Habsburgs to sway the political stance of foreign bishops under threat of sanctions.

The most intriguing case is Salzburg, the metropolitan see for most of southern Germany. This city which, under its formidable prince-archbishop Paris Lodron, *Primas Germaniae*, adopted a position of heavily-fortified neutrality during the Thirty Years War; which refused entry to the Jesuits and opened a rival university, based on its ancient Benedictine community of St. Peter's, and specializing in canon law, Thomism, and history; which evolved a distinctive high-Italianate culture and tolerated Protestants longer than any surrounding territory: Salzburg was clearly no puppet. But behind the grand façade it gradually resembled more and more the piece of provincial Austria which in the end—after Napoleon had wiped the slate clean of clerical immunities—it was destined to become. For the cathedral chapter of St. Rupert's foundation was filled almost exclusively with Austrian families; the university and the city's publishers depended

---

[10] Above, pp. 135–61 f. H. E. Feine, *Die Besetzung der Reichsbistümer vom Westfälischen Frieden bis zur Säkularisation* (Stuttgart 1921), 92 ff.; H. Raab, *Die Concordata Nationis Germanicae in der kanonistischen Diskussion des 17. bis 19. Jahrhunderts* (Wiesbaden 1956), confirms Feine's findings. On Constance: R. Reinhardt, *Die Beziehungen von Hochstift und Diözese Konstanz zu Habsburg–Österreich in der Neuzeit* (Wiesbaden 1966).

on a satisfied, fee-paying Austrian clientele; the culture drew on trading profits impossible to sustain without imperial goodwill. And Salzburg's rulers, a little like Transylvania's, needed no Habsburg to teach them the ways of domestic courtly absolutism. At length their Protestants suffered a fate still crueller—because more anachronistic—than those in Austria and Bohemia. When Archbishop Leopold Anton Eleutherius Firmian expelled 20,000 Lutherans in 1731–2 even Emperor Charles VI felt mildly embarrassed.[11]

Altogether there was much mutuality—migration of persons and ideas—within the body ecclesiastic, particularly among the regular clergy. Let us consider one special case: Germany's very own Catholic order of chivalry, the *Deutscher Orden*. The name 'Teutonic knights' has a good medieval ring and historians are apt to forget that only the order's Prussian and north German possessions were secularized at the Reformation.[12] The rest lived on and established a much closer relation with the emperors, to their common profit. The knights moved their headquarters to Mergentheim in Franconia, while the grand masters spent considerable time in Austria, where they had many estates besides the so-called *Deutsches Haus* behind St. Stephen's cathedral in Vienna. The whole centre of gravity of the order shifted southwards: it is symbolic that the final loss of the bailiwick of Utrecht at the beginning of the Thirty Years War was promptly compensated for by the purchase of lands in Moravia and Silesia. From 1590 to 1618 Archduke Maximilian, brother of Rudolf and Matthias, ruled as *Hoch- und*

[11] There is an admirable history of Salzburg, rich in detail, by Widmann, op. cit. iii; much information also for this period in Hansiz, op. cit. ii, 650 ff. For Salzburg University see Widmann, loc. cit. 303–6, 374 f., 378–84, who is suitably cool about its achievements; M. Sattler, 'Die 'Benediktiner'-Universität Salzburg', *Stud. u. Mitt.* ii (1881), 1, 61–74; 2, 273–87; 3, 90–100; 4, 282–96; iii (1882), 83–96; A. J. Hammerle, 'Ein Beitrag zur Geschichte der ehemaligen Benediktiner-Universität in Salzburg', ibid. xv (1894), 249–70, 445–61, 561–94, with membership of Marian sodalities there; V. Redlich in Tausch (ed.), op. cit. 79–97; and various articles in *Universität Salzburg 1622–1962–1972* (Salzburg 1972). Salzburg's printers, who published such authors as Sancta Clara and Lebenwaldt (below, p. 384), are noted in Benzing, op. cit. 376 f.
[12] J. Voigt, *Geschichte des deutschen Ritter-Ordens in seinen zwölf Balleien in Deutschland*, i–ii (Berlin 1857–9), ii, covers this period dourly, but archivally. Otherwise literature on the late 16th and 17th centuries is very thin; cf. K. H. Lampe, *Bibliographie des Deutschen Ordens bis 1959*, ed. K. Wieser (Bonn–Bad Godesberg 1975). The German knights of Malta are less important in this context, but their development ran parallel; cf. above, p. 222.

Deutschmeister (he was simultaneously regent of the Tyrol); then his cousin Karl; between 1641 and 1662 Leopold Wilhelm, brother of Ferdinand III, held the post, and he was succeeded by another archduke. Otherwise the nominally elective office was bestowed on nobles from the *Reich* who acted in the imperial interest, such as the Alsatian, Johann Kaspar von Stadion (1627–41), who died fighting for the Catholic cause in Germany, antecedent of better-remembered nineteenth-century Stadions in the Habsburg employ, and the Swabian, Johann Kaspar von Ampringen (1664–84). Ampringen's career illustrates a further aspect of this new role of the Teutonic knights: service against the Turks. They were continually active in Hungary from the 1560s and Ampringen (who had been born there) himself led his troops in the field; hence his appointment as governor of the country, though a wild miscalculation, has its logic.[13]

The Teutonic order thus developed strong Austrian associations, but (what should be stressed in this context) it remained a *Reich* institution, with rich property in Germany, like the superb Baroque residence at Ellingen, near Weissenburg in Franconia, and nobles from the *Reich* made up most of its personnel. While no coenobites for the most part—more like a worldly warrior caste—they proved conspicuous upholders of the Catholic faith at an elevated social level. Lower down the social scale the shared experience of Counter-Reformation and its conjoined difficulties tended to create a sense of common purpose, while the movement of popular piety and sacramental devotion, both in Bavaria and elsewhere, manifested much the same temper as in Austria.[14] A confident Catholic Church with firm imperial loyalties is one major formative feature of attitudes throughout middle Germany after 1648, in the great

---

[13] On the estates of Eulenburg (or Eulenberg; Czech: Sovinec) and Freudenthal (Czech: Bruntál), cf. above, p. 222, n. 63 (Zuber, Wieser). For Archduke Maximilian: Hirn, *Erzherzog Maximilian.* Voigt, op. cit. ii, 327–42, on Stadion, and 382 ff. on Ampringen, who seems to have attracted no other literature at all, except a brief notice (by K. H. Lampe) in *NDB*, s.v.; cf. above, pp. 237, 261. H. von Zwiedineck-Südenhorst, 'Über den Versuch einer Translation des Deutschen Ordens an die ungarische Grenze', *AÖG* lxvi (1878), 405–45, adds little to the history of the order in Hungary, where it later (1700–31) held extensive lands on the Great Plain.

[14] This is a very large subject; see, in general, L. A. Veit and L. Lenhart, *Kirche und Volksfrömmigkeit im Zeitalter des Barock* (Freiburg 1956), *passim*; cf. Gugitz, op. cit.

swathe of territories we have identified from Swabia in the south-west to Saxony in the east.

*

Mention of Saxony may surprise: the centre of Luther's revolt and senior secular electorate, a crucial area for the course of recent German history. Both its confession and its size would seem to exclude it from this context. But how had the power of the most populous state of the *Reich* been deployed? Ever since the famous clash between Maurice of Saxony and Charles V, in studied deference to the Habsburgs. The lumbering conservatism of Duke August was inherited, after the short-lived Christian I, by his grandson Christian II—sober, perhaps, only in his politics. Saxony's close contacts with the kingdom of Bohemia culminated at the time of crisis in 1618; but they almost always buttressed the side of authority. The principal spokesman for the Dresden court, Matthias Hoë von Hoënegg, was far more virulent in condemning Calvinists (among them the Czech leader, Budovec) than Catholics, and he had a major part in the new elector's decision to refuse the Bohemian crown. Not, however, from nonchalance towards Austrian affairs: for the *Hofprediger* Hoë was a Viennese himself, son of an aulic councillor ennobled by Rudolf II, and had acted as overseer of the Prague Lutherans between 1611 and 1613.[15] As reward for supporting the emperor, Saxony received Lusatia, Ferdinand II's willingness to part with it suggesting—besides his dire straits—his confidence in loyalty from that quarter; then a short period of unwilling belligerence during the early 1630s was followed by a swift return to the imperial fold. Saxon political theorists (the most prominent is Veit Ludwig von Seckendorff) firmly defended the old constitution and the Habsburgs' role within it. The most perceptive and sympathetic of serious contemporary lives of Leopold I came from a scholar of Leipzig, Eucharius Gottlieb Rinck.[16]

---

[15] B. Jenšovský, *Politika kurfiřta saského v Čechách v posledních letech vlády Rudolfa II* (Pr. 1913), is broader than the title suggests. On Hoë (1580–1645), see the extensive article in *ADB*, s.v.

[16] V. L. von Seckendorff, *Teutscher Fürsten-Staat* (Frankfurt 1656). The most renowned conservative constitutional lawyer of the early 17th century, Dietrich Reinking (1590–1664), was also a Lutheran, who served the landgrave of Hesse-Darmstadt. See his *Tractatus de regimine saeculari et ecclesiastico* (Giessen 1619), the butt of Chemnitz's radical critique. On Rinck, cf. Eisenberg, art. cit. 387–405.

Such filial attitudes naturally attracted the attention of the Jesuits. They mounted a long campaign to recover the souls of the house of Wettin, and then of their subjects, which eventually reaped its harvest in the conversion of the young elector, Friedrich August, at Baden bei Wien in 1697. The move was prompted by political considerations: now Saxony could successfully claim the throne of Poland. But that does not affect the significance of the case—Poland, after all, had itself evolved through the seventeenth century from a bastion of free-thought to an enfeebled servant of Roman intolerance closely linked with the Habsburgs. Now King Augustus, 'Augustus the Strong', as the contemporary epithet absurdly proclaimed (pointing to his physical, not mental prowess) was able to import a riotous Central European Baroque to his two capitals of Dresden and Warsaw.[17] Catholicism made captures too among collateral lines of the Wettin family: Christian August of Sachsen-Zeitz, Augustus's cousin, we have encountered as primate of Hungary; his nephew became a Bohemian bishop. The Lutheran Ernestines in Thuringian duchies like Gotha displayed conspicuous friendship towards Vienna during the later seventeenth century. There was a clutch of converts in the branch which ruled the small north German duchy of Lauenburg: Julius Heinrich (Balbín's patron and Bohemian landowner), his two brothers, and his son.[18]

Other sovereign houses of central Germany exhibit a similar trend. The Guelphs of Brunswick had a twofold ambition: the English succession demanded staunch Protestantism; advancement within the Empire made them faithful retainers of the Habsburgs. Thus while Ernst August of Hanover married the future Stuart heiress Sophia and gained an electoral hat in 1692, his elder brother, Johann Friedrich, converted and married off his daughter to the

---

[17] A. Theiner, *Geschichte der Zurückkehr der regierenden Häuser von Braunschweig und Sachsen in den Schooss der katholischen Kirche* (Einsiedeln 1843), 105 ff. and documents, nos. 51 seqq. Evidence of earlier Jesuit activity in *Nuntiaturberichte*, i, pp. 615, 625, 627, 778, 784, 789 f., 796 ff. On Poland: below, pp. 424–6. There are sardonic comments from the British minister at Vienna during the 1690s about the young Saxon elector as a good-for-nothing commander in Hungary: *The Lexington Papers*, ed. H. Manners Sutton (London 1851), 65, 73 f., 85, 93 f., 101 f.

[18] On Christian August: Kelemen, op. cit.; H. Gerig, *Der Kölner Dompropst Christian August von Sachsen-Zeitz* (Bonn 1930). For Gotha see below, pp. 289, 368. On the Saxe-Lauenburgs: Balbín, *Miscellanea Historica*, i, bk. 1, 101, 130; Räss, op. cit. v, 139–71; Frind, *Erzbischöfe*, 218, 228; Bilek, *Dějiny konfiskací*, ii, 1168 f., and cf. above, p. 201.

future Emperor Joseph I. Later Anton Ulrich, ruler of the closely-related Wolfenbüttel lands, having persuaded his granddaughter to turn Catholic and marry Leopold I's other son, Charles, at length took the same step himself, apparently under the influence of the Viennese agent of the *émigré* Stuarts, a Theatine called Amadeus Hamilton.[19] Whereas some landgraves of Hesse occupied an exposed position as Calvinists during the Thirty Years War, the family produced several colourful renegades as well: Friedrich of Hesse–Darmstadt ended his career as cardinal bishop of Breslau; Ernst of Hesse-Rheinfels turned into a fierce Catholic controversialist and intimate of Valerian Magni; three brothers of Hesse-Darmstadt converted at the end of the century. There was even backsliding in the ranks of the *Reich*'s most determined Calvinist crusaders: Christoph Wilhelm of Brandenburg, who apostatized at Wiener Neustadt after being captured in battle, and his fickle niece Katharina, married first to Bethlen Gábor and later to Franz Karl of Saxe-Lauenburg; two princes of Nassau and several offspring of the Winter King.[20]

Indeed, the Rhineland–Palatinate proved accident-prone throughout the seventeenth century from the Protestant point of view. It was not sufficient to have launched the Thirty Years War and proved abysmally unable to pursue it: in 1685 the line of electors palatine died out altogether in male descent. Disputes over the succession produced a new war; Heidelberg and its hinterland suffered renewed and still more thorough devastation. The victorious claimants were a junior branch of the same Wittelsbach family, based at Neuburg on the Danube, which had recently inherited the rich lands of Jülich and Berg in Westphalia. The outcome was a double triumph for the emperor: not only did he help a fervent Catholic prince to power in the Rhineland, but a prince very much in the Habsburg orbit. For although Wolfgang Wilhelm of Neuburg had been converted back in 1613 by his Munich cousins, the spectacular advance of his descendants led

---

[19] Theiner, op. cit. 3 ff., and documents, nos. 13–35.
[20] Räss, op. cit. v, 466–515 (Friedrich of Hesse-Darmstadt); cf. W. Dersch, 'Beiträge zur Geschichte des Kardinals Friedrich von Hessen', *ZVGAS* lxii (1928), 272–330. Räss, op. cit. vi, 465–500 (Ernst of Hesse-Rheinfels); cf. *ADB*, s.v. Räss, op. cit. vii, 459–71 (more Hesse-Darmstädters); ibid. v, 404–33 (Christoph Wilhelm); ibid. vi, 526–35; vii, 534–50 (Nassauers).

them towards rivalry with Bavaria and alliance with Austria.[21] Wolfgang Wilhelm's son, Philipp Wilhelm, born in 1615 in the tiny ancestral duchy, died at Vienna in 1690 as elector palatine and ruler of half the Rhineland; his eldest son and heir married Leopold's younger sister, the rest filled high dignities in the Church: two as bishops of Breslau, two as grand masters of the Teutonic order. Franz Ludwig of Neuburg (1664–1732), who held both those offices, was one of the greatest pluralists of the day, encountering resistance only in his last, distinctly sanguine project for ruling both electoral archdioceses of Mainz and Trier at the same time. Among Philipp Wilhelm's daughters, Eleonora became the third wife of Leopold, and others married kings of Spain and Portugal.[22] An interesting and parallel case, on a smaller scale, involves yet another branch of the Wittelsbachs (there were anything up to eight in the period): the palsgraves of Sulzbach, between Nuremberg and the Bohemian border. There Christian August, a convert to Rome in 1656, brought his diminutive court close to Austria, both in spirit—as we shall see—and in contacts: his sister married Václav Eusebius Lobkovic; his daughter, originally betrothed to the last archduke of Tyrol (who died young), then married the last prince of Saxe-Lauenburg and shared his large Bohemian estates.[23]

We should not make too much of the mere fact of conversion in high places. It represented an act of partly political, partly spiritual calculation, well illustrated, for example, by the long justificatory writings of Ernst of Hesse and Anton Ulrich of Brunswick. Rather,

[21] On the conversion of Wolfgang Wilhelm see Räss, op. cit. iv, 223–53. It was a *cause célèbre* during the years before the war: cf. ibid. v, 1–73, 195–237, 257–309; *Knihopis*, no. 14662; and H. Sturmberger, *Adam Graf Herberstorff* (Munich 1976).

[22] Philipp Wilhelm of Neuburg, one of the more important of German 17th-century political figures, has long been neglected. But see now H. Schmidt, *Philipp Wilhelm von Pfalz-Neuburg*, i: 1615–58 (Düsseldorf 1973), which will, when complete, be the definitive, though dry, biography; K. Jaitner, *Die Konfessionspolitik des Pfalzgrafen Philipp Wilhelm von Neuburg in Jülich-Berg von 1647–1679* (Münster 1973); id., 'Reichskirchenpolitik und Rombeziehungen Philipp Wilhelms von Pfalz-Neuburg von 1662 bis 1690', *Annalen des Historischen Vereins für den Niederrhein*, clxxviii (1976), 91–144. On Franz Ludwig: L. Petry, 'Das Meisteramt in der Würdenkette Franz Ludwigs von Pfalz-Neuburg', in *Acht Jahrhunderte*, ed. Wieser, 429–40; his elder brother, Wolfgang Georg, actually died before installation as bishop of Breslau.

[23] K. Salecker, *Christian Knorr von Rosenroth* (Leipzig 1931); Wolf, *Lobkowitz*, 40 ff.; and see below, pp. 291 f. Ironically the little Sulzbach family later inherited both the Palatinate and Bavaria.

conversion was symptomatic of a set of attitudes shared by many who remained Lutheran: a deeply conservative, defensive mentality; genuinely enhanced respect for tradition, established rights, and hierarchical forms; perhaps also vague ideas of material and confessional unity under imperial aegis. Similarities with the social situation in the Habsburg lands are not far to seek: princes, after all, were the magnates of Germany. So, *qua* temporal powers, were the imperial bishops and abbots with their sixteen aristocratic quarterings, and the chapters which elected them. So, at least when taken collectively, were the exclusive patriciates of Nuremberg or Augsburg, steeped in noble privilege, quite withdrawn from trade, and jealous masters of their own civic latifundium.[24] Smaller territorial rulers occupied much the same position as the great landowner of Austria, Bohemia, or Hungary, and they considered the latter to be equal in rank, as the Wittelsbach–Lobkovic match shows, or Christoph Wilhelm of Brandenburg's marriages with Martinices and Waldsteins; most of the free *Reichsritter* in Swabia and Franconia fell far short of a Trautmannsdorf, Černín, or Batthyány in wealth. The oligarchy of the Empire pursued the same search for social control by example and prescription, by ordered relations on the land and officially-inspired sentiments among the population at large.

The Saxon model of a patrimonial administration was based on a watered-down version of the imperial aulic departments, courtly dominance cemented by a state Church. Saxon Lutheranism, manipulated by the elector through a tame consistory, hidebound and fossilized like the peculiar Calvinism of Transylvania, ironically recovered some animation only when the Wettins converted. Moreover, its extreme conservatism extended to doctrine and observance: auricular confession and quasi-conventual religious houses (one headed by Elizabeth of the Palatinate), some whole services in Latin, vestments and liturgical colours, sacring-bells and incense, elevation of the Host and fine Church plate, even a residue of canon law. It is symbolic that the Saxon lands of the

---

[24] On social exclusiveness among the higher clergy: Feine, op. cit. 10 ff., 66 ff., and table pp. 406 f. There is, of course, a large literature on the towns; cf. H. Mauersberg, *Wirtschafts- und Sozialgeschichte zentraleuropäischer Städte in neuerer Zeit* (Göttingen 1960), especially on Munich and Frankfurt; and Aubin–Zorn (eds.), *Handbuch*, 475, 576, and *passim*.

Teutonic knights were not confiscated, but managed by the Wettins on payment of a ground-rent.[25] Far from encouraging heresy in Bohemia, Saxon orthodoxy was terrified of discovering advanced Protestant sentiments at home, and relations with Czech immigrants were sometimes strained; only Swedish intervention at Westphalia and Altranstädt preserved the rights of sorely-tried Lutherans in Silesia.

★

These attitudes found support and confirmation in the ranks of Germany's intellectuals.[26] Again, not simply in areas of pure Catholic allegiance: among the Jesuits of Ingolstadt, and more especially their non-Bavarian brethren at Würzburg, Bamberg, and a host of other places in the valleys of Rhine, Main, and Danube; among the learned circle around Johann Philipp von Schönborn and his convert friend, Boineburg; among the secular and regular clergy, the printers and publicists of Cologne, the one large free city which contained no Protestants. Such centres were important— they produced major scholars, like Schott and Kircher, who enjoyed immense respect in Central Europe; but much of their *Weltanschauung* was common to substantially Protestant regions as well.

Consider Luther's own university of Wittenberg, bound hand and foot by the syllabuses of theology, heavily Aristotelian in its leanings, with systematic study of traditional physics and metaphysics. Originally a domestic growth from the later sixteenth century, reacting against the Reformation's dislike of abstract speculation in general and ontological constructions in particular, this philosophical current drew much strength from the neo-scholasticism of Spain as transmitted through Catholic Germany: editions of Vitoria, Cano, Soto, Fonseca, above all Suarez,

---

[25] Zeeden, op. cit. 81–94, for a general survey; cf. *Realencyklopädie für Protestantische Theologie und Kirche*, ii (Leipzig 1897), 533–41 (confession). Elizabeth's convent at Herford (cf. Benecke, op. cit. 104–8) was in neighbouring Lower Saxony. Voigt, op. cit. ii, *passim*. Compare the critique of the Saxon Lutheran establishment in Gottfried Arnold, *Unparteyische Kirchen- und Ketzer-Historie*, i–ii (Frankfurt 1699–1700), esp. i, bk. 17, ch. 5 ('Viel Lutheraner sind ärger als heyden . . .'); and in J. B. Neveux, *Vie spirituelle et vie sociale entre Rhin et Baltique au XVIIe siècle* (Paris 1967).

[26] Parts of this section overlap with my article 'Learned Societies in Germany in the seventeenth century', *European Studies Review*, vii (1977), 129–51. There are some general remarks about converts among German intellectuals in Arnold, op. cit. i, pt. 2, 451–5.

supplemented with a large number of domestic commentators on the standard texts.[27] Similar concerns predominated at the other two Saxon universities, Jena and Leipzig (quite the largest in the Empire), not to speak of Mainz-controlled Erfurt, and the situation was much the same at smaller Lutheran academies like Giessen, Rostock, Strasbourg, or Tübingen, and at the *Gymnasia* patiently tended by their alumni. The only exceptions, outside a few Calvinist high schools, appear to have been Helmstedt in Brunswick and Altdorf near Nuremberg, each of which had its own reasons for avoiding any kind of openly disloyal stance.[28]

There is much in the career of Gottfried Wilhelm Leibniz which betrays this environment. Born in Leipzig of a legal family, he began his philosophical studies by reading Suarez. For all the originality and modernity of his thought, Leibniz remained deeply indebted to the traditions of German Humanism and devoted to the imperial heritage. Having settled first in Mainz as Boineburg's secretary, he then moved to the court of another prominent convert, Johann Friedrich of Brunswick, and cultivated an extensive correspondence with Catholic scholars. Throughout his life he hatched plans for academic reform based, if possible, on Vienna, and supported political initiatives to strengthen the constitution of the *Reich*. These efforts culminated in his Austrian stay between 1712 and 1714 and his friendship with Prince Eugene of Savoy; though little came of the projects but a patent of nobility, the ageing Leibniz still showed deference to the idea and the reality of Habsburg sovereignty. At one point, rather as an ambitious Saxon jurist might have petitioned for one of the half-dozen Protestant places on the Aulic Council, the learned *Freiherr* even offered

---

[27] K. Eschweiler, 'Die Philosophie der spanischen Spätscholastik auf den deutschen Universitäten des 17. Jahrhunderts', *Spanische Forschungen der Görresgesellschaft*, i (Münster 1928), 251–325, esp. 283 ff.; E. Lewalter, *Spanisch-jesuitische und deutsch-lutherische Metaphysik des 17. Jahrhunderts* (Hamburg 1935); M. Wundt, *Die deutsche Schulmetaphysik des 17. Jahrhunderts* (Tübingen 1939). These three writers air many intricate and sometimes technical problems which have not yet been properly resolved. Cf., on the influential Arriaga, below, pp. 319 f.

[28] Much detail on these universities in A. Tholuck, *Das akademische Leben des 17. Jahrhunderts*, i–ii (Halle 1853–4), a work with the confusing alternative title of *Vorgeschichte des Rationalismus*, pt. 1. On Helmstedt and Altdorf cf. below, pp. 306, 291. Again, the contemporary Gottfried Arnold has some acid criticisms (op. cit. i, bk. 16, ch. 10, etc.).

himself as a suitable person to take over the chancery of Transylvania![29]

Leibniz's colleagues adopted the same general position: the polymath Erhard Weigel, for example, one of his teachers, acted as willing propagandist for the imperial crusade against the Turk; the writer and schoolmaster Christian Weise maintained cordial links with Bohemian Jesuits.[30] Leibniz's friend, Job Ludolf became the literary cynosure of the court at Gotha which, under Duke Ernst the Pious, was the model of a small, paternalistic German state thoroughly loyal to the Habsburgs. Though he could not approve of his pupil Wansleb, who apostatized to join the Dominicans, Ludolf had close contacts in Austria and was named first president of a short-lived 'Collegium Imperiale Historicum'.[31] Shortly after the conclusion of the Peace of Westphalia local physicians at Schweinfurt in Franconia founded Germany's first scientific society. This *Academia Naturae Curiosorum* was a pioneer institution for the Europe of the day, but its existence remained tenuous until it turned decisively in the direction of authority and intellectual tradition. By 1670, when it began to publish an annual record of its discoveries under the title *Miscellanea Curiosa*, it had acquired a distinct imperial tinge, with privileges of which it was inordinately proud and protection from the Habsburg court, all duly symbolized on ornate title-pages.[32]

A cultural initiative in the opposite direction, from Vienna to the

---

[29] The standard life is by G. E. Guhrauer, *Gottfried Wilhelm Freiherr von Leibnitz*, i–ii (Breslau 1846). See also, on his Viennese connections, O. Klopp, 'Leibniz' Plan der Gründung einer Societät der Wissenschaften in Wien', *AÖG* xl (1869), 159–255 (195 f. for the Transylvanian incident). Cf. P. Riley (ed.), *The political writings of Leibniz* (Cambridge 1972), esp. 121–63 (defences of imperial sovereignty).

[30] H. Schüling, *Erhard Weigel, Materialien zur Erforschung seines Wirkens* (Giessen 1970), nos. 94, 101–2, and *passim*. Christian Weise, *Epistolae selectiores*, ed. C. G. Hoffmann (Bautzen 1715), pt. 1, nos. 14–15, 19, 21, 28, 31–3, 35–6, 43, 48–9, 53, 55, 91–2; pt. 2, nos. 6–24; mostly to and from Balbin.

[31] On Gotha: A. Beck, *Geschichte des gothaischen Landes*, i–iii (Gotha 1868–76), i, esp. 319 ff. On Ludolf: C. Juncker, *Commentarius de Vita, Scriptisque ac Meritis . . . Iobi Ludolfi* (Leipzig–Frankfurt 1710); and cf. below, p. 429. For the 'college', which may never have assumed any physical form, see Guhrauer, op. cit. ii, 70–3, 85 f.; Klopp, 'Leibniz' Plan', 170–2; H. Gerstenberg, 'Philipp Wilhelm von Hörnigk', *Jbb. f. Natö. u. Stat.* cxxxiii (1930), 813–71, at 859 f.

[32] A. E. Büchner, *Academiae . . . Leopoldino-Carolinae Naturae Curiosorum Historia* (Halle 1755), esp. 169–270 on privileges; cf. R. Herrlinger, 'Das Collegium Naturae Curiosorum von 1652 . . .', in *Steno and Brain Research in the 17th century*, ed. G. Scherz (Oxford 1968), 261–72, esp. 266–8.

Reich, was focused on the great Rhineland publishing centre of Frankfurt am Main. There an imperial book commission, first established in the 1560s, fought a series of rather dilatory Catholic campaigns against subversive and abusive literature during the decades before the war, and also served as collecting station for accessions to the court library. The war lamed both book fair and commission, though the Habsburg agent, Johann Ludwig von Hagen, stayed ineffectually at his post.[33] After Westphalia a new commissioner appeared, Ludwig von Hörnigk (claimed by some sources to be the illegitimate son of a prince of Hesse), who had just converted under the guidance of Jodocus Kedd, issued the proper apologia for his action, and thrown himself on the mercy of the emperor. Hörnigk and his successors reactivated their office and struggled to enforce restraints on the publishing trade. All in all, it is striking what they managed to accomplish in often hostile surroundings, and the achievement might have been greater but for their own internecine feuding.[34]

A leading backer of the book commissioners was the large publishing house of Endter at Nuremberg, an imperial city as firmly Lutheran as Frankfurt. The Endter dynasty divided into two lines, one printing Protestant works, the other—without any serious hindrance—Catholic ones; each issued a wealth of material which supported, either directly or by implication, the Habsburg presence in Germany. Among their authors we find, for example, Joachim von Sandrart, preferred artist of the imperial family in the later seventeenth century, and the popular poet, Sigismund von Birken,

---

[33] On this commission's activities before 1620 see Evans, *Wechel Presses*, 29–31. Hagen: HHStA, Reichshofrat, Miscellanea, Bücherkommission im Reich, fasc. 2, esp. 'konv. 4' and 'konv. 5'; R. Becker, 'Die Berichte des kaiserlichen und apostolischen Bücherkommissars J. L. von Hagen an die römische Kurie (1623–49)', *Quellen und Forschungen aus italienischen Archiven*, li (1971), 422–65.

[34] *Zwanzig Ursachen umb welcher willen Ludovicus von Hörnigk ... der uralten Catholischen Religion und Kirchen zugetretten* (V. 1648; this 1st edn. (Mayer, op. cit. i, no. 1626) is very rare; I have seen another: [Cologne] ?1649); reprinted by Räss, op. cit. vi, 238–59. Hörnigk as commissioner: HHStA, loc. cit., esp. 'konv.5', fols. 18 ff.; and his letters to Lambeck in ÖNB, MS. 9712, fols. 237, 239 f., 253 f.; ibid. MS. 9713, fols. 13 f., 19 f., 22, 29 f., 35 f., 39, 60 f., 72, 74, 103, 129; cf. ibid. 58 f. On the commission after the 1650s: H. Raab, 'Apostolische Bücherkommissare in Frankfurt a.M.', *HJ* lxxxvii (1967), 326–54, at 335 ff.: U. Eisenhardt, *Die kaiserliche Aufsicht über Buchdruck, Buchhandel und Presse im Heiligen Römischen Reich Deutscher Nation* (Karlsruhe 1970), 79 ff.; and HHStA, loc. cit., fasc. 3. Some of the tension stemmed from the political rivalry between Vienna and Mainz.

who edited (indeed positively recreated) one of the most important accounts of medieval Habsburg history.[35] Sandrart and Birken are typical representatives of educated society at Nuremberg, like the lawyers who went to serve on the *Reichshofrat*, the physicians who played an active role in the *Academia Naturae Curiosorum*, the amateur poets who sustained the arcadian *Pegnesischer Blumenorden*, even the academics who staffed the moderately liberal, but thoroughly reliable little university at nearby Altdorf.[36]

Two further examples may help to clinch the argument that, in south Germany at least, considerable confessional coexistence survived among intellectuals on the basis of firm loyalty to the imperial past and to Austria as its embodiment. The worthy *literati* of Augsburg, no match for their brilliant cosmopolitan predecessors of a century earlier, busied themselves now with quaint observations for the *Miscellanea Curiosa* or allusive pageantry to greet the coronation of the young Archduke Joseph as king of the Romans in 1690. But their efforts were not entirely negligible: witness the remarkable visual Lutheran Baroque of Johann Ulrich Krauss and other engravers.[37] Further east the little town of Sulzbach under its

---

[35] F. Oldenbourg, *Die Endter, eine Nürnberger Buchhändlerfamilie, 1590–1740* (Munich–Berlin 1911), is rather slight. The Endters' loyalist stand at Frankfurt appears from ibid., appendix 3; F. Kapp, *Geschichte des deutschen Buchhandels*, i–iv (Leipzig 1886–1913), i, 676–714; and some documents in HHStA, loc. cit. J. von Sandrart, *Academia nobilissimae Artis Pictoriae* (Nuremberg 1683), a Latin version of the *Teutsche Academie* of 1675, with a life of the author (appendix); Sandrart also executed many commissions in Austrian churches. J. J. Fugger, *Spiegel der Ehren des ...Erzhauses Oesterreich*, ed. S. von Birken (Nuremberg 1668); cf. ÖNB, MS. 9712, fols. 220 f., 227–9; ibid. MS. 9713, fols. 99, 116–19, 126 f., 157 f., 178, 183, 192–7, 200 f., 210, 243. Birken was a native of Eger in Bohemia. Nádasdy's *Mausoleum* (above, p. 257, n. 54), was published by the Endters with a German translation from Birken (cf. Gy. Rózsa in *ItK* lxxiv (1970), 477; ÖNB, MS. 9713, fols. 53 f., 56 f.); although not a work of Habsburg panegyric, it—like Sandrart's travel-guide to the Danubian lands—bespeaks Nuremberg's interest in the area.

[36] R. van Dülmen, 'Sozietätsbildungen in Nürnberg im 17. Jahrhundert', in *Gesellschaft und Herrschaft ... Festgabe für K. Bosl* (Munich 1969), 153–90; [J. Herdegen], pseud. Amaranthes, *Historische Nachricht von des löblichen Hirten- und Blumen-Ordens an der Pegnitz Anfang* (Nuremberg 1744). On the general question of appointing Protestants to the Aulic Council see Gschliesser, op. cit. 258–60, 271–3, 279 ff. *passim*. One of the more interesting was a native of nearby Regensburg, the *littérateur* J. A. Portner von Theuren (cf. N. Conrads in *Beiträge zur neueren Geschichte Österreichs*, ed. H. Fichtenau and E. Zöllner (V.–Cologne–Graz 1974), 115–29).

[37] L. Lenk, *Augsburger Bürgertum im Späthumanismus und Frühbarock* (Augsburg 1968), 22 ff., 113–17, 150–2, and *passim*; U. Thieme and F. Becker, *Allgemeines Lexikon der bildenden Künstler*, i–xxxvi (Leipzig 1907–47), s.v. 'Kraus'.

ruler, Christian August, sheltered an odd collection of scholars, among them Abraham Pöhmer from Nuremberg, once a Utopian dreamer and comrade of Comenius, now a convert like the prince, and Joachim Hübner, also an old friend of Comenius.[38] The prime occupation of this court was Hebrew language and philosophy, its leading personality the Cabalist, Christian Knorr von Rosenroth. Knorr, as his biographer informs us, came from Silesia, wrote gratulatory poetry for Leopold I, and received a barony from him in 1677. In fact the family's Habsburg connection was stronger than that, for Laurenz Knorr had been one of the first doctors on the Prague court of appeal, and Paulus Knorr was court chaplain at Graz in the years of Counter-Reformation there.[39] During the 1660s and 1670s the printing-press at Sulzbach issued a series of other works by authors with strong Austrian and Bohemian links, the most striking case in all Germany (and one too easily overlooked by historians) of an accommodation between Lutheran and Catholic learning.[40]

★

The strongest pointer to the attractiveness of Austria is the number of Germans recruited into service in the Habsburg lands. We have already seen some of them in religious orders: Kedd from the Rhineland, Procopius from Brandenburg, Sancta Clara from Bavarian Swabia via the Ingolstadt Jesuits and the Salzburg Benedictines; more are still to be introduced, like Christoph Scheiner or Simon Wagnereck. Aristocrats continued to take up high positions at court, especially as presidents of the *Reichshofkanzlei* and *Reichshofrat*, and as privy councillors. Swabia was the main source, yielding the same parade of south-west Germany's catholic nobility after the 1620s as before: Fürstenbergs, Hohenzollern-

[38] Pöhmer: Dülmen, art. cit. 162, 168–70; M. Blekastad, *Comenius* (Oslo 1969), 151, 247 f., 261, 303 n., 349 f., 380; cf. Zíbrt, *BČH* v, nos. 28648–55. Hübner: Blekastad, op. cit. 249 ff., 274 f., 328 f., 342 f., 397, 432, 605; cf. Zíbrt, *BČH*, v, nos. 28017–92.

[39] Salecker, op. cit.; Zedler, xv, cols. 1163–6; *ADB*, s.v. 'Knorr'. On the family: Zedler, loc. cit.; Auersperg, op. cit. i, 15; Schuster, op. cit. 628–41; *Status Particularis*, 110. Another 'Dr. Knorr' is mentioned in Austria in 1636 (Czerny, *Tourist*, 41–8). For Hebrew studies see below, pp. 350 f.

[40] Examples are Thomas Carve, *Lyra seu Anacephalaeosis Hibernica* (1666); Amandus Hermann, *Sol Triplex in eodem Universo: id est, Universae Philosophiae cursus integer* (1676); Michael Pexenfelder, *Apparatus Eruditionis ... per omnes artes et scientias* (1680); and, somewhat later, Středovský, op. cit.

Hechingens, Sulzes, were followed by Ernst von Oettingen-Wallerstein and his son Wolfgang, who together ran the Aulic Council for all but thirteen of the sixty years after Westphalia, and Leopold Wilhelm von Königsegg, longest-serving imperial vice-chancellor in the seventeenth century.[41] But the most spectacular instance is Franconian: the extravagant dynasty of the Schönborns, greatest palace builders of the Baroque, one of whom, Karl Friedrich, the nephew and brother of archbishops, served three decades as vice-chancellor (he it was—predictably—who commissioned the new *Reichskanzleitrakt* in Vienna) and confirmed his family's possessions as among the most extensive in Europe, stretching into remote corners of the Carpathians where Schönborns, in succession to Rákóczis, ruled over a forested and rock-strewn empire of bears, wolves, and Ruthenes.[42] And German generals: peace was never long enough, or the Habsburg army strong enough, to make them redundant—Wolfgang Julius of Hohenlohe and Ludwig Wilhelm of Baden are among the most celebrated.

These well-born administrators and soldiers helped broaden the choices available to the Habsburgs. More significant indicators in the same direction are the commoners and members of the lower nobility who made a career in Austria. They likewise continue a tradition; we may recall the jurists who had entered the inner councils of the emperor in the later sixteenth century and at the beginning of the seventeenth, and had been well rewarded: Giffen, Melander, Volmar, almost all the earlier vice-chancellors.[43] But that was a time when such careers still lay open to the citizenry of Vienna or Prague, to the purveyors of a native Humanism. Now hierarchy stifled advance at home, and the import of capable

---

[41] Gross, op. cit. (esp. 341–5 on Königsegg); Gschliesser, op. cit. (esp. 237, 257, 268, on the Oettingens); Schwarz, op. cit., appendix; Vann, *Swabian Kreis*, 47 ff.

[42] H. Hantsch, *Karl Friedrich Graf von Schönborn* (Augsburg 1929); A. Sas, 'Ein Latifundium fränkischer Kirchenfürsten in den Nordostkarpathen 1728–46', *Vjschr. f. S.u.WGesch* xxiv (1931), 410–48, criticized by O. Paulinyi in *Sz.* lxvi (1932), 459–65; A. Schröcker, 'Besitz und Politik des Hauses Schönborn vom 14. bis zum 18. Jahrhundert', *MÖStA* xxvi (1973), 212–34, a *compte-rendu*; cf. above, p. 177. The prime Schönborn *Schloss* in Austria is at Göllersdorf (the former Puchheim estate), just north of Vienna; another line of the family settled in Bohemia.

[43] Above, p. 106; Gross, op. cit. 307 ff. Of the first nine *Reichsvicekanzler* (1559–1626), six were bourgeois or recent nobles (*Briefadel*) from southern Germany; the others a member of the Tyrolese gentry (Kurz), an obscure Italian (Coraduz), and a converted knight from Mecklenburg (Stralendorf).

newcomers from Germany preserved opportunity without conceding real mobility, allowed the exercise of talent without disturbing the system. Startling arrivistes after 1650 usually hailed from the *Reich*.

Most flamboyant of them was Joachim Enzmillner, a lawyer, born in 1600 at Babenhausen in Swabia, who took a leading part in the Counter-Reformation of the Austrian countryside and achieved the title Count of Windhag from an estate which he purchased a little east of Linz. There he proceeded to surround himself with all the trappings of a Baroque *grand seigneur*: he built a new castle, full of books, coins and *objets d'art*; he reconstructed the existing castle as a convent for Dominican nuns with his only daughter as prioress; he financed lavish volumes, issued at Frankfurt, to describe his properties. In one respect alone did Enzmillner perhaps retain a sense of the more liberal Germany of his youth: when he died in 1678 he bequeathed his library to the Dominicans of Vienna as a public collection. With an equally Baroque feeling for the large gesture, his daughter had the new castle demolished immediately afterwards.[44]

A more orthodox channel for advancement lay through the Austrian chancery; there is some irony in the fact that this department, quite as much as the *Reichshofkanzlei*, was taken over by a sequence of able newcomers from the Empire. The first, Johann Paul Hocher, born in 1616 at Freiburg im Breisgau, pursued the family profession as a lawyer; his expertise gained him posts in Tyrolean government, then from 1667 the appointment as chancellor. A *protégé* of Lobkovic, he did not scruple to encompass the fall of his patron, and acted as effective chief minister to Leopold until his death in 1683: an absolutist, perhaps, by persuasion, though not by achievement.[45] Hocher was succeeded by Theodor Heinrich Strattmann (died in 1693), a petty noble from the Rhineland and adviser to the house of Neuburg, who passed from them into Habsburg service and became one of the most formidable

---

[44] *Topographia Windhagiana, das ist eigentliche Delineation beyder Herrschaften Windhag und Reichenau* (Frankfurt 1656, reissued in expanded form ibid. 1673); F. X. Pritz, 'Beiträge zur Geschichte von Münzbach und Windhaag in Oberösterreich', *AÖG* xv (1856), 133–84; *Handbuch der historischen Stätten*, i, 142. Visitors noticed the library: Baur, 'Passer', 357, 363, 366; Freschot, op. cit. 27–30.

[45] *ADB* and *NDB*, s.v.; Gross, op. cit. 52–6; Schwarz, op. cit. 247–9; Bérenger, *Finances*, 49–52. On the Austrian chancery in general, cf. above, pp. 147 f.

figures in Viennese public life. The third strong man of the Austrian chancery took a similar route to power: Johann Friedrich Seilern (1646–1715) was not only a German commoner (the son of a dyer from the Rhenish Palatinate) but also a convert. Imperial diplomat, chancellor from 1705, he was the *spiritus rector* of the Pragmatic Sanction.[46]

It need hardly be added that the politicians, though originating outside the system, were happy to be embraced by it: Hocher died as a baron with a small Swabian estate and a huge Austrian fortune (belying the legend of his incorruptibility?); Strattmann married his daughters off to a Stubenberg, a Collalto, and a Batthyány, and placed his sons high in Church, state, and army. While his family proved short-lived, the Counts Seilern, propagated through the chancellor's son-in-law, himself Austrian chancellor in the 1740s, proved more resilient. Overall the hierarchical establishment gained marked profit at minimal cost by encouraging such men: the most outstanding Habsburg diplomat of the period, Franz Paul Lisola, was a resentful citizen of French-occupied Besançon who expended his considerable energies on orchestrating resistance to Louis XIV without ever striking root in Austria. And the same formula continued to be used in the eighteenth century; Maria Theresa's intimate adviser and minister Bartenstein, for example, was born of Protestant burgher stock at Strasbourg (likewise French-occupied) in 1689.[47]

Two instances may suffice to illustrate the scope for ecclesiastical preferment through a move from Germany to the lands of direct Habsburg rule. At the higher level Wilderich von Walderdorff was a member of the lesser immediate nobility (*Reichsritterschaft*) which regularly filled middling clerical positions in the Rhineland. Having acted as Counter-Reforming vicar-general for the archbishop of Mainz, he then settled in Austria as an ineffective imperial vice-chancellor quite overshadowed by the architects of the temporary French alliance in the 1660s, Auersperg and Lobkovic. Crossing the divide between temporal and spiritual a second time, he ended his

---

[46] Strattmann: Zedler, s.v. (not entirely accurate); *ADB*, s.v.; Jaitner, *Konfessionspolitik*, 63–5, 231 ff. *passim*; cf. above, p. 242 and n. 15. G. Turba, *Reichsgraf Seilern... als kurpfälzischer und österreichischer Staatsmann* (Heidelberg 1923).

[47] A. F. Pribram, *Paul Freiherr von Lisola und die Politik seiner Zeit* (Leipzig 1894). On Bartenstein see A. Arneth in *AÖG* xlvi (1871), 3 ff.

life as bishop of Vienna.[48] Andreas Fromm came from a very different background. Court preacher to the Great Elector of Brandenburg, he recanted his Protestantism and moved to Bohemia in 1668 where he issued one of the most circumstantial of all the apologies for conversion. Fromm's *Wiederkehrung zur Catholischen Kirchen*, much reprinted, reiterates all the arguments from authority, unity, continuity of tradition, and morality which we have seen to be the common coin of this genre. More than a mere *succès d'estime* in his new homeland, it earned him the lush pasture of a canonry at Litoměřice.[49]

A third kind of career, beside the political and ecclesiastical, might open itself to the scholar—a category which, of course, embraced some clerics, and also some physicians in the continuing procession of *Leibärzte*. The best case is that of the learned Peter Lambeck, whose conversion and appointment as imperial librarian in 1662 both discomfited Protestant academics and did much to establish the intellectual *bona fides* of Leopold's court.[50] A dramatic translation this, since Lambeck came from Hamburg, the most progressive city in the Empire; but it did not blunt his erudition, as the eight volumes of his *Commentarii* demonstrate, one of the great monuments of contemporary bibliography. We can form some impression of Lambeck's importance by means of his rich correspondence (still, like that of Blotius a century before, largely unpublished). There are international contacts—from London's Royal Society to Constantinople, from Rome to Danzig—along with material of internal, Central European concern and interesting evidence of Lambeck's political influence; but most notable is the *Hofbibliothekar*'s vast acquaintanceship in Germany: Birken and

---

[48] Zedler, s.v. 'Wallendorf'; Gross, op. cit. 340 f.; cf. Veit, *Reformbestrebungen*, *passim*.

[49] A. Fromm, *Wiederkehrung zur Catholischen Kirchen davon er die Historiam und Motiven im Druck zu geben nöthig erachtet* (Pr. ?1668); there were several other Prague edns.—I have encountered 1713, 1730, and 1762—as well as Cologne ones (1669, 1717), and other polemical tracts: e.g. *Entdeckung der nichtigen Künste* [of E. S. Reinhart] (Pr. 1669); *Knihopis*, no. 2604. Cf. Räss, op. cit. vii, 333–62; Balbín, 'Relatio', ed. Rezek, 219 f.

[50] The latest *compte rendu* on Lambeck, who lacks any full biography, is by L. Strebl in Stummvoll (ed.), op. cit. 165–84. He describes his move to Vienna, with lavish praise of the emperor, in *Commentarii de augustissima Bibliotheca Caesarea Vindobonensi*, i–viii (V. 1665–79, I have used the 2nd edn., ed. A. F. Kollár, V. 1766–82), i, cols. 8 ff.

the Endters in Nuremberg; Velschius in Augsburg and J. J. Fuchs in Regensburg; Seckendorff and Ludolf in Saxony, and Andreas Müller in Berlin; printers like G. P. Finck and Matthias Merian; organizers of the *Academia Naturae Curiosorum*; a string of bishops and abbots; Renatus Slusius in Liège and Boineburg in Mainz, who sends enthusiastic recommendations of the twenty-two-year-old Leibniz . . .[51]

Among Lambeck's correspondents are some less easily-classifiable newcomers to Austria. Boineburg's friend Heinrich Julius Blume is one, a highly cultivated, formerly Lutheran lawyer from Brunswick who became vice-president of the appeal court at Prague.[52] Then follows a trio with a remarkable family resemblance: the mercantilists Becher, Hörnigk, and Schröder. At least, we remember them as mercantilists, though they were known in their own day rather as scientists and inventors with a predilection for alchemy. All three immigrated from middle Germany; all three were converts. Hörnigk, son of Ludwig the book commissioner, moved to Austria in the 1660s, making his literary début by translating from Spanish the biography of a sixteenth-century archduchess-nun, and becoming a staunch secretary to two of Leopold's diplomat-bishops: Rojas y Spinola and Johann Philipp Lamberg. His exact contemporary, Schröder, son of Ernst the Pious's chancellor at Gotha, entered Leopold's service in 1673, though he was given only limited opportunities to use those talents which had earned him election to the Royal Society as a very young man, and his absolutist theories found little response.[53] The eldest,

[51] Lambeck's correspondence is in ÖNB, MSS. 9712–16. Among the few published items are those relating to Bohuslav Balbín (whom Lambeck supported against the censors), printed by Menčik (above, p. 104, n. 60), and the letters to and from the secretary of the Royal Society, printed in R. M. and M. B. Hall (eds.), *The Correspondence of Henry Oldenburg*, i– (Madison–Milwaukee 1965–), nos. 520, 1310, 1390. Evidence of political activity in (e.g.) ÖNB, MS. 9716, fols. 74 f., 137 ff. Boineburg's letters about Leibniz are ibid. MS. 9713, fols. 227 f., 302–4; cf. ibid. MS. 9714, fol. 1.

[52] Räss, op. cit. vi, 558–71; *ADB*, s.v.; Weise, op. cit., pt. 1, nos. 20, 82–3; pt. 2, no. 25; ÖNB, MS. 9713, fol. 111; ibid. MS. 9714, fols. 223–37. Blume was rewarded with a barony.

[53] Hörnigk: Gerstenberg, art. cit.; F. Posch, 'Philipp Wilhelm von Hörnigk, Werdejahre und österreichisch-steirische Beziehungen', *MIÖG* lxi (1953), 335–58; cf. above, p. 163. His translation is presumably the work which Leopold I wanted to see in 1677 (ÖNB, MS. 12757, fol. 66). Schröder: H. Srbik, 'Wilhelm von Schröder', *Sb. d. k. Akad.d.Wiss., ph.-h.Kl.* clxiv (1910), Abh. 1; W. Roscher, 'Österreichische
(continued)

the most formidable, and also the most wayward, was Becher (1635–1682), a native of Speyer. Like Hörnigk, who was his brother-in-law, Becher worked first at Mainz, pouring out an extraordinary flood of ideas which continued all his life: projects for manufactories and trading companies, for currency and educational reform, for elixirs and the *perpetuum mobile*, for submarines and new languages. He attracted the attention of the imperial court, settling at Vienna from 1670, though all his undertakings were dogged by failure and clouded by the hectic workings of an unstable fantasy.[54]

Adventurers achieving even a modicum of success must have been far outnumbered by those who got nowhere and have left few scraps of documentation: like one Peter Meisner from Zörbig in Saxony, who offers religious edification to Leopold in the hope of a travel grant; or his compatriot and fellow-convert, Heinrich Jacoberer, who reports—as strong presumption of merit—how the font shattered at his first, Lutheran baptism; or the Swabian, Johann Kircher, who died soon after the fanfare for his apostasy.[55] Many other hard-working immigrants have left only collective traces, like the Franconian and Bavarian architects, masons, and decorative artists who made such large contributions to the mature Bohemian Baroque—the Dientzenhofer family of architects and the sculptor, Matthias Bernhard Braun are outstanding examples. But enough has been said to show how, despite the implications of the political settlement in 1648, no clear boundary can yet be drawn between Monarchy and *Reich*.

★

The German periphery of the Habsburg lands themselves affords further evidence of interplay. The *Erblande*, especially the *Vorlande*, were, after all, still part of the Holy Roman Empire, if only (as Pufendorf shrewdly observed) *in favorabilibus* rather than *in odiosis*.

Nationalökonomik unter Leopold I', *Jbb.f.Natö.u.Stat.* ii (1864), 25–59, 105–22, at 111–22. He was married to another convert, from a family of *émigré* Austrians.

[54] Hassinger, *Becher*; Roscher, art. cit. 38–59; cf. above, pp. 163 f., 276; below, pp. 366 f. Some of Becher's last schemes are outlined in *Catalogue of State Papers: Domestic, 1.9.1680–31. 12.1681* (London, 1921), 205, 339, 425; and ibid., *1682* (London 1932), 612. There are good reflections about the cameralists—especially Becher—as theorists of a harmony of political and economic forces in the *Reich*, in Walker, op. cit. 145 ff.

[55] ÖNB, MS 11671: 'Christliche Betrachtung … entworffen von Petro Meisnero', esp. fols 3 f.; ibid. MS. 8250: 'Relation von mir Heinrich Reinhard Maximilian Jacoberer', 1690s. On Kircher, cf. above, pp. 250 f. and n. 35. .

The Swabian possessions of the dynasty, not integrated with Austria but essentially loyal to it, allowed a kind of symbiosis: imperial protection, ideals, Catholic Church, coexisting with local industriousness and social freedoms.[56] Such sons of the area as Hocher illustrate how potent the combination could be, while by a process of capillary attraction citizens from neighbouring non-Habsburg petty states might be placed on the ladder leading to imperial preferment.

The Bohemian crown too had its large German minority and adhered—in some vague sense—to the *Reich*: in 1708 it actually regained a voice at the imperial diet. Its borders were not hermetically sealed; how could they be with such limited civil power? The region around Eger, on the north-west frontier, retained into the eighteenth century the form of a mortgaged fief of the *Reich*, with separate estates, which duly assembled to accord their own personal recognition to the Pragmatic Sanction in 1712. Within the Egerland's diminutive confines such German princes as Brandenburg-Bayreuth owned property by an irredeemably complex process of subinfeudation. So confused was the status of Asch, a tiny territory projecting northwards into Saxony, that it even managed to avoid the Counter-Reformation; its possessors, the Barons Zedwitz, walking a confessional tight-rope for a century and a half with assistance from some ingenious imperial lawyers.[57]

The main case of interaction here, worth dwelling on more fully, is Silesia, a part of the Bohemian lands since the fourteenth century—and earlier subject to Poland—but peopled predominantly by Germans and communicating most directly down the Oder towards the North German Plain. Silesia, or rather the Silesias, Upper and Lower, each containing its jumble of duchies with distinct privileges, continued to assert a large measure of independence, both from the rest of the crown of St. Wenceslas and from the authorities in distant Vienna. The Habsburgs employed a governor for the whole province (normally the bishop of Breslau) and lieutenants at local level; but diet and Chamber preserved their powers, and administration was only really possible by accommodation with vested interests. The long-suffering Ampringen, fresh

[56] Pufendorf, op. cit. 29–37. Vann, *Swabian Kreis*, esp. ch. 7.

[57] On Eger see the detailed article by J. Čelakovský in *OSN*, xii, 111–22. On Asch: ibid., and a long section in Zedler, s.v. 'Zetwitz'.

from total failure in Hungary, scarcely had an easier job when put out to grass as *Oberhauptmann* of Silesia in 1682![58] Again the system rested on magnates, Catholic Church, and a wider attractiveness of Counter-Reformation culture.

Aristocratic bonds with the rest of the Monarchy were certainly strengthened by the grants of duchies to Liechtensteins at Troppau and Jägerndorf (where they supplanted the cavalier Calvinist rebel, Johann Georg of Hohenzollern), to Lobkovices at Sagan, and to Auerspergs, who occupied the fief of Münsterberg so conveniently vacated in 1647 by the extinct Poděbrads. On top of this, large estates at Oderberg and Beuthen were entailed on the successors of Lazarus Henckel (1550–1624), an Upper Hungarian burgher and the only Habsburg subject who, in the last mobile years of the Humanist age, permanently founded the fortunes of his family as a financier and entrepreneur.[59] Otherwise the government relied on a few great native clans: initially the Dohnas, Abraham and his son, Karl Hannibal (1588–1633), for a time the only lay Catholic in the highest stratum of Silesian society, a man as zealous in prosecuting his faith as were his Calvinist cousins from Prussia who served Brandenburg and the Palatinate; then above all the Schaffgotsches, who provide a further instance of disgrace redeemed. Hans Ulrich Schaffgotsch went to the block in 1635 as a too-faithful ally of Wallenstein, but his convert son, Christoph Leopold (1623–1703) recovered and extended the family estates, serving as diplomat, royal commissioner, and president of the Silesian Chamber. The Schaffgotsches also settled in Bohemia, like the Oppersdorfs, who controlled the countryside around Glogau, and the ubiquitous

[58] Nicolaus Henelius, *Silesiographia Renovata*, ed. and expanded by M. J. Fibiger, i–ii (Breslau–Leipzig 1704), is the fullest contemporary account of Silesia's geography (i, chs. 1–5), and its administration (ii, ch. 12, on the diet; 1193 ff. on the Chamber). Rachfahl, op. cit., is an exemplary survey of the earlier period. There were non-episcopal governors (the office is variously called *Oberhauptmann* or *Oberlandeshauptmann*) between 1609 and 1664 (mostly local Piast princes in these years of greatest friction), in 1671–4 (Lobkovic, *qua* duke of Sagan), and 1682–4 (Ampringen, *qua ad hominem* prince of Freudenthal).

[59] Cf. above, pp. 171–3, 205. The Liechtenstein takeover of Troppau and then Jägerndorf is described in Chr. d'Elvert, *Die Verfassung und Verwaltung von Österreich-Schlesien in ihrer historischen Ausbildung* (Brünn 1854), 82–140. There is no proper history of the highly interesting clan of Henckels von Donnersmarck (i.e. Csütörtökhely, or Spišský Štvrtok, in the Zips region), who became counts in 1661 and Catholics in the Beuthen line in 1700. Cf. *NDB*, viii, 516–19; and, for Lazarus, *Rudolf II*, 76, n. 2.

Nostitzes. The ring of dominant Catholic families is closed with the descendants of a prominent middle-German *condottiere*, Melchior Hatzfeld, ensconced in Silesia from 1641.[60]

Silesia's Counter-Reformation, as we saw, proceeded ruthlessly, belatedly, and incompletely. But within its limits it made for a genuine recovery of Catholic values, especially in the south and east of the area. It fed on the international movement, and the cosmopolitan bishops of Breslau, culminating in Friedrich of Hesse (1671–82) and Franz Ludwig of Neuburg (1683–1732), did much to reassert the Church's authority in the centre of the province, where they owned the large duchy of Neisse. New religious orders dug themselves in, notably the Jesuits, who advanced strongly from mid-century, deploying impressive intellectual and dramatic talents. They came into direct, protracted confrontation with the Protestant council of Breslau over plans for a university: founded in 1702, this was eventually built from 1728 with a long façade, both elegant and grandiose, gazing out in studied triumph across the river Oder.[61]

At the same time Counter-Reformation increasingly tapped indigenous sources, reviving venerable sites of cult and monasticism. Again, one kind of coenobite was particularly characteristic of Silesia; whereas Benedictines, canons regular, Premonstratensians, and Crusaders with a Red Star had a few wealthy houses in the province,[62] it was seven well-endowed Cistercian abbeys which represented the liveliest native tradition: Leubus, Heinrichau, Kamenz, Rauden, Himmelwitz, Grüssau, and the aristocratic nunnery at Trebnitz guarding the relics of St. Hedwig. By the end of the seventeenth century the largest of them, Leubus, had begun reconstruction on a scale as sumptuous as any in Austria or Bohemia; the main front is over 200 metres long, and behind it rose

---

[60] On the Silesian aristocracy: Henelius, op. cit. ii, ch. 8. For Schaffgotsch: Wurzbach and *OSN*, s.v.; cf. above, p. 210 and n. 33; below, p. 392. The Hatzfelds came from Hesse; Melchior's brother was bishop of Bamberg and Würzburg.

[61] Cf. above, pp. 284 f., on the bishops; above, pp. 120, 125, on the Jesuits. Grünhagen, *Geschichte*, ii, 374–82, for their dispute with the city.

[62] Benedictines at Wahlstatt, revived from Bohemia in the years around 1700 (Blücher, it may be recalled, was created prince of Wahlstatt in 1814, after its secularization); canons regular at Breslau and Sagan (Henelius, op. cit. i, 447–500); Premonstratensians at St. Vincent in Breslau (Backmund, op. cit. i, 334–7); Crusaders at Breslau (Bělohlávek–Hradec, op. cit. ii, esp. 48 ff.).

up pompous rooms for the monks and their distinguished visitors. The community at Grüssau, fortified by the spiritual leadership of Bernardus Rosa (abbot from 1660 to 1696), financed two major churches: one a votive offering to St. Joseph, the other a completely rebuilt abbey church which became the most important ecclesiastical monument in Silesia.[63]

Catholicism's wider intellectual resonance is demonstrated firstly by conversions. Examples are Gottfried Ferdinand Buckisch (1641–99), a lawyer and antiquarian ennobled for his defence of Habsburg positions; another legal writer, Samuel Butschky, son of a preacher, who joined the Leopoldine administration; and the poet, Andreas Scultetus, tempted across by Jesuits at Breslau in 1644. A more famous literary figure than any of these is Andreas Scheffler (1624–77), known as Angelus Silesius, not only the greatest German lyricist of the period, but also the author of no less than thirty-nine tracts of Counter-Reformation theology. Scheffler's career spanned two worlds, from student days at Strasbourg and Leiden to a parting from life in the venerable calm of the abbey of the Crusaders at Breslau.[64] Another fine artist likewise found himself irresistibly drawn to the old monastic houses of Silesia: Michael Willmann (1630–1706), a native of Königsberg, abandoned his comfortable position as *Hofmaler* to the elector of Brandenburg and became (along with his stepson, J. K. Liška) the resident painter at Leubus and Grüssau. His work reveals a remarkable blending of individualistic talent (his title of 'Silesian Rubens', for all its exaggeration, is not entirely *mal à propos*) with the anonymity of the cloistered ideal.[65]

Meanwhile the very survival of Lutheranism, not to speak of a Calvinist leaven at certain princely courts, was fruitful. It provides the key to Silesia's unique role as mediator. On the one hand it

[63] Sartorius, op. cit. 1111–28; Henelius, op. cit. i, 648–709; P. Wintera, 'Leubus in Schlesien', *Stud.u.Mitt.* xxv (1904), 502–14, 676–97; G. Grundmann, *Dome, Kirchen und Klöster in Schlesien* (Frankfurt 1963), 109–11, 191–2, 201–3, 207–11, 241–3; A. Rose, *Kloster Grüssau* (Stuttgart–Aalen 1974); Meyer, *Gemeinde*, 102–19 (Kamenz); H. Grüger, *Heinrichau 1227–1977* (Cologne-V. 1978).

[64] Buckisch: Räss, op. cit. vi.i, 115–18; cf. R. Samulski in *ZVGAS* lxvi (1932), 155–61. Butschky: Räss, op. cit. vii, 575–83. Scultetus: Dziazko, 'Der Übertritt des Dichters Andreas Scultetus von Bunzlau zum Katholicismus', *ZVGAS* xii (1875), 439–53; *ADB*, s.v. Scheffler: *ADB* and *NDB*, s.v., summarize the biography; cf. Sommervogel, iv, cols. 968 f.

[65] E. Kloss, *Michael Willmann* (Breslau 1934).

mediated between confessions, such that the impact of Counter-Reformation on the province's sophisticated culture brought more original creativity than anywhere else in the *Reich* during the seventeenth century.[66] Opitz, Logau, Gryphius, Hofmannswaldau, Lohenstein, were all influenced by Jesuit drama and Catholic imagery, and a genuine Protestant Baroque emerged with parallels only in those few parts of Germany, such as Augsburg and Sulzbach, where a similar religious balance obtained (and it will be recalled that Knorr von Rosenroth was a Silesian). Neoscholasticism and universality worked through Lutheran ideology to produce the philosophical system of Leibniz's popularizer, Christian Wolff; and the mingling of two atmospheres yielded nebulous profundities of mysticism and prophecy from Jakob Boehme, through Czepko and Frankenberg (both highly respectable members of the nobility), to the arch-eccentric Quirinus Kuhlmann, who ended at the stake for seeking to convert the Muscovites to Luther's gospel.[67] On the other hand Silesia mediated between the Habsburg lands and Germany precisely because the high qualities of its intellectual life were generally recognized. Earlier traditions formed by the vigorous Humanist movement, when Silesia had been a refuge of moderation, suffered severely in the war. But they lived on in an attenuated way through late representatives like John Jonston (a sort of honorary Polish noble, despite his name); and bonds were now sustained by new generations of authors, students, and professional men: witness, for instance, Breslau's close associations with the young *Academia Naturae Curiosorum*.[68]

[66] H. Schöffler, *Deutsches Geistesleben zwischen Reformation und Aufklärung* (2nd edn. Frankfurt 1956), is very good, dealing only with Silesia, despite its title. There is, of course, a large literature on individual authors. Cf. the interesting *aperçu* of Protestant Silesia's vernacular Baroque architecture by G. Grundmann, 'Hirschberg in Schlesien', *Festschrift H. Aubin*, i–ii (Wiesbaden 1965), ii, 495–510.

[67] Cf. below, p. 395. On Kuhlmann: G. Liefmann, *Dissertatio de fanaticis Silesiorum et speciatim Quirino Kuhlmanno* (Wittenberg 1698); the life by W. Dietze (Berlin 1963); and below, loc. cit.

[68] For 16th-century Silesian culture see *Rudolf II*, ch. 4, *passim*. Jonston (1603–75), whose parents had emigrated from Scotland, was a well-known polymath in his day, author of such works as *Thaumatographia Naturalis* (Amsterdam 1632), translated into English as *An History of the Wonderful Things of Nature* (London 1657). On his life see Zedler, s.v. 'Johnstone'; the biography by T. Bilikiewicz (1931), summarized in *Polski słownik biograficzny*, xi (1964–5), 268–70; Blekastad, op. cit., index, s.v. Büchner, op. cit., esp. 57 ff., 82–4, 127–30, 258 ff., for the *Academia*; cf. below, p. 373.

Thus we find in Silesia the kind of synthesis which does not eliminate either thesis or antithesis: on the surface continued friction, but at a deeper level much interconfessional common ground, with Catholicism defining more of it than Lutheranism. And there was a serious Habsburg dimension to this outlook. What a perfect symbol of the aethereal secular and religious aspirations of Central European Baroque is the opulently symbolical imperial hall at Leubus, constructed during the 1730s to welcome sovereigns who had not set foot in Silesia for a hundred years! In 1740 the allegiance abruptly snapped. Alongside all economic and strategic considerations, all high politics and dynastic pride, a cultural world was lost when Frederick the Great marched against the well-nigh defenceless province. The abbot of Leubus, whose artists and masons had scarce put the finishing touches to their *chef d'œuvre*, fled to Moravia before the plundering Prussian armies. Of course, a different cultural world was *won*; the contest for Silesia's soul had lasted unabated into the eighteenth century, and internal opposition, as in Hungary, extended right up the social scale to embrace some magnates, like the Hohbergs (later princes of Pless), Rederns, or Calvinist Schönaichs, once the foremost patrons of Silesian Humanism, who sided with Frederick so promptly that they were made Prussian princes of Schönaich-Carolath as early as 1741. But these formed a minority; hence the extra vehemence of Maria Theresa in refusing to swallow any definitive cession of her patrimony. Notwithstanding the quaint solace of retaining within rump Austrian Silesia the very duchy (Jägerndorf) to which the Hohenzollerns could lodge a genuine—albeit weak—hereditary claim, the empress set to work paying the Prussians back with far-reaching reforms conceived by a recent Catholic convert from Silesia, Count Friedrich Wilhelm Haugwitz.[69]

*

In this outcome Silesia is a microcosm of the *Reich* at large, whose bonds with the Austrian Monarchy became so weakened in the age of Frederick the Great as completely to obscure the character of previous development. For nearly a century after the Peace of Westphalia the Habsburgs could entertain realistic political and

---

[69] On Haugwitz (1702–65, converted in 1725) see the long article in *ADB*, s.v. He came from a Lusatian–Silesian family on the edge of magnate status, his father being created count in 1733.

spiritual hopes of sustaining, indeed enhancing the imperial position in Germany. Their political prospects were shown in the years after 1680, with the solidarity of almost all middle Germany in an anti-French alliance and much enthusiasm for a crusade against the Turks. Evidently much manœuvring went on, and temporary reverses could not be avoided, even with close associates like Neuburg and Brunswick. But broad support was forthcoming, and in some cases it extended to total commitment: the ruler of Baden-Baden, Margrave Ludwig Wilhelm, spent almost all his time in conspicuously successful direction of imperial armies (and his uncle Hermann was president of the War Council during the crucial decade of the 1680s). Smaller Protestant principalities, such as Hesse-Darmstadt or Ansbach-Bayreuth, sheltered well inside the Habsburg orbit, and their larger neighbours rarely stepped far out of line—one duke of Württemberg confusingly christened all his sons 'Eugen' after the Austrian commander-in-chief. Even Brandenburg was held on a tight rein by negotiations over the Prussian crown, though the logic of its development rendered the accommodation a temporary one.[70]

The spiritual prospects are best illustrated by Bishop Spinola's missions to the *Reich*. Cristóbal de Rojas y Spinola (1626–95) was a typical Habsburg adviser of the period: though Spanish by descent, he grew up in the Netherlands and the Rhineland, moving to Austria by the 1660s. There he combined the roles of cleric and secular intellectual: a Franciscan friar, he gained a diocese, first *in partibus infidelium*, then in Wiener Neustadt (as successor to Kollonich); a cameralist spokesman (like his friend Hörnigk), his sense of the Empire's economic unity was always underwritten by universalist religious convictions.[71] Spinola became the approved agent of Leopold in plans for reunion of the confessions within the *Reich*, and his overtures were widely discussed at Lutheran courts

---

[70] On the military cohesion of the Empire see especially Wines, art. cit.; P.-C. Storm, 'Militia imperialis–Militia circularis. Reich und Kreis in der Wehrverfassung des deutschen Südwestens (1648–1732)', Vann–Rowan (eds.), op. cit. 79–103; Vann, *Swabian Kreis*, ch. 7. For Ludwig Wilhelm ('Louis' to his contemporaries): O. Flake, *Türkenlouis* (Berlin 1937). On Württemberg: T. Mayer, 'Schwaben und Österreich', *Zeitschrift für Württembergische Landesgeschichte*, xvi (1957), 261–78, at 272.

[71] S. J. T. Miller and J. P. Spielman, *Cristobal Rojas y Spinola, cameralist and irenicist* (Philadelphia 1962); Bog, *Reichsmerkantilismus*, 100–6.

and universities. The most fertile soil was Brunswick, with its convert duke, Johann Friedrich and his circle, and its university of Helmstedt, more liberal and flexible than any other in Germany. The chief Protestant figures in the dialogue were Leibniz, to whom oecumenical ideas represented one expression of the search for philosophical unity, and Gerhard Molanus, abbot of a Lutheran monastery and leading advocate of the eirenical wing within Protestantism. Both of them tried to build upon the 'syncretist' positions already elaborated by the most celebrated of Helmstedt theologians, Georg Calixtus.[72] In the end Spinola's visits failed: the gulf was too wide, the suspicion of established Churches—not least at Rome—too great. But plenty of evidence exists that others also desired religious reconciliation under a broad imperial aegis: Mainz Catholics around Schönborn and Boineburg; moderate Lutherans at Altdorf; Daniel Ernst Jablonski in Berlin; compromise thinkers in Silesia; Prince Eugene's coterie at Vienna. Some extraordinary cases of practical ecclesiastical co-operation could be encountered in Germany after 1648, like the mixed chapter at Osnabrück, with its alternate elections of Catholic and Protestant bishops, and even a convent which housed equal numbers of Catholics, Lutherans, and Calvinists.[73]

We may conclude that the new Habsburg 'system' was by no means restricted to the lands of direct rule; it influenced, and interacted with, a complex of surrogate systems in the rest of the *Reich*. Of course, there were grave weaknesses in the emperor's position. I have not laboured the obvious constitutional ones: only self-interest could now really bring German rulers to play Vienna's game. Compulsion being removed, neither the Habsburgs nor the Catholic Church could dictate terms (hence the ultimate failure of

[72] Guhrauer, op. cit. i, 340 ff.; ii, 21–34, 231 ff.; Beck, op. cit. 351 f.; J. Baruzi, *Leibniz et l'organisation religieuse de la terre* (Paris 1907), 246 ff.; Neveux, op. cit. 667–93. Cf. J. O. Fleckenstein, *Gottfried Wilhelm Leibniz, Barock und Universalismus* (Munich 1958). On Calixtus: E. L. T. Henke, *Georg Calixtus und seine Zeit*, i–ii (Halle 1853–60); H. Schüssler, *Georg Calixt, Theologie und Kirchenpolitik* (Wiesbaden 1961), for his ideas; cf. Arnold, op. cit. i, bk. 17, ch.11; and Kantzenbach, op. cit. 230–44.

[73] Examples of practical oecumenism in Zeeden, op. cit., 72–80. On Osnabrück: Benecke, op. cit. 81–95; on Molanus's 'monastery' of Loccum: *Loccum vivum: Achthundert Jahre Kloster Loccum*, [ed. E. Ruppel and D. Andersen] (Hamburg 1963), 30–58.

Spinola's negotiations); as in Bohemia or Hungary, loyalty became a calculation, not a sort of disembodied idealism. Moreover, contact is of necessity a two-way process; where the virtues of hierarchy and authority, the collective and the sacramental, penetrated beyond the Monarchy, some scope was given for rival notions: radical, tolerant, individualist, iconoclastic, to move in the opposite direction. The early Enlightenment did filter into Central Europe from staging posts in the *Reich*; in one important set of attitudes, those of Pietism, it even grew up from a profoundly Lutheran base.[74]

Yet Counter-Reformation had definitely established a Habsburg predominance; and Austro–Catholicism (a larger and directer force than Papal Catholicism) commanded at times a genuine spiritual ascendancy, with that lively, slightly insecure self-assertion so characteristic of the Central European Baroque. Just contrast— among members of the house of Guelph—the convert Johann Friedrich with his staid brother, Ernst August, or the convert Anton Ulrich with Ernst August's desperately wooden son, George I of England. Brandenburg-Prussia may have stagnated militarily and diplomatically under the pro-Habsburg Frederick I, as naïve historians often used to lament, but it gained ample intellectual compensation in the blend of cultures to which its first king showed himself receptive.[75] Altogether much of the ethos of German courts and governments derived in this period from an Austrian model. The impact of Versailles came later, mainly after 1714 (earlier examples, like Christian Ludwig of Mecklenburg (1623–92), converted under Parisian influence, are isolated cases), and it has frequently been exaggerated: it tended to remain superficial, an affair rather of mode than of mood. On top of everything else, Vienna could more easily strike a national note; perhaps the strongest contemporary assertion of German patriotism was penned by an Austrian tutor to the future Emperor Joseph I.[76]

Above all, the unitary imperial ideal was still attractive (even the

---

[74] Cf. the argument of E. Winter, *Frühaufklärung* (Berlin 1966), whose thesis is important, though at times unduly strained.

[75] Arnold, op. cit., dedication, praises the 'ungekränckte Gewissens-Freyheit' in Brandenburg; and the circumstances of the foundation of Halle University and the Berlin Academy of Sciences confirm the point in various ways.

[76] W. Bauer on Hans Jakob Wagner and his *Ehren-Ruff Teutschlands* in *MIÖG* xli (1926), 257–72.

terse, hostile Bryce admits its continuing power of moral suasion[77]). Not only did it operate on many levels in Germany: it cast a residual shadow over parts of Italy. That large subject would lead us too far from the present context; suffice it to make two points. In political terms the designs on the peninsula advanced by Austrian armies during the War of the Spanish Succession issued not only from dynastic ambition, but from a reassertion of long-standing imperial claims. Latter-day Habsburg predominance over the North Italian Plain and beyond belongs in a seamless evolution from medieval notions of *imperium*. And this evolution has its corollary: the long line of the Habsburgs' Italian servants. They included generals, like Annibale Gonzaga and Raimondo Montecuccoli, both president of the War Council under Leopold; intellectuals, like the first four court librarians of the eighteenth century; physicians and lawyers; priests and artists; architects and musicians. Most famous of them was Prince Eugene, as he was also the greatest exponent of the imperial mission, and Eugene enshrines something of the whole ambivalent relationship between Italy and the Habsburg lands: the supreme ornament for Central Europe's Baroque culture, he never quite formed an integral part of it.[78]

With these reflections on the wider horizons of Habsburg influence we have reached the threshold of the third and last main theme of this book: the intellectual milieu of resurgent Catholicism. As will be seen, German thinkers contributed abundantly to the mind of the Habsburg Counter-Reformation, and an Italian dimension was inseparable from it. But that is not all, for where the political power of the system became most attenuated, there—in the *Reich*—its cultural and ideative base stands most clearly revealed. In Austria, Bohemia, and Hungary things are more difficult to unravel, and earlier chapters have charted many fluctuations in the extent and nature of the dynasty's control. There too, however, we shall discover that the imperial programme rested at least as much upon a set of attitudes as upon a set of policies.

---

[77] J. Bryce, *The Holy Roman Empire* (London 1903), esp. 454 f.

[78] O. Aretin, 'Kaiser Josef I zwischen Kaisertradition und österreichischer Grossmachtpolitik', *HZ* ccxv (1972), 529–606. On Montecuccoli see, most recently, T. M. Barker, *Raimondo Montecuccoli and the Thirty Years War* (Albany, N.Y. 1975), a military study. On the librarians (Gentilotti, Garelli, Riccardi, and Forlosia): Stummvoll (ed.), op. cit. 191–228. On Eugene, cf. above, p. 141, n. 64); below, pp. 326 f.

Part Three

THE INTELLECTUAL FOUNDATIONS

CHAPTER 9

The anatomy of Catholic learning

For all the diversity of its territories and institutions the Habsburg Monarchy, by the later seventeenth century, basically supported a single culture. That was truer among educated than among uneducated people, and much could be found at all levels which resisted the unifying mould. Nor can the generalization be pressed to yield clear terminology—any more than the word 'Baroque' can be made to fit at all tightly round the mental structures of the age. Yet the common cultural bond was a crucial element in enhancing the cohesion of Central Europe under the dynastic aegis. In some measure this homogeneity was imposed by political developments and by the associated socio-economic trends which we have already examined. But the phenomenon has an intellectual dimension which demands analysis on its own terms.

In Counter-Reformation culture, as in Counter-Reformation politics and society, a narrow ruling stratum dominated the rest, and the gap between privileged and unprivileged grew ever wider: we have already seen how the new establishment tamed a rising generation of intellectuals in the earlier seventeenth century. Higher culture became divorced from lower, not so much in that they pursued different themes, but in that the former had scope for self-expression while the latter suffered increasing regimentation. Indeed, we shall see that the very factor which lent scope to the one was the chief means of regimenting the other: the world of occult science and superstition. Again, as with the political and social evolution, a condition of comparative equipoise emerged by 1700 through a mixture of controls and autonomous process. Catholic dogma was the *sine qua non*, but whereas the bulk of the population observed a code of Church discipline, the élite observed one of self-discipline. The educated Catholicism to be introduced in this chapter was both assertive and self-conscious, and also a distinctive Central European amalgam; it no more followed a Papal blueprint than did the rest of the Habsburg Counter-Reformation.

'Introduction' is certainly the *mot juste* for what follows: the subject has till now barely received any attention from historians. Reading standard accounts of the period, one might well wonder whether erudition existed at all.[1] Yet there was nothing particularly crude about the learned standards of seventeenth-century Austria: they were just very different from our own. We can distil a sophisticated set of views and discern surprising freedom of thought, given the constraints willingly imposed on themselves by contemporaries. The first, of course, was confessional orthodoxy in matters where the ecclesiastical authorities laid down unambiguous precepts. The second was deference to the constituted order, which provided the tools and organization of scholarship. The third was Latinity. We have seen how vernaculars had their place in the Counter-Reformation scheme, but it was a subordinate one. Even Pázmány laces his Hungarian-language works with Latin dedications to the magnates; Latin is the badge of a mind which can be trusted. While no longer the Latin of the Humanists—heavier, more discursive, more pedestrian—it still afforded refuge for a privileged, even liberal academia against philistine critics. Lambeck associated himself very much with the earlier traditions of the *Hofbibliothek*; Leopold I was anxious not to commit any solecism in the language of scholarship.[2] Behind its defences men had the chance to debate, and perhaps to publish with official backing. Much more was committed to paper in manuscript for private study and circulation—a mass of material which still awaits proper evaluation.

*

Even in strife-torn Hungary nobles and religious orders had well-stocked libraries covering all aspects of traditional learning: theology in its many guises; law and medicine; history, sacred and profane; antiquities and coins; philosophy, mathematics, and the sciences of nature; ethics, politics, and philology. The beleaguered Benedictines of Pannonhalma, scarcely returned to their devastated monastic buildings, registered over 2,000 books in 1658, especially recent devotional literature. The Jesuits developed holdings from slender beginnings, as at Tyrnau and Kassa. The Observant Franciscans in

---

[1] For example, Denis–Vančura, op. cit. i, 1, 258 ('All moral life, all intellectual questioning, went into exile . . .').

[2] Lambeck, *Commentarii*, i, cols. 63 ff. ÖNB, MS. 12757, fols. 61, 78. Cf. above, pp. 114 f.

Szakolca, hardly one of the country's larger municipalities, possessed more than a thousand volumes in Latin and a variety of modern languages when the first catalogue was drawn up in 1662.[3] Magnates' libraries covered the same terrain with more of a secular emphasis. While some owners clearly limited their vision, like Simon Forgách, who seems to have collected mainly improving Catholic literature and Hungarian history, others had greater intellectual ambitions. Pál Esterházy displayed a wide range of interests, particularly medical; Miklós Zrinyi specialized in Italian political writers and possessed such multi-volumed sets as the *Magnum Theatrum Vitae* of Laurentius Beyerlinck; Ferenc Nádasdy's library was so rich that Emperor Leopold requisitioned some two hundred titles to be added to the *Hofbibliothek* after his fall.[4]

Austria and Bohemia had a less troubled evolution. While major collections were being built up by families like Lobkovic, Liechtenstein, and Eggenberg (Hans Ulrich Eggenberg found time to annotate many of his new acquisitions), monasteries generated the need for extra space which was met by their fine Baroque interiors constructed towards the end of the period.[5] Not just the great names were involved: Josef Ignaz von Kirchberg, a representative member of Lower Austria's provincial nobility, left a library with

[3] *Catalogus Librorum Omnium Conventus S. Martini . . .*, ed. V. Récsey (Bp. 1902). The Tyrnau collection later became the core of the university library (Egy. Kt.) in Budapest; its resources were described by G. Pray, *Index rariorum librorum Bibliothecae Universitatis Regiae Budensis*, i–ii (Buda 1780–1). OSzK, MS. 23 fol. lat., is a catalogue of the Kassa collection from the 1660s; ibid. MS. 2119 quart. lat.: 'Cathalogus seu Inventarium perpetuum Librorum Conventus Szakolczensis . . .', continued into the 18th century.

[4] OL, Forgách cs. lt., P. 287, ser. II, fasc. FF, cs. 41: 'Registrum Librorum . . . Comitis Simonis Forgacs'. OSzK, MS. 2149 fol. hung.: 'Catalogus Librorum in Arce et Bibliotheca Fraknó repositorum' (Esterházy); *Bibliotheca Zrinyiana, die Bibliothek des Dichters Nicolaus Zrinyi* (V. 1893), esp. 51–84. A. Sitte, 'Gróf Nádasdi Ferenc művei és könyvtára', *MKSz* x (1902), 142–57; cf., for Nádasdy's works requisitioned by Vienna, ÖNB, MS. 9715, fol. 141; ibid. MS. 9716, fols. 106–15, 155 ff. There has been much miscellaneous information about Hungarian library holdings printed in *MKSz* since 1876.

[5] O. Brunner, 'Österreichische Adelsbibliotheken des 15. bis 18. Jahrhunderts', in *Neue Wege*, 155–67, is a brief sketch. No printed catalogue exists of the vast and important Lobkovic library (though the UK has a MS. one). H. Bohatta, *Katalog der in den Bibliotheken . . . des fst. Hauses von und zu Liechtenstein befindlichen Bücher*, i–iii (V. 1931). On Eggenberg: J. V. Polišenský, *Der Krieg und die Gesellschaft in Europa, 1618–48*, tr. A. Urbanová (Pr. 1971), 50 f.

over 3,800 books, strongest in Catholic theology, but well balanced overall; even the austere Capuchin house at Linz possessed more than 5,000 volumes by the early eighteenth century.[6] Sometimes the work of accumulation took generations, but we have plenty of evidence of individual initiative. Ignaz Karl Sternberg had a special catalogue drawn up for his extensive holdings in mathematics and astronomy. Gabriel von Selb, an ennobled jurist and member of the *Hofkammer*, brought together a large collection particularly strong in history, politics, and law. Johann Crane, a typical aulic councillor whose only memorable act was to sign the Peace of Westphalia as one of the Austrian plenipotentiaries, owned some thousand miscellaneous books, mostly in Latin.[7]

The largest repository of books belonged to the dynasty and occupied premises inside the Hofburg. The *Hofbibliothek* expanded continuously during the seventeenth century, acquiring the Fugger library from Germany, that of the Marquis of Cabrega from Spain, manuscripts and printed works from agents in Italy, France, and Frankfurt.[8] There is excellent information for the reign of Leopold about how its resources were actually used. Lambeck's *Commentarii* I have already mentioned: a vast project, supervised by the emperor, to advertise its treasures to the scholarly world. Only a fraction could be published (twenty-five volumes were planned), but this suffices to show the emperor's close concern for the legacy of Greek theological, legal, medical, philosophical, and historical manu-

---

[6] ÖNB, MS. 14878: the Kirchberg family collection, as inventoried in 1698. H. Paulhart and J. Voglsam (eds.), *Die Bibliothek des Linzer Kapuzinerklosters St. Matthias*, i–ii (Linz 1968–71).

[7] Sternberg: Str., MS. DH V 27, prepared 'Anno 168' (*sic*), and listing over 200 titles; cf. above, p. 208 and n. 27. Selb: ÖNB, MS. 14787, prepared in 1673, with over 3,000 titles in alphabetical order. Selb was at one time the friend and later the enemy of *Hofkammerpräsident* Sinzendorf (Wolf, 'Hofkammer', 479; Bérenger, *Finances*, 369–71), which may explain his evident wealth. Crane: ÖNB, MS. 14860, prepared (by the owner?) in 1658; cf. Gschliesser, op. cit. 230 f. Another example of the individual collector would be Windhag (above, p. 294).

[8] Stummvoll (ed.), op. cit., gives a general survey. For the library of Cabrega (Pedro de Navarra y de la Cueva), cf. *Privatbriefe*, ii, nos. 228, 235, 251, and pp. 65, 69, 91, 105; ÖNB, MS. 12757, fol. 22; there are catalogues of it ibid. MSS. 12601 and s.n. 4289. More on accessions policy ibid., MS. 12757, *passim*; HHStA, Obersthofmeisteramt, SR 46, esp. fol. 32; and esp. ÖNB, MSS. 9713–16, *passim*; cf. above, pp. 289 f., on the book commission. The dynasty maintained subordinate libraries at Ambras, near Innsbruck (Lambeck transferred some of its books to Vienna), and at Graz (ÖNB, MS. s.n. 3791, is a catalogue of works there which are lacking in the main *Hofbibliothek*).

scripts. Leopold consulted his librarian on a wide range of learned topics, especially antiquarian, and received precise reports about his expenditure.[9] Equally revealing are Lambeck's catalogues of the emperor's private library, a shifting collection of some thousand recent works which must have formed his daily reading. They include, of course, a goodly slice of Catholic apologetics and controversy; but also natural philosophy with a practical bent; much history, from the *acta* of favourite saints to contemporary polemic; classical, neo-Latin, and Italian literature; and a variety of manuscripts. And there is no doubt that some of them were thoroughly perused, even such tomes of pure erudition as the letters of the Bohemian Humanist, Bohuslav of Lobkovic.[10] We learn precisely what books lay to hand on 12 July 1674 in the emperor's oratory and closet: devotions and alchemy cheek-by-jowl; even what books were ready to accompany him when he travelled: Leopold's servants might have been less than enthusiastic about transporting the complete works of Lipsius in six volumes, or Bartholinus's *Historiae Anatomicae* in three.[11]

These titles give us a remarkable insight into the Habsburg intellectual world of the later seventeenth century. They also introduce us to some of its representative local authors, the writers who elaborate the serious core of Central Europe's *Weltanschauung*. Most are clerics, the majority in regular orders: Jesuits predominate, followed by Dominicans and Franciscans, Benedictines, Augustinian canons and Premonstratensians, and a goodly sprinkling of lawyers and physicians.[12] The same names reappear in all kinds of

---

[9] On Lambeck, cf. above, pp. 296 f., nn. 50–1. Leopold's relations with him are documented in ÖNB, MS. 12757 (18th-century copies of the emperor's letters); HHStA, loc. cit. (some letters from Lambeck, esp. fols. 16–20: precise accounts of expenditure in 1666); ÖNB, MS. 8011 (*aides-mémoire* for audiences). The latter in particular were well used by Th. G. von Karajan, 'Kaiser Leopold I und Peter Lambeck', *Almanach der k. Akademie der Wissenschaften*, xviii (1868), 103–56.

[10] ÖNB, MS. 12590, prepared in 1666, amended in 1674, lists mostly books published since 1648, a total of 1,086 vols. ÖNB, MS. 12592, is mainly a fair copy of the revised (i.e. 1674) catalogue, with an index and the additions cited in the next note. ÖNB, MS. 12757, fol. 18, for how Leopold devoured Lobkovic.

[11] ÖNB, MS. 12592, pp. 157–8: 'Bücher . . . in der Röm. Kays. Maj. Betzimmer'; ibid. 161–3: 'Bücher, welche in der . . . Retirade auff dem Tische gelegen'; ibid. 165–9: 'Bücher, welche in der Röm. Kayserl. Maj. Reisekasten sich befunden'. Lipsius, *Opera Omnia* is cited as a 1627 edn., presumably an error for 1637 (though that contained only 4 vols.).

[12] For the Jesuits see the bibliographical *chef d'œuvre* by Sommervogel (*et al.*), and
(continued)

disciplines, exhibiting the virtues and weaknesses of Baroque-Catholic polyhistory. In fact the most prominent polymaths often spent little time at Vienna itself. Caramuel, born in Madrid, worked in the Netherlands before moving to Austria, then soon concentrated his activities on Bohemia (where his father had once served Rudolf II) and ended his life in Lombardy. Magni, brought up at Prague, pursued a restless career with missionary and political assignments throughout the Empire. Marci was a provincial Czech who hardly set foot outside his native kingdom, though his intellectual heir, Dobrzensky, displayed slightly more *Wanderlust*. Self-effacing Jesuits passed their lives in periodic transfer from one remote college to another: Stansel, Kochański, Scheiner, Moretus, Lana-Terzi, Conrad, Menegatti . . .[13]

Two key figures never went to Vienna at all, though they became closely associated with it, and erected the nearest thing to a thoroughgoing philosophical rationale (or rather irrationale) for it. Athanasius Kircher (1601 or 1602–80), born near Fulda in Franconia, taught at various Jesuit houses of middle Germany during the testing years of war. Then he moved to Rome, where he received a permanent professorship at the Collegium Romanum in 1635 when on the point of accepting a post in the Habsburg capital, and where most of his thirty-eight books were first published. Kircher's colleague, Kaspar Schott (1608–66), likewise a native of Franconia who spent many years in Italy, later established himself at Würzburg, and his writings appeared there and in neighbouring Nuremberg (under the auspices of the Endters) during a single

---

a useful earlier compendium for the Habsburg lands: [J. N. Stoeger], *Scriptores Provinciae Austriae S. J.*, i (V. 1855). Some other orders are also well served; see especially J. Quétif and J. Echard, *Scriptores O.P.*, i–ii (Paris 1719–21); L. Wadding, *et al.*, *Scriptores O.F.M.* (Rome 1806); M. Ziegelbauer, *Historia rei literariae O.S.B.*, i–iv (Augsburg–Würzburg 1754); B. O. Černik, *Die Schriftsteller der noch bestehenden Augustiner Chorherrenstifte Österreichs von 1600 bis auf den heutigen Tag* (V. 1905); J. F. Ossinger, *Bibliotheca Augustiniana* (Ingolstadt–Augsburg 1768); Horányi, op. cit. (Piarists).

[13] On Caramuel: L. Ceyssens, 'Autour de Caramuel', *Bulletin de l'Institut Historique Belge de Rome*, xxxiii (1961), 329–410; R. Ceñal, 'Juan Caramuel; su epistolario con Atanasio Kircher', *Revista de Filosofia*, xii (1953), 101–47; *OSN* v, 138 f. For him and Magni see above, pp. 119, 217. On Marci: W. R. Weitenweber, 'Beiträge zur Literärgeschichte Böhmens', *Sb. d. k. Akad. d. Wiss ph.-h. Kl.* xix (1856), 120–56, at 122–44; and on Dobrzensky: ibid. 144–56. Brief biographies of Jesuits are appended to the entries in Sommervogel.

hectic decade from 1657.[14] The massive tomes of Kircher, Schott, and the rest, which must have been expensive even when printed with the financial backing of dynasty and Church, were purchased all over the Monarchy. Leopold's personal library contained thirteen of Kircher's and seven of Schott's; the Liechtensteins possessed thirty-one Kirchers; Sternberg had twenty-three works by Kircher and thirteen by Schott, Kirchberg over ten titles by each; even the more modest Crane owned eleven Kirchers by 1658. The monastery of Heiligenkreuz bought his huge *Oedipus Aegyptiacus* for thirty-five florins within a year of publication.[15]

The latest products of this scholarship would be discussed among educated circles in Vienna, Prague, and all the smaller centres of the Monarchy. Often they were interpreted and transmitted by lesser men who themselves wrote little: the Silesian, Godefrid Alois Kinner, provost of All Saints church on the Hradschin and tutor to Leopold's younger brother, Archduke Karl Josef; Philipp Müller, Leopold's secretive Jesuit preceptor and confessor, who smoothed the path of Lambeck to Vienna; Johann Maximilian Lamberg, Bernard Ignác Martinic, Pál Esterházy, and other aristocratic patrons; prominent members of the professions, like J. W. Mannagetta.[16] It is not too hard to imagine *conversazioni* amid the fine bindings of the *Hofbibliothek*, as described and illustrated by the English traveller, Edward Browne, or in the groves of Archbishop

---

[14] K. Brischar, *Athanasius Kircher, ein Lebensbild* (Würzburg 1877, separatum from *Katholische Studien*, iii); Sommervogel, iv, cols. 1046–77. Cf. UK, MS. XIV C 12: 'Vita Reverendi Patris Athanasii Kircheri à semetipso conscripta'. I have encountered several other copies of this brief life, and there exists a printed German translation; but it does not appear (*pace* Zedler and Sommervogel (iv, col. 1070)) to be included in the *Fasciculus Epistolarum ... Athanasii Kircheri*, ed. H. A. Langenmantel (Augsburg 1684). Cf. below, pp. 433–5 and *passim*. On Schott: *Notice raisonné des ouvrages de Gaspar Schott, Jésuite ... par M. l'Abbé M[ercier]* (Paris 1785); Sommervogel, vii, cols. 904–12.

[15] ÖNB, MS. 12590, *passim*. Bohatta, op. cit. ii, 1056–8; Str., MS. DH V 27; ÖNB, MS. 14878, *passim*; ÖNB, MS. 14860, fol. 53ᵛ. 'Die Handschriften-Verzeichnisse der Cistercienser-Stifte', *Xenia Bernardina*, ii (V. 1891), 119 (Heiligenkreuz).

[16] Very little information seems to be available about Kinner; see Zedler, s.v. (brief); Zibrt, *BČH* v, no. 16912; L. Thorndike, *History of Magic and Experimental Science*, vii–viii (New York 1958), viii, 310; and below, n. 61, and p. 361, n. 36. Cf. also his *Stella Matutina ... sive Laudatio Funebris ... in funere ... Caroli Josephi Archiducis Austriae* (V. 1664). On Müller (or Miller): Stoeger and Sommervogel, s.v.; Krones, *Universität Graz*, 382; cf. ÖNB, MS. 9712, fol. 171; ibid. MS. 9713, fols. 7, 12, 15, 18, 33; OL, Eszterházy cs. lt., P. 125, cs. 658, nos. 3184–6. For Mannagetta see above, p. 109.

Lippay's celebrated garden at Pozsony, carefully tended by his horticulturalist Jesuit brother; in the courts and interminable corridors of Prague's Clementinum, or in cloistered walks at Klosterneuburg and St. Florian.[17] And the outcome of such discussions was a recognizable set of opinions and credences which, for all their inconsistencies, for all the lacunae in our understanding of them, we may call an intellectual system.

*

Let us try briefly to analyse this system of ideas. Its foundation was firmly Aristotelian. From Aristotle derived the categories of its logic, the qualities of its physics, the substance of its metaphysics, the duality of matter and form, the unity of creation and the chain of being, the four kinds of causation, the teleological view of gravity, medicine, and so forth. A mass of surviving evidence bears witness to that, mainly university textbooks and manuscript notes by students. It is a genre of utterly predictable accounts of the physical world, of man's place in it and his duties, whether the writer be a Jesuit active in court service, like Philipp Müller, or a retiring Minim like Antonius Mandl. And a genre not restricted to clerics: one of the imperial *Leibärzte*, Johann Conrad Wechtler, laboured for many years on a colossal tome of the most amazing obscurantism and sterility.[18]

Such Aristotelianism had been refracted, of course, through the scholastics. It would be a difficult task to discover how far the great medieval *summae* were now actually read, though Martinic certainly prided himself on the ability to defend the heritage of Anselm and Aquinas.[19] More immediately relevant was the great revival in

---

[17] Browne, *Account*, 90–5; the illustration appears only in later edns. (e.g. *Durch Niederland, Teutschland, Hungarn, Serbien ... Reisen* (Nuremberg 1686), facing p. 242). János Lippay's *Posoni kert*, describing the archiepiscopal pleasure-grounds, appeared at Tyrnau and Vienna in 1664–7. Cf. J. Ernyey, *Természettudományi mozgalmaink a 17.–18. században* (Bp. 1912), separatum from *Természettudományi Közlöny*); R. Rapaics, *A pozsonyi kert* (Bp. 1938, separatum from ibid.); E. Gombocz, *A magyar botanika története* (Bp. 1936), 135 ff. An Italian polyhistor called Giovanni Bonanus (Bonanni?) seems to have been the leading light of the Lippay-circle; see also Mayer, op. cit. i, no. 1302; and the confused observations by E. Browne, *A Brief Account of some Travels in Hungaria ...* (London 1673), 95 f.

[18] ÖNB, MSS. 10503–5, compilations by Müller; A. Mandl, *Templum Sophiae L Columnis constructum* (V. 1662), though he does mention Mersenne, Kepler, Galileo, and Kircher. J. C. Wechtler, *Homo Oriens et Occidens* (Frankfurt 1659—though the frontispiece is dated '1660' (and the imperial privilege '1648'!)).

[19] ÖNB, MS. 9713, fols. 91 f., 97 f.; ibid. MS. 9715, fol. 155. Cf. Kalista (ed.), *Korespondence*, no. 27.

study of Aristotle during the later sixteenth century, which—as we have already seen—spilled over into Protestant Germany and Hungary. The neoscholastic movement of Suarez, Fonseca, Soto, Toletus, showed that traditional Catholic philosophy had regained its nerve. It represented also an accommodation with some of the large challenges which had threatened the Church since the age of Aquinas: nominalism, Humanist critique, Protestant redefinition of theological verities. Thus the doctrine was not pure, even in its inception. Consider the conceptual influences on the young Pázmány, as a persuasive new lecturer at the University of Graz about the year 1600. He knew the Thomist school of Salamanca, the Jesuit philosophers at Coimbra and Rome, the Averroists of Padua, especially Zabarella and Piccolomini, and a wide range of other Humanist writers. They were all combined by the strongly practical and decisive personality of Pázmány in a distinct effort of synthesis.[20]

Structural modifications are still clearer with Arriaga in the next generation. Rodrigo Arriaga (1592–1667) was a Spanish Jesuit who settled at Prague from the 1620s until his death, and not only played a major part, as rector of the Carolinum for many years, in rebuilding Bohemian education, but also gained recognition as one of the leading Catholic thinkers of the period. A fully international figure, standing close to the dynasty (he taught the young Ferdinand III the Spanish he must have needed during the Nördlingen campaign), Arriaga's *Cursus Philosophicus* first appeared on the Plantin presses at Antwerp in 1632 and went into numerous editions.[21] There is no doubt that this formidable folio of 900 pages was designed to uphold established Catholic wisdom under the aegis of benign Habsburg rulers. Its elegant frontispiece illustrates a 'hortus philosophiae' which, as the dedication explains, is entrusted to the king of the Romans and his wife, and where the true logic, physics, and metaphysics of Aristotle can flourish anew.

---

[20] I. Gerencsér, *A filozófus Pázmány* (Bp. 1937); Őry, op. cit. *passim*. Pázmány's Latin works (mostly lecture-courses) are printed in *Opera Omnia, series latina*, i–vi (Bp. 1894–1904). On neoscholasticism in general: L. Giacon, *La seconda scolastica*, i– (Milan 1944–).

[21] K. Eschweiler, 'Roderigo de Arriaga SJ', *Spanische Forschungen der Görres-gesellschaft*, iii (Münster 1931), 253–85; cf. H. Bosmans, 'Théodore Moretus SJ, mathématicien', *De Gulden Passer*, N.R. vi (1928), 57–163, *passim* (Moretus was the cousin of Arriaga's printer). There were further edns. of the *Cursus* at Paris 1637, 1639, 1647, 1669; and at Lyons 1644, 1651, 1653, 1669.

But the text reveals a less rigid adherence to authority, while a preface to the reader explicitly requests him to be prepared for novelty, since the ancients must be 'non domini, sed duces', and the experience of our senses may enable us to improve on them. At several important points Arriaga shows himself more of an Occamist than a Thomist.[22]

For such thinkers as Arriaga Aristotelianism became a practical vehicle, so much so, indeed, that its old metaphysical dimension—where that was felt problematical—tended to be separated out as a distinct study of ontology, leaving the rest of the edifice to find new supports.[23] One aspect of this was the revival of other medieval scholastic systems, particularly the doctrines associated with Duns Scotus. Scotism was championed by the Franciscans and established one of its main seventeenth-century homes at Prague, helped by the Irish friars who, as one admirer claimed, dissolved the pitch-black clouds of ignorance and heresy much as St. Patrick had once cleared their fatherland of serpents. It found weighty and verbose expositors in Bernhard Sannig and Amandus Hermann, whose approach, less advanced than Arriaga's, shows no gleam of modernity; how could it when two-thirds of Hermann's metaphysics are devoted to angels![24] Nevertheless it cast fresh light on Aristotle, as did a continuing preoccupation with certain notions drawn from the classical Renaissance, especially the doctrines of neo-stoicism.

The idea of man's dignity, so central to Humanism, was not, as people frequently imagine, some idle paean to the human spirit, but a precise evaluation of the place of man, being microcosm, in the macrocosm of nature. That theme—expounded before 1600 by such Central Europeans as Lascovius—dominates a curious compendium published by Antonio Zara, Bishop of Pedena in Istria and protégé

---

[22] Cf. S. Sousedík, 'Teorie zhušt'ování a zředování v díle Rodriga Arriagy', *Filosofický Časopis*, xvi (1968), 673–98; Thorndike, op. cit. vii, 399–402.

[23] The theme of a difficult but rewarding book by P. di Vona, *Studi sulla scolastica della Controriforma* (Florence 1968), esp. 184–95 on Arriaga; cf. Wundt, op. cit.

[24] B. Jansen, 'Zur Philosophie der Scotisten des 17. Jahrhunderts', *Franziskanische Studien*, xxxii (1936), 28–58, 150–75 (152–4 on Sannig); Thorndike, op. cit. vii, 465–476; C. M. Balic, 'Wadding the Scotist', *F. Luke Wadding Commemoration volume* (Dublin 1957), 463–507. On Prague Hibernian Scotists: Millett, op. cit. 468–73, 479 f., 482–5, and esp. 152 n. Hermann, *Sol Triplex*, 828–967; cf. above, p. 128. Other orders too had their Scotists; see, for a trivial example, OL, Eszterházy cs. lt., P. 125, cs. 705, no. 11960, a thesis printed on silk.

of Ferdinand II.[25] Zara surveys the gamut of human activity: body, imagination, intellect, memory, in a way which must strike us as rather learned than logical, since we have lost the key to his theoretical organization of the material. But it is the same kind of schema which natural philosophers from the Habsburg lands adopted later in the century: Johann Ferdinand Hertodt, for example, the town physician of Brno, in his poem, *Opus Mirificum sextae diei*; even the uncompromising (not to say unpromising) Aristotelian, Wechtler. It is a view of nature still close to Aristotle and Pliny and wide-eyed medieval attitudes towards the wonders of creation (not by accident was the very last edition of Bartholomaeus Anglicus, that rag-bag of credulity, prepared at St. Vitus's in Prague on the threshold of the seventeenth century), married with some prime insights of Renaissance speculation: the work of Telesio, Cardano, Porta.[26]

Thus orthodox philosophy, the overall philosophy of classroom and seminary, exhibits several strata. At the level of the university arts curriculum, a crude Aristotelianism survives until the end of the century and beyond. When J. J. Scharz and his Jesuit master sought to demonstrate the twin provinces of intellect and will in a Linz dissertation of 1676, they simply hitched Aristotelian assertions about logic, universal physics, particular physics, and metaphysics to the four cardinal virtues and left it at that. When F. S. Schott defended some theses with the good Renaissance title, *Cosmus in Micro-Cosmo*, under the Viennese Jesuits twenty-five years later, he based his text overwhelmingly on Aristotle, Pliny, the Fathers, and early medieval writers. And we should not necessarily be persuaded by any claim to eclecticism or reappraisal. The Austrian Cistercian, Georg Neupauer, for example, reveals in his treatises some familiarity with recent authors: Arriaga, Kircher, Caramuel, and

[25] On Lascovius: above, pp. 32, 34. A. Zara, *Anatomia Ingeniorum et Scientiarum* (Venice 1615), with some autobiographical information at 16 ff. That Zara was no aulic hanger-on, but a proper Tridentine bishop who resided in his humble and distant diocese, is proved by the book's colophon.

[26] J. F. Hertodt, *Opus Mirificum sextae diei, id est Homo physicè, anatomicè, et moraliter...dissectus* (Jena 1670); Wechtler, op. cit. (whose frontispiece depicts, *inter alia*, Hermes Trismegistus). Bartholomaeus Anglicus, *De Genuinis Rerum Coelestium, Terrestrium et Inferarum Proprietatibus*, ed. G. B. Pontanus of Breitenberg (Frankfurt 1601), with no suggestion that the work might be antiquated. For Pontanus, provost of Prague cathedral, see *Rudolf II*, 158–61 (where I have wrongly made him a Jesuit).

Marci among them, and he makes some play with his own opinion; but the outcome is only a conventional *réchauffé*.[27]

On a somewhat more elevated plane, we are faced with a deep-rooted polymathic habit which simply adds new knowledge more or less mindlessly to received views. Part of Caramuel's *œuvre* falls into this category: his *Trismegistus Theologicus*, or the quaintly-titled *Mathesis Biceps*, which Leopold I studied. So do such popular textbooks as Pexenfelder's *Apparatus Eruditionis*, a catch-all of traditional wisdom.[28] The genre was pursued long into the eighteenth century in Hungary, where the Catholic religion, being most vulnerable, proved least adventurous. Martin Szentiványi, a leading professor at Tyrnau, produced three volumes, neatly divided into nine parts and ninety chapters, which he called *Curiosiora et Selectiora Miscellanea*, though they are really a classic instance of the inability to select, a sort of *reductio ad absurdum* of the Baroque striving for completeness.[29] The reader is made to skip alarmingly from cosmography to chronology by way of doggerel verses on the state of the harvest; from geography to ecclesiastical history via the works of Thomas à Kempis. A section on 'discoveries and inventions' passes rapidly from sunspots to the uses of rhubarb; the next one, about 'things lost', embraces both Paradise and genuine cinnamon; the next describes things which have never existed at all, like Copernican motion.

Yet Szentiványi has some merits, even if they are not those of

---

[27] J. J. Scharz, *Gemella Philosophia intellectus et voluntatis* (Linz 1676); F. S. de Schott, *Cosmus in Micro-Cosmo, hoc est: Mundus Opere Sex Dierum Creatus* (V. 1701). These are two examples taken at random from the large dissertation literature; Schott quotes a few 17th-century authors, even Robert Fludd, but they are quite marginal. Neupauer: Schlierbach, MS. 65 (81): 'Metaphysica Eclectica'; ibid. MS. 69 (86): 'Logica Eclectica'; ibid. MS. 76 (93): 'Physiologia Eclectica'; all dated in the 1690s.

[28] J. Caramuel Lobkovic, *Trismegistus Theologicus latine Ter-Maximus*, i–iii (Vigevano 1679); id., *Mathesis Biceps vetus et nova*, i–ii (Campagna 1670). ÖNB, MS. 12757, fol. 19 (Ebersdorf, 8 Oct. 1670), acknowledges imperial receipt of the latter, or perhaps only of vol. 1, since in 1672 one of Lambeck's agents still seems to be trying to secure the second part, which is 'molto bizarra' (ÖNB, MS. 9714, fol. 150); cf. Karajan, op. cit. 127. Pexenfelder, op. cit.

[29] M. Szentiványi, *Curiosiora et Selectiora variarum scientiarum Miscellanea*, i–iii (Tyrnau 1689–1709), all the parts have separate pagination. Full list of his writings in Sommervogel, s.v. (they include the anti-Lutheran tracts collected together as *Opuscula Polemica*, i–ii (2nd edn. Tyrnau 1718–30). On Szentiványi's life see Serfőző, op. cit. esp. 17 ff.

organization. He is definitely not a 'simple' Aristotelian: only the most mediocre writers of the day could be called that. All the better ones—the Pázmánys, the Arriagas—show flexibility and some willingness to disagree. Others again were by no means concerned just to add: they were equally eager to subtract.

*

The most obvious alternative to Aristotle was Plato. Again it is not easy to assemble evidence as to how far the classic texts were actually read, though they are well represented in libraries. Lambeck purchased Platonic manuscripts for Leopold from Venice and Rome in 1671, and Lamberg had a high regard for Marsilio Ficino.[30] We stand on firmer ground with three curious and significant thinkers who were much influenced by the Platonic tradition: Marci, Magni, and Caramuel.

Jan Marcus Marci (1595–1662), from Landskron in Bohemia, had one foot firmly in the post-1620 establishment: he was a professor at the Carolinum from 1626 and a friend of the Jesuits, whose order he joined on his deathbed; a successful doctor, *Leibarzt* to the Habsburgs, and ennobled by Ferdinand III with a special salary; a respected scholar, whose works appeared with priestly approbations and dedications to the emperor. But he was also controversial: his first book, *Idearum Operatricium Idea*, left incomplete, contains highly speculative discussion of the principles of biological propagation, drawing on the animistic armoury of Neoplatonism. Marci felt bound to defend himself against the charge of believing in eternal ideas, independent of the Creator. Some thirty years later, having conducted novel research in mechanics and optics, he returned to the issue of substantial generation and to the criticism of Aristotle, or at least of his interpreters.[31]

---

[30] ÖNB, MS. 9714, fols. 108 f., 116, 120, 127, 129, 153, 163; ibid. MS. 9713, fol. 83 (Lamberg).

[31] Weitenweber, art. cit.; B. Ryba, 'Originál posledního pořízení Jana Marka Marci v diplomatáři strahovském', *Str. Kn.* iv (1969), 95–108; Zíbrt, *BČH* v, 15915–62. The *Acta historiae rerum naturalium necnon technicarum*, special issue 3, ed. J. Smolka (Pr. 1967), are given over to Marci, and add a few new insights (cf. also the (incomplete) bibliography ibid. 39–50). J. M. Marci, *Idearum Operatricium Idea sive Hypotoposis et detectio illius occultae Virtutis, quae Semina faecundat . . .* (Pr. 1635), esp. pref. to reader, sig. (+ + +)ʳ – A2ᵛ; a second volume was announced, but never

(continued)

Valerian Magni (1585–1661) was still more contentious. We have seen something of his role as a politician. He proved no less original and intransigent as a theorist, and there has probably been more recent discussion of him than of anyone else who appears in this chapter (though it amounts to no more than a few articles). Proceeding from the belief that the human understanding is a kind of divine illumination (not for nothing had he lived in Prague at the same time as Johannes Kepler), Magni moved to attack both Aristotelian physics, especially on the subject of the vacuum, and the moral validity of the whole Aristotelian philosophy. From his publication, at Warsaw in 1647, of a brief tract, *De Atheismo Aristotelis*, he fought running battles with the Jesuit censorship.[32]

Both Marci and Magni made enemies; yet both remained an integral part of the intellectual scene. By the end of his life Marci's reputation was secure throughout Central Europe, from Kircher in Rome to Morhof in Kiel. And although Magni, at the end of his, suffered brief imprisonment at the hands of the Papal nuncio, he was soon delivered from his arrest in an imperial carriage.[33] Neither destroyed the framework of knowledge: Marci, in the end, still identified light with the Aristotelian quintessence; Magni's highly personal Christian philosophy could create no new school. It is the same with the extraordinary Caramuel Lobkovic (1606–80), more famous than either in his own day. Child prodigy, master of twenty-

-----

published. Id., *Philosophia Vetus Restituta, omnia in omnibus* (Pr. 1662, reissued Frankfurt 1676), with another interesting preface (sig. *3ˇ ff.). Cf. below, pp. 330 f., 337 (mechanics and optics).

[32] Above, pp. 119, 133 n. 43, 139 n. 59, 217; below, p. 426. General appreciations of his thought in A. de Corniero, 'Capuchinos precursores del P. Bartolomé Barberis en el estudio de S. Buenaventura: P. Valeriano Magni de Milán', *Coll. Franc.* iii (1933), 67–80, 209–28, 347–83, 518–70; and A. Boehm, 'L'augustinisme de Valeriano Magni', *Revue des sciences religieuses*, xxxix (1965), 230–67. Cf., more briefly, *Dictionnaire de théologie catholique*, ix (1926), cols. 1553–65 (good); Winter, *Frühaufklärung*, 164–7; Blekastad, op. cit., index, s.v., who repeatedly compares him with Comenius. Complete bibliography of Magni's works by G. Cygan in *Coll. Franc.* xlii (1972), 119–78, 309–52. See below, p. 337, on his physics.

[33] Marci, *Philosophia Vetus Restituta*, sig. *4ˇ (letter from Kircher); D. G. Morhof, *Polyhistor*, i–iii (Lübeck 1695–1708), ii, bk. 2, pt. 2, 39 f., 259 f., 298 f., 308, 313, 331, 335, 367, etc. *Dictionnaire de théologie catholique*, ix, col. 1556. It has regularly been stated that only one copy survives (in Prague's UK) of Magni's last philosophical work, *Opus Philosophicum* (Litomyšl 1660), which was confiscated by the censors; but that does not appear to be true: one is listed in Paulhart–Voglsam (eds.), op. cit. litt. O, no. 148.

four languages, author of over one hundred books, 'prince of the casuists', Caramuel's Cistercian contemporary, Sartorius, described him as 'a Name worthy to be spelled out in letters of gold, a very Sun among intellects'.[34] There is no doubting his encyclopaedic learning and his eclectic method: it is just difficult to penetrate the bombast of the one and reach any clear statement of the other. Best, perhaps, are the preface to the *Rationalis et realis Philosophia*, where Plato is explicitly preferred to Aristotle, and some letters to Kircher, Marci, Bernard Ignác Martinic, and other friends.[35] Caramuel possessed a highly diffuse and discursive mind: the *Trismegistus Theologicus*, his penultimate book, represents an amazing jumble of erudition, a kind of *Finnegans Wake* of Baroque philosophy. For all his innovatory forays he was certainly no radical, seeking instead to refurbish and rehouse the existing principles of Christian thought.

Marci, Magni, and Caramuel all display, besides their Platonism, some awareness of the contemporary Western debates which we have learned to call the 'scientific revolution'. Those debates penetrated Central Europe in two further ways. Protestant intellectuals in Hungary—and to a lesser extent in Silesia, among pupils of Daniel Sennert (1572–1637)—opened their minds to influences from the Dutch universities and from modernists in Germany; eager readers could be found at Debrecen or Kolozsvár for Bacon and Descartes, Gassendi and the atomists. I mention (but this is not the place to dwell on them) Johannes Bayer (1630–74), who showed empiricist leanings; his Upper Hungarian compatriot and fellow-student at Wittenberg Isaac Zabanius (1632–1707), who wrote on the existence of atoms; and the Transylvanian scholar, János Pósaházi (c. 1630–86), who brought back Cartesian ideas from

---

[34] Cf. above, n. 13 (Ceyssens, Ceñal); and earlier H. Hurter, *Nomenclator Literarius*, i–iii (Innsbruck 1871–86), ii, 529–34. Sartorius, op. cit. 547–50; cf. Morhof, op. cit. i, bk. 1, 209. Caramuel was one of the most redoubtable polyscriptors on record. Ferdinand III once spent the day at his monastery, examining the *œuvre*. The emperor said he could not be the judge of its quality, but he would never have believed, had he not seen it, that one pair of hands and one pen could write so much about so many things. That, adds Caramuel, was twenty years ago, and he only saw the first bookcase full! (*Mathesis Biceps*, i, sig. *3ᵛ).
[35] J. Caramuel Lobkovic, *Rationalis et realis Philosophia* (Louvain 1642), esp. sig. aiii–aiv ('negare non potero eius [Plato's] doctrinam proprius ad Christianam accedere, quam Peripateticam'). A series of these letters is published in *Mathesis Biceps*, i, 415–86, 711–14; cf. Ceñal, art. cit. 122–47.

Utrecht. Puritan authors, like János Apáczai (1625–59), naturally sought to widen such breaches in the traditional firmament.[36] Meanwhile an independent spirit made itself evident within certain immigrant Catholic circles. There were elements of full-scale libertinism around Prince Eugene and his library, housed in Vienna by 1712, with its rich collection of free-thinking literature. Something similar grew up in the entourage of the prickly but gifted second-generation Bohemian, Count Sporck, that peculiar blend of penitent Baroque *seigneur* and enlightened dilettante.[37] More important was an atmosphere of fairly down-to-earth criticism associated especially with the numerous Irish settlers in the Monarchy. Some of it came from men of religion: the Prague Franciscans and their robust instruction, which so offended local Jesuits; the learned Nicholas Donellan, vicar-general of the Augustinian hermits and professor of canon law at Vienna University, travelling companion with Edward Browne on the latter's Royal Society visit to Austria; or the argumentative military chaplain, Thomas Carve.[38] Others were lay intellectuals, like the splendid William O'Kelly, a successful doctor. O'Kelly is the author of a forthright guide to practical philosophy 'methodo parisiensi

---

[36] On Sennert: Thorndike, op. cit. vii, ch. 7. S. Felber, *Ján Bayer, slovenský baconista XVII storočia* (Bratislava 1953), is demolished by D. Tschižewskij, 'Johannes Bayer, ein deutscher Philosoph in der Slowakei', *Südostforschungen*, xv (1956), 471–7. J. Mikleš, *Izák Caban, slovenský atomista XVII storočia* (Bratislava 1948), is again rather misconceived, though Zabanius's *Existentia Atomorum* (Wittenberg 1667), is a significant little work; cf. above, p. 267 (Sachs). On Pósaházi: E. Makkai, *Pósaházi János élete és filozófiája* (Kolozsvár 1942). J. Apáczai Csere, *Magyar Encyclopaedia* (Utrecht 1653); cf. I. Bán, *Apáczai Csere János* (Bp. 1958).

[37] Braubach, op. cit. v, 92–115, 169–95; Winter, op. cit. 118 ff. Cf. Montesquieu, *Voyages*, i–ii (Bordeaux 1894–6), i, 5 ff., 281–4. It is quaint that the two most stimulating companions Montesquieu found at Vienna were both generals (Eugene and Guido Starhemberg); then he moved on to Venice to enjoy the company of a third: the renegade Austrian commander Bonneval. On Sporck, cf. above, p. 216.

[38] Above, pp. 221, 320. For other Hibernians in Central Europe, cf. Millett, op. cit. 356, 366–8, 372 f., 479 f. It was an Irishman, Antonius Donillius (Donnelly?) who reissued Marci's *Philosophia Vetus Restituta* in Germany in 1676 (cf. 1662 edn., sig. **3ʳ). On Donellan (died in 1679): Ossinger, op. cit. 297 f.; Janetschek, op. cit. 292 ff.; J. J. Gavigan, 'A letter from Nicolas Donellan', *Aug.* xix (1969), 291–320; K. Hörmann, 'Nikolaus Donellan, ein Ire auf dem moraltheologischen Lehrstuhl der Universität Wien', *Festschrift F. Loidl*, i, 65–95. Donellan apparently converted Ferenc Nádasdy (Fallenbüchl, op. cit. 67; Gavigan, *Austro-Hungarian Province*, i, 99), though their later relationship is unclear (cf. Pauler, op. cit. i, 281 ff.). He corresponded with Lambeck from Eperjes in Hungary (ÖNB, MS. 9714, fols. 43,

pertractata', aimed as an antidote to dryasdust scholastic primers and an introduction to the useful discoveries of recent Western scientists: Galileo, Gassendi, Descartes. He proudly acknowledges a line of distinguished Irish (or honorary Irish) iconoclasts stretching from Scotus through Occam to Robert Boyle.[39] Yet none of this goes very far to alter the general picture. Hungarian Protestants were isolated and basically conservative, heavily indebted to Aristotle and less radical than some admirers have claimed. Eugene and Sporck were also isolated, an élite of the élite, only toying with erudite sedition. Though the *libertins* received at Vienna represent an interesting chapter in the prehistory of the Enlightenment and the troubled story of Habsburg–Papal relations (the Italian anticlerical fugitive, Pietro Giannone, actually became a pensionary of Emperor Charles VI), their impact on the country at large was extremely slight. The letters of Eugene's protégé, J. B. Rousseau, show how distant that French salon poet remained from the Austrian milieu.[40] Much of the Catholic criticism was linked to power struggles within the ecclesiastical establishment, usually campaigns against the Jesuits. Even O'Kelly is more striking for irreverence than for novelty. No new framework of analysis was constructed; indeed, the elaboration of new logical systems, one aspect of an anti-Aristotelian approach, proved largely a Jesuit preserve. Caramuel—needless to say—had views on that, as on everything else, but the main debate was pursued by Kircher and Schott, Caspar Knittel in Prague and Szentiványi at Tyrnau, and

71 f.; ibid. MS. 9715, fols. 40, 48), and seems to have accompanied Count Leslie's regiment thither. For other Irish Augustinians in Central Europe, cf. Ossinger, op. cit. 363 f., 735; Gavigan, *Austro-Hungarian Province*, 10–14. Carve (died after 1672), from Tipperary, wrote a lively travel-diary: *Itinerarium*, ed. M. Kerney (London 1859, 1st edn. 1639–46); as well as books on Irish history which involved him in a marvellous slanging-match with a Hibernian friar called Bruodin (T. Wall, 'Bards and Bruodins', in *Wadding Commemorative volume*, 438–62).

[39] O'Kelly, op. cit.; cf., for some details of his life, Schmid, op. cit. 21 ff.

[40] On the Viennese exile of Giannone (1676–1748), who was a friend of Eugene and the court librarian Garelli, see most recently G. Ricuperati, 'Libertinismo e deismo a Vienna: Spinoza, Toland e il Triregno', *Rivista Storica Italiana*, lxxix (1967), 628–95. Jean-Baptiste Rousseau, *Lettres sur differens sujets*, 2 vols. in 3 (Geneva 1749); he began by feeling at home ('Tous les Princes et tous les Seigneurs parlent notre langue, et la pluspart en connoissent les agréments mieux que nous-mêmes'—a palpable exaggeration, though cf. above, p. 214, n. 45), but soon grew disillusioned.

involved a thoroughly backward-looking rediscovery of the *Ars Magna* of Ramon Lull.[41]

The most fundamental opponents of orthodox learning belonged to a tradition almost as old as Christianity itself: Augustinianism, a thorn for complacent scholastics in Counter-Reformation no less than in Reformation. Again the doctrine was espoused by a clear faction within the body of the Church: canons regular, Premonstratensians, Augustinian friars. Partly they taught a timeless scepticism. Nebridius of Mündelheim, from the abbey of Klosterneuburg, made no bones about it in the preface to his *Philosophia … S. Augustini*: "Aristotle", he tells us, "was a man heathen and false, profane and arrogant, obscure and slippery, who neither knew nor worshipped the one God or true wisdom; for that reason he now resides with the inhabitants of the nether regions, quibuscum desperatè Deum summè bonum blasphemat et execratur." Then the good canon proceeds to a Baroque *tour-de-force* of quotations drawn entirely from St. Augustine.[42] Similar sentiments can be found on occasion in Caramuel, while the vehemence of Magni betrays the influence of Augustine and Bonaventura, as do the mystical leanings of some Franciscans and the odd mild flirtation with Cornelius Jansen.[43] At the same time there exists a particular debt to Renaissance sceptics, most evident in the writings of Hieronymus Hirnhaim (1637–79), the Premonstratensian abbot of Strahov. Hirnhaim was the author of some fairly unremarkable devotional literature, but his *De Typho Generis Humani* is one of the

---

[41] S. Sousedik, 'Diskrétni logika Jana Caramuela z Lobkovic', *Filosofický Časopis*, xvii (1969), 216–28; cf. below, pp. 353–5.

[42] Nebridius à Mündelheim, *Philosophia … S. Augustini … Christiana* ([V.] 1654); cf. his *De vita et virtutibus … S. Augustini* (V. 1648), with reflections on ethics. It would be helpful to know more about the intellectual life of the Augustinian canons in this period. The general level of study among Augustinian friars does not appear to have been very high (Gavigan, *Austro-Hungarian Province*, ii, 98–161, 213–26, 313–33).

[43] J. Caramuel Lobkovic, *Thanatosophia nempe Mortis Museum in quo demonstratur esse tota Vita … vanitas vanitatum …* (Brussels 1637). For Magni: Corniero, art. cit.; Boehm, art. cit. Amandus Hermann, *Desertum Pharan mystice explicatum …* (Pr. 1687), sermons for passiontide. On Central European readers of Jansen: L. Ceyssens, 'Fiorence Conry, Hugh de Burgo, Luke Wadding, and Jansenism', in *Wadding Commemorative volume*, 295–404, at 331–55; S. Dolezel, 'Frühe Einflüsse des Jansenismus in Böhmen', in Seibt (ed.), op. cit. 145–53; cf. Rezek (ed.), 'Idea gubernationis ecclesiasticae'.

most provocative books to have come out of seventeenth-century Central Europe. Learning is evil, it insists, conducive only to vanity; no real knowledge is possible and scholars never agree; the works of the Creator are inscrutable. The message can be summed up in a simple—albeit rather paradoxical—chapter-heading: 'de vano libros conscribendi studio'.[44]

Once more, however, the picture is not completely negative. Nebridius and Hirnhaim, like Magni and Caramuel, are seeking a genuine Catholic philosophy. Hirnhaim especially was a man of real erudition, besides being a considerable public figure; despite his reflections on the vanity of books, he showed much concern for the well-being of his monastery's library and the archbishop of Prague's seminary. His *De Typho* represents more than just a paean to *docta ignorantia*—as the Emperor Leopold perhaps perceived when he recorded qualified approval of it. Rather Hirnhaim takes up a similar position to his spiritual ancestor, Agrippa of Nettesheim, in the *De Incertitudine et Vanitate Scientiarum*: both would dearly embrace pansophy, but they are baffled by the complexities of the world and human opinion. And Hirnhaim leaves no doubt of a residual sympathy for the pious, even mystical Neoplatonism of his teacher, Marci.[45] A very interesting postscript to this appears in a manuscript compiled for private use by an Augustinian friar down the Petřín hill in the Old Town of Prague. The anonymous writer stresses the weaknesses of Aristotle—he has little time for Peripatetic qualities, humours, or elements. Instead, he tries to build up a new doctrine based on recent philosophers of nature: Kircher, Schott, Caramuel, above all Marci. His very title launches a manifesto of both critique and reconciliation: *Nova, vel potius Antiqua, Philosophia, Naturalis,*

---

[44] H. Hirnhaim, *De Typho Generis Humani sive Scientiarum Humanarum inani ac ventoso tumore* ... (Pr. 1676); the title-word 'typhus', as he explains, is derived from Augustine: 'Huic inflanti et evertenti vento, Divi Augustini vestigiis insistens, exitiosam hujus mundi scientiam comparo'. Hirnhaim also says that this work presents a view of science parallel to that of religion expressed in his *Sermo S. Norberti* (Pr. 1676). C. S. Barach, *Hieronymus Hirnhaim* (V. 1864), is an interesting study, though it makes excessive claims for its subject's modernity.

[45] Str. MS. DJ III 3 is an autobiographical account of Hirnhaim's public activities; cf. above, p. 221. Hirnhaim drew up the first *Leges Bibliothecae Strahoviensis* (1671), ed. P. Kneidl (Pr. 1971). For Leopold: ÖNB, MS. 12757, fol. 57 (4 Feb. 1676), where the emperor says that *De Typho* is 'not bad'. In the Kirchberg library catalogue (ÖNB, MS. 14878, fols. 10ᵛ, 22ᵛ) there is an inspired miscopying of Agrippa's title: 'De incertitudine et *varietate* omnium *Senten*tiarum'.

*Fundamentalis,   Realis,   Christiana,   Catholica,   Selecta,   Anti-
Aristotelica.*[46]

★

Thus we have a thread of dissent. But, in intention at least, it was
usually a creative dissent. The larger instinct was a desire for the
synthesis of old and new. Let us follow it now into two areas of
crucial contemporary intellectual concern. The first is astronomy.
As everyone knows, cosmological speculation in much of Europe
was seriously affected by successive Roman condemnations of
Galileo and the Copernican system in 1616 and 1633; but we need
to keep the impact of these judgments in perspective[47] Besides its
own highly mythopoeic contribution, the Galileo-affair has fostered
two widespread legends about seventeenth-century astronomy:
firstly, that Catholic countries were forced to suspend cosmological
investigations; secondly, that everywhere a straight contest took
place henceforth between Ptolemaic reactionaries and Copernican
progressives. The truth is more subtle.

In Central Europe both practical and theoretical work continued.
Galileo even retained some unrepentant admirers: the truculent
Magni, not altogether surprisingly, still backed his views, while the
military architect Pieroni had plans for a German translation of the
Dialogo dei due massimi sistemi del mondo and actually enlisted the
help of Cardinal Dietrichstein.[48] But that is not the real point:
Magni thought the earth's rotation only probable; Pieroni was a
shadowy figure, not a true radical mind. More important, the new
discoveries engendered much Catholic analysis of celestial problems
which was unexceptionable and unexceptioned. In the 1640s
Caramuel and the Tyrolean Capuchin, Antonius Schyrl de Rheita,
debated the number of Jupiter's satellites, Caramuel and Marci the

---

[46] UK, MS. XIV G 21, written in 1661, with later additions evidently influenced
by the publication of Marci's *Philosophia Vetus Restituta* (cf. UK, loc. cit. fols. 8ᵛ–
11ʳ).

[47] T. S. Kuhn, *The Copernican Revolution* (Cambridge, Mass. 1957) is an intelligent
and intelligible general survey of a complex issue. It should be remembered that the
condemnations were specifically and crudely directed at a few crucial (and anyway
well-known) passages. Cf. Reusch, op. cit. ii, 394–400.

[48] J. Cygan, 'Das Verhältnis Valerian Magnis zu Galileo Galilei und seinen
wissenschaftlichen Ansichten', *Coll. Franc.* xxxviii (1968), 135–66, a somewhat
inconclusive article. On Pieroni: Galileo, *Opere*, i–xx (Florence 1890–1909), xvi,
188–90, 300 ff., 358–60, 393 f., 397 f., 419 f.; xviii, 268; cf. *Rudolf II*, 194 n. 3; and
above, p. 202.

relation between the motion of a pendulum and the earth's centre of gravity. Of course, it was easier to discuss some things than others: the incorruptibility of the heavens formed a far more dispensable piece of the Aristotelian scheme than the immobility of the earth. Yet little evidence exists that those who tended to criticize the former rather than the latter were anything but free agents; and we have every sign of genuine intellectual enthusiasm for the inquiry.[49]

The Jesuit order was especially active, its practical astronomy already a lively tradition in Central Europe by 1600, with Christoph Clavius from Bamberg, who settled at Rome and attracted the Tyrolean Grienberger (1564–1636) to join him. A series of important instrument-makers and observers followed, like Scheiner, known for his work on sunspots; Behm, Stansel, and Hartmann, who wrote on comets and planets; and others more concerned with ancillary questions of mathematics and mechanics, horology and optics. The quality of their technical competence is illustrated by a Prague manuscript based entirely on Jesuit authorities, as well as in more modest compilations, and the interest lasted into the eighteenth century, as the researches of Maximilian Hell (1720–92) demonstrate.[50] Moreover, it was never divorced from theories of the world-systems: J. B. Riccioli's massive *Almagest*, quite the largest cosmological treatise of the period, contains a long section on the Copernican hypothesis and Galileo's opinions. Standard courses of lectures, such as Hirnhaim's, seem also to have embraced this issue, albeit in much briefer compass.[51]

---

[49] J. Caramuel Lobkovic, *Novem Stellae circa Iovem, circa Saturnum sex, circa Martem non-nullae* (Louvain ?1643); id., *Perpendiculorum Inconstantia ... examinata et falsa reperta* (Louvain 1643), with a dedication to Bernard Ignác Martinic. J. M. Marci, *Otho-Sophia seu Philosophia Impulsûs Universalis*, op. posth. ed. J. J. W. Dobrzensky (Pr. 1683), 127 ff., with further reference to Martinic as intermediary and the opinions of Kinner *et al*. One instance of constraint may be Théodore Moretus, who seems to have argued for the immobility of the earth without complete conviction (Bosmans, art. cit. 98 f.).

[50] On these Jesuits, all born in the Habsburg lands except for Scheiner, who came from Mindelheim in Bavaria, see Sommervogel, s. vv. UK, MS. XII G 3: 'Gnomonice sive Horologiographia ex diversis ... Scriptoribus ... Operâ F. F. S.', a careful piece of work and well illustrated. Heiligenkreuz, MS. 470, is a typical monastic MS. Good 18th-century observatories were constructed by the Benedictines at Kremsmünster and the archbishop of Eger.

[51] J. B. Riccioli, *Almagestum Novum*, 1–11 (Bologna 1651) i, pt. 2, 290–500, including Galileo's recantation. Str., MS. DB VI 37, based on Hirnhaim's lectures, esp. pp. 35–7 (on Copernicus) and 147 ff. (appendix on instrument-making).

Perhaps the best-known textbook in the Habsburg lands was Kircher's *Itinerarium Exstaticum*, an epitome of Riccioli commissioned by Ferdinand III and first published at Rome in 1656, then reissued with commentaries from Kaspar Schott at Würzburg in 1660. While offering an orthodox general account of planetary science, Kircher and Schott stress its experimental base and the great body of recent discoveries about the heavens which have radically altered older notions.[52]

There was, then, an evident need to steer between the Scylla of an outmoded Ptolemy and the Charybdis of Copernicus (viewed as fact, rather than as idle hypothesis). Riccioli, Kircher, and the rest thought they had found a perfectly satisfactory compromise candidate: Tycho Brahe, who in the years around 1600 evolved a mixed system where sun and moon circle a stationary earth and the other planets circle the sun. Jesuits readily espoused the Tychonic system, with certain modifications (often they preferred one or two more planets to revolve around the earth); so did Caramuel, who while promising, as usual, 'multa contra veterem Philosophiam', really offered 'multa *Caramuelaeam* verae doctrinae *restitutionem* propugnantia' (my italics), and even sought to cling to the solidity of the heavenly spheres; so did thinkers throughout the *Reich*. From the Capuchin Schyrl came a thorough exposition, modelled on Tycho but including distinctly generous references to Copernicus too, all backed by his own observations and prefaced with an elaborate illustrated dedication to Ferdinand III.[53]

Schyrl's association of his book with the Habsburgs is no mere genuflection; the dynasty had long shown interest in astronomy. Of

[52] I have used the 2nd edn., entitled *Iter Extaticum Coeleste* (Würzburg 1660); see esp. 1–10 (Schott's dedication to the abbot of Fulda), 11–18 (Kircher's preface to the reader), 485 ff. (Schott's defence against certain critics). There was a 3rd edn. (Würzburg 1671), and two more followed in 18th-century Hungary.

[53] Ibid., esp. 36–9. Caramuel, *Novem Stellae*, ded. (quoted); id., *Mathesis Biceps*, 271–83, 415–86, 1389 ff.; cf. Hermann, *Sol Triplex*, 565 ff., for another defender of the spheres. See also, in general, D. Stimson, *The Gradual Acceptance of the Copernican Theory of the Universe* (2nd edn. New York 1971), 77 ff. (sketchy). Antonius Maria Schyrl de Rheita, *Oculus Enoch et Eliae sive Radius Sidereomysticus* (Antwerp 1645), esp. the interesting preface, which emphasizes how the Index has suppressed only a few passages of Copernicus, *donec corrigantur*; cf. G. Schott, *Technica Curiosa sive Mirabilia Artis*, i–ii (Würzburg 1664), i, 397 ff. Schyrl (also known as 'Rheita') is said (by Heimbucher, op. cit. i, 741) to have converted Christian August of Sulzbach.

course, its greatest protégé was Kepler, but that is to judge by the standards of a more distant posterity. Tycho had also been patronized by Rudolf II at Prague, where he died in 1601, and he was the right kind of figure for court consumption: an aristocratic cavalier, exiled from the Protestant north. His descendants remained in Central Europe during the seventeenth century, as did his instruments and manuscripts; it is not too important for our purposes that the former were largely engaged in securing a profitable sale of the latter.[54] From the 1640s Ferdinand III and Leopold supported a Jesuit, Albrecht Kurz, or Curtius, in his project to publish the great series of Tycho's observations of the heavens recorded between 1582 and 1601. Kurz was well suited to the task, being not only the brother of an imperial vice-chancellor and a Bavarian major-domo, but also a relative of the Rudolfine courtier who had done most to attract Brahe to Prague. His edition of the *Historia Coelestis* eventually appeared on a thousand folio pages at Augsburg in 1666, with full recognition of the stimulus given by the Habsburgs and Georg Martinic and reflections on the continuity of the Tychonic tradition. This work duly found its way into Leopold's private library; and we know that Ferdinand III sponsored other publications of a similar hue.[55] Some aspects of the case are not clear to me—why did Kurz always hide behind the pseudonym 'Lucius Barrettus' (a transparent anagram of 'Albertus Curtius')? On the other hand we possess one piece of information which very few contemporaries can have known: by a piquant turn of fate the original manuscript of Copernicus's *De Revolutionibus* lay all the time in the library of one of Bohemia's magnates.[56]

[54] On Tycho Brahe's life see, most recently, W. Norlind, *Tycho Brahe, en levnadsteckning* (Lund 1970), who offers no real reinterpretations. His heirs were the offspring of a somewhat devious son-in-law and bore the family name Gansneb Tengnagel vom Kamp.

[55] Tycho de Brahe, *Historia Coelestis* (Augsburg 1666, apparently reissued at Regensburg in 1672). This Georg Martinic (ibid., p. cxxiii) is presumably the elder brother of Bernard Ignác, acting chancellor of Bohemia during the 1640s, who died in 1651. Kurz seems to have published a trial run of his work at Vienna in 1657 (Mayer, op. cit. no. 1804, not in Sommervogel). On Kurz (1600–71) see the scattered information in Balbin, *Bohemia Docta*, i, bk. 2, 408 f.; Riccioli, op. cit. i, pt. 1, pp. xxix, xlv f.; Sommervogel, ii, cols. 1742–4; Norlind, op. cit. 320–2; Schmidt, *Pfalz-Neuburg*, 39 f., 42. Cf., on Jakob Kurz von Senftenau, *Rudolf II*, 71, 136. ÖNB, MS. 12590, p. 38, lists the *Historia Coelestis*; cf. HHStA, RHR, Misc., Bücherkommission im Reich, fasc. 2, 'konv. 5', fols. 70–3, 78 f.

[56] On the pseudonym, cf. below, n. 84. N. Copernicus, *Complete Works*, i (London–
(continued)

*

Thus astronomical views in the Habsburg lands were not merely benighted; they show how the Central European environment could adapt and accommodate novel ideas. It is worth pursuing this theme further, into the field of terrestrial science. Concern for measurement meant an interest in mathematics. Among members of the dynasty it is most pronounced with Ferdinand III. Having been forced into the unwelcome career of soldiering, which he abandoned at the earliest opportunity, Ferdinand began by studying military geometry—a popular subject at the Habsburg court—then turned to more general problems and drew up a set of exercises, even preparing an instrument (a kind of prototype slide-rule) to help solve them. The emperor's brain-child was edited for publication, first (pseudonymously) by Kurz, then by Schott.[57] Mathematical enquiry reached wider circles via imperial favourites such as Kinner and its partisans among the Jesuits, one of whom, the Belgian Grégoire de St. Vincent, proved the most gifted local exponent of the art. St. Vincent, like the emperor, was drawn into the theatre of war: during the Saxon invasion of Prague many of his manuscripts were destroyed. Fortunately enough could be rescued by his colleague Arriaga to allow publication of his huge *Opus Geometricum*, which included important theorems about circles and conic sections as well as a suitably intricate dedication to the dynasty.[58]

Undoubtedly mathematics became the serious pursuit of a learned élite which operated in an international framework. Links were provided with the Low Countries by such men as St. Vincent and the mobile Belgian Jesuit, Théodore Moretus; with Germany by Caspar Ens, Schott, and the equally mobile Polish Jesuit, Adam

Warsaw–Cracow 1972) is a facsimile of this MS., which once belonged to Comenius, then passed to the younger Otto von Nostitz, and remained the *pièce de résistance* of the Nostitz Library in Prague for nearly 300 years.

[57] G. Schott, *Mathesis Caesarea sive Amussis Ferdinandea* (Würzburg 1662), esp. the preface; Kurz's edn. appeared at Munich in 1651. The Viennese interest in military architecture is evidenced by copies of MSS. by Joseph Furtenbach (1591–1667): ÖNB, MSS. 10834, 10842, 10847–8, 10884–5, 10918, 10960, 11026; cf. MS. 11015.

[58] G. de St. Vincent, *Opus Geometricum Quadraturae Circuli* (Antwerp 1647). On the author see H. Bosmans in *Biographie Nationale ... de Belgique*, xxi (1911), cols. 141–71. Sommervogel and others perpetuate the myth that St. Vincent (1584–1667) was seriously wounded in Prague during the *Swedish* siege: by that time he had long returned to Belgium.

Kochański. Becher looked still further afield and presented his work on exact timekeeping to the Royal Society of London in 1680. Even standard monastic treatises refer to French textbooks.[59] But no decisive move ensued to enthrone quantity in the place of existing qualitative assumptions. The most debated part of St. Vincent's tome was its culminating section, a vain claim to have finally solved the age-old riddle of how to square the circle. Moreover, this riddle is actually described as *the* 'problema Austriacum', both by St. Vincent and by his friend Kinner, who (with the approval of Caramuel, Marci, and others) issued a simplified version of one of his proofs at Prague in the 1650s.[60] Now it was still perfectly reasonable for contemporaries to discuss the possibility of quadrature—like the philosophers' stone, no one could yet demonstrate it to be a phantasm. But the Austrian obsession with it begins to look old-fashioned; more important, it goes with an attachment to mathematics as a learned amusement, a game of fancy rather than an iron discipline. Kircher, Schott, and Kinner devised for the dynasty a species of calculating machine with keyboard (or tabulator) to simplify the operations of arithmetic and geometry, fortification and astronomy, and much else besides. Though no doubt an ingenious project, it owed more to an environment of courtly diversion, backed by a belief in some pristine harmony of knowledge, than to the spirit of Barrow and Newton, or even of Leibniz.[61]

Another fascinating issue, even more central, where we can

---

[59] On Moretus (1602–67): Bosmans, 'Moretus'; G. Schott, *Cursus Mathematicus* (Würzburg 1661), with ded. to Leopold. Adam Kochański (1631–1700) was born in Poland, taught at Bamberg, Würzburg, and Mainz, and also in Bohemia, where he died. J. J. Becher, *Theoria et Experientia de nova Temporis Dimetiendi Ratione …* (London 1680). Heiligenkreuz, MS. 470, pp. 175 f. and *passim*, using the *Cursus seu Mundus Mathematicus* of Claude François Milliet de Chales (Lyons 1674).

[60] G. A. Kinner, *Elucidatio Geometrica Problematis Austriaci sive Quadraturae Circuli* (Pr. 1653, colophon says '1654'). Cf. J. M. Marci, *Labyrinthus in quo via ad circuli quadraturam plurimis modis exhibetur* (Pr. 1654); and other Central European examples in Schott, *Technica Curiosa*, ii, bk. 8.

[61] G. Schott, *Organum Mathematicum libris IX explicatum* (Würzburg 1668), esp. the dedication (to Johann Kaspar Ampringen) and preface; cf. A. Kircher, *Specula Melitensis encyclica* (Naples 1638), reprinted in Schott, *Technica Curiosa*, i, 427–77. Western Europeans interested in quadrature included Henry Oldenburg, who sought a copy of Kinner's book in 1668 (R. M. and M. B. Hall (eds.), op. cit. iv, no. 891); but St. Vincent's claims were disputed by Descartes and Mersenne, Huygens and Leibniz.

observe Central Europeans wavering between old and new, trying to espouse the latter in order to confirm the former, is the empirical approach to knowledge. As with astronomy, so with natural philosophy as a whole, thinkers from the Habsburg lands were not behindhand in asserting the authority of the senses. Observation of the heavens could be paralleled by close study of nature. Kircher's *Itinerarium Exstaticum* formed the prelude to a much larger book called *Mundus Subterraneus*, very celebrated in his lifetime, an account of geology which possesses some genuine originality and claims to be founded on experience, both the author's own and that of his helpers. These range from fellow-Jesuits to emperors, through the elector of Mainz and Friedrich of Hesse-Darmstadt, Archbishop Lippay and Bernard Ignác Martinic. When Becher took up the same subject, he claimed to be more practical still, incorporating schemes to derive useful minerals from the mud of the Danube, and so forth.[62] Similar concerns exercised local physicians and clergy who went around collecting evidence of natural phenomena. Some of it was published in the proceedings of the *Academia Naturae Curiosorum*; some provided scope for disputes at home, like that between two Moravian doctors, J. F. Hertodt and Wenceslaus Ardensbach, who argued heatedly about the properties of the flora and minerals in their province.[63]

At the same time both astronomy and physics called for the testing of hypotheses and the construction of new instruments with which to conduct experiments. Two particular areas of investigation found favour in Central Europe. The first was optics, continuing the work of Kepler and of Scheiner, whose *Oculus*, printed at Innsbruck in 1619 with a dedication to Ferdinand II, discusses both theoretical and practical aspects of vision. The properties of light

[62] A. Kircher, *Mundus Subterraneus*, i–ii (Amsterdam 1665), esp. the two prefaces. J. J. Becher, *Physica Subterranea* (2nd edn. Frankfurt 1681, first published ibid. 1669); id., *Experimentum novum ac curiosum de Minera Arenaria Perpetua* (Frankfurt 1680); cf. H. von Srbik, 'Abenteurer am Hofe Kaiser Leopold I', *Archiv für Kulturgeschichte*, viii (1910), 52–72, at 67 f. See also the evaluation of these works by Thorndike, op. cit. vii, 567–83.

[63] J. F. Hertodt, *Tartaro-Mastix Moraviae* (V. 1669); id., *Opus Mirificum*; id., *Crocologia seu curiosa croci regis vegetabilium enucleatio* (Jena 1671); W. M. Ardensbach von Ardensdorff, *Tartaro Clypeus, excipiens Tartaro Mastigem* (etc.) *Hertodianum* (Pr. 1671). The latter—a pupil of Marci and assiduous reader of Kircher—appears to prevail, especially since he makes some use of Western sources (Harvey, Boyle, Willis, Nathaniel Highmore, Swammerdam, etc.).

fascinated Marci, and his *Thaumantias* of 1648 contains notable new observations on the spectrum; after Marci's death a Styrian Jesuit took up similar themes.[64] In optics too the largest compendium came from the pen of Kircher—once again at the instigation of Ferdinand III. Kircher's *Ars Magna Lucis et Umbrae* tells us much about colour, lenses and mirrors, the construction and application of telescopes and magic lanterns (of which he has some right to be called the inventor). Its decidedly practical flavour is confirmed elsewhere in Kircher's *œuvre*: witness the beautiful illustrations of what a microscope reveals, reproduced in the posthumous guide to his museum; it was passed on to students like Jan Rakolupský of Szakolca, whose careful manuscript handbook of optics draws on Kircher, Schott, Scheiner, and other Jesuit writers.[65]

One of the classic seventeenth-century problems, atmospheric pressure, was likewise widely debated in Central Europe. During the 1640s Magni became a leading demonstrator of the possibility of a vacuum, and he revelled in the resultant controversy; his novel experiments, along with those of Guericke, Boyle, Torricelli, and Maignan, were fully reported there. Schott wholly gave over the early books of his *Technica Curiosa* to an approving discussion of their conclusions.[66] Similar ingenuity was devoted to hydraulics, especially by Dobrzensky, who wrote a treatise on the properties of water, illustrating the kinds of machine which could be used to harness them. Further elaborate mechanisms employing water-

[64] J. M. Marci, *Thaumantias Liber de Arcu coelesti* (Pr. 1648, reissued, ed. J. Marek, ibid. 1968); Zacharias Traber, *Nervus Opticus* (V. 1675). Cf. also S. Hartmann, *Catoptrica illustrata propositionibus Physico-mathematicis* (Pr. 1668).

[65] A. Kircher, *Ars Magna Lucis et Umbrae* (Rome 1646), with a dedication to the 'rising sun' of Archduke Ferdinand (IV), and a preface describing the emperor's part in the project. Excerpts from this work in J. S. Kestler, *Physiologia Kircheriana Experimentalis* (Amsterdam 1680), bk. 3. For the microscope: Philip Bonanni, *Musaeum Kircherianum* (Rome 1709), sect. 11. Rakolupský: Str., MS. DS V 19, written in the 1660s, with careful drawings, and based on a range of printed sources. Cf., for more optical constructions, Schott, *Technica Curiosa*, ii, bk. 11.

[66] V. Magni, *Admiranda de vacuo et Aristotelis philosophia* (Warsaw 1647); id., *Philosophiae pars prima* (Warsaw 1648); id., *Vacuum pleno suppletum* (V. 1650). Schott, *Technica Curiosa*, i, bks. 1–4; cf. id., *Mechanica Hydraulico-Pneumatica* (Würzburg 1657); Caramuel, *Rationalis et realis Philosophia*, 442–9; J. J. W. Dobrzensky, *Nova et Amaenior de admirando fontium genio* ... *Philosophia* (Ferrara 1659), 26 ff. Even Hermann (*Sol Triplex*, 504–7) was ready to be persuaded; cf. Marci, *Philosophia Vetus Restituta*, 208–22; UK, MS. XIV G 21, pp. 192–5; F. S. Schott, op. cit. 31.

power adorn the pages of Kircher, Schott, and other Jesuit investigators of nature, and some of them were no doubt actually constructed in order to probe the secrets of the visible world. The magnificent contrivances described by the German inventor, Georg Andreas Böckler, enjoyed widespread fame throughout the Empire, and one of them was consulted in manuscript by Leopold I.[67]

How far were these scientists genuinely scientific? How far, in other words, were they aware of the conditions necessary for controlled physical experiment? Kircher's protestation at the beginning of his *Magnes* may stand for the attitude of many of his contemporaries: "I have introduced nothing, however small, into this book which could not be, so far as lies within my power, personally tested and established (propriis experimentis comprobatum, stabilitumque)". The *Magnes* indeed offers (as its author also claims) a marriage of theory with practice, and—despite criticizing Gilbert and Kepler—it has serious insights into the working of magnetism.[68] One of Kircher's fellow-Jesuits went further: Francesco Lana-Terzi, from Brescia in northern Italy, compiled a massive three-volume survey of physical demonstrations and machines, some invented by himself, among them a visionary project for an airship as well as more standard thermometers and microscopes. He also published an introductory *Prodromo*, dedicated—like the main work—to Leopold, whose preface issues a real manifesto of the new philosophy, the more forcible for being written in Italian, not Latin. It is always wrong (Lana-Terzi assures his readers) to build on speculation and universal axioms instead of 'isperienze certe, ed accuratamente fatte', to follow authority or

[67] Dobrzensky, op. cit.; his book first appeared at Ferrara in 1657. Bonanni, op. cit. sect. 9; G. Schott, *Technica Curiosa*, i, bk. 5; cf. id., *Anatomia Physico-Hydrostatica Fontium* (Würzburg 1663). G. A. Böckler, *Theatrum Machinarum Novum* (Cologne 1662, and Ger. trans. Nuremberg 1673), takes much from his Renaissance predecessors Ramelli and Rudolf II's antiquary Strada. His 'Machina Universalis', listed as belonging to the emperor in ÖNB, MS. 12590, p. 87, is presumably the present ÖNB, MS. 10993: 'Machina universalis, Das ist eine neu erfundene ... anrichtung eines mechanischen Wercks, das man ... zu unzehlig vielen ... Sachen ... gebrauchen kan'.

[68] A. Kircher, *Magnes sive De Arte Magnetica* (3rd edn. Rome 1654), esp. reverse of title-page and preface to reader: 'Ego Artem trado Magneticam, eamque ita quidem pertracto, ut in ea tamen nec praxin Theoria, nec Theoriam praxis unquam destituat...'; ibid. 383 ff. on Gilbert and Kepler. Cf., for a positive view of this work, E. Benz, 'Theologie der Elektrizität', *Mainz, Akademie der Wissenschaft und der Literatur, Geistes- und Sozialwissenschaftliche Klasse*, 1970, no. 12.

popular appeal instead of induction; learning must be reformed so that it serves common human needs.[69]

Here again, however, the overall mood of Habsburg intellectuals, even of Lana-Terzi himself, was much less radical than these sentiments might suggest. The mood is well mirrored in the rag-bag writings of Schott, with their boundless curiosity and lack of discrimination, their privileged and comfortable world of garrulous clerical erudition. A practical bent certainly existed—Caramuel, amid all his other activites, managed to practise as an architect[70]—but it grew less, rather than more pronounced as time went on, and it does not appear to have involved contact with any true artisanate; a courtly, not an urban milieu defined it: the isolated and playful circles of imperial patronage. Just as mathematics could be put to work in arithmetical toys for Ferdinand III and his sons, so the highest purpose of mechanics might be found in stagecraft for the Hofburg theatre, of hydraulics in water-machines for the palace gardens. Significantly physics provided its own equivalent to quadrature of the circle, its own (as it were) archduke's head: the quest for perpetual motion, a pursuit not so much disreputable as definitely unprofitable. *Perpetuum mobiles* were continually discussed and described by Kircher, Schott, Dobrzensky, Becher, and their fellows, their causative principle related sometimes to magnetism, sometimes to atmospheric variation, sometimes to water-power. Lana-Terzi also devoted his best energies to demonstrating them.[71]

Thus empiricism had its proper, but subordinate place in the philosophical priorities of Central Europe. Experiment served ultimately to prove old assumptions; it was part of a preconceived harmony of knowledge. That may help us understand why music, the embodiment of practical and theoretical harmony, played such

---

[69] F. Lana [-Terzi], *Prodromo overo saggio di alcune inventioni nuove* ... (Brescia 1670), 1–17, stressing how few there are who 's'impieghino nelle lettere per esercitar il lume dell'intelletto ottenuto da Dio a fine di giovare al genere humano'. The main work, *Magisterium Naturae et Artis*, i–iii (Brescia—Parma 1684–92), received long and flattering reviews in Germany (*Acta Eruditorum*, 1685, 31–7; 1688, 35–9; 1693, 145–50). Lana-Terzi's other writings are listed in Sommervogel, s.v.

[70] D. de B. Ferrero, 'Il Conte Ivan Caramuel di Lobkowitz.., architetto e teorico dell'architettura', *Palladio* N.S. xv (1965), 91–110.

[71] Kircher, *Magnes*, 238 ff.; Schott, *Technica Curiosa*, i, bk. 6; ii, bk. 10; Dobrzensky, op. cit. 113–20; Becher, *De nova Temporis Dimetiendi Ratione, passim*; cf. R. M. and M. B. Hall (eds.), op. cit. i, nos. 87, 97, 108–9, 112, 119, 223. Lana-Terzi, *Prodromo*, chs. 9–14, and much more in his *Magisterium*.

a great role in the seventeenth-century Austrian Baroque. The achievements of composers and performers were underpinned with deeper reflections on the purpose of the art. The first full musical lexicon appeared at Prague in 1701. Kircher devoted perhaps the best of all his monumental treatises to the science of music, and he counted as an international expert both on its actual techniques and on its metaphysical foundations.[72] It is hardly an accident that Habsburg scholars were so interested in constructing an 'organum', which might be just the king of musical instruments—Dobrzensky devised one for Leopold at Prague in 1668—and might also carry the connotation, familiar to generations of schoolmen, of a logical or mathematical key to the universe. Not for nothing does the peroration to Kircher's *Musurgia* describe the entire world as an organ played by the Creator.[73]

★

Although the instruments might be new, the tunes were old. New, potentially disruptive forces were held within a traditional intellectual matrix: a mental stance by no means entirely inflexible, but embattled. Having established that, we are in a position to address the crucial problem of this Baroque world-view: its occultism. While natural philosophy clearly represented the most exposed flank of existing Catholic orthodoxy, contemporaries could turn to a defence already elaborated during the later Renaissance. As I have tried to explain elsewhere, tension between received authorities and advancing knowledge is an important root of sixteenth-century magic, and the combination of realism and irrationality formed an essential element in Mannerism.[74] Now the terms were reformulated

---

[72] T. B. Janovka, *Clavis ad Thesaurum magnae artis musicae* (Pr. 1701). A. Kircher, *Musurgia Universalis sive Ars Magna Consoni et Dissoni*, i–ii (Rome 1650), with dedication to Archduke Leopold Wilhelm. An epitome of this work, by one Andreas Hirsch, was published as *Kircherus ... Germaniae redonatus ... Das ist Philosophischer Extract und Auszug ...* (Schwäbisch Hall 1662); and extracts from it appeared in German and English translation. U. Scharlau, *Athanasius Kircher als Musikschriftsteller* (Marburg 1969), is detailed and technical. Cf. briefly above, p. 153 for practising musicians; but that subject lies outside the purview of this book.

[73] Dobrzensky: ÖNB, MS. 10051: 'Philomela Veris Quaerens non iam rivulos, sed mare Gratiarum Desideransq. suaviter sub umbra Vel alarum, vel Aquilarum suarum Augustissime Caesar Leopolde sedere: seu Vocale Organum ...' Cf. Schott, *Organum Mathematicum*; Kircher, *Musurgia*, bk. 10, repeated in Hirsch, op. cit., bk. 6.

[74] *Rudolf II*, ch. 7; cf. above, pp. 33–6.

for the Counter-Reformation context: intellectually more vulnerable, emotionally and spiritually more stable; Mannerism heightened into the paradox and mystery of Baroque. Against such a
background learning could actually be designed to demonstrate
wonders, the occult invoked as a form of quasi-scientific explanation.
  This process was not always conscious, but Kircher lets slip the
premise when he tells us that his treatise on astronomy will show
"how the fabric of the world is constituted according to principles
far more recondite than either the simple minds of former ages or
the vulgar philosophers of our own time have persuaded themselves". Schott is equally explicit in his first major work, *Magia
Universalis Naturae et Artis*, which treats 'universal magic' as a
dimension of all other branches of knowledge, as man's contact
with the underlying divine wisdom. Indeed, Schott's whole *œuvre*
offers the best introduction to this literature of secrets and mysteries,
whose title-pages and chapter-headings throb with the promise of
hidden intellectual treasure: of *mirabilia, curiosa, abdita, arcana,
rara, recondita, prodigiosa, exotica* . . .[75] The same enthusiasms appear
in the proceedings of the *Academia Naturae Curiosorum*; in the
work of Bohemians like Hertodt and above all Balbín, ever on the
look-out for curiosities of nature with a patriotic flavour; in
Hungarian compendia of wonders surviving through Szentiványi
and beyond: a typical late product is Antonius Gabon's *Physica
Exotica* of 1717 which, setting its face against the sceptic, appeals to
the 'ardens ad arcanissima quaeque ingenium'.[76] The mood was
easily coloured with mysticism: Schyrl's astronomy aimed to help
our minds rise to contemplation of God; Caramuel developed
analogies between Mother Church and the order of the heavens,
nature, and the elements; visionary inspirations guided some of the

---

[75] Kircher, *Iter Extaticum*, 15. G. Schott, *Magia Universalis* . . ., i–iv (Würzburg
1657–9), with a 2nd edn. at Bamberg 1674–7; id., *Physica Curiosa sive Mirabilia
Naturae et Artis* (Würzburg 1662), with an expanded edn. ibid. 1667, reissued in
1697. These works were designed, with the *Technica Curiosa*, to form a trilogy; cf.
Mercier, *Notice raisonné*, 6–34, 36–49, 51–63.
[76] A. Gabon, *Physica Exotica sive Secreta naturae et artis* (Tyrnau 1717), intro.: a
text based on Kircher, with mentions of Schott, Porta, Paracelsus, Ca:dano,
Agrippa, Mizauld, and others. Cf., for a further example, A. Felker, *Arcana naturae
et artis* (Kassa 1734–5). On the genre in general see Thorndike, op. cit. vii, ch. 21;
viii, ch. 31.

work of Kircher and Magni; Hirnhaim laid sceptical stress on the ineffability of natural mysteries.[77]

All this amounted to renewed apostrophe of a vitalist universe with its hidden correspondences and sympathies. Of course, many Europeans took symbols seriously in the seventeenth century (though their great age was drawing to its close); educated men everywhere were frequently credulous. Spain, in particular, was not markedly different from the *Reich*, as the career there of the German Jesuit Nieremberg indicates.[78] But Catholic Central European philosophy presents us with a pervasive habit of mind which invested even commonplace phenomena with 'magical' workings: a mentality standard enough among Aristotelians, still more standard among the Platonists and syncretists who went beyond Aristotle. It is almost as though its proponents were making a plea (reasoned enough, in its anti-rational way) for *nebulous* and *indistinct* ideas, by contrast with the revolutionary slogan of Cartesianism—a contrast the more pointed if we recall that Descartes claimed to have discovered his new method while a mercenary wandering through the Habsburg lands in the precise years around 1620 when they were made safe for Catholicism.[79]

Thus far, occult philosophy yielded an admirable establishment creed, for it seemed to confirm both Catholic truth and social order. Learning must not conflict with dogma, but room existed for interplay between the two. While natural magic demonstrated grounds for the miraculous and mysterious aspects of belief, Catholic doctrine offered scope for the activities of the natural magicians. How different was the rigid disapproval by official

[77] Schyrl, op. cit., pt. 2; J. Caramuel Lobkovic, *De Ecclesiae Romanae Hierarchia* (Pr. 1653), pref. and 17–35; Kircher, *Iter Extaticum*, 4 f.; Hirnhaim, *De Typho*, *passim*.

[78] Nieremberg (1595–1658) was born in Madrid of south-German parents. Sommervogel, v, cols. 1725–66, lists over fifty books by him; some appeared in several languages, including Czech (*Knihopis*, nos. 6188–91), and they were republished as far afield as Hungary (*RMK* ii, no. 1020). Among the best known were his *Curiosa y occulta philosophia*; and the *Historia Naturae* (Antwerp 1635), which was read by Leopold (ÖNB, MS. 8011, fol. 101ʳ). Austro-Spanish cultural relations in this period are—so far as I know—largely untrodden terrain. Another interesting case would be Caramuel, some of whose works, even late in his life, were written in Spanish.

[79] Descartes, *Discours de la méthode*, esp. pt. 2. The episode when he fell into a trance while seated by the stove of an overheated room seems to have taken place in 1619 at Neuburg, home of the newly-converted palsgraves.

Calvinism of all meddling with the supernatural! How evidently do the German Lutherans, here as elsewhere, occupy a middle position, with their vogue for *mirabilia* and sympathetic cures.[80] Undoubtedly Catholic advocates of the occult thought themselves to combine unconstrained curiosity with total orthodoxy. Kircher interprets some crosses found on people's clothes after an eruption of Vesuvius as prodigies of the Almighty, the fall of the walls of Jericho as an instance of 'musical magic'; Balbín recounts many stories of beneficial supernatural agencies—uncorrupted corpses and the like; the *Academia Naturae Curiosorum* prints descriptions of 'rarities of nature': the name of Christ incised in a stone or an image of the Virgin in a mineral, and thanks Emperor Leopold for sending them[81] Both Schott and Szentiványi edified their fascination with letter-mysticism by compiling long sets of bizarre anagrams on the *Ave Maria*; Szentiványi (characteristically) managed to cobble together one for each day of the year.[82]

At the same time this was erudition which sought to conform as well as confirm. That lay in the nature of its patronage; but it went deeper. There is a mystic strain in the symbolic forms of Habsburg culture, displayed in repeated dedications and frontispieces which liken the imperial dynasty—from a sense, not of idle simile, but of some real correspondence—to the sun, the magnet, the fount of harmony, the prime mover.[83] Moreover, the whole endeavour played itself out in a closed fraternity, esoteric and exclusive, studying things 'a vulgi captu aliena', an admiring coterie of

[80] Cf. below, esp. pp. 373, 385, 389 f.

[81] A. Kircher, *Diatribe de prodigiosis Crucibus* (Rome 1661), with dedication to Archduke Leopold Wilhelm, reprinted in Schott, *Joco-Seria* (below, n. 84), 313–63; Kircher, *Musurgia*, ii, 231 f; Balbín, *Miscellanea Historica*, i, bk. 3, 168 ff. *passim*; *Miscellanea Curiosa Medico-Physica Academiae Naturae Curiosorum*, i (1670), 261 ff. and *passim*.

[82] Schott, *Mathesis Caesarea*, filling up the last pages; Szentiványi, *Curiosiora . . . Miscellanea*, i, pt. 2, 27–37. In both cases the text used: 'Ave Maria, gratia plena, Dominus tecum', yields such pearls as 'Te puram sine macula genitam adoravi'. Examples of similar anagrams, chronosticha, and so on, are legion. Cf. below, p. 351 and n. 15.

[83] Kircher, *Magnes*, dedication: 'Quicquid demum in abditis politici mundi arcanis, solis Regibus notis, conditum est: id totum magnes in se, veluti in divinae cuiusdam ideae architypo, uti ex totius huius praesentis Operis decursu patet, implicitum tenet; Regiae prorsus mentis symbolum, virtutum heroicarum in magnis hominibus elucescentium norma vera, amussis omnis fallaciae expers . . .' Cf. Kircher, *Ars Magna Lucis et Umbrae*, ded.; Lana-Terzi, *Prodromo*, ded.; J. M. Marci, *De Proportione Motus* (Pr. 1639), ded.; ÖNB, MS. 10051, fol. 1.

initiates, protected by courts and aristocrats. Emphasis lay always
on the passive, contemplative side of life, the philosophy of
acceptance. Even when concerned with 'operative magic', practitioners tended to remain playful and allusive, as in the *Jocoseria
Naturae et Artis*, a collection of tricks and improbable effects issued
by Schott under another of those punning Jesuit pseudonyms whose
significance (though an open secret to contemporaries) seems lost
on us.[84]

*

Yet not all magic was either Christian or licit. The occult also posed
an immense threat both to Catholic truth and to the Catholic social
order. As everyone recognized, there existed another sort of magic:
the black magic of superstition, drawing on the hidden powers, not
of God, but of the devil. The whole system was potentially steeped
in demonology. Equally evidently there existed a vast mass of the
common population, easily attracted into active pursuit of the
supernatural. The operative magic of the unprivileged had immediate practical implications: wizardry and divination, witchcraft
and sorcery. The ordinary man's need to satisfy his physical wants
by occult means was a far cry from the reflective arcana of the well-
to-do.

The enormous challenge from this paganism was felt by all
Churches: at a local level it absorbed a large part of their energies
during the sixteenth and seventeenth centuries. Recent literature
emphasizes the similarity of response on the part of Catholic and
Protestant reformers alike to deep-rooted survivals of pre-Christian
attitudes, and their parallel attempts to impose a new morality and
culture, especially in the countryside.[85] Yet there were also major

---

[84] Schott, *Magia Universalis*, i, sig. †††††† 1–4; cf. his statement (ibid. i, 57) that
the magical part of optics is that 'quae ... quidquid in scientia illa universa rarum,
reconditum, prodigiosum, ac paradoxum est, atque à communi Opticorum sensu ac
usu remotum, rimatur, atque ad aliorum utilitatem, liquidissimamque voluptatem,
Principum praesertim et Magnatum, producit in medium, non sine intuentium
admiratione ac stupore'. *Joco-Seriorum Naturae et Artis sive Magiae Naturalis
centuriae tres*, issued, without place or date of publication (in fact Würzburg or
Nuremberg 1666), under the name of 'Aspasius Caramuelius'. It is transparently a
work of Schott's (cf. Mercier, *Notice raisonné*, 70–5), and even features in a list (at
the end of *Mathesis Caesarea*) of his books soon to be printed. Leopold had a MS.
copy of it (ÖNB, MS. 12590, p. 87). But the reason for the pseudonym—as for
Kurz's (above, p. 333)—escapes me, unless it be some parody of Caramuel Lobkovic.
[85] Cf. above, p. 140 and n. 62.

differences between faiths, quite apart from the distinctive features of a Central European evolution where Catholicism reasserted itself slowly and belatedly against particularized religious communities and amid constant pressure from local heresy. At a profounder level the Catholic Church was different precisely because it built on the miraculous and the sacramental, and laid such weight on the supernatural. Having harnessed white magic in the cause of holiness, the Counter-Reformation required a clear definition of black magic and a fierce campaign against it.

That definition was, in the nature of things, impossible—since the phenomena which it sought to define existed merely as mental constructs, blended of learned and popular credulity; but the quest for it was vital to the success of seventeenth-century Catholicism. And not only of Catholicism, for the definition had social as well as spiritual reference: most magic was permitted to the educated, proscribed for the uneducated. Thus the outcome was fruitful to state as well as Church: while the compromise with white magic allowed an élite to maintain its integral Catholic *Weltanschauung*, the attack on superstition enforced hierarchy and subordination. One face of Janus was the servant of the political nation, the other dictated to society at large. As the next two chapters will seek to show, the intellectual synthesis of Central Europe's Counter-Reformation needed to approve magic; its social actualization needed to condemn it.

CHAPTER 10

The compromise with
educated magic

In the days of Maximilian II and Rudolf the Central European intellectual had speculated much as he pleased. Counter-Reformation, provided he accepted its political, social, and doctrinal rules, made surprisingly little difference to that freedom. The new apparatus of Catholic authority, engaged in a day-to-day war against superstition, failed to pronounce on the awkward question of occultism as such. The Council of Trent, so explicit in matters of organization and discipline, offered hardly any philosophical clarification. The Roman Index concerned itself in the first instance with tangible Protestant heresy, and banned its magicians accordingly; though later it notoriously widened its scope, it did not inquire into the niceties of academic debate quite as often as critics are apt to suggest. Nor did the Inquisition, which was in fact barely used to harry reputable scholars who showed the necessary modicum of respect for it, a few grievous exceptions notwithstanding. More important, where Papal positions lacked precision, Habsburg ones were even less clear-cut. The Tridentine decrees had no measurable official backing; while (by contrast with Spain) no separate Index was even printed during the seventeenth century, let alone observed.[1] Thus authors denounced at Rome, who included Magni and Hirnhaim, were not automatically prohibited in Austria, and we find very little sign of the Inquisition beyond the Alps. No doubt the censorship—severe enough *vis-à-vis* the population at large— took a hand on occasion, but it operated more through the play of personalities than by any consistent implementation of policy, and it could be moulded correspondingly, as Lambeck, Lamberg, and

[1] On Trent: above, pp. 59 f. On the Inquisition: Caesar Carena, *Tractatus de Officio Sanctissimae Inquisitionis et modo procedendi in causis fidei* (Cremona 1641), policy; and below, esp. pp. 381, 406, for the practice. On the Index: Reusch, op. cit. i, 344–6, 543 f.; ii, 63–5. The Roman Index was printed at Prague in 1596 and again in 1726. Not until 1729 did Antonín Koniáš (on whom see A. Podlaha in *SbHKr* ii (1893), 3–48) belatedly produce a list of prohibited works tailored to local Bohemian conditions.

Kinský intervened to rescue Balbín's *Epitome* during the 1670s.[2]
None the less magic *was* magic, a word suspect to Christian
opinion since the time of Simon Magus, and serious explorers of the
art felt exposed: the very fact that no line separated mild
mystification or innocent wonderment from thoroughly nefarious
studies rendered them vulnerable. So they covered themselves with
fulsome, and sincere, protestations of orthodoxy. For Marci any
view which offends Mother Church is to be deemed 'unsaid and
revoked'; Schott apologizes if his scholarly moderation should seem
to condone 'superstitious, impious, or delirious things'. Other
authors submit their work, in a more or less standard formula, to
the better judgment of the Holy Catholic Church.[3] Of course, the
more disclaimers are employed, the more evidently is the ground
felt to be dangerous; which did not keep educated men from
traversing it, usually with impunity. They certainly had no shortage
of suggestive reading, and many of those we shall encounter in the
next chapter fulminating against popular superstition show an
uncanny familiarity with its character and devotees.[4]

Whether banned by the Index or not, books of most of the great
European magicians were readily available: Agrippa and Paracelsus,
Khunrath, Fludd, Maier, and the rest.[5] General Montecuccoli

[2] Reusch, op. cit. ii, 289 (Magni), 416 (Hirnhaim); even Caramuel seems to have
had certain difficulties in Rome, though only because of his moral writings (ibid.
501 f.). On the Balbin case, see above, p. 104 and n. 60, pp. 230 f. Str. MS. DJ III 3,
fols. 477–85, contains a censure of Hirnhaim's *De Typho* by the University of
Louvain on the grounds of its scepticism, anti-Aristotelianism, and vain curiosity
(influenced even by English models) in matters physical and chymical, together
with the author's defence of his positions, both dated 1679.

[3] Marci, *Philosophia Vetus Restituta*, sig. **2ʳ. The passage is worth quoting
further: 'Ex hac hypothesi [about generation] atque his quae in libro idearum pro
fundamento assumpsi [cf. above, p. 323], omnia naturae arcana, occultas rerum vires
et agendi modos, sympathias et antipathias, coelestes influxus, totiusque magiae
naturalis rationem, atque infinitas in rebus chimicis perplexitates summa facilitate
assequi licebit: quae via vulgari impervia sunt. Haec tamen uti reliqua omnia ex his
quacunque ratione collecta eousque valere volo, dum nihil ex his S. Matris Ecclesiae
sensum offendit. Quòd si quid tale praeter mentem mihi excidisset, pro non dicto et
à me revocato habeo ...'. Schott, *Magia Universalis, prooemium*; Kircher, *Oedipus
Aegyptiacus* (full title below, p. 435, n. 41), ii, 3 f.; UK, MS. VI F 9, intro. and
fol. 5; UK, MS. XIV G 21, fols. 336, 440.

[4] The Jesuit Benedictus Pereira actually recommends this course: *De Magia, de
observatione somniorum et de divinatione astrologica* (Cologne 1598, 1st edn. Ingolstadt
1591), 97–101.

[5] The authors mentioned were all—except apparently Khunrath—on the Index
in respect of some works at least (Reusch, op. cit. i, 121, 497; ii, 177 f.). Austrian and

(continued)

apparently knew Robert Fludd's writings almost by heart; Leopold
I possessed such prohibited works as Guillaume Postel's *Cosmographia*. Count Sternberg's library mixed down-to-earth texts on
military engineering with highly arcane treatises; so did that of the
Habsburg servant, Friedrich Hirsch. Lists of contemporary magical
literature, one of them prepared by Lambeck for the emperor,
reveal the volume of material published during the 1660s and 1670s
and its availability in Central Europe.[6]

★

Let us therefore consider some of the markedly speculative areas
ventured into by Habsburg thinkers. We may begin with astrology,
a fundamental component in the philosophy of an internally related
cosmos. Belief in the influences of heavenly bodies involved belief
in the predictability of earthly events. Now prediction—for reasons
which I shall examine later—was gravely mistrusted by official
Catholicism in the seventeenth century. Despite this, some of its
scholars displayed a zealous attachment to portions of the astrological
heritage. 'Provided it remains within limits', says Schott, 'and does
not assault the citadel of free will, then it is praiseworthy.'[7] But how
was free will to be defended? That riddle never found a proper
answer. Still, it was fairly common ground among the educated that
natural astrology could be distinguished from judicial; whereas the
latter meant the superstitious determination of horoscopes, the
former sought only to understand a divine plan, God working
through His created effects.

German bishops had general powers to dispense from its prohibitions (ibid. i,
186 f.); I do not know how far those powers were appealed to in practice.
  [6] E. Vehse, *Memoirs of the Court, Aristocracy and Diplomacy of Austria*, tr. F.
Demmler, i–ii (London 1856), i, 487, for Montecuccoli; cf., on the general's overall
reading: R. Montecuccoli, *Ausgewählte Schriften*, ed. I. Veltzé, i–iv (V. 1899–1900),
I, 113 ff. His immediate predecessor as president of the War Council, Gonzaga, is
said to have protected a priest-magician called Palemon (Wiedemann, *Reformation*,
v, 112); while the Hungarian general, Miklós Bercsényi, seems to have collected
similar books (K. Thaly in *MKSz* vi (1881), 275–89, esp. 281, 284 f.). ÖNB, MS.
12590, p. 41 (Postel). Str., MS. DH V 27 (Sternberg); on Hirsch see below, p. 371.
ÖNB, MS. 13522: 'Catalogus Librorum Medicorum, Chymicorum, Chymico-
Medicorum, Physicorum, Metallicorum, Mathematicorum et Magicorum impres-
sorum, à Cl. Dño Lambecio consignatorum', prepared *c.* 1677. Schlierbach, MS. 93
(110): 'Chymische Buecher Cathalogus', prepared *c.* 1683, either a library catalogue
or a notional list.
  [7] Schott, *Organum Mathematicum*, 630–94, deals with the zodiac, the tempera-
ments, medical astrology, etc.

Such a definition, like all definitions of white versus black magic, rested more on assumption than proof, and ultimately only lent words their own power to legitimize. It became permissible to predict 'natural' phenomena, more obviously those closely harmonized with astronomical calculations: celestial portents, harvests, and similar outdoor things; but also other implications of an occult universe, as the individual writer thought fit.[8] Indeed, the possibilities were quite extensive: chiromancy and metoposcopy or physiognomy (roughly what the Victorians would later christen 'phrenology') seem to have been widely studied by erudite circles in Central Europe. In 1667 Leopold received a treatise on the techniques of palmistry from the titular bishop (very titular, one imagines) of Budva in Dalmatia, and Schott—as might be expected—speaks of the subject with sympathy.[9] In a broader way astrology was often invoked as a factor in medical theory: analysis of cosmic forces yielding remedies for the human microcosm. The point may fairly be made that the astrologers of early modern Europe, in their use of measurement and their search for physical laws, exhibit a quasi-scientific attitude, however wrong-headed the assumptions. Yet in the Habsburg lands it was almost exclusively the *mysteries* of nature which dominated, and which exercised on their devotees a squarely religious appeal. Nowhere is the truth more clearly demonstrated that Counter-Reformation learning committed itself heavily in the illicit arts, the better to find out how illicit they really were.

Astrology stood in close relation to another occult discipline with disreputable associations: the Cabala, the secret wisdom of the Jews,

---

[8] Typical discussions in Zara, op. cit. 116–22, 261–76; Adam Tanner, *Astrologia Sacra* (Ingolstadt 1615), esp. 32–56; Carena, op. cit. 227–35; Szentiványi, op. cit. i, pt. 1, 84- 156, 294–319. Cf. the monumental reference-book by Laurentius Beyerlinck, *Magnum Theatrum Vitae Humanae*, i–viii (Lyons 1665, a Catholic reworking of Zwinger (cf. above, p. 33)), lit. A, 546–86; lit. D, 192–343, *passim*; Thorndike, op. cit. vii, ch. 5; viii, ch. 32; and below, pp. 394–9.

[9] ÖNB, MS. 12625: 'Discorso di Fisonomia con la Chiromantia . . .' The writer, F. L. Paolono da Camerino, says this science has been abused by some, and hence attacked as divinatory, and the Church prohibits it outside medical use. Yet it should be viewed as a practical, physical science, with no claim to infallibility. Schott, *Magia Universalis*, iv, 637–69. Sternberg (Str., MS. DH V 27) owned thirteen books on chiromancy. Cf., for Lutheran opinions, the *Cheiromantia* of Johann Rottmann, first published at Erfurt in 1595; and the works by Praetorius cited below, p. 385, n. 8.

a range of magical beliefs all founded on a speculative cosmology which professedly gave its initiates power to interpret the world and—in some degree—to predict its workings. Both brands of Cabalism had formed an integral part of Renaissance occult studies in Central Europe, and there is some evidence that the operative kind continued to have its secretive following among the nobility.[10] More remarkably, official Catholic spokesmen saw merits in the theoretical Cabala, although almost all Hebrew literature nominally stood on the Index. Schott offers his usual lengthy exposition, with a characteristic inclination to give the subject the benefit of the doubt. Like Kircher he displays wide reading in the field.[11] Caramuel's case is more complex, for he combines a deep interest in Cabalist ideas with ritual condemnation of Jewish superstition. Probably he found the matter too hot to handle in print. He tells us with evident chagrin that his youthful involvement in genuine Hebrew mysteries was soured by the blasphemies of the rabbis, while the book he announced on the 'purified' Cabala seems never to have been published.[12]

Meanwhile, just beyond the Austrian border at Sulzbach, a more conscientious and still less orthodox scholar, Christian Knorr von Rosenroth, was raising up the greatest monument to seventeenth-century philosemitism with two massive volumes whose title speaks for itself: *Kabbala Denudata seu Doctrina Hebraeorum transcendentalis et metaphysica atque theologica*.[13] Knorr not only translated and

[10] ÖNB, MS. 11419, crude soothsaying by Gaetano Volpi for Franz Ehrenreich Trautmannsdorf (1662–1719), dated 1707–9. At this level there was a heavy overlap with astrology (and with alchemy, for Trautmannsdorf also wants to know whether he will ever be able to make the philosophers' stone). Other MSS. of the same kind have pseudo-Cabalistic passages. On the 16th-century Cabala see *Rudolf II*, 236–42; cf. Mayer, op. cit. i, nos. 680, 682.

[11] Schott, *Technica Curiosa*, ii, bk. 12 (pp. 896–1044): 'Mirabilia Cabalistica' (in fact more astrological than anything else, but it is Schott's definition which matters); for Kircher's Cabalism see below, p. 438. General regulations against Hebrew literature were introduced by the Council of Trent and tightened by Clement VIII: Reusch, op. cit. i, 45–53, 148–50; cf. Menčik, 'Censura', 115 f.

[12] Caramuel discusses the Cabala during a listing of his works in *Mathesis Biceps*, i, sig. *1–3. He apparently published an *Excidium Cabalae Theologicae* (Rome 1656); I have not found a copy. He planned to compose a book under the title: 'Cabala, hoc est, Secretior Interpretatio Sacrae Paginae'; it would have been 'liber curiosus', in which, 'rejectis Rabbinorum Commentis', he would show 'modos multos et varios inveniendi et exponendi in Bibliis sententias occultas'.

[13] Sulzbach 1677–84. Vol. i, in some 1,500 folio pages, contains the 'Apparatus' of

edited the prime Cabalist text, the book of Zohar; he compiled a whole lexicon to accompany it, and assembled such relevant Hebrew and Christian commentaries as were available. Even Knorr had to exercise discretion, and the *Kabbala Denudata* appeared anonymously. That it appeared at all is very revealing of a Central European atmosphere which, within its general intolerance, licensed so many flights of esoteric fancy. In the earlier eighteenth century the Habsburgs lent firm support to David Oppenheimer (1664–1736), the rabbi and bibliophile nephew of their court banker, Samuel.[14]

One very standard feature of Cabalism is gematria: letter-magic, an obsession which accorded well with the larger Baroque passion for word-play, anagrams, chronosticha, and the like.[15] That mentality could hardly ignore the temptation of occult writing: the notorious *Steganographia* of Abbot Trithemius of Sponheim, a treatise on the art of secret communication which cited all manner of arcane formulae and drew heavily on the principles of astral sympathy and antipathy. It is all very well for us to dismiss the *Steganographia* as a set of trivial exercises in cipher which masquerade as grotesque hocus-pocus; contemporaries attributed to it a much deeper significance. Throughout the sixteenth century, abominated by all Churches, this work of the learned Franconian monk circulated only in manuscript. When it was eventually printed in 1606 by Protestants, Rome rose to the provocation and slapped

lexicon, commentaries, and explanations; vol. ii contains the book of Zohar, in Latin and Hebrew, with more commentaries, and some observations (especially in an appendix) about how the Jews should be tolerated, understood, and peacefully converted. Cf. Salecker, op. cit.; O. Muneles, *Bibliographical survey of Jewish Prague* (Pr. 1952), nos. 160–1; Francis Mercurius van Helmont, *Kurtzer Entwurff des eigentlichen Natur-Alphabets der Heiligen Sprache* (Sulzbach 1667, also issued in Latin), on the powers of the Hebrew language; above, pp. 285, 291 f., on links with Austria.

[14] On Oppenheimer: *Encyclopaedia Judaica*, i–xvi (Jerusalem 1973–4), s.v. 'Oppenheim'. The *Hofbibliothek* continued to buy Hebrew Bibles in the 17th century, though it exchanged the Talmud and other rabbinical works to do so: HHStA, OMeA, SR46, fol. 14.

[15] Even a highly esteemed Carmelite friar used such techniques to date his sermons: W. Krause, 'Chronosticha und Chronico-Cabalistica bei P. S. Andreas à S. Theresia OCarm.' in *Sacerdos et Pastor semper ubique*, Festschrift F. Loidl (V. 1972), 333–46. Further examples among many: Hertodt, *Crocologia*, sig.)º(6ᵛ–7ʳ; Schottenstift, MS. 535.

the book firmly on the Index.[16] But Trithemius's spiritual successors in southern Germany and Austria now took up his cause. First came a number of Bavarian Jesuits and Benedictines, who claimed the *Steganographia* for their own idealized brand of natural magic; then the young Caramuel whose lengthy commentary, published with ecclesiastical approval and warmly greeted by Ferdinand III and Martinic, develops the same theme, praising the 'ars ingenua ab omnique superstitionis notā libera' and its overtones of holy Cabala. Kircher and his faithful pupil, Schott, likewise devoted much time to an investigation of steganography, and they reached the same conclusion: this is a wonderful new artifice for probing and harnessing the mysteries of nature. As late as 1721 their opinion was reinforced with a benediction from the archbishop of Mainz.[17]

In fact Kircher, Schott, and their colleagues were fascinated mainly by the practical side of occult writing, by those methods of coding messages which Trithemius had worked up into a less controversial textbook called *Polygraphia*. Many of their 'secrets of communication' turn out to be little more recondite than pigeons or invisible ink. Kircher's own 'polygraphy' was a shorthand cipher, based on Latin but applicable to any language, provided both correspondents possessed the key and wrote simply; he sent holograph copies of it to the emperor, Archduke Leopold Wilhelm, and Bernard Ignác Martinic. Becher advanced a similar project, while earlier a Habsburg secretary, Rafael Mnišovský, even adapted Trithemius's work as a means of teaching Czech to the young Ferdinand III.[18] Nevertheless it was the arcane associations of

[16] J. Trithemius, *Steganographia* (Frankfurt 1606), including two 'Claves Steganographiae'; the whole reissued ibid. 1608 and at Darmstadt 1621. Cf. Reusch, op. cit. ii, 182 f.; and, on Trithemius himself, K. Arnold, *Johannes Trithemius* (Würzburg 1971).

[17] [Sigismund, Abbot of Seeon], *Trithemius sui ipsius vindex: sive Steganographiae ... Apologetica defensio* (Ingolstadt 1616); A. Tanner, op. cit. 1–20; A. Dürrwächter, 'Adam Tanner und die Steganographie des Trithemius', *Festgabe H. Grauert* (Freiburg 1910), 354–76. J. Caramuel Lobkovic, *Steganographiae ... genuina, facilis, dilucidaque declaratio* (Cologne 1635); cf. id., *Theologia Regularis*, i–ii (Lyons 1665), ii, 432–5. G. Schott, *Schola Steganographica* (Würzburg 1665), mainly derived from Kircher; id., *Organum Mathematicum*, 695–751; cf. Lana-Terzi, *Prodromo*, chs. 1–4. W. E. Heidel, *J. Trithemii ... Steganographia ... vindicata, reserata et illustrata* (Nuremberg 1721).

[18] A. Kircher, *Polygraphia* (Rome 1663); ÖNB, MS. 9545: 'Nova Steganographia', with ded. from Kircher to Ferdinand III (1 Jan. 1650); ibid. MS. 11388, the same

cryptography which attracted these writers; behind it they descried the lineaments of a universal language, a total representation of occult reality.[19]

*

The Baroque intellect needed a grammar, as well as a vocabulary of harmony. Like Trithemius, the Catalan philosopher Ramon Lull was still (quite literally) a name to conjure with in the seventeenth century; he too, though a good Catholic according to his own medieval lights, did not enjoy favour at Rome. Lull's claim to fame or infamy rested on the *Ars Magna* or *Combinatoria*, a logical key to understanding which aimed at penetrating beyond language and uncovering the real essence of things.[20] His method held obvious attraction for minds weaned on the synthetic ambitions of the neoscholastics, and the Jesuits paid special attention to it. One of its chief propagators was Kircher, apparently encouraged by the ever-curious Emperor Ferdinand III. Kircher founded his polygraphy on Lullist principles and built up a 'universal art' of his own. While the cool modern observer must adjudge the latter an overblown scheme intoxicated with a certain specious consistency, it attracted the notice of Lutherans like Leibniz and Kuhlmann, and came to be expounded by pedestrian pupils in Bohemia and Hungary, Caspar Knittel and Martin Szentiványi, who applied it

text sent to Leopold Wilhelm; ibid. MS. 9536: 'Linguarum Omnium nova arte ad unam Reductio', dedicated to Martinic as Grand Burgrave, n.d. J. J. Becher, *Character pro Notitia Linguarum Universali* (Frankfurt 1661); C. Davidsson, 'Johannes Trithemius' Polygraphia als tschechisches Lehrbuch', *Scando-Slavica*, v (1959), 148–63. For Mnišovský (1580–1644), a pupil of the Jesuits, agent of Ferdinand II and stadholder in Carniola for a time, see also below, pp. 360 f.; his letters from Graz to Zdeněk Vojtěch Lobkovic (1619–29) in the archive of Litoměřice, filial at Žitenice, LRRK, B 213; and a report in Hrubý (ed.), *Moravské korespondence*, i, no. 156. Mnišovský was one of those associated with a bizarre and apparently indecipherable MS. attributed to Roger Bacon, which passed from Rudolf II to Marci, who sent it to Kircher in 1665 (W. M. Vojnich in W. R. Newbold, *The Cipher of Roger Bacon* (Philadelphia–London 1928), 31 f.; cf. *Rudolf II*, 239 n.).

[19] Even Becher concludes his severely practical little treatise by telling us that his method 'singulari Harmoniâ in universum linguas unit' (*Character*, sig. N3ʳ). Cf. below, p. 437 and n. 46. Similar problems exercised some Central European Protestants at this time, among them Comenius, Bisterfeld, and Cyprian Kinner; cf. Morhof, op. cit. i, bk. 4, 10 ff.; above, n. 13 (Helmont), and below, n. 36 (Kinner).

[20] Lull hovered on the brink of the Index (Reusch, op. cit. i, 27–33). On his 'art', too complicated to enter into here: T. and J. Carreras y Artau, *Historia de la filosofía española*, i–ii (Madrid 1939–43), ii, 304 ff.

to all the subjects they could think of, from theology to agriculture.[21]

This kind of 'analogy of all the sciences', as Caramuel called it, was a version of the general occult striving for unity of knowledge, and it could take a quantitative form. Its numerate equivalent was Pythagorean mysticism, a doctrine very close to the Cabala, as even the lumbering Knittel managed to observe. Kircher took up Pythagoreanism strongly in a book dedicated with effusion to Ferenc Nádasdy: having reviled its blasphemous side—the sigils, talismans, and so on—he argues the great importance of number both for Catholic theology and for a natural, occult revelation of the divine.[22] Kircher's root figure is a mystic 'one' or, to use the initiate's term, a 'monad', out of which grow all more complicated aggregations and which will therefore, like a hieroglyph, actually manifest the nature of the created world. Some evidence suggests that Kircher was not alone in his quest for the monad. Several manuscripts of the time describe and illustrate a figure of this type. The most intriguing and suggestive of them affords an unsuspected link with England, albeit with an earlier England of Elizabethan Humanism and symbolism. The most extraordinary speculations about the monad had been written by the learned and famous Dr. John Dee of London and presented with a long, highly flattering, and suitably incomprehensible dedication to Maximilian II at Pozsony in 1564. A hundred years later Dee's memory was held in little honour by his own countrymen, who widely condemned him as a conjurer. His ideas must have left a more lasting echo in Central Europe, for we now find a Silesian subject of the Habsburgs

---

[21] The categories in Kircher's arrangement owe much to Lull: e.g. in ÖNB, MS. 9536, fols. 20–4. P. Friedländer, 'Athanasius Kircher und Leibniz', *Atti della Pontificia Accademia Romana di Archeologia, Rendiconti*, xiii (1937), 229–47; Qu. Kuhlmann, *Epistolae Duae ... cum responsoria Athanasi Kircheri* (Leiden 1674): two interesting exchanges, in which Kircher somewhat moderates his claims (Pierre Bayle characteristically thought Kircher's praise of the wild enthusiast Kuhlmann feigned and ironical (*An Historical and Critical Dictionary*, i–iv (London 1710), iii, 1860 f. nn.)—but irony is one of the Baroque's weakest suits!). C. Knittel, *Via Regia ad omnes scientias et artes* (Pr. 1687), with ref. to Ferdinand III on p. 64; Szentiványi, op. cit. iii, pt. 2, esp. 22 ff. Another Central European Lullist was George Raguseus (V. Filipović in *Südostforschung* xvii (1958), 39 f.). Cf., in general, Morhof, op. cit. i, bk. 2, chs. 5–6.

[22] Caramuel, *Rationalis et realis Philosophia*, 457 ff.; Knittel, op. cit. 38–49. A. Kircher, *Arithmologia sive De abditis Numerorum mysteriis* (Rome 1665); the dedication praises Nádasdy's great gifts, zeal, and intellect. Cf. below, pp. 436–40, on the superstitious aspect.

returning to his *Monas Hieroglyphica*, preparing a German translation with commentary, and offering it to the Cistercian abbot of Grüssau.[23] What the impeccably respectable Bernardus Rosa made of this gift is not recorded, but the donor evidently cannot have thought it conspicuously heretical. Had not a wise emperor inspired it and pronounced in its favour?

All such occultizing currents were long-established traditions of secret wisdom. Indeed, the older the tradition, the more esoteric do its manifestations become during the period. That is true of Platonism and Neoplatonism: still a pervasive, if indefinable, influence in the seventeenth century, via so many Renaissance thinkers; still, given the inner flexibility of Catholic learning, perfectly orthodox in some contexts. But Platonism was regularly associated with more advanced magic, like astrology and the Cabala, and writers deeply affected by it (Marci, for instance) could easily be led into wilder fancies about emanation or the archeus. The esoteric cult appears even more clearly in what claimed to be the oldest tradition of all: the Hermetic or Egyptian mysteries, supposedly handed down from Hermes Trismegistus, the supreme mage, priest, and lawgiver of ancient Egypt. Since the 'Hermetic' texts—*Pymander* and *Asclepius*—were in fact only strung together during the second and third centuries A.D., they naturally betray much similarity with avowedly Neoplatonist ideas, and many Central European writers were familiar with them. The whole subject was fraught with especial danger: Marci, after telling us how he first took up Hermetic studies, goes on to recount the story of an old Prague Dominican who had been reduced to complete spiritual confusion by pursuing them. Even more disclaimers than usual needed to be issued.[24]

---

[23] Schlierbach, MS. 8: 'Monas Hieroglyphica Joannis à Dee. Londinensis; dass ist: Nachdenckliches Zeichen des Mercurii ...', *c.* 1680, by one Friedrich Geissler of Freiburg in Silesia. His lengthy title (fol. 1ʳ) and dedication (fols. 112–15ʳ) make play with the original dedication to Maximilian. On Dee: *Rudolf II*, 218–28; on his 17th-century reputation: F. A. Yates, *The Rosicrucian Enlightenment* (London 1972), *passim*. I have no evidence to suggest that a cult of Dee persisted in Central Europe, and the bold arguments of Dr. Yates must be rated a fragile hypothesis. But the kind of Renaissance learning for which he stood lingered on in a Catholic, conservative, and (as we shall see) heavily alchemized guise. On Rosa, cf. above, p. 302. Other 'monads' in ÖNB, MS. 11291, esp. fol. 21ᵛ; ÖNB, MS. 15449, esp. fol. 3ʳ; Str., MS. DH III 25, p. 552.

[24] Marci, *Philosophia Vetus Restituta*, 280 f. 'Authentic' Christian Hermetism is

(continued)

Yet the Egyptian arcana had a key role to play in the Habsburg-
Catholic occult synthesis, and Athanasius Kircher, that oracle of
the Viennese court, was the single most considerable Hermetist of
seventeenth-century Europe. How and why Kircher endeavoured
to reinterpret an apparently irreducible paganism in the light of its
conformity with Christian theology I shall consider below, in
chapter twelve. His interests were undoubtedly shared by Leopoldine intellectuals. Dee's translator describes himself as 'der
hermetischen Philosophie beflissen' and makes extensive reference,
not only to Kircher, but to the advanced Hermetist, Khunrath. A
fascinating unpublished treatise by some Bohemian Augustinian
friar during the 1670s seeks to reconcile Catholic doctrine with the
universal Hermetic philosophy. Its author, fortified in his own mind
by the work of such unexceptionable scholars as Kircher, Hirnhaim,
and Becher, subjects the main Christian dogmas to what can only
be described as a thorough Hermetic transformation. Other
manuscript titles display similar concerns: *Saturna Regna sive
Magisterium Sapientum per Hermeticas Positiones digestum*: or
*Compendiosa spiegazione ... del Subietto delli veri Adepti Filosofi nel
hermetica scienza*.[25] And if the approach of these two texts proves
woefully crude on inspection, they were evidently not beyond the
pale: both bear dedications to Habsburg emperors. It is worth
remembering that the most massive available edition of the
Pymander was issued by a Franciscan in the Catholic capital of
Poland during the 1580s and reprinted in the largest Catholic city
of Germany forty years later.[26]

---

closely analysed by A. Festugière, *La Révélation d'Hermès Trismégiste*, i–iv (Paris
1949–54).
[25] UK, MS. VI F 9: 'Theologia naturalis posterior, ad hypothesin Hermeticam
analogizata', etc., dated 1676–9; the author was probably a Discalced Augustinian
from the New Town of Prague. Other authorities cited include Beyerlinck, Delrio,
Helmont, Willis, Bartholinus, Sendivogius, Digby, Schott, Boyle, Dobrzensky,
Croll, Becher, a Dr. Oswald Grembs in Salzburg, and the *Miscellanea Curiosa
Academiae Naturae Curiosorum*. Some of the ideas are remarkably bold, such as
comparing the sacraments to 'seven philosophical operations' (though the writer is
at a loss to find any Hermetic analogy for matrimony!). ÖNB, MS. 11291: 'Saturna
Regna ...', by 'P. (or 'R.') F.T.M.S.' (anagrammatized (fol. 4ᵛ) as: 'Fis Paracelsus
rubeam intus tincturam sequens'), dated 1649, and allegedly based on a printed
work by a Moravian Minim called Gabriele Gotifredus. ÖNB, MS. 15449:
'Compendiosa spiegazione ...', in Italian, and addressed to Leopold I.
[26] *Pymander cum commentariis Hannibalis Rosselii*, i–vi (Cracow 1585–90),
reprinted, i–vi (Cologne 1630).

*

From Hermetism it is but a short step to the final branch of learned occultism, one cultivated more extensively in Central Europe than all the rest: alchemy. Alchemy was not only a widespread interest; it left a mass of evidence, printed and unprinted, most of which has never even been sifted, let alone seriously studied. That might in itself be sufficient reason for devoting the rest of this chapter to it. There is another: for alchemy seemed to many of its practitioners the culmination of the whole magic-encrusted system so far introduced. Examination of it will illustrate many points already made. I shall sketch these recurrent features at the outset, to help the reader's orientation in an otherwise forbidding jungle with few places of vantage. They may be subsumed, roughly and readily, under four heads.

In the first place, alchemy, like the mentality which encouraged it, rested on instinctively Aristotelian principles, heavily modified by other traditional philosophies, and developing in a strongly supernatural direction since the Renaissance. Transmutation of metals might be somewhat difficult for orthodox Aristotelians to swallow, but it was an effort not different in kind from that long demanded (from Catholics) by transubstantiation. Certainly adepts are happy to number Aristotle—like Aquinas, Lull, and many others—among their ancestors. While drawing on Neoplatonism and Cabalism in its imagery, alchemy stood especially close to two further occult sciences: astrology and Hermetism. With astrology it shared a structure (not, significantly, any presumption of predictability): the general scheme of correspondences and the symbolism of the seven planetary metals, along with the theory of microcosm which underlay the metallic cures preached by iatro-chemists. From Egypt it took—as contemporaries believed—its actual historical origins and a number of obscure principles enshrined in the so-called *Tabula Smaragdina*. In fact the debt lay rather in the other direction, since much of the seventeenth century's vogue 'Hermetism' was fairly straightforward alchemy dressed in peculiarly arcane language, as was much hunting of the 'hieroglyphical monad'.[27]

---

[27] The already-mentioned Dee-commentary; UK, MS. VI F 9; and ÖNB, MSS. 11291 and 15449, fall largely into this category; cf. ÖNB, MS. 11267. So, I suspect, does Marci, who acquired the working library of George Barschius 'rerum

(continued)

Secondly, alchemy evinced experimental activity encapsulated in a spiritual quest. It linked, that is to say, very practical metallurgy with very speculative metaphysics. There were plenty of stimuli to operative chemistry in the Habsburg lands: mines and their exploitation, especially the Hungarian ones, famed throughout Europe for the strange phenomena observed in them; physicians wedded to the iatrochemical techniques of Paracelsus, who lay buried in the little cemetery beneath the Capuchins' rock at Salzburg; or just warlords like Wallenstein, hungry for gold.[28] But any forward-looking implications were amply neutralized by a contemplative, irrational environment which aimed at things abstruse, esoteric, and ultimately mystical. Here, as in the overall *Weltanschauung*, physics yielded to metaphysics. While mines declined from a surfeit of quackery and a want of true entrepreneurship, the later Paracelsans evolved a heavy chemical philosophy whose intellectual attraction proved inversely proportional to its clinical usefulness.[29] Perhaps the alchemists' growing obsession with the elixir of life tells a tale: they served the ideal of preservation rather than creation.

Thirdly, alchemy, like learned Catholic attitudes in general, was not a rigid orthodoxy, but a debate within tacitly agreed limits. Alchemists were divided amongst themselves on key issues, such as the number of elements, and their disputes (naturally) lacked nothing in vitriol; at the same time their science came under sharp attack from a series of domestic critics. But the objections were

chymicarum peritissimus' (*Philosophia Vetus Restituta*, 280). For alchemical interpretations of Dee's *Monas* see J. J Becher, *Oedipus Chimicus* (Amsterdam 1664), 175; L. de Comitibus in J. J. Manget (ed.), *Bibliotheca Chemica Curiosa*, i–ii (Cologne–Geneva 1702), ii, 840–5; and cf. F. Roth-Scholtz, *Deutsches Theatrum Chemicum*, i–iii (Nuremberg 1728–32), iii, 4–13, with life of Dee.

[28] There are many descriptions of the mines at Neusohl, Kremnitz, and Schemnitz which could turn iron into copper (by transmutation or replacement, according to the visitor's taste): e.g. J. B. Morin, *Nova Mundi Sublunaris Anatomia* (Paris 1619), 116–44; Browne, *Brief Account*, 85 ff.; R. M. and M. B. Hall (eds.), op. cit. v, nos. 1023, 1046, 1097, 1145, 1182; Kircher, *Mundus Subterraneus*, ii, bk. 10, *passim*; M. Cranston, *John Locke, a biography* (London 1957), 84, 90; M. Boas, *Robert Boyle and 17th-century Chemistry* (Cambridge 1958), 174–80; Montesquieu, op. cit. ii, 241–4, 253–6. For Wallenstein: Ernstberger, 'Wallenstein und "Chimicus" Eckhardt', *Gesammelte Aufsätze*, i, 327–49.

[29] In general: W. Pagel, *Paracelsus* (Basle 1958); R. P. Multhauf, *The Origins of Chemistry* (London 1966); id. and A. G. Debus, *Alchemy and Chemistry in the 17th century* (Los Angeles 1966).

traditional ones, and the objectors often spoke from deep within the system—foremost among them none other than Athanasius Kircher. It is not surprising that protagonists of the philosophers' stone gave as good as they received until the end of the century. Moreover, while a line of recognizably progressive chemists: Libavius, Hartmann, Sennert, Glauber, Kunckel, Stahl, wrote in Germany and were far from unknown in the Habsburg lands, their own steps towards modernity proceeded more hesitantly, even unwittingly, than hindsight might suggest: all still believed in transmutation. The prominent and original writer, J. B. van Helmont, was influential in Austria rather for his mystical philosophy (Knorr von Rosenroth edited his work) than for novelties in experiment.[30] The spell of an alchemical Utopia was not broken in the mind of the educated public. That is the crucial point, for it affords another sign of major intellectual divergence from Western Europe, where some, of course, still explored alchemy, but the subject gradually ceased to be *respectable*. Oldenburg seeks information from Lambeck on behalf of the Royal Society about alchemical manuscripts in the *Hofbibliothek*, but he professes himself very cautious about their merits. The difficulty is summed up by another of Lambeck's correspondents, the French doctor, Charles Patin, who describes his Central European counterparts as 'full of extraordinary secrets and miracles'. The remark might be extended to the upper echelons of Habsburg society at large.[31]

Lastly, alchemy reveals with especial clarity the privileges of an

---

[30] A. Libavius, *Syntagmata Arcanorum Chymicorum*, i–iii (Frankfurt 1613–15), esp. iii (entitled *Appendix necessaria . . .*). Hartmann: W. Ganzenmüller, *Beiträge zur Geschichte der Technologie und der Alchemie* (Weinheim 1956), 314–22. Sennert: above, p. 326, n. 36. Glauber: K. F. Gugel, *Johann Rudolph Glauber 1604–70, Leben und Werk* (Würzburg 1955); cf. MS. references to him in (e.g.) ÖNB, MS. 11439, *passim*; OSzK, MS. 3 duod. slav., fols. 43'–56'; UK, MS. XI B 8, fol. 1. Kunckel began his career in Bohemia, working for the Saxe-Lauenburgs: Ganzenmüller, op. cit. 46–51, 105–15,192–203; J. R. Partington, *A History of Chemistry*, ii (London 1961), 361–77. Stahl: ibid. 653–88; and D. Oldroyd in *Ambix*, xx (1973), 36–52. J. B. van Helmont, *Aufgang der Artzney-kunst*, i–ii (Sulzbach 1683, reissued by W. Pagel, Munich 1971).

[31] Oldenburg's letter is ÖNB, MS. 9714, fol. 3, London 10 Feb. 1970, printed in R. M. and M. B. Hall (eds.), op. cit. vi, no. 1390. Patin, *Travels*, 52. Many letters from this son of Guy Patin, 1669–78, often about numismatics, in ÖNB, MSS. 9713–16. Cf., on progressive Western chemists in general, Boas, op. cit., though her book lacks nuance: she sees things in terms (as an alchemist might put it) of *nigredo* and *albedo*.

élite, headed by the dynasty itself, and the tolerance of the Counter-Reformation towards a magic which it believed could be harnessed to Christian purpose. By contrast with official disapproval in many Protestant countries, the Catholic Church took a markedly benign view: Trent forbade only alchemical fraud; the Index banned hardly any alchemical books, and although the huge collectioℓ of texts entitled *Theatrum Chymicum* did appear on it, prohibition only commenced fifty years after its publication at Strasbourg in 1659.[32] Delrio and Pereira both except alchemy from their strictures, albeit neither is happy about its practical workings or the ever-present danger of charlatanry. Therefore they make their favour conditional on the art's being handled by some authorized figure, either a prince or magnate.[33] That suited the Habsburgs' book admirably: alchemy manifestly involved them and continued to link them with the heyday of the occult under Rudolf II. It displayed their willingness to indulge Rudolfine traditions, protect them against the cold winds of seventeenth-century scepticism, harmonize them with a new-found religious orthodoxy by stressing their spiritual features. Not that later emperors were convinced conjurers in the Rudolfine mould; gone are the most esoteric aspects of Rudolf's patronage. Now they conduct something much more like an open debate. Yet the documentation—given all the received views about a lacklustre and hidebound dynasty—is intensely surprising.

★

The survival of this acceptable face of occultism even through the turmoils and dogmatism of the 1610s and 1620s could be demonstrated by such things as book dedications.[34] More striking—because quite unconstrained—evidence comes in the private correspondence of Ferdinand II: a letter to the emperor in 1630 from his Czech secretary and confidant, Rafael Mnišovský, about

---

[32] K. V. Thomas, *Religion and the Decline of Magic* (London 1971), 245, on the official prohibition of alchemy in England. *Enciclopedia Cattolica*, i (1948), cols. 723–726; Reusch, op. cit. ii, 179. The *Theatrum* was probably not banned because of its alchemical contents; similar works had anyway been printed in the earlier 17th century. Carena, op. cit., has nothing on alchemy.

[33] Martin Delrio, *Disquisitiones Magicae*, i–iii (Louvain 1599–1600), i, 63–101, esp. 100; Pereira, op. cit. 69–86; cf. Beyerlinck, op. cit. ii, lit. C, 203–6.

[34] One example is Philip Müller, *Miracula et Mysteria Chymico-Medica*, with ded. to Archduke Maximilian of Tyrol,which (for all the obscurity of the author) went through four edns., ?all at Wittenberg, between 1610 and 1623.

the celebrated Polish alchemist, Michał Sędziwój, or Sendivogius, whose checkered career had included a long stay at the court of Rudolf II. It is sufficiently interesting to hear that Ferdinand has made provision for Sendivogius to live out his old age as the owner of a Silesian estate. But the writer now goes on to reveal that he (Mnišovský) has been studying alchemy for thirty years, seeking out manuscripts associated with Rudolf, and working in monastery libraries at Braunau and Kremsmünster. More than that: he professes unbounded admiration for Sendivogius, calls him the most remarkable person he has ever met, and recounts how the Pole can explain the greatest mysteries of nature and expound the obscurest of texts.[35] If anyone is to achieve the 'great work' of transmutation under Habsburg protection, that man will be Sendivogius. And Ferdinand evidently shared this respect for Sendivogius's opinions, even if the elderly maestro failed to realize Mnišovský's larger hopes. Not only does a persistent tradition credit him with receiving a barony from the emperor, but the young chemist Glauber and the young Silesian enthusiast, Cyprian Kinner, both gained entrée to the Viennese court on his recommendation.[36]

After the accession of Ferdinand III alchemy blossomed again in the open. Its best-publicized practitioner was Johann Konrad Richthausen, son of an Austrian mine-owner and tutor to Ferdinand's heir, the king of Hungary. Many contemporaries reported Richthausen's conversion of mercury into gold before the emperor in 1648 and his subsequent elevation into the peerage with

[35] HHStA, Hausarchiv, Fam. Korr. A Kart. 8, fols. 279–84, from Troppau, 22 Sept. 1630. The printed sources disagree about Sendivogius's last years: N. Lenglet du Fresnoy, *Histoire de la philosophie hermetique*, i–iii (The Hague 1742), i, has him dying in Poland in 1646 as a pauper (pp. 334–49), or in Silesia in 1636 as a baron (350–69). Cf. Becher, ·*Physica Subterranea*, 662. On his earlier career: *Rudolf II*, 211 f.; on Mnišovský, cf. above, n. 18.

[36] Gugel, op. cit. 13 f.; G. H. Turnbull, *Hartlib, Dury and Comenius* (London 1947), 384, who says that Kinner's invitation came from 'Baron Michael Scudivogius' (sic) and 'Count Gaschinus' (the Gaschins were old nobility of Silesia). On Kinner's life, cf. ibid. 384 ff.; Blekastad, op. cit. 402 ff. Besides corroborating the Sendivogius-saga, this information raises the interesting possibility that Cyprian Kinner—known as a friend of Comenius—may have been related to Godefrid Alois Kinner: both came from Silesia; both showed interest in a universal language (Schott, *Organum Mathematicum*, 740 ff.; V. Salmon, *The Works of Francis Lodwick* (London 1972), 17, 26); both corresponded with Kircher (cf. Cyprian's letter in BL, Sloane MS. 649, fols. 17 f.; the MS. also contains evidence of alchemical interests).

the flippant (though also Helmontian?) title of Baron von Chaos. No mystery surrounds the rest of Richthausen's career either: he became master of the mint—which struck a large medal from 'transmuted' gold to commemorate his achievement; then army paymaster, and finally superintendent of the royal mines in Hungary.[37] Other operators are more enigmatic, among them the intriguing 'Baron Wagnereck', who puts in a first appearance during these years in the company of his eminently respectable Jesuit uncle, Simon.[38] Ferdinand III did not hide his willingness to investigate the possibilities of alchemy, and he found no shortage of helpers. Straightforward metallurgists, like the Carinthian, Johann Jakob Menschor, are outnumbered by would-be adepts: Hieronymus Damean, 'Artista et Chy [mista]', sends Paracelsan tracts from Ghent; Helvicus Otten attends the Regensburg diet in 1654 to present his plea for the philosophical tincture to be used as a universal medicine; anonymous Italians, one apparently supported by a son of Rudolf's friend Wolf Unverzagt, offer brief chymical wisdom attributed to the Emperor Justinian, or more extended rules for the *aurum potabile*.[39] The court library was quarried for Greek '*chrysopoei*', whose writings were rendered into Latin and supplemented with a lexicon of alchemical terminology.[40]

---

[37] Monconys, op. cit. ii, 378–80; J. Zwelfer, *Pharmacopoeia Regia* (Nuremberg 1668), 328 f.; Becher, *Oedipus Chimicus*, 196; Schröder in Roth-Scholtz, op. cit. i, 232 f.; Lenglet du Fresnoy, op. cit. ii, 35–44; K. C. Schmieder, *Geschichte der Alchemie* (Halle 1832), 397–403. Cf. A. Bauer, *Die Adelsdocumente österreichischer Alchemisten* (V. 1893), 23–6, 52–6; Srbik, 'Abenteurer', 56; Thorndike, op. cit. viii, 361 f.; and two letters from Philip von Mansfeld, 26 Feb. and 18 Mar. 1648, in HHStA, Hausarchiv, Fam. Korr. A 10.

[38] Simon Wagnereck (1605–57) was a scholar, called by Ferdinand III to catalogue coins in the imperial collection (see Sommervogel, s.v. 'Wangnereck'). According to Kalista (ed.), *Korespondence*, no. 11, his nephew came with him as a 'chimico', and made 'una prova rara con una sua tintura', but was subsequently sent to the galleys. H. Kopp, *Die Alchemie in älterer und neuerer Zeit*, i–ii (Heidelberg 1886), i, 207 n. thinks that Simon also knew something of alchemy, but the whole affair is very misty. Cf. below, p. 370.

[39] Menschor: ÖNB, MS. 11360, dated 1650, with attack on 'conjurers' (fols. 168 ff.). Damean: ibid. MS. 11343, also dated 1650. Otten: ibid. MS. 11429, fols. 1ᵛ– 13ʳ, who claims the architect Joseph Furtenbach as one of his witnesses. ÖNB, MS. 11339: two tracts dedicated to Ferdinand III by Wolfgang Sigismund Unverzagt, presumably a son (cf. Zedler, s.v.) of Wolf Unverzagt; ibid. MS. 11298, also in Italian, and almost identical with MS. 11339, fols. 47–9; ibid. MS. 11387, in Italian and Latin, dated 1640.

[40] ÖNB, MS. 11453: 'Graeci Chrysopoei Veteres quicunque ... in S.ᵃᵉ Caesᵃᵉ

Ferdinand's brother, Leopold Wilhelm, engaged in the adventure more passionately. In his alchemy, as in his art-collecting, he overstepped the bounds of moderation always observed by the emperor. His name appears in dedications of published treatises on the subject; indeed, he was probably better remembered by contemporaries as an authority for transmutation recipes than as a servant of Church or state. At all events, ecclesiastical office seemed no handicap: Leopold Wilhelm's chief collaborator was his chamberlain, Wilhelm Leopold von Tattenbach, Grand-Prior of the Maltese order in Bohemia, president of the Styrian War Council, and—incidentally—uncle of the small-time rebel, Count Erasmus.[41] One manuscript records twelve alchemical processes for which the archduke paid goodly sums of money (2,000 thalers changed hands on a single occasion). From it we learn that he and the grand-prior, each with technical assistants, conducted experiments wherever their court found itself, especially at Vienna, Brussels, and Laibach in Carniola, using everything from the arcana of Rudolf II to the 'secret medical and chymical writings' of van Helmont.[42]

Especially fascinating is an entirely unpublished correspondence which survives for the earlier 1640s between Ferdinand and Leopold Wilhelm.[43] Amid all the alarms of desperate campaigns against the Swedes, they employ a miniature army of adepts to examine

Mai[is] Bibliothecâ ... asservantur', texts and lexicon of terms; ibid. MS. 11465 is another copy of the 'Dictionarium Chymicum'. ÖNB, MS. 11249 (below, n. 78) is also dedicated to Ferdinand III, and there are further references to him in J. J. Becher, *Chymischer Glücks-Hafen* (Frankfurt 1682), 260–4; Bod., Canonici Misc. MS. 122, fols. 275 f.; ÖNB, MS. 11469, fols. 204 f.; ibid. MS. 11433, fols. 357–8[r].

[41] Ludovicus de Comitibus, 'De liquore Alchaest', in Manget (ed.), op. cit. ii, 764–81. Many mentions of Leopold Wilhelm in the MSS. cited below, nn. 54–5, 75; cf. UK, MS. XI B 8, fol. 25[v]. On Tattenbach: Schwarz, op. cit., appendix, s.v.; cf. J. Kedd, *Paraenesis ad Lutheranos Dominos Academicos aberrantes* (V. 1655), ded.; and above, p. 180, for his nephew.

[42] ÖNB, MS. 11365: 'Ihre Ertzherzogl: durchl: Leopoldi Wilhelmi Labores chymici', in German, perhaps by J. F. von Rain. Cf. *Miscellanea Curiosa*, i (1670), 73 f.; Lhotsky, *Sammlungen*, i, 371.

[43] HHStA, Hausarchiv, Fam. Korr. A 10–11: 31 letters from Leopold Wilhelm, 1634–50; 142 from Ferdinand, 1627–45; almost all early 1640s, German and m.p. 102 further letters from Leopold Wilhelm, 1644–6, in Stockholm, Riksarkivet, Extranea 195, are noted by E. Schieche, 'Umfang und Schicksal der von den Schweden ... erbeuteten Archivalien', *Bohemia-Jahrbuch*, viii (1967), 113–33, at 131. I have not consulted them. Many more letters must be lost.

congelation and the properties of sulphur, to fix silver and sublimate antimony. 'So much for public affairs,' runs the typical letter from the emperor in Vienna, 'Iam ad Chymica...' 'I can tell you today', writes Leopold Wilhelm at Querfurt in January 1642, 'that I have begun the New Year with chemistry', and he goes on to describe the visit of a Dr. Agricola from Leipzig who is 'in sein secretis gar tenax', but may be persuaded to reveal the 'verum aurum potabile'. His brother replies with alchemical poems and details of the activities of 'Dr. Fortonio' and 'Manriquez'. Small wonder that the archduke's forces suffered crushing defeat a few months later! But the experiments were not long interrupted.

★

With the death in 1657 of Ferdinand III and in 1662 of Leopold Wilhelm (given over at the last, as the Venetian ambassador reported, to 'pictures, curiosities, poets, and delights'[44]) a different atmosphere seemed to prevail in Vienna. The gayer, more open, less complicated character of the young Leopold's court was not immediately favourable to alchemy. The lull in activity coincided with a blast against the sophistry of the art from the highly-esteemed Athanasius Kircher, whose *Mundus Subterraneus*, though written in Rome and published at Amsterdam, must have spoken for attitudes familiar also in Austria. Kircher devotes a whole long section to condemning the charlatanry of adepts, revealing their trickery, exploding their mummery and empty jargon. If transmutation has ever taken place, he asserts (striking below the belt), then the unnatural change involved must surely be the work of the devil.[45]

The alchemists, however, stood poised to reassert themselves. Kircher, after all, was hardly a sceptic or a progressive, and the mantle of demonologist ill became him, as his opponents soon realized. One of them, under the alias 'Salomon de Blawenstein', published in Vienna a spirited and well-argued tirade which, besides citing Richthausen and the 'great Sendivogius', pointed out how many things in Kircher's own books were less plausible than alchemy (a sentiment with which the modern reader will heartily

[44] *Relationen Venetianischer Botschaften*, ed. Fiedler, 50–2.
[45] Kircher, *Mundus Subterraneus*, ii, bk. 11; bk. 12, 419 ff. There were new edns. in 1668 and 1678, and a German trans. in 1688. The section on alchemy is reprinted in Manget (ed.), op. cit. i, 54–112; and extracted in Kestler, op. cit. 36 ff.

concur). Similar vindications came from Blawenstein's colleague, Johann Zwelfer, and from the eminent Saxon physician, Gabriel Clauder.[46] Meanwhile Leopold's interest began to grow. He had, it seems, already witnessed experiments by a mysterious wandering adept known as Monte Snyders, and perhaps also by others who claimed to possess the powder of projection. Soon we find him reading Goldmayer (whom his father had created count palatine), Glauber, even the recipes of that notorious Rudolfine magus, Edward Kelley, as well as Blawenstein and a certain 'Solinus Salzthal'.[47]

By the 1670s a broader debate ensued. The learned Moravian Dr. Hertodt, for example, took issue with his fellow-alchemists on some technical matters, but was attacked by his Kircherite colleague Ardensbach over the general principle of transmutation. These were good times for any Central European claimants to the tincture, like the combative Silesian, Franz Gassmann, who traded under the peculiar name of Pantaleon and purveyed a kind of graduated introduction to the 'Hermetic wisdom'.[48] The Viennese court heard about the majority of them—Leopold certainly sought the writings of Pantaleon—and the most colourful figure of the decade was definitely an imperial protégé. Johann Wenzel Seiler's classic career deserves to be described: if his story has been embroidered in some details by popular chroniclers, the substance of it is fully authentic.

Seiler was a young Moravian friar who learned alchemical secrets from an aged fellow-Augustinian at Brno and fled his monastery

[46] Salomon de Blawenstein, *Interpretatio brevis ad Philosophos pro Lapide Philoso-phorum* (V. 1667); reprinted in Manget (ed.), op. cit. i, 113–19. Kircher calls 'Blawenstein' a 'defrocked monk' and a 'fictitans Bubo' (*Fasciculus Epistolarum*, ed. Langenmantel, 35). Zwelfer, *Pharmacopoeia Regia*, 324–30, who nevertheless allows Kircher to be 'vir incomparabilis doctinae ac talenti'; G. Clauder, *Dissertatio de Tinctura universali* (Altenburg 1668), reprinted in Manget (ed.), op. cit. i, 119–68.

[47] Monte Snyders may have been in Vienna in 1660 (Schmieder, op. cit. 403–8 on his career), and—more certainly—in 1666 (ÖNB, MS. 11370, pp. 90 ff., 118 f., 125 ff.; ibid. MS. 11486, pp. 11 f.; confirmed by Valvasor, *Krain*, i, 415 f.). He wrote *Metamorphosis Planetarum* (Amsterdam 1663), which was in the court library (ÖNB, MS. 13522, fol. 19ʳ), and other works listed by J. Ferguson, *Bibliotheca Chemica*, i–ii (Glasgow 1906), ii, 104–6; cf. Monconys, op. cit. ii, 371; ÖNB, MS. 11266, fols. 150ᵛ–3ʳ. For Leopold's reading: ÖNB, MS. 12590, fols. 25 f., which includes Goldmayer's *Harmonia Chymica* and an anonymous *Centuria Chymica* also p.obably by him (cf. Ferguson, op. cit. i, 335 f.); ÖNB, MS. 12592, fol. 161 (Kelley); ibid. MS. 8011, fol. 35ʳ (Blawenstein).

[48] Hertodt, *Tartaro-Mastix, passim*; and in Manget (ed.), op. cit. ii, 697–9;

(continued)

with what purported to be the genuine powder of projection. Despite that unorthodox start and the glaring irregularities in his private life, Seiler gained the favour of several aristocrats, among them Prince Liechtenstein, who may even have engineered his escape. Leopold promptly showed interest, and when Seiler appeared at court (probably in 1674) he was received with great partiality, provided with a laboratory in one of the gatehouses of the Hofburg, then knighted with the predicate 'von Reinburg'. For a time all went well: Seiler plied the emperor with choice texts, including a superb vellum manuscript in heavy binding, protected by iron lock and key, which contains fulsome praise of his patron and gaily coloured drawings of furnaces.[49] In 1677 he produced a large Habsburg medallion and claimed to transmute it—on St. Leopold's day—from silver into gold. Eventually disenchantment set in; the baseness both of Seiler's tincture and of his morals could not be indefinitely concealed. Nevertheless the emperor was content to post him back to Bohemia with a remunerative office in the royal mint (shades of Sendivogius and Richthausen). He appears to have died at Vienna in 1681.[50]

If Seiler proved the most feckless of Leopold's alchemists, he was defended by the most serious: Johann Joachim Becher. From an early age Becher showed an obsessive concern with the philosophers' stone; he launched into a succession of open apologies for the art,

---

Ardensbach, op. cit. 115 ff. Pantaleon, *Tumulus Hermetis Apertus* (Nuremberg 1676); *Bifolium Metallicum seu Medicina duplex* . . . (Nuremberg 1676); cf. below, p. 374, and ÖNB, MS. 8011, fol. 279ᵛ.

[49] ÖNB, MS. 11532, with dedication (pp. 1–4) and standard alchemical text, by 'Johann Wenzel von Reinburg'. Cf. ÖNB, MS. 11456, Greek alchemists in translation, an almost exact copy of ibid. MSS. 11453 and 11465 (above, n. 40), dated 15 Nov. 1677, with a new dedication from Seiler in the hand of Lambeck.

[50] There were many contemporary accounts of Seiler's adventures; a very substantial one by Becher, who knew most of the story well, even appeared in English: *Magnalia Naturae or the Philosopher's Stone lately exposed to publick Sight and Sale* (London 1680). The standard modern source is Bauer, op. cit. 26–8, 57–60, but it needs some correction and expansion. Seiler was already well known to Leopold— at least in name—by 1674 (ÖNB, MS. 8011, fols. 213ᵛ, 214ʳ, 225ʳ, 228ᵛ, 248ʳ; ibid. MS. 11472, fol. 53ʳ). He was not disgraced until early 1679, as Lambeck reveals, along with other corroborative evidence (ÖNB, MS. 9716, fols. 2–5, 237 f., 269), shows that 'Reinburg' was the title of his maternal grandfather, and that his laboratory was in the Michaelertor (cf. Srbik, 'Abenteurer', 53 f. and n., who suggests 'Wasserkunstbastei')). The death of 'Der Kayserl. bissher berühmt geweste Goldmacher' is noted by Bauer, 'Passer', 314, on 4 Dec. 1681.

each weightier than the last and all much read in their day. He was an equally irrepressible practical metallurgist.[51] His views must have been known to Leopold before he settled in Austria (for it is Becher who hides behind the palpable pseudonym 'Solinus Salzthal' in the imperial private library); and from 1670 to 1676 he served as a kind of semi-official Habsburg alchemical counsellor. Becher's published works contain some references to this activity, and I have drawn on them elsewhere in the present chapter.[52] Unpublished evidence yields more explicit information about his relations with Leopold. Especially important is his long memorandum on the claims of an adept called Daniel Marsali—an operator who recognizably hailed from the same stable as Seiler—submitted to the emperor at Laxenburg palace outside Vienna during May 1674. Becher quickly disposes of the pretext: Marsali's process for the tincture looks sound enough on paper, some minor contradictions aside, although its practitioner should learn to live as befits a philosopher. He now turns to a more congenial exercise, a substantial theoretical statement which, for all its ritual mystification, represents a considerable intellectual performance. Becher stresses that the alchemical art is natural and ultimately simple in its essence: the tincture is a 'child of nature', transmutation is a 'natural generation', a 'perfectio materiae'; yet its ways demand profound study, technical expertise, and goodness of intent.[53] All in all Becher shows himself a thoughtful and sophisticated alchemist, blending Aristotelian and Paracelsan traditions with a strong empirical element and wide reading in the literature of his own time.

[51] Becher, *Oedipus Chimicus* (1664); *Physica Subterranea* (1669), with two supplements, entitled *Experimentum Chymicum Novum* and *Theses Chymicae veritatem ... transmutationis metallorum in aurum evincentes* (1675), all reprinted together in 1681; *Chymischer Glücks-Hafen* (1682). J. Juncker, *Conspectus Chemiae Theoretico-Practicae* (Halle 1730), draws heavily on Becher; while Bod., Canonici Misc. MS. 122, contains copies of printed works and some new experiments. Cf. above, p. 336. On his theories cf. Hassinger, *Becher*, 59 ff.; and Partington, op. cit. ii, 637–52.

[52] 'Dedit enim Sacr. Caes. Maj. commissionem mihi, Chymicis hisce invigilandi et incumbendi': *Physica Subterranea*, 687. Becher's identity with Salzthal is revealed by the list of his works in *Minera Arenaria*, sig. M2ʳ. His first contact with the Habsburgs seems to have been with Ferdinand III in 1655.

[53] ÖNB, MS. 11472: 'Gutachten über Daniels Marsalii Process ...' Marsali may well be the man instanced by Seiler as a deceiver (ibid. MS. 11532, fols. 15 f.). Cf. BL, Sloane MS. 2867, fols. 2–7; and the closely related material in Becher, *Physica Subterranea, supplementum secundum* (1675 edn.), sig. A2–7ʳ, ded. to Leopold; and id., *Chymischer Glücks-Hafen*, 25–107.

One scholar yet more learned than Becher, though seemingly much less credulous, likewise played a part in the Seiler affair: the court librarian, Lambeck. Lambeck's involvement is very odd, for whereas in the 1660s he sneers at the pretensions of the 'most vain art of chymistry' with all the venom of one who has already condemned the Hermetic texts as worthless frauds, a decade later we discover him engaged in a sort of arcane correspondence worthy of the died-in-the-wool spagirist. Not only does he recount the history of Seiler, but he claims a long and intimate acquaintance with him, asserts that his tincture—part of Rudolf II's treasure— had been discovered by means of a crystal-ball, and recommends other recipes and occult books as to the manner born.[54]

What provoked this remarkable *volte-face*, quite unknown (I fancy) to all previous writers on Lambeck? The proximate cause was his new correspondent, Duke Friedrich of Saxe-Gotha, an evidently hard-bitten alchemist who wrote in search of secrets from the Austrian court.[55] Friedrich, eldest son of Ernst the Pious of Gotha whom we met earlier, was a dutiful subject of the emperor and ruler of one of the smaller Thuringian duchies whose links with Vienna were close. The rewards for satisfying his curiosity would range from an extra contingent in the imperial army (actually promised at one point) to enhanced prestige for Lambeck himself and significant donations for the *Hofbibliothek*—a large Lutheran Bible was one quaint quid pro quo. Such political and social advantages induced the librarian to swallow his intellectual scruples; or perhaps he even took to heart the comment of a bookseller friend that Germany offered a much better market for alchemy than for catalogues of Greek manuscripts![56]

---

[54] ÖNB, MS. 9713, fols. 93–5 (deprecating comments about an alchemist-Lullist from Danzig called Böhm von Böhmfelden; cf. ibid. MS. 9714, fol. 246). On Hermetism: Lambeck, *Prodromus*, esp. 134–43 (first published at Hamburg, 1659). Drafts of his alchemical correspondence: ÖNB, MS. 9715, fols. 223, 244, 259, 267; ibid. MS. 9716, fols. 2–5, 21, 30, 46, 26 (out of order), 85, 99 f., 116, 237 f., 241, 256, 269. Cf. above, n. 50.

[55] Friedrich's letters (German and mostly m.p.): ÖNB, MS. 9715, fols. 206–8, 222, 224, 229, 246 f., 270 f.; ibid. MS. 9716, fols. 1, 36ª, 39, 59ª, 95, 247, 282. On Friedrich (1646–91) see *ADB*, s.v. (brief); and Beck, op. cit. i, 342 ff. (with mention of more alchemical MSS.); and cf. above, pp. 283, 289.

[56] Friedrich sent the so-called Weimar or Ducal Bible, commissioned by his father. ÖNB, MS. 9714, fols. 267–9, a letter from Georg Philipp Finck in Freising, 8 Apr. 1673.

Thus the episode casts light on the frailty of scholars, as well as on the complicated reciprocal contacts—discussed in a previous chapter—which underlay the continuing Habsburg role in the *Reich*. Yet there is rather more to the tale than that. However tongue-in-cheek some of Lambeck's alchemical patter may have been he seems to have fallen genuinely under the spell of his royal protectors and their occult leanings: why else should he prepare documents from Seiler for presentation to the sovereign? His errands for Duke Friedrich included seeking out the arcana of Ferdinand III, Archduke Leopold Wilhelm, and Tattenbach, and trying to persuade Leopold to disgorge his personal elixir.[57] Overall some belief in alchemy was perfectly respectable, and on occasion even *de rigueur*, in mid-Leopoldine Vienna. When the emperor married for the third time in 1677, Knorr von Rosenroth thought it appropriate to celebrate the event in an elaborate and abstruse *Chymisches Prachtspiel*, an extravaganza which blends a mythological plot with the *magnum opus* of transmutation. The scenes of his drama are expounded in an erudite preface, though their subtitles alone would give the game away, beginning with 'the universal Harmony and the Antipathy and Sympathy of nature', and proceeding through many weary hexameters to the final 'preparation, amalgamation, and augmentation of the stone'.[58]

So great was the favour shown to aspiring alchemists—sincere or bogus—during these years that one of them, Johann Friedrich von Rain, drew an extreme conclusion. His pretext was the plague year of 1679 and a natural preservative recommended against infection by Dobrzensky, whose pamphlet expressed doubts about the existence of any philosophers' stone, especially if it could not be made available at such a moment of crisis. Rain had already been

---

[57] Above, n. 49; cf. ÖNB, MS. 13522, presumably drawn up for Leopold; and ibid. MS. 8011, fol. 288ʳ, with mention of a list of chemical works from the Fugger library. ÖNB, MS. 9715, fols. 224, 244, 259; ibid. MS. 9716, fols. 2–5, 26, 85, for the errands.

[58] Chr. Knorr von Rosenroth, *Conjugium Phoebi et Palladis oder die, durch Phoebi und Palladis Vermählung erfundene Fortpflanzung des Goldes* (Sulzbach 1677). Lambeck, for one, actually lists this as a real work of alchemy (ÖNB, MS. 13522, fol. 7ᵛ). It may owe its inspiration to the famous *Chymische Hochzeit* by J. V. Andreae, which—if Dr. Yates is right (op. cit., ch. 5)—celebrated the marriage of Leopold's grandfather's rival, the Winter King. Another example of this mythologizing approach is Monte Snyders, *Metamorphosis Planetarum*.

flooding the emperor with tracts of secret wisdom for some time, and he promptly issued a furious rejoinder to assert, not merely that alchemists possess a panacea, but that disbelief in it must actually be *lèse-majesté*, an affront to the dynasty which has espoused their art, and which with their remedies will dominate the world. Leopold's reaction to this bizarre act of homage is unknown; but friends of Dobrzensky (himself no stranger in court circles) hastened to vindicate the Prague doctor's professional dignity, and the subsequent polemic seems to have brought Rain little comfort.[59]

The Dobrzensky–Rain controversy is revealing also for what it does not say. While Rain had plainly suggested the flimsiness of his own position by a *reductio ad absurdum*, his opponents are careful not to deny the possibility of transmutation.[60] In fact a gradual decline set in for court alchemy after 1680, though it stemmed rather from the upheavals of war than from any sudden official change of mind. The activities of Becher, both practical and theoretical, were continued by Schröder, who (like Richthausen) ended his life as a mining official, and to some extent by Hörnigk.[61] Schröder's *Nothwendiger Unterricht vom Goldmachen*, first published in 1684 and several times reprinted, gives us—besides his own defence of the art—a glimpse of some of the rivals and successors to Seiler and Marsali: Colonel Schellenberg, with his expensive furnace for purifying silver; a wayward Dutchman called Sommer, specialist in experiments with mercury; even 'Baron Wagnereck', who apparently returned to Austria and Bohemia before his death in the early 1680s, and whose recipes passed surreptitiously from hand to hand. As late as 1704 Leopold and his courtiers proved very susceptible to overtures from a certain Count Caetano, or Ruggiero,

---

[59] J. J. W. Dobrzensky, *Praeservativum universale naturale* (Pr. 1680); J. F. von Rain, *Praeservativum universale naturale a natura et arte depromptum* (Laibach 1680), an exceedingly rare book (I have used the Str. copy; there is another in Ljubljana); J. V. von Schwartzenwald, *Epistola novi praeservativi universalis naturalis Nunciatoria ... Vindicatoria* (n.p. 1681); 'Didacus Germanus', *Judicium Philosophico-Ethico-Chymico Medicum* (n.p. 1682). Cf. Valvasor, op. cit. ii, 363 f.; ÖNB, MS. 11370, pp. 39, 113–15, 146 ff., 234–8; ibid. MS. 11486, ded. and p. 51. There may have been further publications on the issue; Rain tells us he had another apology printed in 1685.

[60] Even Dobrzensky's original *Praeservativum* only queries the philosophers' stone *en passant*. His own chemical MSS. (*olim* Str. MSS. DD IV 26–35) have been lost.

[61] Srbik, 'Schröder', esp. 41 f., 75–85; ÖNB, MS. 11439*, fol. 283; UK, MS. XI B 8, fol. 30ʳ(?). It may be recalled that Schröder came from Gotha.

really a peasant's son and one of the more spectacular charlatans of his age.[62]

There is an undated postscript to Habsburg alchemy in the seventeenth century. Sometime around 1650 an imperial valet de chambre (*Kammerdiener*) named Friedrich Hirsch died, and an inventory was drawn up of his effects.[63] They included some 300 books and manuscripts, many relating to chemistry, metallurgy, pharmacy, and astrology. More remarkably, they included also a complete alchemical laboratory, occupying seven rooms, with at least a dozen furnaces, one of which incorporated both an 'athanor', or self-firing oven, and a *fauler Heinz* (whatever that may have been). The contents are minutely described: alembics, hundreds of retorts, crucibles and *ova philosophica*, all manner of minerals and chemicals, mathematical instruments and miscellaneous equipment. I have not found any further reference to Hirsch; but if many others like him worked in the Habsburgs' employ, then their alchemy merits even more space than I have accorded it here.

★

The alchemical concerns of the ruling dynasty were, predictably, shared by some of its aristocratic supporters, particularly by those with court appointments and—perhaps—large Viennese town houses to stage the work. Leopold's high marshal, Franz Augustin Waldstein (died in 1684), favoured Seiler; so did Count Schlick and two of the Paars, at least one of whom enjoyed considerable contemporary fame as an initiate. On his death during the 1670s, Paar's manuscripts fell into the hands of the president of the *Hofkammer*, Sinzendorf, who favoured both Seiler and Marsali.[64] Count Karl Ernst Rappach, commander of Vienna, was mixed up

---

[62] Schröder's *Nothwendiger Unterricht* appeared separately in 1684 and 1727; it was also—significantly—issued as an appendix to editions of his mercantilist treatise, *Fürstliche Schatz- und Rentkammer*; I have used the reprint in Roth-Scholtz, op. cit. i, 219–88. Schellenberg: ibid. 282–5; cf. Srbik, 'Abenteurer', 63–7. Sommer: Schröder, loc. cit. 240–4. Wagnereck: ibid. 234–9; cf. Schmieder, op. cit. 438–42; ÖNB, MS. 11319*, fols. 113–17ʳ, 127ʳ [1680]; ibid. MS. 11321, fols. 1–19; ibid. MS. 11433, fol. 282(?). 'Caetano': Schmieder, op. cit. 484 ff.; Bauer, op. cit. 29.

[63] ÖNB, MS. 8041: 'Inventarium über Weylandt Friderich Hirschen gewesten Kayl. Cammer Diener Seel: Verlassenschaft'. The books suggest a *terminus post quem* of *c.* 1640 (they include the 1st edn. of Kircher's *Magnes*), but there are mentions in the text of Glauber and Richthausen. The inventory later speaks of a 'Sigfridt Hirsch von Plessiberg' (fols. 20–1ʳ), but they were presumably one and the same person.

[64] Becher, *Magnalia Naturae*, who hints that Franz Augustin Waldstein's brother,

(continued)

with some experiments which also involved Franz Trautmannsdorf and the wife of the Bohemian chancellor. Can he have been the fabricator of the 'Tinctur Rapach' which Leopold took on his death-bed? Count Volkra certainly put forward metallurgical proposals to the emperor in 1682.[65] At Prague we hear of Baron Přehořovský and Baron Gottfried Daniel Wunschwitz, who received a long alchemical treatise from his father-in-law in 1713. In Moravia the Petřvaldskýs at Buchlov were serious students of chemistry, while Count Julius Hoditz and Petrus de la Fosse (perhaps his brother-in-law) witnessed transmutations by one 'Petrus della Bono', described as a colonel in the imperial army and pupil of Helmont. Unfortunately references to noble patrons of the art tend to be laconic and imprecise. Such figures as Franz Weickard von Hoffmann und Lichtenstern and Wolfgang Julius von Hardeck (Hardegg?) may now be impossible to trace. Even worse are loose mentions of 'Lobkowitz', or the unspecified count who conducted an intimate alchemical correspondence during the 1690s, or our friend 'Baron' Wagnereck, whose title could conceivably be genuine.[66]

More easily identifiable in the scattered writings I have consulted are prominent *Leibärzte*, who frequently championed alchemy and formed an important link between these aristocrats and the court.

Karl Ferdinand, has also witnessed transmutations; id., *Chymischer Glücks-Hafen*, 126 ff. (Peter Paar); Monconys, op. cit. ii, 371, 376–8, 382; ÖNB, MS. 9716, fols. 2–5, 116; ibid. MS. 11472, fols. 53^r, 55^v.

[65] ÖNB, MS. 11433, fol. 308 (Rappach). This probably dates from between 1683 and 1699, since the chancellor was a Kinský, and Wenceslaus Ecker (below, p. 378) was also involved; but Schmieder (op. cit. 494–7) records a transmutation at the house of the same Rappach in 1716. On Trautmannsdorf, cf. above, n. 10. F. Menčik, 'Die letzten Tage Kaiser Leopolds I', *MIÖG* xix (1898), 518–20, at 519. Srbik, 'Abenteurer', 69, n. 3 (Volkra).

[66] Přehořovský: ÖNB, MS. 11439*, fols. 289 f., dated 1688 (either Christoph Karl (died in 1695), or his son, Franz Karl, who became chief justice of Bohemia). Wunschwitz (1678–1741): Str., MS. DH III 25 (son of Matthias Gottfried, the first baron). Petřvaldskýs: Hertodt, *Tartaro-Mastix*, 8, 25, 31 (presumably including Johann Sigismund (died in 1688), *hejtman* of Hradiště). Hoditz, etc.: ÖNB, MS. 11439*, fols. 148, 153–5 (dated 1678), 260. Hoffmann: ibid. 178 (he was a member of the *Hofkammer*); Hardeck: Becher, *Chymischer Glücks-Hafen*, sig.) (iv^v. Lobkowitz: ÖNB, MS. 11321, fols. 83 ff.; ibid. MS. 11433, fols. 339 f. For the 'count': ÖNB, MS. 11393, fols. 36–65, with interesting details; cf. ibid. MS. 9715, fols. 271–4. Another magnate worth attention as an alchemist would be Franz Ludwig Zinzendorf (1661–1742); cf. *ADB*, xlv, 339.

Not that all Vienna's physicians favoured occult remedies: the dean of the university medical faculty, Sorbait, was a moderate progressive who took a distinctly strait-laced view of Paracelsus and, like a few of his colleagues, embraced Harvey's theory of the circulation of the blood.[67] But others were openly sympathetic to transmutation, among them Johann Zwelfer—clearly a reputable doctor, despite his penchant for withering invective; Georg Sebastian Jungius, who wrote a work called *Malum Aureum* for Leopold; Friedrich Ferdinand Ilmer, whom the emperor ennobled as 'von und zu Wartenberg'; Wolf Carolus Lebzelter, apparently an expert on poisons; even the ultra-scholastic Wechtler.[68] In the provinces physicians exhibited similar enthusiasm, from the Hertodts, father and son, in Moravia, to the enterprising Philipp Jakob Sachs and Johann Jenisch at Breslau, or the shadowy Doctor Scheidenberger who practised first at Villach and later at Tyrnau. Most of these men had connections with the *Academia Naturae Curiosorum*, the professional forum for Central European doctors in the later seventeenth century (Sachs was its secretary), and there is no doubt about that academy's commitment to alchemical debate. The commitment was confirmed by the activities of its members elsewhere, like the Saxons Clauder, Balduin, and Wedel, or Volcamer in Nuremberg, or Cnöffel at the Polish court.[69]

Evidently the prospect of some sort of universal medicament

[67] E. Lesky, 'Paul de Sorbait', in *Science, Medicine and Society in the Renaissance, essays to honour W. Pagel*, ed. A. G. Debus, i–ii (London 1972), ii, 1–11; cf. above, p. 109 and n. 71.

[68] J. Zwelfer, *Pharmacopoeia Regia*, 314–418, *passim*; id., *Pharmacopoeia Augustana reformata* (Gouda 1653), 737–810; cf. his *Discursus Apologeticus*, a violent polemic against Otto Tachenius. Jungius, *Malum Aureum* (V. 1673); ÖNB, MS. 12592, p. 161. Ilmer (or Illmer): ÖNB, MS. 11433, fol. 250; ibid. MS. 11439*, fols. 286 f., 289 f.(?), 293, 294(?). He published an *Oratio in honorem SS. Cosmae et Damiani* at Vienna in 1655, was a member of the medical faculty by the 1660s, and still held the post of *Leibarzt* in 1698 (Nyáry, op. cit. 80). Lebzelter: ÖNB, MS. 11433, fol. 118; ibid. MS. 11366(?). Wechtler, op. cit. i, 321 f.; ii, 11–13, 39 f. (unsympathetic to the *aurum potabile*); cf. his general views of the occult, ibid. ii, 240–85; and Zwelfer, *Pharmacopoeia Regia*, 329.

[69] J. F. Hertodt (the son): above, p. 365; ÖNB, MS. 11433, fols. 106, 166ʳ. Sachs: *Miscellanea Curiosa*, i (1670), 65–75; cf. ibid. iv–v (1676), 1–76. Jenisch: ÖNB, MS. 11393b, fols. 54 f. Scheidenberger: ibid. MS. 11472, fol. 53ʳ; Becher, *Chymischer Glücks-Hafen*, 73. Clauder: above, p. 365. Texts by Balduin and Cnöffel in *Manget* (ed.), op. cit. ii. Wedel: BL, Sloane MS. 2853; and the interesting printed works listed by Ferguson, op. cit. ii, s.v. Volcamer: ÖNB, MS. 11439*, fols. 286 f. More evidence about all these men in *Miscellanea Curiosa, passim*.

could attract both doctors and aristocrats. It is a common assumption too that the chance of wealth may have drawn the improvident noble to alchemy. The Hungarian correspondence of Ádám Forgách reveals a chronic absence of both good-health and money; hence probably his recorded interest in metallurgical experimentation.[70] The rapacious Sinzendorf presumably obeyed the same urge. Yet alchemical patronage by magnates, like that by Habsburgs, had deeper roots. Forgách's neighbour, Pál Esterházy, one of the country's richest men, seems to have pursued chemistry from an early age: his library contained a good collection of books and manuscripts relating to the subject, and Becher credited him with possessing the 'prima rotatio' in the process of transmutation.[71]

The best example of a compulsive alchemist from the ranks of the highest-born is Karl Eusebius Liechtenstein. Though on his own admission deceived by a long succession of adepts whom he invited to his Austrian and Moravian estates, the prince continued to believe in the *lapis philosophorum* until his death in 1684.[72] It can have been small comfort for Liechtenstein that Pantaleon (himself not above suspicion of duplicity) dedicated to him a tract entitled: *Examen Alchymisticum quo . . . Adeptus à Sophistâ et verus Philosophus ab Impostore dignoscuntur.* This little book is, in fact, intended explicitly 'for the benefit of magnates and others who . . . do not fully understand the workings of chemistry'; and its brief (or rather, lapidary) injunctions, specious in a more straightforward way than usual, reinforce the impression of a social élite privileged to investigate such matters—the very state of affairs positively encouraged by Counter-Reformation theorists of occultism.[73] Liechtenstein's chief helper at Feldsberg was one Maurus Waibel,

---

[70] OL, Forgách cs. lt. loc. cit. (above, p. 260, n. 60), esp. P. 1883 for his debts. Becher, *Minera Arenaria*, 35 f., and *Chymischer Glücks-Hafen*, 430; repeated by J. Juncker, op. cit. 993; and by L. Szathmáry, *Magyar alkémisták* (Bp. 1928), 303–12, who describes Forgách as a 'great alchemist'.

[71] OSzK, MS. 2149 fol. hung., s.v. 'Medici'; OL. Eszterházy cs. lt., P. 125, cs. 705, nos. 11942–52. Becher, *Chymischer Glücks-Hafen*, 73; ÖNB, MS. 11472, fol. 53'.

[72] BL, Sloane MS. 1378, fol. 10: letter from Jacobus Pragestus offering his services; ibid. fol. 57: Liechtenstein replies, 29 Aug. 1682, sending 100 thalers, but no more 'cum in hanc diem semper de continuo et ab omnibus turpissime deceptus fuerim'. Nevertheless Lambeck still thought Liechtenstein's 'arcanum' worth acquiring (ÖNB, MS. 9716, fol. 241).

[73] Pantaleon, *Examen Alchymisticum ,. . .* (Nuremberg 1679); we know that this work was consulted by Leopold (ÖNB, MS. 8011, fol. 279'). Cf. above, p. 360.

whose brother, Johann Martin, acted as physician and apothecary to the duke of Sulzbach—another link between Austria and the circle of Knorr von Rosenroth. Others recorded there include the Habsburg cast-off, Schellenberg, and a professed Lutheran called Kling.[74]

The most voluminous alchemical writer of all in the Habsburg lands was a baron from Carniola, a man known to both Esterházy and Liechtenstein: Johann Friedrich von Rain. In the last decades of the seventeenth century Rain, about whose background I have been able to discover very little, gave to Emperor Leopold more than fifty carefully prepared and sometimes illustrated treatises on the philosophers' stone. They are not rewarding to read. Turgid and repetitive, full of arcane rhetoric, they present a mass of macaronic gibberish with interchangeable titles which announce the 'Apocalypse of Hermes', the 'Theory and Practice of the Stone', the 'Seven Seals of the Philosophers', or even a 'Natural Hermetico-Chymico-Magical Philosophy' in no less than twenty-eight volumes (this last being intended presumably as a *magnum opus* in both senses). They forever harp on the wisdom of the true initiate by contrast with the fraudulence of 'pseudo-chymists'.[75]

Rain was quite clearly a crank; his *lèse-majesté* thesis alone would suggest that. Yet there are several reasons for drawing attention to this curious and unregarded legacy in Vienna's former *Hof-*

---

[74] ÖNB, MS. 11469: 'Alchymia Magna seu Suppellex Alchymica operosissima . . .', dated (by a complex number-acrostic) 1677, with many hundreds of recipes, all apparently written down by Waibel, and deriving from Rudolf II, Paracelsus, Sendivogius, Francis Anthony, and many others. Ibid. fols. 57ʳ, 116ᵛ–17, 237ʳ–46ʳ, not only provide information about Waibel's brother, but also show that the latter was a friend of the adept De Comitibus, a fact confirmed by the text reprinted in Manget (ed.), op. cit. ii, 840–5, and by Becher, *Chymischer Glücks-Hafen*, sig.)(ivᵛ. Falke, op. cit. 318, mentions the existence of other alchemical MSS.; cf. Wiedemann, *Reformation*, v, 145, 153. Karl's son, Johann Adam, is supposed to have abandoned alchemy, though he is mentioned in ÖNB, MS. 11433, fol. 361; and another member of the family, Anton Florian, was taken in by 'Count Caetano' (Bauer, op. cit. 29).

[75] The historian of Carniola, Valvasor, who knew Rain, calls his family only knights (op. cit. iii, 116), but Rain regularly styles himself 'Freiherr', and other sources confirm this (e.g. ÖNB, MS. 11439*, fols. 278 f.). He would hardly don peacock's feathers when addressing the emperor (although the estates in his predicate, Radlseck and Stermol, seem to have been alienated from the family (Valvasor, op. cit. iii, 459, 561)). Links with Esterházy: OL, loc. cit. (above, n. 71), no. 11950; with Liechtenstein: ÖNB, MS. 11486, pp. 48–50. The MSS. sent to Leopold are ÖNB, MSS. 11323d, 11370, 11395–8, 11406, 11458, 11473–516, some m.p., some by a scribe.

bibliothek. For one thing, Rain held fairly prominent public office: he calls himself 'imperial counsellor and assessor in the duchy of Carniola' (and one of his enemies pities the province if it has any more assessors like him!). For another thing, he does not seem to have been personally spurned by his sovereign: Leopold was reading Rain's work at least as early as 1674, while much later the baron's son still thought it worth presenting a posthumous volume to the emperor.[76] Again, Rain displays real knowledge of the alchemical literature; besides referring constantly to the Strasbourg six-volume *Theatrum Chymicum* of 1659, he cites most leading authors from Paracelsus to Monte Snyders and Becher. He is, in other words, no mere noble dilettante, as the extraordinary trouble taken with his presentation copies confirms.

Lastly and most significantly, Rain stands firmly on the spiritual wing of his beloved science. He defines alchemy as 'the occult part of natural philosophy, and therefore a most necessary part of physics or natural investigation', and although he claims to possess the philosophers' stone, he evidently expects few material benefits from it. His *lapis philosophorum* is a sacrament, or the third person of the Trinity (formed from father mercury and son sulphur), the Resurrection, even the creation of the world and the birth of Christ. As an elixir it is 'plasmator primarius Deus' and incorporeal: 'a substance never fabricated in the alembics and furnaces of the Chymists'. Precisely the same sentiments appear in the memorandum to Leopold from Becher, for whom 'the contemplation of alchemy is a hundred times more pleasant than gold itself'.[77] Becher too saw transmutation as regeneration, and stressed that the tincture could only be acquired through divine grace. We have here something markedly different from the sales-talk of mountebanks or the project-making of mercantilists; at one point Rain even offers his secrets to the emperor in the service of Counter-Reformation. If he and Becher are fanatics, then their fanaticism is inseparable from the symbols of Catholic religion.

[76] ÖNB, MS. 12592, p. 158; ibid. MS. 11516, with ded. from Wolfgang Weickard von Rain.
[77] For Rain's personal statements see esp. ÖNB, MS. 11370; ibid. MS. 11395, fols. 2–5; ibid. MS. 11406; ibid. MS. 11488, pp. 1–38; and cf. the symbolic frontispieces to the set of MSS. 11488–515. Becher: ibid. MS. 11472, fols. 11 ff. (quoted from fols. 12^v–13^r).

★

These reflections prompt a final question: how far was the Church directly involved in Central European alchemy? That is difficult to establish, not only because of a natural fear of publicity and misrepresentation, but because of the timeless mythical role attributed to churchmen by adepts and exemplified in the legendary 'Basil Valentine', believed to be a fifteenth-century Benedictine, really the invention of a recent German author, whose arcana even penetrated into Slovak translation. Thus it is hard to know what to make of the actual provenance of a manuscript with secret recipes allegedly found (or perhaps compiled?) in the Swabian monastery of Weingarten by one of the Kurz family—probably an uncle or cousin of Albrecht—and later presented to Ferdinand III; or of one supposed to have been dug out of a grave at Breslau and written down for the benefit of Bohemian Benedictines.[78] More important is a readiness of contemporaries to accept such accounts, and in that sense we have no reason to doubt that these are genuine documents of Benedictine alchemy. In fact Liechtenstein's associate, Waibel, was also a member of the order, seconded to serve as chaplain at Feldsberg, and he must have felt himself a legitimate 'successor' to Basil Valentine.[79] Similar evidence survives from other monasteries. We may recall the Cistercian dedicatee of Dee's alchemized translation, and experimental activity in the Cistercian houses of Lower and Upper Austria is strongly suggested by some extant materials, among them a copy of the spurious correspondence of Sendivogius and several collections of tinctures and medical arcana.[80] The canons regular of St. Florian owned alchemical

[78] OSzK, MS. 3 duod. slav., fols. 57–115ᵛ, 121ʳ–48ᵛ (Basil Valentine). ÖNB, MS. 11249, dated 1650, Latin, with a dedication signed by Joannes Baptista à Willenbroch, a Swabian official of the Aulic Council, who says he has it from his relation, Baron Karl Kurz von Senftenau. ÖNB, MS. 11266, fols. 154–71, with a note by Christoph Kraus SJ, dated Klatovy in Bohemia '169.' (? or 1669).

[79] A loose address-slip in ÖNB, MS. 11469 calls him 'Fürst. Liech. Herzog zu Troppau (etc.) HoffCapellan in Veldsberg', and several of his recipes are taken from ecclesiastical sources: e.g. ibid. fol. 79ʳ, 'sincerissimè communicatum â duobus religiosis gallico et italico pro mea Discretione'; and fols. 261–6, from a Benedictine MS. Cf. Vienna, Schottenstift, MSS. 533, 539, 559, 577, 580.

[80] Heiligenkreuz, MS. 377: 'Apographum seu Copia Epistolarum hactenus ineditarum Michaelis Sendivogii'. This careful MS. seems to be identical with the printed form of the letters in Manget (ed.), op. cit. ii, 493–516, who also says that they are 'hactenus ineditae'. The MS. includes other metallurgical and alchemical material, with more references to Sendivogius, and to Monte Snyders. Heiligenkreuz,

(continued)

manuscripts, while the chronicle of Strahov notes the death in 1655 of Chrysostom Kynast, who was 'skilled in pharmacy and versed with such hope and fame in the ways of alchemy that he found favour with many lords of the realm, even with the emperor'.[81] That was, perhaps, all in a pastoral day's work for a Premonstratensian.

Friars too showed interest: Seiler, after all, learned his trade from fellow-Augustinians at Brno, though the historian of the house wisely avoids mention of him. Other recorded Augustinian alchemists include a confessor at the imperial court, while Dominicans, Carmelites, and Minims are mentioned with varying degrees of obfuscation. Abraham a Sancta Clara, suspicious of most spagirical pretensions, believed Paracelsus and Thurneysser had possessed the philosophers' stone.[82] The position of the Jesuits remains more problematical. Kircher's views may reflect a generally frosty official attitude, and Becher tells us of a young Jesuit who hesitated to participate in experiments because he feared the censure of his superiors. But the order cannot have prohibited alchemy: Lana-Terzi wrote about it with enthusiasm, Szentiványi thought it might be true, Kochański received correspondence about transmutation, Wenceslaus Ecker actually practised it, and so on.[83] Further research could no doubt fill out the picture.

MSS. 402–3: 'Alchimey Biechl', etc., dated 1674, with no clear evidence of provenance, but much mystical alchemy, some domestic accounts, and mention of the monastery of Rein in Styria. Schlierbach, MSS. 86–8 (103–5) and 94 (111): 'Quodlibetum Alchymicum', practical alchemy, probably 17th-century.

[81] A. Czerny, *Die Handschriften der Stiftsbibliothek St. Florian* (Linz 1871), nos. xi, 623: 16th-century alchemy, which belonged to the provost in 1654; xi, 644: Rudolfine recipes passed on to the monastery in 1617; xi, 647: Basil Valentine, etc. Str., MS. DJ III 2, p. 484 (Kynast).

[82] Seiler does not feature in Janetschek, op. cit. ÖNB, MS. 11469, fol. 208ʳ: a secret from Joannes Chrysostom de S. Petronella, OESADisc., 'damahls gewester Khayl. Beichtvatter'. Ibid. MS. 11395, fols. 2–5: Carolus de Assumptione B.V.M., OESADisc.; cf. above, n. 25 (UK, MS. VI F 9). ÖNB, MS. 11266, fols. 154 ff.: Franciscus de la Pietre OP, prior of Klatovy; cf. Becher, *Chymischer Glücks-Hafen*, 126 ff. (Pater Spiess OP of Cologne). ÖNB, MS. 11267, fols. 210–22: Giovanni Battista di S. Theresa OCarm., at Gorizia. Ibid. MS. 11393b, pp. 55 ff.: Gabriel ?Lieffray OMinim, 1673; cf. above, n. 25 (Gabriele 'Gotifredus'—perhaps the same man?). On Sancta Clara: Loidl, *Menschen im Barock*, 270.

[83] Becher, *Physica Subterranea*, 600 ('quoniam regula Societatis Alchymiam prohibet'). Lana-Terzi, *Prodromo*, 105–23; Szentiványi, op. cit. ii, pt. 1, 249; *Miscellanea Curiosa*, iii (1673), 439–50, letter to Kochański from the Bohemian

A full list of priests attached to alchemy would embrace also secular clergy, from the occasional parish incumbent—though most of these probably lacked either the education, the wherewithal, or the approbation of their seniors—to the ranks of higher prelates.[84] While the strict Bishop Brenner of Seckau castigated his cathedral provost early in the century for the latter's notorious pursuit of alchemy, some of Brenner's ecclesiastical successors—and not only the hedonist Archduke Leopold Wilhelm—took a different line. Pötting of Passau seems to have been involved with both Wagnereck and Pantaleon; Waldstein of Prague perhaps learned from his brother, Franz Augustin; Friedrich of Hesse at Breslau had alchemical books and a laboratory.[85] György Lippay, the primate of Hungary, dedicated to Leopold a beautiful manuscript on the four elements of the philosophers, based 'in part on the inspiration of divine clemency, in part on long years of continued experience and interpretation of the most eminent authors'.[86]

Thus alchemy was permitted some role within the Church, and ecclesiastical criticism of it tended to be distinctly muted. The one exception, Kircher's diatribe, betrays by its very stridency, not to say its excellent information on the subject, both the author's uneasiness about this awkward condemnation of 'superstition' and

military architect, Philip Talducci, in 1671. Ecker (not in Sommervogel) is mentioned as an alchemist by J. F. Hertodt (Manget (ed.), op. cit. ii, 698), and he must be the 'Wenceslaus E.S.I.' who writes to Count Rappach in ÖNB, MS. 11433, fol. 308. Cf. Christoph Kraus SJ (above, n. 78); and the Martin Santinus SJ, whom Marci (*Philosophia Vetus Restituta*, 280 f.) calls an eager chemist.

[84] One parish priest who appears in the literature is Dr. Andreas Jehlin of Waizenkirchen (near Eferding in Upper Austria): ÖNB, MS. 11472, fol. 53'; Becher, *Chymischer Glücks-Hafen*, 73; Schmieder, op. cit. 440.

[85] Brenner: Schuster, op. cit. 569. Pötting: ÖNB, MS. 11319*, fol. 127', where Wagnereck's tincture is left to the bishop of Passau, presumably in the 1680s; Schmieder, op. cit. 442–5. Rain includes him in his list of those possessing the vulgar tincture (ÖNB, MS. 11486, pp. 48–50), who include also the late Wittelsbach archbishop of Cologne. Waldstein: ÖNB, MS. 11439*, fols. 289 f.; cf. above, p. 371. Friedrich of Hesse: Dersch, art. cit. 299, 301 f.

[86] ÖNB, MS. 11280: 'Mons Magnesiae ex quo Obscurum sed Verum Subiectum Philosophorum effoditur et Expresse denominatur', esp. fols. 2–5; the beautifully calligraphed text is standard theoretical alchemy with references mainly to Sendivogius and the *Theatrum Chymicum*. Becher (ÖNB, MS. 11472, fol. 53'; *Chymischer Glücks-Hafen*, 73) oddly refers to the archbishop as 'Count Georg Lippay in Pressburg', and seems to suggest that he is still alive in the 1670s; but there can hardly have been another 'Georgius Lippay de Zombor' (except the prelate's insignificant artist-nephew).

the popularity of his chosen target. A satirical oration as late as 1708 is more typical in failing to deliver the *coup de grâce*: 'Quis nam Aasoth?', asks the speaker; then decodes his chemical anagram to reveal 'Thomas Aquinas' as the true quintessence, apparently oblivious of Aquinas's positive association with the traditions of transmutation.[87]

Yet the Church did not need to implicate itself very far, since the larger service of alchemy, and of occultism as a whole, was to consolidate Catholicism's intellectual and spiritual grip over secular society. Zwelfer may have erred monstrously in fact when he asserted that many great monasteries grew through donations made possible by the philosophers' stone, but his words may be true in a transferred, symbolic sense which he could hardly have apprehended.[88] For alchemy now boasted good imperial, aristocratic, Catholic credentials. Of course, neither it nor other branches of learned magic were restricted to the Catholic world; but only there, and in the conservative Lutheran circles which—I have suggested— represented a half-way house on the way to that world, was discussion of such things still a central theme of intellectual life, rather than an increasingly outmoded sideshow. The very fact that no objective breakthrough in chemistry took place anywhere in seventeenth-century Europe serves perhaps to highlight the growing differences of mentality and emphasis across the continent.

Moreover, for all its experimental fumes and recipes, alchemy had become in the Habsburg lands the least revolutionary of techniques, stressing a preservative rather than a transformatory function, a potable gold, *aurum potabile*, which claimed to afford spiritual as much as physical release. The descendants of Rain and Liechtenstein a hundred years later were not Lavoisier, or even Scheele, but the reactionary Rosicrucian mystagogues of the early Romantic age.[89] Along with the other kinds of occultism we have considered in this chapter, alchemy formed part of a hierarchical Baroque culture where social transmutation was hardly easier to achieve than the laboratory gold of the enthusiasts. Now we are ready to turn to baser metals: to popular magic and its fate.

[87] J. G. J. Rings, *Universalis Aasoth. Medicina Catholica D. Thomas Aquinas è solidioribus Alchymiae fundamentis demonstratus* (Pr. [1708]).
[88] Zwelfer, *Pharmacopoeia Regia*, 329.
[89] Multhauf, *passim*; Kopp, op. cit. ii, esp. 223–39.

CHAPTER 11

The attack on popular magic

We have seen how the educated could dabble in almost everything, so long as they respected conventions. It is instructive to consider just two among the small number who overstepped the mark. The first, Giuseppe Francesco Borri, was a European celebrity, one of the most potent mages of the day. Facing trial for heresy in his native Italy, he fled the country and toured the continent during the 1660s as scientist, occultist, Paracelsan physician, and alchemist, winning golden opinions for his learning.[1] Among those intrigued by his undoubted talents were the Habsburgs: he spent some time at the Innsbruck court, then was received by Leopold in 1670; his alchemical remedies grew familiar in Central Europe. This is an extraordinary career indeed for one accused of flagrant heterodoxy at Rome, where he was regarded as a kind of latter-day Giordano Bruno. In the event, the nuncio at length managed to persuade Leopold that Borri should be delivered to the Inquisition, largely, it seems, because he fell under suspicion of complicity in the Hungarian troubles. Even so, the emperor insisted that his life be spared, and many believed that Borri's last wizardry had been to save Leopold from poisoning by none other than Ferenc Nádasdy.[2]

[1] Borri's life and religious opinions in: *Vita, processo e sentenza di Francesco Borri* (n.p. 1671), of which there is a German version, *Relatio Fidei ... das ist eine Erzehlung des Glaubens, Thaten und Leben des ... Franciscus Joseph Burrhi,* dated 1670; 'Breve relazione...', in *La Chiave del Gabinetto del Cavagliere ... Borri* ('Cologne' (*rectè* Geneva?) 1681), 337–80; E. Ferrario, *La vita di Francesco Giuseppe Borro* (Milan 1858), adds little. There is an account of his 1661 trial in Bod., Mendham MS. 36, fols. 135ᵛ–61. For his philosophical-medical ideas see *Chiave del Gabinetto*; and his *Epistolae Duae ... ad Th. Bartholinum* (Copenhagen 1669). For his alchemy see *Chiave del Gabinetto,* 124–91; and his *Hyppocrates Chymicus* (Cologne 1690); cf. Roth-Scholtz, op. cit. i, 123–9. Borri was approved of by, among others, Monconys, op. cit. ii, 74, 82, 135, 137, 143 ff., 154 f.; Oldenburg in R. M. and M. B. Hall (eds.), op. cit. i, no. 234; ii, no. 283; Arnold, op. cit. i, pt. 2, 315; ii, pt. 3, 188–90. Through some remarkable oversight his works did not appear on the Index (Reusch, op. cit. ii, 187).

[2] Austrian connections in *Nuntiaturberichte,* i, nos. 128, 132, 134–5, 146, 150, 152–153, 165, 189, 195–7, 202, 265, 484, 486, 489; ii, 1–8; Bauer, op. cit. 28 f., and cf. id., *Chemie und Alchemie in Österreich* (V. 1883), 49 f.; *Chiave del Gabinetto,* 376–8; ÖNB, MS. 11393b, pp. 64–6; ibid. MS. 11433, fols. 255–6ʳ, 306ʳ, 337 f.

Borri fell because he flouted Catholic doctrine and compounded it by political intrigue. The Hungarian magnate László Liszti represents a rather different case. The Liszti family rose to prominence in the sixteenth century through a self-made Humanist bishop who became close adviser to Maximilian II, and the dynasty's favour still rested on László: he lived at the castle of Köpcsény outside Pozsony, and was created count in 1655. But the noble lord's life was the very reverse of exemplary: having begun by forging legal documents, he then turned to murder, slander, arson, sodomy, alchemy, black magic. For good measure he sought to poison his uncle and pass off a Viennese foundling as his own son. The authorities brought him to trial, but Liszti's high station in Hungary preserved him from serious molestation until the Lower Austrians arraigned him on a political charge of counterfeiting coin which brought him to the block in 1662 or 1663.[3]

Liszti's sensational life, like Borri's, points a clear lesson: how difficult it was for those established in polite society—whether by rank or by erudition—to fall foul of authority on intellectual issues. In both cases a manifest political risk and extreme threat to orthodox Catholic values needed to be shown. Did Leopold hazily remember, when signing the death-warrant for Ferenc Nádasdy, that his grandmother (*née* Erzsébet Báthory) had been one of the most bloodthirsty of all Renaissance occultists—and even she had been spared the extreme penalty?[4] But while the privileged orders were presumed harmless, the rest of the population faced secular or ecclesiastical penalties from the start; no presumption existed of their innocence in either sphere. I have already suggested that what could be embraced on an elevated plane by the seventeenth-century intellectual was progressively denied to the people. A greater wedge than ever before was driven between the two cultures, and it is now time to investigate the place of the uneducated in the general

---

[3] A. Komáromy (ed.), *Listi László munkái* (3rd edn. Bp. 1891), an edn. of Liszti's mediocre poems with good introductory life by Komáromy, who is however surely wrong to make his subject's magic a mere pretext (the references to Agrippa of Nettesheim, etc., are genuine enough). Amazing to relate, one of László's uncles likewise practised alchemy and was executed as a forger. Cf. above, p. 17.

[4] The story of Erzsébet Nádasdy, née Báthory, who had maidens slain in order to bathe in their blood, is well authenticated. See R. A. von Elsberg, *Elisabeth Bathory* (2nd edn. Breslau 1904); cf. ÖNB, MS. 13328. She ended her life under what might be called 'castle-arrest'.

scheme. It must be stressed at the outset: the world of Baroque popular magic is even more intractable and neglected than the learning of the refined, which at least often found its way into books (however little they may have been read since their own day). All suggestions must be tentative; much more documentary evidence will need to be produced to substantiate firm conclusions. Still, the main lines of this part of my argument seem obvious enough, for they are a corollary of the previous chapter: those who could not be trusted to interpret the world for themselves must have their opinions handed down by the Church. The more prone they are to superstition and error, the more guidance they require in Christian magic and orthodoxy.

★

Some, of course, accounted simple-mindedness a blessing. Great preachers and moralizers address themselves to the common people with sympathy, as subjects unencumbered by intellectual pride. Martin van Cochem's life of Christ, an enormously influential work (and his first to be translated into Czech), requests the pious reader 'not to measure the words of this book according to the rules of philosophy and theology'—though it does in fact insert references. Sancta Clara praises the capabilities of peasants and artisans, and there are strains in the published sermons by Hirnhaim of the same *docta ignorantia* which we have already encountered in his philosophical writings. Growing quantities of devotional literature catered specifically for the 'meaner sort'.[5] But the lower classes would need unshakeable faith and saintly patience to endure their deteriorating socio-economic position, and many Catholic intellectuals were not so confident of their loyalty. Most treatises written either directly for a wider public or for those who ministered to it paint a gloomy picture of its temptations. They draw on deep fears of a recrudescence of heresy and a sense of diabolism which is enhanced precisely because its expositors know so much about the supposed manifestations of the devil. The majority of these works were a product of international Catholic attitudes—published indifferently at Rome or Lyons, Cologne or Ingolstadt. Let us take

---

[5] Cochem, op. cit., preface to reader; Loidl, *Menschen im Barock*, 218–46. H. Hirnhaim, *S. Norberti ... Sermo* (Pr. 1676); *Richtiger Weg des Lebens* (Pr. 1698); etc.; cf. above, p. 328 f. B. Balbin, *Přepodiwná Matka Swato-Horská Marya* (Litomyšl 1666), dedication.

just two examples, for the beginning and the end of the seventeenth century, of authors particularly associated with Austria.

Martin Delrio was a Spaniard who lived in the Netherlands and, rather like his friend Lipsius, forsook the world of late Humanism for the embattled certainties of Rome. He joined the Jesuit order and spent the years after 1600 at Graz as a colleague of Lamormaini and Pázmány. While in Styria he revised his recently published *Disquisitiones Magicae*, perhaps the most notorious and widely publicized of all the demonologies of its age.[6] In uncompromising language Delrio excoriates every imaginable folk superstition with a severity quite unaffected by the theoretical admission that the devil's powers are only derived from the Almighty, his wiles only deceptions. In Delrio's eyes almost all uneducated occult beliefs stand condemned, not because they are occult (for that would endanger cardinal principles of the faith), but because they are uneducated.

From the famous to the obscure; from erudite Latin tome to colloquial German tract for the times: eighty years after Delrio, Adam von Lebenwaldt, a Styrian physician, wrote a pithy and entertaining summary of the same material. In the *Acht Tractätel*, published at Salzburg and dedicated to various Austrian monks, the dangerous follies of popular credulity are itemized—kabbalists, casters of horoscopes, and so on—and contrasted with the wise forbearance of civilized men. Like a good disciple of Kircher, Lebenwaldt does not exclude alchemy from his strictures, though (equally characteristically) he is not consistent: local patriotism induces him to defend the name of Paracelsus, even against his revered Jesuit mentor, while his own medical practice accorded thoroughly with the spirit of the *Academia Naturae Curiosorum* to which he belonged.[7]

Such attitudes could largely be matched among the ruling

[6] Delrio, op. cit. There were at least fourteen further printings by 1650; where indicated I have also used the Cologne 1633 edn. On the rest of his *œuvre* see Sommervogel, ii, cols. 1894–905. Delrio's friendship with Lipsius appears from the latter's correspondence (*Opera Omnia*, ii, 160 and *passim*).

[7] A. à Lebenwaldt, *Acht Tractätel von dess Teuffels List und Betrug*, i–viii (Salzburg 1680–2); alchemy in iv, esp. 80–110 on Paracelsus,—Lebenwaldt's criticism of the art does not touch its basic principles. For his life and other works: R. Peinlich, 'Dr. Adam von Lebenwaldt, ein steirischer Arzt und Schriftsteller des 17. Jahrhunderts', *MHVSt.* xxviii (1880), 42–105.

echelons of Lutheranism, which had, after all, been terrified by the threat from the devil since the first days of the Reformation. The most important Lutheran writer about popular superstition, Johann Praetorius (or Schulze), spent his career pouring scorn on primitive aberrations while upholding all the supernatural inferences of the learned. Praetorius pursued the mirage of a watertight distinction between divine and diabolical knowledge through a vast range of topics from chiromancy to witchcraft.[8] He was particularly attracted by stories of Rübezahl, the mountain sprite from the Riesengebirge on the borders of Saxony and Bohemia, which were perhaps a folk creation of considerable antiquity but first appeared in print in 1618 and gained wide fame during the sevententh century. Was Rübezahl, with his shades of Eulenspiegel and Robin Hood, a chivalrous righter of wrongs or a minion of hell? While few educated men on either side of the frontier entertained any doubts about his existence, they tended to take the censorious view.[9]

Considerable correspondence between the mentalities of educated Lutherans and Catholics did not, however, hinder the latter from building on the Counter-Reformation as a popular programme even when the Protestant menace had become a historical myth. Certainly, doctrinal priorities must form the starting-point for any account of the relation between popular magic and the Catholic Church. It was common ground among its theorists that Lutherans had been directly inspired by Satan. Pázmány wrote repeatedly and at length, quoting a wealth of sources, in support of the assertion that the founder of Protestantism was literally born of an incubus. Delrio devotes a whole preface to equating heresy, just as literally, with the impulse to black magic.[10]

*

[8] On Praetorius (1630–80) see the lengthy article and bibliography (by F. Zarncke) in *ADB* xxv, 520–9. Good examples of his curious work are the *Ludicrum Chiromanticum* (Jena 1661), a huge rag-bag of opinions on chiromancy; and homely vernacular pieces like *Philologemata abstrusa de Pollice* (Sagan–Leipzig 1677), and *De Coscinomantia, oder vom Sieb–Lauffe* (Hof a.d. Saale 1677), on magic or divination by means of thumbs and sieves.

[9] J. Praetorius, *Daemonologia Rubinzalii Silesii* (Leipzig 1662); Balbín, *Miscellanea Historica,* i, bk. 1, 11–22; J. Kolář, 'O Rybecoulovi', *ČL* v (1896), 439–52; cf. further arts. ibid., esp. V. Tille in vii (1898), 173–80, 257–64, 347–52, 439–43; and Zíbrt, *BČH* iii, nos. 10813–989.

[10] Pázmány, *Levelei,* i, no. 6; id., *Kalauz,* 177–99; id., *Összes munkái,* i, 397 ff. Delrio, op. cit. (1633 edn.), sig.):(4 –):():(2.

The first campaign was engaged on a level of persuasion: in favour of the holy magic of ancient Mother Church. The restoration of liturgy and ritual went hand-in-hand with an attack on Lutheran survival and folk superstition. Jesuit missionaries in Bohemia confiscated magical recipes and amulets along with heretical literature.[11] In return they offered the seven sacraments, buttressed by an ever more elaborate symbolism.

Central among them stood the Eucharist, surrounded with that veneration for the mystery of the Host whose converse—as we shall see—was the heinous sin of sacrilege. Scarcely less prominent appeared the rites of passage into and out of this world: baptism and extreme unction. Countless tales were told of stillborn infants marvellously revived long enough for them to be marked with the sign of the cross, or of old men reached by the viaticum and the oil-bearing priest despite all obstacles of weather and natural hazard. Penance, with its finely-calculated gradations of self-abasement and the formal requirement of confession, created a key bond between the ecclesiastical and the civil community.[12] Confirmation and matrimony received more-or-less conventional treatment, but the sacrament of holy orders was accorded a very significant place. The priest did not just mediate between God and man; by virtue of ordination he was also a sanctifier. Thus natural objects, once blessed by him, might take on magical properties. Consecrated water for the stoup; consecrated soil for the crops of the faithful; consecrated wood to resist fire: all such materials, indistinguishable in form from their unregenerate counterparts, stood on the very borderland of superstition, always particularly liable to abuse, but always peculiarly attractive to the populace. Catholicism's complicated rites for seasons, festivals, processions, and the like, with all their half-comprehended associations, left the individual priest as

---

[11] Č. Zíbrt, 'Albrecht Chanovský... o výročních obyčejích, pověrách a slavnostech staročeských', *VKČSN*, 1895, no. 24, 2–7: Podlaha, 'Z dějin katolických missií', 106 f., 116, 118 f., 124, 126 f., 130. Cf. below, n. 29 (Balbín-Rezek).

[12] Veit–Lenhart, op. cit. 23 ff., 209–15; Loidl, op. cit. 49 ff.; much in Gugitz, op. cit., *passim*. The great contemporary work on this subject is J. B. Thiers, *Traité des Superstitions qui regardent tous les Sacremens*, i–iii (Paris 1704), who freely admits (e.g. ii, 25–30) that the only arbiter of superstition is the actual practice of the Church, which may authorize no firm view on a particular point (when it is superstitious to insist on one), and may change with time. Thus superstition is a less serious thing than outright Protestant heresy (the Orthodox Churches are full of it), and the more enlightened Frenchman reaches a definition quite different from that of Delrio.

arbiter, having power to create a little heaven on earth whenever he uttered the formulae of benediction.[13]

This sort of magical activity by representatives of the Church relied on the intervention of spirits, the beneficent agents of Catholic occultism. Hence great stress was laid by propagators of Counter-Reformation on the spiritual hierarchy and great efforts were made to demonstrate its validity. One important method of confirmation seemed to lie in the apparition of the souls of the dead, which dwelt—as the Church believed—in purgatory. Their dealings are reported by many of our authorities: we find ghost stories in Balbín and Beckovský, in Sancta Clara and Procopius, in monastic chronicles; while Delrio tackled the matter with his usual ingenuity.[14] A curious (but symptomatic) episode took place in 1651, when two recently-buried Augustinian friars sent back messages to their friends in Vienna through the medium of a novice. The case was seen as popular evidence of Catholic truth—one of the revenants being made to speak his native Czech rather than Latin, thereby—presumably—to establish his bona fides the better.[15]

Best proof of the spirit world came always from the supernatural powers of saints, an unfailing *topos* of Counter-Reformation magic. We have already seen something of their cult in Central Europe, which reached its apotheosis with Jan Nepomuk, that martyr to the mystique of confession and the sanctity of priestly office. Whatever the regional associations of given saints, their relics uniformly inspired holy awe and accounts of their efficacy were allowed to multiply.[16] While the authorities made some attempt to eliminate

[13] Veit–Lenhart, op. cit. 130–80 and *passim*, who seem at times to be themselves confused where 'superstition' began.

[14] Balbín, *Miscellanea Historica*, i, bk. 3, 184 ff.; id., 'Relatio', ed. Rezek, 207; Beckovský, op. cit. pt. 1, 283, 369 f., and *passim*; Procopius, *Iudiciale*, 232–49, 292 ff., 554–70; Loidl, op. cit. 253–6; Wiedemann, *Reformation*, v, 171 f.; Šimák, 'Chotěšovské zprávy'; F. Dvorský, 'Historické příspěvky k dějinám pověr ...', *ČL* xi (1902), 194–6, 248 f., 328–30, 490–2; xii (1903), 277, at 248 f.; C. Straka, 'Pověsti strašidelné ze Strahovských letopisů', *ČL* xxv (1925), 15–22. Delrio, op. cit. i, 248 ff.; cf. Pázmány, *Kalauz*, bk. 14.

[15] UK, MS. XI E 12: 'Enarratio Casuum Praeteritorum Viennae Austriae in Conventu Lauretano ...', fols. 10–43ʳ (narrative); 44–76 (interpretation). One commentator (ibid. fols. 1–9) is a 'sceptic', preferring the view that the manifestations were *evil* spirits—no doubt a reader of Delrio.

[16] Good examples are the saints in Prague cathedral, described by Wenceslaus Coelestinus a Blumenberg, *Devota ac debita veneratio ad Sanctos Patronos in Sacra Metropolitana Ecclesia Pragensi* (Pr. 1654), and J. I. Dlouhoveský, *Podivín s Přibislavou*

(continued)

accretions of legend around the popular observance of saints, as of the Eucharist, no one could proceed far without the risk of falling into crypto-Protestant error. Thus the pious stories were encouraged and the picturesque customs embroidered, reaching their peak in the mid-eighteenth century at a time when enlightened criticism of them began to spread from above, whence the cults themselves had originally been fostered. Everywhere devotion and superstition blended in a mixture the more bewildering for resting—at least until after 1700—so much on oral tradition.[17]

Invocation of saints leads us logically to the fundamental category of Counter-Reformation magic: miracle. A miracle was a divine intervention, a response to the prayers of the faithful. Since Satan could draw on similar occult resources, it had to be sharply distanced from the automatic, and therefore diabolical, workings of charms or books of incantations, widely employed in Central Europe and fiercely attacked—albeit with only limited success—by the priesthood. The devil, argues Delrio in his robust but equivocal way, works 'mira' or 'mirabilia', not true 'miracula', and such distinctions were a commonplace of the theologians.[18] However that might be, the need for thaumaturgy was not far to seek among the population at large. Insecurity and helplessness in face of a fickle universe, so admirably described for contemporary England by Keith Thomas,[19]

(Pr. 1673, both reprinted, ed. A. Podlaha, Pr. 1931); the latter treatise lists different relics to be worshipped on some 250 days throughout the year. Cf. the treatment in Pázmány, *Kalauz*, bk. 13; id., 'Felelet az Magyari ... könyvére' in *Összes munkái*, i, at 153–77, and 'Keresztyéni felelet ...', ibid. ii, 321–501.

[17] Veit-Lenhart, op. cit. 58 ff., 109–13, 234 ff., for critics; and much in Thiers, op. cit., and Loidl, op. cit. 86 ff. and *passim*. Cf. above, pp. 223 f.

[18] For incantations see V. Houdek, 'Moravská kniha o zaklínání duchův', *ČL* i (1892), 267–73; J. Čižmář, 'Moravské knihy zvané 'Krištofky' ...', *ČL* ix (1900), 395–403. Heiligenkreuz, MS. 530 is a typical example, presumably confiscated. Cf. Delrio, op. cit. ii, bk. 3, pt. 2; below, n. 26 (Kameníček). In 1644 pupils at one of the Jesuit schools in Prague were tried on charges of conjuration and only released after lengthy hearings which were reported to the emperor (J. Kočí, *Čarodějnické procesy ... v českých zemích v 16.–18. století* (Pr. 1973), 69–81). For discussion of the powers of the devil—who harnesses local motions and all manner of deception—see Delrio, op. cit. i, 124 ff.; Zara, op. cit. 154–92; Carena, op. cit. 217 f.; Pereira, op. cit. 30 ff.; Schott, *Magia Universalis*, i, 27–44; Loidl, op. cit. 249–53. Cf., for a Lutheran view, J. Praetorius, *Alectryomantia, seu, Divinatio Magica cum Gallis Gallinaceis peracta* (Frankfurt-Leipzig 1680), 56 ff.

[19] Thomas, op. cit., ch. 1.

is yet more evident in the Habsburg lands, which had neither strong reserves of urban self-help nor a genuinely caritative movement within their restored Catholicism to compensate for the ravages of war and depression.

Little material succour existed even for distressed burghers: a few hospitals, some run by municipalities, others by the clergy and communal enterprise. Prague, for example, possessed ten or so by the eighteenth century, and Vienna had a *Bürgerspital* financed through a monopoly on the brewing and retailing of beer.[20] The poor in the towns and the mass of the peasantry could expect less still: religious orders did what they could, above all the handful of houses belonging to the Brothers of Mercy and some wealthy old monasteries with long experience in basic pharmaceutics. A few institutions were set up for war-wounded and invalids.[21] But all remained primitive, and scarcely extended beyond the cities; the great plague of 1679–80, recrudescent periodically in the next years, and the Turkish onslaught of 1683 brought catastrophe to hundreds of thousands.[22]

Nor was there much guidance for the great mass of humanity about how to cope with routine problems of everyday life. One source alone seems to have been available, at least to those who could read, and predominantly in German-speaking areas: the so-called *Hausväterliteratur*. This 'paterfamilias literature' comprised advice on the management of households and estates, on growing crops and raising animals, on medicine—with remedies against plague, and so forth. The genre originally belonged to Lutherans: its greatest exponent, Johann Coler, was a Silesian pastor who died in 1636. But Coler's *Oeconomia* and the other standard texts were readily tolerated and reprinted in Catholic territories, while

[20] Bílek, *Statky*, 406–14: Prague had common spitals, infirmaries attached to the Strahov and Crusader monasteries, and an Italian, with associated French, hospice (on which see Rigetti, op. cit. 163 ff.). *Geschichte der Stadt Wien*, v, 323–30; L. Sailer, 'Das Bierbrau- und Schankmonopol des Wiener Bürgerspitals', *MVGStW* vi (1926), 1–35. A typical small-town *Bürgerspital*, at Waidhofen an der Ybbs, is described in Friess, 'Soziale und wirtschaftliche Lage', 182 f.

[21] Sobel, op. cit.; and cf. above, p 132. Str., MS. CR I 7, is a printed medical compendium with annotations by Hieronymus Hirnhaim which display an extensive knowledge of practical cures. *Feldzüge des Prinzen Eugen*, 290–7.

[22] *Geschichte der Stadt Wien*, vi, 260 f., with an improbable figure of 50,000 dead in 1679; F. Mareš, 'Veliký mor v letech 1679 a 1680', *SbH* (Rezek), i (1883), 397–419; V. Schulz, *Příspěvky k dějinám moru v zemích českých z let 1531–1746* (Pr. 1901).

Catholics produced similar compendia, like the *Opus Oeconomicum* by a Bohemian Jesuit, Christoph Fischer—a genuine friend of the common man—which even attained translation into Czech, and the works of János Lippay in Hungary.[23] Such writing presented no threat to the Church's intellectual dominance over the lower classes: thoroughly conservative and full of semi-occult information, from weather-prediction to distillation, from iatrochemical remedies to the interpretation of dreams, *Hausväterliteratur* shaded off into the vernacular compilations of natural magic which were so popular in Central Europe and varied little between Hildebrand at the beginning of the seventeenth century and Andreas Glorez at the end. Below it came primitive calendars firmly controlled by the ecclesiastical censorship.[24]

Many peasants evidently remained untouched by any veneer of acculturation. They could do no more than pray to the Virgin or some other intercessor when they needed relief of suffering. Poignant testimony to such hopes of cure or release appears in the 'miracle-books' kept at most of the shrines visited by simple people throughout the Habsburg lands and recording wonders vouchsafed to their faith. The Marian image at Mikulov, for example, not in

---

[23] J. Coler, *Oeconomia oder Haussbuch*, first published in the 1590s, later expanded; by 1680 it appears at Frankfurt as *Oeconomia Ruralis et Domestica ... in 1,150* folio pages. Hohberg's *Georgica Curiosa* (above, p. 178) was a more sophisticated handbook, likewise by an Austro-Silesian author. Fischer's work appeared in Latin at Prague, 1679–83, and in German at Nuremberg–Frankfurt, 1690; cf. *Knihopis*, nos. 2542–4; he appended practical glossaries in Latin, Czech, and German. In 1680 Fischer displayed sympathy for the peasants (Schulz, *Korrespondence jesuitů*, nos. 111–69, *passim*; Kašpar, *Nevolnické povstání*, 164). On Lippay, cf. above, p. 318, n. 17; and J. Barta, *Mezőgazdasági irodalmunk a XVIII században* (Bp. 1973), ch. 1. His *Calendarium Oeconomicum Perpetuum* was also translated into Hungarian.

[24] On the whole genre see W.-E. Peuckert, *Gabalia, ein Versuch zur Geschichte der magia naturalis im 16. bis 18. Jahrhundert* (Berlin 1967), an absorbing, but peculiar book. Glorez announces himself as the 'Moravian Albertus Magnus' in his *Eröffnetes Wunderbuch von Waffensalben* (Regensburg–Stadtamhof 1700) and *Neuangeordnete vollständige Haus- und Land-Bibliothec* (Nuremberg 1719); but cf. Peuckert in *Europäische Kulturverflechtungen ... Festschrift B. Schiers* (Göttingen 1967), 73–81. The great interest shown by later 17th-century Germans in sympathetic medicine can only be noted here *en passant*. There are fascinating lists of popular calendars, including some by Dobrzensky, in *Knihopis*, nos. 950, 990–6, 1285–97, 1373–85, 1723–45, 1788, 1809, 1820–39, 2006–37, 2181, 2376–7, 2622–3, 2637–48, 2728–32, 2765–81, 2845–51, 3052, 3112–34, 3141, 3236–9, 3455–7, 3513–4, 4394–400, 4500–50, 4576–82, 5966, 6142–7, 6574–605, 6696–7, 6932–5, 15145–6, 15762–4, 16395, 16967–81, 16996, 17058, 17233–4, 17583, 17588–90 (cf. the 18th-century series, nos. 2471–2537).

the front rank of sanctuaries, healed 150 miscellaneous patients between 1625 and 1675, some from Vienna and farther afield. Mariastein in the Tyrol saw a larger stream of satisfied clients, freed from maladies as diverse as toothache and insanity, happy to manifest their recovery by pilgrimage and reading of Masses, by prayer on the steps of the church and gifts of votive tablets or wax replicas of the Madonna.[25]

*

Ordinary people, then, had no adequate protection against the advances of the devil. Once they were ensnared by Satan, only a single avenue of rescue could be attempted: exorcism. Some Protestants retained formulae for the official casting-out of evil spirits, and they belonged in the uneasy half-way house of state Lutheranism; but Counter-Reformation made them an integral part of its campaign to recover men's souls. That involved problems not at all easy to settle on a theoretical level—exorcism could come dangerously close to the sort of mindless incantation which the Church most feared.[26] None the less we find examples of it from the early days of Central Europe's Catholic revival. The first *cause célèbre* in Austria took place in 1584, when a girl brought to Vienna's burgher hospital was delivered of 12,652 demons by the Jesuit, Georg Scherer. Scherer describes the case vividly in one of his sermons (as well as revealing his mathematical calculations, based on the value of a 'legion' of devils): the wicked grandmother who summoned the nether powers; the helpless suffering of the girl; the release through prayer and the sacraments, holy water and the *Benedicite*.[27]

This exorcism, coinciding with another conducted in Bavaria at

---

[25] Ignatius Wohlhaubter, *Miracul oder Wunderzeichen, welche Gott der Allmächtige ... in ... Nicolsburg ... gewürcket* (V. 1675), with a Baroque ded. to the emperor and an approbation from the bishop of Olomouc. H. Bachmann, *Das Mirakelbuch der Wallfahrtskirche Mariastein in Tirol als Quelle zur Kulturgeschichte, 1678–1742* (Innsbruck–Munich 1973). Many miracle-books are listed and used by Gugitz, op. cit. Cf. *Knihopis*, nos. 6280, 6285–6, 6288.

[26] As with the later case described by F. Kameníček in *ČL* ii (1893), 674–9, though the MSS. in question claimed to be copies of a Jesuit work. Cf. above, n. 18 (esp. Koči); and, for Anglican and Puritan reactions to exorcism, Thomas, op. cit. 477–92.

[27] G. Scherer, *Christliche Erinnerung bei der Historien ... einer Jungkfrawen, die mit zwölfftausent, sechshundert, und zwey und fünfftzig Teuffeln besessen gewesen* (Ingolstadt 1584, reprinted in *Opera*, ii, 179–96). Cf. Bibl, 'Eder', 133, 135; Beckovský, op. cit., pt. 1, 341; Socher, op. cit. 281–4.

the same time and likewise widely reported, set a pattern for the future; in fact the decades of the 1580s and 1590s saw a sudden wave of manuals for exorcists, some later to be prohibited by the Index on the grounds of superstition.[28] In the next century their procedures were widely applied, and carried into the front line by missionaries who, working with the active help of the authorities, released their converts from demons of recognizably Protestant hue. Both Archduke Leopold of Styria and Cardinal Dietrichstein tried their hand at driving out devils, and the Roman religion was declared the only true insurance policy against Satan. When the penitent Silesian aristocrat, Christoph Leopold Schaffgotsch, had a chapel built atop the highest summit of the Riesengebirge, he was not only celebrating his personal acceptance of Catholicism but also seeking to exorcise his estates from Rübezahl.[29]

The *modus operandi* as approved for Hungary is described in a lengthy section of the ritual of Esztergom. Priests should beware, it says, of confusing possession with mere melancholy or illness: its symptoms are an ability to speak or comprehend unfamiliar tongues, to display mysterious or abnormal powers, and so on. It is combated by prayer and fasting, and by the Church's own invocation of supernatural assistance, which must not, however, fall into crude or illicit magic. 'The exorcist must not indulge in high-sounding or superfluous chatter or curious questionings, especially about future and occult things.'[30] The practical implications of that advice are well brought out by an episode which took place at Pozsony in 1642

---

[28] *Erschröckliche gantz warhafftige Geschicht, welche sich mit . . . Hannsen Geisslbrechts . . . Haussfrawen . . . verlauffen hat* (Ingolstadt 1584). An important collection of manuals, compiled mainly by north Italian friars, was twice issued at Cologne by the Protestant publisher Zetzner: *Thesaurus Exorcismorum atque Conjurationum Terribilium* (1608, 1626); cf. Reusch, op. cit. ii, 218–23; H. C. Lea, *Materials towards a History of Witchcraft*, i–iii (New York 1957), 1049–69.

[29] Balbin, 'Relatio', ed. Rezek, 216 f., 224 f., 236, 247, 250, 254; Dvorský, 'Příspěvky', 195 f., 249; Schuster, op. cit. 628–41; F. Bischoff and Chr. d'Elvert, *Zur Geschichte des Glaubens an Zauberer, Hexen und Vampyre in Mähren und Österreich-Schlesien* (Brünn 1859), 76; E. Tomek, op. cit. 407 n.; Koči, *Čarodějnické procesy*, 59 f. Scherer, *Christliche Erinnerung*, 55–63; Pázmány, *Kalauz*, 127 ff.; cf. Beyerlinck, op. cit. ii, lit. D, 1–18. A curious case of temporary possession during a dream, warded off by faith, is recorded by the late 16th-century Catholic academic, Marek Bydžovský: UK, MS. XVII G 22, fols. 444ᵛ–6ᵛ. For Schaffgotsch: W. Roesch, 'Die Geschichte der Kapelle auf der Schneekoppe im Riesengebirge', *Archiv für Schlesische Kirchengeschichte*, viii (1950), 105–16; cf. above, p. 300.

[30] *Rituale Strigoniense* (Tyrnau 1715), 250–'256' (*recte* 274).

and which combines elements of spiritualism and possession. A twenty-year-old woman staying in the Hungarian capital was tormented by the uneasy ghost of a local man, recently converted to Catholicism before his death. As the unfortunate victim's struggles increased and preternatural manifestations multiplied, priests were called in, who ascertained that certain pious wishes of the deceased had not been fulfilled. After implementing them, they could exorcise the spirit from the girl and send the disquieted soul from purgatory to heaven.[31]

This bizarre but typical story has particular interest. For one thing it involves a highly authoritative *démarche*: thirty-two witnesses to the events were examined by an official tribunal before the account was published under the name of Mihály Kopcsányi— shortly to become bishop of Vác—with an approbation from the newly-installed primate, Lippay; and Kopcsányi's tract promptly appeared in German and Italian translation. Moreover, it sparked off a controversy with Protestants which extended beyond the borders of Hungary. Not only did the exorcism earn a swift refutation from the Lutheran, Zacharias Láni of Trencsén, whose anti-Catholic tirade likewise came out in more than one language. The Calvinists, after some delay, produced a stronger counterblast by sending the materials to the prince of orthodox Dutch theologians, Gisbert Voet, for thorough disproof.[32] And these Protestant attacks on exorcism are themselves revealing, for whereas Láni views the spirit as real, but evil (simply Satan cunningly transmuted into an angel of light!), Voet couches his critique in terms of biased evidence and a deluded patient. Once more, Luther's heirs stand intellectually much nearer to the Catholic position than Calvin's.

*

[31] M. Kopcsányi, *Narratio Rei Admirabilis ad Posonum gestae* (Pozsony 1643). Even the ghost of Miklós Pálffy (died in 1600) was reported to have reappeared.

[32] Kopcsányi translations: Apponyi, op. cit. nos. 832 (German); 2034 (Italian). Z. Láni, *Pseudo Spiritus Posoniensis* (n.p. 1643); cf. *RMK*, ii, no. 634 (in Slovak). This tract is dedicated in sorrow to Thomas Belavius, canon of Pozsony, evidently a fellow-countryman of Láni's fallen into error. Cf. on Belavius: *RMK* ii, 649, a refutation of his theology. G. Voet, *Selectarum Disputationum Theologicarum pars secunda* (Utrecht 1655), 1133–93, including reprint of Kopcsányi, whose work reached the Netherlands via Benjamin Szilágyi, rector of the school at Nagyvárad, and the Puritan, Péter Bacca (on whom cf. Zoványi, *Puritánus mozgalmak*, 232 ff.). For Láni see also above, pp. 250 f.

It would be difficult to say who came off best from this contest
between the Catholics and the local priests of Baal. Certainly, their
opponents made points awkward for Counter-Reformation demonologists: could the Church really be sure of the credentials of its
apparitions? Could it parry the objection that exorcism was
indistinguishable from mumbo-jumbo? Often it must have appeared
safer to take the line advocated by Delrio and Lebenwaldt and
oppose almost all spontaneous popular appeals to the supernatural.
That meant moving beyond flexible persuasion to stern prohibition.
Fortunately there existed one large terrain where prohibition of
occultism could actually be combined with a forward policy against
Protestants: prophecy and divination. The subject is difficult and
hardly explored by historians; I can only hazard here a brief
interpretative sketch.

With the breakdown of the universal Church of the Middle Ages
and the universal magical scheme of the Renaissance, different parts
of the latter were appropriated by different branches of the former.
The lion's share tended—as we have already seen—to pass into the
Catholic world-view, but notions of revelation and predictability of
the future fitted more readily with the Protestant tradition, at least
in a Central European context. Thus prophecy became to Lutherans,
and more especially to Calvinists, what miracle was to Catholics: an
occult principle which they seized on to justify themselves, but
which laid them open to condemnation from confessional rivals.

There seem to have been various reasons for this development.
Protestant faith in the Bible conduced to a fundamentalist view of
its prophets, while the general spiritual enthusiasm of the sixteenth
century inclined supporters of the Reformation (for all the sobriety
of most of its leaders) towards chiliasm, particularly by their
identification of the Pope with Antichrist and of Rome with Babylon
in the book of Revelation. Whereas Catholics retreated into
conservative postures which laid all weight on the continuity of
Church tradition, many Protestants (if not their leaders), having
experienced one great religious change, felt temperamentally
committed to religious change for its own sake: they looked
forward, not back. Whereas Catholics emphasized the freedom of
the human will, many Protestants turned towards determinist
creeds which, like astrology, implied that the future might be
foreknown; a fact which the frenzied attacks on astrology by some

of their leaders, comparable to Catholic condemnation of superstitious 'quasi-miracles', should only superficially conceal.[33]

Protestantism's prophetic mood only increased in intensity as its Churches became better established. The evolution is ironical rather than surprising; for widespread disappointment that things had not yet been taken far enough (an ultimately sectarian attitude heartily discouraged by authority), mingled with fears of Catholic revival in the years after the Peace of Augsburg and the Council of Trent. From 1600 millenarianism in Central Europe rose to a flood-tide: Rosicrucian mystics are one classic manifestation of it. It formed an important concomitant to political events in Bohemia, both before and after the White Mountain, then assumed ever wilder proportions abroad among the *émigrés* of the 1620s: Comenius, Habernfeld, Partlicius, Stoltzius, Felgenhauer, Melisch ...[34] In the only two regions of the Monarchy where Protestantism survived openly, Silesia and Hungary, prophetic intimations survived with it. Jakob Boehme and his disciples, Kotter and Poniatowska, Caspar Thym and Cyprian Kinner, Quirinus Kuhlmann and the forerunners of Pietism, are matched by the Hungarian Puritans with their German mentors Alsted and Bisterfeld, by Drabík and Otrokocsi.[35]

---

[33] Thomas Erastus, *Defensio libelli Hieronymi Savonarolae de Astrologia divinatrice* (n.p. 1569, reprinted Hanau 1610), launches an assault against astrologers in the name of Aristotle and the Calvinist Bible, but his preface (p. 6) freely admits that Germany is full of them, much more so than Italy. Cf. the good discussion in Thomas, op. cit., esp. 358 ff., and some related points made by J. Delumeau, 'Les reformateurs et la superstition', *Actes du colloque l'amiral de Coligny et son temps* (Paris 1974), 451–87.

[34] Arnold, op. cit. ii, pt. 3, 196–284; J. Volf, 'Bratří Růžového Kříže v zemích českých a proroctví jejich na rok 1622', *ČL* xvii (1908), 145–9, 161–5, 209–12, 257–61, 305–9, 353–5; xviii (1909), 52–5, 132–4, 185–7, 356–60; xix (1910), 217–21, 261–7 (on Felgenhauer), 338–41, 362–6, 401–12; id., 'Zima zimu bude stihati, v kožišich budou žinati', *ČČM* xcvi (1922), 102–25; Blekastad, op. cit., *passim*. Habernfeld: ibid. 68, 112, 335, 337, 376; H. R. Trevor-Roper, *Archbishop Laud* (2nd edn. London 1963), 395, 420. S. Partlicius, *Astronomici apologetici pars prior* (n.p. 1623); id., *Metamorphosis Mundi* (n.p. ?1626); both highly chiliastic works, though Partlicius later returned to Bohemia (cf. *Knihopis*, nos. 6873–92).

[35] Cf. above, p. 303. Kotter and Poniatowska: below, n. 43; Thym: Peuckert, *Gabalia*, 449 ff.; Kinner: above, p. 361, n. 36. Qu. Kuhlmann, *Mysterium viginti unarum Septimanarum Kotterianarum ... apertum* (London 1682); cf. above, p. 303, n. 67. A typical instance of moderate Hungarian eschatology is Alexis János Kecskeméti, *Prédikációs Könyv*, ed. L. Szuromi and O. Lábos (Bp. 1974, original edn. 1621); cf. the earlier examples cited ibid. 27 ff., and in *Humanista történetírók*, ed. P. Kulcsár (Bp. 1977), 1188–93. The view of Bocskai as a divine liberator (cf.

(continued)

I am concerned here to investigate, not Protestant futurology (though a survey is richly needed and recent insights into English Calvinist millenarianism could profitably be extended to the continent) but Catholic responses to it. The Habsburg Counter-Reformation was well satisfied with this trend—quite apart from the fact that the very process of Counter-Reformation had helped create the extremer, panic-stricken climate. Catholics mistrusted prediction from the start, and the more Protestants stressed it, the more they could assail it with an easy conscience. It had directer subversive implications than did their own learned occultism. Moreover, despite its communal political message, prophecy rested on a distinctly individual base: ultimately all revelation was *personal*, and it carried over into the concept of purely personal providences, with the corollary of a belief in divination (or in 'artificial' rather than 'natural' *manteia* as the ancient distinction described it). A detailed comparison would surely confirm that judicial astrology found more practitioners among committed Protestants than committed Catholics in this period.

Catholicism did not deny the validity of all vaticination, just as it could readily accept certain strictly theoretical and erudite principles of astrology. Clearly the Roman Church had to allow some Scriptural and medieval instances, as well as (normally) some approved kinds of dream and heavenly portent. It took comfort from prognoses of victory for the Habsburg house and its religion, both during the difficult years of 1618–20 and more broadly during the belated crusade against the Ottomans. Earlier supernatural inklings of Turkish collapse were seized on by seventeenth-century commentators like the Hungarian Jesuit Szántó, and new expectations became attached to the reign of Leopold.[36] The most famous

---

Benda, 'Kálvini tanok') lies in this tradition. Drabík (see below, p. 399) and Otrokocsi (*Furor Bestiae contra Testes Jesu Christi in Hungaria*, ed. S. Csikesz (Debrecen 1933), etc.; cf. above, p. 250 and n. 34) belong among its later, extremer manifestations.

[36] Above, p. 67, n. 64 (Beckovský). ÖNB, MS. 12415: 'Confutatio Alcorani', by István Szántó, 1611, esp. fols. 124–30; ibid. MS. 10602: 'Otium in Otio seu Reflexio Historico-Politica ac... Prognosticon ad Hunc Annum bissextilem 1688', by Baron(?) Ignatius Franciscus Haase, with presages of Ottoman downfall and acrostics pointing to Habsburg triumph; ibid. MS. 12620, miscellaneous prophecies, mostly for the 1680s, apparently compiled in Silesia; ibid. MS. 12775, esp. fols. 91–6. On the general issue see also Pázmány, *Kalauz*, 57–61; and the references cited below, n. 39 and n. 44 (Balbin).

Catholic prophecy of the day was reliably attributed to a man of unimpeachable respectability, Martin Stredonius (Středa), rector of the Jesuit college at Brno. Before his death in 1650 Stredonius made a series of accurate predictions: that Ferdinand IV would not live long; that his brother Leopold would succeed to the imperial title and defeat the Turks and the French. His utterances circulated widely with the evident sanction of the dynasty.[37] This evidence could doubtless be multiplied, but it would still be conspicuous for its relative scarcity. Even the infidel polity of the Turks and its nemesis were more fully incorporated into Protestant eschatology, while Vienna's style was cramped by the scorn which it always affected for the large role played by soothsayers in Ottoman decision-making. Though Matthias is the dedicatee of an extraordinary Cabalist-prophetic treatise by Johann Faulhaber and Ferdinand II flirted briefly with Campanella, Rudolf's heirs definitely forswore his absorption in astrology. No court stargazers surrounded Leopold, although the odd forecaster might try his luck.[38]

In the early seventeenth century a chorus of official theologians denounced the art. The Jesuit Benedictus Pereira spread the orthodox line in Germany: if divination proves false, then it is trickery; if true, then it is diabolical. For him prediction bears the mark of Satan and he lays his curse on almost all of it. So do Delrio, with loving attention to every detail of mantic superstition, and the Dalmatian professor at Padua, George Raguseus, author of a large

[37] The prophecy appears in ÖNB, MS. 10602, fol. 27ʳ; ibid. MS. 12620, fols. 10ʳ, 11ʳ, 19ʳ; ibid. MS. 1ʼ775, fols. 91, 95ʳ-6; Arnold, op. cit. ii, pt. 3, 240; Rinck, op. cit. 132-4; J. Cacavelas, *The siege of Vienna by the Turks in 1683*, ed. F. H. Marshall (Cambridge 1925), 162-7; and in other MSS. (Sommervogel, vii, col. 1640; *OSN*, s.v. 'Středovský'). On Stredonius (1587 or 1589-1649) see Balbin, *Miscellanea Historica*, i, bk. 1, 14 f.; bk. 4, pt. 2, 118-23; J. Tenora, *Život sluhy Božího P. Martina Středy* (Brno 1898), a hagiography. The Papal mistrust of Leopold's fatalism, noted earlier (p. 136), may be recalled in this context. We still find occasional Lutheran support for Habsburg victories as the fulfilment of prophecy, even from a minister at Sopron (above, p. 122, n. 14 (Barth)).

[38] J. Faulhaber, *Magia arcana Coelestis sive Cabalisticus, Novus, Artificiosus et Admirandus Computus de Gog et Magog* (Nuremberg 1613, also in German); Faulhaber was a man admired by the young—though presumably not by the mature—Descartes. J. Kvačala, 'Thomas Campanella und Ferdinand II', *Sb. d. k. Akad. d. Wiss., ph.-h. Kl.* clix (1907), Abh. 5. ÖNB, MS. 11371, is a horoscope for Leopold I, *c.* 1700, by one 'Giberti Veneto', predicting his deeds up to the year 1714 (!).

treatise about the subject.[39] Their views were corroborated by the Roman Inquisition, whose rules were tightened in 1631, and the Index, which pronounced global anathemas. For the Bavarian Jesuits, Adam Tanner trod slightly more circumspectly—as an astronomer he meditated on the possible meaning of new celestial discoveries; but his rejection of divination is for all practical purposes complete. The same can be said of later commentators like Sancta Clara and the layman Lebenwaldt, who anyway addressed a simpler audience. There is the trivial, but revealing little case of a Jesuit pupil in the 1660s who turns to his Hungarian mother-tongue to record a primitive prophecy, but covers himself with the marginal gloss: 'huic nulla fides habenda'.[40] Pázmány decried reliance on astrology as a characteristically Lutheran aberration; he and Scherer offered forceful refutations of the Protestants' belief in a contemporary Antichrist and imminent judgment, seeking at the same time to refute also the underlying principle on which that interpretation rested. Throughout the period Catholic authors were at pains to deny any millenarian exegesis of Biblical or medieval prophecy.[41]

With this prompting from theorists went a firm campaign to curb popular faith in divination. The authorities rightly enough saw a link between prophecy and revolt. Thus in Austria they suppressed such weird enthusiasts as Martin Laimbauer and his followers, who fed on visions and hoped to resurrect Frederick Barbarossa; in

---

[39] Pereira, op. cit. 156–236; Delrio, op. cit. ii, bk. 4; G. Raguseus, *Epistolae Mathematicae seu De Divinatione* (Paris 1623). Cf. Stobäus, *Epistolae*, 114 f.; and the huge section in Beyerlinck, already cited (above, p. 349, n. 8).

[40] Carena, op. cit. 228–34 (Inquisition); the ninth of the *Regulae Tridentinae* prohibited this literature and was strengthened by Pope Clement VIII. A. Tanner, op. cit. 21–64, esp. 21–31, 57–64; cf. Schott, *Magia Universalis*, iv, 541 ff. Loidl, op. cit. 271 ff., on Sancta Clara (who sees certain extenuating circumstances); Lebenwaldt, op. cit. ii, iii, v, with much picturesque detail. UK, MS. I G 25: 'Porta Philosophiae' by Ambrosius Gabrieli, fol. 599ᵛ ('Halalrol valo jövendölis' (*sic*)).

[41] Pázmány, 'Felelet az Magyari ... könyvére', in *Összes munkái*, i, at 106 f.; id., *Kalauz*, bk. 10; G. Scherer, *Eigentliche Abcontrafehung einer newen unerhörten Monstrantzen* (Ingolstadt 1588), esp. 19–21; id., *Bericht ob der Bapst zù Rom der Antichrist sey* (Ingolstadt 1585), esp. 134 ff.; etc. Even the wayward occultist Paul Skalich (on whom cf. *Rudolf II*, 117 f.), once returned to the Catholic fold, wrote a perfectly orthodox and non-chiliastic commentary on the vaticinations of Joachim of Fiore, with a dedication to Maximilian II: *Primi tomi Miscellaneorum de Rerum causis ... effigies ac exemplar* (Cologne 1570). At the other end of the period, Gregorius Coelius, *Collectanea in Sacram Apocalypsin ...* (Tyrnau 1682), is an exhaustive historical explanation of the Book of Revelation by a Hungarian Pauline.

Bohemia they seized on any nationally-tinged presages by opposi-tional groups—as during the 1620s or the peasant unrest of 1680.[42] In Hungary they combated violently the whole stance of the Calvinists and found their most pathetic victim in Mikuláš Drabík, a minor seer exiled from Moravia, whose prognoses of Habsburg doom—fervently supported and publicized by Comenius—made an impact on rebel movements. The eighty-year-old Drabík was brought to trial and executed at Pozsony in 1671, and during the next decade other chiliasts like Otrokocsi were sent to the galleys.[43] On a more mundane level, cunning men and women of the countryside: fortune-tellers, treasure-seekers, and the rest, suffered official reprisals, and cautionary tales circulated as a deterrent to others.[44]

At least divination on its own involved a set of fairly passive beliefs; but it merged imperceptibly with the most dangerous brands of folk occultism. As prohibition of it passed organically into suppression we enter the world of operative black magic, against which Church and state acted with all available weapons. In that world small-time predicters of the future occupied only a minor place. Its real criminals were the witches.

---

[42] On Laimbauer, executed in 1636: Czerny, *Tourist*, 53 f.; F. Wilflingseder, 'Martin Laimbauer und die Unruhen im Machlandviertel 1632–6', *MOöLA* vi (1959), 136–207, esp. 191–202. On Bohemia: Baur, 'Passer', 285, 293; Kašpar, *Nevolnické povstání*, 70; and cf. above, pp. 97 f., 110 f.

[43] Drabík's prophecies appeared in English, along with those of Kotter and Poniatowska, as *Prophecies of Christopher Kotterus, Christiana Poniatovia, Nicholas Drabicius* . . . (2nd edn. London 1664), 91–115 for Drabík. On his life and death see Arnold, op. cit. ii, pt. 3, 236–9; O. F. Grünenberg, *Ex Historia Ecclesiastica, de Nicolao Drabicio neotropheta in Hungaria delirante et turbulento* (Altdorf 1721), more sympathetic than the title suggests; Pauler, op. cit. ii, 377–89; J. Kvacsala in *Sz.* xxiii (1889), 745–66; L. Szimonidesz in *MKSz* lxvi (1942), 176–81; Blekastad, op. cit. 473–5, 482 f., 497 ff. *passim*. Though many Protestants were critical of him, the submission by P. Špička in *SbHKr* iv (1895), 3–84, that Drabík was a mere charlatan represents a piece of manifest Catholic special pleading. His writings were studied— not without some censure—by Ferenc II Rákóczi's lieutenant, Bercsényi (K. Thaly, *Irodalom- és miveltségtörténeti tanulmányok a Rákóczi-korból* (Bp. 1885), 86–9).

[44] Austrian example in Strnadt, art. cit., 394–6. Bohemian examples: A. Podlaha in *ČL* iv (1895), 289–91; J. Teige ibid. vii (1898), 283–5; V. Ráž ibid. xxi (1912), 371; E. Šebesta, ibid. xxii (1913), 184 f.; Verbik (ed.), op. cit. 181–4. Hungarian examples: A. Komáromy (ed.), *Magyarországi boszorkányperek oklevéltára* (Bp. 1910), 149 f., 354 ff., and index, s.v. 'tátos'; F. Schram (ed.), *Magyarországi boszorkányperek 1529–1768*, i–ii (Bp. 1970), ii, 71–6, 469 f., 563. Cf. Balbín, *Miscellanea Historica*, i, bk. 3, 168 ff., esp. 174–6; though Balbín's own interest in Czech prophets sailed close to the wind on occasion (ibid. 217 ff.; A. Patera (ed.), *Dopisy*, 153 f., 158 f.).

*

'Witchcraft' is a term of convenience. For a seventeenth-century contemporary it could mean any sinister or inexplicable work of evil. The historian tries to be more precise: defining it as the activity of black, i.e. illicit magic, the *crimen magiae* of civil law. But it still covers a multitude of forms and designations, including conspicuously different use of terminology from language to language, not least in the Central European vernaculars.[45] By no means did it embrace merely a category of supposedly malignant old women; rather the definition was (as our previous discussion should have indicated) supplied by the mental presuppositions of early-modern Europeans in their view of the occult world. Thus the social and intellectual dimensions of the charge were inseparable.

Two conditions were necessary for the persecution of witchcraft; we may think of them as the lower and upper spheres of credulity. At the lower level witch-beliefs were handed down from time immemorial in rural societies: belief in the power of an enemy to do harm by means of evil spirits (*maleficium*), for example make storms, damage property and stock, injure and kill humans, make love-potions and cause impotence. This was strictly local fuel for *individual* accusations, and probably fairly constant within the same society, though yielding considerable differences in emphasis *between* societies. It might rest on a real grievance: sorcerers often used actual poisons, stuck pins in wax images, and so on; but basically it involved an *ir*rationalization of complex tensions within comparatively primitive communities. At the upper level we have a disposition of the authorities at a given moment to judge and punish such cases, their identification of witches' supernatural talents with the power of the Christian Satan, and their elaboration

---

[45] Most languages have a term for 'witch' which—like Latin 'striga', etc.—is not semantically related to 'magic' *vel sim.* Thus German *Hexe* as against *Zauber(ei)*, where 'wizard' is *Zauberer* (or *Schwarzkünstler*). Czech possesses the pair *čarodějník/čarodějnice* (male or female), words associated with *čarování* or *čáry* (= operative magic): '*čarodějník*' describes Faust in the early Czech translation of the *Faustbuch* (*Knihopis*, nos. 3012–13); *kouzelník* had much the same meaning. Hungarian uses *boszorkány*—which can also be masculine—and the general notions of *varázs* ('magic', from a Slavonic root connoting evil, whence also Romanian *vrajitoare/vrajitor* for witch/wizard) and *bűbáj*. There is fascinating information now in Attila T. Szabó, *Erdélyi magyar szótörténeti tár*, i: A–C (Bucharest 1976), s.vv. 'boszorkány', 'bűbáj', 'bűvös-bájos', and cognates. But the whole subject needs a separate treatment.

of a fantasy world of sabbaths, covens, salves, nocturnal rides, and blasphemies, all based on a pact with the devil and confirmed by his mark on the body of the accomplice. That again might embrace 'real' elements, at least in the sense that victims on trial actually believed what they admitted; but basically their confessions form a stereotype induced by torture and the common opinion of mankind. The intersection of the two spheres produced a full witch-craze, with extreme penalties demanded and secured, with educated people giving shape to the inchoate and variegated prejudices of the uneducated, with society sacrificing its weakest links, which snapped under pressure from above.

A large body of writing exists on the witch-craze in Western Europe and Germany.[46] Extensive printed documentation is available and there has been much recent interest. Though considerable scope remains for differing interpretations, the main lines of development are clear. Persecution was very sporadic indeed throughout most of the Middle Ages. It only gained ground during the fifteenth century, fanned by the work of Dominican inquisitors, who crusaded against heresy especially in Alpine regions, where pre-Christian superstition still had deep roots. In the sixteenth century, after a brief lull, it was resumed by Protestants and Catholics alike through an era of confessional strife which also saw the spread of Roman law with its formalized procedures. During the fifty years around 1600 a climax was reached, wars and plague adding to its ferocity, most of all in France and Germany. By mid-century the craze began to die away, not from any direct intellectual challenge to the core beliefs, but from practical scepticism, revulsion against the trials and their cruelty; somewhat more humane attitudes came to be cultivated in the upper sphere, and perhaps rather less reliance was placed on magical explanations among the lower orders.

---

[46] I have found the following particularly useful: W. G. Soldan, H. Heppe, and M. Bauer, *Geschichte der Hexenprozesse*, i–ii (Munich [1911]); Lea, op. cit. (documents); J. Hansen, *Quellen und Untersuchungen zur Geschichte des Hexenwahns und der Hexenverfolgung im Mittelalter* (Bonn 1901); and N. Cohn, *Europe's inner demons* (London 1975), for the medieval period; H. R. Trevor-Roper, *The European witch-craze of the 16th and 17th centuries* (London 1969); R. Mandrou, *Magistrats et sorciers en France au XVIIe siècle* (Paris 1968), for France; Thomas, op. cit. chs. 14–18, for England; H. C. E. Midelfort, *Witch-hunting in south-west Germany* (Stanford, Cal. 1972); and the works cited below, n. 65, for Germany. There is a good modern bibliography by Midelfort in *Papers of the Bibliographical Society of America*, lxii (1968), 373–420.

Where do the Habsburg lands fit into this picture? They have as yet attracted hardly any outside attention, while few native historians have devoted themselves to the question for many years and the one major recent archival contribution is from an ethnographer.[47] Thus there are great lacunae in the published evidence, quite apart from the larger problem (which cannot yet be resolved) of how much relevant material has perished. Nevertheless the overall chronology of witchhunting in the Habsburg Monarchy may be outlined as follows.

The *Erblande*[48] were first to be affected, as their Alpine regions became drawn into the original ecclesiastical campaign against sorcery. In the 1480s Heinrich Institoris, co-author of the notorious *Malleus Maleficarum*, led an inquisition in the valleys of the Tyrol. But little came of it: Institoris, not the witches, retreated in disarray and we have next to no evidence of systematic burnings, either then or for many years afterwards.[49] Throughout most of the sixteenth century Austria—with the partial exception of certain Habsburg territories in Swabia[50]—remained free of any craze; isolated accusations of *maleficium* carried no weight in an atmosphere of Humanism, tolerance, and comparative urbanity. In these years the leading continental opponent of witch-finding (though a highly learned magician), Johann Wier, was writing for the Catholic duke of Cleves and his Habsburg wife. Only from the very end of the

[47] Schram (ed.), op. cit. (hereafter 'Schram'), with a minimum of editorial apparatus. On the other hand the Austrian novelist Heimito von Doderer, a pupil of the *Institut für Österreichische Geschichtsforschung*, produced what must be the most accurate and extended reconstruction of a witch-trial in all imaginative literature (*Die Dämonen* (Munich 1957), 757–806 and *passim*).

[48] Two good monographs by F. Byloff, *Das Verbrechen der Zauberei, ein Beitrag zur Geschichte der Strafrechtspflege in Steiermark* (Graz 1902), and *Hexenglaube und Hexenverfolgung in den österreichischen Alpenländern* (Berlin–Leipzig 1934), subsume almost all the earlier work. Most major Austrian trials are probably known about in some degree, at least the Inner Austrian ones.

[49] A few trials spilled over from northern Italy into southern Tyrol; but even for neighbouring areas the 'Alpine' witch phenomenon can be exaggerated. Cf. L. Rapp, *Hexenprozesse im Tirol* (Innsbruck 1874), 5 ff.; Byloff, *Hexenglaube*, 31 ff.

[50] Further Austria experienced some purges around Constance in the early 16th century, and large witch-trials between the 1570s and the 1620s (Midelfort, *Witch-hunting*, 90 ff., 125 ff.) which fit the Swabian pattern better than the distant Austrian one (they ran parallel too with serious panics on the Franconian lands of the Teutonic knights at Mergentheim and Ellingen). As in ch. 5 above, I leave the *Vorlande* out of account in what follows.

century did the mood begin to change, with a growing number of trials which each implicated a growing number of people: sixteen executions at Bregenz in 1609 for example, at least as many at Hainburg, on the eastern edge of the area, a few years later. After 1650 persecution reached its height, especially in Inner Austria, which experienced twenty major outbreaks in the space of four decades. While writers lamented Satan's hold over the population, special criminal prosecutors (*Bannrichter*) sought to squeeze a livelihood out of the status of witchcraft as a *crimen exceptum*—only now fully accepted to be such in local law—and elicited snowball-confessions under torture from children as well as adults.[51] By the early eighteenth century Habsburg government began to restrict the scope of the panic, leaning on judges to moderate their sentences. Even so, large-scale convictions persisted into the 1730s and smaller trials into the 1750s.

The Bohemian lands[52] were more tainted with heresy in the fifteenth century than anywhere else in Europe (and Institoris actually died there), yet no known witch-burnings took place before the 1540s, and punishment continued to be very occasional for several more decades, usually following accusations of love-charms, miscellaneous rural *maleficium*, and perhaps poison. The one serious case, at Velká Byteš between 1571 and 1576, seems to rest on accusations of poisoning. At the end of the century courts became distinctly tougher, as at Poděbrady and Nimburk.[53] Nevertheless

---

[51] Lebenwaldt, op. cit., and Sancta Clara (cf. Loidl, 256–64) have much discussion of witches. On the *Bannrichter*: Byloff, *Verbrechen*, 156 ff.; id., 'Johannes Wendtseisen, ein steirischer Hexenschriftsteller und Hexenverfolger', *ZHVSt* xxvi (1931), 218–230; Strnadt, art. cit. 209 ff. and appendices 2–3; Grüll, *Bauer, Herr . . .*, 64–70. Although these sources reveal details of their acquisitiveness and willingness to protract proceedings, we should not exaggerate the motive of reward as a general cause of witch-trials. On Ferdinand III's criminal code, enacted for Lower Austria in 1656 and also applied elsewhere, cf. Bischoff–d'Elvert, op. cit. 78–80, 114–16.

[52] The main sources—antiquated and incomplete—are J. Svátek, *Culturhistorische Bilder aus Böhmen* (V. 1879), 1–40, for Bohemia; and Bischoff–d'Elvert, op. cit., for Moravia and Silesia. Koči, *Čarodějnické procesy*, adds little new. A number of shorter communications (I shall cite them without titles) were published in the periodical *Český Lid* (*ČL*); while a few *smolné knihy* (records of trials involving torture) have been edited: e.g., recently, *Smolná kniha velkobítešská*, ed. A. Verbik and I. Štarha (Brno 1973). But the evidence is still far from complete, especially for Silesia.

[53] J. Tiray in *ČL* xii (1903), 26–31, 149–52 (Velká Byteš); V. Schulz, ibid. ix (1900), 34 f.; and A. Podlaha, ibid. xii (1903), 314–16 (Poděbrady); Svátek, op. cit. 19 ff. (incl. Nimburk). Cf. Bischoff–d'Elvert, op. cit. 74 ff.

notions of diabolism and pact with the devil barely crept in before 1620—their first coherent literary rehearsal is by Matouš Konečný in 1616; an age of cultivated burgher and Renaissance intellectual found little time for them, while German and Roman law made only limited inroads.[54] The real craze was imported towards the end of the Thirty Years War, and German-speaking areas seem to have felt it most severely. Whereas at Buchlov (south Moravia) we find individual convictions for such things as raising up mice and wolves, in Silesia the whole gory apparatus of fearsome torture and mass delation brought perhaps 250 people, including children, to the stake in the 1640s at Neisse, Zuckmantel, and Freiwaldau. The epidemic reached a peak of notoriety during the 1680s on various north Moravian estates with a *Bannrichter* called Boblig, whose methods yielded full details of nearby sabbaths and their attendant crudities.[55] By 1700 the worst blood-letting was over; it was replaced with isolated trials, mainly in Moravia. There seem to have been no more executions after 1740.

In Hungary and Transylvania[56] the whole span of the rise and fall of witchhunting is set even later. Hardly any trials at all appear to have occurred before 1600 and only a handful of victims were executed. Numbers begin to increase during the seventeenth century, though cases still involve no more than two or three

---

[54] M. Konečný, *Theatrum Divinum, to jest: Divadlo Boží* (Pr. 1616), chs. 1–2; cf. Č. Zíbrt in *ČL* xiii (1904), 293–7, on a harangue of 1561 (by one Aleš Knobloch) against witches as the bearers of *maleficium*. There are scarcely any prosecutions of them in the surviving records of the town jurisdiction of Olomouc (V. Prasek (ed.), *Tovačovská Kniha ortelů olomuckých* (Olomouc 1896)).

[55] Verbík (ed.), *Černé knihy*, 67–72, 77 f., 192–9, 209–11; most such accusations at Buchlov before 1630 were not proven. B. Šindelář, 'Příspěvek k dějinám slezských procesů s čarodějnicemi se zvláštním zřetelem k procesům frývaldovským v letech 1651–84', *Slezský Sborník*, xliv (1946), 65–80; Koči, *Čarodějnické procesy*, 82 ff.; cf. Lea, op. cit. iii, 1075, 1081, 1131, 1231 f. For Boblig's chain of trials, which lasted seven years: Bischoff–d'Elvert, op. cit. 11 ff. Cf. *Knihopis*, nos. 6256–8, 6260, etc.; 6306, etc.

[56] Komáromy (ed.), *Boszorkányperek*, and Schram offer a remarkably—and perhaps uniquely—thorough coverage of the archives (over 900 trials, many communicated in full), including Transylvania, for which there is also a helpful earlier study by F. Müller, *Beiträge zur Geschichte des Hexenglaubens und des Hexenprocesses in Siebenbürgen* (Brunswick 1854), and a recent sketch, with certain new material, by C. Göllner, *Hexenprozesse in Siebenbürgen* (Cluj 1971). But very many records must have gone astray (particularly for the :6th century?), quite apart from all the fragments without any judgment, and the subject needs a new evaluation.

accused, and many are let off with light punishment. Hungary, like England but unlike the rest of Europe, never recognized witchcraft as a *crimen exceptum* to be brought before special courts, and it concentrated attention on the aspect of *maleficium*. Hence procedures tended to be milder, concern with diabolism less explicit, inquisition less ramified, and acquittal commoner. But whereas in England prosecutions fell away sharply after about 1650, in Hungary they only seriously multiplied from that date. Not until the early decades of the eighteenth century was the high-point reached, with a series of *autos-da-fé*, mainly in the south of the country and especially around Szeged, where torture forced defendants to admit a pact with Satan, nocturnal concourses, networks of accomplices, and the rest (although their confessions retain a certain homespun quality too). Elsewhere trials were instigated quite intensively and with continuing executions until the 1750s, when they suddenly lost steam, or backfired so that plaintiffs faced a counter-charge of slander.[57] Here, as throughout the Habsburg lands, the belated sea-change of an enlightened mentality among the educated anticipated radical legal reforms under Maria Theresa. In 1756 a forensic doctor—perhaps the only one in the annals of Hungarian witchcraft prosecutions—advised drily that 'these days physicians leave supernatural matters to the clergy'. In 1768 one of the very last cases was quashed by personal fiat of the empress.[58]

★

This distinctive evolution of the witch-craze in Austria, Bohemia, and Hungary fits neatly enough with the evidence from surrounding areas. To the west we have Bavaria, whose epidemic reached rampant proportions a little earlier, and Salzburg, which staged the largest, most brutal of all trials in the region, the so-called

[57] F. Möstl, *Ein Szegediner Hexenprocess* (Graz 1879). Komáromy (ed.), op. cit., rather understates and postdates the accusations of diabolism. The main diabolical cases in Schram are i, 229–97, 333–45, 392–4, 463–73, 487–96; ii, 80–100, 147 f., 163–172, 188–206, 219–29, 250–7, 335–41, 442–53, 454–9, 475–505, 696 f. Cf. R. Horna, *Monsterproces s čarodějnicemi v Šamoríně koncem XVII. stoleti* (Bratislava 1934), who describes a large trial held in 1691 at a small town near Pozsony, with many confessions of nocturnal flights (across the Austrian border!), covens, etc.; overlooked by Schram. Horna also unearthed a much earlier (1602) example of diabolism: *Zwei Hexenprozesse in Pressburg zu Beginn des XVII Jahrhunderts* (Bratislava 1933). For Transylvania, cf. Müller, op. cit. 36 ff.; Edmund Chishull, *Travels in Turkey and back to England* (London 1747), 105.

[58] Schram, ii, 298–302, 534–43.

'Zauberjackel' affair from 1675 to 1681, and executed its last devil-worshipper in 1750. To the east we have Poland, a little tardier even than Hungary, where 70 per cent of all witches were condemned after 1675, a full 32 per cent of them between 1701 and 1725.[59] Central Europe contrasts not only with France and England (leaving most of Germany, including the Lutheran lands, in a middle position) but also with the Papacy, whose enthusiasm for the hunt waned markedly after 1600 until by the 1670s a nuncio, told that Leopold's empress had sickened from suspected sorcery, could reply 'che a Roma non si credeva a simili incanti'.[60]

At the same time there is evidently a good fit with the Habsburg Counter-Reformation. The first Austrian persecutions for full-scale pact with the devil date from the 1580s, when Catholicism started to reassert itself; indeed, one victim was the wicked grandmother of the girl exorcized by Scherer in 1582. Then, at the beginning of the next century, Archduke Ferdinand, with Delrio as his adviser, turned the screw on malignant heresy in Styria.[61] By the 1630s the craze fed on the tensions of a Bohemia wrenched forcibly back into the Catholic orbit; it is striking how the worst outbreaks are found on the militant perimeter, following teams of Jesuits to the still hostile villages of Silesia and northern Moravia after 1650. Finally the inquisition moved to join the belated Counter-Reformation of Hungary, where it enjoyed a final fling in the first half of the eighteenth century, especially on the newly-recovered territories where confessions were still locked in bitter struggle. Moreover, there were close links in some trials between witchcraft and secret Protestantism, which certainly lived on most strongly among the lowest orders: conventicles could easily enough look like covens, while some of the extremer sectarians—we know all too little about

[59] S. Riezler, *Geschichte der Hexenprozesse in Bayern* (Stuttgart 1896); the isolated Bavarian executions after 1700, often cited, conceal a marked general diminution of activity from about 1650. For Zauberjackel: Byloff, *Hexenglaube*, 116–18. B. Baranowski, *Procesy czarownic w Polsce w XVII i XVIII wieku* (Łódź 1952), esp. statistics at 29 f. The *Malleus Maleficarum* was translated into Polish in 1614.

[60] *Nuntiaturberichte*, ii, no. 183 (15 Mar. 1676). Cf. *S^{mi}D.N.D. Gregorii Papae XV Constitutio adversus Maleficia, seu Sortilegia committentes* (Rome 1623), ordering punishment only for diabolism and severe *maleficium*; Carena, op. cit., esp. 240 ff., with various caveats about procedure; C. Ginzburg, *I benandanti, ricerche sulla stregoneria . . .* (Turin 1966), 135 ff.; Lea, op. cit. ii, 942–1038.

[61] Cf. above, p. 391. Delrio (1633 edn.), v, appendix 2 (pp. 830–98): advice to a 'certain prince', dated Graz 1602. Cf. Wiedemann, 'Wiener Neustadt', 261.

them—may actually have perpetuated pagan fertility rituals.[62] The cult of the *Springer* (i.e. leapers) among Slovene peasants, apparently founded in the 1580s and perhaps related to the strange *benandanti* of Friuli, engaged in suspicious nocturnal rites and was mercilessly hounded by the Catholic authorities.[63]

Yet to make the main point of this chapter we must go a little further, beyond the 'accident' that Central Europe's brand of religious intolerance happened at the crucial time to be Catholic. After all, Protestant ministers were just as threatening during their period of influence in the sixteenth century: Lutherans led the agitation for action against witches in Styria and Transylvania; Hungary's first recorded victim was burned at Calvinist-dominated Kolozsvár in 1565, and the next decades brought several more executions there.[64] Might they not have behaved in the same spirit as Catholics, given the chance, when real persecution came in vogue? Or was rather Baroque Catholicism, as it developed through the seventeenth century, peculiarly sensitive to the threat from witchcraft, precisely because of its dependence on a rival occult world? Some general evidence from Germany, where rough comparisons are possible, suggests that Catholics, after about 1600, harried witches more brutally and over a longer period than Protestants. They launched the wildest purges during the Thirty Years War; they maintained their pressure while trials gradually died out in the Protestant north-west and south-west, leaving the quasi-scholastic demonologists of Saxony as the chief official backers of witchhunting, with a decline by 1700 even there, especially in practice.[65] Perhaps there are pointers inside the Monarchy too, in

---

[62] Examples in Podlaha, 'Z dějin katolických missií', 121 f., etc.; id., *Posvátná místa*, i, 90, and *passim*; A. Rezek, 'Mikulášenci v Čechách po třicetileté válce', *ČČM* lxv (1891), 412–16.

[63] On the *Springer*: Hurter, op. cit. iv, 235–7, 523; Dimitz, op. cit., pt. 3, 212–15; Schuster, op. cit. 615–22; Byloff, *Hexenglaube*, 15–17. For the *benandanti*, operating just across the Venetian border, see Ginzburg, op. cit.

[64] Byloff, *Hexenglaube*, 44 ff.; Müller, op. cit. 17–24; Komáromy (ed.), op. cit. 1–74. Cf. the trials at Debrecen: ibid. 23, 88 f., 91 f., 100–4; and Attila T. Szabó, loc. cit.

[65] Riezler, op. cit., esp. 149–230; H. Zwetsloot, *Friedrich Spee und die Hexenprozesse* (Trier 1954), 95 f., 102; Midelfort, op. cit. 31–3 and *passim*, and the summary of this book published as 'Witchcraft and religion in 16th-century Germany...', *Archiv für Reformationsgeschichte*, lxii (1971), 266–78. J. Diefenbach, *Der Hexenwahn vor und nach der Glaubensspaltung in Deutschland* (Mainz 1886), tries to show that Protestants

(continued)

so far as Protestant and Catholic parts of Hungary can be distinguished—though the continuing impact of Counter-Reformation there, and the very hidebound nature of its Lutheranism and Calvinism, make the evidence difficult to evaluate.[66]

Best testimony to the Catholic view of the *crimen magiae* appears in the key concept of sacrilege, profanation of holy things, upon which the Counter-Reformation, with its reverence for the sacramental, called down particular anathemas. Sacrilege, as many believed, would be punished by divine displeasure anyway: thus with an old woman in 1578 who set fire to altars, then three days later found her crops destroyed by hail; with an Austrian officer executed for cowardice, whose brother had stolen the Marian image of Stará Boleslav exactly a year earlier; with the rural Czech legend of a woman turned into stone for abusing the Host.[67] But that was a fallible method—in the last case rustics soon started to worship the statue!—and firm earthly retribution was called for too.

Many witch-trials in the Habsburg lands either begin with alleged desecration of the holy wafer, usually accompanied by blasphemy, or incorporate it as an important part of the crime. We may assume not only that the authorities thought this a particularly

---

were more bloodthirsty than Catholics, but without any success. F. Merzbacher, *Die Hexenprocesse in Franken* (2nd edn. Munich 1970), tries to show that both sides were equally bloodthirsty, but his figures do not seem to support this assertion either (for some places, e.g. Schweinfurt, his cases hardly square with those listed by Diefenbach). Cf. Lea, op. cit. iii, 1394 ff. and *passim*; Soldan–Heppe–Bauer, op. cit. ii, esp. 1–130 and 245 ff. This is very difficult ground: some Catholic writers were milder on the procedural side than Lutherans in the earlier 17th century, especially the Jesuits Adam Tanner, Laymann, and Spee (Duhr, op. cit. ii, pt. 2, ch. 10, esp. 516 ff.; Zwetsloot, op. cit., on Spee—whose *Cautio Criminalis* had a Sulzbach edn. in 1696 and Polish translations in 1680 and 1714); perhaps Roman influence was at work. But that does not invalidate the larger point.

[66] Compare, for example, Bihar and Szabolcs (mainly Protestant counties) with Sopron, Csongrád, and Tolna (mainly Catholic ones) in Schram, for trials involving diabolism. But the test is not conclusive (N.B.: ibid., Vas or Zala). A source used by Müller (op. cit. 54 f.) suggests the same point for Transylvania, but the worst trials of all there were staged at Saxon Schässburg. Two Calvinist disputations presided over by G. Komáromi Csipkés, *Disputatio[nes] Theologica[e] de Lamiis Veneficiis* (Nagyvárad 1656), strongly hint that the real crime of the witches is not *maleficium* but an offence against God.

[67] Bibl, 'Eder', 101 f.; J. Seidler, *Das Prager Blutgericht 1633* ([Memmingen] 1951), 19–22, 34–7; A. Rezek, 'Pověst o zkamenělé ženě', *ČČM* lxv (1891), 416–18. On sacrilege in general: Thiers, op. cit. i, 22 f., 68 ff., 111 f., 252, 272 f., 335–9, 353–358, 365–71 (black mass); ii, 201 ff., 307–9; iii, 412 f., 453 ff., 483 ff., 504 ff., 567 ff.

incriminating circumstance—the hard-pressed Bohemian religious commissioners in 1629 found time for an impassioned letter on the subject—but that witnesses knew it to be an accusation which would stick. If the defendant had spat out the Host, then he must be a secret Protestant (if not a notorious one); if he had retained it in his mouth, then he was still more evidently intent on black magic, since he could use it to cause *maleficium*. The great purge at Szeged in 1728 started thus.[68] At other times conviction rested on abuses little less offensive to Catholic sensibilities, like necrophilia (interfering with the dead), which made an obvious parody of the reverence for relics.[69] Imputations of sacrilege could occasionally come to involve priests (they had the readiest opportunity to commit it), though presumably only those already unpopular enough to be cited by scandalmongers and regarded as dispensable by their clerical colleagues. *Bannrichter* Boblig's terrible witch-hunt at Ullersdorf in the 1680s began with accusations of sacrilege, culminating in a five-year trial and the eventual burning of the local dean. Clergy were implicated, but acquitted, in the great Styrian purge at Feldbach in the 1670s.[70]

Two qualifications need to be made here. All witchcraft clearly meant abandonment of God, and we must distinguish sacrilege as a real source of condemnations for magic from sacrilege as the ritual desecration or 'black mass' celebrated at the sabbath by those already initiated. Moreover, Protestants had their own line of theological argument which stressed the crime against God rather than the power of witches to harm (the devil could anyway do quite enough mischief unaided), and this was a line which led eventually

---

[68] Podlaha (ed.), *Dopisy*, 156 f. (commissioners); Komáromy (ed.), op. cit. 395 (Szeged). Austrian examples: Byloff, *Verbrechen*, 123–5, and *passim*; id., *Hexenglaube*, 53, etc.; and especially the Zauberjackel imbroglio (Soldan–Heppe–Bauer, op. cit. ii, 123–6). Bohemian examples: V. Schulz in *ČL* viii (1899), 177–80; Dvorský, 'Historické příspěvky', 328–30, 490; Koči, *Čarodějnické procesy*, 57 f.; cf. *Knihopis*, nos. 6274, 14496 seqq. *passim*. More Hungarian examples: Schram, i, 333–45; ii, 241–50; but less frequent there.

[69] Examples: J. Šimek in *ČL* iv (1895), 26–31, 110–14; Dvorský, 'Historické příspěvky', 491 f.; H. Gross in *ČL* xv (1906), 299 f.; V. Medek in *Acht Jahrhunderte* ... ed. Wieser, 387–93; Koči, *Čarodějnické procesy*, 55 f.; Schram, ii, 36–9. *Per contra*, Č. Zíbrt, in *ČL* xvi (1907), 361, prints an order from Rudolf II (1608) to collect moss from the skulls of hanged men.

[70] Bischoff–d'Elvert, op. cit. 11–55; Byloff, *Verbrechen*, 50–4, 173–5. Cf. Merzbacher, op. cit. 187–9; Schram, ii, 522.

to more moderate and humane positions.[71] The point about the Catholic view is its close association of sacrilege with *maleficium*— trials without the latter are always rare—and the very long life enjoyed among educated people throughout the Habsburg lands by a core belief in supernatural powers conferred upon ill-doers through pact with the devil. Even the learned Dr. Haen, who advised Maria Theresa against persecuting witches, devotes the central portion of his treatise, written in 1774, to defending the possibility of their existence.[72]

★

The whole witch-craze in Central Europe outlasted any mere identification with Counter-Reformation, even with the self-doubting, overwrought Habsburg version of Counter-Reformation, whose problematical spirituality was shot through with Christian occultism. It must have answered a social, and perhaps also a political need. Who then instituted the trials? Most were heard in district courts: the *Landgerichte* of Austria and Bohemia; the lords' and county tribunals in Hungary; some urban jurisdictions. They thus came firmly under the aegis of the provincial establishment, and little difference appears between secular and ecclesiastical landowners. The Church played no significant role as prosecutor, but many trials, including some of the largest, were held on its estates: bishops of Olomouc and Breslau, abbots of Rein, St. Lambrecht, and Kremsmünster—all exercised the same harshness as the one fully sovereign cleric in the area, the archbishop of Salzburg. The solidarity of noble and priest is mirrored in the opinions of legists and theologians: Roman and case law as expounded by men like Frölich von Frölichsburg in the Tyrol, Beckmann in Styria, Weingarten in Bohemia, Kitonics in Hungary,

---

[71] Midelfort, op. cit. 34–66; E. W. Monter, 'Witchcraft in Geneva 1537–1662', *Journal of Modern History*, xliii (1971), 179–204. A Bohemian representative of this position is Jan Štelcar Želetavský, writing in the 1580s, on whom see J. J. Hanuš in *ČČM* xxxviii (1864), 262–87, 343–52.

[72] Thus, for example, the trial of Johann Grillenberger, executed in Upper Austria in 1731 for sacrilege, diabolism, and bestiality, on the testimony of his niece and others (printed in Strnadt, art. cit. 321–54), would hardly have been possible in a Protestant country by that date. Antonius de Haen, *De Magia liber* (Leipzig 1774), esp. pt. 2, ch. 3, and pt. 3, ch. 1. Cf. the Theatine monk, Sterzinger, in Bavaria (Riezler, op. cit. 298 ff.); and other opinions in Lea, op. cit. iii, 1447 ff.

marched with the delusions of demonologists following the Delrio tradition. The fount of this law, and the ultimate sanction for demonology, was the dynasty; but in fact few appeals were made to its judgment, either through high courts or through university faculties. Only after 1700 did government begin to intervene directly in the proceedings.[73] All the more initiative came from below, as villagers, singly and collectively, denounced local black-magicians, though their denunciations, of course, if not their underlying beliefs, were part-conditioned by their social superiors. The court strengthened them in their prejudices; and they told the court what it expected to hear.[74]

It is impossible to descry simple social motivations in Central European witchhunts, while the absence of full harmony between these different persecutors accounts for some unevenness and irregularity about the procedure and outcome of trials, as also for cases where better-to-do citizens found themselves accused. But the latter are uncommon,[75] and one pattern emerges fairly clearly: witchhunts challenged superstition in order to enhance conformity. Social control, to go with religious control, lay in the interests of all those with a position to preserve, from the solider kind of peasant upwards. It forms another aspect of the pursuit of settled hierarchy.

Now it is a commonplace of witchcraft literature that accusations were often directed, consciously or unconsciously, against noncon-formists: that was one reason for lighting on importunate widows and spinsters, as on women of loose morals, especially at times of misfortune when their supposed powers of malicious damage, arson, and such like, might more readily be believed. A wealth of proof for such a hypothesis could be assembled from the Habsburg lands, notably from Hungary, where the diabolical side anyway played a less central role and misfortune was more than usually

---

[73] For the involvement, or non-involvement, of the ruler: Bischoff–d'Elvert, op. cit. 9 f.; Svátek, op. cit. 17–22, 35–9; Strnadt, art. cit. 223 ff.; Byloff, *Verbrechen*, 271 ff.; id., *Hexenglaube*, 143 ff.; Eckhart, *Büntetőbiráskodás*, 138; Koči, *Čarodějnické procesy*, 86–97.

[74] One good instance, among many, in Schram, i, 441–6.

[75] Respectable people, including priests, suffered in the Ullersdorf and Feldbach purges (above, n. 70). Further cases in Byloff, *Verbrechen*, 67–74; id., *Hexenglaube*, 58, 63, 75; Schram, i, 132–5; ii, 308. The chief accused at the Szeged trial of 1728 was a prominent burgher, unlike his 'rough' accomplices.

prevalent.[76] The victims' crime would then be expiated almost as well by banishment from the community as by death; expulsion was indeed a particularly regular sentence in Hungary. Everywhere defendants stood on the margin of an integral society; or perhaps they reflected its disintegration. One kind of witch-trial began with something akin to the feudal challenge (*Absage*): a vindication of honour against slanders. The declining efficacy of this resource goes with an unwillingness on the part of villagers to testify in favour of the accused person: again we have the breakdown of communal solidarity.[77]

This approach is attractive, but difficult to pursue. Did nationality frictions, for example, contribute to tension?[78] Its major relevance for Central Europe appears to lie in the category of society's real outsiders: the vagrants. The reader may recall my earlier discussion of the seventeenth-century increase in vagrancy; he may refer back also to the broad definition of 'witch' suggested by the argument of the present chapter. The two are connected, for the ranks of male witches were especially large in the Habsburg area. One Styrian defendant in three was a man; elsewhere the proportion increased throughout the period. Many of these people were luckless misfits, the dregs of village life: shepherds, idle farmhands, unemployable youths like the miserable paupers harried to imprisonment and death in Bavaria around the year 1720.[79] But they seemed suspicious enough, and they shaded off into a world of threatening strangers,

---

[76] Telling examples in Schram, i, 143–53, 169–214 (which must be one of the most voluminous trials ever printed, involving the depositions of no less than 167 witnesses to misdeeds perpetrated at Miskolc during the Rákóczi rebellion), 536–43. Cf., in general, the comments of Thomas, op. cit. 526–34.

[77] The traditional challenge seems to have been especially frequent in Transylvania: Müller, op. cit. 65 ff. There is a striking case (from Kolozsvár in 1568) in Komáromy (ed.), op. cit., 13–15. Cf., on the *Absage*, above, p. 107.

[78] Probably not much, except perhaps in the south of Styria and the Tyrol (cf. Byloff, *Hexenglaube*, 40 f.). The predominance of German over Czech victims in the Bohemian lands appears to stem from different causes. Nationality resentments are rare in Hungarian trials (but cf. below, n. 80). See also below, p. 424.

[79] Above, pp. 99 f. Byloff, *Verbrechen*, 86; id., *Hexenglaube*, 46 ff.; cf. the figures in E. W. Monter, 'Patterns of witchcraft in the Jura', *Journal of Social History*, v (1971–1972), 1–25, esp. 14. For the Bavarian case: *Ausführliche Erzählung des Verhörs und der Hinrichtung des im Jahre 1722 der Hexerey beschuldigten Georg Pröls* (n.p. 1806); cf. Schram, ii, 36–9; and the Poděbrady examples cited above, n. 53 (Schulz, Podlaha). Instances of shepherds in, e.g., T. Antl in *ČL* ix (1900), 293–9; V. Schulz, ibid. xii (1903), 110 f.; H. Gross, ibid. xv (1906), 299 f.; Schram, ii, 45–50, 196–206.

sturdy beggars, outlaws, and bandits. Contemporaries must have taken more seriously than can we the likes of the aged roué Ferenc Bangó, rounded up with his fading female accomplices on the Great Hungarian Plain in 1734 and charged with *maleficium* and immorality. Certainly they feared the bands which roamed the eastern Alps: the 'Lauterfresser' in the Tyrol, convicted of making storms and plagues of rats, of divination and lewdness, of sacrilege and diabolatry; or 'Zauberjackel', the ne'er-do-well son of a knacker, and his confederates in Salzburg.[80]

Of course, such desperadoes were answerable to the courts on ordinary criminal charges, particularly theft; but it is significant of the official mentality that it attributed (or connived in attributing) magic powers to them. Sorcery not only became an extra measure of their guilt: it indicated the diabolical origin of all their misdeeds, including their responsibility for otherwise inexplicable disasters like plague. Thus a campaign could be launched against the 'wizard' Petrovskýs in Bohemia after 1648, much as openly insurrectionist leaders could be tarred with the brush of Satanism and suspected of subversive prophecy. In fact vagabonds and rebels were easily lumped together for these purposes: a play about beggars printed in Bohemia at the time of the great revolt depicts its chief character with the sinister eye-patch of the Hussite general, Žižka.[81] Once again we have an uneasy marriage between approval and disapproval of magic. Accusations of witchcraft demanded that people credit outlaws with supernatural powers for evil; the trouble was that deprived and discontented elements within organized society might well invest them with a beneficent occult role. Oleksa Dovbuš and Juro Janošik are famous examples of charismatic banditry, not to mention mythical folk heroes like Rübezahl.[82]

Still, we should not glamorize the bandits; the popular estimate

---

[80] Schram, ii, 430–40 on Bangó, a seventy-eight-year-old Calvinist who had been present at the siege of Buda in 1686. Cf. ibid. 505–11, and i, 366–9, for two similar cases involving suspects who had come originally from Bohemia. Byloff, *Hexenglaube*, 63 ff., 81 f., 103–5, 116–18, 125 f.

[81] On the Petrovskýs (the Czech plural is *petrovští*) see literature above, p. 100, n. 48. Cf., for the Lower Austrian rebellion of 1596, Feigl, *Bauernaufstand*, 32 f. 'Hra žebráčí, z polské řeči do češtiny přeložená 1619', *ČL* xx (1911), 364 ff. (Žižka).

[82] E. Hobsbawm, *Bandits* (London 1969), 51 f. and *passim*, makes interesting comments on this phenomenon. A more openly political Hungarian instance would be Ferenc Rákóczi's general, 'blind' Bottyán (Thaly, op. cit. 95 ff.).

of them probably often coincided in practice with the official stereotype, even where fears overlay a residue of secret admiration. At all events, the ordered society of the Baroque found no place whatever for the core group among vagabonds: the gipsies. Gipsies had been established in Central Europe since the 1420s (some reached Hungary a little earlier) and they appear to have had a special affiliation with the area, to judge by the designation 'Bohemians' which for unexplained reasons attached to them from an early date. It is impossible to determine whether the number of true Romanies grew during the seventeenth century; but it is clear that many others joined them, or else set up their own quasi-zingari communities: forced or voluntary outcasts from society, driven by the ravages of war, economic depression, and legal subjection. The French traveller Patin encountered several hundred in a near-naked state beside the Elbe in 1670.[83]

This development appalled contemporaries. The plague of gipsies was condemned from professorial chairs down to the widely-circulated *Liber Vagatorum* with its cautionary but fascinated insights into a forbidden world. The authorities acted vehemently: a series of decrees after 1650 proscribing gipsies culminated at the end of the century, in Bohemia at least, with an edict which allowed them to be killed on sight, and fearful massacres ensued.[84] An important part of their crime, in the eyes of both writers and legislators, was superstition. The *Zigeuner* of German-speaking lands were also *Gauner*, criminals and swindlers, whose deceptions rested on illicit magic: mostly small-time divination, especially palmistry; but also perhaps a full pact with the devil and consequent powers of active *maleficium*. Thus gipsies were assimilated to witches, and many shared the same fate.[85] Just as suggestive was the

---

[83] Charles Patin, *Relations Historiques et curieuses* ... (Amsterdam 1695), 224. On the gipsies in general: A. F. Pott, *Die Zigeuner in Europa und Asien*, i–ii (Halle 1844–1845), i, esp. 1–63; F. C. B. Avé-Lallemant, *Das deutsche Gaunerthum*, i–iii in 4 pts. (Leipzig 1858–62), i, pt. 1, esp. 25–36.

[84] Critics: Ahasuerus Fritsch, *Tractatus theologico-nomico-politicus de Mendicantibus Validis* (Jena 1659); id., *Diatribe historico-politica de Zygenorum Origine, Vita ac Moribus* (Jena 1660); Jakob Thomasius, *Dissertatio philosophica de Cingaris* (Leipzig 1671): both these authors see most gipsies as an able-bodied rabble of local provenance. On the *Liber Vagatorum*: Avé-Lallemant, op. cit. i, pt. 1, 136–206. Persecution: Weingarten, op. cit. 409 f., 537 f., 564 f., 595 f.; Svátek, op. cit. esp. 288 ff.; Frauenstädt, art. cit.; Grüll, *Bauer, Herr* ... 56.

[85] Fritsch, *Diatribe*, sig. B3ᵛf.; Thomasius, op. cit. sig. B1ᵛ, C1ᵛ-3; Lebenwaldt,

word 'gipsy' itself: while no one at that time seriously investigated the origins of the Romany people, they counted as 'Aegyptiaci', who had brought their evil snares from Egypt, the home of all paganism. Yet Egypt, as the cradle of the Hermetic tradition and birthplace of Moses, was also the source of wisdom. To a learned Catholic the gipsies' profanation of those divine mysteries might have been the greatest of their sins. Certainly it testifies once more to the complementary relationship, within the intellectual world of Counter-Reformation, between educated and uneducated occultism.

One final category of untouchables remains to be discussed: Jews. Some overlap may have existed between them and witches, though the subject is a tricky one. Can it be more than coincidence that the village which later (in the 1880s) staged Hungary's most notorious ritual murder trial was still burning women for *maleficium* in the mid-eighteenth century?[86] A more definite overlap appears between Jews and vagrants. Both belonged nominally under the jurisdiction of the imperial high marshal; Yiddish formed a strong element in the cant of the underworld: the *Rotwelsch* of Germany, the *hantýrka* of Bohemia; Jews and gipsies were even parodied together at court entertainments.[87] Moreover, Jews in the Habsburg lands enjoyed reasonably mild treatment (some temporary expulsions apart) during the Renaissance, when Prague became one of their foremost intellectual centres; but while the legacy of toleration survived into the early seventeenth century—Ferdinand II set up a privileged ghetto across the Danube from Vienna and showed favour to moneyed communities in Bohemia—a different mood was now spreading.[88]

op. cit. v; Delrio, op. cit. (1633 edn.) 585–9; Avé-Lallemant, op. cit. i, pt. 1, 95–8; cf. ibid. pt. 2, 20–5, 245 ff.

[86] The village was Tiszaeszlár: evidence in Schram, ii, 312–14, 321–5, 384–402. The medieval municipal law of Buda prescribed quasi-Jewish degradation for witches (Lea, op. cit. iii, 1253, 1260). Cf., on this topic, Trevor-Roper, *Witch-craze*, 34–7.

[87] On argot: Avé-Lallemant, op. cit. ii–iii (=pts. 3–4); A. J. Puchmayer, *Románi Čib, das ist Grammatik und Wörterbuch der Zigeuner Sprache* (Pr. 1820); and the early discussion in Bonaventura Vulcanius, *De Literis et Lingua Getarum* (Leiden 1597), 105–9. Baur, 'Passer', 278 f. (court entertainment).

[88] Jews were briefly exiled from Bohemia in 1541, and local burghers forced some pogroms in earlier 16th-century Hungary. On Vienna: *Geschichte der Stadt Wien,*
(continued)

Again popular friction blended with official suspicion. Mass anti-Semitism never lay far beneath the surface: witness occasional sixteenth-century pogroms and the expulsion in 1596 of the (admittedly inconsiderable) Upper Austrian communities. During the 1640s it was focused in the imperial capital by the affair of a lapsed and vicious convert to Christianity called Engelberger, who added sacrilege to the catalogue of his other crimes. Resentment now swelled apace, with growing approval from secular and ecclesiastical authorities; Jews were widely blamed for outbreaks of fire and disease. At length Leopold was persuaded by his entourage and his conscience to expel them totally from Lower Austria as a votive act.[89] In Prague, the largest community of Central Europe, things did not go so far, but tension built up unmistakably after 1620, to reach a climax by the 1690s in another scandal, when a Jewish boy convert was murdered by his father and quickly invested with all the miraculous apparatus of Christian martyrdom. During the next century the Prague ghetto very nearly suffered the same fate as the Viennese one.[90]

Jews could particularly easily be branded as living in unregenerate superstition. Their version of prophecy was messianism, and no 'messiah' of modern times received such universal acclaim in Jewish communities everywhere as Sabbatai Ṣevi, for all that the meteoric career of this visionary from Smyrna lasted only eighteen months (1665-6). Central Europe took an active part in propagating the Sabbatian message, and Vienna became a centre for distributing reports of the saviour.[91] Can we not see here one cause of the expulsion which took place four years later, especially since the

---

v, 49 ff.; H. Tietze, *Die Juden Wiens: Geschichte, Wirtschaft, Kultur* (V. 1933), 43 ff. On Bohemia: *Rudolf II*, 236–42; M. Popper, 'Les juifs de Prague pendant la Guerre de Trente Ans', *Revue des Études Juives*, xxix (1894), 127–41; xxx (1895), 79–93.

[89] D. Kaufmann, *Die letzte Vertreibung der Juden aus Wien und Niederösterreich* (V. 1889), a very full account for the years 1625–70. Cf. Loidl, op. cit. 290–3, for Sancta Clara's anti-Jewish venom.

[90] Beckovský, op. cit. pt. 3, 303 f., 401 f., 420 f. (who tells us that almost as many Jews (over 11,000) as Christians lived in the Old Town). *Knihopis*, nos. 2186, 2213, 6218, 6301 (cf. earlier nos. 2977–80); Muneles (ed.), op. cit. nos. 183, 186–7, 241, 247. The *cause célèbre* of the 1690s is reproduced in G. Freytag, *Bilder aus der deutschen Vergangenheit*, i–v (Leipzig [1920s]), iv, 354 ff. See also S. Schweinburg-Eibenschitz, 'Une confiscation de livres hébreux à Prague', *Revue des Études Juives*, xxix (1894), 266–71; and—for the 18th century—Stern, op. cit. 202–7.

[91] G. Scholem, *Sabbatai Ṣevi, the mystical messiah 1626–76* (London 1973), esp. 469 f., 559–66, 636 f.; Kaufmann, op. cit. 91–4.

Prague ghetto, whose conservative rabbinate resisted Sabbatai's claims, fared better than the Viennese one? Messianic enthusiasm was generated by other occult studies, much pursued in the Habsburg lands, particularly at Vienna which possessed its flourishing school of Cabalists. As with gipsies, so with Jews: their magic seemed more heinous when Catholic scholars wished themselves to legitimize quasi-Cabalist brands of occultism. The dichotomy recurs: the privileged may dabble, just as the occasional court Jew, like Samuel Oppenheimer, may grow rich; the odd convert may still enjoy official favour; a few commercial families may gain the protection of high aristocrats. But the popular message is one of rejection and intolerance.[92]

*

Much has been said in the latter half of this chapter about persecution. The conclusion should, however, be a qualified one. The total of known executions for witchcraft is perhaps 1,500 in the *Erblande*, 1,000 in Bohemia, less than 500 in Hungary. The real figures must be twice, if not three times as high, and there were many victims who received lesser sentences. Even so the numbers punished remain moderate by comparison with some parts of Europe.[93] Other methods of control: persuasion and prohibition, had their effect. The point is made in a picturesque accidental juxtaposition of two cases by a Benedictine visitor to Austria: the first, a woman who took her own life because she feared the curse of a spurned beggar; the second, a woman cured of suicidal mania through wearing an *Agnus Dei*.[94] Evidently Church magic exerted its attraction.

---

[92] Ibid. 81–4; the ranks of Cabalists were swelled by *émigrés* from the pogroms in Poland after 1648. On Oppenheimer, cf. above, pp. 164, 351. One example of a successful convert would be the imperial court painter, Ferdinand Renati (died in 1701). Jewish traders served the aristocracy in Bohemia (Klíma, op. cit. 23, 26 f., 78, 81, 83–6, 132); in Hungary seven communities of Jews were protected by the Esterházys, with autonomous privileges from the 1680s (*Encyclopaedia Judaica*, s.v. 'Burgenland', 'Eisenstadt', 'Mattersburg'). For the parlous state of other Hungarian Jews see E. Marton, 'The family tree of Hungarian Jewry', *Hungarian-Jewish Studies*, i (1966), 1–59, at 16 ff.

[93] Most of the standard works (above n. 46) venture some approximate totals, though they must evidently be received with great caution. Estimates for neighbouring areas are 1–2,000 in Bavaria (Riezler, op. cit. 240–2) and 10,000 in Poland (Baranowski, op. cit. 30).

[94] Czerny, *Tourist*, 102–4.

And in the view of the most generous and idealistic protagonists of Counter-Reformation, things were really very hopeful indeed. Christian magic would win out entirely in the end; the spiritual and intellectual world of the Baroque would conquer. They indulged an unrealistic but—in its way—a grandiose vision that faith would ultimately subsume superstition; that the relation between learned and primitive occultism was a dialectical one. We must now explore this last and most nebulous leading idea, the Utopian substratum, in the making of the Habsburg Monarchy.

CHAPTER 12

The universal enterprise

One of the most intriguing features of the Habsburg Counter-Reformation is its nice blend of insecurity and confidence. This is not simply a case of stout hearts replacing faint at a certain point in the proceedings; rather the two coexisted, such that a rising sense of certainty lent renewed emotional weight to lingering feelings of uncertainty. What began as the febrile assertiveness of the first seventeenth-century generation gradually took wing, most of all in the clerical mind, drawing encouragement first from the events of the 1620s—when Jesuits at Olomouc, for example, stood ready not only to act in Germany, but even to embark for Scandinavia—then from the further successes which I have chronicled in all parts of the Monarchy. Catholic expansion somehow always found reserves of strength, as late as the 1690s and beyond in Transylvania and the Hungarian Plain. The need produced the deed, and if the struggle was uphill, it still looked uncommonly like the measured tread of progress. Whereas the secular arm better knew how much the achievement owed, if not to brute force, at least to subtle social and political pressures, intellectuals in the Church tended to discern providence illumining the mind of the heretic.

The lessons of this development persuaded many Catholic thinkers in favour of a mild approach which married with their hope of some all-embracing spiritual solution and did not rule out certain gestures of conciliation. The first targets continued to be the Protestants. We have already encountered the mission to Germany of Rojas y Spinola, which yielded only a very limited harvest of individual converts, mainly well-born: useful gains politically, but no vindication of the eirenical programme with its goal of reunion by mutual consent.[1] During the 1680s Spinola turned his attention to Hungary, where both he and the Dutch representative at the Habsburg court espied the seeds of a possible patriotic religious

[1] Above, pp. 305 f.

compromise. But while Hamel Bruynincx negotiated defensively for a political accommodation, the Franciscan friar issued a printed appeal to the diet at Sopron and sought discussions with Protestant leaders about dogma. In 1691–2 Spinola tried again, still convinced—as he explains in a long letter to Pál Esterházy—that goodwill exists, that common ground can be found in Scripture and revelation, and that success in Hungary will be followed by agreement in the *Reich*.[2] Once more, however, the ideals were outflanked even on the Catholic side by mercenary considerations and achieved little: only a few non-committal replies came from Lutheran and Calvinist congregations, along with the odd apostate like Otrokocsi, who speedily passed through eirenism to furious denunciation of his former co-religionists.[3]

Not all the non-Catholics who could be approached within the Monarchy were Protestants. Two widespread heathen groups seem, indeed, to have been written off almost unanimously at an early stage. Hopes of persuading Jews into the faith by a mixture of forced attendance at Christian sermons, edifying literature from *conversos*, and material incentives, though entertained briefly in the early seventeenth century, soon lapsed, and philosemitism retreated into the scholar's study. Catholics naturally could not share the conviction of some Calvinists that the recovery of the Jews would represent a fulfilment of millenarian prophecy.[4] Gipsies—whether true Romanies or not—appear likewise to have been cast aside as hopeless reprobates without the ministrations of missionaries, and a last echo of gentler counsels sounds in some instructions of 1724

---

[2] Antal–Pater (eds.), op. cit. i, esp. 260–305. Spinola's conciliatory approach of 1681: *Regni Hungariae Augustanae et Helveticae Confessionis Status et Ordines... Quod inter tantos Praelatos, omnium minimus DD. VV. hisce accedat* ([V.] 1681), is described in *OSzK Évkönyve*, 1963–4, 139. OL. Eszterházy cs. lt., P. 125, cs. 658, no. 2888 (Wiener Neustadt, 30 July 1691); see also nos. 2889–90. Cf. the interesting earlier (1667) feelers in OL. Forgách cs. lt., P. 287, ser. II, fasc. CC, cs. 40, fols. 311, 307.

[3] Lampe, op. cit. 500–2, 506–15; W. Neuser in Barton–Makkai (eds.), op. cit. 144–146. F. F. Otrokocsi, *Sententia Media ac Pacificatoria... Fratres ad pacem et concordiam mutuam invitans* (Amsterdam 1690); id., *Strenae cujusdam Discussio Pacifica ...* (Amsterdam 1690); the latter work especially has a strong oecumenical flavour. But cf. above, pp. 250 f., 395.

[4] For efforts at persuasion see Kaufmann, op. cit. 21 ff.; Tietze, op. cit. 58; Mayer, op. cit. i, nos. 680, 682, 996, 1009. Wallenstein set up a foundation for young Jewish converts (Popper, art. cit. 140 f.). Cf. above, pp. 349–51. On prophetic views of Jewry, primarily in England: P. Toon (ed.), *Puritans, the Millennium and the future of Israel* (Cambridge 1970).

for Silesia sparing Catholic converts among them from banishment.[5] But much better prospects opened up on another front: among the populations of Greek Orthodox religion scattered around the periphery of the Hungarian state.

In the eyes of Rome it was not clear that all the Orthodox communities of Eastern Europe had ever been fully schismatic. With some special pleading a case could be made that they never stood very firmly under Constantinople, that Catholic bishoprics had been established in several areas during the Middle Ages, and that the reunion negotiated at Ferrara and Florence in 1438–9, widely though temporarily approved by the Eastern Churches, remained valid. These were murky waters, further muddied when sixteenth-century Lutherans put forward their own theological feelers towards the patriarchs. But the Counter-Reformation took the plunge more boldly and offered membership of the Roman Church to any Orthodox who would acknowledge the supreme authority of the Pope and a few other central Catholic tenets. Such 'Uniate' status[6] would permit them full use of their traditional ritual and liturgical language. It promised too, since the operation could scarcely advance far without support from a sympathetic ruler, social and political betterment for unprivileged groups, especially for their priesthood.

The first modern Uniate Church was founded among the Ruthenes (Ukrainians) of Poland by the synod of Brest in 1596. That accord spurred Catholics to seek a corresponding agreement with the Ruthenes who lived across the Carpathian mountains inside Hungary. The campaign was initially led by an aristocratic convert, György Drugeth of Homonna, who brought Jesuits to his estates around Ungvár (Užhorod) and began negotiations with the local bishop of Munkács (Mukačevo) in 1613–14. Sabotaged by Orthodox militants, the cause revived in the 1640s and 1650s with the aid of the Drugeth family, Hungarian prelates (including the primate, Lippay), and the dynasty. A certain Basil Tarasovič, who took over the unreliable see in 1633, and his even flightier successor,

---

[5] Frauenstädt, art. cit. 505 f.
[6] The Uniates were (and are) also widely known as 'Greek-Catholics', in Hungarian always so. The usual requirements, besides obedience to the Pope, were addition of the *filioque* clause in the creed, belief in purgatory, and use of unleavened bread at the Eucharist.

Peter Parthenius, seem to have accepted the Union for themselves and their fellow-priests, though the endeavour was hindered by counter-ploys, especially from the Calvinist Rákóczis, who owned much land in the area, including the episcopal seat. Things could be consolidated a little after the death of György II Rákóczi in 1660, but progress remained slow and the commitment to Union shallow. Only further missionary work led by a Jesuit, Joseph de Camillis, secured a permanent arrangement at the end of the century with De Camillis himself as the first dependable bishop of Munkács.[7]

Among the Serbs, the other Orthodox Slavonic race of the Monarchy, a Uniate movement blossomed earlier, but failed to bring forth as much lasting fruit. Turkish advance through the Balkans caused large numbers of Serbs to migrate into southern Hungary during the sixteenth and seventeenth centuries. In 1611 their bishop at the monastery of Marča in Croatia, Simeon Vretanija, together with his monks and flock, accepted overtures made to him by the Jesuits at Zagreb and Cardinal Bellarmin in Rome. That episode is well documented; thereafter the story becomes obscure. The Union survived, particularly among Serbs in the military district of Sichelburg (Žumberak) on the borders of Croatia and Carniola; in the 1670s Bishop Zorčić set up a seminary for Greek-Catholic priests at Zagreb. Yet its impact must have been restricted: what are we to make of an episcopal see whose incumbent was regularly styled 'bishop of Svidnica' when no such place as Svidnica exists? During the 1690s, following the triumph over the Turks, Habsburg authorities on the military frontier and local Jesuits tried to reanimate the Union. This purpose, however,

---

[7] There is a surprisingly rich literature on these confusing events, much of it highly partisan: A. Hodinka, *A munkácsi görög-szertartású püspökség története és okmánytára, 1458–1715*, i–ii (Bp. 1909–11); J. Fiedler, 'Beiträge zur Geschichte der Union der Ruthenen in Nord-Ungarn . . .', *Sb. d. k. Akad. d. Wiss., ph.-h. Kl.* xxxix (1862), 481–524; J. Duliškovič, *Istoričeskia čerty Ugro-Russkich*, i–iii (Ungvár 1874–1877), ii, 52 ff.; iii; N. Nilles, *Symbolae ad illustrandam historiam Ecclesiae Orientalis in terris Coronae S. Stephani*, i–ii (Innsbruck 1885), 821–914 (documents); M. Lacko, *Unio Užhorodensis Ruthenorum Carpaticorum cum Ecclesia Catholica* (Rome 1965, also in English ibid. 1966), very thorough on events into the 1660s; O. Baran, 'Tserkva na Zakarpatti v rokach 1665–91', *Bogoslovia*, xxxii (1968), 77–145, with an equally thorough account of the next years. Cf. Szentiványi, 'Dissertatio Chronologico-Polemica, de Ortu, Progressu, ac diminutione Schismatis Graeci', in *Opuscula Polemica*, ii, 137–93; Kazy, op. cit. i, 116 f.; ii, 113 f.; Krones, 'Jesuitenorden 1645–71', 303–6; Fraknói, *Kegyúri jog*, i, 388–90.

inevitably fell foul of another: the offers simultaneously being made to the loyalist Arsenius Crnojević, Patriarch of Peć, and his fellow-refugees, as encouragement for them to settle on the empty *neo-acquistica* lands of central Hungary. Guarantees of undisturbed Orthodox worship and personal freedom left little material inducement for Serbs to turn to Catholicism, and what survived of the Union had to be buttressed by oppressive means in the eighteenth century.[8]

More important in numerical terms than either Ruthenes or Serbs were the Romanians (contemporaries would have called them Wallachians) who inhabited large parts of Transylvania and formed about half its population. Evidently Catholics could do little while the principality remained independent; rather its rulers, following their own miniature programme of expansion, sought to convert the Romanians to Calvinism and made some superficial impact, mainly on the organization of the Orthodox Church.[9] When the Habsburgs took over in the 1690s they promptly put in a higher bid: the government tempted the downtrodden, semi-nomadic Orthodox community with promises of social amelioration and political influence; Jesuit missionaries, co-ordinated by Kollonich, pressed the spiritual merits of Union. Metropolitan Athanasius of Alba Iulia (Gyulafehérvár) and the majority of his clergy swore allegiance in 1698, and were rewarded with a Leopoldine diploma guaranteeing their position and a statute to regulate the affairs of the new Church.

[8] The fullest account is J. Šimrak, *De relationibus S. Romanae Sedis Apostolicae et Slavorum meridionalium saeculo XVII, XVIII* (Zagreb 1926). See also Nilles, op. cit. 703–818 (documents); G. Hofmann, 'Il B. Bellarmino e gli Orientali', *Orientalia Christiana*, viii (1927), 261–305, at 274 f., 290–8, with material on the 1611 Union; J. Fiedler, 'Die Union der in Ungern zwischen der Donau und Drau wohnenden Bekenner des griechisch-orientalischen Glaubens', *Sb. d. k. Akad. d. Wiss., ph.-h. Kl.* xxxviii (1861), 284–97, and id. in *AÖG* xxxvii (1867), 105–45, on the 1690s. J. H. Schwicker, 'Zur Geschichte der kirchlichen Union in der croatischen Militärgränze', *AÖG* lii (1875), 275–400, is mainly about the 18th-century struggles, and fiercely critical. Cf. Fraknói, *Kegyúri jog*, i, 390–3. The whereabouts of 'Svidnica' are inconclusively discussed by Nilles, op. cit. 739–43; the see was also sometimes called 'Vretanija' (after its founder?), or even—quaintly—'Britanija'. At the end of the 18th century it was reconstituted at Križevci (Ger.: Kreutz; Hung.: Körös) in north-east Croatia. The episcopal residence at Marča was burned down by schismatics in 1739.

[9] Compare I. Révész, *La Réforme et les Roumains de Transylvanie* (Bp. 1937), and Ş. Meteş, *Istoria bisericii şi a vieţii religioase a Românilor din Transilvania şi Ungaria*, i (Sibiu 1935), for two very different views of this programme. Cf. A. Grana, *Instituţile Calvineşti în biserica română* (Blaj 1895).

During the eighteenth century Uniates played a dominant part in the ecclesiastical and cultural life of the Monarchy's Romanians. Neither the troubled internal history of this Union, nor the question whether its initiators acted out of conviction, calculation, or compulsion, belongs to the present discussion: from the standpoint of Counter-Reformation it was a notable victory.[10] And a bloodless one: it is an interesting detail that the Romanians and Ruthenes of Eastern Europe both appear to have stayed free of witchcraft persecutions.[11]

One further Uniate group, Transylvanian-based and very small, needs to be mentioned: the Armenians. By the seventeenth century numbers of Armenians, dispossessed from their Anatolian and Caucasian homeland, had become scattered through Eastern Europe, bearing with them their distinctive kind of Oriental Christianity. In 1672 some thousands fled across the mountains from Moldavia and Wallachia and were allowed to settle in the principality by Apafi. As early as 1686 their Orthodox bishop, on his death-bed, acknowledged the supremacy of Rome, and the work of Union was soon accomplished by an active priest, Oxendius Verziresky, whom the Pope named vicar-apostolic over all his fellow-countrymen in Transylvania. The speed and completeness of this accommodation—helped, no doubt, by a similar agreement already reached in Poland—brought clear advantages to local Armenians. Mainly traders and artisans, they were allowed to found three towns for their own exclusive residence; the largest was even officially styled 'Armenopolis'.[12]

*

Ideals of mission did not stop short at the frontiers of the Monarchy or the *Reich*. Their most obvious extension led into Poland. During

---

[10] Nilles, op. cit. 127–390, offers a comprehensive collection of documents for the years 1697–1711. See also J. Fiedler, 'Die Union der Walachen in Siebenbürgen unter Kaiser Leopold I', *Sb. d. k. Akad. d. Wiss., ph.-h. Kl.* xxvii (1858), 350–82; cf. Szentiványi, 'Dissertatio . . .' in *Opuscula Polemica*, loc. cit. The continued polemic about these events is illustrated by—for the Uniates—*Biserica română unită*, ed. P. Cârnaţiu *et al.* (Madrid 1952), esp. 29–66; and—for the Orthodox—D. Stăniloae, *Uniatismul din Transilvania, încercare de dezmembrare a poporului român* (Bucharest 1973). K. Hitchins, *The Rumanian national movement in Transylvania, 1780–1849* (Cambridge, Mass. 1969), indicates some of the 18th-century consequences.

[11] Müller, op. cit. 52; Baranowski, op. cit. 27 f.

[12] Ch. Lukácsi, *Historia Armenorum Transsilvaniae* (V. 1859), 64 ff. Armenopolis is Hungarian Szamosújvár, Romanian Gherla, north of Cluj (Kolozsvár).

the seventeenth century the previous rivalry between Austrian and Polish crowns was replaced by close political co-operation, several times cemented with bonds of marriage. But whereas at the beginning of the period Poland seemed an equal partner in the alliance (King Sigismund III sent crucial reinforcements to his brother-in-law Ferdinand II in 1619), by the end she had manifestly become a client state, dependent on Habsburg support for whatever limited independence she could still sustain.[13] The process reached its climax with the accession in 1697 of Augustus II, 'the Strong', that former Habsburg commander in Hungary and Catholic convert at Austrian instigation, who took with him to Warsaw the long Saxon tradition of subservience to Vienna. Only one Polish ruler seriously tried to halt this development: Jan Sobieski. It is a fine irony that his reign is remembered for the greatest single act of Habsburg–Polish solidarity: the relief of Vienna. In fact the stirring events of 1683 fall in years of comparative antipathy; witness the notorious coolness between Sobieski and Leopold on the morrow of the Ottoman defeat.[14]

Underlying tendencies were not disturbed by the temporary diplomatic manœuvrings of Sobieski. Poland's Counter-Reformation ran a course similar to that in the Habsburg lands and over much the same span of time. It too rested on the court and the territorial magnates, on the intolerance of a revived national hierarchy whose shades of patriotism mirrored those of its counterpart in Hungary, and on the weakness of a divided Protestant opposition. Again, however, the balance gradually shifted. Earlier in the seventeenth century Poles played an expansive role: they were the first to woo Greek Orthodox Christians; they were active across the Habsburg border, especially in Bohemia as priests who

---

[13] Sigismund (Zygmunt) III (1587–1632) married two sisters of Ferdinand II; Władisław IV (1632–48) married a daughter of Ferdinand II; Michael (Michał) Wisniowiecki (1669–73) married a sister of Leopold I. Between 1644 and 1666 the duchies of Oppeln and Ratibor in Silesia were pledged to Poland: W. Konopczyński, *Dzieje Polski nowożytnej*, i–ii (2nd edn. London 1958–9), i, 324 f.; ii, 63–5. In addition sixteen towns of the Zips region in Upper Hungary were continuously mortgaged to the Polish crown from the 15th until the 18th century.

[14] On Augustus, cf. above, p. 283. For Austro–Polish political links: Konopczyński, op. cit. i, 241–3, 253–6, 274 f., 301–4, 321–5; ii, 30 ff., 72 f., 86 ff. *passim*; O. Forst de Battaglia, *Jan Sobieski, König von Polen* (Einsiedeln–Zurich 1946), esp. 157–237; Redlich, *Weltmacht*, 53–76.

could communicate (after a fashion) with the native Czech population or—like Balbín's teacher, Lancicius—raise up a new generation of Catholic intellectuals. Between 1625 and 1655 a Vasa prince held the bishopric of Breslau.[15] But later influences and transfers of personnel tended to proceed in the opposite direction. Polish Uniates studied at Olomouc and Prague, and the progress of their Church was keenly observed from the Habsburg lands, by Valerian Magni for example, a key figure in the counsels of King Władysław IV, who was also involved with the feeble eirenical overtures made to Protestants at the colloquy of Thorn in 1645. Jesuits looked increasingly to the leadership of Vienna.[16] Even the shrine of Częstochowa, with its famous black Madonna which allegedly halted a Swedish invasion and saved the country in 1655, belonged to hermits from the Hungarian-based Pauline order.

So firmly Romanized was Poland, so successful seemed its Union of the Orthodox population, that proselytizers gained confidence for a further advance of Catholicism in Eastern Europe through the gentle arts of persuasion. Some looked to Muscovy, where Juraj Križanić (1618–83), the visionary canon of Zagreb, pursued his single-minded mission of Slav reconciliation, and where a Czech-speaking Jesuit community was organized from the 1680s with the backing of the Habsburgs, who had a status as the official protectors

---

[15] Cf. above, p. 123, n. 18. On the Polish Uniates: J. Pelesz, *Geschichte der Union der ruthenischen Kirche mit Rom*, i–ii (V. 1878–80), ii; and the vast collection of printed sources in A. Theiner (ed.), *Vetera Monumenta Poloniae et Lithuaniae … historiam illustrantia*, iii (Rome 1863), *passim*. Lancicius (Lęczycki): Tanner, *Societas Jesu …Imitatrix*, 773–91; *Knihopis*, nos. 4761–6. Another significant Jesuit example would be Adam Kochański (cf. above, pp. 316, 334 f. and n. 59, p. 378). The bishop was Karol Ferdynand, son of Sigismund III.

[16] A. V. Florovský, *Čeští jesuité na Rusi* (Pr. 1941), 3–107. For Magni: Z. ab Haarlem, *Unio Ruthenorum a morte Sigismundi III usque ad coronationem Ladislai IV* (Tartu 1936); J. Cygan, 'Zum Übertritt des kalviner Pastors Bartholomäus Nigrin zur katholischen Kirche (1636–43)', *Coll. Franc.* xxxix (1969), 282–303 (Nigrin was a Silesian Lutheran, later Calvinist, and later still Catholic convert, who played a prominent part at Thorn); A. Jobert, *De Luther à Mohila, la Pologne dans la crise de la Chrétienté* (Paris 1974), 375–400. Cf. also L. Pastor, *History of the Popes*, xix (London 1938), 165 ff.; Melchior a Pobladura, 'Disceptatio historica de Cardinalatu Valeriani Magni (1634–48)', *Coll. Franc.* xxxix (1969), 104–71; and A. Gába, 'Kontakty Władysława IV ze szlachcicem morawskim', *Sobótka*, vi (1951), 26–9, on the role of Valerian's brother, Francesco Magni, as governor of Oppeln and Ratibor (cf. above, n. 13) during the 1640s. Some of Magni's vacuum experiments (above, p. 337, n. 66) were carried out at Warsaw. The standard work on Polish Jesuits is S. Załęski, *Jezuici w Polsce*, i–v (Lemberg 1900–6).

of all Catholics resident in Russia.[17] Others, echoing political overtures made by the imperial government, tried to nurture the tender growth of Papal allegiance within the Romanian principalities, which had some hazy medieval antecedents; various religious orders worked there intermittently from about 1580 to spread the Word.[18] Neither of these attempts bore much fruit: endless friction ensued in Russia, though Jesuit educational methods proved influential throughout the eighteenth century; little response was evoked in Wallachia or Moldavia, despite the benevolent neutrality of some of the *hospodar* rulers (one appears to have been created Hungarian count and prince of the Empire by Leopold). Even direct Habsburg sovereignty over Oltenia (western Wallachia) between 1718 and 1739 brought few conversions.[19]

My concern here is to illustrate an ambitious mentality, not to chart the modest returns which that mentality can be seen, with hindsight, to have yielded. What worlds might be opening up for the faith as the young, impressionable, and Westernizing Tsar Peter listened to the oratory of Kollonich and the imperial confessor Wolff (the latter holding forth in a macaronic blend of Czech and Polish) during his Austrian visit in 1698!?[20] Thus Habsburg intellectuals now also devoted increasing attention to the Ottoman Empire, a concern dictated both by practical needs of the moment and by larger plans for conversion, perhaps even political hegemony, in the Near East. Activities began long before 1683—indeed, they may be traced back to the Humanist curiosity of men like Busbecq and Lewenklau, Hieronymus Megiser and Peter Kirsten of Breslau.[21] They expanded considerably by the mid-seventeenth

---

[17] On Križanić: P. Pierling, *La Russie et le Saint-Siège*, i–v (Paris 1896–1912), reprinted The Hague 1967), iv, 3–39; *Enciklopedija Jugoslavije*, v (1962), 416–18, with full bibliography. On the Czech Jesuits: Pierling, op. cit. iv, 77 ff. *passim*; Florovský, op. cit. 111–356.

[18] R. Cândea, *Der Katholizismus in den Donaufürstentümern* (Leipzig 1916), collects together the scattered evidence; cf. Krones, 'Jesuitenorden 1645–71', appendix 2; L. Pásztor in *Archivum Franciscanum Historicum*, xlii (1949), 257–77. For the diplomatic contacts see O. Brunner, 'Österreich und die Walachei während des Türkenkrieges von 1683–99', *MIÖG* xliv (1930), 265–323.

[19] Cândea, op. cit. 101–6. On the whole Oltenian episode: Ș. Papacostea, *Oltenia sub stăpînirea austriacă* (Bucharest 1971).

[20] Pierling, op. cit. iv, 126–64, esp. 138 f.; cf. Nyáry, op. cit. 91–8.

[21] Cf. above, p. 29 and n. 67 (Evans). Kirsten (1577–1640) was a Silesian doctor and one of the greatest pioneer Arabists, whose main works appeared at Breslau between 1608 and 1611 (Zedler and *ADB*, s.v.).

century, with a series of embassies to the Porte which culminated in Count Walter Leslie's mission after the battle at Szentgotthárd, where Habsburg troops inflicted a first major defeat on the Ottoman army. They coincided also with early projects for Austrian commercial penetration into the Balkans.[22] In the 1660s two men commenced serious study of Oriental languages in Vienna. One of them, Franz Meninski à Mesgnien, a Lorrainer ennobled in the service of the Polish king, set up his own press to print a pioneering Arabic–Persian–Turkish dictionary. The other, Giovanni Battista Podestà, rose as imperial interpreter and agent to become a university professor, and compiled several volumes on the languages and traditions of the Ottoman realm. Both maintained close connections with the court: Meninski, a member of the War Council, helped produce a catalogue of the Oriental manuscripts in the *Hofbibliothek*; Podestà was one of Lambeck's most loyal correspondents.[23] While their initiative proved far from harmonious—a flaming public row broke out between them worthy of their immigrant contemporaries, the stage Irishmen, Carve and Bruodin—it led on to outstanding Austrian achievements in Oriental scholarship during the eighteenth and nineteenth centuries.[24]

Some schemes of religious mission usually accompanied the

---

[22] R. Neck, 'Andrea Negroni', *MÖStA* iii (1950), 166–95; P. Meienberger, *Johann Rudolf Schmid zum Schwarzenhorn als kaiserlicher Resident in Konstantinopel, 1629–43* (Bern–Frankfurt 1973); above, p. 208, n. 26, for Černín's mission in 1644. On Leslie's embassy: P. Taverner, *Caesarea Legatio* (V. 1668), a work which appeared the following year at Litomyšl in Czech translation (*Knihopis*, no. 16052: Leslie possessed estates nearby). On commercial plans: H. Hassinger, 'Die erste Wiener orientalische Handelskompagnie', *Vjschr. f. S. u. WGesch.* xxxv (1942), 1–53.

[23] Meninski (1623–98): Mayer, op. cit. i, pp. 302–4; F. Babinger, 'Die türkischen Studien in Europa bis zum Auftreten J. von Hammer-Purgstalls', *Welt des Islams*, vii (1919), 103–29, at 114–16, esp. 115 n. Podestà: Mayer, op. cit. i, pp. 319 f. and nos. 1839, 1901–3, 1921, 1929, 2197; Babinger, art. cit. 113 f. and 115 n. Podestà prepared an abstract of Turkish grammar, based on the Jesuit approach to Latin, at the express command of Leopold: ÖNB, MS. 9644, in Latin, m.p., and dated 1666. His surviving letters to Lambeck cover the period 1667–79 and were written on travels in Hungary, Italy, and Turkey: ÖNB, MS 9713, fols. 173, 186–8, 212, 286; ibid. MS. 9714, fols. 170, 207, 309; ibid. MS. 9715, fol. 258; ibid. MS. 9716, fols. 211, 236, 285.

[24] F. Meninski, *Veritas defensa* ... (V. 1675); G. B. Podestà, *Theriaca contra viperinos malesuadae invidiae morsus, sive dissertatio de Meninskiano scommatum et execrationum Orco* ... (V. 1677); cf. the comment (presumably by Meninski) in the front of ÖNB, MS. 9644. On Carve and Bruodin see above, p. 327, n. 38. For the Viennese Oriental Academy, founded in 1753, whose first director was a Jesuit: V. W. von Starkenfels, *Die k.-k. orientalische Akademie zu Wien* (V. 1839).

practical soundings. They were not clearly articulated for the Balkans themselves, beyond a generalized hope of reunion with Orthodoxy: the Habsburgs had suffered too much from pretenders and adventurers to risk any firm commitment on such treacherous terrain.[25] More excitement was aroused—despite their small numbers—by the Copts, the surviving Christian population of the Nile valley. Kircher made a protracted study of their language, whose antiquity and links with the hieroglyphics he correctly divined.[26] Since (as we shall shortly see) he revered ancient Coptic as vehicle for the occult wisdom of Hermes Trismegistus, the scientific content of his work necessarily remained rather exiguous; but its religious purpose was correspondingly enhanced. Other Germans took up the theme, among them Leibniz and especially Ludolf at Gotha, the first important European writer on the history and language of the Ethiopians. Ludolf, the careful and modest Lutheran, was a very different kind of person from Kircher, yet his devotion to the imperial cause stands beyond question: he became a good friend of Lambeck and received the personal encouragement of Leopold. Confessional *arrière-pensée* emerges more obviously in Ludolf's errant pupil Wansleb, who disappointed his master not only by staying put in Egypt when sent to explore Ethiopia and by some lamentably imprecise Amharic scholarship, but also by converting to the Church of Rome.[27]

---

[25] Cf. *Rudolf II*, 77, 108 f. Another in the same mould was presumably the author of ÖNB, MS. 11660, in which one Matteo Nicolao, Duke of Rulmia (or Kulmia?), who styles himself 'hereditary Count of Illyria and Dalmatia' and claims descent from the king (!) of Sheba (described as one of the Three Wise Men), offers the emperor a confession of Christian faith written in Arabic.

[26] A. Kircher, *Prodromus Coptus sive Aegyptiacus* (Rome 1636); id., *Lingua Aegyptiaca Restituta* (Rome 1644), with dedication to Ferdinand III, 'Regi Trismegisto'. He also translated the ritual of the Egyptian Church.

[27] Baruzi, op. cit., esp. 5–45. Leibniz looked first to the French for an initiative in Egypt. Job Ludolf, *Lexicon Aethiopico-Latinum* (London 1661, revised Frankfurt 1699); id., *Historia Aethiopica* (Frankfurt 1681, also English and French edns.); id., *Ad ... Historiam Aethiopicam .. Commentarius* (Frankfurt 1691); id., *Appendix ad Historiam Aethiopicam* (Frankfurt 1693). Cf. Juncker, *Commentarius*, 105 ff.; J. Flemming, 'Hiob Ludolf', in *Beiträge zur Assyriologie*, ed. F. Delitzsch and P. Haupt, i (1889), 537–82; ii (1891–2), 63–110; and above, p. 289. Ludolf's letters to Lambeck (1676–9) are in ÖNB, MS. 9715, fols. 167, 188 f., 196 f., 239–42, 272–5; ibid. MS. 9716, fols. 38^{a-b}, 104, 120, 149, 208, 217, 223, 227, 252, 296. Johann Michael Wansleb (or Wansleben) wrote *The Present State of Egypt* (London 1678, also in French); and *Histoire de l'Église d'Alexandrie fondée par S. Marc* (Paris 1677). He is

(continued)

Christian communities in the Asiatic Near East looked equally ripe for Habsburg protection. There too Austria possessed certain traditions: the *editio princeps* of the Syriac New Testament, for example, had been published at Vienna in 1555 (it was reissued by Knorr von Rosenroth at Sulzbach in 1684) and long-standing, albeit desultory contacts existed between the imperial court and Persia.[28] The most interesting developments in this direction were overtures made to Armenians, which evoked a remarkable response from one Peter Bedik, a noble *émigré* from the Caucasus who studied at the Jesuit college in Rome before moving to Vienna. In reality the prospects for a genuine ecclesiastical Union in Armenia, that embattled mountain fastness pressed by Turks and Persians, never stood very high; yet who could imagine that when reading Bedik's curious treatise of 1678 entitled *Cehil Sutun*? Not only are Armenians, for him, spiritually at one with Catholic Europe; the whole of Persia may be ripe for conversion. The Holy Roman Emperors have a mission to rebuild the fabled but decaying temple of King Cyrus: they are the great light of Eastern Christianity, and Bedik feels like one of the wise men of old in making his pilgrimage to the rising star of Austria.[29]

Such Oriental flattery must have had its effect on minds already directed towards Asiatic horizons. Still farther afield lay the greatest prize of all: China. The conversion of the Chinese tempted Italian and Spanish clergy from the early years of the Counter-Reformation; the initiatives of St. Francis Xavier were taken up by the next energetic generation of Jesuits, especially the formidable Matteo Ricci. The Society's real period of influence at the imperial court

---

claimed as the inspirer of *A Brief Account of the Rebellions and Bloudshed occasioned by the Anti-Christian Practices of the Jesuits … in the Empire of Ethiopia* (London 1679), though it is not clear whether the sentiments were really his. He also arranged the first, and faulty, edition of Ludolf's *Lexicon*. Cf., on him, Räss, op. cit. vii, 271–5. Later a Czech, Jakub Rímař, became head of the Franciscan mission in Egypt and Ethiopia (Z. Kalista, *Cesty ve znamení kříže* (2nd edn. Pr. 1947), 228–37).

[28] Cf. *Rudolf II*, 77 f. In 1676 Albertus ab Holten offers Leopold his Syrian grammar with some Baroque reflections as to its usefulness: ÖNB, MS. 9715, fols. 217 f., 225.

[29] Peter Bedik, *Cehil Sutun, seu Explicatio utriusque celeberrimi, ac pretiosissimi Theatri Quadraginta Columnarum in Perside Orientis* (V. [1678], date only in a chronogram). The two works published in Vienna at this time by Paul Piromallus, a Dominican who became archbishop of Nakhichevan in Armenia, are relevant to this theme (Mayer, op. cit. i, nos. 1372–3; cf. Bedik, op. cit. 363 ff.).

and among the mandarin caste began in the mid-seventeenth century under the new Manchu dynasty and reached its climax in the 1690s. It coincided with the arrival of a number of adventurous missionaries from Central Europe.[30] Bernhard Diestel and Johann Grueber, both Austrians, were first to reach Peking by journeying through Persia; the mathematician Grueber, accounted by some the outstanding land traveller of the century, even made his way back to Rome across the uncharted wastes of Central Asia and ended an eventful life wrestling for souls in eastern Hungary. The Tyrolese Martin Martini translated a series of theological and philosophical works into Chinese as part of the campaign of persuasion. Others, like Christian Herdricht from Graz and Karel Slaviček from Moravia, continued the undertaking. Adam Schall of Cologne and his successor, the Fleming Ferdinand Verbiest, transmitted their Jesuit contemporaries' fascination with astronomy and instrument-making.[31]

At home Catholic intellectuals propagated the achievements of these pioneers and placed them in a larger Utopian context. Yet again Kircher played a crucial part: not only did he chronicle the stories of Grueber, or of the Augsburger, Heinrich Roth, from whom he received the first specimens of Sanskrit to be published in Europe. He also constructed a whole spiritual history of China in which Christianity is claimed as an abiding force there since the early centuries A.D., the improbable (but typical) argument resting on his interpretation of an eighth-century 'Nestorian' monument dug up in Shansi province in 1625.[32] And Habsburgs were more

---

[30] See, in general, A. H. Rowbotham, *Missionary and Mandarin, the Jesuits at the court of China* (Berkeley–Los Angeles 1942); L. Pfister, *Notices biographiques et bibliographiques sur les Jésuites de l'ancienne mission de Chine*, i–ii (Shanghai 1932–4). The first Central European in China was Václav Kirwitzer (died in 1626).

[31] Biographical information about all these Jesuits in Pfitzer, op. cit., and Sommervogel (not always quite accurate). On Grueber also C. Wessels, *Early Jesuit travellers in Central Asia, 1603–1721* (The Hague 1924), 164–204; B. Zimmel, 'Der erste Bericht über Tibets Hauptstadt Lhasa aus dem Jahre 1661', *Biblos*, ii (1953), 127–45; and *NDB*, s.v. On Martini also W. Schrameier in *Journal of the Peking Oriental Society*, ii (1888), 99–119. On Slaviček also Kalista, *Cesty*, 137–66. On Schall and Verbiest also Rowbotham, op. cit., chs. 5–7. Such Central Europeans formed a small proportion of all the Jesuits in China, but some were important, and my purpose here is anyway not to analyse that mission as such.

[32] A. Kircher, *China Monumentis ... Illustrata* (Amsterdam 1667); B. Szczesniak in *Osiris*, x (1952), 385–411, adds little. The excavated tablet was perfectly genuine, though it would not bear Kircher's Catholicizing exegesis.

than willing to back the enterprise. Kircher's book appeared under their aegis. A Polish Jesuit, Michał Boym, could publish at Vienna his remarkable treatise on China's flora with a dedication (1655) to the young Leopold. In the same year Martini presented Archduke Leopold Wilhelm with his atlas of the country, which includes a highly positive view of Chinese civilization and the sanguine prediction of a speedy triumph for Catholicism. Later a French Jesuit, François Noel, settled at Prague, where several of his important works on Chinese culture were issued.[33] An imperial-sponsored *chinoiserie* took root in the Reich—witness Sandrart's descriptions of Chinese art, Fischer von Erlach's of Chinese buildings—and attracted earnest speculations from the Lutheran camp. Leibniz positively welcomed the success of his Jesuit friends as part of some larger scheme for reconciliation between Christian and Chinese philosophy, while a lesser scholar like Andreas Müller of Berlin sought to interest Lambeck and Kircher in elaborating a *clavis sinica* or 'key to the Chinese language'.[34]

*

All these endeavours represent an ultimately spiritual mission conceived *sub specie universi*. They even came to embrace America, not so much through the steady flow of Central European emigrants thither (such as the astronomer Valentin Stansel, observing comets in the clear skies of the New World; J. V. Richter, murdered by Indians on the Andes; or František Boryně, ministering to the Moxos of Peru[35]) as through the prospect, so dear to Habsburgs between the 1660s and 1714, that Austria would inherit the vast Spanish Empire, overseas as well as Iberian, Italian, and Nether-landish. 'Counter-Reformation' now becomes subsumed in some-thing far broader: a drive to conquer for Mother Church all those who, precisely because they were not Protestants, were free of the trammels of open and refractory heresy. Superstition, especially

[33] M. Boym, *Flora Sinensis* (V. 1656); cf. Pfister, op. cit. i, 269–76. For Martini's work: ibid. i, 256–62; and G. Hamann, 'Das Leben der Chinesen in der Sicht eines Tiroler Missionars des 17. Jahrhunderts', *AÖG* cxxv (1966), 96–120. On Noel: Sommervogel, v, cols. 1791–4.

[34] G. W. Leibniz, *Novissima Sinica* (2nd edn. n.p. 1699); Baruzi, op. cit. 77 ff. Leibniz hoped also to work through Russia towards China. Müller: ÖNB, MS. 9715, fols. 7 f., 126 f.; he published a number of works on Oriental subjects. Cf. Morhof, op. cit. ii, bk. 2, pt. 1, ch. 5.

[35] Kalista, *Cesty*, 55–97, 124–33, and *passim*. On Stansel: Balbín, *Bohemia Docta*, i, bk. 2, 425 f.; and Sommervogel, s.v.

that of the Eastern Churches, might be a set of scandalous, primitive errors; it was not necessarily—on a generous view—incapable of correction.[36] The mission emanated above all from Rome, the fulcrum of world Catholicism, with its direction of the international religious orders, its Oriental colleges, and so on. But it was also Catholicism in a markedly imperial guise, growing (as we saw) out of circumstances within the Monarchy and the *Reich*, hence able to embrace even some eirenically-minded Lutherans like Leibniz.

And universalism was not merely a spiritual need. It went with the search for intellectual synthesis already outlined in chapters nine and ten above: seventeenth-century system-building in a characteristically Catholic and irrational matrix. The programme of global evangelism gave those studies in universal logic, universal language, universal harmony, universal science, an extra dimension, or rather a further duality in need of reconciliation. For while Unions among the Orthodox raised mainly theological problems (besides the political ones), the question of the status of non-Christians involved major philosophical issues too. Modern Chinese, like ancient Greeks, could not be dismissed as crude heathens, not at least by men who aimed at a total view of the divine purpose in the world. The effort to embrace pagans as well as Christians in a kind of Catholic theodicy illustrates both the grandeur and the instability of the Baroque scholastic edifice in Central Europe.

One author and one work form the culmination of this intellectual tradition: Athanasius Kircher and his *Oedipus Aegyptiacus.* A closer analysis of the *Oedipus* should help draw together the threads of interplay between faith and learning which we have been examining. But is it not odd to select Kircher as spokesman? Surely he spent most of his life in Rome? And was he not, more or less, a charlatan? The first objection has already been met in part. Not only did Kircher keep abiding links with his German homeland, corresponding prolifically with Catholic pupils and Protestant sympathizers like Duke August of Brunswick (to whom he sent gifts ranging from Syriac gospels to stones for protecting dogs against snakebite).[37] He was also intimately bound to the Habsburg court and

---

[36] Cf. above, p. 386, n. 12; and Pázmány, *Kalauz*, 676–82.
[37] *Fasciculus Epistolarum*, ed. Langenmantel, mainly letters to the editor and to Lucas Schröck the Younger of Augsburg; J. Burckhard, *Historia Bibliothecae*

(continued)

Monarchy. Although he did not take the post offered him at Vienna by Ferdinand II (hardly surprisingly, given the political uncertainties of the 1630s) Kircher readily accepted copious signs of imperial favour. Ferdinand III paid for the publication of his books: 3,000 ducats were necessary to cover the *Oedipus Aegyptiacus* with its many strange type-faces; and he added an annuity of 100 ducats, maintained by Leopold, besides following Kircher's advice in such matters as musical composition.[38] The Jesuit responded with a stream of dedications, gifts, inventions, suggestions. Habsburg *literati*, prelates, and aristocrats consulted him, visited him in Italy, exchanged books and manuscripts. Ferenc Nádasdy even had the scholar's portrait painted, to hang among the *objets d'art* in one of his Hungarian castles.[39]

The second objection is more substantial, yet not decisive. Kircher certainly went in for self-advertisement, and posterity has tended to judge his huge output severely, dismissing it as unoriginal compilation, a grandiloquent pursuit of the trivial or the misguided, even as a fraud perpetrated from mixed motives of piety and ambition.[40] The truth is far more complex, because Kircher was as greatly celebrated in his own time and among his own kind as he has been decried since. That renown demands to be explained, and reappraisal of his standing in the history of thought is long overdue. He needs to be placed, not in any genealogy of modernism, for there

---

Augustae quae Wolfenbutteli est, i–ii (Leipzig 1744–6), i, 209 f., 232–42, 72–4; ii, 123–52, where a large number of letters from Kircher to the duke and his agent (most in Latin, a few in German) are excerpted.

[38] Brischar, op. cit. 68, 87; Scharlau, op. cit. 41, 347–51; cf. above, pp. 316 f.

[39] Rózsa, op. cit. 129 (Nádasdy). Kircher left a voluminous correspondence. A few of his own letters have been published, mainly by Langenmantel and Burckhart (above, n. 37); cf. the interesting single letters communicated by Kuhlmann and Friedländer (above, p. 354, n. 21). Those sent to him fill fourteen large MS. volumes in the archive of the Gregorian University in Rome. They are introduced by G. Gabrieli, 'Carteggio Kircheriano', *Atti della Reale Accademia d'Italia, Rendiconti della classe di scienze morali e storiche*, ser. VII, ii (1941), 10–17 (who is, however, surely wrong to suggest (pp. 13 f.) that Kircher ever travelled in the Orient); and they must contain much valuable information. But Kircher's published writings are so prolix as to reveal enough for my purposes. Like many another Baroque author, he is not shy of reproducing private comments—usually favourable ones—on the printed page.

[40] Thus, for example, the entirely negative view by 'Erman' in *ADB*, s.v., and a similar estimation in Winter, *Frühaufklärung*, 96 f. The *Dictionnaire de théologie catholique* has nothing on him at all; other Catholic encyclopedias are more generous, but brief. Cf. below, next n. and n. 57 (Bayle).

is little advantage in seeking out the occasional progressive nuggets in his writing (like the experiments with lenses or magnets), but at the end of an intellectual tradition, in an age and an area which gave him his reputation and shared his failings. Kircher's subtlety and vainglory, insights and confusions, mirror the whole credulous *élite* culture of Central European society.

The *Oedipus Aegyptiacus*[41] is Kircher's *magnum opus* and also—in retrospect—his most preposterous error: a flawed masterpiece of 2,000 folio pages, published at Rome in 1652–4, devoted to the twin theses that the hieroglyphics were occult representations of Christian truth, and that the subsequent history of civilization has been a contest between two faces of a single Egyptian coin, the black magic of superstition and the white magic of the Church. He first took up its themes while a seminarist and worked on them concertedly from the early 1630s. Indeed, Egyptology was a prime reason why he settled permanently at Rome, where he made a particular study of the obelisks which had been brought to the city during the Renaissance.[42] The *Oedipus* begins with a pompous display of mutual admiration between the Habsburgs and their Jesuit protégé-propagandist: Kircher's dedication to Ferdinand III is followed by imperial testimony to the shining merits of the author ('Imperii nostri subditus') who has opened the way to a rediscovery of primeval wisdom, then by a prodigious apotheosis of Ferdinand in twenty-four different languages. Jaunty German stanzas by Harsdörffer of Nuremberg and pungent English verses by the eccentric exile J. A. Gibbes rub shoulders with a Chinese tribute from Boym and, as the *pièce de résistance*, a hieroglyphical inscription

---

[41] *Oedipus Aegyptiacus, hoc est Universalis Hieroglyphicae Veterum Doctrinae temporum iniuria abolitae Instauratio*, 3 vols. in 4 (Rome 1652–4 (*rectè* –5?)). Some sympathetic discussion of Kircher's place in Egyptology by E. Iversen, *The Myth of Egypt and its Hieroglyphs in European tradition* (Copenhagen 1961), 89–98; and in the decipherment of ancient scripts by M. V.-David, *Le Débat sur les écritures et l'hiéroglyphe aux XVIIe et XVIIIe siècles* (Paris 1965). D. P. Walker, *The ancient Theology* (London 1972), does not deal with Kircher, but he is very illuminating on some aspects of the same topics; cf. also F. A. Yates, *Giordano Bruno and the Hermetic tradition* (London 1964), 416–23.

[42] The autobiography (UK, MS. XIV C 12, fols. 8 ff.) acknowledges particularly the help of Peiresc in France. *Obeliscus Pamphilius* (Rome 1650), is a preliminary study; *Obelisci Aegyptiaci ... interpretatio Hieroglyphica* (Rome 1666), and *Sphinx mystagoga, sive Diatribe Hieroglyphica* (Rome 1676), are consequential works. Cf. above, n. 26.

from Kircher himself.[43] Next, Kircher's combative preface (he calls it *Propylaeum Agonisticum*) defends the validity of the undertaking and sketches out the ground: no knowledge is so difficult that the 'subtlety of the human intellect' cannot penetrate it, none so extinct that no trace of it remains. Thus the wisdom of the ancient Egyptians survived among the Greeks and even among the Jews, whose Cabala is a kind of Hebraizing of the hieroglyphical message. But it was always wrapped in obscurity, the province of a few learned men, as Kircher's *fidus Achates*, Kaspar Schott, stresses in another foreword to the reader. At length, after one further assertion of his scholarly bona fides, Kircher is ready to unravel the mysteries of antiquity.

*

Immediately after the Flood, says Kircher, the Egyptian state was founded, or perhaps revived, by Cham, alias Osiris, son of Noah.[44] A sophisticated and well-ordered polity, with a firm official religious ethos, it nevertheless faced from the outset one fundamental duality: God's revelation to men, handed down from Adam to Noah, was continually perverted by those who sought to use the power it conveyed in the service, not of spiritual wholeness, but of operative magic. The greatest profaner of this true and universal faith was Cham himself; its greatest vindicator his grandson, Hermes (or Mercurius) Trismegistus, whom Kircher reveres as statesman, lawgiver, and author of the hieroglyphics. Under Hermes the battle-lines were already drawn up: a learned and sagacious priesthood was forced by the devilish machinations of its enemies to veil the divine message in symbolic forms. Can we not already descry in this antithesis the contours of seventeenth-century Central European culture too, and its Baroque interplay of light and darkness?

Kircher now discusses the notorious superstitions of the Egyptians: their polytheism and idolatry, their sacrifices and animal

[43] Georg Philipp Harsdörffer was a friend of Sigismund von Birken and pillar of the *Pegnesischer Blumenorden* (see above, p. 291). Gibbes was an English Catholic convert, a doctor by profession, a poet by predilection, but mainly in Latin; he received the title of *poeta laureatus* from Leopold I in 1667 (*DNB*, s.v.). Needless to say, Hungarian, Czech, Croatian, and Serbian are also represented in this eulogy, along with most of the main Oriental languages.

[44] There may, it appears, have been earlier rulers. Kircher quotes such an inextricable jumble of sources that in what follows I have had to try to abstract the really salient thesis and antithesis.

rituals, often more imaginative than decent. These cults passed to the classical peoples, as (for instance) Osiris was transmogrified into Dionysius; and not only to Greeks and Romans, for the same shibboleths were transmitted throughout the ancient world: among Jews, who received them via the progeny of Cham—'primi omnis superstitionis ac idololatricae (*sic*) impietatis Authores'—and the concubines of Solomon; among Chaldeans, Arabs, Persians; among Chinese, Japanese, Tartars, Indians, Africans, Americans. All had their gods of Baal, their golden calves, their Molochs . . . Most of the first volume of the *Oedipus* is given over to a survey of the Mephistophelean works contrived by the spirit of negation, the 'Ape of the Lord', and Cham manifestly assumes some of the features of Lucifer and Prometheus. In volume two Kircher redresses the balance, launching into a monumental exposition of the overwhelming positive contribution of Hermes and his followers: for they, by contrast, apprehended sublime spiritual and metaphysical truth. I shall follow his ground-plan, though it abounds in vagaries.

He starts with an analysis of the notion of symbol, 'which by its nature leads our mind through a kind of similitude to an understanding of something very different from the things which offer themselves to our external senses; whose property is to be hidden under a veil of obscurity'. Here again we enter the world of occult explanation which the Baroque has inherited from the later Renaissance, a debt underlined in Kircher's account of emblems and *imprese*.[45] Next he reflects on the origins of language, trying to prove the primacy of Hebrew, as the language of Adam: a theme common enough during the seventeenth century, but which bears in the *Oedipus* a characteristic impress of symbolism and evidently relates to the author's work on 'steganography' and 'polygraphy'.[46] Kircher then returns, in a section meaningly superscribed *Sphinx mystagoga* (with a dedication to the future imperial major-domo,

[45] *Oedipus*, ii, 1, *classis* 1, quoted at p. 6. Cf. above, pp. 340–4.

[46] Ibid. ii, 1, *classis* 2. Cf. above, pp. 351–3. The subject seems rather inconsequentially placed here, though it is consolidated later with a discussion of scripts and alphabets (iii, 8 ff.). Cf. Salmon, op. cit., for an interesting presentation of other 17th-century views and the contrast between the search for a 'universal character', found, *inter alia*, in Kircher, and the 'philosophical language' of Wilkins and more scientific thinkers. A curious letter from Kircher to Archduke Leopold Wilhelm about some ancient script is printed in Lambeck, *Commentarii*, i, cols. 192–4.

Lamberg) to the sphere of ancient arcana, finding parallels between the Egyptian mysteries and Zoroaster, Orpheus, Pythagoras, the fables of the gods, and the Neoplatonic interpretation of the *furor poeticus*.

From this point we can begin to make sense of Kircher's extraordinary main argument. Absolute truths, he tries to show, were handed down by God in two stages: first to Adam as Hebrew wisdom, yielding the Jewish or Cabalist esoteric tradition; secondly through Hermes to the Egyptians, who perpetuated them in the still more inscrutable guise of hieroglyphics. Section four, which carries a dedication to Bernard Ignác Martinic, considers the Cabala. Of course, much of it is rabbinical perversion, and Papal anathemas are perfectly just, but true, uncorrupted Cabbalism tells the mysteries of the world and its creation.[47] It enshrines both spiritual revelation, especially in the *tetragrammaton*, or holy name of God, and natural revelation, as large parts (though by no means all) of the Cabala's cosmic scheme can be squared with Catholic science. A bridge passage on Arabian imitators of Jewish thought leads us to the philosophers of Egypt. Their cosmology, as expounded by Kircher (and dedicated to a Polish bishop), appears like a Christian Aristotelianism *avant la lettre*, complete with angelic world of intelligences, solar system, and elements. Indeed, Aristotle himself recounted these scholastic verities 'not from his own ideas, but from those of the ancient Egyptians and according to their recondite hieroglyphic doctrine'.[48]

The seventh section, longest of all and the heart of the *Oedipus*, has correspondingly weighty Central European dedications: to the emperor and his confessor Gans, to one of the Liechtensteins, Auersperg, and Johann Friedrich of Brunswick. It treats of mathematics and physics among the Egyptians, who invented them. Again these subjects are not quite what they seem, but always bear symbolic significance, even arithmetic 'with which by some occult analogy the arcaner part of Theology is concluded'. We learn about the hidden meanings of numbers and the mysteries of geometrical figures, about Hermetic music, astronomy, and measurement of time, as well as about the astrological abuses introduced by Cham

---

[47] *Oedipus*, ii, 1, *classis* 4: a long section (pp. 209–360). Cf. above, pp. 349–51.

[48] Ibid. ii, 1, *classis* 6, esp. 437–40. Cf. Kircher's own scheme, above, p. 332 and *passim*.

and his offspring.[49] Physics leads on to mechanics, a predilection not only (as we have seen) of the author, but evidently also of his dedicatee, Archbishop Lippay. Kircher describes the marvels of Egyptian construction: their pyramids, temples, labyrinths, machines for raising weights and conducting water, above all their experiments in pure thaumaturgy, like the talking statue of Memnon. They worked, he insists, not by diabolical agency, but through natural, and thus Christian magic, of the kind which Schott was to exploit in his *Technica Curiosa* or Lana-Terzi in his *Magisterium*.[50]

The next 'Hermetic' theme is medicine, introduced with a dedication to the elector of Mainz. Here Kircher reiterates his set purpose throughout the *Oedipus*: 'our one intention [is] to extirpate those false arts which, sown by the devil, have spread their roots into our own times; and to reveal, by true interpretation, the secrets of hieroglyphic doctrine'. Thus, while the common people resorted to amulets and similar superstitions, Hermes Trismegistus taught a spiritual healing derived from Adam, resting on natural sympathies and antipathies, and confirmed by prayer—in other words, a genuine Christian therapy.[51] The reader is transported in imagination to an Egypt dotted with the whitewashed pilgrimage churches which Kircher would have encountered in his south-German youth. What follows is still more intriguing: hieroglyphical alchemy. For Kircher shows that his condemnation of the vulgar claim to transmute metals, later so fiercely repeated in the *Mundus Subterraneus*, is only one pole of a larger dualism. Most alchemists are impostors, and the Egyptians were right to put them to death, but there existed also a pure art reserved by them for kings, priests, philosophers. It involved some sort of spiritual and bodily refining—Kircher seems to suggest the possibility of an *elixir vitae* or even a monad—and lived on as an esoteric tradition through the medium of hieroglyphs, allegorical stories, and other symbols. There are then, after all, elements in Kircher of seventeenth-century Catholic alchemy.[52]

---

[49] Ibid. ii, 2, *classis* 7 (pp. 3–278). Cf. above, pp. 334 f., 353 f.

[50] Ibid. ii, 2, *classis* 8. Cf. above, pp. 336–9.

[51] Ibid. ii, 2, *classis* 9, quoted at p. 346. Cf. above, pp. 386–91.

[52] Ibid. ii, 2, *classis* 10, esp. 399 ff. on the 'Hermetic cross'. Cf. above, pp. 357 ff. This argument can be found also in the *Mundus Subterraneus* (esp. ii, 234–6, 311 ff.), but there it is quite outweighed by the attack on charlatanry.

Two concluding sections in volume two afford a kind of summary (albeit a highly diffuse one) of the double occultism bequeathed to men by the Egyptians of old. On the one hand black magic—astrology, divination, charms, idolatry—descended from Cham to all the races of the ancient world and still flourishes today. On the other hand 'theosophia metaphysica'—the sacramental insights of thrice-great Hermes into the divine properties, the Trinity, the origins of creation, angels and demons, became (when suitably insulated against the depravities of the profane) the foundation of philosophical and theological thinking in all later civilizations.[53] And now, at last, the arcane truths vouchsafed to Egyptians may be presented in detail. The rest of the *Oedipus* forms in fact a glorified documentary appendix. It is Kircher's actual 'decipherment' of hieroglyphic inscriptions: the Bembine Table, the Lateran Obelisk, and the rest, punctuated with dedications to Ferdinand III and IV, Leopold Wilhelm and Leopold I, Marci and Lazarus Henckel, Archbishop Harrach, Ferenc Nádasdy, and others.[54] While some monuments yield genuine wisdom, others primarily illustrate debased practices and beliefs like the wearing of amulets or metempsychosis. Altogether they leave us, by implication at least, with a positive message: that 'knowledge of ideal things', which Kircher has found embedded in the mysteries of the pre-Christian world, surely confirms the universal teachings of contemporary Catholic scholarship.

*

By this time the sceptic may well think I have devoted too much space to the *Oedipus Aegyptiacus*. Yet scepticism will never be able to penetrate the Counter-Reformation mentality which Kircher so eminently represented. He stood in a long tradition and wrote for a like-minded (if not an equally imaginative or erudite) audience. He personifies the whole Catholic reformulation of the Christian Humanist thought of the Renaissance; and his Egyptian fantasies unconsciously hold up a mirror to the seventeenth-century Habsburg Monarchy, with its clash of good and evil supernatural forces. With Kircher we have reached the summit of the Counter-

---

[53] *Oedipus*, ii, 2, *classes* 11–12.

[54] Ibid. iii; cf. the *Obeliscus Pamphilius* of 1650. This is Lazarus Henckel the Younger (1573–1664), who corresponded with Kircher about music (Scharlau, op. cit. 351 f.). The rest of the list should by now be familiar to the reader.

Reformation's intellectual ambition. His writings, most especially the *Oedipus Aegyptiacus*, form a sort of phenomenology of the occult or—to employ a phrase which he could perhaps have recognized— a *Summa Magiae* for the neoscholastic age.

From the summit the intellectual path led steeply downwards. Even as men like Kircher elaborated their ideas, the European climate was turning against them. They sought to link theology and philosophy through a common ground in magic; but in the long run their theology did not help their philosophy, nor their philosophy their theology, while their magic only weakened both. Counter-Reformation was threatened by the stirrings of Enlightenment and the new-found assertiveness of the Atlantic and Baltic powers; the final overthrow of Aristotelian physics and method gathered pace; occult explanations yielded to common sense and natural laws. Even the Latin of their learned discourse became an increasingly outmoded vehicle, which may gradually have heightened the atmosphere of unreality and ritual. And their 'universal language'—we can recall—proved a set of empty formulae.

Moreover, the political moment was lost; the spiritual programme of Catholicism began to diverge decisively from the foreign political programme of the Habsburgs. By the 1680s the dynasty had to see religious universalism as an international liability. Whereas England and Holland represented the most advanced spokesmen of a rival *Weltanschauung*, Leopold was forced—for all his qualms of conscience—to seek their support against Louis XIV; while the creation of an Austrian sphere of influence in Eastern Europe owed more to calculation and material inducement than to spiritual conquest.[55] On a wider front the trans-continental enterprise found itself crippled from within by a struggle which culminated, with the so-called Rites Controversy over Jesuit methods in China, in an attack on the whole accommodating approach to non-Christian civilizations.[56]

[55] The debates which went on in Vienna during 1688–9 before the alliance with William of Orange are particularly instructive: Antal–Pater (eds.), op. cit. i, 390 ff.; *Life of Leopold*, 188–96; Klopp, *Haus Stuart*, iv, 423–37, 512–22, including an approving memorandum from Father Menegatti. On top of the doubtful means sometimes employed to promote ecclesiastical Union, there were also unedifying clashes between Catholics and Uniates over allegiance and jurisdiction.

[56] Rowbotham, op. cit., chs. 9–12. The controversy was mainly fought out in France, but it had echoes in Central Europe too (e.g. Kalista, *Cesty*, 25 f.). It is

(continued)

Thus the Kircherian scheme proved, in European terms, to be hollow. It achieved its ingenious refraction of the Renaissance occult universe through the prism of Catholic orthodoxy just when elsewhere the presuppositions of that universe were being discarded. Indeed, its collapse proved all the more complete since the dismantling process had started considerably before. By the early eighteenth century Kircher himself was a forgotten writer, and with the Hermetic texts now generally recognized as spurious the pivot of his Utopia crumbled away—the *Oedipus Aegyptiacus* can rarely have been opened since.[57] There remained only the *disjecta membra* of a grandiose construction: much as the contents of Kircher's museum of rarities in Rome (catalogued by his pupil Bonanni) were henceforth celebrated merely as 'curiosities', bones without flesh.[58] By Western European standards, Kircher and his friends had piped a *danse macabre*, raising to life once more the skeletons of a decaying world-order before the midnight hour.

By *Western* European standards. That is a vast subject which does not belong to my present purpose. Yet in *Central* European terms they stand for something very different and far more durable. For even if the summit could not be held, the set of attitudes and aspirations which flanked it cemented the Habsburg cultural *imperium* as it developed through the seventeenth century in the ways I have already described. They made an important contribution, in other words, not only to the Monarchy's intellectual consolidation within, but to its differentiation from rivals abroad. That dual role was confirmed in the sphere of activity where the rising Habsburg lands achieved their most outstanding and distinctive memorial: in Baroque art.

*

Here is not the place for any serious discussion of the Baroque, still

---

evidently not unrelated to the swelling criticism of the Jesuits' laxist moral teachings, voiced especially by the Jansenists, whose ideas began to reach the Habsburg lands with mounting force from the early decades of the 18th century.

[57] Kircher receives no separate entry in Bayle's *Dictionary*, that Bible of scholars in the Enlightenment. The *Hermetica* had first been declared unauthentic by Isaac Casaubon, *De rebus sacris et ecclesiasticis Exercitationes XVI* (London 1614), 70–87; his view soon gained wide credence in the West and was followed by some Germans, among them Conring, Ursinus, and Lambeck (cf. above, p. 368.).

[58] Bonanni, op. cit. On the frontispiece of Daniel Nessel's catalogue of the Greek and Oriental MSS. in the court library (i–ii in 7 parts, V.–Nuremberg 1690), Leopold is seen pointing to a text which is attributed (ibid. pt. 7, p. 168) to Ozymandias.

less for any definition of a word whose meaning can be, at best, gradually and imperfectly sensed from the social and cultural context which gave it birth.[59] Yet we must make some approach to it, however briefly, since it is no accident that the ideals of the Central European Counter-Reformation found their fullest realization in art. One might even say: its whole mentality aspired unwittingly to the condition of art, and only there could its scheme be coherent. Only there could the synthesis of classical and Christian traditions still be successfully sustained. Only there could the gulf between high and low cultures be bridged: esoteric visual and literary programmes joining with popular creativity and a mass response. Only there could genuinely native idioms be evolved, which nevertheless show an unmistakable family likeness. Only there could the religious and the secular truly complement one another. Thus the arts, above all painting, sculpture, and architecture, richly and extravagantly combined, became themselves a kind of thaumaturgy. They celebrated dynasty, Church, and aristocracy in a great magical apotheosis, orchestrated by the élite, accomplished by the people (for while the forms might come from above, the content was in large measure supplied from below). Nothing better conveys the effect than the majestic *Kaisersäle*, imperial halls, of the monasteries along the Danube, which link the worldly triumph of the Habsburgs with a learned but universal decorative message.

Splendour and panache, however, are only half the story. The other spring of Baroque art lay—to return to the first premise of the present chapter—in insecurity, not confidence. It drew on illusion and allusion: on *trompe l'œil* and indirect symbolical expression; it strove desperately after completeness; it longed for medieval reassurance. The style has a nervous power which derives precisely from the essential fragility of its socio-political base in Central Europe. It is fantastic and intricate by comparison with France, where that base was so much more stable; tense and propagandist compared with Spain and Italy, where no taint of heresy or rebellion

---

[59] Some good general works exist on Baroque art in the region, and there is a vast specialized literature (cf. below, nn. 63–5). But very little relates it securely to its historical base. O. Redlich, 'Über Kunst und Kultur des Barocks in Österreich', *AÖG* cxv (1940–3), 331–79, though often cited, is a slight sketch, almost exclusively about the *Erblande*. V.–L. Tapié, *The Age of Grandeur*, tr. A. R. Williamson (London 1960), chs. 9–10, offers perhaps the best introduction; cf. also E. Angyal, *Theatrum Mundi* (Bp. 1938).

remained. The artist with his otherworldly and supernatural terms of reference (rather like Kircher with his view of superstition as merely the dark side of true revelation) could resolve conflicts, but only by sublimating the harsh realities which engendered them.

In many a market square throughout the lands of the old Habsburg Monarchy one can still see an imposing stone column, usually erected during the late seventeenth or the early eighteenth century, and elaborately contrived. These columns served several religious purposes: penitence for an attack of the plague, and thanksgiving for deliverance, together with a taut confidence in the unseen Christian verities, above all the cult of the Virgin and, most mysterious and ineffable, the symbol of the Trinity. They are perfect witnesses to the depths and heights of Baroque self-questioning. The most famous of them, the huge *Pestsäule* on the Graben in Vienna, conveys a further trinitarian notion: it depicts also the triune Habsburg realms of Austria, Bohemia, and Hungary—not surprisingly, since the design was conceived by Leopold I and his Jesuit confessor.[60]

The art of the period reflects and summates too the threefold articulation of this book, and we may take it as a peg on which to hang a few conclusions. In the first place, it expressed the power and anxieties of the new civil and ecclesiastical establishment. The dynasty marches firmly but a little incongruously across the set-piece ceilings of its palaces or monasteries. In the end only the eye of the beholder could supply them with a third dimension, just as the proud new buildings being added to Vienna's Hofburg concealed the absence of any corresponding extension of governmental authority. The aristocracy made full play with the eminence of its situation: witness, for instance, the later seventeenth-century Liechtensteins indulging their three passions of architecture, alchemy, and riding, even housing their horses in a monumental stable-block constructed by Fischer von Erlach. Again, however, an undercurrent of doubt remains, as in the ancestor worship of families like the Althans at Frain, or the eccentricity of so many

[60] Cf. the fine passage in V.-L. Tapié, *Monarchie et peuples du Danube* (Paris 1969), 158–60. For the emblematical significance of such sculptuary: G. Kapner, *Freiplastik in Wien* (V. 1970), *passim*; id., 'Inschriften an Wiener Heiligenstatuen—ein Beitrag zur Untersuchung barocken Frömmigkeitsstils', *Sacerdos et pastor semper ubique, Festschrift F. Loidl* (V. 1972), 299–323.

noble patrons.[61] The Church entered an age of frenzied ostentation, building and rebuilding with unexampled haste throughout the Monarchy, its myriad calvaries and pilgrimage churches, votive altars and statuary creating a dense ecclesiastical landscape in country as well as town. It used the plastic arts, like the literary dramas enacted in its colleges and schools, to emphasize the sacred harmony of the world and its absolute order behind the shifting façade of human frailties.[62]

Secondly, art embodies the qualified accommodation between centre and regions analysed above in part two. By the late seventeenth century a cosmopolitan Italianate style was giving way to the creations of a new generation of native-born artists who harnessed indigenous traditions of craftsmanship and subject-matter. In Austria this was the era of Fischer von Erlach (from Graz), Prandtauer, Munggenast, and Troger (from the Tyrol), Donner (from Lower Austria), Gran (from Vienna), Rottmayr (from Salzburg), and many lesser talents.[63] In Bohemia individuals such as Brandl and Santini-Aichel, Jäckl and Kaňka, competed with entire families like the Dientzenhofers, Brauns, and Brokoffs.[64] Even in Hungary naturalized foreigners and their domestic pupils

[61] On the Liechtensteins: V. Fleischer, *Fürst Karl Eusebius von Liechtenstein als Bauherr und Kunstsammler* (V.–Leipzig 1910), printing the text of Karl Eusebius's own 'Werk von der Architektur'; cf. above, pp. 374 f. Eccentric patrons include Sporck at Kuks (above, pp. 216, 326), and Johann Adam Questenberg at Jaroměřice (*Jaroměřická kronika 1700–52*, ed. A. Plichta (Jaroměřice nad Rokytnou 1974)); many others were wildly spendthrift. Cf. the examples of follies and historicism in Kotrba, op. cit. 59 ff.

[62] Duhr, op. cit. iii, 459–66 and *passim*; Tibal, op. cit. 61–83; Angyal, *Theatrum*, esp. ch. 4; K. Adel, *Das Jesuitendrama in Österreich* (V. 1957); J. Takács, *A jezsuita iskoladráma 1581–1773* (Bp. 1937). Many examples of new churches in the pages of Podlaha, *Posvátná místa*.

[63] Among the major monographs are H. Sedlmayr, *Johann Bernhard Fischer von Erlach* (V. 1956); H. Hantsch, *Jakob Prandtauer, der Klosterarchitekt des österreichischen Barock* (V. 1926); A. Pigler, *Georg Raphael Donner* (V. 1929). I have omitted Hildebrandt (on whom see B. Grimschitz, *Johann Lucas von Hildebrandt* (V. 1959)) from this list only on the technicality that he was born at Genoa and did not settle in Vienna until the age of twenty-eight. The Viennese academy of painting was founded in 1692. See also H. Sedlmayr, *Österreichische Barockarchitektur, 1690–1740* (V. 1930), and the Austrian volumes in Dehio's series of *Kunsthandbücher*.

[64] Important recent works include O. J. Blažíček, *Baroque art in Bohemia* (London 1968); id., *Sochařství baroku v Čechách* (Pr. 1958); J. Neumann, *Malířství XVII století v Čechách* (Pr. 1951); H. G. Franz, *Bauten und Baumeister der Barockzeit in Böhmen* (Leipzig 1962); *Petr Brandl 1668–1735*, ed. J. Neumann (Pr. 1968); Kotrba, op. cit., esp. 124–78 (on Santini-Aichel).

began to produce work with distinctive local characteristics.[65] Yet the basic idiom, of course, remained international. Artists still crossed frontiers without a second thought, and such painters as Kupecký or—later—Maulpertsch cannot be identified with anything less than the whole culture of Central Europe in their day. Fullest possibilities for the future lay in the art with the most universal forms of expression: music, especially in Bohemia and the Austrian duchies where many a village cantor or monastery organist of the Baroque age contributed to the great eighteenth-century flowering of composers and performers.[66]

Finally and most obviously, art belonged to the intellectual atmosphere of Counter-Reformation, seeking the same synthesis and reconciliation of opposites, employing the same contrived vocabulary of metaphor to baffle and amaze, displaying the same morbid obsession with evil in all its guises, indulging the same tendency towards the antiquarian and the obscure. The one could not long survive the other, and both were condemned to remain incomplete. The projects of the Baroque outran its resources, as with the dozens of exuberant buildings left unfinished when mood and circumstances changed. Posterity has been no more able to reconstruct its grander schemes than to conclude the last *contrapunctus* in Bach's Art of Fugue. The Baroque Monarchy of the house of Habsburg appealed to forces which were not only supranational but also, on any sober reckoning, well-nigh supernatural; they could provide at best only an uneasy foundation for lasting and effective sovereignty.

[65] See especially K. Garas, *Festészet a XVII században*; ead., *Magyarországi festészet a XVIII században* (Bp. 1955); M. Aggházy, *A barokk szobrászat Magyarországon*, i–iii (Bp. 1959); Margit B. Nagy, *Reneszánsz és barokk Erdélyben* (Bucharest 1970).

[66] Charles Burney, *The present state of Music in Germany*... (London 1775), i, 201–372 *passim* (Austria); ii, 1–25 (Bohemia).

Epilogue

It remains only to sketch some implications which this view of the making of the Habsburg Monarchy may hold for its subsequent history. I have argued that unity was fostered during the seventeenth century by the political implementation of the Counter-Reformation, by social and economic evolution, above all by a set of common mental habits which (at least at the end of this period) we can describe as a distinctive culture. While the dynasty and its advisers pressed fairly consistently for stronger central control, conformity grew more out of consent, the fruit of a process not necessarily understood by those who participated in it, certainly not imposed by any single group. The result was a complex and subtly-balanced organism, not a 'state' but a mildly centripetal agglutination of bewilderingly heterogeneous elements.

On this base the Habsburg lands achieved the status of a Great Power during a series of wars against the Turks and the French between 1683 and 1719. All the historians since Ranke who have seen the rise of Austria in terms of its military triumphs during those decades essentially put the cart before the horse. Indeed, the war-chariot of a largely unmilitarist dynasty now moved relentlessly forward in a way unparalleled before or after, but it was sustained by the logic of domestic political relations within the Monarchy, and drawn by a combative ideology already formulated. The siege of Vienna and the battle of Blenheim lent great psychological impetus, but (rather like the débâcle at Königgrätz before the Compromise of 1867) they did not alter the direction of change or the terms of the debate. With territorial expansion and diplomatic influence went the fullest unfolding of Baroque civilization: buildings, fine arts, display, popular piety, all reached their largest extent—ironically—during the reign of the least colourful of Habsburg emperors, Charles VI (1711–40). Here too the roots of advance lay in a previous development. Central Europe in the early eighteenth century has at last become, to outward appearances, an ordered, reasonably prosperous, culturally and politically harmonious realm.

Appearance concealed major weaknesses, of two overlapping kinds. The first kind we have already examined: those flowing from the incomplete consolidation of the Counter-Reformation establishment. On the one hand, the Viennese government could never wholly command the supranational religious and political loyalties of its peoples: 'ultramontanism'—at least as a tactical reflex—was never eliminated, especially in Hungary, as the Kollár affair would show. On the other hand, localist sentiments survived, even enhanced on occasion through a faith which set such store by patron saints, immemorial traditions, and the associations of particular places. Thus the middle-ground between provincialism and cosmopolitanism tended to remain unoccupied, either institutionally or emotionally. Earlier allegiances might be heavily overlaid with Monarchical ones; but they rarely became transmuted by them (imperial alchemy, after all, was ever an abortive science). Worse, there were areas in private, even in public life which stood outside the whole scope of the Baroque polity. A large Protestant minority in Hungary and Silesia, and pockets of entrenched heresy elsewhere, though by no means untouched by the ruling ethos, bred sullen resentment of a power system from which they were excluded by the very philosophy of state. Silesia predictably started the rot in the 1740s; Hungary continued it a few decades later. The fatal gap between a theory, according to which the Protestant heritage was anathematized, and a practice, where it could not be altogether eliminated, left a potent focus for opposition: both Hungarian and Czech nationalism grow directly out of it. Beside the Protestant threat, the danger posed by discontents of the socially unprivileged appears far less immediate: eighteenth-century *jacqueries* still served on balance (but only just) to confirm the need for solidarity within the ruling alliance. Events in 1790–1 represent perhaps the last demonstration of that.

A second set of weaknesses was revealed during the eighteenth century by the challenge from new circumstances and ideas. We may sum them up as 'Enlightenment' or *Aufklärung*, though the terms have drawbacks, and 'modernism', while vaguer, is also more neutral. Enlightenment penetrated first (logically enough) to Protestant or quasi-Protestant circles, via the legacy of the Puritans and the fervour of the Pietists. But it also entered the body of the

Catholic faithful, from France, Germany, and Italy, above all from the newly-acquired Southern Netherlands, in the guise of a generalized 'Jansenism' and the kind of critical temper which had already undermined the cohesiveness of the Baroque scholastic system. By mid-century a new spirit was at work in the Church, not among the commonalty in the Baroque order of things, but among its senior echelons: some bishops and abbots, university professors and court literati. Slowly the Monarchy began to come to terms with a novel cast of mind and to forswear its reliance on tradition, metaphysics, symbols, and mysteries.

Only against this background can we properly understand the revolution from above attempted in eighteenth-century Austria by Empress Maria Theresa, and more especially by her son Joseph II, from whom it takes the convenience title of 'Josephinism'. By the 1740s old institutions and their ideologies showed themselves unable to compete with other modern, centralized, and proto-national states. The dynasty's response was to reform, rightly perceiving that the only hope for an enduring Habsburg realm lay in a new identity, backed by an organized administration and an efficient economy. Yet Maria Theresa and Joseph did not *dismantle* the existing edifice: they possessed no other. Rather they sought to *redirect* it, maintaining their alliance with Church, nobles, and intelligentsia, but turning it from a conservative-universalist hierarchy into an enlightened-absolutist one, imbuing it with a philosophy of action rather than reflection. Josephinism did not seek to dethrone the Catholic religion, but to refurbish it in the name of a state Church; even the famous Patent of Toleration, that final death-blow to the ideology of the Baroque, may be viewed as the first step towards a new conception of official spiritual conformity. Joseph II did not so much break with the past as turn the past on its head: a purpose perhaps most aptly described as *counter*-Counter-Reformation.

The vast and heady reform movement, more ambitious than any other in Europe before 1789, achieved a contemporary success whose extent can easily be overlooked. It was enough to see the Monarchy into the nineteenth century; not enough to guarantee its future stability. In the event the two distinct enemies of traditionalism and modernism combined to defeat it. Josephinism succumbed to the structural inadequacies of the Baroque system: those elements not so bound to the Habsburg destiny as to acquiesce without a fight in this change of course. Thus many Hungarian and Bohemian nobles, clerics, and conservative pamphleteers joined the ranks in opposition on the right, and issued their manifestoes of nascent Romanticism or Federalism. And it succumbed, of course, though only gradually, to pressure from more advanced positions on the left, the stirrings of Liberalism in Central Europe. Here Maria Theresa and Joseph, by their authoritarian stance, alienated groups who might have co-operated with them, rather as the régime of the Counter-Reforming Habsburgs deliberately made enemies of its Protestant subjects. Ultimately orthodoxy *forced* dissent: Baroque Catholicism and reforming Josephinism had that much in common; and the latter, by its extra dynamism, threw into sharper relief some grievances which previously were only latent. But by the same token orthodoxy created unorthodoxy *in its own image*, and responses to the age of Baroque paradoxically perpetuated much of the Baroque's own intellectual equipment: its categories, if not its content. Central Europe's secular *Aufklärung* was well populated with former seminarists and owed much to a network of Freemasons coloured by illuminist or mystificatory tendencies. Liberals were first and foremost anticlericals, and we can sense a strong measure of high-handedness in the vendetta against the claims of the Church; while nationalist movements grew up as equal and opposite reactions to the immobile ideology of supranationalism.

Thus a curious negative legacy survived from the era of Habsburg Counter-Reformation. Yet its larger lasting significance was more active, for the stamp of the Baroque permeated the Austrian monarchy and its territories until the very end. Catholicism remained a crucial binding force in all its spiritual and social ramifications. The great aristocratic families retained immense prestige and influence, and the ethos of *Herrschaft* still lived on after 1848. Intellectuals betrayed their common heritage even by the language in which they expressed themselves (for the vernaculars of Central Europe—so diverse in their family origins—have many similarities of vocabulary, idiom, and structure), not to say by habits of thought and patterns of creativity. Altogether the rise of the Habsburg Monarchy by the early eighteenth century must hold many lessons for students of its subsequent decline. And even beyond the decline, since that which has once been joined together can never entirely, and without residue, be put asunder.

Political and military chronology

1526 Battle of Mohács. Ferdinand I elected king of Bohemia and Hungary; János Zapolya (Szapolyai) anti-king in Hungary

1540s Turks occupy Buda and consolidate hold over central Hungary. Establishment of a separate Transylvanian state under Zapolya's widow, Isabella, and son, János Zsigmond

1546–7 War of Schmalkalden: Charles V defeats the German Protestant estates at Mühlberg; Ferdinand disciplines their Bohemian sympathizers

1556–64 Ferdinand I Holy Roman Emperor

1564–76 Maximilian II Holy Roman Emperor

1564–95 Archduke Ferdinand ruler of Tyrol

1564–90 Archduke Karl ruler of Styria

1566 Last campaign of Suleiman the Magnificent in Hungary; siege of Szigetvár

1568–78 Limited constitutional guarantees secured for Protestant nobles and burghers in the Austrian provinces and Bohemia

1571–86 Stephen Báthory prince of Transylvania and (1576–86) king of Poland

1576–1612 Rudolf II Holy Roman Emperor

1588–97/1602 Zsigmond Báthory prince of Transylvania

1591/3–1606 Fifteen years war with Ottoman Empire

1596 Archduke Ferdinand (II) becomes ruler of Styria

1604–6 Rebellion of István Bocskai

1606 Peace of Zsitvatorok (with the Turks) and Vienna (with Bocskai)

1608 Archduke Matthias elected king of Hungary; full guarantees for Hungarian Protestants

1609 Bohemian estates extract Letter of Majesty from Rudolf

1610–11 Passau invasion; Matthias elected king of Bohemia

1612–19 Matthias Holy Roman Emperor

1613–29 Bethlen Gábor prince of Transylvania

1614 General diet of Central European estates at Linz

1617–18 Archduke Ferdinand (II) elected king of Bohemia and Hungary

1618 Defenestration of Prague. Beginning of Bohemian revolt and Thirty Years War

1619 Frederick of the Palatinate elected king of Bohemia

1619–37 Ferdinand II Holy Roman Emperor

1619–22 First campaign of Bethlen Gábor; peace of Mikulov

1620 Battle of the White Mountain; collapse of Bohemian revolt

1623–4 Second campaign of Bethlen Gábor

1625–30 Wallenstein as imperial commander-in-chief; Habsburg victories in Germany

1626 Third campaign of Bethlen Gábor

1627 Renewed Constitution (*Obnovené zřízení zemské*) for Bohemia

1630–48 György I Rákóczi prince of Transylvania

1631 Imperial defeat by Swedes at Breitenfeld; Saxon invasion of Bohemia

1632 Recall of Wallenstein; inconclusive battle of Lützen; recovery of Bohemia

1634 Assassination of Wallenstein. Victory of Archduke Ferdinand (III), king of Hungary, and the cardinal *infante* of Spain at Nördlingen

1635 Peace of Prague signed by most German princes

1637–57 Ferdinand III Holy Roman Emperor

1639–48 Swedish invasions of Bohemia and parts of Austria

1643–8 Negotiations at Münster and Osnabrück leading to Peace of Westphalia

1644–5 War with Transylvania; peace of Linz

1648–58/60 György II Rákóczi prince of Transylvania

1657/8–1705 Leopold I Holy Roman Emperor

1658–62 Turkish invasion and subjugation of Transylvania; Mihály I Apafi named prince

1664 War with Ottoman Empire; Habsburg victory at Szentgotthárd; peace of Vasvár

1664–71 Wesselényi conspiracy in Hungary; execution of Nádasdy, Zrinyi, and Frangepan

1668–73 Secret treaty with Louis XIV for partition of Spanish empire; pro-French policies of Lobkovic

1671–81 Military rule in Hungary; constitution abrogated and *Gubernium* installed

1673–8 War with Louis XIV; fall of Lobkovic; peace of Nijmegen

1678–83 Rebellion of Imre Thököly

1680 Peasant revolt in Bohemia

1681 Diet of Sopron; restoration of Hungarian constitution

1683 Ottoman invasion of Habsburg Hungary and Austria; siege and relief of Vienna

1684–9 Turks driven from Hungary; recovery of Buda; Habsburg victory at Nagyharsány (Mohács)

1688–97 War of the League of Augsburg against France; peace of Rijswijk

1690–1 Annexation of Transylvania; Leopoldine Diploma

1690–9 Continuing war against the Turks; Habsburg victories at Slankemen and Zenta. Peace of Karlowitz: Habsburgs confirmed in the possession of most of historic Hungary (including Transylvania)

1701–14 War of Spanish Succession against France; Battle of Blenheim (Höchstädt); Eugene's campaigns in Italy

1703–11 Rebellion of Ferenc II Rákóczi

1705–11 Joseph I Holy Roman Emperor

1711–40 Charles VI Holy Roman Emperor

1711 Peace of Szatmár with Hungarian rebels; exile of Rákóczi

1712–23 Pragmatic Sanction, proclaiming indivisibility of Habsburg realm, accepted by diets throughout the Monarchy

1714 Peace of Rastatt with France; acquisition of Southern Netherlands, Milan, Naples, and Sardinia (exchanged in 1720 for Sicily)

1718 Peace of Passarowitz with Ottoman Empire; acquisition of Serbia, Oltenia, and the Banat of Temesvár

The House of Habsburg
in the sixteenth and seventeenth centuries

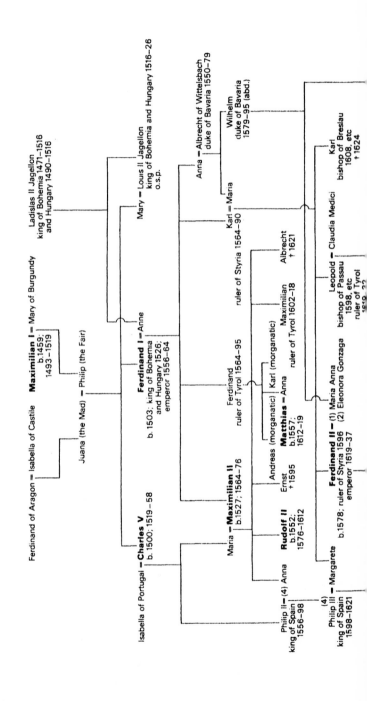

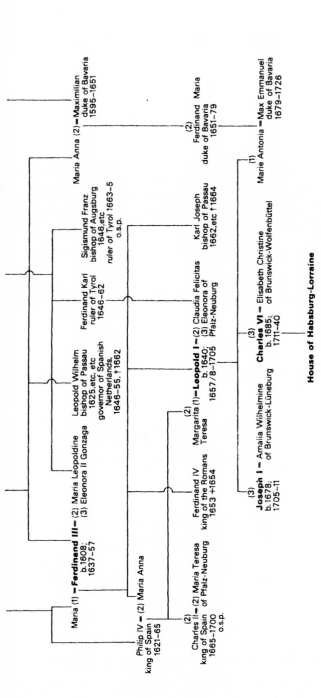

House of Habsburg-Lorraine

Maria (1) = **Ferdinand III** = (2) Maria Leopoldine
b.1608;   (3) Eleonora II Gonzaga
1637–57

Maria Anna (2) = Maximilian
    duke of Bavaria
    1595–1651

Philip IV = (2) Maria Anna
king of Spain
1621–65

Leopold Wilhelm
bishop of Passau
1625,etc, etc
governor of Spanish
Netherlands,
1646–55, †1662

Ferdinand Karl
ruler of Tyrol
1646–62

Sigismund Franz
bishop of Augsburg
1646,etc
ruler of Tyrol 1663–5
o.s.p.

Ferdinand   Maria
duke of Bavaria
1651–79

Charles II = (2) Maria Teresa
king of Spain of Pfalz-Neuburg
1665–1700
o.s.p.

(2)
Margarita (1) = **Leopold I** = (2) Claudia Felicitas
Teresa   b.1640;   (3) Eleonora of
     1657/8–1705   Pfalz-Neuburg

Ferdinand IV
king of the Romans
1653 †1654

Karl Joseph
bishop of Passau
1662,etc †1664

(3)   (3)
Joseph I = Amalia Wilhelmine   **Charles VI** = Elisabeth Christine
b.1678;   of Brunswick-Lüneburg   b.1685;   of Brunswick-Wolfenbüttel
1705–11   1711–40

(1)
Marie Antonia = Max Emmanuel
    duke of Bavaria
    1679–1726

Holy Roman emperors are indicated in bold type, with their dates of rule as emperor. From Maximilian II onwards, all were simultaneously kings of Bohemia and Hungary, though the coronations at Prague and Pozsony usually took place in the lifetime of their predecessors: thus, for example, Ferdinand II notoriously took over Bohemia in 1617; Ferdinand III became king of Hungary as early as 1625. Marriages with the Polish Vasas (cf. above, p. 425, n. 13) and certain other dynastic alliances have, for convenience, been omitted.

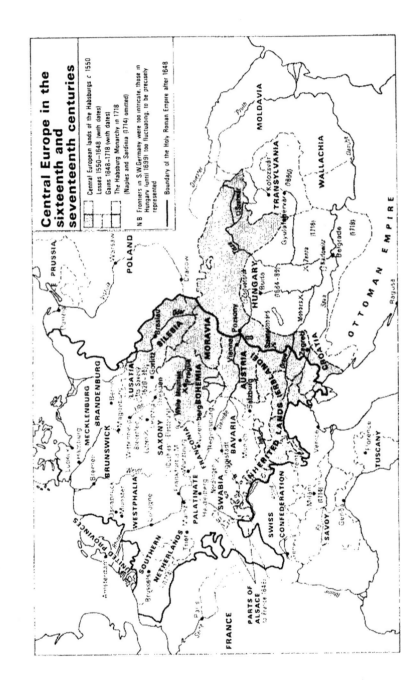

Central Europe in the sixteenth and seventeenth centuries

Central European lands of the Habsburgs c 1550

Losses 1550–1648 (with dates)

Gains 1648–1718 (with dates)

The Habsburg Monarchy in 1718 (Naples and Sardinia (1714) omitted)

N.B. Frontiers in S.W Germany were too intricate, those in Hungary (until 1699) too fluctuating, to be precisely represented

—— Boundary of the Holy Roman Empire after 1648

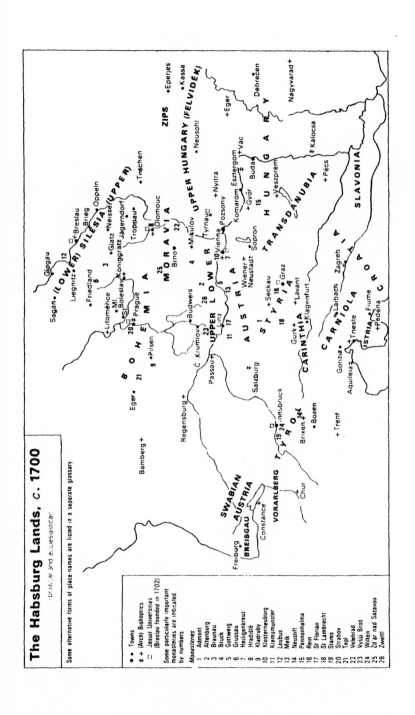

The Habsburg Lands, c. 1700

(Political and ecclesiastical)

Some alternative forms of place-names are listed in a separate glossary

• • Towns
‡ + (Arch) Bishoprics
☐ Jesuit Universities
(Breslau founded in 1702)

Some particularly important monasteries are indicated by numbers

Monasteries

1 Admont
2 Altenburg
3 Braunau
4 Bruck
5 Gottweig
6 Grüssau
7 Heiligenkreuz
8 Hradiště
9 Kladruby
10 Klosterneuburg
11 Kremsmünster
12 Leubus
13 Melk
14 Neustift
15 Pannonhalma
16 Reun
17 St Florian
18 St Lambrecht
19 Slams
20 Strahov
21 Tepl
22 Velehrad
23 Vyšší Brod
24 Wilten
25 Žďár nad Sázavou
26 Zwettl

Glossary of the more important place-name variants

The form used in the text is indicated by CAPITALS
Present-day official names are indicated by asterisks

1. Austria

German	Italian	Slovene/Croat	Other
BOZEN	Bolzano*		
BRIXEN	Bressanone*		
FELDSBERG			Valtice* (Czech)
St. Veit am Flaum	FIUME	Rijeka*	
Görz	GORIZIA*		
LAIBACH		Ljubljana*	
Piben	PEDENA	Pićan*	
Mitterburg	PISINO	Pazin*	
Trient	Trento*		TRENT (Eng.)
Triest	TRIESTE*	Trst	

2. Bohemia

Czech	German	Polish
MLADÁ*/STARÁ*) BOLESLAV*	(Jung/Alt) Bunzlau	
Broumov*	BRAUNAU (in Böhmen)	
Vratislav	BRESLAU	Wrocław*
Břeh	BRIEG	Brzeg*
BRNO*	Brünn	
Louka*	(KLOSTER) BRUCK	
(České*) Budějovice*	BUDWEIS	
Cheb*	EGER	
Kladsko	GLATZ	Kłodzko*
Hlohov	GLOGAU	Głogów*
Krnov*	JÄGERNDORF	
	JAUER	Jawor*
JIČÍN*	Gitschin	
JINDŘICHŮV HRADEC*	Neuhaus	
Jáchymov*	JOACHIMSTHAL	

Hradec Králové*	KÖNIGGRÄTZ		
(ČESKÝ*) KRUMLOV*	Krum(m)au		
Kutná Hora*	KUTTENBERG		
Lehnice	LIEGNITZ	Legnica*	
LITOMĚŘICE*	Leitmeritz		
MIKULOV*	Nikolsburg		
Minstrberk	MÜNSTERBERG	Ziębice*	
	NEISSE	Nysa*	
	ÖLS	Oleśnica*	
OLOMOUC*	Olmütz		
Opolí	OPPELN	Opole*	
Plzeň*	PILSEN		
Ratiboř	RATIBOR	Racibórz*	
Liberec*	REICHENBERG		
Zahán	SAGAN	Żagań*	
	SCHWEIDNITZ	Świdnica*	
Těšín*	TESCHEN	Cieszyr.*	
TŘEBOŇ*	Wittingau		
Opava*	TROPPAU		

3. Hungary (including Transylvania)

Hungarian	German	Slovak	Other
Bártfa	BARTFELD	Bardejov*	
EGER*	Erlau		Agria (Lat.)
Kismarton	EISENSTADT*		
EPERJES	Preschau	Prešov*	
ESZTERGOM*	Gran		Strigonium (Lat.)
GYÖR*	Raab		Jaurinum (Lat.)
GYULAFEHÉRVÁR	Weissenburg (later Karlsburg)		Alba Iulia* (Rom.)
Karlóca	KARLOWITZ		Sremski Karlovci* (Serb.)
KASSA	Kaschau	Košice*	Cassovia (Lat.)
KOLOZSVÁR	Klausenburg		Cluj, Cluj-Na-poca* (Rom.); Claudiopolis (Lat.)
KOMÁROM*	Komorn	Komárno*	
Körmöcbánya	KREMNITZ	Kremnica*	
Löcse	LEUTSCHAU	Levoča*	

MUNKÁCS			Mukačevo* (Ruth.)	
NAGYVÁRAD (Várad)	Grosswardein		Oradea* (Rom.)	Mare
Érsekújvár	NEUHÄUSEL	Nové Zámky*		
Besztercebánya	NEUSOHL	Banská Bystrica*		
NYITRA	Neutra	Nitra*		
	PASSAROWITZ		Požarevac* (Serb.)	
PÉCS*	Fünfkirchen			
POZSONY	Pressburg	Bratislava* (earlier Prešporok)	Posonium (Lat.)	
Selmecbánya	SCHEMNITZ	Banská Štiavnica*		
SOPRON*	Ödenburg			
SZAKOLCA	Skalitz	Skalica*		
SZATMÁR*			Satu (Rom.)	Mare*
TRENCSÉN	Trenschin	Trenčin*		
Nagyszombat	TYRNAU	Trnava*	Tyrnavia (Lat.)	
UNGVÁR			Užhorod* (Ruth.)	
VÁC*	Waitzen			
VAS* (VASVÁR*)	Eisenburg			
Zágráb	Agram		ZAGREB* (Cr.)	
Szepes(ség)	ZIPS	Spiš*		
ZSOLNA	Sillein	Žilina*		

Guide to pronunciation

The chief languages of the sixteenth- and seventeenth-century Habsburg Monarchy, besides German, Latin, and (in some measure) Italian, were Czech and Hungarian, and the uninitiated reader might appreciate a few brief hints about the pronunciation of the last two of these. Both Czech and Hungarian have a consistent scheme of pronunciation, with no silent letters; and both invariably stress the first syllable only of any word, however long. The acute accent (´) indicates a long vowel. Sounds which differ materially from their English equivalents are as follows:

Hung. *a* and *á*: somewhat idiosyncratic letters, the former very short, almost like *o* in *hot* (or the Dutch *a* in *Amsterdam*); the latter long, fuller than German *ah* in *Hahn*

Cz. and Hung. *c*: *ts* as in *lots* (and *ck* = *tsk*)

Cz. *ch*: Scottish *ch* as in *loch*

Cz. *č* and Hung. *cs*: *ch* as in *church*

Cz. *d'* and Hung. *gy*: soft *d* as in *adieu*

Cz. *ě*: *ye* as in *yell*

Cz. and Hung. *j*, and Hung. *ly*: *y* as in *yard*

Cz. *ň* and Hung. *ny*: soft *n* as in *new*, or French *gn* as in *champignon*

Hung. *ö*: as in German *Hölle*

Hung. *ő*: a long vowel, like German *öh* in *Höhle*

Cz. *ou*: a diphthong, rather like *ow* in *own*

Cz. and Hung. *r* is rolled

Cz. *ř*: a difficult sound, roughly *r* and French *j* (as in *jour*) pronounced simultaneously; familiar from the name of the composer Antonín Dvořák

Cz. *š* and Hung. *s*: *sh* as in *shoot*

Hung. *sz*: simple *s* as in *soot*

Cz. *t'* and Hung. *ty*: soft *t* as in *tune*

Cz. *ú*: a long *u*, like *oo* in *loom*

Hung. *ü*: as in German *füllen*

Hung. *ű*: a long vowel, like German *üh* in *fühlen*

Cz. *y* is identical with *i*; Hung. *y* survives only in proper names (below), and in the letter combinations *gy*, *ly*, *ny*, *ty* (above)

Cz. *ž* and Hung. *zs*: French *j* as in *jour*

Some Hungarian family names preserve antiquated spellings, still quite standard in the written language until the nineteenth century. Commonest are *ch* for *cs*, *cz* for *c*, *th* for *t*, and *w* for *v*. *i* and *y* are used almost indifferently at the end of surnames in Magyar (e.g. Bocskai or Bocskay), though *y* has often been thought to contribute a more aristocratic flavour. In a few cases the name is conventionally written with *-ly* or *-lyi*, but pronounced as *li*: thus Thököly is spoken 'Tököli', and Károlyi the Bible-translator 'Károli' (whereas Károlyi the family of magnates sounds as it is written). At least one proper name encountered in this book seems to defeat all the rules: Dessewffy is pronounced 'Dezsőfi'.

Select bibliography

The majority of works consulted for this book have been cited once only, in the appropriate footnote. The following list contains those to which repeated reference is made. Standard modern encyclopedias are omitted.

Abgottspon, P. G., *P. Valerianus Magni, Kapuziner* (Olten 1939)
Acht Jahrhunderte Deutscher Orden in Einzeldarstellungen, ed. K. Wieser (Bad Godesberg 1967)
Acta Sanctorum, ed. J. Bolland *et al.*, i–   (Antwerp, etc. 1643–   )
Andritsch, J., *Studenten und Lehrer aus Ungarn und Siebenbürgen an der Universität Graz, 1586–1782* (Graz 1965)
Angyal, E., *Theatrum Mundi* (Bp. 1938)
Antal, G. von, and Peter, J. C. H. de (eds.), *Weensche Gezantschapsberichten van 1670 tot 1720*, i–ii (The Hague 1929–34)
Apponyi, A., *Hungarica: Ungarn betreffende, im Ausland gedruckte Bücher*, i–iv (Munich 1903–27)
Ardensbach, W. M., *Tartaro Clypeus, excipiens Tartaro Mastigem Hertodianum . . .* (Pr. 1671)
Arneth, A., *Prinz Eugen von Savoyen*, i–iii (V. 1858)
Arnold, Gottfried, *Unparteyische Kirchen- und Ketzer-Historie*, i–ii (Frankfurt 1699–1700)
Aschbach, J. von, *Geschichte der Wiener Universität*, i–iii (V. 1865–88)
Aubin, H., and Zorn, W. (eds.), *Handbuch der deutschen Wirtschafts- und Sozialgeschichte*, i (Stuttgart 1971)
Auersperg, J. C. von, *Geschichte des königlichen böhmischen Appellationsgerichtes*, i–ii (Pr. 1805)
Avé-Lallemant, F. Ch. B., *Das deutsche Gaunerthum*, i–iii (Leipzig 1858–1862)

Backmund, N., *Monasticon Praemonstratense*, i–iii (Straubing 1949–59)
Bagyary, S., *A magyar művelődés a XVI–XVII században Szamosközy István történeti maradványai alapján* (Esztergom 1907)
Balbín, Bohuslav, *Epitome historica rerum Bohemicarum quam . . . Boleslaviensem Historiam placuit appellare* (Pr. 1677)
— *Miscellanea Historica Regni Bohemiae*, decas I, i–viii; decas II, i–ii (Pr. 1679–88)
— *Bohemia Docta*, ed. R. Ungar, i–ii (Pr. 1776–80)
— 'Relatio progressus in extirpanda haeresi 1661–78', ed. A. Rezek, *VKČSN*, 1892, 203–57

Baranowski, B., *Procesy czarownic w Polsce w XVII i XVIII wieku* (Łódź 1952)

Bártfai Szabó, L., *A Hunt-Pázmán nemzetségbeli Forgách család története* (Esztergom 1910)

Barton, P. F., and Makkai, L. (eds.), *Rebellion oder Religion?* (Bp. 1977)

Baruzi, J., *Leibniz et l'organisation religieuse de la terre* (Paris 1907)

Batthyány, Ignác, *Leges Ecclesiasticae Regni Hungariae*, i–iii (Alba Julia–Kolozsvár 1785–1827)

Bauer, A., *Die Adelsdocumente österreichischer Alchemisten* (V. 1893)

Baur, L., 'Berichte des hessen-darmstädtischen Gesandten J. E. Passer . . . über die Vorgänge am kaiserlichen Hofe und in Wien von 1680 bis 1683', *AÖG* xxxvii (1867), 273–409

Bayle, Pierre, *An Historical and Critical Dictionary* (Eng. edn. London 1710)

Becher, J. J., *Character pro Notitia Linguarum Universali* (Frankfurt 1661)

— *Oedipus Chimicus* (Amsterdam 1664)

— *Magnalia Naturae, or the Philosopher's Stone lately exposed to publick Sight and Sale . . .* (London 1680)

— *Experimentum novum ac curiosum de Minera Arenaria Perpetua* (Frankfurt 1680)

— *Theoria et Experientia de nova Temporis Dimetiendi Ratione* (London 1680)

— *Physica Subterranea* (2nd edn., Frankfurt 1681)

— *Chymischer Glücks-Hafen* (Frankfurt 1682)

Beck, A., *Geschichte des gothaischen Landes*, i–iii (Gotha 1868–76)

Beckovský, Jan, *Poselkyně starých příběhův českých*, ii (in 3 pts.), ed. A. Rezek (Pr. 1879–80)

Békefi, R., *Zirc . . . története*, i–v (Pécs 1901–2)

Bělohlávek, V., and Hradec, J., *Dějiny českých křižovníků s červenou hvězdou*, i–ii (Pr. 1930)

Benda, K., 'A kálvini tanok hatása a magyar rendi ellenállás ideológiájára', *Helikon*, xvii (1971), 322–9

— 'Absolutismus und ständischer Widerstand in Ungarn am Anfang des 17. Jahrhunderts', *Südostforschungen*, xxxiii (1974), 85–124

Benecke, G., *Society and politics in Germany, 1500–1750* (London 1974)

— *Ein Benediktinerbuch*, ed. S. Brunner (Würzburg n.d.)

Benger, N., *Annalium O.S.P.P.E. volumen secundum* (Pozsony 1743)

Benkő, J., *Transilvania*, i–ii (V. 1778)

Benzing, J., *Die Buchdrucker des 16. und 17. Jahrhunderts im deutschen Sprachgebiet* (Wiesbaden 1963)

Bérenger, J., *Les 'Gravamina', remontrances des diètes de Hongrie de 1655 à 1681* (Paris 1973)

— *Finances et absolutisme autrichien dans la seconde moitié du XVIIe siècle* (Paris 1975)

Berni rula, ed. K. Doskočil *et al.*, i–iii, x–xiii, xviii–ix, xxiii, xxvi–viii, xxxi–xxxiii (Pr. 1950–5)

Beyerlinck, L., *Magnum Theatrum Vitae Humanae*, i–viii (Lyons 1665)

Bibl, V., 'Die Organisation des evangelischen Kirchenwesens im Erzher-zogtum Österreich under der Enns 1568–76', *AÖG* lxxxvii (1899), 113–228

— 'Erzherzog Ernst und die Gegenreformation in Niederösterreich, 1576–90', *MIÖG*, Erg.-Band vi (1901), 575–96

— 'Die katholischen und protestantischen Stände Niederösterreichs im XVII Jahrhundert', *Jb.f.Lk.v.NÖ*, N. F. ii (1903), 165–323

— 'Die Berichte des Reichshofrates Dr. George Eder an die Herzoge Albrecht und Wilhelm von Bayern über die Religionskrise in Nieder-österreich, 1579–97', *Jb.f.L.k.v.NÖ* N. F. viii (1909), 67–154

Bidermann, H. I., *Geschichte der österreichischen Gesammt-Staats-Idee, 1526–1804*, i–ii (to 1740) (Innsbruck 1867–89)

Bílek, T. V., *Dějiny konfiskací v Čechách po r. 1618*, i–ii (Pr. 1882–3)

— *Reformace katolická neboli Obnovení náboženství katolického v království českém po bitvě bělohorské* (Pr. 1892)

— *Statky a jmění kolleji jesuitských, klášterů, kostelů, bratrstev a jiných ústavů v království Českém od císaře Josefa II zrušených* (Pr. 1893)

Bischoff, F., and D'Elvert, Chr., *Zur Geschichte des Glaubens an Zauberer, Hexen und Vampyre in Mähren und Österreich-Schlesien* (Brünn 1859)

Blekastad, M., *Comenius* (Oslo 1969)

Boas, M., *Robert Boyle and 17th-century Chemistry* (Cambridge 1958)

Bod, Peter, *Historia Hungarorum Ecclesiastica*, ed. L. W. E. Rauwenhoff *et al.*, i–iii (Leiden 1888–90)

Boehm, A., 'L'augustinisme de Valeriano Magni', *Revue des sciences religieuses*, xxxix (1965), 230–67

Bog, I., *Der Reichsmerkantilismus* (Stuttgart 1959)

— (ed.), *Der Aussenhandel Ostmitteleuropas 1450–1650* (Cologne–V. 1971)

Bogišić, V. (ed.), *Acta coniurationem P. a Zrinio et F. de Frankopan nec non F. Nadasdy illustrantia* (Zagreb 1888)

Bohatcová, M., *Irrgarten der Schicksale* (Pr. 1966)

Bohatta, H. (ed.), *Katalog der in den Bibliotheken ... des fürstlichen Hauses von und zu Liechtenstein befindlichen Bücher ...* i–iii (V. 1931)

Böhl, E., *Beiträge zur Geschichte der Reformation in Österreich* (Jena 1902)

Bojani, F. de, *Innocent XI, sa correspondance avec ses nonces*, i–iii (Rome–Roulers (Belgium) 1910–12)

Bonanni, Philip, *Musaeum Kircherianum* (Rome 1709)

Borový, K., *Antonín Brus z Mohelnice* (Pr. 1873)

Bosmans, H., 'Théodore Moretus SJ, mathématicien', *De Gulden Passer*, N. R. vi (1928), 57–163

Braubach, M., *Prinz Eugen von Savoyen*, i–v (Munich 1963–5)

Braumüller, H., *Geschichte Kärntens* (Klagenfurt 1949)

Brischar, K., *Athanasius Kircher, ein Lebensbild* (Würzburg 1877)

Browne, Edward, *A Brief Account of some Travels in Hungaria ...* (London 1673)

— *An Account of Several Travels through a great part of Germany* (London 1677)

Brummel, L., *Twee ballingen 's lands tijdens onze opstand tegen Spanje* (The Hague 1972)

Brunner, O., 'Das Archiv der niederösterreichischen Kammer und des Vizedoms in Österreich unter der Enns und seine Bedeutung für die Landesgeschichte', *Jb.f.Lk.v.NÖ* xxix (1944–8), 144–66

— *Adeliges Landleben und europäischer Geist* (Salzburg 1949)

— *Neue Wege der Sozialgeschichte* (Göttingen 1956)

— *Land und Herrschaft* (5th edn. V. 1965)

Bubics, Zs., *Eszterházy Pál Mars Hungaricusa* (Bp. 1895)

Büchner, A. E., *Academiae … Leopoldino-Carolinae Naturae Curiosorum Historia* (Halle 1755)

Bucsay, M., *Geschichte des Protestantismus in Ungarn* (Stuttgart 1959)

Burbury, J., *A Relation of a Journey … from London … to Constantinople* (London 1671)

Byloff, F., *Das Verbrechen der Zauberei, ein Beitrag zur Geschichte der Strafrechtspflege in Steiermark* (Graz 1902)

— *Hexenglaube und Hexenverfolgung in den österreichischen Alpenländern* (Berlin–Leipzig 1934)

Cândea, R., *Der Katholizismus in den Donaufürstentümern* (Leipzig 1916)

Carafa, Carlo, *Commentaria de Germania Sacra Restaurata* (Cologne 1639)

— 'Relatione dello stato dell'Imperio e della Germania', ed. J. G. Müller, *AÖG* xxiii (1860), 103–449

Caramuel Lobkovic, J., *Rationalis et realis Philosophia* (Louvain 1642)

— *Novem Stellae circa Iovem …* (Louvain ?1643)

— *Mathesis Biceps vetus et nova*, i–ii (Campagna 1670)

Carena, Caesar, *Tractatus de Officio Sanctissimae Inquisitionis et modo procedendi in causis fidei* (Cremona 1641)

Ceñal, R., 'Juan Caramuel, su epistolario con Atanasio Kircher', *Revista de Filosofia*, xii (1953), 101–47

Čermák, D. K., *Premonstráti v Čechách a na Moravě* (Pr. 1877)

Chanovský, Albert, *Vestigium Boemiae Piae* (Pr. 1659)

La Chiave del Gabinetto del Cavagliere Gioseppe Francesco Borri (?Cologne 1681)

Chlumecky, P. von, *Karl von Zierotin und seine Zeit*, i–ii (Brünn 1862)

— *Ein Chorherrenbuch*, ed. S. Brunner (Würzburg–V. 1883)

Chyba, K., 'Dobrovická tiskárna', *Ročenka Universitní Knihovny v Praze*, 1958, 54–97

— *Ein Cisterzienserbuch*, ed. S. Brunner (Würzburg 1881)

Cochem, Martin van, *Život Pána Nasseho Gezisse Krysta*, tr. E. Nymburský (Pr. 1698)

Constant, G., *Concession à l'Allemagne de la communion sous les deux espèces*, i–ii (Paris 1923)

Coreth, A., 'Job Hartmann von Enenkel', *MIÖG* lv (1944), 247–302

— *Österreichische Geschichtschreibung in der Barockzeit* (V. 1950)

— *Pietas Austriaca* (V. 1959)

Corniero, A. de, 'Capuchinos precursores del P. Bartolomé Barberis en el estudio de S. Buenaventura: P. Valeriano Magni de Milán', *Coll. Franc.* iii (1933), 67–80, 209–28, 347–83, 518–70
Csapodi, Cs., *Eszterházi Miklós nádor* (Bp. ?1942)
Czerny, A., *Bilder aus der Zeit der Bauernunruhen in Oberösterreich* (Linz 1876)
— *Der zweite Bauernaufstand in Oberösterreich, 1595–7* (Linz 1890)
— (ed.), *Ein Tourist in Österreich während der Schwedenzeit* (Linz 1874)
Czerwenka, B., *Die Khevenhüller, Geschichte des Geschlechts* (V. 1867)

Dalnerus, Andreas, *Tractatus de Seditione* (V. 1599)
Delrio, Martin, *Disquisitiones Magicae* (Louvain 1599–1600; Cologne 1633)
Denis, E., *Čechy po Bílé Hoře*, tr. and expanded by J. Vančura, i–ii (3rd edn. Pr. ?1921)
Dersch, W., 'Beiträge zur Geschichte des Kardinals Friedrich von Hessen', *ZVGAS* lxii (1928), 272–330
Dillon, K. J., *King and estates in the Bohemian lands, 1526–64* (Brussels 1976)
Dimitz, A., *Geschichte Krains*, i–ii (Laibach 1874–6)
Dobrzensky, J. J. W., *Nova et Amaenior de admirando fontium genio ... Philosophia* (Ferrara 1659)
Dudik, B., *Bibliothek und Archiv im fürsterzbischöflichen Schlosse zu Kremsier* (V. 1870)
— (ed.), 'Correspondenz Kaisers Ferdinand III und seiner erlauchten Familie mit P. Martinus Becanus und P. Wilhelm Lamormaini kaiserlichen Beichtvätern', *AÖG* liv (1876), 221–350
Duhr, B., *Geschichte der Jesuiten in den Ländern deutscher Zunge*, i–iii (Freiburg–Regensburg 1902–21)
Dülmen, R. van, 'Sozietätsbildungen in Nürnberg im 17. Jahrhundert', in *Gesellschaft und Herrschaft, Festgabe für K. Bosl* (Munich 1969), 153–90
Dvořák, M. (ed.), 'Briefe Kaiser Leopold I an Wenzel Euseb Herzog in Schlesien ...', *AÖG* lxxx (1893), 463–508
Dvorský, F., 'Historické příspěvky k dějinám pověr ...', *ČL* xi (1902), 194–6, 248 f., 328–30, 490–2; xii (1903), 277

Eder, Karl, *Glaubensspaltung und Landstände in Österreich ob der Enns 1525–1602* (Linz 1936)
Egger, J., *Geschichte Tirols von den ältesten Zeiten bis in die Neuzeit*, i–iii (Innsbruck 1872–80)
Eisenberg, N., 'Studien zur Historiographie über Kaiser Leopold I', *MIÖG* li (1937), 359–413
Eckhart, F., *A földesúri büntetőbiráskodás a XVI–XVII században* (Bp. 1954)
Ember, Gy., *Az újkori magyar közigazgatás története Mohácstól a török kiűzéséig* (Bp. 1946)

Erdélyi, L. and Sörös, P., *A pannonhalmi Szent Benedek-Rend története*, i–xii (Bp. 1902–12)
Ernstberger, A., *Franken–Böhmen–Europa, gesammelte Aufsätze*, i–ii (Kallmünz 1959)
Evans, R. J. W., *Rudolf II and his World* (Oxford 1973)
— *The Wechel Presses* (Oxford 1975)

Falke, J., *Geschichte des fürstlichen Hauses Liechtenstein*, ii (V. 1877)
Fallenbüchl, F., *Az Ágostonrendiek Magyarországon* (Bp. 1943)
Feigl, H., *Die niederösterreichische Grundherrschaft vom ausgehenden Mittelalter bis zu den theresianisch-josephinischen Reformen* (V. 1964)
— *Der niederösterreichische Bauernaufstand 1596/7* (V. 1972)
Feine, H. E., *Die Besetzung der Reichsbistümer vom Westfälischen Frieden bis zur Säkularisation* (Stuttgart 1921)
Feldzüge des Prinzen Eugen von Savoyen, ser. I, i (V. 1876)
Fellner, Th. and Kretschmayr, H., *Die österreichische Zentralverwaltung*, Abt. I: 1491–1749, i–ii (V. 1907)
Ferguson, J., *Bibliotheca Chemica*, i–ii (Glasgow 1906)
Flégl, O., 'Relace kardinála Harracha o stavu pražské arcidiecése do Říma', *VČAVSlU*, xxiii (1914), 185–97, 227–43
Florovský, A. V., *Čeští jesuité na Rusi* (Pr. 1941)
Fragmen Panis Corvi Proto-Eremitici seu Reliquiae Annalium O.S.P.P.E. (V. 1663)
Fraknói, V., *Pázmány Péter és kora*, i–iii (Bp. 1868–72)
— *A magyar királyi kegyúri jog Szent Istvántól Mária Teréziáig*, i–ii (Bp. 1895–9)
— *Magyarország egyházi és politikai összeköttetései a Római Szent-Székkel*, iii: 1526–1689 (Bp. 1903)
Frankl (= Fraknói), V., *A hazai és külföldi iskolázás a XVI században* (Bp. 1873)
Frauenstädt, P., 'Bettel- und Vagabundenwesen in Schlesien vom 16. bis 18. Jahrhundert', *Preussische Jahrbücher*, lxxxix (1897), 488–509
Freschot, Casimir, *Mémoires de la cour de Vienne* (Cologne 1705)
Friess, E., 'Zur sozialen und wirtschaftlichen Lage der gutsherrlichen Leute am Fuss des Ötschers nach dem Bauernsturme', *JbfLk.v.NÖ*, N. F. xxi (1928), 2, 172–88
Friess, G. E., 'Geschichte des Benediktiner-Stiftes Garsten in Oberösterreich', *Stud.u.Mitt.* ii (1881), 4, 251–66
— 'Geschichte der österreichischen Minoritenprovinz', *AÖG* lxiv (1882), 79–245
Frind, A., *Die Geschichte der Bischöfe und Erzbischöfe von Prag* (Pr. 1873)
Fritsch, A., *Diatribe historico-politica de Zygenorum Origine, Vita et Moribus* (Jena 1660)
Fuxhoffer, D., *Monasteriologia Regni Hungariae*, i–ii (3rd edn. V.–Esztergom 1869)

Galla, F., *A Pálosrend reformálása a XVII században* (Bp. 1941)
— 'A püspökjelöltek kánoni kivizsgálásának jegyzőkönyvei a Vatikáni Levéltárban', *LK* xx–xxiii (1942–5), 141–86
— 'Magyar tárgyú pápai felhatalmazások, felmentések és kiváltságok a katolikus megújhodás korából', *LK* xxiv (1946), 71–169
Ganzenmüller, W., *Beiträge zur Geschichte der Technologie und der Alchemie* (Weinheim 1956)
Garas, K., *Magyarországi festészet a XVII században* (Bp. 1953)
Gavigan, J. J., *The Austro-Hungarian province of the Augustinian friars, 1646–1820*, i–iii (Rome 1975–7)
Gebauer, J., *Die Publicistik über den böhmischen Aufstand von 1618* (Halle 1892)
Gellner, G., *Životopis lékaře Borbonia a výklad jeho deníků* (Pr. 1938)
Gerstenberg, H., 'Philipp Wilhelm von Hörnigk', *Jbb.f.Natö.u.Stat.* cxxxiii (1930), 813–71
Geschichte der Stadt Wien, ed. H. Zimmermann, *et al.*, 6 vols. in 8 (V. 1897–1918)
Gindely, A., *Rudolf II und seine Zeit*, i–ii (Pr. 1862–5)
— *Geschichte des dreissigjährigen Krieges*, i–iv (Pr. 1869–80)
— *Geschichte der Gegenreformation in Böhmen* (Leipzig 1894)
Ginzburg, C., *I benandanti, ricerche sulla stregoneria* (Turin 1966)
Gooss, R., *Österreichische Staatsverträge: Fürstentum Siebenbürgen, 1526–1690* (V. 1911)
Greiderer, V., *Germania Franciscana*, i–ii (Innsbruck 1777–81)
Grisar, H., 'Vatikanische Berichte über die Protestantisierung und die katholische Restauration in Böhmen zur Zeit Ferdinand II', *Zschr.f.Kath.Theol.* x (1886), 722–37
Gross, L., *Die Geschichte der deutschen Reichshofkanzlei von 1559 bis 1806* (V. 1933)
Grüll, G., *Die Robot in Oberösterreich* (Linz 1952)
— *Bauer, Herr und Landesfürst* (Linz 1963)
Grünberg, K., *Die Bauernbefreiung und die Auflösung des gutsherrlich-bäuerlichen Verhältnisses in Böhmen, Mähren und Schlesien*, i–ii (Leipzig 1893–4)
Grünhagen, C., *Geschichte Schlesiens*, i–ii (Gotha 1884–6)
— 'Schlesien unter Rudolf II und der Majestätsbrief', *ZVGAS* xx (1886), 54–96
Gschliesser, O. von, *Der Reichshofrat, 1559–1806* (V. 1942)
Gugel, K. F., *Johann Rudolph Glauber 1604–70, Leben und Werk* (Würzburg 1955)
Gugitz, G., *Österreichs Gnadenstätten in Kult und Brauch*, i–v (V. 1955–8)
Guhrauer, G. E., *Gottfried Wilhelm Freiherr von Leibnitz*, i–ii (Breslau 1846)
Guillot, G., 'Léopold I et sa cour (1681–4)', *Revue des Questions Historiques*, xli (1907), 401–46
Gulyás, P., *A könyvnyomtatás Magyarországon a XV és XVI században* (Bp. 1931)

Gutkas, K., *Geschichte des Landes Niederösterreich* (4th edn. St. Pölten 1973)

Hall, R. M. and M. B. (eds.), *The Correspondence of Henry Oldenburg*, i– (Madison–Milwaukee 1965–)

Hammer, J. von, *Khiesls, des Cardinals ... Leben*, i–iv (V. 1847–51)

Handbuch der historischen Stätten: Österreich, ed. K. Lechner and F. Huter, i–ii (Stuttgart 1966–70)

Hansiz, Marcus, *Germania Sacra*, i–ii (Augsburg 1727–9)

Hanzal, J., 'Vesnická obec a samospráva v 16. a na počátku 17. století', *Právněhistorické Studie*, x (1964), 135–47

— 'Jiři Ignác Pospichal a jeho doba', *ČsČH* xix (1971), 229–57

Harant, Jan Jiři, *Paměti*, ed. F. Menčík (Pr. 1897)

Hassenpflug, E., 'Die böhmische Adelsnation als Repräsentantin des Königreichs Böhmen (1627–1740)', *Bohemia-Jahrbuch*, xv (1974), 71–90

Hassinger, H., *Johann Joachim Becher 1635–82* (V. 1951)

— 'Die Landstände der österreichischen Länder: Zusammensetzung, Organisation und Leistung im 16.–18. Jahrhundert', *Jb.f.Lk.v.NÖ* xxxvi (1964), 989–1035

Házi, J., *Die kanonische Visitation des Stefan Kazó ... in den Jahren 1697–8* (Eisenstadt 1958)

Heckenast, G. (ed.), *Aus der Geschichte der ostmitteleuropäischen Bauern-bewegungen im 16.–17. Jahrhundert* (Bp. 1977)

Heimbucher, M., *Die Orden und Kongregationen der Katholischen Kirche*, i–ii (Paderborn 1933–4)

Henelius, N., *Silesiographia Renovata*, ed. and expanded by M. J. Fibiger, i–ii (Breslau–Leipzig 1704)

Herepei, J., *Adattár XVII. századi szellemi mozgalmaink történetéhez*, i–iii (Bp. 1965–71)

Hermann, Amandus, *Sol Triplex in eodem Universo: id est, Universae Philosophiae cursus integer* (Sulzbach 1676)

Hertodt, J. F., *Tartaro-Mastix Moraviae* (V. 1669)

— *Opus Mirificum Sextae Diei, id est Homo physicè, anatomicè, et moraliter ... dissectus* (Jena 1670)

— *Crocologia seu curiosa croci regis vegetabilium enucleatio* (Jena 1671)

Herzog, P., 'Cosmographia Franciscano-Austriacae Provinciae Sancti Bernardini Senensis', *Analecta Franciscana*, i (Quaracchi 1885), 41–213

Heydendorff, W. E., *Die Fürsten und Freiherren zu Eggenberg und ihre Vorfahren* (Graz 1965)

Héyret, M. (ed.), *P. Marcus von Aviano, sein Briefwechsel ... ii* (Munich 1938)

Hirn, J., *Erzherzog Maximilian, der Deutschmeister*, i–ii (Innsbruck 1915–1936)

Hirnhaim, Hieronymus, *De Typho Generis Humani* (Pr. 1676)

Hirsch, A., *Kircherus ... Germaniae redonatus ... Das ist Philosophischer Extract und Auszug ...* (Schwäbisch Hall 1662)

Hoffmann, A., *Wirtschaftsgeschichte des Landes Oberösterreich*, i (Salzburg 1952)

Holub, J., *Istvánffy Miklós Históriája hadtörténelmi szempontból* (Szekszárd 1909)

Hóman, B. and Szekfű, Gy., *Magyar történet*, i–v (Bp. 1935–6)

Hopf, A., *Anton Wolfradt, Fürstbischof von Wien* . . . i–iii (V. 1891–4)

Horányi, A., *Scriptores Piarum Scholarum liberaliumque artium magistri*, i–ii (Buda 1808–9)

Hrejsa, F., *Česká Konfesse, její vznik, podstata a dějiny* (Pr. 1912)

— *Dějiny křest'anství v Československu*, v–vi (Pr. 1948–50)

Hrubý, F., 'Z hospodářských převratů českých v století XV a XVI se zvláštním zřetelem k Moravě, *ČČH* xxx (1924), 205–36, 433–69

— 'Selské a panské inventáře v době předbělohorské', *ČČH* xxxiii (1927), 21–59, 263–306

— (ed.), *Moravské korespondence a akta z let 1620–36*, i–ii (Brno 1934–7)

Hurt, R., *Dějiny cisterciáckého kláštera na Velehradě*, i–ii (Olomouc 1934–8)

Hurter, F., *Geschichte Kaiser Ferdinands II und seiner Eltern*, i–xi (Schaffhausen 1850–67)

Illyés, András, *Megrövidittetet Ige az-az: Predikatios Könyv*, i–iii (Nagyszeben–V. 1691–2)

Imre, S., *Alvinczi Péter kassai magyar pap élete* (Hódmezövásárhely 1898)

Ipolyi, A., *Bedegi Nyáry Krisztina* (Bp. 1887)

Irmscher, J. (ed.), *Renaissance und Humanismus in Mitteleuropa und Osteuropa*, i–ii (Berlin 1962)

Iványi, B., *Könyvek, könyvtárak, könyvnyomdák Magyarországon 1331–1600* (Bp. 1937)

— and Gárdonyi, A., *A királyi magyar Egyetemi Nyomda története, 1577–1927* (Bp. 1927)

Jaitner, K., *Die Konfessionspolitik des Pfalzgrafen Philipp Wilhelm von Neuburg in Jülich-Berg von 1647–1697* (Münster 1973)

Janetschek, C. d'E., *Das Augustiner-Eremitenstift S. Thomas in Brünn*, i (Brünn 1898)

Jarnut-Derbolav, E., *Die österreichische Gesandschaft in London, 1701–11* (Bonn 1972)

Jedin, H., *Kirche des Glaubens, Kirche der Geschichte*, i–ii (Freiburg 1966)

Jöchlinger, W., 'Andreas Weissenstein, erwählter Propst von Klosterneuburg, und sein Kampf gegen das Staatskirchentum', *Jb.d.St.Klnb.* N. F. vi (1966), 7–135

Juncker, Ch., *Commentarius de Vita, Scriptisque ac Meritis . . . Iobi Ludolfi* (Leipzig und Frankfurt 1710)

Juncker, Johann, *Conspectus Chemiae Theoretico-Practicae* (Halle 1730)

Kadich, H. von, *Der mährische Adel* (Nuremberg 1887)

Kaindl, D., *Geschichte des Zisterzienserstiftes Hohenfurt in Böhmen* (Hohenfurt 1930)

Kalista, Z., *Čechové, kteří tvořili dějiny světa* (Pr. 1939)

— *Cesty ve znamení kříže* (2nd edn. Pr. 1947)

— *Česká barokní gotika a její žd'árské ohnisko* (Brno 1970)

— 'Bedřich Bridel, kontext života a díla', *Annali dell'Istituto Universitario Orientale*, sezione slava, xiv (1971), 13–46

— (ed.), *Korespondence císaře Leopolda I s Humprechtem Janem Černínem z Chudenic*, i (Pr. 1936)

Kalousek, J., *České státní právo* (2nd edn. Pr. 1892)

Kantzenbach, F. W., *Das Ringen um die Einheit der Kirche im Jahrhundert der Reformation* (Stuttgart 1957)

Kapihorský, S. E., *Hystorya Klásstera Sedleckého* (Pr. 1630)

Karajan, Th. G. von., 'Kaiser Leopold I und Peter Lambeck', *Almanach der kaiserlichen Akademie der Wissenschaften*, xviii (1868), 103–56

Károlyi, Á., 'Az ellenreformáció kezdete és Thurzó György nádorrá választása', *Sz* liii–liv (1919–20), 1–33, 124–63

Kašpar, J., 'Dvě studie k dějinám nevolnického povstání roku 1680', *AUC*, *Phil.et Hist.*, 1958, 1, 55–81

— *Nevolnické povstání v Čechách r. 1680* (Pr. 1965)

Kathona, G., *Fejezetek a török hódoltsági reformáció történetéből* (Bp. 1974)

Kaufmann, D., *Die letzte Vertreibung der Juden aus Wien und Niederösterreich* (V. 1889)

Kazy, F., *Historia Regni Hungariae*, i–iii (Tyrnau 1737–49)

Keiblinger, I., *Geschichte des Stiftes Melk* (V. 1851)

Kelemen, A., *Keresztély Ágost herceg katolikus restaurációs tevékenysége a győri egyházmegyében* (Pannonhalma 1931)

Kestler, J. S., *Physiologia Kircheriana Experimentalis* (Amsterdam 1680)

Kink, R., *Geschichte der kaiserlichen Universität zu Wien*, i–ii (V. 1854)

Kircher, Athanasius, *Ars Magna Lucis et Umbrae*, i–ii (Rome 1646)

— *Musurgia Universalis, sive Ars Magna Consoni et Dissoni*, i–ii (Rome 1650)

— *Oedipus Aegyptiacus*, 3 vols. in 4 (Rome 1652–4)

— *Magnes sive De Arte Magnetica* (3rd edn. Rome 1654)

— *Iter Extaticum Coeleste*, ed. G. Schott (Würzburg 1660)

— *Mundus Subterraneus*, i–ii (Amsterdam 1665)

— *Fasciculus Epistolarum*, ed. H. A. Langenmantel (Augsburg 1684)

Kisbán, E., *A magyar Pálosrend története*, i–ii (Bp. 1938–40)

Klabouch, J., *Osvícenské právní nauky v českých zemích* (Pr. 1958)

Klíma, A., *Manufakturní období v Čechách* (Pr. 1955)

Klingenstein, G., *Staatsverwaltung und kirchliche Autorität im 18. Jahrhundert* (V. 1970)

— *Der Aufstieg des Hauses Kaunitz* (Göttingen 1975)

Klopp, O., 'Leibniz' Plan der Gründung einer Societät der Wissenschaften in Wien', *AÖG* xl (1869), 159–255

— *Der Fall des Hauses Stuart ... im Zusammenhange der europäischen Angelegenheiten von 1660–1714*, i–xiv (V. 1875–88)

Knihopis českých a slovenských tisků, ed. Z. Tobolka and F. Horák, II: 1501–1800, i– (Pr. 1939–)

Knittel, Caspar, *Via Regia ad omnes scientias et artes* (Pr. 1687)

Koch, M., *Quellen zur Geschichte des Kaisers Maximilian II*, i–ii (Leipzig 1857–61)

— *Geschichte des deutschen Reiches unter der Regierung Ferdinands III*, i–ii (V. 1865–6)

Koči, J., *Boje venkovského lidu v období temna* (Pr. 1953)

— *Odboj nevolníků na Frýdlantsku 1679–87* (Liberec 1965)

— *Čarodějnické procesy ... v českých zemích v 16.–18. století* (Pr. 1973)

Köhler, J., *Das Ringen um die tridentinische Erneuerung im Bistum Breslau, 1564–1620* (Cologne–V. 1973)

Kohn, Samuel, *Die Sabbatarier in Siebenbürgen* (Bp. 1894)

Kolár, J. (ed.), *Zrcadlo rozděleného království* (Pr. 1963)

Kollár, A. F., *Historia Diplomatica Iuris Patronatus apostolicorum Hungariae Regum* (V. 1762)

— *De Originibus et Usu perpetuo potestatis Legislatoriae circa sacra Apostolicorum Regum Ungariae* (V. 1764)

Komáromy, A. (ed.), *Magyarországi boszorkányperek oklevéltára* (Bp. 1910)

Konopczyński, W., *Dzieje Polski nowożytnej*, i–ii (2nd edn. London 1958–1959)

Kopp, H., *Die Alchemie in älterer und neuerer Zeit*, i–ii (Heidelberg 1886)

Kosáry, D., *Bevezetés a magyar történelem forrásaiba és irodalmába*, i–iii (Bp. 1951)

Kosch, W., *Deutsches Literatur-Lexikon* (Bern–Munich 1963)

Kotrba, V., *Česká barokní gotika* (Pr. 1976)

Krásl, F., *Arnošt hrabě Harrach, kardinál ... a kníže arcibiskup pražský* (Pr. 1886)

Krebs, R., *Die politische Publizistik der Jesuiten und ihrer Gegner in den letzten Jahrzehnten vor Ausbruch des dreissigjährigen Krieges* (Halle 1890)

Kroess, A., *Geschichte der böhmischen Provinz der Gesellschaft Jesu*, i–ii (V. 1910–38)

Krofta, K., *Přehled dějin selského stavu v Čechách a na Moravě* (2nd edn. Pr. 1949)

Krones, F. von, *Geschichte der Karl Franzens-Universität in Graz* (Graz 1886)

— 'Zur Geschichte des Jesuitenordens in Ungarn, 1645–71', *AÖG* lxxix (1892), 280–354

— 'Zur Geschichte Ungarns (1671–83) mit besonderer Rücksicht auf die Thätigkeit und die Geschichte des Jesuitenordens', *AÖG* lxxx (1893), 353–455

Kubinyi, M., *Bethlenfalvi Gróf Thurzó Imre* (Bp. 1888)

Květoňová-Klimová, O., 'Styky Bohuslava Balbína s českou šlechtou pobělohorskou', *ČČH* xxxii (1926), 497–541

Lambeck, Peter, *Prodromus Historiae Literariae* (2nd edn. Leipzig–Frankfurt 1710)

— *Commentarii de augustissima Bibliotheca Caesarea Vindobonensi*, i–viii (2nd edn. V. 1766–82)

Lampe, F. A. [really Debreceni Ember, P.], *Historia Ecclesiae Reformatae in Hungaria et Transilvania* (Utrecht 1728)
Lana-Terzi, Francesco, *Prodromo overo saggio di alcune inventioni nuove* (Brescia 1670)
— *Magisterium Naturae et Artis*, i–iii (Brescia–Parma 1684–92)
Lascovius, Petrus, *De Homine Magno illo in rerum natura miraculo et partibus* (Wittenberg 1585)
Lea, H. C., *Materials towards a History of Witchcraft*, i–iii (New York 1957)
Lebenwaldt, Adam à, *Acht Tractätel von dess Teuffels List und Betrug*, i–viii (Salzburg 1680–2)
Lehmann, M., 'Die Kalvarienberganlagen im Donauraum', *Festschrift F. Loidl*, i–ii (V. 1970), i, 113–59
Lenglet du Fresnoy, N., *Histoire de la philosophie hermetique*, i–iii (The Hague 1742)
Lhotsky, A., *Die Geschichte der Sammlungen*, i–ii (V. 1941–5)
The Life of Leopold late Emperor of Germany (London 1706)
Lipsius, Justus, *Opera Omnia*, i–iv (Antwerp 1637)
Litterae Annuae Societatis Jesu (various places and dates)
Liva, V., 'Jan Arnošt Platejs z Platenštejna', *ČMM* liv (1930), 15–78, 293–336
Loesche, G., *Zur Gegenreformation in Schlesien*, i–ii (Leipzig 1915–16)
— *Geschichte des Protestantismus im vormaligen und im neuen Österreich* (3rd edn. V.–Leipzig 1930)
Loidl, F., *Menschen im Barock* (V. 1938)
Lorenz, W., *Die Kreuzherren mit dem roten Stern* (Königstein i. Taunus 1964)
Loserth, J., *Die Reformation und Gegenreformation in den innerösterreichischen Ländern im XVI Jahrhundert* (Stuttgart 1898)
— *Geschichte des altsteirischen Herren- und Grafenhauses Stubenberg* (Graz–Leipzig 1911)
— (ed.), *Acten und Correspondenzen zur Geschichte der Gegenreformation in Innerösterreich unter Karl II und Ferdinand II*, 2 vols. in 3 (V. 1898–1907)
Luijk, B. A. L. van, *Le Monde augustinien du XIIIᵉ au XIXᵉ siècle* (Assen 1972)
Luschin-Ebengreuth, A., *Studien zur Geschichte des steirischen Adels im 16. Jahrhunderte* (Graz 1875)
— *Geschichte des älteren Gerichtswesens in Österreich ob und unter der Enns* (Weimar 1879)
— *Österreichische Reichsgeschichte* (Bamberg 1896)

Macek, Jaroslav, and Žáček, V., *Krajská správa v českých zemích a její archivní fondy* (Pr. 1958)
Machilek, F., 'Die Zisterzienser in Böhmen und Mähren', *Archiv für Kirchengeschichte von Böhmen–Mähren–Schlesien*, iii (1973), 185–220
Macůrek, J., *České země a Slovensko, 1620–1750* (Brno 1969)
Magyar országgyűlési emlékek, ed. V. Fraknói and A. Károlyi, i–xii (Bp. 1874–1917)

Magyary-Kossa, G., *Magyar orvosi emlékek*, i–iv (Bp. 1929–40)
Makkai, László, *Histoire de Transylvanie* (Paris 1946)
— *A magyar puritánusok harca a feudalizmus ellen* (Bp. 1952)
— 'Az abszolutizmus társadalmi bázisának kialakulása az osztrák habs-
 burgok országaiban', *TSz* iii (1960), 193–223
— 'Die Hauptzüge der wirtschaftlich-sozialen Entwicklung Ungarns im
 15.–17. Jahrhundert', *Studia Historica*, liii (1963), 27–46
Maksay, F. (ed.), *Urbáriumok, XVI–XVII század* (Bp. 1959)
Manget, J. J. (ed.), *Bibliotheca Chemica Curiosa*, i–ii (Cologne–Geneva
 1702)
Mann, Golo, *Wallenstein*, tr. Ch. Kessler (London 1976)
Marci, J. Marcus, *Idearum Operatricium Idea* (Pr. 1635)
— *Philosophia Vetus Restituta* (Pr. 1662)
Marsina, R. and Kušík, M. (eds.), *Urbáre feudálnych panstiev na Slovensku*,
 i–ii (Bratislava 1959)
Matějek, F., 'Bílá Hora a moravská feudální společnost', *ČsČH* xxii (1974),
 81–103
Mayer, A., *Wiens Buchdruckergeschichte*, i–ii (V. 1883)
Mecenseffy, G., *Geschichte des Protestantismus in Österreich* (Graz 1956)
Mell, A., *Die Lage des steirischen Unterthanenstandes seit Beginn der neueren
 Zeit bis in die Mitte des 17. Jahrhunderts* (Weimar 1896)
Menčík, F., 'Censura v Čechách a na Moravě', *VKČSN*, 1888, 85–136
Meraviglia-Crivelli, R. J., *Der böhmische Adel* (Nuremberg 1886)
Mercier, B., *Notice raisonné des ouvrages de Gaspar Schott, Jésuite* ... (Paris
 1785)
Merzbacher, F., *Die Hexenprocesse in Franken* (2nd edn. Munich 1970)
Meszlényi, A., *Szelepcsényi primás és Északmagyarország rekatolizálása,
 1671–5* (Bp. 1935)
Metz, F. (ed.), *Vorderösterreich, eine geschichtliche Landeskunde* (2nd edn.
 Freiburg 1967)
Meyer, W., *Gemeinde, Erbherrschaft und Staat im Rechtsleben des schlesischen
 Dorfes vom 16. bis 19. Jahrhundert* (Würzburg 1967)
Midelfort, H. C. E., *Witch-hunting in south-west Germany* (Stanford, Cal.
 1972)
Mika, A., 'Majetkové rozvrstvení české šlechty v předbělohorském období',
 SbH xv (1967), 45–73
— 'K národnostním poměrům v Čechách po třicetileté válce', *ČsČH* xxiv
 (1976), 535–60
Millett, B., *The Irish Franciscans 1651–65* (Rome 1964)
Miscellanea Curiosa Medico-Physica Academiae Naturae Curiosorum (various
 places, 1670–)
Mohl, A., *Der Gnadenort Loreto in Ungarn* (Eisenstadt 1894)
Monconys, B. de, *Journal des Voyages*, i–ii (Lyons 1665–6)
Monte Snyders, J. de, *Metamorphosis Planetarum* (Amsterdam 1663)
Montesquieu, Ch.-L. de Secondat de, *Voyages*, i–ii (Bordeaux 1894–6)
Morhof, D. G., *Polyhistor*, i–iii (Lübeck 1695–1708)
Mout, M. E. H. N., *Bohemen en de Nederlanden in de zestiende eeuw* (Leiden
 1975)

Muk, J., *Po stopách národního vědomí české šlechty pobělohorské* (Pr. 1931)
Müller, Friedrich, *Beiträge zur Geschichte des Hexenglaubens und des Hexenprocesses in Siebenbürgen* (Brunswick 1854)
Multhauf, R. P., *The Origins of Chemistry* (London 1966)
Muneles, O., *Bibliographical survey of Jewish Prague* (Pr. 1952)

Nagy, Iván, *Magyarország családai*, 13 vols. in 8 (Pest 1857–68)
Németh, L., *A Regnum Marianum állameszme a magyar katolikus megújhodás korában* (Bp. 1941)
Neveux, J. B., *Vie spirituelle et vie sociale entre Rhin et Baltique au XVIIᵉ siècle* (Paris 1967)
Nilles N., *Symbolae ad illustrandam historiam Ecclesiae Orientalis in terris Coronae S. Stephani*, i–ii (Innsbruck 1885)
Norlind, W., *Tycho Brahe, en levnadsteckning* (Lund 1970)
Novák, J. B., *Rudolf II a jeho pád* (Pr. 1935)
Nuntiaturberichte vom Kaiserhofe Leopolds I, 1657–79, ed. A. Levinson, i–ii *AÖG* ciii (1913), 549–830; cxvi (1918), 497–728
Nyáry A., *A bécsi udvar a XVII század végén* (Bp. 1912)

Odložilík, O., *Jednota Bratrská a reformovaní francouzského jazyka* (Philadelphia 1964)
Oestreich, G., *Geist und Gestalt des frühmodernen Staates* (Berlin 1969)
O'Kelly, William, *Philosophia Aulica, juxta veterum ac recentiorum philosophorum Placita* (Pr. 1701)
Okolicsányi, P., *Historia Diplomatica de Statu Religionis Evangelicae in Hungaria* (n.p. 1710)
Oldenbourg, F., *Die Endter, eine Nürnberger Buchhändlerfamilie, 1590–1740* (Munich–Berlin 1911)
Őry, M., *Pázmány Péter tanulmányi évei* (Eisenstadt 1970)
Ossinger, J. F., *Bibliotheca Augustiniana* (Ingolstadt–Augsburg 1768)
Ott, E., *Beiträge zur Receptions-Geschichte des römisch-canonischen Processes in den böhmischen Ländern* (Leipzig 1879)
Österreichische Weistümer, various eds., i– (V. 1870–)

Pach, Zs. P., 'The role of East-Central Europe in international trade, 16th–17th centuries', *Études Historiques*, 1970, 217–64
Palaeologus, Jacobus, *Catechesis Christiana Dierum Duodecim*, ed. R. Dostálová (Warsaw 1971)
The Particular State of the Government of the Emperour, Ferdinand the Second (London 1637)
Partington, J. R., *A History of Chemistry*, ii (London 1961)
Paschini, P., *Storia del Friuli*, i–ii (2nd edn. Udine 1953–4)
Patera, A. (ed.), 'Dopisy B. A. Balbína k opatu teplskému . . . a knězi téhož kláštera Aloisovi Hackenschmidtu z l. 1664–7', *VKČSN*, 1888, 143–226
Patin, Charles, *Travels through Germany, Bohemia . . . and other parts of Europe* (London 1696)

Pauler, Gy., *Wesselényi Ferenc nádor és társainak összeesküvése*, i–ii (Bp. 1876)

Paulhart, H. and Voglsam, J. (eds.), *Die Bibliothek des Linzer Kapuzinerklosters St. Matthias*, i–ii (Linz 1968)

Pázmány, Péter, *Isteni Igazságra vezérlő Kalauz* (Pozsony 1613)
— *Összes munkái, magyar sorozat*, i–vii (Bp. 1894–1905)
— *Összegyűjtött levelei*, ed. F. Hanuy, i–ii (Bp. 1910–11)

Pekař, J., *České katastry 1654–1789* (2nd edn. Pr. 1932)
— *Kniha o Kosti, kus české historie*, i–ii (2nd edn. Pr. ?1936)

Pereira, B., *De Magia, de observatione somniorum et de divinatione astrologica* (Cologne 1598)

Pescheck, C. A., *The Reformation and Anti-Reformation in Bohemia*, i–ii (London 1845)

Péterfy, C., *Sacra Concilia Ecclesiae Romano-Catholicae in Regno Hungariae celebrata*, i–ii (Pozsony 1741–2)

Petráň, J., 'Matouš Ulický a poddanské povstání na Kouřimsku a Čáslavsku roku 1627', *AUC*, 1954, no. 7, 43–64
— 'Pohyb poddanského obyvatelstva a jeho osobní vztahy v Čechách v době předbělohorské', *ČsČH* v (1957), 26–58, 399–447
— *Poddaný lid v Čechách na prahu třicetileté války* (Pr. 1964)

Peuckert, W.-E., *Gabalia, ein Versuch zur Geschichte der magia naturalis im 16. bis 18. Jahrhundert* (Berlin 1967)

Pexenfelder, M., *Apparatus Eruditionis ... per omnes artes et scientias* (Sulzbach 1680)

Pfister, L., *Notices biographiques et bibliographiques sur les Jésuites de l'ancienne mission de Chine*, i–ii (Shanghai 1932–4)

Pickl, O. (ed.), *Die wirtschaftlichen Auswirkungen der Türkenkriege* (Graz 1971)

Pierling, P., *La Russie et le Saint-Siège*, i–v (Paris 1896–1912, reprinted The Hague 1967)

Pirchegger, H., *Geschichte der Steiermark*, ii (Graz 1931)

Pirnát, A., *Die Ideologie der Siebenbürger Antitrinitarier in den 1570er Jahren* (Bp. 1961)

Placht, O., *Lidnatost a společenská skladba českého státu v 16.–18. století* (Pr. 1957)

Podlaha, A., 'Z dějin katolických missií v Čechách r. 1670–1700', *SbHKr* iv (1895), 104–31
— *Posvátná místa království Českého*, i–vii (Pr. 1907–13)
— *Dějiny arcidiecése pražské, I: 1694–1710*, i (Pr. 1917)
— (ed.), *Dopisy reformační komisse v Čechách z let 1627–9* (Pr. 1908)

Polišenský, J. V., *The Thirty Years War*, tr. R. Evans (London 1971)

Popper, M., 'Les juifs de Prague pendant la Guerre de Trente Ans', *Revue des Études Juives*, xxix (1894), 127–41; xxx (1895), 79–93

Pribram, A. F., 'Die niederösterreichischen Stände und die Krone in der Zeit Kaiser Leopold I', *MIÖG* xiv (1893), 589–652

Privatbriefe Kaiser Leopold I an den Grafen F. E. Pötting, ed. A. F. Pribram and M. Landwehr von Pragenau, i–ii (V. 1903–4)

Procházka, R. von, *Genealogisches Handbuch erloschener böhmischer Herrenstandsfamilien* (Neustadt a. d. Aisch 1973)

Procopius a Templin, *Iudiciale, Purgatoriale et Infernale, Das ist … Discursen oder Predigen vom Jüngsten Tag und Gericht …* (Munich 1666)

Pufendorf, Samuel, *De statu Imperii Germanici* ('Geneva' 1667)

Rachfahl, F., *Die Organisation der Gesamtstaatsverwaltung Schlesiens vor dem dreissigjährigen Kriege* (Leipzig 1894)

Rácz, István, *A hajdúk a XVII században* (Debrecen 1969)

Radvánszky, B., *Magyar családélet és háztartás a XVI és XVII században*, i–iii (Bp. 1879–96)

Räss, A., *Die Convertiten seit der Reformation*, i–xiv (Freiburg 1866–80)

Redlich, O., 'Das Tagebuch Esaias Pufendorfs (1671–4)', *MIÖG* xxxvii (1916), 541–97

— *Die Weltmacht des Barock* (4th edn. V. 1961)

— *Das Werden einer Grossmacht* (4th edn. V. 1962)

Regele, O., *Der österreichische Hofkriegsrat, 1556–1848* (V. 1949)

Régi magyarországi nyomtatványok, ed. G. Borsa *et al.*, i (Bp. 1971)

Rejzek, A., *Bohuslav Balbín, jeho život a práce* (Pr. 1908)

Relationen Venetianischer Botschaften über Deutschland und Österreich, ed. J. Fiedler, ii (V. 1867)

Reusch, F. H., *Der Index der verbotenen Bücher*, i–ii (Bonn 1883–5)

Révai, S., *Káldi György életrajza, Biblia-forditása és Oktató Intése* (Pécs 1900)

Révész, I., 'Debrecen lelki válsága 1561–71, *Sz* lxx (1936), 38–75, 163–203

— *Magyar református egyháztörténet*, i (Debrecen 1938)

Rezek, A., *Dějiny prostonárodního hnutí náboženského v Čechách*, i (Pr. 1887)

— *Děje Čech a Moravy za Ferdinanda III až do konce třicetileté války* (Pr. 1890)

— *Dějiny Čech a Moravy nové doby*, i–ii (Pr. 1892–3)

— 'Dva příspěvky k dějinám selských bouří a selského poddanství v XVII století, *VKČSN*, 1893, no. 2

— 'Tak-zvaná 'Idea gubernationis ecclesiasticae' z času kardinála Harracha', *VKČSN*, 1893, no. 3

Riccioli, J. B., *Almagestum Novum*, i–ii (Bologna 1651)

Richter, K., 'Die böhmischen Länder von 1471 bis 1740', in *Handbuch der Geschichte der böhmischen Länder*, ed. K. Bosl, i–iv (Stuttgart 1966–74), ii, 97–412

Riezler, S., *Geschichte der Hexenprozesse in Bayern* (Stuttgart 1896)

Rigetti, P., *Historische Nachricht sowohl von der Errichtung der Wellischen Congregation als auch des dazu gehörigen Hospitals* (Pr. 1773)

Rinck, G. E., *Leopolds des Grossen … wunderwürdiges Leben und Thaten* (Leipzig 1709)

Röhrig, F., 'Protestantismus und Gegenreformation im Stift Klosterneuburg und seinen Pfarren', *Jb.d.St.Klnb.* N. F. i (1961), 105–70

Roscher, W., 'Österreichische Nationalökonomik unter Leopold I', *Jbb.f.Natö.u.Stat.* ii (1864), 25–59, 105–22

Roth-Scholtz, F., *Deutsches Theatrum Chemicum*, i–iii (Nuremberg 1728–1732)

Rowbotham, A. H., *Missionary and Mandarin, the Jesuits at the court of China* (Berkeley–Los Angeles 1942)

Rózsa, Gy., *Magyar történetábrázolás a 17. században* (Bp. 1973)

Rudolf II, see Evans, above

Rukověť' humanistického básnictví v Čechách a na Moravě, ed. J. Hejnic and J. Martínek, i– (Pr. 1966–)

Salecker, K., *Christian Knorr von Rosenroth* (Leipzig 1931)

Salmon, V., *The Works of Francis Lodwick* (London 1972)

Sartorius, A., *Cistercium Bis-Tertium, seu Historia Elogialis* . . . (Pr. 1700)

Scharlau, U., *Athanasius Kircher als Musikschriftsteller* (Marburg 1969)

Schellhass, K., *Der Dominikaner Felician Ninguarda und die Gegenreformation in Süddeutschland und Österreich*, i (Rome 1930)

Scherer, G., *Christliche Erinnerung bei der Historien . . . einer Jungkfrawen, die mit zwölfftausent, sechshundert, und zwey und fünfftzig Teuffeln besessen gewesen* (Ingolstadt 1584)

— *Opera oder alle Bücher, Tractätlein, Schrifften und Predigen*, i–ii (Munich 1613–14)

Schlenz, J. E., *Geschichte des Bistums und der Diözese Leitmeritz*, i–ii (Warnsdorf 1912–14)

— *Das Kirchenpatronat in Böhmen* (Pr. 1928)

Schmid, L., *Irští lékaři v Čechách* (Pr. 1968)

Schmidl, J., *Historia Societatis Jesu Provinciae Bohemiae*, i–iv (Pr. 1747–59)

Schmidt, Hans, *Philipp Wilhelm von Pfalz-Neuburg*, i (Düsseldorf 1973)

Schmieder, K. C., *Geschichte der Alchemie* (Halle 1832)

Schott, F. C., *Cosmus in Micro-Cosmo, hoc est Mundus Opere sex dierum Creatus* (V. 1701)

Schott, Gaspar, *Magia Universalis Naturae et Artis*, i–iv (Würzburg 1657–1659)

— *Mathesis Caesarea sive Amussis Ferdinandea* (2nd edn. Würzburg 1662)

— *Technica Curiosa sive Mirabilia Artis*, i–ii (Würzburg 1664)

— *Physica Curiosa sive Mirabilia Naturae et Artis* (2nd edn. Würzburg 1667)

— *Organum Mathematicum libris IX explicatum* (Würzburg 1668)

Schram, F. (ed.), *Magyarországi boszorkányperek 1529–1768*, i–ii (Bp. 1970)

Schulz, V. (ed.), *Korrespondence hr. Václava Jiřího Holického ze Šternberka* (Pr. 1898)

— *Korrespondence jesuitů provincie české z let 1584–1770* (Pr. 1900)

Schuster, L., *Fürstbischof Martin Brenner, ein Charakterbild aus der steirischen Reformations-Geschichte* (Graz–Leipzig 1898)

Schwarz, H. F., *The Imperial Privy Council in the 17th century* (Cambridge, Mass. 1943)

Schyrl de Rheita, A. M., *Oculus Enoch et Eliae sive Radius Sidereomysticus* (Antwerp 1645)

Seibt, F. (ed.), *Bohemia Sacra* (Düsseldorf 1974)
Serfőző, J., *Szentiványi Márton munkássága a XVII század küzdelmeiben* (Bp. 1942)
Šimák, J. V., 'Chotěšovské zprávy o selské bouři r. 1680', *VKČSN*, 1900, no. 10
— (ed.), *Zpovědní seznamy arcidiecése pražské z r. 1671–1725*, i, ix–xiii (Pr. 1918–38)
Skála ze Zhoře, Pavel, *Historie Česká, 1602–23*, ed. K. Tieftrunk, i–v (Pr. 1865–70)
Sobel, J. de Deo, *Geschichte und Festschrift der österreichisch-böhmischen Ordensprovinz der Barmherzigen Brüder* (V. 1892)
Socher, A., *Historia Provinciae Austriae Societatis Jesu*, i (V. 1740)
Soldan, W. G., Heppe, H., and Bauer, M., *Geschichte der Hexenprozesse*, i–ii (Munich 1911)
Sommervogel, C., continuing Backer, A. and A. de, *Bibliothèque de la Compagnie de Jésus*, i–x (Brussels–Paris 1890–1909)
Sörös, P., 'Forgách Ferenc a biboros', *Sz* xxxv (1901), 577–608, 690–729, 774–818
Srbik, H. von, *Der staatliche Exporthandel Österreichs von Leopold I bis Maria Theresia* (V.–Leipzig 1907)
— 'Abenteurer am Hofe Kaiser Leopold I', *Archiv für Kulturgeschichte*, viii (1910), 52–72
— 'Wilhelm von Schröder', *Sb.d.k.Akad.d.Wiss.,ph.-h.Kl.* clxiv (1910), Abh. 1
Stanka, R., *Die böhmischen Conföderationsakte von 1619* (Berlin 1932)
Status Particularis Regiminis ... Ferdinandi II (n.p. 1637)
Steinhuber, A., *Die Geschichte des Collegium Germanicum in Rom*, i–ii (Freiburg 1895)
Stepischneg, J., 'Georg III Stobaeus von Palmburg, Fürstbischof von Lavant', *AÖG* xv (1856), 71–132
Stern, Selma, *The Court Jew* (Philadelphia 1950)
Stieve, F., *Der oberösterreichische Bauernaufstand des Jahres 1626*, i–ii (Munich 1891)
Stobäus, Georg, *Epistolae ad diversos* (Venice 1749)
Stoeger, J. N., *Scriptores Provinciae Austriae S.J.*, i (V. 1855)
Stölzel, A., *Die Entwicklung des gelehrten Richterthums in deutschen Territorien*, i–ii (Stuttgart 1872)
Stránský, Pavel, *Respublica Bojema* (Leiden 1643)
Středovský, J. G., *Sacra Moraviae Historia sive Vita SS. Cyrilli et Methudii* (Sulzbach 1710)
Strnadt, J., 'Materialien zur Geschichte der Entwicklung der Gerichtsverfassung und des Verfahrens ... des Landes ob der Enns', *AÖG* xcvii (1909), 161–520
Stülz, J., *Geschichte des Cistercienser-Klosters Wilhering* (Linz 1840)
Stummvoll, J. (ed.), *Geschichte der österreichischen Nationalbibliothek*, i (V. 1968)
Sturmberger, Hans, *Georg Erasmus Tschernembl* (Linz 1953)

— *Kaiser Ferdinand II und das Problem des Absolutismus* (Munich 1957)
Sturminger, W. (ed.), *Die Türken vor Wien in Augenzeugenberichten* (Düsseldorf 1968)
Svátek, Josef, *Culturhistorische Bilder aus Böhmen* (V. 1879)
Svátek, Josef, 'Organizace řeholních institucí v českých zemích a péče o jejich archivy', *SbAPr* xx (1970), 503–624
Svoboda, Josef, *Katolická reformace a marianská Družina v království Českém*, i–ii (Brno 1888)
Szabó, Attila T., *Erdélyi magyar szótörténeti tár*, i: A–C (Bucharest 1976)
Szabó, Gy. P., *Ferencrendiek a magyar történelemben* (Bp. 1921)
Szekfű, Gy., *Bethlen Gábor* (Bp. 1929)
Szentiványi, Márton, *Curiosiora et Selectiora variarum scientiarum Miscellanea*, i–iii (Tyrnau 1689–1709)
— *Opuscula Polemica*, i–ii (2nd end. Tyrnau 1718–30)

Tanner, Adam, *Astrologia Sacra* (Ingolstadt 1615)
Tanner, Matthias, *Societas Jesu usque ad Sanguinis et Vitae profusionem Militans* ... (Pr. 1675)
— *Societas Jesu Apostolorum Imitatrix sive Gesta praeclara et virtutes eorum qui ... per totum Orbem terrarum speciali zelo desudârunt*, i (Pr. 1694)
Tausch, H. (ed.), *Benediktinisches Mönchtum in Österreich* (V. 1949)
Thaly, K., *Irodalom- és miveltségtörténeti tanulmányok a Rákóczi-korból* (Bp. 1885)
Theiner, A., *Geschichte der Zurückkehr der regierenden Häuser von Braunschweig und Sachsen in den Schooss der katholischen Kirche* (Einsiedeln 1843)
Thiel, V., 'Die innerösterreichische Zentralverwaltung 1564–1749', *AÖG* cv (1916), 1–209; cxi (1929–30), 497–644
Thiers, J. B., *Traité des Superstitions qui regardent tous les Sacremens*, i–iii (Paris 1704)
Thomas, K. V., *Religion and the Decline of Magic* (London 1971)
Thomasius, Jakob, *Dissertatio philosophica de Cingaris* (Leipzig 1671)
Thorndike, L., *History of Magic and Experimental Science*, vii–viii (New York 1958)
Tibal, A., *L'Autrichien, essais sur la formation d'une individualité nationale* (Paris 1936)
Tietze, H., *Die Juden Wiens; Geschichte–Wirtschaft–Kultur* (V. 1933)
Timon, Á., *Ungarische Verfassungs- und Rechtsgeschichte* (Berlin 1904)
Toldy, F. (ed.), *Galántai Gróf Esterházy Miklós munkái*, i–ii (Pest 1853)
Tomek, Ernst, *Kirchengeschichte Österreichs*, ii (Innsbruck 1949)
Tomek, V. V., *Geschichte der Prager Universität* (Pr. 1849)
— *Sněmy české dle obnoveného zřízení zemského Ferdinanda II* (Pr. 1868)
Történelmi atlasz, ed. S. Radó et al. (7th edn. Bp. 1965)
Tremel, F., *Der Frühkapitalismus in Innerösterreich* (Graz 1954)
— *Wirtschafts- und Sozialgeschichte Österreichs* (V. 1969)
Trevor-Roper, H. R., *The European witch-craze of the 16th and 17th centuries* (London 1969)

Trócsányi, Zs., *Az erdélyi fejedelemség korának országgyűlései* (Bp. 1976)
Trophaeum ... Domus Estorasianae [i.e. Esterházy] (V. 1700)
Tumpach, J. and Podlaha, A., *Bibliografie české katolické literatury náboženské, 1828–1913*, i–v (Pr. 1912–23)
Turner, Robert, *Posthumae Orationes* (Cologne 1615)
Turóczi-Trostler, J., *Magyar irodalom, világirodalom*, i–ii (Bp. 1961)

Vacek, F., 'Diecésní synoda pražská z r. 1605', *SbHKr* v (1896), 25–45
Válka, J., *Hospodářská politika feudálního velkostatku na předbělohorské Moravě* (Pr. 1962)
Valvasor, J. W. von, *Die Ehre des Hertzogthums Crain*, i–iv (Laibach 1689)
Vann, J. A., *The Swabian Kreis* (Brussels 1975)
— and Rowan, S. W. (eds.), *The Old Reich* (Brussels 1974)
Vanyó, A. T., *A katholikus restauráció Nyugatmagyarországon* (Pécs 1928)
— *A bécsi nunciusok jelentései Magyarországról 1666–83* (Pannonhalma 1935)
Varga, E. (ed.), *Úriszék: XVI–XVII századi perszövegek* (Bp. 1958)
Varga, János, *Jobbágyrendszer a magyarországi feudalizmus kései századaiban 1556–1767* (Bp. 1969)
Vašků, V., *Studie o správních dějinách a písemnostech moravského královského tribunálu z let 1636–1749* (Brno 1969)
Veit, A. L., *Kirchliche Reformbestrebungen im ehemaligen Erzstift Mainz unter Erzbischof Johann Philipp von Schönborn* (Freiburg 1910)
— and Lenhart, L., *Kirche und Volksfrömmigkeit im Zeitalter des Barock* (Freiburg 1956)
Velics, L., *Vázlatok a magyar jezsuiták múltjából*, i–iii (Bp. 1912–14)
Venetianische Depeschen vom Kaiserhofe, Abt. 2, vol. i, ed. A. F. Pribram (V. 1901)
Verbík, A. (ed.), *Černé knihy práva loveckého na hradě Buchlově* (Brno 1976)
Vlasák, F., *Der altböhmische Adel und seine Nachkommenschaft nach dem dreissigjährigen Kriege* (Pr. 1866)
Vlček, J., *Dějiny české literatury*, i–ii (3rd edn. Pr. 1940)
Voigt, J., *Geschichte des Deutschen Ritter-Ordens in seinen zwölf Balleien in Deutschland*, i–ii (Berlin 1857–9)
Volf, J., *Geschichte des Buchdrucks in Böhmen und Mähren bis 1848* (Weimar 1928)

Father Luke Wadding Commemorative volume (Dublin 1957)
Walker, Mack, *German Home Towns* (Ithaca 1971)
Wechtler, J. C., *Homo Oriens et Occidens* (Frankfurt 1659)
Weingarten, J. J. von, *Codex Ferdinandeo-Leopoldino-Josephino-Carolinus* (Pr. 1720)
Weise, Christian, *Epistolae selectiores*, ed. C. G. Hoffmann (Bautzen 1715)
Weitenweber, W. R., 'Beiträge zur Literärgeschichte Böhmens', *Sb.d.k.Akad.d.Wiss.,ph.-h.Kl.* xix (1856), 120–56
Wenzel, G., *A Fuggerek jelentősége Magyarország történetében* (Bp. 1882)
Wesener, G., *Das innerösterreichische Landschrannenverfahren im 16. und 17. Jahrhundert* (Graz 1963)

Weszprémi, I., *Succincta Medicorum Hungariae et Transilvaniae biographia*, i–iii (Leipzig–V. 1774–87)

Widmann, H., *Geschichte Salzburgs*, i–iii (Gotha 1907–14)

Wiedemann, Th., 'Beiträge zur Geschichte des Bisthums Wiener Neustadt', *ÖVjschr.f.Kath.Theol.* vii (1868), 241–66; viii (1869), 67–118; ix (1870), 359–74

— 'Die kirchliche Büchercensur in der Erzdiöcese Wien', *AÖG* l (1873), 215–520

— *Geschichte der Reformation und Gegenreformation im Lande unter der Enns*, i–v (Pr.–Leipzig 1879–86)

Williams, G. H., *The Radical Reformation* (London 1962)

Wines, R., 'The imperial circles, princely diplomacy and imperial reform 1681–1714', *Journal of Modern History*, xxxix (1967), 1–29

Winter, Eduard, *Frühaufklärung* (Berlin 1966)

Wolf, Adam, 'Die Hofkammer unter Kaiser Leopold I', *Sb.d.k.Akad.d.Wiss.,ph.-h.Kl.* xi (1853), 440–84

— *Fürst Wenzel Lobkowitz* (V. 1869)

— *Geschichtliche Bilder aus Österreich*, i–ii (V. 1878–80)

Wundt, M., *Die deutsche Schulmetaphysik des 17. Jahrhunderts* (Tübingen 1939)

Wurm, H., *Die Jörger von Tollet* (Linz 1955)

Wurzbach, Constant von, *Biographisches Lexikon des Kaiserthums Oesterreich*, i–lx (V. 1856–91)

Yates, F. A., *The Rosicrucian Enlightenment* (London 1972)

Zara, Antonio, *Anatomia Ingeniorum et Scientiarum* (Venice 1615)

Zedler, J. H. (ed.), *Grosses vollständiges Universal Lexicon*, i–liv (Halle–Leipzig 1732–50)

Zeeden, E. W., *Entstehung der Konfessionen* (Munich 1965)

Zelený, V. V., 'Tomáš Pešina z Čechorodu', *ČČM* lviii (1884), 1–22, 250–69, 471–97; lix (1885), 90–108, 226–43; lx (1886), 102–21, 331–57, 554–82

Zerlik, A., 'Das Stift Tepl in der Zeit der Glaubensspaltung', *Anal.Praem.* xxxvii (1961), 262–81; xxxviii (1962), 93–110; xxxix (1963), 70–131, 257–66

Zíbrt, Č., *Bibliografie české historie* (= *BČH*), i–v (Pr. 1900–12)

Ziegler, H., *Die Gegenreformation in Schlesien* (Halle 1888)

Zimányi, V., *A rohonc-szalonaki uradalom és jobbágysága a XVI–XVII században* (Bp. 1968)

Zoványi, J., *Puritánus mozgalmak a magyar református egyházban* (Bp. 1911)

— *A magyarországi protestantizmus 1565-től 1600-ig* (Bp. 1977)

Zsilinszky, M., 'Lippay György és a tokaji tanácskozmány', *Sz* xx (1886), 400–24

Zwelfer, Johann, *Pharmacopoeia Regia* (Nuremberg 1668)

— *Discursus Apologeticus* (V. 1668)

Zwetsloot, H., *Friedrich Spee und die Hexenprozesse* (Trier 1954)

Index

Substantive material in footnotes is indexed as part of the text. Localities entered in CAPITALS appear on the maps (above, pp. 456–7) and/or in the glossary of place-name variants (pp. 459–61); less significant and less divergent alternative forms are indicated below in brackets. Persons entered in CAPITALS appear on the genealogical table of members of the dynasty and related rulers (above, pp. 454–5). Aristocratic families are shown with their predicates where relevant, with the titles they bore during the period, and—in certain cases—with subsequent elevations (cf. above, pp. 170 and n. 27, 175 n. 35; below, s.v. 'aristocracy'). I have employed the following abbreviations: b. = baron(s); c. = count(s); pr. = prince(s); d. = duke(s). The styles for houses and members of religious orders observe the abbreviations listed above, p. xix, and the following additional abbreviations are used: abp.(ric) = archbishop(ric); bp.(ric) = bishop(ric); can. = canonry; card. = cardinal; coll. = college; fr. = friary; mon. = monastery.

Gordon, John, 202

GORIZIA, province and town in S. Austria, 139, 159, 161, 378; coll.S.J., 64, 124

Gotha (Saxe-Gotha), duchy in Thuringia, 283, 289, 370, 429; Ernst the Pious, d. of, 289, 297, 368; Friedrich, d. of, 368–9

Gotifredus, Gabriele, O.Minim., 356, 378

GÖTTWEIG, mon.O.S.B. in Lower Austria, 4, 64, 181, 184, 193

government and administration: Austrian, 164–8; Bohemian, 198–200, 212–14; Hungarian, 238–40, 245–6; imperial, 146–52, 191–2, 276–7; Silesian, 299–300; Transylvanian, 268

Gradisca, county in Friuli, 172, 178

Gran, Daniel, 445

Grassalkovich of Gyorok, Hungarian family (c. 1751, pr. 1784), 246

GRAZ, capital of Styria, 12, 36, 43, 60, 104, 133, 139, 150, 153, 159, 164–5, 172, 191, 292, 314, 431, 445; coll.S.J./university, 41, 44, 50, 73, 101, 114, 124–5, 139, 187, 319, 384

Greiffenberg, Katharina von, 187

Greillenstein, castle in Lower Austria, 177

Grembs (Krems?), Oswald, 356

Gremonville, Jacques Bretel de, 262

Greysing, Martin, O.Praem., 220

Grienberger, Christoph, S.J., 331

Gries, mon.Can.Reg. in Tyrol, 183

Griffen, castle in Carinthia, 162; can.O.Praem., 183

Grillenberger, Johann, 410

Grindal, Edmund, abp., 19

Gröbming, estate in Styria, 161

Gross-Enzersdorf, town in Lower Austria, 162

Grotius, Hugo, 31, 268

Grueber, Johann, S.J., 431

Grumbach, Wilhelm von, 107

Grünberg, K., German historian, 91, 234

Grundner, Christoph, 31

GRÜSSAU (Krzeszów), mon.O.Cist. in Silesia, 301–2, 355

Gruter, Jan, 23

Grynaeus, Johann Jakob, 9

Gryphius (Greif), Andreas, 303

Gualdo Priorato, Galeazzo, c., 152

Guarinoni, Bartholomew, 22

Gubernium: in Austria, 165; in Hungary, 237, 452

Guericke, Otto, 337

Guevara, Antonio de, 114, 244

Guldin, Paul, S.J., 126

Günther (Vintiř), St., 225

GURK, bp.ric in Carinthia, 135, 183

Güssing (Németújvár), castle in W. Hungary, 93–4

Gustavus Adolphus, king of Sweden 1611–32, 74

Gutenstein (Gutštein), Bohemian family (c.), 210

Gutsherrschaft, see demesne (farming)

GYŐR, town and bp.ric in W. Hungary, 122, 161, 248, 251, 256; coll.S.J., 125

GYULAFEHÉRVÁR, residence town of Transylvania, 268; Catholic bp.ric, 51, 270–1, 273; Uniate bp.ric, 423

Gyulaffi(-y) of Ráthót, Transylvanian family (c. 1693), 269

Gyulai, Pál, 23, 33–4

Haase, Ignatius Franciscus, 396

Habernfeld, Andreas Hoberweschel von, 395

Hackenschmidt, Alois, O.Praem., 228

Haen, Antonius, 410

Hagen, Johann Ludwig von, 290

Hainburg, town in Lower Austria, 403

hajducks, 55, 97–100, 258

Hajnal, Mátyás, S.J., 72

507

Kirchberg, Josef Ignaz, b., 313, 317, 329
Kircher, Athanasius, S.J., 231, 287, 316–18, 321, 324–5, 327, 329, 332, 335–43, 350, 352–4, 356, 359, 361, 364–5, 371, 378–9, 384, 429, 431–2, 433–42, 444
Kircher, Johann, 250, 298
Kirsten, Peter, 427
Kirwitzer, Václav, S.J., 431
Kisalföld (lesser Hungarian Plain), 236
Kisl (Kh-) von Gottschee, Austrian family (b. 1590, c. 1623), 179
Kitonics, János, 106, 410
Kitzbühel, town in Tyrol, 161
KLADRUBY (Kladrau), mon.O.S.B. in Bohemia, 218, 224
KLAGENFURT, capital of Carinthia, 139, 159, 167; coll.S.J., 64, 124
Klatovy (Klattau), coll.S.J. in Bohemia, 138, 377; fr. O.P., 378
Klein-Mariazell, mon.O.S.B. in Lower Austria, 181
Kleinwechter, Martin, 102
Kleist, Heinrich von, 108
Kling, Johann, 375
KLOSTERBRUCK, *see* Bruck
Klostergrab (Hrob(y)), town in Bohemia, 65
Klösterle (Klášterec nad Ohří), town in Bohemia, 203
KLOSTERNEUBURG, mon.Can.Reg. in Lower Austria, 4, 61, 112, 183–4, 189, 193, 318, 328
Klosterrat (in Lower Austria), 61
Knittel, Caspar, S.J., 327, 353–4
Knobloch, Aleš, 404
Knorr von Rosenroth, Christian, b., 292, 303, 350–1, 359, 369, 375, 430; Laurenz, 292; Paulus, 292
Kobersdorf (Kabold), estate in W. Hungary, 168
Kochański, Adam Adamand, S.J., 316, 334–5, 378, 426
Kocín of Kocinét, Jan, 23–4, 105
Koháry of Csábrágh and Szitnya,

Hungarian family (b. 1616, c. 1685, pr. 1815), 246; Péter, 246
Kollár, Adam Franz, 273, 448
Kollonich (-itz), Croatian–Austrian family (b., c. 1637), 251–2; Leopold, card., abp., 146, 238, 248, 251–2, 257, 260, 272, 305, 423, 427; Johann Sigismund, card., abp., 252
Kolovrat of Libštein and Krakovec, Bohemian family (b., c. 1624/60), 93, 137, 208, 212, 215; Franz Karl, 208, 213; Ferdinand Ludwig, 208; Johann Wilhelm, 208; Ulrich Franz, 208
KOLOZSVÁR, chief town of Transylvania, 270, 325, 407, 412; coll.S.J., 114
KOMÁROM, town in W. Hungary, 145, 251
Komáromi Csipkés, György, 408
Konečný, Matouš, 404
Koniáš, Antonín, S.J., 346
KÖNIGGRÄTZ, district and town in Bohemia, 82, 102, 122, 195, 212; battle of (1866), 447; bp.ric, 134, 218; coll.S.J., 138; fr.O.F.M.Conv., 129
Königsberg, town in E. Prussia, 302; university, 27
Königsegg-Rothenfels, Leopold Wilhelm, c., 293
Königsmarck, Hans Christoph, c., 76–7
Königstetten, town in Lower Austria, 91
Königswart (Kynžvart), castle in Bohemia, 201
Kopcsányi, Mihály, bp., 393
Köpcsény (Kittsee), castle in W. Hungary, 382
Körmend, castle in W. Hungary, 93
Kornis of Gönczruszka, Transylvanian family (c. 1714), 269, 271
Kost, castle in Bohemia, 90–1
Kotter, Christoph, 395, 399

miracles, 388, 390–1; *see also* saints, cult of
Miskolc, town in C. Hungary, 412
Miskolci Csulyak, István, 30
Mizauld, Antoine, 341
Mizera, Andreas, 102–3
Mnišovský of Sebuzín, Rafael Soběhrd, 352–3, 360–1
MOHÁCS, battle of, xxii, 93, 451; *see also* Nagyharsány
Möhner, Reginbald, O.S.B., 186
Molanus, Gerhard, 306
MOLDAVIA, principality, 424, 427
Mollart, Austrian family (b. 1571, c. 1652), 246
Molnár, Albert Szenci, 28
monad, 354–5, 357, 439
monasteries, *see* orders, religious
Monau, Jakob, 23–5
Mondsee, lake and region in Upper Austria, 161; mon.O.S.B., 181
Monoszlói, András, bp., 18
Montecuccoli, Italian–Austrian family (c., pr. 1689), 173, 179; Raimondo, 144, 150, 308, 347–8
Monte Snyders, Johannes de, 365, 376–7
Montesquieu, Charles-Louis de Secondat, b., 326
Montfort, Swabian family (c.), 176
Montserrat, mon.O.S.B. in Catalonia, 218, 226
MORAVIA (Morava, Mähren), margravate, 10, 46–8, 52, 71, 120, 123–4, 133, 195, 198–9, 209–10, 212–13, 336, 372, 399, 403–4, 406; *see also* Bohemia
Moravian Brethren, 194
Moravský Krumlov (Mährisch-Krumau), mon.O.S.P. in Moravia, 133
Moravský Šternberk (Mährisch-Sternberg), mon.Can.Reg. in Moravia, 219
Moretus, Théodore, S.J., 125, 316, 319, 331, 334
Morhof, Daniel Georg, 324

Mornay, *see* Duplessis-Mornay
Morzin, Camillo, c., 203; Paolo, c., 203
Mossóczy, Zacharias, bp., 17
Muelen, Baptista van der, 29
Muffat, Georg, 153
Mühlberg, battle of, 451
Mühlviertel, division of Upper Austria, 159
Müller, Andreas, 297, 432
Müller (Miller), Philipp, S.J., 145, 317–18
Munggenast, Josef, 445
MUNKÁCS, bp.ric in N.E. Hungary, 421–2
MÜNSTER, bp.ric in Westphalia, 77, 278, 452
MÜNSTERBERG, duchy in Silesia, 172, 196, 300
Muscovy, *see* Russia
music and musicians, 47, 135, 153–4, 263, 339–40, 434, 438, 440, 446
Myllner (Milner) of Milhauz (Mühlhausen), Jan, 59
mysticism, 78, 110, 303, 341–3, 354

Náchod, castle and town in Bohemia, 202
Nádasdy of Nádasd and Fogarasföld, Hungarian family (b., c. 1625), 38, 178, 242, 247; Ferenc (died 1604), 242; Ferenc (died 1671), 242–3, 245–7, 249, 257, 262–3, 265, 291, 313, 326, 354, 381–2, 434, 440, 452
Nagy, Iván, Hungarian genealogist, 240–1
Nagyharsány, battle of (second battle of Mohács), 452
NAGYVÁRAD, town and bp.ric in E. Hungary, 12, 97, 235, 249, 256, 261, 393
Náprági (-ágyi), Demetrius, bp., 18, 51, 65
Nassau, German dynasty, 205, 284
nationalities and nationalism, 15,

518

Printed in the United Kingdom
by Lightning Source UK Ltd.
109027UKS00001B/137